Reading
and Learning from
Text

Second Edition

This book is dedicated to the memory of *Harry Singer*—husband, father, scholar, colleague, friend.

READING AND LEARNING FROM TEXT

Second Edition

Harry Singer
Dan Donlan

UNIVERSITY OF CALIFORNIA,
RIVERSIDE

LAWRENCE ERLBAUM ASSOCIATES, PUBLISHERS
1989   Hillsdale, New Jersey   Hove and London

Lawrence Erlbaum Associates, Inc., Publishers
365 Broadway
Hillsdale, New Jersey 07642
Production and interior design by Robin Marks Weisberg

Library of Congress Cataloging in Publication Data
Singer, Harry.
   Reading and learning from text / Harry Singer and Dan Donlan. —
2nd ed.
      p.   cm.
   Bibliography: p.
   Includes index.
   ISBN 0-89859-789-7
   1. Content area reading. 2. Reading (Elementary) I. Donlan,
Dan. II. Title.
LB1573.75.S56 1988
372.4—dc19
Printed in the United States of America   87-35110
10 9 8 7 6 5 4 3 2   CIP

Contents

Preface

The first edition of this text was aimed at content area teachers and reading- and learning-from-text specialists. It emphasized single and multiple text strategies to meet the wide range of individual differences in reading achievement in each grade level and content area without stigmatizing any student. This revised edition contains several additions. We made the text more relevant to elementary school instruction by incorporating explanations of oral, silent, and schema-interactive reading instruction in our chapter on Theories and Research on Reading and Learning from Text (chap. 4). We also added relevant elementary school information in each chapter.

We constructed an instructional model that integrates the text (see model at end of chap. 4 and beginning of chap. 6). The model explains that the instructor can vary the text characteristics (chap. 5), develop or activate reader resources (chap. 6, 11, 13, 14, 15, 16), and control the difficulty level of the goal of instruction, often defined by a test (for information on tests, see chap. 9— section on Study Questions—and chap. 15—section on Table of Specifications). Even the instructor varies in the model in several ways, such as phasing out and phasing in student resources. We explain this model and the phase-out, phase-in strategy in greater detail in chap. 12, ''An Instructional Blueprint.'' If instructors make the necessary adjustments in the components depicted in the model, then all students, regardless of their level of development, can make successful progress in reading and learning from text.

We wrote a new chapter on text features that includes an inventory for evaluating the friendliness of texts. The inventory enables the teacher to determine the degree to which the text has features that facilitate instruction. We also constructed another inventory for evaluating the text-friendliness of teachers. It assesses the degree to which teachers make use of the instructional model in their classroom instruction.

We include information on elementary curricula in each content area chapter. **vii** We also updated all of the chapters by incorporating in them recent research and developments in the field. We still explain how to teach students to participate in groups through discussion and how to conduct a classroom discussion that can develop students' thinking to higher levels of abstraction, generalization, and problem solving (chap. 8). We have an entire chapter on "Letting the Students do the Writing" (chap. 9). We also have added sections on teaching students how to listen.

The greatest change in the content area chapters is in the chapter on English. The change reflects the emphasis in theory and research in English, particularly in writing and responses to literature, that has occurred over the last 5 years. Indeed, the boundary between writing and reading is beginning to disappear as professors, researchers, and teachers have begun to be concerned with the broader category of "literacy."

Although this edition has more chapters in it, we are not too concerned that the text will be unduly long because we recognize that teachers can select appropriate chapters for their courses. Some teachers may skim over the introductory chapters 1–3 and perhaps not be interested in a chapter on theory (chap. 4) or text characteristics (chap. 5). They may want to focus their beginning emphasis on a chapter on strategies for reading and learning from text (chap. 6) and their application to teaching a chapter in a text (chap. 7). Some instructors may have students exercise a choice over content area chapters according to their interests in English (chap. 13), social studies (chap. 14), science (chap. 15), and mathematics (chap. 16). Other teachers who are only concerned with classroom instruction in the content areas may not stress the last two chapters that focus on the role of the reading specialist in diagnosis, operating a lab or center, and involving the faculty in a schoolwide inservice program in reading and learning from text. Thus, through judicious selection, instructors can make the text fit their course objectives.

We wrote, tested, and have been using this text in our own classes over the past 10 years. The text enables us to teach our students the way we want them to teach their classes. We lecture on chapters 1–5, point out the organizing questions for the text toward the end of chapter 1, then explain our model and show them how chapters 4 (Theory), 5 (Text Features), 6, 7, and 11 (Single and Multiple Text Strategies), 8 and 9 (Discussion, Listening, and Writing), 10 (Readability), 11 (Instructor's Phase-in/Phase-Out), and 12 to 16 (Domain specific strategies in the content areas of English, social studies, science, and mathematics) give them the knowledge to manipulate the variables in the model. Then we demonstrate through whole class instruction how to employ a single text strategy, such as an Reading and Learning from Text Guide (RLFT) to a chapter in a content area text that students will use either in student teaching or in their own classrooms (see chap. 7, "Teaching Students to Learn from a Chapter"). Next we divide the class into content area groups and have each group construct its own RLFT Guide for another chapter in the content area text. Finally, students in the class are ready for the assignment of preparing a unit for teaching three chapters from their own content area text and incorporating in it single (chap. 6) and multiple text strategies (chap. 11), just as we have done in our content area chapters. They also have to explain how they will teach their students to listen, discuss, and write as prerequisites for working in groups, particularly in the project method strategy for handling individual differences.

In the last part of our course, we explain how to diagnose an entire class and improve students' abilities for reading and learning from text in classrooms and in schoolwide programs (chap. 17 and 18). Thus, we cover all the information in our text in a 10-week course (one quarter) during the academic year and in a more intensive 6-week course during the summer session.

We are most gratified that students who complete the course report that they continue to use the text as a manual for ideas and procedures for teaching their own classes. We also appreciate the suggestions we have received for this revision from reviewers, professors, and students throughout the country who have been using the first edition, and from Lawrence Erlbaum, Carol Lachman, Robin Weisberg, Hollis Heimbouch, and other members of the Erlbaum staff. As a result of all the changes we have made in this edition—with the help of our secretaries, Wendy Shipley, Jean Hara, Chriss Jones, and Linda Faulkner—we hope that professors and students in other colleges and universities who are in curriculum courses at the elementary, junior, and senior high school levels, reading and learning from text courses, reading specialist programs, and teacher-inservice groups will find the second edition even more useful for knowledge and strategies on how to teach all students to read and learn from text.

Harry Singer
Dan Donlan

Introduction

The ideas in this book are depicted in the graphic organizer on page xiii. It shows that the text has two parts: (a) problems in reading and learning from text and (b) solutions to the problems. By following the arrows you can see the organization of the text and the interrelationships among its ideas. The problems pertain to (a) changes in schools and student characteristics, (b) teachers' attitudes toward teaching reading and learning from text, and (c) students' individual and intraindividual differences in ability to read and learn from text (chapter 3).

The text provides three solutions to the problems:

1. It provides you with knowledge of theories and research on reading and learning from text (chapter 4) that you can use to understand problems in reading and learning from text and generate your own solutions;

2. It explains an instructional model for teaching students to read and learn from text that you can use to enable students to learn text features (chapter 5), develop their resources by having them learn single-text strategies (chapter 6) and their applications to social studies and other content areas (chapter 7), skills (discussion, chapter 8; writing, chapter 9, and listening, also in chapter 9), multiple-text strategies (chapter 11), and achieve the goal of independence in reading and learning from text by phasing yourself out and phasing students in to the use and internalization of these strategies and skills (a blueprint for instruction, chapter 12). Examples show teachers how to apply these strategies to content specific domains, such as English Language Arts (chapter 13), social studies (chapter 14), science (chapter 15), and mathematics (chapter 16); and

3. It contains information and a questionnaire with anticipated answers for a schoolwide program under the principal's direction that consists of a representative faculty committee that learns the limitations of current reading labs and centers (chapter 17), decides to employ a specialist who will develop a reading

and learning from text center that will teach content area reading acquisition and comprehension plus learning from text strategies, and conducts an inservice training program that will teach all the teachers in the school how to teach students to read and learn from text and enable them to progress successfully in all their text-based courses (chapter 18).

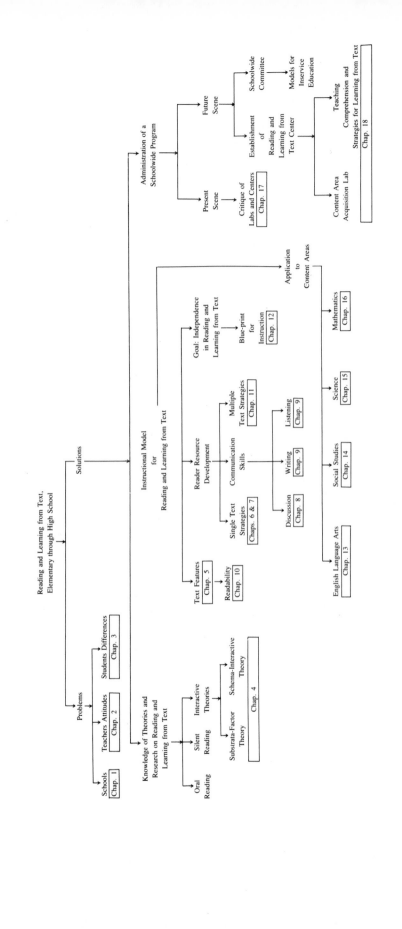

Reading and Learning from Text, Elementary through High School

Problems

Solutions

Schools
Chap. 1

Teachers Attitudes
Chap. 2

Students Differences
Chap. 3

Knowledge of Theories and Research on Reading and Learning from Text

Oral Reading

Silent Reading

Interactive Theories

Substrata-Factor Theory

Schema-Interactive Theory
Chap. 4

Instructional Model for Reading and Learning from Text

Text Features
Chap. 5

Readability
Chap. 10

Reader Resource Development

Single Text Strategies
Chaps. 6 & 7

Communication Skills

Multiple Text Strategies
Chap. 11

Goal: Independence in Reading and Learning from Text

Blue-print for Instruction
Chap. 12

Discussion
Chap. 8

Writing
Chap. 9

Listening
Chap. 9

Application to Content Areas

English Language Arts
Chap. 13

Social Studies
Chap. 14

Science
Chap. 15

Mathematics
Chap. 16

Administration of a Schoolwide Program

Present Scene

Future Scene

Critique of Labs and Centers
Chap. 17

Establishment of Reading and Learning from Text Center

Schoolwide Committee

Models for Inservice Education

Content Area Acquisition Lab

Teaching Comprehension and Strategies for Learning from Text
Chap. 18

1 Problems and Solutions in Reading and Learning from Text in the Schools

CHAPTER OVERVIEW

The ability to learn from text starts to develop at the first-grade level. As students progress through school, teachers' expectations increase for students to learn from text on their own. At the elementary school level, students in the primary grades search for answers to questions from their own and from library texts. At the intermediate grades, the curriculum drastically expands. Teachers now have textbooks in each area of the curriculum and use them for instruction. However, they only group students for instruction during the reading period where students receive further instruction in reading narrative materials. But teachers expect the entire class to read and learn from the same level texts in social studies, science, and mathematics. At the junior and senior high school level, teachers assign chapters to students for homework. At the college level, the expectation is that students will study (learn from texts) 2 hours outside of class for each hour they spend in the classroom. Thus, as students progress through the grades, they spend an increasing amount of time on learning from texts outside the classroom.

Although some students are able to learn from texts, other students in today's classrooms can't seem to learn from the materials the teachers assign. Even students who have been "pulled out" for special reading instruction return to their content classroom unable to understand their textbooks. These students may know the fundamentals of reading, but they can't apply their reading skills to gain information from their classroom texts. In other words, they have *learned to read,* but they can't quite *read to learn*. By the time you have finished this chapter you will (a) have a clearer understanding of the two phases of reading instruction—learning to read and learning from text, (b) learn how schools have traditionally handled reading instruction, and (c) discover the problems schools must solve in order to provide equality of educational opportunity for all students and produce students who are independent and active readers and learners.

1

GRAPHIC ORGANIZER

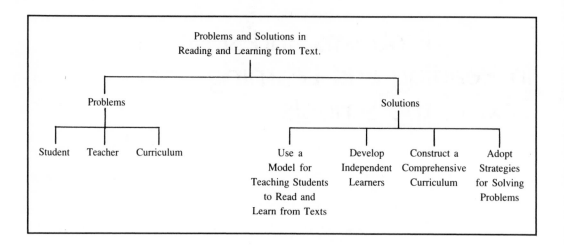

PREPOSED QUESTIONS

1. State three problems that students have manifested in reading and learning from text at each school level.
2. List one problem in reading and learning from text in the content areas of arithmetic, social studies, science, and literature.
3. Can you cite any evidence that teachers today are being prepared to teach students how to read and learn from texts in the content areas at each school level?
4. What changes have occurred in schools, students, and content that require changes in the curriculum and instruction?
5. What are the major components and their interrelationships that are involved in teaching students to read and learn from texts?
6. What are the four major categories of difficulties in reading and learning from text? What are their symptoms and remedies?
7. What are the major problems that administrators and teachers need to solve in order to integrate instruction in reading and learning from text into the curriculum at each school level and in each course?

PROBLEMS IN TEACHING STUDENTS TO READ AND LEARN FROM TEXTS

To introduce the text, we start with four instructional problems that teachers need to solve in teaching students to read and learn from text. The text provides solutions to these and other instructional problems in reading and learning from text.

Student Problems

CLASSROOM SITUATIONS
Individual Differences

Henry Wyatt is a seventh-grade social studies teacher at Ratter Junior High School. The school district has adopted only one textbook that he can use for these seventh-grade classes. Although all of the students are the same appropriate chronological age, Henry is concerned about the wide range of differences in the classes. For instance, the test scores that he has received from the central office indicate that in his third-period class, there is a 10-year span of achievement: One student in his class reads at the third-grade level whereas another student reads at Grade 12. In addition, two thirds of the students in the class read below the seventh-grade level, the level at which the textbook is written. Henry wonders how he can teach this group of students to learn social studies content from the one textbook. HENRY COULD FIND POSSIBLE SOLUTIONS TO HIS CLASSROOM PROBLEMS BY READING CHAPTERS 3, 5, 6, 7, and 14 OF THIS BOOK. Chapter 3, "Individual and Intraindividual Differences Among Students," explains why Henry, and many teachers like him, teach classes with students of widely varying achievement and ability levels. Chapter 5, "Text Features," provides Henry with guidelines on what features a good textbook has and how to adjust to using a text that isn't so good. Chapter 6, "Single-Text Strategies," provides Henry with a number of useful classroom strategies for teaching a heterogeneous class such as his how to learn from a common text [by providing for the individual differences among the students]. Chapter 7, "Teaching Students to Learn from a Chapter," provides Henry with a rich variety of lesson materials for teaching his seventh graders to learn from their social studies text. Finally, chapter 14, "Social Studies," describes a complete instructional plan for teaching students to learn from the various kinds of textual material in social studies.

Word Problems in Arithmetic

Hedy Davis teaches fifth grade at Driscoll Elementary School. She is currently trying to teach fractions to a group of nine children. Their diagnostic tests indicated they are ready for such instruction. She is frustrated because most of these children can work the problems when they are in number form. However, when she assigns word problems, the students cannot seem to make the transfer. What is particularly bothersome to Hedy is that the students' reading scores indicate that they can all read at grade level or better. HEDY WOULD FIND

SOME ANSWERS TO THIS PROBLEM BY READING CHAPTERS 2, 4, and 16. Chapter 2, "Teachers' Attitudes," explains the difference between knowing how to read and knowing how to learn from text in a specific content area, such as mathematics. Chapter 4, "Theories and Research on Reading and Learning from Text," further clarifies the difference. Chapter 16, "Mathematics," provides Hedy with a number of helpful teaching strategies for getting students to learn from mathematics texts, including the comprehension of word problems.

Motivating Students

Bill Mara teaches seventh-grade English at Monroe High School. Most of the students in Bill's classes are of average or below-average ability. They tend not to turn in homework, fail to read required reading assignments from the literature text, and tend to have problems writing clearly, and most are content not to participate in classroom activities, particularly discussion. They are complaining either that the work is too hard or that it is too boring. Bill has tried to interest them in reading and creative writing, but he feels that he is fighting an uphill battle. BILL CAN LEARN SOME INSTRUCTIONAL PROCEDURES AND ACTIVITIES FROM READING CHAPTERS 8, 9, and 13 that would enable him to motivate his students. Chapter 8, "Letting the Students Do the Talking," describes a series of classroom-tested methods for involving students in responding to their text readings in discussion and other small-group activities. Chapter 9, "Letting the Students Do the Writing and Listening," shows Bill how to plan motivational writing activities that can get the student actively involved in learning from the textbook. In addition, this chapter describes activities for increasing students' active listening and note-taking skills. Finally chapter 13, "The English Language Arts," provides Bill with a master plan for planning sequences of reading, writing, and speaking activities that will help students comprehend their literature text.

Variety and Interesting Instruction

Carol Willbanks has been teaching high school science for 30 years. In that time she has always been on the lookout for innovative ways of presenting content to her students. She likes to assign library projects, but has some difficulty directing the students' work once they get to the library. Also, she would like to learn new teaching strategies that would make her textbooks more useful to the students. CAROL SHOULD READ CHAPTERS 11, 12, 15, 17, and 18. Chapter 11, "Multiple-Text Strategies," shows Carol three ways to make library projects work for students. Chapter 12, "An Instructional Blueprint," provides Carol with a year-long plan for varying her teaching techniques to ensure that by the end of the year her students will be independent learners. Chapter 15, "Science," describes a variety of single- and multiple-text strategies that Carol can use to make her students learn from their science texts more effectively. Finally, chapters 17, "The Present: Centers for Reading," and 18, "The Future: A

School-wide Program,'' suggest some ways in which Carol and teachers like her can receive useful in-service education in getting students to learn from text.

If you are like Henry, Hedy, Bill, or Carol, you will find this book informative and helpful. If you haven't begun teaching yet, you will find that this book will prepare you to deal effectively with classroom problems that result from students' inability to learn from their textbooks. AND WHAT ABOUT THE STUDENTS?

In the next section, we introduce problems in reading and learning from text in a classroom situation from the viewpoint of students. What problems do they face?

CASE STUDIES

Joe, Jo-Ann, and Jerry have a lot in common. First, they are graduates of a K–12 educational system. Second, they are venturing into the world of college or work. Third, they are frustrated by their inability to function. Fourth, presumably literate, they are hampered by inadequate reading and learning skills. These three teenagers are not unlike many others who have learned to read, yet they can't make their reading work for them. In addition, large numbers of students can't even function in the classroom itself, let alone outside the classroom. Is the high school, then, failing those students it is supposed to educate?

Comprehending College Textbooks

Joe graduated from high school with honors. His high grade point average earned him a scholarship to a local university. Once enrolled in classes, Joe became frustrated. The reading assignments were frequent and lengthy. The lectures supplemented rather than repeated the assigned reading material. Joe, accustomed to As and Bs, continually received Cs and Ds. No matter how long he labored over the books, his grades remained low. After his first semester, the university placed him on probation and his counselor recommended a remedial reading program or some tutorial assistance that would help Joe to comprehend college textbooks.

Literacy in the Workplace

Between her 11th and senior year, Jo-Ann decided to seek a summer job. A newly opened department store was hiring part-time salesclerks. At the store's personnel office Jo-Ann was handed several forms to fill out in advance of an interview. The forms confused her. First of all, there were words she didn't understand: *residence, employment history, reference, title of position, verification.* Second, she wasn't always sure whether she should be writing above or below the lines. Third, she filled in areas of the application form reserved for the interviewer. Fourth, when asked to describe her strengths and weaknesses she didn't know what to write. In frustration, she tore up the forms and left the store without an interview.

Literacy in Each Content Area

Jerry had a part-time job at his uncle's garage. He wanted to work into a full-time position now that he was a high school graduate. Only one aspect of the job bothered Jerry: He found using the computerized parts catalog tremendously difficult. Occasionally, Jerry's uncle, working on an engine, would send Jerry to the catalog to get information. Jerry could never find anything. Finally, the uncle told Jerry that if he wanted a full-time job at the station he would have to learn how to use the catalog.

Just 2 years ago, Jerry was an 11th-grade student at Monroe High School, which you will learn about in chapter 2. Like many students at Monroe, Jerry took a number of courses that used textbooks for homework reading assignments. On a given day, Jerry might have to complete as many as four homework reading assignments in order to be prepared for classes the next day. Here are some short excerpts from textbooks that Jerry had to learn from:

English

Stealthily, the twisted, surly crone made her ritualistic, gruesome journey into what may have been the darkest edges of consciousness, relieved only by the thought that some day she could wreak vengeance on the source of her physical and emotional misshapenness.

American History

Newcomers to the American shores brought with them the remnants of their past, specifically, their religious customs. Some colonies, reputed for religious tolerance, housed diverse religions with little turmoil. Inhabitants of other colonies, however, were treated with a disdain reminiscent of their past European experiences.

Science

The simple household experiment you have just read about illustrates two scientific principles: chemical change and osmosis. The acetic acid of the vinegar combined chemically with calcium of the eggshell, causing the shell to dissolve. Subsequently, the water (thinner) is drawn through the membrane of the egg into the albumin (thicker) causing the egg to expand.

Mathematics

George has a limited amount of money to spend on a used car. Dealer A offers to sell George a given car under these conditions. George is to put $300 down and make 12 equal monthly payments of $100, including interest. Dealer B offers to sell George the same kind of car for $200 down and 18 monthly payments of $75, including interest. Dealer C, for the same kind of car, will charge no interest but will require $100 down and 24 monthly payments of $35. Which dealer is giving George the best deal? How would you prove it to George's satisfaction?

Confronted with these assignments, Jerry is perplexed. He knows that he learned to read in elementary school, but, somehow, words he comprehends are patterned into sentences and paragraphs that have no meaning for him. Anyhow, if he could manage to struggle through his English assignment there would be no guarantee that he could understand the history or science chapters, let alone solve the mathematics problems. Faced with frustration, Jerry, basically a conscientious teenager, closed his books and either turned on the television or went out to work on his car. It is no surprise that, 2 years later, Jerry, an able mechanic, couldn't hold down a job in his uncle's garage. He had not learned how to get meaning from printed text.

Teacher Problems

OVERCOMING LACK OF TRAINING

Many content area teachers are now being prepared by their education and training to know and apply instructional strategies designed to foster students' development in reading and learning from texts. In 1973, only nine states required prospective high school teachers to have had a course in reading instruction (Estes & Piercey, 1973), but in 1984 the number of states requiring such a course had increased to 37 (Farrell & Cirrincione, 1984). Apparently, these states have recognized the need to prepare content area teachers for the wide range of individual differences in the ability of students to read and learn from text that they will encounter in their classrooms.

NEED TO TEACH BOTH PHASES
OF READING DEVELOPMENT

Reading development has two overlapping phases (a) Learning how to read and (b) using reading to learn from texts. Elementary school teachers have long been providing instruction in the first phases of reading development: teaching students how to read (Hill, 1971; Smith, 1965a). But high school teachers have not been systematically teaching students to improve in the second phase of reading development: using reading to learn from texts in content areas.[1]

Learning how to read is mastered by most students prior to the eighth grade, but reading to learn from text or any printed material of any length is an ability that continues to develop throughout a person's lifetime (Bloom, 1971; Cronbach, 1971).[2] Teachers in such content areas as English, social studies, science, and math, who do teach students how to read and learn from texts, contribute to both phases of reading development, but mostly to the second. They teach technical vocabulary and concepts, background information, patterns of writing, unique symbols, particular literary devices (allusions, similies, metaphors, personifications), and specialized modes of inquiry characteristic of their content areas (Moore, 1969; H.A. Robinson, 1975; Russell & Fea, 1963; Singer, 1973b; Smith, 1964a, 1964b).

---

[1]The word *text* in the singular refers to any printed material of any length; the word texts in the plural refers specifically to textbooks.

[2]Complete references are located at the back of the book.

In this book we stress classroom instructional strategies in reading and learning from texts for content areas and an instructional blueprint for their use in each content area. This blueprint emphasizes a systematic progression from student dependence on teachers to independence in reading and learning from texts.

TEACHING TODAY'S STUDENTS: PLUGGED IN AND TURNED OFF

The stereotype of the American teenager either staring mindlessly into a television tube or plugged into a stereo headset is partially supported by research. Goodlad (1983), for instance, found that in an average week, students spend more time watching television than they do attending school. Telfer and Kann (1984) noted that 11-grade students spend an average of over 2 hours a day listening to music, whether by radio, record, or tape. Electronic media, no doubt, compete favorably for a student's out-of-class time. The question is whether heavy exposure to these media negatively affects achievement. Common sense would argue that the effect is harmful. However, research evidence is ambivalent. Gough (1979) found that 89% of 595 students in Virginia had been motivated to read at least one book because of a commercial television broadcast. Salomon (1981) reviewed research which revealed that the amount of television viewing done at early ages positively affected the amount of reading done in later years. Less supportive were the findings of Moldenhauer and Miller (1980), which indicated that television had no effect, either positive or negative, on reading achievement. Both Neuman and Prowda (1982) and Telfer and Kann (1984) found slightly negative correlations between the amount of time exposed to electronic media and reading achievement. Because Telfer and Kann discovered that as children grow older they spend less time watching television and more time listening to music, they suggest that teachers make positive use of these media in their instructional planning. Likewise, Shoup (1984) sees television as the teacher's friend, supplying both instructional programming and useful commercial offerings.

RAISING STUDENT AND CURRICULUM STANDARDS

During the decade 1975–1985, the American high school was buffeted by two contradictory movements aimed at making high school graduation difficult to achieve. The first movement was reflected in a growing national trend to require competency tests for high school graduation. In addition to meeting school district course-of-study demands, students were to pass tests of "minimum competency" or "proficiency" in basic skills areas, such as reading, mathematics, and writing. In some states, students unable to pass these tests by high school graduation are denied a diploma, though they may have completed all other graduation requirements and maintained a respectable grade point average. Although programs in proficiency in basic skills were being implemented, a series of school reform reports (Boyer, 1983; National Commission on Excellence in

Education, 1983; National Science Board Commission on Precollege Education in Mathematics, Science, and Technology, 1983; Task Force on Education for Economic Growth, 1983) emphasized the "lack of excellence" in contemporary high schools. Among the collective recommendations that caught public fancy were (a) an increase in graduation requirements in English, mathematics, science, and social studies, (b) establishment of programs in computer literacy, (c) an increase in the school day and school year, and (d) an enhancement of the professional image of teachers, particularly with substantial salary increases. Whereas the proficiency text curriculum was a response to the amorphous "back-to-basics movement," the parallel "move to excellence" was a response to scholars and academicians who decried the alleged intellectual flabbiness of high school curricula. Some critics lamented the physical and emotional climate of the public high school. Goodlad (1983), for instance, found many high schools to be lackluster and oppressive places where too much time is consumed dealing with noninstructional matters, such as record keeping, routine, and order. Just as Goodlad views maintenance of order as only one area of misdirected energy, Cusick (1983) views school administrators' concern for "keeping the lid on" as overshadowing attention to teacher effectiveness, student welfare, campus violence, and instructional appropriateness. Whereas Cusick sees no solution to the problem, Sizer (1984), more optimistically, recommends curricular reforms that will cause teachers to teach more effectively and students to learn more effectively. One such recommendation is to limit high school departments to four: (a) inquiry and expression, (b) mathematics and science, (c) literature and the arts, and (d) philosophy and history. Some states acted quickly in response to these bids to reform. California, for instance, has legislation mandating both proficiency testing and, subsequently, more rigorous academic requirements for high school graduation. Although many schools throughout the country have undergone incidental change in the past three decades, instruction and the curriculum have remained fairly traditional. However, the small student population of high ability and achievement for whom instruction and curriculum were originally intended now exists mostly in the college preparatory program. Remember Joe, Jo-Ann, and Jerry. They are examples of the large student population of wider range in ability who are now completing high school. Therefore, teachers have two major problems to solve: (a) acquisition of instructional strategies for teaching students with a wider range of abilities and achievement to satisfy the higher standards and (b) modification of the curriculum to enable students to function more effectively in response to the demands of modern society.

Curricular Problems

EMPHASIS ON PROCESSES

Generally, high schools, and many junior high schools, are departmentalized into areas of content—history, mathematics, English, and so on. Each content area is divided into segments and assigned to certain grade levels. The teacher's perceived function is, understandably, to make sure the content is absorbed by the students. When students come to class knowing how to read, write, and speak, the teacher's task is relatively easy. The teacher can become frustrated when students lack these skills: they may not be able to read the textbook independently, may not be able to discuss the course content in class, and may not be able to write reports or take examinations. As a result, students are labeled *deficient*. In effect, these students enter class as predetermined failures.

The role of the teacher as dispenser of knowledge or content worked well while the population was more homogeneous. However, the current times demand that teachers do more than teach content, especially now since Public Law 94–142 has required that many exceptional children be mainstreamed, that is, returned to regular classrooms. Understandably, teachers feel pressured to cover the curriculum, even at the expense of student comprehension, but perhaps, as Alvin Toffler suggested over a decade ago in *Future Shock* (1970), students need to be taught processes for learning the expanding content rather than just remembering the content itself.

CURRICULUM MODERNIZATION

The revolution wrought by the advent of personal computers may eventually require schools to develop a curriculum in computer literacy. This curriculum is likely to become another basic skill with its own proficiency levels, assessment, and requirements for a high school diploma (Singer, Dreher, & Kamil, 1982). Throughout this text, we incorporate computer information in appropriate chapters; for example, use of computers for composition is discussed in chapter 13, "The English Language Arts."

EDUCATION FOR THE PRESENT
AS WELL AS THE FUTURE

Five years ago, a high school graduate who could read, write, and calculate was considered at least minimally proficient in learning skills. Today, students need computer literacy, not only because computers are increasingly affecting the way we shop, pay bills, and bank, but also because computers are becoming a significant instructional resource. Consider, again, the so-called basic skills. Computer software has the potential for making teaching and learning more effective and efficient (Benfort, 1983; Guthrie, 1981; O'Donnell, 1983). In fact, software is becoming as much a part of classroom texts as is the traditional textbook. With respect to the teaching of writing, computers have the potential for reducing writer's block through word processing programs that make editing and revising relatively painless (SWRL reference). Mathematics software has made the learning of difficult concepts more pleasurable.

Knowledge of computers will help the student deal with the present. But what about the future? Neuman (1984) suggests that *teletext,* the telecasting of printed text by way of one's own television set, has the potential for replacing traditional written text. Fortier (1983) predicts that the printed symbol may sometime soon be replaced by electronic impulses that bypass the eyes and move directly to the brain. Evidence supports the notion, then, that in some areas the computer may well be obsolescent. It becomes imperative, therefore, that schools teach students to take advantages of current technology as well as providing them with strategies for dealing with rapid technological change.

NEED FOR A FOCUS

Solutions to the many problems facing today's high school will not come easily. Some problems with which education is expected to deal often lie outside the school's sphere—de facto segregation, inflation, recession, unemployment, and intolerance. By graduation, a young person may have salable skills, read well, and communicate clearly in speech and writing, but still be unemployable because of social and economic conditions outside the school's control. In other words, Jerry could learn to use the computerized parts catalog but his uncle might not have the money to hire him. However, if education has taught Jerry to be an independent learner, he will at least be able to cope intelligently with the outside wold. He will be able to learn new skills readily and convince prospective employers that he has something valuable to offer. Perhaps teaching students to be independent learners should be the focus of the school's curriculum so that students can adapt to a continually changing world (Buswell, 1956).

SOLUTIONS

Use of a Model for Teaching Students How to Read and Learn from Text

A model for teaching students how to read and learn from text is depicted in Figure 1.1. This model contains four factors: (a) student resources, (b) text features, (c) goal(s), often defined by tests, and (d) the role of the teacher. The model indicates that students interact with a text to achieve a goal, such as construction of meaning based on their interaction with the text; attainment of this goal provides information or feedback to the instructor and to the students. This feedback may influence the instructor who may then provide instructional input to enhance students' resources, such as explanation of vocabulary or clarification of information needed for making an inference; modify the text, perhaps by inserting some additional material students might need to organize the information in the text (Flood, Lapp, Singer, & Mathison, 1985); or modify the goal(s) of instruction. Thus, the instructor influences each of the factors in the model; in turn, the other factors in the model also influence the instructor.

FIGURE 1.1. Model for Teaching Students How to Read and Learn from Text.

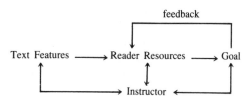

We explain in greater detail in chapter 4 students' resources and how they interact with text to attain reading and learning from text goals, such as the construction of meaning for the text. Chapter 5 explains text features. Chapter 12 has a blueprint for instruction that explains the role of the instructor in our model. Throughout the text are strategies for teaching students how to read and learn from text and attain the goal(s) of instruction from single texts (chapter 6) and multiple texts (chapter 11) and in each content area (chapters 11–15). Thus, almost the entire text explains the factors in the model.

Chapter 17 explains the role of the Reading and Learning-from-Text Specialist and a Center for Reading and Learning from Text. The last chapter contains information on a program and sequence for in-service education that will enable a school to phase in reading and learning from text throughout the school.

Develop Independent Learners

Whether you argue that school is preparation for life or a part of life, you might agree that educated people are independent: they can adjust, they can adapt, they can accommodate, they can cope, they can control their lives. The independent person, in effect, is always learning and altering behavior as a result of what is learned.

English teachers can teach students how to use language effectively and how to appreciate literature. Social studies teachers can show them how knowledge of the past helps individuals deal with the future. Mathematics teachers can demonstrate how people can cope with the world of measures and economics. Science teachers can explain the order of the universe and arouse curiosity to find out more. Physical education teachers indicate how people can be healthy. And the list goes on. Teachers use content as a means to develop independence. If students cannot comprehend the content or learn how to use it, they will not function independently. It is hoped that students like Joe, Jo-Ann, and Jerry can become independent learners.

All teachers want their students to be independent learners. What teacher, for example, would reject a class of students who complete every homework reading assignment and come prepared to discuss it the next day? The problem often is that teachers *expect* students to be independent learners before instruction begins. This assumption results in the students ''covering'' content without understanding it. In addition, many students function independently in one area of content, but not in another. For example, students who can read a novel or build an engine by reading a set of instructions can be deemed by science teachers to be non-readers.

Every secondary school teacher is a content specialist. As a content specialist, the teacher is most knowledgeable in the thinking processes related to that content and the types of discussion and writing that students must perform to function well in that content area. No reading specialist can know mathematics, science, industrial arts, and history well enough to teach any student to read independently in all of those areas. No English teacher should be expected to teach students how to write science reports and social studies term papers. Likewise, no content teacher has time or experience enough to teach students reading acquisition skills or the basic fundamentals of sentence and paragraph construction. As a result, because 95% of the high school students can read, talk, and write minimally, the content teacher's responsibility is to show the student how to write about it. If students can process information independently, it matters less that they "cover the text."

Many schools have attempted to retrain their teachers to teach process as well as content. Institutions of teacher education offer preservice courses in content area reading. Articles in professional journals such as *Language Arts, English Journal, The Reading Teacher,* and *Journal of Reading* deal with the teaching of reading in different content areas. Professional organizations plan conferences that focus on the problems of teaching from text materials. School workshops train teachers in the use of specific strategies, such as Directed Reading Activity (DRA), survey, question, read, recite, review (SQ3R), and in the development of reading guides. Many times these efforts pay off with increased student motivation and performance. But too often, strategies are employed without a system, either a classroom system or a schoolwide system.

Construct a Comprehensive Program

If schools decide to deal with the task of trying to teach all students to be independent learners, they must develop a comprehensive program. If a school's goal is student independence, then each teacher's classroom goal must be to promote student independence. Teachers must not relegate the responsibility of teaching textual reading to the reading teacher. Nor must teachers expect students to come to class fluent readers, proficient speakers, and competent writers. Furthermore, teachers must not expect all students to perform at the same level. Instead, teachers must be willing to offer guidance where needed, to individualize class assignments, and to know when to withdraw aid. In effect, an organized program for handling individual differences in the ability to read and learn from text must integrate a student's determination to learn independently, the teacher's instructional framework, and the administration's willingness to support this teacher-student effort.

Adopt Strategies for Solving Problems

DEFICIENCIES, DEFECTS, DISRUPTIONS, AND DIFFERENCES (4 Ds)

Actually, high schools need different strategies or programs for dealing with four types of difficulties that make up the range of individual differences in ability to read and learn from text. Special classes or reading laboratories for learning to read are necessary for some high school students. But these classes are not sufficient for meeting the instructional needs of high school students who have one of these types of difficulty in reading and learning from text:

1. Some of these students have a *deficiency* in reading; they are still unable to pronounce many of the words, general as well as technical, in their texts. The percentage of these students varies from school to school. Some schools, particularly schools with a large number of bilingual students, have a much higher percentage of students who are still in the acquisition phase of reading development.

Another deficiency may affect students who are beyond the acquisition stage of reading development, but have not done much reading, or students who did not learn to read till late in their school careers: they may have a *knowledge deficiency*. They may not have read as widely or as deeply as the average student. Hence, they do not have adequate prior knowledge to draw upon for making inferences and interpretation. Consequently, they have a more difficult reading task than their peers because they have more *new knowledge* to acquire. This knowledge deficiency may be reflected not only in range and depth of knowledge stored in memory but also in a vocabulary level that is lower than expected according to the students' mental ability.

2. A small percentage of students may have physical or physiological *defects,* such as visual or auditory handicaps, that may interfere with ability to read.

3. A third group of students, also relatively small, may experience severe *disruptions,* such as social or emotional disturbances, that adversely affect their ability to concentrate on reading and learning from text. However, varying degrees of social or emotional disturbances can affect any reader. For example, factors within the social situation may result in emotional disturbances during oral reading. Readers who are susceptible to such disturbances are likely to perform better in silent than in oral reading. Factors within individuals such as lack of confidence may also adversely affect reading performance (Athey, 1985; Athey & Holmes, 1967), particularly when readers have both difficult text and questions to answer on the text (Dreher & Singer, 1986; Singer & Bean, 1982a, 1982b).

4. Most of these students are beyond the reading acquisition stage of development; they do not have any defects or any serious emotional disturbances; yet they may still have difficulties in reading and learning from texts in the content areas because their assigned texts do not match their ability. Some students read at the 8th-grade level but their texts are at the 10th-grade level or higher. Or their reading abilities may be at the same level as the general difficulty level of the text but the students lack the specific ability to learn from the text in a particular content area; they may not have the specific skills for interpreting graphs or charts in social studies, comprehending symbols and manipulating them in chemistry, understanding irony and satire in English, or transforming and applying formulae in mathematics. These students do not have deficiencies, or defects, or disruptions; they have a *difference,* a mismatch between their abilities and the demands of their assigned texts (Nicholson, 1985; Samuels, 1970; Wiener & Cromer, 1967).

These four types of difficulties can be labeled the 4 Ds of reading difficulties. They cover the entire range of difficulties in reading and learning from text at the high school level. These difficulties, with definitions, examples, suggested remedies, and high school programs for ameliorating them, are summarized in Table 1.1.

The classroom teacher's responsibility is to refer students with three of the four types of difficulties listed in Table 1.1 to a reading specialist or a school counselor. The reading specialist should be called upon to diagnose students with deficiencies in reading, the first type, and to provide improvement programs that will help them read materials in their content area classes. (See chapter 18 for teaching reading acquisition using content area materials.) Although the content area teachers will use strategies in the classroom that will help students with deficiencies (see chapter 6, "Single-Text Strategies" and chapter 11, "Multiple-Text Strategies"), these students need additional and more concentrated instruction in learning how to read than can be offered in a content area course.

Students with defects, the second type of difficulty, should also be referred to

TABLE 1.1. Four Types of Difficulties in Reading and Learning from Texts

Type of Difficulty	Definition	Example	Remedy	Program
1. Deficiency	Inadequacy in skill development.	Inability to identify printed words.	Teach word recognition skills.	Reading acquisition classes.
2. Defect	Physical or physiological difficulty.	Visual difficulty, such as astigmatism.	Medical screening and referral to appropriate specialist or agency for correction.	Individual diagnosis and referral.
3. Disruption	Emotional interference in reading and learning.	Anxiety over inability to achieve in school.	Eliminate cause for disruption.	Individual diagnosis and referral to guidance or counseling staff.
4. Difference	Mismatch between instruction and student capability or mode of learning.	Texts in content area that are too difficult for some or most students.	Adjust instruction to individual students.	Classroom instruction strategies for handling individual differences.

the reading specialist for screening and perhaps medical referral. But content area teachers and classmates can also help some of these students. Those who have hearing problems can be seated in the center of the room so they are equidistant from all sources of sounds and hence more likely to hear their class-mates' recitations as well as their teacher's oral instruction. In the case of students with severe hearing difficulties, including deafness, classmates may volunteer to be buddies. The task of the buddy is to communicate missed infor-mation by repeating it orally during or after class, by providing the information in writing, or by sharing notes; some buddies may even want to learn to commu-nicate through sign language.

Students with the third type of difficulty, persistent emotional interferences in learning, should be referred to counselors for diagnosis and intervention. Con-comitantly, classroom teachers (in consultation with the school counselor) can make appropriate classroom adjustments in order to relieve classroom stress upon these students.

For the fourth type of difficulty, differences, the classroom teacher has the main responsibility. The emphasis in this book is on helping the classroom teacher handle this type of difficulty by providing strategies that the classroom teacher can use to teach all students to read and learn from texts in the content areas.

We perceive that the differences difficulty is the greatest problem confronting classroom teachers at all grade levels and in all content areas. The magnitude of the problem is described and analyzed in chapter 3. However, solutions to the four types of difficulties listed in Table 1.1 are not solely the responsibility of the classroom teacher; the entire high school staff has to be involved. To resolve the difficulties, the entire staff will need to have answers to the questions in the following section.

SPECIFIC PROBLEMS AND SOLUTIONS
To undertake a comprehensive program to teach reading and learning from texts, a high school staff will need to deal with specific problems:

1. What are the conflicting attitudes of content area teachers toward teach-ing students to learn from text? (chapter 2)
2. How can teachers assess individual differences in achievement levels in the classroom? (chapter 3)
3. What changes in definition, instruction, and assessment of reading have occurred over the past 75 years? (chapter 4)
4. What are the major features of texts and how can they be evaluated and written so that they can be friendly to students, that is, facilitate learning? (chapters 5 and 10)
5. What strategies are useful in teaching students to learn from text in each content area? (chapters 6, 7, and 10)

6. How might teachers use discussion and writing activities to facilitate students' response to text? (chapters 8 and 9)

7. What sort of instructional framework can teachers develop to encourage students to become independent learners? (chapter 12)

8. What particular instructional problems arise in individual content areas, and how must teachers deal with these problems? (chapters 13 through 16)

9. How do schools currently teach students who are referred because of defects, deficiencies, disruptions, and low reading achievement? (chapter 17)

10. How can students with deficiencies learn how to read in ways consistent with their content area courses? (chapter 17)

11. How can administrators encourage development and maintenance of an all-school reading program? (chapter 18)

The purpose of this book is to show teachers and administrators how to find answers to these questions. Chapters in this book deal with the eleven problems in sequence.

Therefore, this book has value for the student teacher who will soon be joining a faculty, as well as for the seasoned teacher, reading specialist, department chairperson, or principal. In the book, we focus on explaining to teachers how to provide for equality of educational opportunity without stigmatizing students and how to encourage and educate secondary school students to become independent learners.

SUMMARY

Many of today's students are unable to learn from text, even though they have learned to read. Part of this problem is caused by the evolving nature of the school system and its curriculum. In effect, students are staying in school longer and are taking courses from a continually expanding curriculum. The result is that today's students have wider differences in ability and achievement than ever before. Schools need, then, to be sensitive to the problems students have in learning from their textbooks, specifically those problems caused by (a) deficiency, (b) defects, (c) disruption, and (d) differences. Teaching students to be independent learners is a schoolwide responsibility. The process begins with changing attitudes.

ACTIVITIES

1. If possible, visit the high school from which you graduated. Describe any changes you observe, focusing on:
   a. course offerings

b. makeup of student body
c. the physical plant
d. special programs
What do you attribute these changes to?
2. Interview a teacher who has taught at a high school for over 20 years. What changes have occurred at this school, as the teacher perceives them? How is the school dealing with these changes?

2 Teachers' Attitudes

CHAPTER OVERVIEW

If a school is to make a comprehensive attack on reading and learning problems, it must first focus on the attitudes that its teachers have concerning the teaching of reading and learning from texts. Primary grade, most intermediate grade and some junior high school teachers have a favorable attitude toward teaching students how to read and learn from texts, but many secondary school teachers, trained as content specialists, are hesitant to teach those reading and learning skills that help students comprehend their textbooks. In this chapter, you examine the attitudes of certain teachers on the Monroe High School faculty. You then see how these attitudes evolved, by studying a brief history of Monroe High's development. (As you read, compare Monroe High School with the high school you attended.) Finally, you examine one specific method of measuring teachers' attitudes concerning teaching reading and learning from texts.

GRAPHIC ORGANIZER

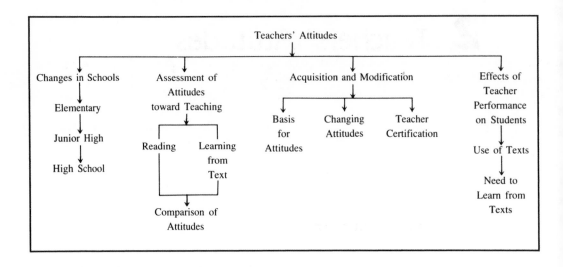

PREPOSED QUESTIONS

1. What are the attitudes of teachers at each school level toward teaching students to read and learn from text?
2. How does your attitude toward teaching reading or teaching students to learn from text differ from junior and senior high school teachers' attitudes?
3. What changes occur in high school teachers' attitudes when they are asked to teach reading versus teaching students to learn from text?
4. What is the basis for teachers' attitudes toward teaching reading?
5. How do teachers' attitudes toward use of textbooks in classes affect students' perceptions and use of textbooks?
6. Are ability and attitude toward learning from text significant factors in achievement at the college level?
7. Can ability to learn from text be improved at the high school and college levels? If so, what strategies will effect this improvement?

CHANGES IN SCHOOLS

In the past century some aspects of the schools have changed and others have not changed at all. Larry Cuban (1984), in his 18-month historical study of how teachers taught between 1890 and 1980, found that despite periodic attempts at school reform, classroom instruction has managed to undergo few changes. In one part of his study, he comments that the schools he observed looked markedly like those schools he had attended in the 1950s.

Whereas Cuban's study focused on instructional practices, constancy and change in curriculum can also be examined. Of the three school structures—elementary school, junior high/middle school, senior high school—the most radical changes over time have occurred at the senior high school level, mandatory education's "Last Chance." Neither the elementary school nor the junior high/middle school have been so strongly affected by external changes in the nature of society.

Driscoll Elementary School: An Example of Minimal Change

Driscoll Elementary School, where Hedy Davis is a fifth-grade teacher, was built in 1962, to accommodate expanding enrollment in the Shelter Views neighborhood of Monroe, California. By 1973, however, student enrollment declined sharply, and Driscoll closed one wing of the school. In 1974, the Monroe Unified School District began using the closed wing for an alternative school for emotionally disturbed elementary school students from the district's 11 elementary schools. Ms. Davis has been teaching at Driscoll since 1964. In the more than two decades she has taught, she has actually seen little change in the curriculum, other than the abandonment of "new math" programs in favor of the more "traditional approaches." Other teachers in the school claim there has been a reduced emphasis on social studies, science, music, and art and a corresponding increased emphasis on reading, arithmetic skills, writing, and language development—a response to the "back-to-basics" movement of the middle and late 1970s. Hedy has noted that "kids are acting up and out" more than they used to and she attributes this, rightly or wrongly, to loss of parental supervision, divorce, single-parent families, and working mothers.

Ratter Junior High: An Example of Surface Change

Ratter Junior High, where Henry Wyatt teaches seventh-grade social studies, was built in 1931, when Monroe City Schools decided to move the seventh- and eighth-grade students in its three elementary schools and the ninth-grade students at Monroe High School to a new common site, in an attempt to reduce crowding at the four affected schools. In 1957, there were so many students at Ratter that the school district built an additional junior high school and then in 1966 a third. As two additional high schools were built in Monroe to accommodate increasing enrollment, the district decided to move the ninth grade back into the high schools and turn the junior high schools into ''middle schools,'' incorporating the sixth grades from the district's elementary schools. In 1976, to ameliorate the declining enrollments in the elementary schools, the district returned the sixth grade, leaving the middle schools with seventh and eighth grades only. In 1980, the term *junior high school* replaced *middle school*. During more than a half century of Ratter's existence, it continued to be staffed by teachers with two distinctly different kinds of preparation. One group of teachers had elementary school background and experience and were prepared to teaching multiple subjects. Another group of teachers were trained in one specific academic area; many of these either moved on to teach at the high school level or expressed interest in doing so. Since Mr. Wyatt, a former fourth-grade teacher, had taught at Ratter since 1970, he experienced some of the district-mandated structural changes. However, he admits that in that time the substance of his seventh-grade social studies curriculum changed very little, except as new editions of traditionally used texts were purchased.

Monroe High School: An Example of Significant Change

As you have seen in chapter 1, both Hedy Davis and Henry Wyatt are concerned about the wide range of differences that exists in their classrooms—and how to deal with these differences by teaching students to learn from a specific text. Generally speaking, teachers who have taught elementary school accept reading and learning from text as part of their teaching responsibilities. High school teachers, on the other hand, tend to be more resistant to the notion that students can benefit from instruction in learning from text.

MONROE HIGH SCHOOL'S PRESENT

Why teach students to learn from texts? Perhaps the best way to answer this question is to let you observe a classroom and faculty lounge in action. This observation has been written in the form of a script for a play, entitled ''Making the Scene.'' Use your imagination to set the scene and then follow the dialogue.

Making the Scene

SCENE ONE: *An English classroom at Monroe High School. It is 2 minutes before the tardy bell rings. Mr. Wallace, the teacher, is standing nervously at the front of the room, watching the students enter the classroom, most of them in rather disorderly fashion—some pushing and shoving, some slinking, a few dropping books and papers at the doorway, some shouting to other students across the room and down the hall. As the tardy bell rings, Mr. Wallace finds himself answering questions from groups of students clustered around his desk: "I was absent yesterday. What was the homework assignment?" "I thought you wanted us to read Carl Sandburg. Joe said you assigned Walt Whitman. I couldn't find him in our textbook." "I couldn't understand the assignment. I thought it was dumb. Do we have to do it?'' Mr. Wallace is desperately trying to free himself from the students clustered around his desk so that he can begin class. Finally, he nervously orders the students to their seats. He notes occasional gliders and wads of papers being passed and thrown around the room. He begins.*

Mr. Wallace: All right, I want you to quiet down. (*The students don't seem to hear him because it is too noisy.*) I said, I want you to quiet down. I am going to give you a quiz on last night's reading assignment. So will you please take out a sheet of paper, write your name in the right-hand corner, and number from one to ten down the red margin.

Joe: I didn't understand the homework assignment.

Jerry: Do I have to take this quiz? I wasn't here yesterday.

Mary: None of us were.

Phil: Do I get an *F* on this if I don't take it?

Chuck: Shut up, you guys. Mr. Wallace is getting mad.

Mr. Wallace: I believe I made last night's reading assignment very clear. Right before you left the classroom to go to third period, I said, ''Read the poems of Carl Sandburg in your textbook.''

Jo-Ann: Yes, but where do you find the poems? They're not all in the same place.

Jim: Yeah, who is this Carl Hamburg?

Phil: Sandburg, you dummy!

Mr. Wallace: First question! (*Groans from the class*) What does it mean to be a hog butcher for the world?

Mary: Hog butcher? What's that? What poem was that in?

Mr. Wallace: Quickly now, so that we can get on to the next question.

Joe: Would you repeat the question?

Mr. Wallace: Second question! What is the city that Sandburg writes most about? (*Time passes as the questions are read; the students groan. Finally, Mr. Wallace collects the papers and begins a discussion on the homework assignment.*)

Mr. Wallace: You will notice that the assignment I gave you was to test your ingenuity in finding the poetry. As Jo-Ann noted, the poems are not in the same place. One of them was on page 54, one of them on page 89, one on page 107, and the last one on page 143.

Barry: Why are we reading about Sandburg?

Ellen: That's what I want to know. He's so boring.

Mr. Wallace: He's one of this country's most distinguished poets.

Joe: Mr. Wallace, I found the poems by thumbing through the book, but I couldn't understand them when I tried to read them.

Jo-Ann: I used the index, but I still didn't like them. What do they mean?

Mr. Wallace: It seems to me that you need a little background, first on the nature of poetry, and second on the life of Carl Sandburg. Take out your notebooks. Please take notes while I talk to you about how to read a poem and how to understand the poetry of a man who has made an invaluable contribution to American literature.

(For the next 20 minutes, Mr. Wallace talks to the class about the nature of poetry and how a student should approach a poem differently from a short story. Then he starts a brief biography of Carl Sandburg and quotes lines from the four poems in the textbooks. Phil is yawning and drumming the desk as if he had heard the lecture before. Joe is doodling in his notebook. Jerry is squinting as if he is trying to understand. Jo-Ann is writing a letter to her boyfriend, who

is in the navy. Other members of the class look as if they are taking notes. But one thing all the students have in common: their eyes are glazed and lifeless.) Now that you have this background information, let's discuss the first poem, "Chicago." Has anyone here been to Chicago? *(No students raise their hands.)* It's a beautiful city—lots of tall buildings. There's nothing in this town to equal it. I had a very scary experience one time when I flew to Chicago and the plane lost power over the airport. *(A few students begin to show signs of interest.)* But I don't want to get into that here. There's a picture of Chicago somewhere in the book. You might want to look at it after class. Is there anyone here who would like to read the poem aloud? Joe, why don't you? *(Joe begins to read and it is obvious that his problems with English prevent him from reading aloud effectively. Several students laugh. Mr. Wallace gets angry, and Joe becomes embarrassed but finishes the poem.)*

Ellen: I still don't understand the poem. Let's do some grammar.

Jim: Let's do English for a change. I'm tired of all this literature and stuff.

Mr. Wallace: (pained but persevering) For tonight's homework I want you to reread all of Sandburg's poetry for a test, not a quiz, tomorrow. In addition, I'd like you to read all of the poetry of Emily Dickinson. Try to profit from last night's problems. There will be a quiz on her poetry tomorrow also. Now, you have one minute before the bell rings. Open your books and start reading. *(When Mr. Wallace said Emily Dickinson, one student said, "She neat." Mr. Wallace's pleasure was dimmed when he discovered that the "she" referred to a movie actress, not to Emily Dickinson.)*

(Curtain)

SCENE TWO: *It is lunch time at Monroe High School. Mr. Wallace has just finished eating in the cafeteria and is proceeding in the direction of the faculty lounge. He enters, goes to the corner to draw a cup of coffee from the large urn.*

Mr. Harris: Well, how'd it go today, Wallace?

Mr. Wallace: Don't ask! I may just have had the worst morning of my professional life.

Ms. Stewart: What else is new?

Mr. Phelps: I never knew English teachers had any problems. You're supposed to be different from the rest of us.

Mr. Wallace: I gave those kids a homework assignment to read last night and you'd think by the response today that they don't know how to read.

Ms. Stewart: They don't, and that's because you guys in the English department don't teach them.

Mr. Wallace: Don't lay that on us. We have to teach them how to write and speak.

Mr. Phelps: Yeah, that's not fair. It's those elementary school teachers that don't teach them anything. They can't even locate the correct page numbers in their lab manuals.

Ms. Jones: Why should they? What's relevant about a lab manual?

Mr. Phelps: Social studies is relevant?

Ms. Jones: It's a matter of motivation. My kids can't read, so I tape all the chapters and have them listen to the tapes as they read.

Ms. Stewart: That may work for you, but what about algebra for my ninth graders? How can I tape math problems?

> *Mr. Wallace:* I read aloud to them a lot. When I mentioned Carl Sanburg, one jerk said "Who's Carl Hamburg?" I'm sure those few bright kids in the class are really frustrated by the dummies—I mean, those kids who can learn but don't want to. I feel sorry for those kids who actually don't know how to read. Why have them all in the same class?
>
> *Ms. Stewart:* Don't you remember, three years ago we made a push to return to ability grouping, but the young radicals on our campus claimed that would be stigmatizing kids. Isn't that so, Ms. Jones?
>
> *Ms. Jones:* You're darned right it's stigmatizing them. How would you like to be grouped in Building C with a group of low-ability teachers?
>
> *Ms. Stewart:* I'm grouped that way now!
>
> *(raucous laughter)*
>
> *Mr. Phelps:* It's just a simple matter. Don't let them out of elementary school until they can pass a reading test at the sixth-grade level.
>
> *Mr. Wallace:* What if they can't? Do we hold them back? Do we continue to read to them? Do we kick them out? Do we show movies and play records 5 hours a day?
>
> *Mr. Harris:* If our budget wasn't so overextended as it is, I would say to use different texts for different kids.
>
> *Mr. Phelps:* That would be jolly! I've got all I can handle teaching out of one text, let alone 30.
>
> *Ms. Jones:* I still say it's motivation. Why should these kids learn to read? What's in it for them when they graduate?
>
> *Mr. Wallace:* Are you saying that you can judge which kids will need reading and which ones won't? I'm glad I'm not in your classes.
>
> *Ms. Stewart:* Well, we're not going to solve this problem, at least not today or even in my lifetime.
>
> *Mr. Wallace:* So what do we do in the meantime?
>
> (Curtain)

Mr. Wallace has his own approach and attitudes toward instruction. Attitudes toward teaching vary considerably. Among members of a faculty, a range of attitudes toward any subject and instructional procedure is to be expected. Attitudes toward teaching have evolved as the high school itself has evolved.

Monroe High School is over 100 years old. Mr. Wallace has been on the faculty for 15 years; Ms. Stewart has been at Monroe for 37 years; Ms. Jones for 4 years. Read now a brief history of Monroe High School to see how its development may have affected the attitudes of its teachers. As you read, compare Monroe with the high school from which you graduated or with a high school you've visited or are teaching at.

MONROE HIGH SCHOOL'S PAST

Monroe High School, located in the older section of Monroe, California, has a student population of 2,156 students. The students represent a cross-section of the city's population. Approximately 10% of the students are bused into school from the outlying rural areas. They are children of prominent ranchers and farmers who have owned land for several generations. Another 10% are Black and walk or drive to school from a de facto segregated neighborhood that lies on the northwest corner of the high school's attendance area. From other de facto segregated neighborhoods come first- and second-generation Mexican Americans, Latinos, and Asians, some bilingual, some speaking only Spanish, Chinese, Vietnamese, or Thai. This group comprises about 15% of the school's population. Approximately 65% of the students are middle- and lower-middle-class White children. A few are children of professionals—doctors, lawyers, teachers—but most are the children of blue-collar workers or small business owners. Twenty-five percent of the students attending Monroe qualify for the free lunch program.

Time has brought many changes to Monroe High School. It was founded in 1875, shortly after the city had become incorporated. At that time, Monroe was a "one main street" community made up of small businessmen and a few professionals, but mainly farmers and ranchers. The community grew slowly. In 1925, the citizens of Monroe felt that a larger, more modern high school was in order; so one was built, farther away from the downtown area, closer to the pleasant tree-lined residential neighborhoods.

Monroe, California, underwent three dramatic growth spurts. World War II brought defense-supported industry to the quiet community. From 1941 to 1945 the population increased by 30%. Two new wings were added to Monroe High. More teachers were hired and more businesses opened. Old-timers soon discovered they didn't know everyone in town by first or even second names. Banks became less friendly about loans. PTA meetings became more formal. Vested interests saw the town's land developers and farmers taking sides in many conflicts. The ethnic nature began to change as Black families, Mexican-American families, and, after the war, Japanese families moved into what were formerly all White neighborhoods, each group forming its own cultural community. In addition, scores of middle-westerners, sometimes crudely referred to as Okies, found employment in the once sleepy, rural town.

In 1946, Monroe High established its first reading class, remedial reading, taught by a junior member of the English department with no prior training in reading. In 1947, so many students were referred to this teacher that additional classes were created to satisfy the demand. In 1948, a course in speed reading was added. By 1950, Room 9 was designated "the reading lab" where five classes in reading were taught. Though the demand increased, no additional resources were added until 1968 when a grant of federal funds under Title I enabled the school to construct a building housing a reading communication center.

In 1953, two prominent packing houses opened up canneries to take advantage of the rich harvests in the area. More people moved to Monroe. A second high school was built to serve the outlying middle-class and upper-middle-class suburban neighborhoods that were expanding. Rivalries developed between the two high schools, both friendly and not so friendly. Teachers at Monroe were somewhat bitter over losing the "better" students to the other high school; yet they coped. Although Monroe sent fewer students to college than did the other high school, Monroe's students scored higher on entrance examinations and made higher grades once enrolled. This was due in part to an intricate tracking system that had been developed in the late 1940s. Students with IQs over 110 were placed in the A-track (college preparation). Those with IQ scores between 90 and 110 were placed into a B-track (community college). Students with scores between 70 and 89 were placed in a C-track (terminal education). The B-track was watered down A-track, with a lower proportion of students taking algebra and chemistry and a higher proportion taking homemaking and industrial arts. C-track students were taught the so-called basic skills and enrolled in shop and home arts courses. If they didn't drop out of school, they graduated, married, went to work, or joined the military.

By 1962, a space industry located in Monroe bringing with it increased opportunities for employment. Again the population increased sharply—a third high school was built and later a fourth. Government money was lavished on the schools in the early post-Sputnik years to improve the quality of scholarship in mathematics, science, and foreign languages and, in the late 1960s, to improve the learning environment for the disadvantaged. As a result of shifting population and urban sprawl, Monroe found itself with a majority of the town's "disadvantaged" students and received huge sums to build a reading and language lab for these students.

In April, 1970, with inflation, public antipathy, and economic recession, Monroe experienced its first student demonstration. Fifty A-track students formed a picket line in front of the school's entrance to protest the dress and hair code. In May, the Black students joined with the Mexican-American students to protest the discrimination of the tracking systems. The following October, a postgame dance was interrupted by a racial incident. In November, vandals entered the Title I reading lab and did damage amounting to $50,000. The faculty, confronted with confusion and strife, argued over whether the school's situation was a result of too much student freedom or too little. During the 1972–1973 school year, Monroe almost lost its accreditation because of its tracking system, its "insensitivity" to student needs, and its inability to deal properly with segments of the community that were demanding reform.

By fall of 1975, Monroe, in its centennial year, had abolished the tracking system and returned to open enrollment. Monroe's handful of university-bound students were bused across town for Latin, physics, and trigonometry. As one teacher commented: "In the 30 years I've been here at Monroe the quality of students has declined. There's no more respect for us or the school. They don't want to learn. Many *can't* learn. Why must we deal with them?" Echoing this teacher's sentiments is a Monroe High student: "I don't know what's happening around here. My father went to this school and got a great education. So did my aunt and uncle. Even my older brother got by here. But I'm not getting anything. The courses are aimed for the slow learners; many of these kids can't speak English. There's no discipline. How am I expected to get an education in this circus?'' Another student comments: ''The teachers, they don't care whether you learn anything or not. I can't read the books. They're dull. Even if I graduate, what do I know to make a living?'' A school administrator offers an explanation: ''The school, like the town, has undergone destructive changes. The town grew without a master plan. Schools were built with little concern for balancing the school population. For instance, the fourth high school we built has a student mean IQ of 109. Monroe's is 95. And even then we have widespread differences. Many of our students want to attend a two-year or four-year college or a university; yet while we are forced to structure watered-down college courses, the courses themselves aren't watered-down enough for most of the students in the classes. Our teachers often get the feeling that we're just putting in our time.''

Vandalism, apathy, disruption, and strife plagued Monroe High School into the 1980s. In effect, the ''back-to-basics'' movement did little to improve Monroe's faculty and student morale. Nor did subsequent attempts to restore ''educational excellence'' by increasing graduation requirements. After a heated faculty meeting, a group of teachers, all department chairpeople, went to the principal with a proposal for an in-depth study of the school's problems: the curriculum; the attitudes of students, faculty, administrators, and community toward the school; and the school's physical and emotional environment. The principal approved the study, schoolwide committees were formed, and the study was implemented. The results, presented at a subsequent faculty meeting, showed the following: (a) the basic curriculum had not substantially changed since 1965; (b) students generally perceived school as not meeting their needs; (c) teachers were frustrated by lack of success; (d) administrators were alarmed at low student and faculty morale; (e) many students were graduating only knowing how to read, write, or perform mathematical operations at a minimum competancy level.

MONROE HIGH SCHOOL'S FUTURE

Monroe High School is facing perhaps the worst crisis in its century-long history. How the administration, faculty, and students handle the crisis will affect the future of Monroe High School. If shortsighted, expedient solutions are sought, the school will undoubtedly remain in chaos and confusion. If, however, a comprehensive program of reform is implemented, the school's future will be brighter. Such a program might well begin with an examination of the varying attitudes of its teachers toward students and learning. Why, for instance, does Ms. Stewart distrust the ''young radicals'' on the faculty? Why does Ms. Jones value ''relevance''? Why does Mr. Wallace continue to lecture about poetry appreciation? By examining differences in values and attitudes, a school may better understand itself and what it is trying to accomplish.

The principal of Monroe High School might want to begin attitude assessment with an instrument that focuses on reading instruction, since reading is at the core of the school's problems. The following section presents such an assessment instrument.

ASSESSMENT OF ATTITUDES TOWARD TEACHING

Attitudes Toward Teaching Reading

To prepare for reading this section, you can begin by determining your own *attitude* toward teaching reading. Follow the directions given in Box 2.1 to complete the "Attitude Inventory Toward Teaching Reading in the Content

---

BOX 2.1. Attitude Inventory Toward Teaching Reading in the Content Area

Directions: Read the statement on the left. Then decide whether you strongly agree, agree, are undecided, disagree, or strongly disagree with the statement. Indicate your response by circling the number on the right under the appropriate column. (If you do not want to write in your book, number 1 to 14 on a separate piece of paper. Then copy down the number you would have circled. Thus, if you strongly disagree with the first statement, you would copy down "5" after the first statement because that is the number you would have circled. The numbers change. So look and copy down the correct number.)

	SA	A	U	D	SD
1. In the secondary school, the teaching of reading should be the responsibility of reading teachers only.	1	2	3	4	5
2. Secondary school teachers can teach reading effectively without special university courses in methods of teaching reading.	5	4	3	2	1
3. The teaching of reading skills can be incorporated into content area courses without interfering with the major objectives of these courses.	5	4	3	2	1
4. Any secondary school teacher who assigns reading should teach his or her students how to read what is assigned.	5	4	3	2	1
5. With rare exceptions, students should know what there is to know about reading before they are permitted to leave the elementary school.	1	2	3	4	5
6. Only remedial reading should be necessary in the secondary school and that should be done by remedial reading teachers in special classes.	1	2	3	4	5

7. Teaching reading is a technical process that secondary school teachers generally know nothing about.	1	2	3	4	5
8. Secondary school teachers cannot teach reading without special materials designed for that purpose.	1	2	3	4	5
9. Teaching reading is a necessary and legitimate part of teaching any content course in secondary school.	5	4	3	2	1
10. Teaching reading takes all the fun out of teaching at the secondary school level.	1	2	3	4	5
11. Every secondary school teacher should be a teacher of reading.	5	4	3	2	1
12. At the secondary school level students want to learn content, not how to read.	1	2	3	4	5
13. Integrating the teaching of reading with the teaching of specific content can be as exciting for the content teacher as teaching content only.	5	4	3	2	1
14. Content area teachers in the secondary school are probably more competent to teach the reading skills needed for their subjects than special reading teachers.	5	4	3	2	1

Key: SA — strongly agree; A — agree; U — undecided; D — disagree; SD — strongly disagree.

Areas'' (Otto & Smith, 1969). The items in the attitude inventory and results, based on this inventory, are discussed in the subsequent sections of this chapter. By taking the attitude inventory yourself, you will not only become aware of your own attitudes, you will also be able to compare your attitudes with other teachers' responses.

SCORING YOUR ATTITUDE INVENTORY

To find your score on the attitude inventory, simply add the numbers you circled. The total is your score. Your score can be interpreted by comparing it with the scores derived from a sample of junior and senior high school teachers shown in Table 2.1.

Otto and Smith, who obtained the scores from the junior and senior high school teachers, computed reliability coefficients of .80 for the junior high and .92 for the high school teachers on this inventory. These coefficients are high enough for groups at the junior high livel and *reliable* enough for indi-

TABLE 2.1. Results of the Attitude Scale
for Teaching Reading in the Content Areas

	Junior High	*High School*
Size of sample	38	48
Range of scores	22 to 65	19 to 54
Average score	42	45

viduals at the high school level. These reliabilities indicate teachers are consistent in their attitudes on this scale. In short, if you filled out the scale again, you would probably circle the same numbers. Because the scale is reliable, it is worthwhile comparing your scores with the sample and interpreting your responses.

INTERPRETING YOUR ATTITUDE INVENTORY

If you responded to each statement and followed the scoring directions correctly, you can compare your results with the sample of junior and senior high school teachers. You can ask yourself whether your score is within the range of scores of junior and senior high teachers and whether your score is above or below the average score. If you have a high score, your attitude is highly favorable toward teaching reading in content areas. If you have an intermediate score, you may agree that reading should be taught in junior and senior high school, but you yourself are not the person to do it. If you have a low score, then you think not only that you should not teach reading but also that reading should not be taught at all after elementary school. If you have an extremely low score, you may even resent the idea of students not being prepared well for junior or senior high school reading by teachers in lower grades. How do you think Mr. Wallace, Ms. Jones, and Ms. Stewart would score?

In general, junior high and senior high school teachers agree on their responses to the scale. However, fewer junior high school teachers believed elementary students should know all there was to know about reading before they left elementary school (item 5) and more junior high teachers believed every teacher should be a teacher of reading (item 11). Apparently junior high teachers, perhaps because they are closer to elementary school, are more willing to be responsible for teaching students to read.

Look at the remaining items. On items 1, 6, 9, and 11, teachers generally disagree that reading should be the responsibility of reading teachers only. But on item 2, teachers also generally disagreed that secondary teachers could teach reading effectively without further training. Apparently secondary teachers would like to teach reading, but believe special training is necessary to do so.

Secondary teachers think they can teach both reading and the content of the course without interfering with instructional objectives (item 3). Moreover, they agree that a teacher who assigns reading should teach students how to read the assigned material (item 4). In addition, they believe that they know something about the teaching of reading (item 7), that they can teach reading without special materials (item 8), that teaching reading would not take the fun out of teaching content (items 10 and 13).

Despite their favorable and agreeable attitudes toward teaching reading, teachers are divided in their attitudes about whether students want both content and reading (item 12); and they believe the special reading teachers are more qualified than they are to teach reading in the content area even though the special reading teachers do not have competence in the content areas (item 14).

Attitudes Toward Learning from Text

Now take the attitude inventory in Box 2.2. This inventory is similar to the previous scale you took, but it does have an essential difference. Read each item carefully and record your response. Then, we will interpret your score.

BOX 2.2. Attitude Inventory Toward Teaching Students to Learn from Texts in the Content Areas

Directions: Read the statement on the left. Then decide whether you strongly agree, agree, are undecided, disagree, or strongly disagree with the statement. Indicate your response by circling the number on the right under the appropriate column.

	SA	A	U	D	SD
1. In the secondary school, teaching students to learn from texts should be the responsibility of reading teachers only.	1	2	3	4	5
2. Secondary school teachers can teach students to learn from texts effectively without special university courses in methods of teaching reading.	5	4	3	2	1
3. Teaching skills in learning from texts can be incorporated into content area courses without interfering with the major objectives of these courses.	5	4	3	2	1
4. Any secondary school teacher who assigns chapters in texts for students	5	4	3	2	1

should teach the students how to acquire information from these chapters.

5. With rare exceptions, students should know what there is to know about learning from texts before they are permitted to leave the elementary school.	1	2	3	4	5
6. Only remedial reading should be necessary in the secondary school and that should be done by remedial reading teachers in special classes.	1	2	3	4	5
7. Teaching students to learn from texts is a technical process that secondary school teachers generally know nothing about.	1	2	3	4	5
8. Secondary school teachers cannot teach students how to gain information from texts without special materials designed for that purpose.	1	2	3	4	5
9. Teaching students how to learn from texts is a necessary and legitimate part of teaching any content course in secondary school.	5	4	3	2	1
10. Teaching students how to gain information from texts takes all the fun out of teaching at the secondary school level.	1	2	3	4	5
11. Every secondary school teacher should teach students how to learn from texts.	5	4	3	2	1
12. At the secondary school level students want to learn content, not how to gain information from texts.	1	2	3	4	5
13. Integrating the teaching of learning from texts with the teaching of specific content can be as exciting for the content area teacher as teaching content only.	5	4	3	2	1
14. Content area teachers in the secondary school are probably more competent to teach the learning-from-text skills needed for their subjects than special reading teachers.	5	4	3	2	1

Key: SA — strongly agree; A — agree; U — undecided; D — disagree; SD — strongly disagree.

TABLE 2.2. Results of Attitude Scales for Teaching Students (a) Reading vs. (b) Learning from Text in the Content Areas

	Sample Size	Mean or Avg. Score
Elementary		
(a) Reading	24	48
(b) Learning from text	21	50
Secondary		
(a) Reading	50	44
(b) Learning from text	57	53

SCORING AND INTERPRETING YOUR ATTITUDE INVENTORY

Add up the circled numbers. If you are an elementary teacher, you are likely to find your score on this scale higher than your score on the previous scale; if you are a secondary teacher, you are likely to have an even higher score. Is your score higher? Compare your score with the mean or average scores shown in Table 2.2. If you are an elementary teacher and your score is above 50 or if you are a secondary teacher and your score is above 53, then you have a more favorable attitude toward teaching students to *learn from text* than the average elementary or secondary teacher.

COMPARISON OF ATTITUDES TOWARD TEACHING READING AND LEARNING FROM TEXT

To know what items teachers respond to move favorably, we can compare the distribution of responses to our two scales: (a) Reading and (b) Learning from Texts in the Content Areas. We compare our secondary teachers' results on each item by a statistical technique known as chi-square. This technique indicates whether the teachers who filled out our attitude scales responded in significantly different ways to the items on the two scales. Look at the results in Table 2.3. The items for each scale are listed in the table. (The underlined phrase in each item appeared in the scale in Box 2.1. The phrase in parentheses in each item appeared in the scale in Box 2.2) The percentage of responses to each item on each scale (Rdg = reading; LFT = learning from text) is shown next to each item.

The first item for the scale in Table 2.3 is "In the secondary school *the teaching of reading* should be the responsibility of reading teachers only." The line of figures next to item 1 that starts with *Rdg* shows that, of the secondary teachers who responded to this item, 2% strongly agreed, 10% agreed, 14% were

TABLE 2.3. Attitudes of Secondary Teachers Toward Teaching Reading
vs. Learning from Text, Tested by Chi-Square
for Significance of Difference

		SA	*A*	*U*	*D*	*SD*	*Significance*
1. In the secondary school, *the teaching of reading* (teaching students to learn from text) should be the responsibility of reading teachers only.	Rdg: LFT:	2.0 0.0	10.0 5.3	14.0 8.8	28.0 43.9	44.0 40.4	ns
2. Secondary teachers can teach *reading* (students to learn from text) effectively without special university courses in methods of teaching reading.	Rdg: LFT:	2.0 0.0	10.0 28.1	22.0 31.6	44.0 35.1	22.0 5.3	*s*
3. *The teaching of reading skills* (teaching skills in learning from texts) can be incorporated into content area courses without interfering with the major objectives of these courses.	Rdg: LFT:	26.0 35.1	42.0 45.6	10.0 17.5	14.0 1.8	6.0 0.0	*s*
4. Any secondary teacher who assigns *reading* (chapters in texts) should teach his or her students how to acquire information from this assignment.	Rdg: LFT:	22.0 59.6	48.0 21.1	8.0 10.5	14.0 8.8	8.0 0.0	*s*
5. With rare exceptions, students should know what there is to know about *reading* (learning from texts) before they are permitted to leave the elementary school.	Rdg: LFT:	30.0 10.5	30.0 28.1	14.0 21.1	12.0 33.3	12.0 7.0	*s*
6. Only remedial reading should be necessary in the secondary school and that should be done by remedial reading teachers and special teachers.	Rdg: LFT:	4.0 1.8	20.0 14.0	14.0 19.3	28.0 36.8	34.0 28.1	ns
7. Teaching *reading* (students to learn from texts) is a technical process that secondary school teachers generally know nothing about.	Rdg: LFT:	8.0 1.8	26.0 22.8	34.0 26.3	26.0 28.1	6.0 21.1	ns
8. Secondary school teachers cannot teach *reading* (students how to gain information from texts) without special materials designed for that purpose.	Rdg: LFT:	8.0 0.0	16.0 10.5	20.0 15.8	38.0 50.9	14.0 22.8	ns

9. Teaching *reading* (how to learn from texts) is a necessary and legitimate part of teaching any content course in secondary school.

	SA	A	U	D	SD	
Rdg:	26.0	32.0	20.0	14.0	6.0	*s*
LFT:	45.6	45.6	1.8	7.0	0.0	

10. Teaching *reading* (students how to gain information from texts) takes all the fun out of teaching at the secondary school level.

Rdg:	0.0	6.0	22.0	36.0	34.0	*s*
LFT:	1.8	1.8	5.3	47.4	43.9	

11. Every secondary teacher should *be a teacher of reading* (teach students how to learn from texts).

Rdg:	12.0	22.0	20.0	22.0	22.0	*s*
LFT:	38.6	33.3	10.5	14.0	3.5	

12. At the secondary school level students want to learn content, not how to *read* (learn from texts).

Rdg:	6.0	26.0	18.0	40.0	4.0	*s*
LFT:	1.8	8.8	19.3	50.9	19.3	

13. Integrating the teaching of *reading* (learning from texts) with the teaching of specific content can be as exciting for the content area teacher as teaching content only.

Rdg:	18.0	30.0	32.0	10.0	4.0	ns
LFT:	28.1	40.4	28.1	1.8	0.0	

14. Content area teachers in the secondary school are probably more competent to teach the *reading* (learning from text) skills needed for their subjects than special reading teachers.

Rdg:	6.0	20.0	20.0	36.0	14.0	*s*
LFT:	12.3	38.6	28.1	19.3	1.8	

Key: SA—strongly agree, A—agree, U—undecided, D—disagree, SD—strongly disagree. Total percentages may be less than 100 because nonresponse percentages are not shown.

Source: Harry Singer, ''Attitudes towards Reading and Learning from Text.'' In M. L. Kamil and A. J. Moe, eds., *Reading Research: Studies and Applications,* 28th Yearbook of the National Reading Conference. West Lafayette, Indiana: The National Reading Conference, 1979. Reprinted by permission.

---

undecided, 28% disagreed and 44% strongly disagreed. What was your response to Item 1 in the scale in Box 2.1?

The first item's alternative states: ''In the secondary school, *teaching students to learn from text* should be the responsibility of reading teachers only.'' As shown on the line next to item 1 starting with LFT, no secondary teacher who responded to this item strongly agreed, 5.3% agreed, 8.8% were undecided, 43.9% disagreed, and 40.4% strongly disagreed. What was your response to this item in the scale in Box 2.2? Were you more or less favorable to this item when it used the term *learning from text* instead of *reading*?

On the extreme right side of Table 2.3 a column is labeled ''significance.'' Two symbols occur in this column. The symbol *ns* (nonsignificant) indicates only a chance difference occurred when responses on the two scales were compared. For example, the *ns* on item 1 indicates that this item, whether it included the words *the teaching of reading* or *teaching students to learn from text,* would not cause teachers to respond differently. In other words, we wouldn't expect teachers to change their attitudes on this item much when we shifted from *reading* to *learning from text.* Thus, on the issue of *responsibility* in item 1, secondary teachers do not differ, whether the wording is *reading* or *learning from text.* But on both scales they disagree with statements that such instruction should be the responsibility of reading teachers only.

Now, if you look down the "significance" column, you will find the symbol *s* beside item 2. An item with an *s* in the last column means that this item elicited significantly different responses when the word *reading* was replaced by the phrase *learning from text.*

On the second item, which focuses on *preparation,* secondary teachers tend to disagree that they can teach reading without special university courses. However, they tend to shift toward agreement that they are prepared to teach students to learn from text. But, even though a significant shift in attitude occurs, a high percentage are still undecided or disagree that they can teach students to learn from text without having a special university course to prepare them for doing so.

The third item focuses on a *conflict in objectives:* teaching content versus teaching skills for learning content. Secondary teachers would have less conflict in integrating skills involved with learning from text in content area classes than they would in incorporating the teaching of reading skills.

The fourth item, *assignment,* indicates that secondary teachers tend to agree that they assign *chapters in text* more than they do reading and that, although they should help students learn how to gain information from either assignment, significantly more of them agree that they should teach students how to gain information from assigned chapters in texts.

The fifth item is on *proficiency standards.* Significantly more secondary teachers agree that students should have mastered reading before being allowed to graduate from elementary school, but they disagree that students should know what they need to know about learning from text when they graduate from elementary school. Apparently, secondary teachers recognize that it is normal for high school students to have to acquire skills they need to learn from texts.

Item 6 concerns *remedial reading.* Both scales had the identical statements. The difference in responses on the two scales, as expected, was not significantly different. Secondary teachers disagree that only remedial reading should be necessary in high school and that it should be the responsibility of remedial reading teachers.

Item 7 emphasizes that teaching reading or learning from text is a *technical process.* Although teachers do not differ on this item, they tend to disagree more that they know nothing about teaching students to learn from text than they do about teaching reading.

Item 8 deals with *materials* for teaching. Although the difference is not significant, secondary teachers disagree more that they need special materials for teaching students to learn from text than they do for teaching reading.

On *legitimacy,* item 9, both scales elicit a favorable reaction, but significantly more teachers agree that teaching students to learn from text is a necessary part of teaching any content course in secondary school.

On *enjoyment* in teaching, item 10, teachers disagree that teaching reading or learning from text takes all the fun out of teaching.

On *slogan,* item 11, secondary teachers agree that every secondary teacher should teach students to learn from text, but disagree that they should be teachers of reading.

On *student objectives,* item 12, secondary teachers indicate their feelings about students wanting to learn content rather than reading skills or skills to gain information from text. But more teachers disagree with the statement that students want to learn content rather than how to gain information from text.

On *integration* of skills, teaching (reading or learning from text) with content, item 13, teachers agree that this integration can be as exciting for the content teacher as teaching content alone.

On item 14, *competence* in teaching reading or learning from text: secondary teachers feel they are significantly more competent than special reading teachers to teach students skills for learning from text (as contrasted with teaching reading skills) for their subjects.

Thus, the phrase *learning from text* elicits a significantly more favorable attitude on 9 of the 14 items. On the other 5, the difference is not statistically significant when *learning from text* is used in place of *reading,* but all 5 of these items on both scales elicit favorable responses toward teaching the skills of learning from text or reading (Singer, 1978b).

Why do we get more favorable attitudes when we substitute the phrase *learning from text* for *reading* in these scales? The answer comes from the definition of the term *reading.* Secondary teachers define *reading* as "learning how to read," something that is taught in the primary grades. They do not see such instruction as their main task. What they do perceive is that their task is to teach students how to learn from text. Hence, they respond much more favorably to this idea. Indeed, in preservice and in-service courses, as well as throughout this text, we emphasize the second phase of reading, "learning from text," and advise high schools to develop "Learning from Text Centers" and employ "Learning from Text Specialists." We also show how such instruction can be accomplished in heterogeneous groups of students, which have recently been made even more heterogeneous with the passage of PL 94-142, the Education for All Handicapped Children Act. This act has led to the return of some handicapped children, including low-achieving students, from special education to regular education classes for at least part of the day. This procedure is known among teachers as "mainstreaming."

ACQUISITION AND MODIFICATION OF ATTITUDES

Basis for Teacher Attitudes

Because elementary teachers prepare to teach all subjects, including reading, they experience no conflict between their preparation, expectations, and attitudes toward instructional requirements in elementary school. Indeed, elementary teachers enjoy teaching students how to read and observing their development in reading throughout the elementary grades. First graders are highly specific in their abilities in reading. Mostly they know only those words and skills they have been taught. But gradually elementary students generalize and integrate their abilities and skills, achieving some convergence by Grade 3 (Guthrie, 1973). By that time, if they do well on one skill such as word recognition, they tend to perform about as well in another skill such as use of syntax or semantics for anticipating words. They are also able to pronounce words that have not been directly taught (Gates, 1961) because they can apply their skills in use of syntax and semantics plus skills in word recognition to identify new words. By the sixth grade, most students have integrated their language abilities (syntactic, semantic, and phonological) with their well-developed responses to graphic stimuli. At this point in their education, they are learning more new vocabulary from reading than from listening (Armstrong, 1953). But they still need help in pronouncing words, particularly in placing accent or stress and in identifying words borrowed from other languages. For example, without help in pronunciation some students might erroneously say /ep' tom/ for /i pit' me/ when they read the word *epitome*.

Although elementary teachers succeed in teaching most students how to read, they do not prepare students well for the reading and study-skill requirements of junior high school (Spache & Spache, 1969). Indeed, in the intermediate grades, teachers may still teach some students how to read, but they usually do not give instruction on reading in the content areas. That is, they usually do not teach students how to learn from texts in social studies, science, mathematics, literature, and other content areas. If students know how to read, teachers in the intermediate grades as well as those in junior high and high school presume students can read in all content areas. Hence, *assumptive* rather than *prescriptive* teaching becomes the rule in reading assignments for students. That is, as students progress through the grades, they are assigned chapters or books to read without any instruction on how to read the chapters or books (Herber, 1970a).

Teachers may engage in assumptive teaching because they have not been taught how to teach reading in content areas nor how to teach students to learn from texts. Consequently, it is possible to observe a class in the intermediate grades during the reading period reading books that are appropriate to their widely divergent reading levels; but during social studies, science, or math period, the students are all reading out of the *same* text without any instruction in how to read or learn from the text. As in junior or senior high school, intermediate grade teachers tend to focus only on the content of the text.

When confronted with the discrepancy between what they know about the range of individual differences in the reading abilities of their students and the reading difficulty of assigned texts, intermediate grade teachers defensively complain they have only one text for teaching a particular subject. But when materials became available for teaching reading in the content areas, such as *The Harper and Row Basic Reading Program: How to Read in the Subject Matter Areas, Strand II* (O'Donnell & Cooper, 1963), and even when these materials are state-adopted and present in the classroom, teachers do not use them, perhaps for the reason cited by junior high and high school teachers: They have not been trained in how to use such materials. Thus, intermediate grade teachers, as well as junior and senior high school teachers, have to learn how to teach students to learn from texts and how to use various strategies for meeting the wide range of individual differences in reading ability.

Teachers in junior and senior high schools largely prepare to teach the subject matter of their major field. If they have not taken a course in secondary reading, they do not identify with the processes of instruction involved in reading, do not feel competent to teach reading, and believe that reading instruction, although necessary, should be taught by a specialist, even in their own content areas!

However, variation in attitudes toward teaching reading in the content areas does exist among content area teachers. Lipton and Liss (1978) found that physical education and fine arts teachers responded least favorably and foreign language teachers most favorably to the question, "How much benefit would students derive if taught reading skills specifically geared to your subject area?" The variation in response may have realistically reflected the import of reading in their classes. O'Rourke (1980) found similar variation: English teachers were favorable while social studies, math, and science teachers were neutral.

Changing Attitudes

Teachers who have had a course in reading have a more favorable attitude toward teaching reading in content areas (O'Rourke, 1980). Apparently the difference in attitude is due to instruction: Vaughan (1977) found a required course changed undergraduate students' attitude from neutral to favorable.

Instruction can also change the attitudes of experienced teachers. Dupuis, Askov, and Lee (1979) found that a year-long biweekly workshop based on a competency format with follow-up supervision by trained supervisors between the sessions improved 57 junior high school teachers' knowledge of reading and their attitudes significantly more than the 72 teachers in the control group who had not volunteered to participate in the project. A pretest showed both groups were similar in their attitudes prior to the workshop. Ratings of teacher integration of reading instruction into their classrooms were significantly higher at the conclusion of the workshop.

Change in attitude and instructional practices persists at least several years after students have completed a course on reading in the content areas. In a survey, following up his course, Steiglitz (1983) found that the graduates of his course when compared with a control group of subject matter specialists still had more favorable attitudes and provided significantly more instruction on reading in the content areas, such as teaching key vocabulary, preparing students for reading assignments, developing higher as well as lower comprehension skills, and assessing students' comprehension, but they did not do as much on restructuring lessons to integrate reading skills with subject matter, use reading guides, instruct students in organization of information, and employ different grouping patterns in the classroom. But Patberg, Dewitz, and Henning (1984) observed that a summer institute for 33 junior and senior high school teachers significantly changed their attitudes and incorporated assessment and reading strategies (ask questions at all levels of cognition, construct reading guides, use directed teaching assignments, teach flexibility techniques, explain SQ3R and other study methods) into their simulated unit and lesson planning; another group of vocational teachers who were rated in a classroom followup used the reading strategies more often in classroom than they had reported they did.

Certification Requirements

Apparently the trend toward a required course in teaching reading in the secondary school is beginning to achieve the goal of making every secondary teacher knowledgeable about strategies for teaching reading in the content areas and enabling them to incorporate some of the strategies in their classrooms. Organized reading instruction began in high schools as early as the 1920s when the public became aware of reading deficiencies in World War I recruits. By 1973 only nine states required prospective secondary school teachers to take a course in reading (Estes & Piercey, 1973; Freed, 1973). In 1984, the number of states that had a reading requirement for all academic content area teachers at the secondary level had increased to 32, with another 5 states having the requirement for English/Language Arts teachers only (Farrell & Cirrincione, 1984).

EFFECTS OF TEACHERS' CLASSROOM PERFORMANCE ON STUDENTS

Use of Texts

Do teachers use texts in content area reading instruction? A team of researchers (Ratekin, Simpson, Alvermann, & Dishner, 1985) tried to answer this question by observing, analyzing documents, and taping the classes of eight experienced teachers of math, science, social studies, and English in Grades 8 to 11. They then contrasted the results of what they observed with what 10 content area methods texts recommended that teachers should do in teaching reading in the content areas. They found that most time (31%) was spent in lecturing in a question-answer format to the whole class and monitoring students as they worked individually at their desks, teachers spent no time in presenting objectives and very little time in previewing concepts, and predominantly used a single textbook. Math teachers used a text the most and social studies teachers used it least. Teachers rarely used multiple copies of a text. Only the English teachers requested reading of various books before writing a report. Fewer than 1% of the observed assignments indicated teachers expected students to develop concepts outside of class. The teacher, not the text, was the primary source of information. Ratekin et al. reached the conclusion that when teachers do not use the textbook much, then it may be futile to teach them how to teach students to learn from a text.

However, Ratekin et al. did not carry out an experimental program to determine what would happen if teachers did learn how to teach students to learn from a text and then observe teacher use of texts and guidance in teaching their students how to learn from texts.

The assumption that it is necessary for students to learn from their texts and that students actually do so has been questioned. F. R. Smith and Feathers (1983) conducted an ethnographic study of two middle school social studies classes and two high school history classes at intervals over a long time period. They observed in the classrooms and interviewed teachers and students. In the classes where the teachers covered the assigned reading with lectures and discussion about half the students in the class were not likely to have read the assigned material because the quizzes and tests were only on the lecture material and class discussion. Interviews of the students revealed they studied for the goals defined by the examinations, which emphasized facts and ideas expressed by the teacher, not the general objectives established for the course. Moreover, the students felt that these courses had little applicability to their lives. However, Smith and Feathers did not make any claim about the representativeness of their sample of schools and teachers nor did they report whether the teachers in their study had taken any preservice or in-service instruction on teaching students how to learn from their texts. However, Rieck (1977) also found that teachers do not teach their students to learn from texts.

Need to Learn From Texts

However, students do need to learn from text and at each level of their education, including the university level, according to a 5-year project conducted on Learning from Text in the University of California and California State University systems (Singer & Bean, 1982a, 1982b, 1982c, 1983a, 1983b). The purpose of the project was to determine whether the ability to learn from text was significantly related to achievement at the university level. The ability to learn from text was assessed by the *Sequential Test of Educational Progress: Reading, Form 1A* (Educational Test Service, 1959). The *California Survey of Study Methods* (Carter, 1957), which contains subtests of "Attitudes," "Mechanics," and "Planning," was used in the battery of tests. The other measures in the battery were Scholastic Aptitude Scores (Verbal and Quantitative) and high school grade point average. Some 3,000 freshmen on four University of California and four California State University campuses participated in the project. The results indicated that three predictors yielded a multiple prediction of .42. The predictors were (a) High School Grade Point Average, which was interpreted as an index of prior knowledge, (b) Attitudes toward Learning, that is, desire to study for the purpose of learning and knowing, and (c) Ability to Learn from Text. These three predictors represent major components in achievement because as students progress through school they increasingly are expected to learn from text. If they have the necessary background knowledge for learning from the text, the desire to learn and remember, and the ability to learn from text, then they are likely to achieve more than other students who are lower or one or more of these factors. The project also demonstrated that students in various university classes such as botany, sociology, history, and psychology could improve their achievement as a result of learning mapping (Ruddell & Boyle, 1984), answering inserted questions in their text (Spring, Sassenrath, Ketellapper, & Neustadt, 1982), and listening to text-based lectures (Flood et al., 1985).

A one-unit elective course on Learning from Text, established at the University of California, Berkeley as a byproduct of the project, enrolled students from a variety of disciplines; enough students elected to take the course that eight sections had to be offered each semester! Apparently some students who have earned at least a B average at high school and could learn well from text at a high school level recognize that they still need to improve their ability to learn from text at a university level of understanding, which entails constructing and reconstructing information drawn from the text and students' background knowledge (Chall, 1983; Singer, 1985).

The project also conducted a longitudinal study at the high school level. Students enrolled in a college preparatory world history course learned to summarize text, use graphic organizers, and apply explanations to predict events. For example, an explanation of the causes of revolutions was inserted into a history text that only had the French, American, and Russian revolutions as exemplars or separate descriptions of revolutions. The explanation and the exemplars formed a hierarchically organized knowledge base that students could use for predicting a revolution they had not studied, namely, the Cuban revolution (Bean, Singer, Frazee, & Sorter, 1983). As a result of his experience in teaching these learning-from-text strategies, the high school instructor for this course changed toward a more favorable attitude on teaching students to learn from text.

Thus attitudes and instruction in teaching reading in the content areas can change as a result of preservice or in-service education. The trend toward more states requiring secondary teachers to take a preservice course in teaching reading in the content areas is likely to make the long-held slogan that "Every secondary teacher is a teacher of reading" into reality. But it would be preferable for the slogan to be "Every secondary teacher teaches students to learn from text" (Singer, 1979). As we have explained, using the results reported in Table 2.3, secondary teachers are more confident teaching students to *learn from text* and are more willing to provide such instruction. The evidence on change in attitudes and performance as a result of taking a course on reading and learning from text indicates that when teachers have acquired single- and multiple-text strategies such as those presented in this text, they will be even more confident and more willing to teach students to learn from texts, but they are also more likely to require students to read and learn from text and be able to teach them how to do so.

CONCLUSION

Whether your high school is like or unlike Monroe High, one fact is clear: High schools are pressured to change as society changes. Today, more students receive a high school education than ever before. As a result, student bodies are more widely varied than ever (in ability, achievement, and culture), as we see in the next chapter. Yet schools often fail to deal with these increasing differences. As a result, both teachers and students become dissatisfied, even frustrated. Because the ultimate goal of education is to produce independent learners, it is each teacher's responsibility to train students to comprehend the text material assigned in class. However, some teachers don't perceive teaching comprehension as their responsibility; other teachers feel inadequate to handle the task. Consequently, high school teachers desiring change must first deal with the disparate attitudes of other faculty members. They can start by investigating and revealing to the faculty the range of individual differences in general reading achievement that exists within each class. In the next chapter, we explain how large this range is and how it can be measured.

SUMMARY

Two scales for assessing teachers' attitudes were used to show that junior and senior high school teachers have a more favorable attitude toward teaching students to *learn from text* than toward teaching students to *read*. The reason for this discrepancy is that teaching *reading* can be defined as an instructional procedure for elementary school whereas teaching students to *learn from text* is consistent with high school instruction. Consequently, when the phrase *learning from text* or *teaching students to learn from text* is used as an aspect of a teacher's role, teachers are likely to respond more favorably. They are also more likely to (a) determine the range of individual differences in their students' abilities to learn from text and (b) acquire the strategies and skills for teaching students to learn from texts in the content areas.

ACTIVITIES

1. Compare your scores on the two attitude scales in this chapter with the scores of other students in your class. Discuss the reasons for any differences on each item.
2. Interview an experienced teacher to find out how this teacher responds to the items on the attitude scales.
3. Compare attitudes of elementary, junior high, and high school teachers on each scale: (a) the attitudes toward reading scale and (b) the attitudes toward learning from text scale.

3 | Individual and Intraindividual Differences Among Students

CHAPTER OVERVIEW

Within a given classroom, differences in learning abilities among students are large. Even before Public Law 94–142 mandated mainstreaming certain exceptional children into regular classrooms, a teacher could expect an ability span equal to two-thirds the average chronological age of the students enrolled in a class. In a 10th-grade history class, for example, where the average chronological age is 15 years, there will be at least a 10-year span of achievement, perhaps from 5th grade to college level. After you read this chapter, you will see why a teacher cannot assume that all students are alike nor that students have ability to learn from text equally well in all content areas.

GRAPHIC ORGANIZER

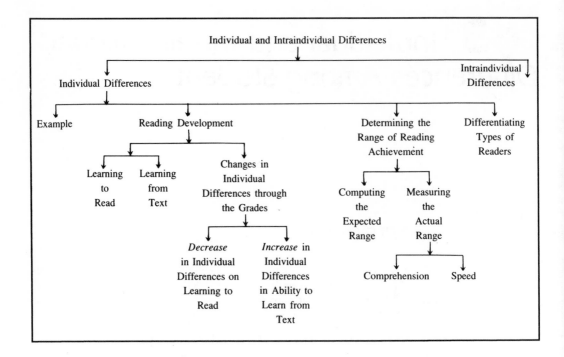

PREPOSED QUESTIONS

1. How would you determine the range of reading achievement in a class?
2. What is the formula for estimating expected range of reading achievement in a regular class?
3. What are the two phases of reading development and the components involved in each phase?
4. What changes occur in individual differences in each phase over the grades? What are the reasons for these changes?
5. What is meant by intraindividual differences in specific content area reading achievement?

INDIVIDUAL DIFFERENCES BETWEEN STUDENTS

Example: A 10th-Grade History Class at Monroe High

Ms. Jones wasn't looking forward to teaching her third period 10th-grade, world history class. From her experience, she realized that 15-year-olds tend to be difficult to motivate. First of all, there would be a wide range of individual differences in ability. In last year's class there were students who were reading 5 years below grade level as well as students reading 4 years above grade level. This year's class would include several mainstreamed students, increasing last year's ability span. Second, the adopted textbook was written at the 11th-grade level, so many of the students in class would not be able to comprehend it. During the first week of class, Ms. Jones received scores on reading tests from the counseling office. The data that Ms. Jones received are compiled in Table 3.1. Ms. Jones used the data to construct the histogram shown in Figure 3.1.

TABLE 3.1. Reading Achievement Scores for Ms. Jones's Class

Student	Reading Grade-Equivalent Scores
Adams, Jane	8.3
Anderson, Bob	12.7
Baker, Fred	5.1
Blotski, Barb	7.2
Carrington, Iris	4.1
Clutzton, Dan	9.3
Davis, Roy	6.4
Dixon, Tabby	13.9
Ebbing, Sasha	9.0
Farthing, Ray	14.5
Fremont, Tony	10.2
Groutinski, Lou	7.1
Hirostad, Myra	11.4
Ibert, Margie	8.0
Jackson, Phil	10.3
Kato, Umeko	11.8
Logan, Mary	2.9
Lysert, Roger	7.3
Mathens, Carter	16.9
Morgan, Rose	9.8
Parker, Joe	9.4
Quodas, Xlicis	—
Romero, Marta	11.3
Smith, Sammy	10.1
Thomas, Tommie	12.3
Victa, Lota	3.3
Young, Iola	8.9

FIGURE 3.1. Histogram of Reading Grade-Equivalent Scores in Ms. Jones's Class.

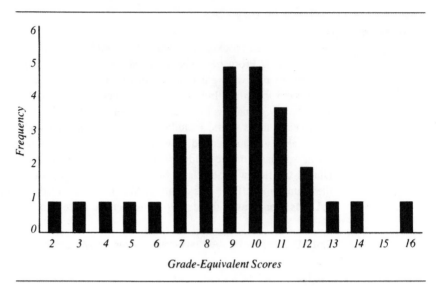

Note that in tallying grade equivalent scores, Ms. Jones dropped the decimal point; for example, she counted 8.9 as 8. She then constructed a bar graph to indicate the number of students who had scores at the same grade equivalent levels. She could then answer the following questions by simply looking at her bar graph:

1. What is the range of reading achievement in this class? (Answer: Grade equivalent 2 to 16, a total of 14 grades.)
2. What are the two most frequently occurring reading grade equivalent scores? (Answer: Grades 9 and 10.)
3. If Ms. Jones has an opportunity to adopt a new text for her class, what grade level of reading difficulty should the text have? (Answer: If the text has a reading grade difficulty of 9 to 10, then Ms. Jones would have the least difficulty in adapting the text to all the students in her class. Do you agree with this answer?)
4. If Ms. Jones uses the text with the 11th-grade reading level, but does not adapt it to the students in the class, which students do you think would give Ms. Jones the most problems in the areas of (a) discipline, (b) attitude, and (c) achievement? Why? What can Ms. Jones do to eliminate or reduce the problems?

Ms. Jones should be aware that there are two overlapping phases of reading development: (a) the *reading acquisition* phase (learning how to read) and (b) the *learning-from-text* phase. Her students at the low end of the range are in the reading acquisition phase whereas those at the upper end are in the learning-from-text phase. Students in the middle range are in-between, with some who are on the verge of mastering the first phase and others who have recently achieved the *mastery level*. The next section explains these two phases of reading development.

Reading Development

Reading development consists of two overlapping phases: learning how to read and ability to learn from text. We explain each phase. Then we will point out how individual difference in each phase changes as students progress through the grades.

LEARNING TO READ

Learning to read consists of an integration of two processes. The first process is use of language abilities, such as syntax and semantics, for anticipating words. Consider this sentence:

The car raced down the _____.

Syntax leads to the expectation of a noun after the noun determiner *the*. The context of the sentence suggests that the noun will be a word such as *hill, highway, street, road, freeway, avenue, track.*

The second process consists of the acquisition and application of letter-to-sound relationships. Students have to learn to relate letters, letter combinations, and words to the sounds they stand for. Hence, if the reader can use language abilities for anticipating words and can relate letters or groups of letters to the sounds they represent, the combination can drastically delimit choices in word identification and can facilitate the process of reading. For example, when the initial consonant is added to the following sentence, the choices for the missing word are limited to one or two words that begin with the sound of *h*:

The car raced down the h_____.

The acquisition of print-to-sound relationships takes time because these relationships are complex. However, the number of print-to-sound relationships that have to be learned is finite.

About 95% of students can learn to read (Bloom, 1971); indeed, many students master the process of reading before they reach the sixth, seventh, or eighth grades. Learning how to read is the first phase of reading development. The range of individual differences in this phase of reading decreases as a group of students progress through school and master the processes involved in learning how to read.

LEARNING FROM TEXT

The second phase of reading development overlaps the first phase and involves the ability to comprehend, or learn from text. Readers learn from text by using their general information, their knowledge of sequences of events, their semantic and conceptual abilities, and their reasoning capacities to interact with information gleaned from the text (R. Anderson, Spiro, & Montague, 1977; Rumelhart, 1976; Schank & Abelson, 1977; Singer, 1977b; Winograd, 1972). They also use their metacognitive ability, their ability to direct and regulate their own cognitive processes and use fix-up strategies whenever their self-evaluation indicates they have made an error in identifying or processing print (Brown, 1980). Thus, a reader and a text interact to produce new knowledge that may get stored in the reader's long-term memory. We refer to this entire process as *learning from text*.

The processes and contents of thinking that underlie a person's ability to learn from text develop most rapidly while a person is in school. Moreover, the contents of thinking (including semantic and conceptual, as well as knowledge about the world) continue to increase throughout a person's lifetime. Hence, the ability to learn from text improves as a person matures. Because the processes and contents of thinking are part of a person's general mental ability, then the capacity to learn from text increases at a rate that correlates with the development of general mental ability (Singer, 1977b).

Thus, reading development consists of two overlapping phases: (a) learning to read and (b) learning from text. Learning to read is mastered by most students prior to eighth grade. However, learning from text is an open-ended process that is never mastered, but continues to develop throughout life as a person gains new information, vocabulary, concepts, and general knowledge of the world in various content areas.

Because increases in general reading achievement or ability to learn from text are correlated with general mental ability, and because the range of individual differences in general mental ability increases as a group of students progress through school, we can expect that the range of general reading achievement will increase from grade to grade. Indeed the range of individual differences in a class does increase as students progress through the grades.

CHANGES INDIVIDUAL DIFFERENCES
THROUGH THE GRADES
Decrease in Individual Differences in Learning to Read

The range of individual differences in learning how to read *decreases* as a group of students progress through the grades. (See chap. 4 for an explanation of this decrease.)

Increase in Individual Differences in Ability to Learn from Text (Reading Achievement)

Students vary in reading achievement as early as the first grade. Durkin (1964) found that 1% of beginning first graders are already able to read at a grade equivalent of 2.3 (second grade, third month). At the other extreme are children who, when tested on a reading readiness test, did not know the names of any letters of the alphabet. In lessons taught as part of a reading readiness test, these same children did not learn sounds for any letters. Nor could they learn even 1 of the 10 sight words taught as part of the same reading readiness test (Murphy & Durrell, 1965).

If we follow the same group of students through school, we will find that the junior high school teacher reports a wider range of reading achievement than the elementary teacher reported for the same class. The high school teacher confronts an even greater *reading range* in this class. For evidence of this rate of increase, look at the graph in Figure 3.2. It shows the actual reading comprehension scores of students in Grades 2 through 8. The scores are reported in age equivalent terms. If a student has an age equivalent score of 10, it means that the student, regardless of his or her *actual* age or grade, has a reading comprehension score equal to the score earned by an average 10-year-old student. In other words, the student has a *reading age* of 10.

Find *Grade 2* on the left side of the graph. You will see the reading ages range from a reading comprehension age of 5.5 to 10.0, a difference of 4.5 years. Notice, as you go up the grades, that the range increases. At Grade 5, the range is from 8.0 to 15.5, a difference of 7.5 years. At Grade 8, the difference has increased to 10 years. In other words, at the eighth-grade level, the lowest achieving student has a reading comprehension age equal to that of an average 9-year-old (a fourth-grade student) whereas the highest reading achiever in the eighth grade comprehends as well as the average 19-year-old—the reading

FIGURE 3.2. Measured Range of Reading Comprehension Ages in Grades 2 Through 8

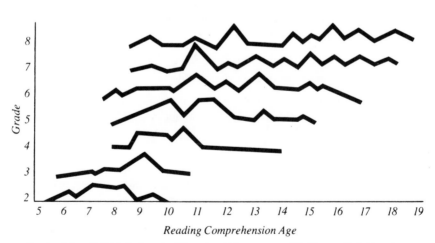

Reading Comprehension Age

Reprinted from E.F. Lindquist, ed., *Educational Measurement* (Washington, D.C.: American Council on Education, 1951), p. 13. Used by permission.

achievement score of an average student one year after graduation from high school! Thus, the range of reading achievement in any class is very wide, at least as wide as the mental age of the group.

Determining Range of Reading Achievement

COMPUTING THE EXPECTED RANGE

Shown below is a formula for computing the *expected reading range* in a class where student IQs range from 67 to 133.

$$\text{Expected reading age range} = \tfrac{2}{3} \times \text{average chronological age of the group}$$

The range in reading achievement for a 10th-grade class, which includes all, or a representative sample of, the students in the 10th grade and which has an average chronological age of 15, is shown here.

$$\text{Expected reading age range} = \tfrac{2}{3} \times 15 = 10 \text{ years}$$

Because the average reading age in the 10th grade is 15, the reading range would vary from 10 to 20 years. Half of the 10-year range would be added to the average of 15 and half would be subtracted from this average age.

Knowing the expected range of reading achievement in their classes, teachers are not likely to believe that all students should be reading up to grade level or that they should try to keep any student from going beyond grade level in achievement. Instead the ideal goal for teachers at successive grade levels would be to increase the range of reading achievement. Why? Because the mental-age range for a group increases each year, and we assume that students should be attaining reading achievement levels equal to their mental-age levels. Nor should junior high or high school teachers complain that elementary teachers should have done a better job of teaching reading, if in fact the group fits the expected

---

BOX 3.1. Some Widely Used Survey Tests
of Reading Achievement in Junior and Senior High School

Gates-MacGinitie Reading Tests, Surveys E, Grades 7–9, and F, Grades 10–12. Published by Teachers College Press, Columbia University, 1970. The test has three subscales: speed and accuracy, vocabulary, and comprehension. Test time: 46 minutes. A reliable and well-constructed test. Uses a multiple choice type of technique for assessing comprehension.

Metropolitan Reading Achievement Test, Advanced Form, Grades 7–9. Published by Harcourt Brace Jovanovich, 1970. Measures vocabulary and comprehension. Test time: 46 minutes. Well-constructed test.

Nelson-Denny Reading Test, Grades 9–16. Published by Houghton Mifflin, 1973.

range in reading achievement. Teachers at each level have to accept the fact that the range in reading achievement increases as students progress through the grades and learn to teach all students within this normal, expected range. Even if students are divided into ability levels, or into achievement groups, or placed into tracks, there would still be a range of reading achievement in each group (Balow, 1962; Cook, 1951) and this range is even likely to increase as a result of downward and upward adaptations of the curriculum (Balow, 1964). Since homogeneous groups, in which all students are alike do not exist, teachers can expect classes made up of students with a wide range of individual differences in reading achievement. Each teacher should determine the range of reading achievement in his or her class.

MEASURING THE ACTUAL RANGE OF INDIVIDUAL DIFFERENCES IN GENERAL READING ACHIEVEMENT

To determine a class's or school's range of individual differences in general reading achievement, teachers can administer a *survey test*. An annotated list of survey tests is given in Box 3.1. Survey tests usually assess reading comprehension, speed, and vocabulary. The Gates-MacGinitie Reading Tests are typical. We use the Gates-MacGinitie as an example of a survey test and explain how it can be employed for determining range of individual differences.

Comprehension

The Gates-MacGinitie assesses comprehension by a multiple-choice type of cloze test.[1] Each paragraph has two key words omitted. Below the paragraph are two rows of five words, one row of choices for each key word omitted. The student reads the paragraph and underlines the one word in each row to indicate his or her choice of one of the missing key words in the paragraph. See the sample paragraph in Box 3.2.

The comprehension paragraphs are arrayed from easy to difficult. As students progress through the test, they find that they have more and more difficulty in filling in the missing blanks. Eventually, the students stop because they realize they have reached their limit in reading achievement or else they run out of time. Some students may find that the entire test is too difficult and do not answer any of the items correctly. Others guess at answers and get only a chance score.

The Gates-MacGinitie Reading Test, like any survey test, spans a wide range of reading achievement. Yet a test standardized for a particular grade level may

---

[1]The cloze type of comprehension test deletes words from a passage that is usually about 250 words long. In the traditional form of the test, every fifth word is deleted. A reader than tries to infer from the meaning and the syntax of the passage what the missing words are and retrieve them from their vocabulary storage. See chapter 10 (''Determining Readability Levels and Their Applications'') for an example of a cloze test. The Gates-MacGinitie modifies the task of deleting only key words in a short paragraph and providing readers with a multiple choice of words for the necessary key words.

BOX 3.2. *Sample Comprehension Paragraph from the Gates-MacGinitie Reading Test*

Directions: Draw a line under the best word in Rows C1 and C2 for each of the blanks.

The Weather Bureau gives each hurricane a girl's name. Each year the first ____C1____ is given a name that begins with A, such as ____C2____

C1. month hurricane name Bureau start

C2. Mary Betsy Linda Susan Alice

---

be too difficult for some students and too easy for others. Students who score at the "bottom" of the test (zero or close to zero items correct) should be retested on a test standardized for a lower grade level, whereas those students who score at the "top" of the test (all or almost all items correct) should be retested on a *standardized test* for the next higher grade level.

Another problem with survey tests is that students who are slow readers may nevertheless be powerful readers. These students may, in fact, be superior in reading comprehension, but time limits on the test prevent them from obtaining a high score in comprehension. Two criteria can be used to detect this type of reader: (a) All or almost all items attempted on the comprehension test are correct, and usually at least 50% of the items have been attempted. (b) On a speed-of-reading test, this type of reader may score in the bottom half of the group. Consequently, a speed-of-reading test has an important function in diagnosing reading.

Speed of Reading

Students have a variety of reading rates, depending on their purpose in reading and the difficulty of the material (Holmes & Singer, 1966). Hence, the speed of reading assessed by the Gates-MacGinitie Reading Test is only one type of speed of reading.

The Gates-MacGinitie determines speed of reading by having the student read relatively easy paragraphs of uniform difficulty. After each paragraph, students answer a simple question. Hence, this speed-of-reading subtest might be called a rate-of-comprehension test for relatively easy material. See the sample paragraph in Box 3.3.

Students who have mastered the first phase of reading development can get all the paragraphs correct on the speed-of-reading subtest, if given enough time. But time for reading and responding to the 36 paragraphs in the test is drastically

---

BOX 3.3. *Sample Paragraph from Speed of Reading Subtest of Gates-MacGinitie Reading Tests, Form F*

Directions: Read the paragraph. Under the paragraph are four words. Draw a line under one of the four words that best answers the question asked in the paragraph.

In the far north, a frozen river winds between two high mountains. It does not melt even in summer. A river like this is found only in places that are

mild   hot   cold   sunny

---

limited to only 4 minutes. Indeed, the time limit was set low so that no student would be able to read and respond to all the paragraphs. Consequently, results on the test will show the range of individual differences in speed of reading.

Differentiating Types of Readers

The results on both the speed and comprehension subtests may indicate that a student is a slow but powerful reader or that the student is a slow reader who has not yet mastered the initial phase of reading. The vocabulary subtest of the Gates-MacGinitie Reading Test helps to differentiate these two types of readers.

The vocabulary subtest of the Gates-MacGinitie Test consists of items in which a key word is followed by a multiple choice of five words. The student's task is to select the synonym closest in meaning to the key word. The list of 50 items of the vocabulary subtest starts with relatively easy, commonly used words; gradually the words become less common and more difficult. See the sample item from the vocabulary subtest in Box 3.4.

If a student gets a relatively high score in vocabulary and a low score in comprehension and speed of reading, the student is a slow reader, but he or she may be a powerful reader if given adequate time to read. However, a student who scores low on all three tests is likely to be in the initial phase of reading development, that is, still learning how to read.

The distribution of survey test scores reveals the magnitude of the class's range of individual differences. The teacher's task, if he or she is to provide for equality of educational opportunity, is to adopt strategies that will handle this range of individual differences. Ideally, this will be done without stigmatizing students, yet all students will have the opportunity to develop toward their level of capability and toward independence in reading and learning from texts. Strategies in the next chapter and throughout this text are aimed at helping teachers achieve these objectives, not only in general reading ability, but also in learning from texts in each content area.

BOX 3.4. *Sample Item from Vocabulary Subtest of Gates-MacGinitie Reading Tests, Form F*

Directions: Read the first word, "rush." Then draw a line under one of the five words that means most nearly the same.

rush

back

grab

grow

hurry

spend

INTRAINDIVIDUAL DIFFERENCES

Students are not homogeneous in their reading abilities. They have intraindividual differences, that is, they have differences within themselves in their various abilities. They differ not only in their subskills, such as their word recognition and vocabulary abilities (Balow, 1962), but also in their ability to learn from text in different content areas. For example, the Sequential Tests of Educational Progress assess ability to learn from text in mathematics, science, social science, and reading (the passages on the reading test for the college level form of the test are drawn from different areas of the curriculum, such as biology, political science, and psychology). The correlation at the college level between reading and mathematics is .25, science, .42, and social science, .55. These correlations indicate that a person can read and learn from a mathematics text very well yet not perform as well on a survey test of reading ability. The same interpretation can be given to the relationship between performance in reading and in science or in social science. In short, if you construct a bar graph of the results of a person who is assessed on reading in the content areas, you will find a profile of reading abilities. The strengths will reflect the courses, experiences, and interests the person has had and the weaknesses will represent the relative lack of courses, experiences, and interests. The implication is that a person has to learn how to learn from text in each content area.

SUMMARY

Reading development consists of two overlapping phases: (a) learning how to read and (b) learning from text.

Learning how to read (reading acquisition) can be mastered by most students. Indeed, many students master the process of learning how to read prior to eighth grade. Individual differences in this first phase of reading development conse-quently *decrease* as a group of students progresses through the grades. But, even though students have mastered the process of reading, they will still have to learn how to prnounce and read technical terms, symbols, and other features of text peculiar to each content area.

Learning from text (general reading achievement) is a process that is highly correlated with general mental ability. In progressing through school, students increase their ability to learn from text as they acquire new information, vocabu-lary, and concepts; as they improve in their reasoning abilities; and as they learn strategies for learning from texts and modes of thinking that are characteristic of each content area. This improvement is related not only to learning and instruc-tion in the content areas, but also to mental age, which increases from grade to grade. Therefore, ability to learn from text, as indicated by a survey test of general comprehension, also *increases* as students progress through school. Hence, the major task of teachers shifts from teaching students how to read toward teaching them how to learn from texts in the content areas.

This chapter also explained how a teacher can determine the range of indi-vidual differences in general reading achievement. Three parts of a survey test, the Gates-MacGinitie, were described and a sample item from each part of the test was provided, along with some directions for administering and interpreting the results of the test.

Knowledge of the range of general reading achievement (an index of ability to learn from text) will make a teacher appreciate the necessity of developing strategies to meet this wide range of individual differences in his or her class. The next chapter describes these strategies.

ACTIVITIES

1. If you are teaching or assisting in a classroom, construct a frequency distribu-tion of the results of a reading achievement test. To do so, use the graph in Figure 3.3. Simply write all the test scores on the horizontal axis. Then, in the box below each test score, write the number of students who earned that score. Next, draw bars above the scores to show the frequency (the number of stu-dents) who earned a particular score. Compare the results with the data shown in the graphs in Figures 3.1, and 3.2. Does your class show more or less variability than is shown on these two graphs?
2. If you teach a public school class, give a norm-referenced test for your grade at the beginning of the year. At the end of the year, give the same test to all students. Analyze results for (a) the total class, (b) only those students who scored between the 25th and the 75th percentile at the beginning of the year, and (c) those students who scored above the 75th percentile and below the 25th percentile. Plot the percentile gains for individual students and for the class means. Which students have gained? Which students have not? What would you recommend for students in either category?

FIGURE 3.3. Frequency Distribution Graph for Results of a Reading Achievement Test

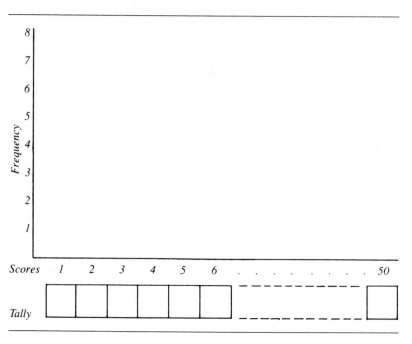

4 | Theories and Research on Reading and Learning from Text

CHAPTER OVERVIEW

Theories and research on reading have changed in a progressive way over the past century (Singer, 1983d). Although thousands of studies on reading have been conducted during this time, there have only been three widely accepted conceptions of reading: oral reading to reconstruct printed words so that meaning could be associated to them, silent reading to reason while reading and extract meaning from print, and text-reader interactions that result in the construction of meaning (Singer, 1984). In this chapter, we explain how each of these conceptions of reading has determined how we teach, assess, and study reading (Singer, 1981a). We also cite the landmark research studies that undergird each conception.

GRAPHIC ORGANIZER

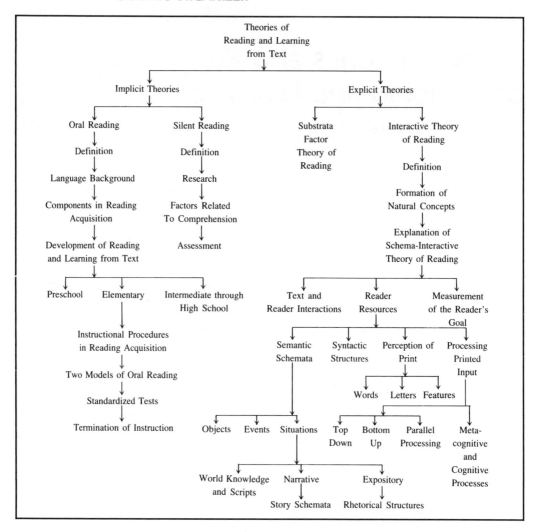

PREPOSED QUESTIONS

1. What are the three conceptions of reading?
2. What is phonemic awareness? Is it necessary for reading acquisition?
3. Can you explain a model of oral reading and show how it is related to assessment of oral reading?
4. What enables readers to comprehend better in silent than in oral reading?
5. Do the different conceptions of reading result in differences in how we teach, assess, and study reading? Give an example of each.
6. Can you explain the schema-interactive theory of reading?
7. What is meant by scriptal comprehension?

ORAL READING

The first definition states that reading is the ability to identify and pronounce printed words. This definition was dominant in American reading instruction from 1642 until about 1920 (N.B. Smith, 1965a). During this time, instruction focused primarily on teaching students how to identify printed words and read them aloud with appropriate intonation.

Intonation consists of the variations in pitch, stress, pause, and sentence contour that occur in speech (LeFevre, 1964). Teachers can determine from a student's use of intonation or lack of intonation whether they are reading the text with understanding and feeling or merely saying the words.

To teach oral reading, you should have some knowledge of children's language abilities, the relationship between these abilities and reading, and principles of teaching reading.

FIRST GRADERS' LANGUAGE BACKGROUND

First graders already know how to make proper intonations. Indeed, intonation with its communication of meaning differentiates out of the early crying expressions of infants and babies. First graders also have well-developed language subsystems: they have a semantic or word meaning system that contains about 5,000 words; a syntactic system that has almost all the syntactic structures, the word order and grammatical forms, that adults know and can use in their speech; and a sound system whose phonological components, rules for pronouncing sounds and words, are adequate for expressing their needs and ideas to their peers and adults (Athey, 1985; Ruddell & Haggard, 1985). In short, you do not have to teach first graders oral language as a prerequisite for reading instruction if they are native speakers and are being taught how to read in their own language.

Phonemic Awareness

However, you do have to teach phonemic awareness, the ability to segment words into their constituent phonemes and manipulate them (Yopp, 1987). Phonemes are minimal units of sound that make for differences in meaning. For example, the words *pin* and *pen* each have three phonemes and these two words differ in only one phoneme. This phonemic contrast in vowel sounds changes the meanings of these two words.

To test for phonemic awareness, ask students to say a word, such as *cat,* and then say the word again leaving off the initial sound. There are actually at least two factors in tests of phonemic awareness (Yopp, 1987). The first factor is called *simple* because it involves only one operation, such as deletion of a sound, blending sounds together, or segmenting a word into its separate sounds. The second factor is *compound* because it requires students to segment a word, hold the first sound in memory, and blend it with the remaining sound. For example, say "stand without the /t/ in it."

You can use a "stretch and snip" method to teach phonemic awareness. First you draw out the pronunciation of a word, such as /*mmmaaannn*/, and then you ask the students to say the word without the /*mmm*/ (Gough, 1985a). You may start the stretch and snip method with compound words, such as *flashlight*, asking students to leave off the morpheme, *flash,* and say the rest of the word. When students understand the easier task of morpheme deletion, you can then request them to delete phonemes in words.

Some students acquire phonemic awareness on their own prior to first grade, probably by abstracting sounds from words, such as /*ch*/ in /*church, touch, satchel*/. They are more successful in learning in the initial steps in reading acquisition in a symbol-sound correspondence program. Success in this initial instruction is significantly related to reading achievement in Grade 1 (H. Yopp, 1987; H. Yopp & Singer, 1985). Thus, phonemic awareness is causally related to reading achievement. In fact, phonemic awareness at the beginning of reading instruction is a better predictor of reading achievement at the end of Grade 1 than general intelligence (Stanovich, 1986).

We also know that the process of instruction in beginning reading develops phonemic awareness in students (Perfetti, 1985; Perfetti & Beck, 1982). For example, in phonics instruction, you can model phonemic awareness when you point to an initial consonant and identify its sound. You are teaching your students to segment and sound the individual letters in a word. Thus, through this and other instructional processes in phonics, your students will tend to learn not only grapheme-phoneme correspondence, but also phonemic awareness. Such grapheme-phoneme instruction means that phonemic awareness is not only a cause of reading acquisition, but also a concomitant of reading instruction. In short, there is reciprocal causation between phonemic awareness acquisition and reading acquisition (Perfetti, 1985).

Language of Instruction

You also have to teach the language of instruction. First graders do not know the meaning of *word, sentence, page,* and so on. These words that direct students' attention and behavior in reading instruction have to be taught directly to students in the initial stage of reading acquisition (Downing & Oliver, 1973-1974).

English as a Second Language

Students who do not speak English or have a language handicap may require oral language instruction prior to learning to read. After you teach them English words and sentences, you can teach them how to identify the corresponding printed version. That is, they do not have to become fluent in English before you initiate reading instruction. However, schools vary in treatment of bilinguals. Some schools believe in complete immersion in English whereas others teach students to read in their native language while they are learning English as a second language and then initiate the transition to instruction in reading in English. Some schools make this transition as early as first grade.

COMPONENTS IN READING ACQUISITION

Although beginning readers may be native speakers of the language, they do not automatically apply their language abilities as they are beginning to learn how to read. At this time they may be concentrating their attention only on learning how to identify printed words. Consequently, you have to teach students how to use their language abilities while they are reading. For example, you can have them complete sentences read to them. You can say: "The painter uses a brush and —."

By the end of first grade, most students are beginning to integrate their identification of printed words with use of their language abilities (Weber, 1970). In short, they have made considerable progress in learning how to read. They have begun to learn (a) how to identify printed words, (b) how to use their language background while reading, and (c) how to integrate both of these processes rapidly, accurately, and in the appropriate sequence (Biemiller, 1970). Which of these components they learn first depends on the method emphasized in instruction (Barr, 1972, 1975): If you stress a language experience method of teaching, your students may first learn to use their language background while reading, but if you start with a phonics method, they will initially learn to sound out printed words.

DEVELOPMENT OF READING
AND LEARNING FROM TEXT

Preschool Level

For some children, reading instruction begins when their parents start to read to them. Some parents may do so as early as age 1 or earlier. During this preschool instruction, they are exposing children to stories. As the children acquire language, they can converse with their parents about the stories (Durkin, 1962). Consequently, they learn that stories can be enjoyable, that pages turn from left to right, and that stories have general characteristics, such as a beginning, middle, and end. If exposure to stories also results in children making repeated responses to printed words, 3- and 4-year-olds can learn to identify some of them (Davidson, 1931).

Elementary School Level

(a) Picture-story method. At the kindergarten level, you can bridge the gap between prior and new knowledge by having children draw a picture and tell you a story about the picture. Usually the story is only one sentence long. You write this sentence under the picture. Then you have the child "read" the sentence. Gradually the child may learn to identify some words at sight, using cues from the printed words. Perhaps the words are *I, you, she, he, see, go, home, tree.* You can combine these words with picture cards to produce a wide variety of sentences, such as "I saw a tree (or any pictured noun)." If the printed word for the noun is on the back of the card so that they have to attend to the print (Samuels, 1967; Singer, Samuels, & Spiroff, 1973-1974), your students can learn it and add it to their sight word repertoire. The students can use these cards to construct their own sentences. When these kindergartners enter first grade, they are ready for the next stage of reading development, the language experience method.

(b) Language experience approach. You start this approach by providing students with a common experience, such as observing goldfish in a bowl. You ask the students what they saw and write their answers on the board. You then have the students read their stories. You can have them not only read the sentences but also identify individual words and even learn the sounds for individual letters in the story. Eventually the students learn to write and read their own and other students' stories. In this method, your students will emphasize their language background. After this language experience approach, students may go into a more formal instructional program consisting of individualized reading or a basal reader, or preferably both.

(c) Individualized reading. Individualized reading consists of self-selection of books with guidance from the teacher. The teacher checks a student's comprehension of a book by having the student recall the story and answer a few questions about the characters, plot, outcome, and the student's evaluation of the book. The teacher also notes word recognition problems and corrects them then or at a later time for a group of students with common word recognition problems. Most teachers next use a basal reader to teach the word recognition, word meaning, and comprehension skills involved in reading. Basal readers provide a systematic way of developing reading. They differ mostly in how they start instruction. Some basal readers, such as the Ginn and Scott Foresman series, begin with whole words; others, such as the Open Court and Lippincott series, emphasize phonics.

(d) Basal reader: Whole-word method. A basal reader is a more systematic way of teaching students to read and learn from text. Its vocabulary is carefully controlled. Each new word is taught by the teacher, used immediately in a story, and then cumulatively with other new words in subsequent stories until students have acquired word recognition techniques for independently identifying novel words.

A teacher's manual that accompanies the basal reader contains prepared lessons for teaching word identification and comprehension. Each comprehension lesson usually consists of five steps by the teacher:

1. Establishes a purpose for reading and arouses students' curiosity for the story.
2. Introduces new vocabulary.
3. Relates the story to students' prior knowledge and experiences.
4. Guides the reading of the story through questions.
5. Directs students to read the rest of the story silently to answer previously posed questions or to prepare for answering questions at the end of the story.

At the end of the comprehension lesson, teachers have skill lesson options. They may have students learn to skim and scan by having them search through the story again to find answers to specific questions. Or they can teach some aspect of word recognition; if word recognition lessons are taught prior to reading a story, students can apply the new skill to identifying words in the story. You should note that although this basal reader starts with whole words, it eventually teaches students all aspects of word recognition, including phonics, context, and structural analysis.

Thus, the basal reader teaches comprehension primarily through questions that direct students to focus attention on important components. If the questions are based on story grammar concepts and teachers ask these questions at appropriate points in the story, students are more likely to learn to segment stories at the junctures. In other words, they become able to classify story content into the relevant story grammar structures and store the content in memory in an organized way. They can subsequently use their story grammar structures to retrieve the story from memory (Beck, Omanson, & McKeown, 1982). (See last section of this chapter for information on story schema.)

Some teachers might not use a language experience approach with its lead-in to individualized reading and/or a whole-word basal reader method. Instead, they might start with a basal reader that emphasizes "phonics first" (Flesch, 1981; Singer, 1983b).

(e) Basal reader: Phonics. Typically in this method of instruction, you proceed from letters to stories. You first teach students individual letters and the sounds for them. For example, you could start with the letter /a/, then add the letters /m/ and /n/, and then have your students blend these letters to make up words, such as /an/, /man/, /ma/. This instruction provides the information for students to construct their own sounds in response to printed words. Subsequently you will have your students learn to identify these words in organized sentences. Then your students progress to reading stories. In this method of reading acquisition, word identification is likely to be learned first and use of language background second. However, as they develop fluency in reading, your students will bypass the phonological process, and perceive words visually as sight words. If they have to respond to a new word, they can fall back on sounding it out (Maclean, 1988).

Although basal readers today include some expository material, they still tend to emphasize narrative reading. However, a gradual shift occurs from narrative to expository texts at the high school level. But narrative and expository texts overlap. Some stories may contain information consisting of facts, concepts, and generalizations. Some expository texts may also contain stories, such as a scientist in a particular setting who is trying to solve a problem and reach a goal.

However, these types of materials differ in structure and content. At the beginning stages of reading acquisition, stories are familiar and frequently within students' own experiential repertoires. Subsequently the students will have to learn to comprehend less familiar stories and even less familiar expository content. As this change occurs, teachers shift from instructional emphasis on teaching students how to read to strategies for teaching students to read silently in order to comprehend or learn from texts.

Intermediate Grade through High School

From the intermediate grades on, you can use a variety of strategies for teaching students how to read and learn from text in the content areas; these strategies are presented in chapter 6. You can also have your students engage in (a) recreational reading, where they read for pleasure or to satisfy their own curiosity, (b) enrichment reading, where they read a variety of books on the same subject and thus learn a topic in depth, (c) applied reading, where they read and use the knowledge gleaned from texts in various ways, such as participating in discussion groups, constructing a model plane, or following directions for baking a cake, and (d) developmental reading, where they systematically learn word recognition, word meaning, and comprehension skills, and practice using them in reading stories and expository texts. Thus, a comprehensive program in elementary school comes under the acronym, READ, for *r*ecreational, *e*nrichment, *a*pplied, and *d*evelopmental reading activities. In the developmental activities, you will be teaching your students how to read and, in the other activities, you will be giving them ways of using their reading ability. This combination is analogous to a swimming coach teaching skills on land and then having students engage in free swimming where they try out and integrate the new skills with those already in their repertoire.

A time line depicting this instructional sequence is shown in Figure 4.1 (Singer, 1981b).

FIGURE 4.1. *Time Line for a Developmental Sequence of Instruction.*

Initiating Instruction	Transition to Formal Reading Instruction		Formal Reading Instruction	
Reading to Children			READ Program (Recreational, Enrichment, Application,	
Exposure and Conversational Methods	Picture Story Method	Rebus Method	Language Experience Approach	Developmental) Basal Reader Dev. skills Appl. skills and Literature Recreational Enrichment Application	Content Area Instruction
Age 3 to 4	5 to 6		6 to 10	10 and up
		Age		

Arrows in the table: Exposure and Conversational Methods → Picture Story Method; Language Experience Approach → Basal Reader; Developmental → Content Area Instruction.

INSTRUCTIONAL PROCEDURES
IN READING ACQUISITION

Under the oral definition of reading, you can use a variety of instructional procedures to teach students how to identify printed words, use their language background while reading, and integrate these two components in order to read aloud with appropriate intonation (Singer, 1981b; N.B. Smith, 1965a). In general, you will be teaching your students these components of reading:

Identification of Letter Features

Letter features consist of the horizontal, vertical, slanted, and circular lines that make up letters; for example, students learn whether the line and circle come before or after each other, as in *b,d,p,q* (Gibson, 1965, 1985; Gibson & Levin, 1975). Students may learn these features through instruction and practice in simultaneous matching of a letter to the same letter among several choices, such as a *b* to be matched to one of these letters: *d, p, b, q.* Because the letter and the choices are on the same page, the student can look back and forth, comparing the features of the letter and the choices to which it is to be matched. The process leads to the development of detectors for the features of letters. Detectors may be neurological circuits within readers that enable them to discriminate letters from each other.

Next, students get delayed matching-to-sample so that they can integrate the features for particular letters. In this exercise students see the sample item, such as the letter *b* on one page and the multiple choices, such as *b,p,d,* and *q,* on the next page. Students have to keep all the features in mind in order to match the sample to the correct choice. Thus students learn to perceive whole letters (Samuels, 1976), perhaps because the practice leads to the development of detectors for whole letters.

Finally, students acquire detectors for whole words. These detectors operate not only in relation to printed words but also in response to higher order processes, such as syntax and semantics. In short, an interaction occurs between printed materials and resources within the reader. An illustration of this interaction is depicted by a current model of word identification shown in Figure 4.2. It indicates that the visual stimulus first progresses through feature, letter, and word detectors. The outputs from these detectors interact with each other and with higher order knowledge sources. These sources include use of orthographic knowledge (correct spelling of words), lexical knowledge (selection of words that exist in an individual's lexicon or dictionary-like entries for words), syntax (word order and organization of words into such structures as noun and verb phrases), and semantics (meanings of words, including the instantiation or the selection of the particular meanings of words called for by the meaning of the entire sentence). Thus, the model shows that perception of printed words is not a simple process (Johnston & McClelland, 1981).

Word identification processes can progress in a bottom-up fashion, from the stimuli in the text through the detectors and on to higher knowledge sources,

FIGURE 4.2. Johnston and McClelland's (1981) schematic diagram of a fragment of proposed hierarchical theory of word identification. Diagram shows hypothetical activation state of the detector network after presentation of the target word READ.

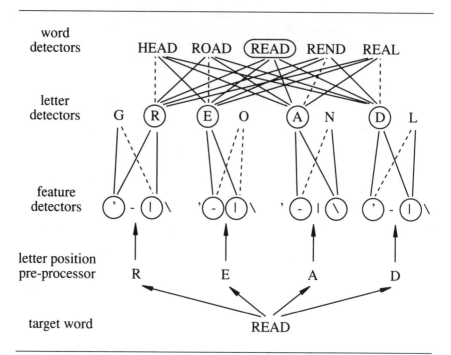

such as syntax, which groups words into noun and verb phrases, and then semantics, which gives them meaning. They can also act in a top-down sequence with the expectancies of the reader propagating downward and influencing the anticipation of the printed stimuli by all the other knowledge sources. The knowledge sources can also each interact with the text data simultaneously, independently, and in compensatory ways (Stanovich, 1980), using direct, analytical processes (Gough, 1976; McConkie & Rayner, 1976) if the words are familiar or contextual, inferential processes if they are unfamiliar (Adams & Huggins, 1985; Au, 1986; Samuels, 1985). In short, all the knowledge sources can act to influence each other in mutual and reciprocal ways and simultaneously in parallel ways with the stimuli in the text (Adams & Collins, 1977/1985). That is why readers can understand a sentence by the time they get to the end of it.

Symbol-Sound Correspondences, Perceiving
Letters and Providing Sounds for Them

Synonyms for symbol-sound correspondence are grapheme-phoneme correspondence and phonics. Venezky (1970) has identified 65 functional units that are the graphemes of the English writing system. They are vowels, consonants, and combinations of vowels and consonants that call for single sounds, such as digraphs (th, ph) and glides (ey, ow). They more than adequately represent the 46 phonemes in English phonology. These functional units are shown in Box 4.1.

BOX 4.1. Functional Units of English Orthography, After Venezky (1970)

Note: Simple consonants, which appear here in initial position, can occur in any position. So can most of the other units.

Consonant and Consonant Combinations
Embedded in Content Area Words

b-biology	k-kinship	s-semicolon	ch-channel
c-congruent	l-legislative	t-teleplay	gh-ghost
d-democracy	m-multiplier	u-ultraviolet	ph-phase
f-factor	n-nonconductor	v-vocal	sh-shares
g-gas	p-pantomime	w-waltz	th-theocracy
h-humanity	q-quartile	y-yoke	th-thin
f-function	r-retrorocket	z-zipper	wh-whether
			dock-ck
			judge-dg
			batch-tch
			six-cks

Vowel and Vowel Combinations

a-antebellum	ai-aim/ray	oa-boast
e-epidemic	au-astronaut/law	oe-cargoes
i-interplanetary	ea-east/eel	oi-oil/Troy
o-optical	ew-dew/deuce	oo-moon
u-upright	ey-whey	ou-outer space/clown
y-cycle	ie-piece	ue-deuce/sluice

Students learn these functional units in isolation and then obtain practice in perceiving them in their whole-word contexts as they read their stories. Immediate use of these skills in the context of relatively easy reading materials enables students to integrate the skills into their word recognition repertoire and use them in the proper time and sequence as they read. This learning process is analogous to learning a swimming skill on shore and then going into a pool to practice it in relationship to all the other skills involved in swimming. Stories in basal readers and the classroom libraries are the swimming pools where reading skills get integrated. As the skills mesh and function smoothly, students attain "psychosynchromeshing facility."

To teach the skills in isolation, you first say the letter's name, then you give the sound for the letter. You can repeat the process for several words that have the same letter sound in them. Students then imitate what you did. You can test whether they have abstracted and can generalize the letter-sound relationship by having them identify the combination in novel words. For example, they can learn /c/ in /cow, cat, cup/ and then you can test them on /cap/ or /cot/. Thus, your students will learn to identify the printed stimuli and hook up sounds to them. In other words, they will be learning to use their phonological system to generate sounds for printed stimuli (Samuels, 1976). The phonological system consists of rules that individuals have acquired that direct their formation of sounds in speech.

Instructional materials usually teach consonants first because they are more stable than vowels and communicate most of a word's identification. Indeed, you can identify a printed word with the vowels missing. For example, you can read this sentence:

N_w _s th_ t_me f_r _ll g_d m_n t_ c_me t_ th_ _d _f th_ r p_rty.

Vowels come next. Sometimes teachers use the principles, shown in Box 4.2, to teach vowel sounds:

BOX 4.2. *Principles for Vowel Sounds*

a. In a word that ends in a vowel, the vowel is usually long.
   Examples: be, say, go, marry.
b. In a single-syllable word that has two adjacent vowels in it, the first vowel is usually long and the second is silent; the beginning vowel is usually pronounced as long.
   Examples: eat, seat, tea.
c. An exception to (b) is that diphthongs, which have two vowels, are neither long nor short, but represent a combination of these two vowels. Other exceptions also occur.
   Examples: oil, how. Others: read, said, lead.
d. In a single-syllable word with a vowel between consonants (CVC or CVCC, or CCVC), the vowel is usually short.
   Examples: cup, last, this.
e. In a single-syllable word ending in a silent e, the middle vowel is usually long (CVCe)
   Examples: cape, like, use.

Blending the Sounds Together (Samuels, 1976)

Beck (1986) has demonstrated that students can more readily blend sounds together if you simplify the task. First, have your students synthesize the small units to form larger units and then add an additional unit. For example, /c-a-t/ becomes /ca/, then /t/ is added. This instruction might enable students to develop *unitizers,* cognitive processes that combine letters and letter-sound relationships into whole words (LaBerge, 1979).

Use of Language Background Through Emphasis on Context Cues for Inferring Unknown Words

Context cues consist of the use of semantics, the cumulative meaning of the sentence, and syntax, the rules governing the order of words in a sentence. Both of these processes are involved in reader expectations for words in a sentence. For example, the semantic and syntactic cues of this sentence enable the reader to predict its final word: "When the girl received the mail, she read the ------." Because the combination of semantics and syntax limits the choice of words that complete the sentence, this process is also known as the use of "sentence constraints."

Readers use context cues for disambiguating homonyms, words that sound alike, but have different meanings, such as "He *led* the army" and "He has *lead* in his bullets." You can teach students to use context cues by having them practice completion of sentences, as in the above example, and by reading relatively easy material, the kind of material students would read for recreation or enjoyment.

Structural Analysis

It includes syllabication, division of words into syllables, and morphemic analysis, division of words into their constituent meanings. A syllable is a combination of letters that contains a heard vowel sound, such as /lit/ and /tle/ in /little/. Morphemes are the minimal units of meaning in words. Hence, morphemic analysis consists of division of words at their meaning boundaries, such as the boundaries between compound words, /shep-herd/), or between words and their affixes, /beauti-ful/. For some words, such as /shepherd/, readers must first use morphemic analysis to divide the word at its morpheme boundaries and then they can use their knowledge of symbol-sound correspondences to sound out each morpheme. This dual process indicates that the English writing system is not strictly an alphabetic, but actually a morphophonemic, system. Indeed, the spelling of morphemes in the English writing system tends to be maintained, even though their sounds might change. For example, in the words /nation/ and /nationality/, note that the sound of the /a/ in the first word changes in the second word.

Systematic instruction and practice in syllabication and morphemic analysis usually begins about third grade when students start to encounter a higher density of multisyllabic words.

English has over 5,000 syllables. To teach all of them would require more time and memory than teaching children to become fluent in reading Chinese characters. However, the principles, shown in Box 4.3, govern the syllabication of a large number of words.

BOX 4.3. Principles of Syllabication

a. When one vowel sound occurs in a word, it usually has one syllable.
    Examples: oak, see, go, try, mate.
b. When a word ends in -le, the -le forms a separate syllable. If a -b precedes the -le, it begins the syllable.
    Examples: pick-le, nick-le. Aud-i-ble
c. When two consonants occur between vowels, divide the word between the consonants.
    Examples: but-ter, mat-ter, ran-ger
d. Prefixes, suffixes, and inflectional elements usually form separate syllables.
    Examples: beau-ti-ful, work-er. go-ing, sand-ed

    Polysyllabic words, words that have more than one syllable, require a combination of these principles. Use the principles by starting with the division of a word into morphemes, then take off the affixes and apply the principles to the remaining parts of the word.
    Examples: circumference = circum-ference =
    circum-fer-ence = cir-cum fer-ence

Identification of Sight Words, Words that can be Recognized Instantly

Beginning readers identify cues for words that enable them to identify the whole word. At this stage they are cue readers. Cues only work till words with similar cues appear, usually after about 15 to 20 words have been introduced (Samuels, 1971). Then readers have to switch to a systematic way of perceiving words, such as symbol-sound correspondence, mapping sounds on to individual letters. This process enables them to learn the alphabetical principle that there is a sound for each letter or letter combination. Then they are in the ciphering stage of word recognition (Gough, 1985a). Later, they can recognize many words instantly because they have developed whole-word detectors (McClelland & Rumelhart, 1981/1985; Rumelhart, 1985) or because they have attained automaticity for the words; that is, they have acquired *unitizers,* an organization of cognitive processes that enables individuals to perceive words as whole words without any or with only minimal conscious attention to them. Consequently, we can say they have developed automaticity in word identification because they only have to give minimal attention to word recognition processes and can allocate maximal attention to processes for comprehending the text (LaBerge, 1979; LaBerge & Samuels, 1985).

Readers develop a repertoire of sight words as a result of repetition, most frequently by perceiving the same words repeatedly in a variety of printed materials. For example, 220 words and 95 common nouns account for 75% of all primary grade words and 50% of words encountered after the third grade (Dolch, 1952). Wide and interesting reading of relatively easy material, such as the series books, for example, *Nancy Drew* or *Tom Swift,* fosters fluency for these words because they appear with high frequency in these materials. These books tend to be handed down from one child to another as part of the ''culture of childhood.'' They are usually not found in libraries because they are not considered by librarians as ''good'' literature. Other series books, such as the *Doctor Doolittle* series that are found in school libraries, will also contribute to development of fluency. In general, students who learn to read early, participate in an environment where peers are also involved in reading books, and have families that support an interest in books may read 100 times as many books per year as students who do not learn to read in the beginning grades. They become the better readers not only because they develop fluency but also because their reading enables them to increase their vocabulary and their range of knowledge, which in turn, enhance their reading speed and comprehension and their enjoyment of reading, leading to even more reading. This cumulative process results in increasing the range of individual differences in reading achievement as a group of students progresses through school (Stanovich, 1986).

Students can also acquire fluency or automaticity for a given list of words, either through repetition of the words via a tachistoscope that flashes the words for some fraction of a second on a screen in a laboratory-type setting, via flash cards in a classroom, or by any procedure that provides frequency of response to the same set of printed words (Dahl & Samuels, 1975; Jenkins, Pany, & Schreck, 1978). However, under these conditions, students develop fluency only for the particular set of words; they do not develop the general fluency or automaticity that accrues from wide and frequent reading of children's literature.

Use of Intonation in Reading

You can teach intonation as a drama coach teaches actors and actresses to read with feeling. The coach explains the situation and stresses the feelings of the characters in the script. Similarly, you can explain to students the emotions involved in the characters and situations students are reading about; then the students are more likely to read aloud with the appropriate intonation.

Round-Robin Method

A widely used method for teaching oral reading is known as the round-robin method. You have one child read aloud while the others follow silently. You correct the word identifications of the oral reader. The assumption in this method is that each child is perceiving and identifying the same word as the oral reader and is thus receiving reinforcement by hearing each word as they read it.

However, Gilbert (1940) found that the method does not work: Good readers have their eye-movement patterns disrupted in trying to follow the oral reading of poor readers and the poor readers cannot keep up with the rate of reading of the good readers. You can probably observe round-robin reading by going into a primary-grade class when the teacher is teaching reading and has a circle of children around her. Notice what the other children are doing when another child is reading. Also, notice what happens when the teacher calls upon a good reader to read and later on, a poor reader.

What is the alternative? Use oral reading only for learning to read aloud to an audience and for diagnosis of individual readers. In this procedure, one student at a time reads aloud while the others in the group listen, but the group does so with questions that the teacher has given them or elicited from them about events in the story that they can respond to in silent ways. For example, the teacher may ask the group to open their mouths wide when the reader says that a door is opening. Thus, the group is purposefully listening to the child who is reading aloud (Singer, 1970).

All of the components and processes for identifying printed words that we have explained above are necessary because of the nature of English orthography: only 50% of English words are regularly spelled (Nelson, 1970). Therefore, you have to teach students multiple ways of identifying them.

Figure 4.3 contains a graphic organization of the relationship between language systems and word recognition components. The figure shows that language systems consist of syntax, semantics, and phonology. Syntax and seman-

FIGURE 4.3. Relationship between language systems and word recognition components. Intonation is another component of language; it draws upon phonology (sound contour for sentences and pitch, stress, and pause for elements within and between sentences) but also communicates meaning.

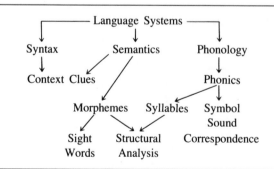

tics form the basis for context clues. Semantics is directly related to morphemes, which, in turn, are directly related to sight words. Phonology is directly related to phonics, which subdivides into syllabication and symbol-sound correspondences. Syllabication and morphemes are both involved in structural analysis. Thus, language systems underlie the four major methods of identifying printed words: context clues, sight words, structural analysis, and symbol-sound correspondences. Combinations of these four components are also used in word identification, for example, morphophonemics involves the use of morphemic analysis and then graphophonemics to identify words that have to be divided at their morpheme boundaries before graphophonemics rules can be used, as in the word /*shep herd*/.

TWO MODELS OF ORAL READING

Gough's Model

A definition of oral reading is assumed in the statement that all the processing of printed materials beyond word identification lies in the domain of thinking. An equivalent statement is that the only difference between reading and listening is that in reading the student has to pronounce the printed words himself; if the student can pronounce all the words, then reading comprehension is not different from listening comprehension (Gough, 1985a). A diagram of this conception of reading is shown in Figure 4.4. However, even if the claim is valid that after oral pronunciation of printed words, reading comprehension is no different than thinking or listening, perception of printed words is still a complex interactive process, as shown by the model in Figure 4.4.

FIGURE 4.4. Diagram of Oral Reading

Printed Words → Oral Pronunciation → Thinking or Listening

Goodman's Model

Another definition of oral reading, formulated by Goodman (1966, 1970), states that reading is a process in which a reader uses syntactic, semantic, and graphophonic systems to reconstruct printed words into their oral equivalents, to which meaning can be associated. The syntactic system is the grammar of a language; it involves the reader's use of word order, inflectional endings (as the endings in big, bigger, biggest), and function words, such as prepositions (to, for, by) and conjunctions (and, but, so). The syntactic cues provide considerable information. For example, read the following sentence, which has artificial words in it, except for the verb and the grammatical elements:

Baf went blajing in the saterm and caught the zavest sihf.

From the information given, you can answer these questions:

1. Who went blajing?
2. Where did Baf go blajing?
4. What did Baf catch?

Semantic information is the reader's meaning for words, drawn from his ideational knowledge. The graphophonic system consists of orthographic (spelling), phonological (rules for expressing words aloud), and phonic information (sounds that correspond with printed letters), and is used to relate visual patterns in the text to corresponding speech sounds in the reader. The reader samples cues from these three sources of information and makes inferences or predictions about the remaining information. For example, you can read this sentence with some print deleted to resemble sampling of the text:

> She went xx xxx store xx buy x xxxx xx bread.
> xxx loaf xx bread xxx long xxx thin.

The result is the oral reconstruction of the message, which is the process that occurs when you are reading and hear yourself mentally saying the words as you read. Then the reading comprehension process is analogous to the way an individual listens and comprehends when he hears spoken words. Sampling partly works because of the redundancy or repetitiousness of language. For example, how many times does this sentence tell you that there is more than one person:

> Three girls are going to do the dance for trios.

The correct answer is four (three, girls, are, trios). Oral language is even more redundant than printed language. If you listen to a taped conversation, you will notice that the speaker frequently repeats information, sometimes even saying the same sentence again.

Next, the reader tests the meaning to determine whether it is consistent with expectations, that is, whether it makes sense to the reader. If it does not make sense, the reader often rereads the passage. If it is consistent and does make sense, the reader continues to read on. The reader can store the message in long-term memory or orally encode it, that is, state the meaning in the reader's own words and express these words aloud. The degree of congruence between the writer's and the reader's ideational knowledge will determine how well the reader understands the writer's message. When the print is orally reconstructed but meaning is bypassed, then the reader is only orally *recoding* the printed message, that is, transforming the printed words into their oral counterparts. For example, recoding probably occurs when a parent is reading the same story to a child for the tenth time; the parent may be saying the words while thinking about something else. This conception of the two modes of oral reading is depicted in the model shown in Figure 4.5.

FIGURE 4.5.   Goodman's Model of Oral Reading

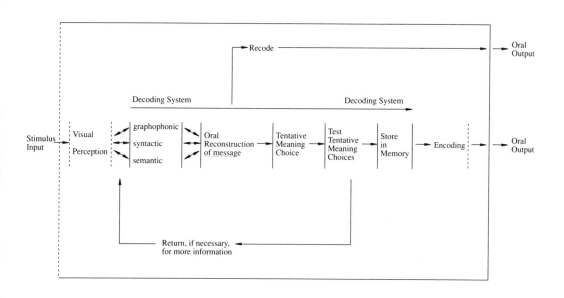

USE OF MODEL FOR DIAGNOSIS

The procedure in using this model for diagnosis is to have a student read a passage ''one level of difficulty beyond his current reading ability.'' To implement this direction, determine the student's current reading level on a test of oral reading, then continue testing until the passage is one grade above the student's current reading level. As the student reads the passage aloud, you can assess word recognition by noting the *miscues,* deviations of the oral responses from the printed words. The deviations are then categorized as being graphically similar (house, horse), phonemically similar (cow, how), semantically similar (house, home), or syntactically appropriate (noun for noun, verb for verb, etc.) to the printed word in the text. Only those miscues that represent changes in meaning require instructional intervention.

If the reader can pronounce the printed words correctly, but has low comprehension, then the reader is probably only ''recoding'' the passage. But if the reader not only orally reconstructs the printed words, but also self-corrects or rereads, then the reader is probably associating meaning to the orally constructed words and testing the meaning given to them; this process indicates that the reader is not only reading aloud but also trying to comprehend the passage.

You can assess comprehension by asking the reader to retell what he read in the text. You record the retelling and then probe the reader with questions to determine whether the reader has stored but did not retrieve essential expository or narrative information in the retelling. The expository information consists of facts, concepts, and generalizations. The narrative information involves identifying the story's characters, setting, plot, and resolution.

CAUTIONS IN DIAGNOSIS

Although this diagnostic procedure, originally used in the *Reading Miscue Inventory* (Goodman & Burke, 1972), provides some useful information, its limitation stems from the lack of norms for interpreting the results. Hence, this approach to diagnosis should be accompanied by results from a standardized oral reading test.

You also have to observe another caution in assessing oral reading and determining whether the reader comprehended the oral reading passage. If you have a student read a passage aloud at sight and then test the student's comprehension, such as having the student answer questions on the passage or recalling it, you will get a lower estimate of the student's comprehension. Why? Because in reading aloud, a reader is concentrating attention on accuracy in word recognition and giving an appropriate intonation for an audience's benefit; consequently, the reader is not focusing attention on comprehension. The procedure that would solve these problems is to have the reader first read the passage for accuracy in oral reconstruction of printed words and then have the reader read the passage again or a parallel passage silently before testing for comprehension. This procedure would obtain an upper estimate of the reader's comprehension.

LIMITATIONS IN THE GOODMAN MODEL

Some readers do not orally reconstruct printed words but bypass this stage and go directly to meaning (Chomsky, 1970). Because the meaning attained influences word identification (Tzeng & Singer, 1982), another modification of the oral reading model would be a feedback loop from meaning to word identification.

STANDARDIZED TESTS OF ORAL READING

Prior to 1920, when teachers did not instruct students in comprehension, they did not assess it. Consequently pioneering tests of oral reading, such as Gray's oral paragraphs, did not assess comprehension. Some current tests of oral reading, such as the *Gates-McKillop-Horowitz Reading Diagnostic Tests,* still do not assess comprehension. However, the *Diagnostic Reading Scales* assess both oral reading and comprehension and also provide information on listening ability. Only one form is available for each test battery. We describe both test batteries.

The *Gates-McKillop-Horowitz Reading Diagnostic Tests* (2nd Ed.) were published by Teachers College Press in 1981. A kit or specimen set contains all the materials for administering, scoring, and interpreting the test. It includes a pupil record booklet, manual of directions, tachistoscopes, and test materials. The tests include oral reading (seven paragraphs graded from 1.5 to 6.9), reading sentences (a quick screening test), words (flashed and untimed), knowledge of word parts (word attack): syllabication, recognizing and blending common word parts, giving letter sounds, reading words (artificial words), naming upper- and lowercase letters, recognizing vowels, auditory blending and auditory discrimination, spelling, and informal writing sample.

The manual reports a .94 test-retest reliability for 27 children. The oral reading test correlated from .68 to .96 with silent reading tests (Gates-MacGinitie and Metropolitan). The normative sample consisted of 600 children in Grades 1 through 6 who attended 10 different schools (65% private and 35% public, divided into 83% urban and 17% suburban schools) and spoke English fluently but were Caucasian (62%), Black (32%), and Oriental (4%); some came from homes where Spanish was spoken (14%). Interrater agreement on the oral reading test for word errors was 94% for paragraphs 1–4 and 91% for paragraphs 5–7.

The 1962 edition included an oral vocabulary test that provided an expectancy level, an estimate of how well a student ought to read. This test was omitted from the 1981 edition. If you cannot obtain the original oral vocabulary test, then use the Stanford-Binet mental age or the listening age from the Spache Diagnostic Reading Scales as an expectancy estimate. However, you should realize that expectancy measures are not infallible.

The *Diagnostic Reading Scales,* devised by George D. Spache, were published by the California Test Bureau/McGraw Hill Book Company in 1963. The specimen set contains an examiner's manual and record booklet and a student's testing booklet. The test battery consists of three word recognition lists to test a pupil's skills at word recognition and analysis and locate level of entry to the reading passages. The 22 reading passages, graded in difficulty, range from mid-first to eighth grade. They include narrative, expository, and descriptive selections drawn from science, social studies, and children's literature. The reading passages yield three reading levels for each student: instructional level (oral reading), independent level (silent reading), and potential level (listening comprehension). Comprehension questions accompany each passage. Rate of reading on passages at each grade level can be determined. Six phonics tests measure specific skills with consonant, vowels, consonant blends, common syllables, blends, and letter sounds.

The manual indicates that for about 50 cases the reliability coefficients are .84 for the instructional level and .88 for the independent level. The reliabilities for the word recognition lists range from .87 to .96. Concurrent validity correlations with the California Reading Achievement Test varied from .71 to .92 for the word recognition scales, .67 to .87 for the instructional level, and .64 to .79 for the independent level, with the lower coefficients being at the upper grade levels. The potential level (listening comprehension) correlated .80 with the verbal section of the Wechsler Intelligence Scale for Children (WISC). Specific information is not given about the normative sample, but the norms are probably based on about 409 students, ranging from 107 in Grade 2 to 24 in Grade 6.

TERMINATION OF READING INSTRUCTION

Under the oral definition of reading, teachers terminated formal reading instruction as soon as students could read aloud accurately and with proper intonation. It takes about 3 years to teach individuals to attain these criteria. For example, students taught in a systematic phonics program learned to identify words accurately after 3 years of instruction (Agnew, 1939). Consequently, reading instruction terminated for many students in the third grade. Teachers than assumed that students who met the termination criteria, without further instruction, could use their reading ability to learn from texts in any content area throughout the rest of the grades.

READING AS REASONING

Although oral reading is still taught, teachers now shift to silent reading as soon as possible. This change is due to Thorndike's (1917) definition of reading as reasoning. His definition was based upon an analysis of the errors made by mature readers' comprehension of a paragraph. Thorndike concluded that comprehending a paragraph is analogous to the various reasoning processes involved in solving a problem in mathematics.

The goals of oral and silent reading instruction are different. The criterion for success in oral reading is whether the message is read correctly and with proper intonation so that the *audience* can comprehend the text. In contrast, silent reading places a premium upon the *reader's* understanding of the message. Because the reader does not need to read aloud, he can allocate more attention to reasoning processes for comprehending the passage.

To shift to silent reading instruction, tests, materials, and procedures had to be developed and evaluated. In this section, we present some of the salient research on silent reading instruction, factors that underlie silent reading, assessment, and conclude with a theory of silent reading.

RESEARCH ON SILENT READING

Initial Questions on Silent Reading Instruction

When silent reading instruction began, teachers wondered how they would know that students were comprehending what they read. Gates (1921) responded by developing a silent reading test for assessing speed and comprehension of reading. This test was widely used and later became the *Gates-MacGinitie Reading Tests*, which we have described in chapter 3. However, it only assesses speed at one grade level. In general, schools do not assess speed of reading because they recognize that students have a variety of rates of reading that vary according to their purposes and the difficulty of the material.

Another question concerned the use of materials for teaching reading silently. Again, Gates (1927) answered the question by developing exercises and materials for teaching reading silently. In research on these materials, he found that the correlations between the type of the exercise and comprehension in the primary grades varied from a low of .10 for motor skills to a high of .90 for matching phrases. In general, the closer the exercise came to the processes used in comprehension, the higher the correlation. He also found that training students on perception of objects, numbers, and words yielded correlations among these activities of about .30; these correlations were so low that Gates (1926) concluded that if you want individuals to learn to perceive words, train them on perception of *words*. In spite of Gates's conclusion, kindergarten teachers have tried to prepare children for reading by having them use Frostig's materials for tracing lines and Manolakes's materials for matching blocks. Few, if any, teachers still use such materials; instead, they rely upon the basal readers, workbook, and seatwork materials that stem from Gates's pioneering research.

The next question was, What materials would motivate children? What would they want to read silently? Terman and Lima (1929) investigated children's interests and found that primary graders like animal stories, intermediate graders enjoy adventure and funny stories, and teenagers prefer stories that deal with male-female relationships and ideal solutions to family and world problems. Thus, they found that the content of reading materials could be age-graded.

Another answer to the question was proposed by Gray and Leary (1935). They tried numerous variables that might predict the difficulty of texts. Their pioneering work resulted in the first readability formula for grading textbooks. Research on text characteristics and readibility has continued; this research is reviewed in chapter 5 where we present the topic of text characteristics and chapter 10 where we review formulas on readability and their applications.

A basic question was whether students would be better readers if they were taught to read silently from the very beginning of reading instruction, instead of starting with oral reading and later switching over to silent reading. Although teachers could talk and give directions to students, they tended to rely on pantomime and have students respond behaviorally to printed directions. The students also used workbook and other types of materials, much of which had been invented by Gates (1927), that called for selection of multiple-choice responses, but not for oral responses to questions and word recognition exercises.

Buswell (1945) evaluated this silent reading instruction, which lasted over the 6 years of the elementary school curriculum in Chicago's public schools. He used two criteria: percentage of students making lip movements while reading and speed of reading in words per minute. Buswell reasoned that if the students were reading silently, they would have less subvocalization and therefore would be able to read more rapidly. Comparing the experimental group with a control group that first had oral reading, Buswell found that the experimental group did have significantly fewer lip movements and read significantly faster than the control group at the end of sixth grade.

However, schools today still teach oral reading and silent reading. Why? Because parents and society in general want students to be able to do both types of reading. However, schools mostly use oral reading for diagnosis and audience situations and teach children as early as the first grade to read silently.

Methods of Reading Instruction.

By the 1960s, a variety of methods had been developed for teaching beginning reading. Researchers wanted to know whether these methods of teaching beginning reading made a difference in reading achievement at the end of first grade. To answer this question, Bond and Dykstra (1967) compared various methods of instruction, including (a) phonics (Sullivan's programmed instruction that is based on contrastive analysis of phonemes, the initial teaching alphabet that attempts to regularize the spelling of all words by introducing some novel alphabet characters, and the Lippincott reader that begins instruction with a consonant and then adds a vowel to make words such as *ma* and *am*); (b) language experience approaches (children dictate and learn to read their own stories); and (c) basal reader instruction (start with high frequency words taught as whole words, repeat these words in stories, and use the words taught cumulatively in successive stories). They found that methods of instruction did not differ significantly in reading achievement at the end of first grade. However, methods that emphasized identification of printed words led to superiority in word attack.

But this initial superiority in word attack had only short-range benefit. When a phonics program (Sullivan's programmed instruction) was compared with basal reader instruction (Harper & Row) over Grades 1–3, the basal reader eventually resulted in superior achievement (Ruddell, 1968). Why? Because the basal reader contained a more comprehensive program that started with whole-word instruction, but went on to phonics and all the other methods of word instruction and taught word meanings and various comprehension strategies. In short, a more comprehensive program was taught that developed not only word attack, but also word meaning and comprehension skills that led to superior achievement on the *Metropolitan Reading Achievement Test* at the end of the second and third grades. At these grade levels, reading achievement tests begin to assess acquisition of new word meanings and more sophisticated comprehension responses, as well as use of word identification skills; consequently, the more broadly based program developed the skills and abilities that enabled students to perform better on these tests than the programs that emphasized mostly word recognition.

Methods of instruction not only make a difference in word attack skills; they also make a difference in routes to the goal of reading achievement. Katz and Singer (1982, 1984) found that supplementary instruction in various word attack skills in Grade 1 would give students significant differences in their patterns of word recognition abilities. In a multiple regression for predicting reading achievement, the differential in instruction was reflected in the predictors. In short, differential emphases in methods of instruction do not make a difference in reading achievement, but do enable students to take different pathways toward attainment of reading achievement.

**Teaching Comprehension: Directed
and Active Comprehension**

Basal readers emphasize directed comprehension that involves a five-step plan. Teachers develop background knowledge for the story, preteach new vocabulary terms, use some initial questions to guide the reader, have students complete the story reading silently, and then monitor their comprehension with postreading questions and discussion. However, in practice, teachers usually only teach students to comprehend by preteaching some vocabulary, giving students teacher-posed questions to answer—mostly literal *wh*-questions (Who, What, Where, When, and How) and not many *Why* questions that require students to use processes of inference and interpretation—and "mentioning" how to obtain the answers and evaluate them (Durkin, 1978–1979). This method of instruction emphasizes comprehension as a *product*.

In contrast, active comprehension teaches students a *process* of comprehension by having them formulate and read to answer their own questions (Singer, 1978a). The knowledge that students bring to their reading task provides a basis for asking a question. For example, knowledge of story schema can be used to generate such questions as "What is the setting? Who are the characters and what do they do in the story? What is the problem that needs to be resolved? What attempts are made to solve the problem? How do the characters in the story react to attempted solutions to the problem? How is the problem finally resolved?" If students make the story schema questions specific to the story by including names and events from the story in the questions, the story-specific words will further help them flag the answers to their questions (Donlan & Singer, 1979). (See explanation of story schemata in next section.)

When students become active comprehenders, they achieve higher comprehension than students who only read to answer teacher-posed questions (Nolte & Singer, 1985; Singer & Donlan, 1982; Wong, 1985; R. Yopp, 1987). The products of their comprehension, that is, the answers to their questions, are then added to their *potential* or knowledge for generating further comprehension questions. Thus, the process of comprehending results in a product that is added to readers' potential for generating further questions. This cyclical process can repeat itself from paragraph to paragraph in a text.

To teach active comprehension, you ask questions that get a question in return. For example, after a title of a story has been read, ask, "What would you like to know about this story?" At the end of the first paragraph, ask, "What would you like to know next?"

You can also model the kinds of questions to ask; for example, if the text is a narrative, then story schema questions are important. If the text is expository, then teach students to detect expository patterns, such as problem-solution, question-answer. (See chapters 5 and 9 for expository patterns and terms that signal these patterns.) You can model these patterns as questions. Then have students ask similar questions of each other in groups, then in pairs, and finally alone. This phase out of the teacher and phase in of the student has been used successfully in several studies (Nolte & Singer. 1985; Singer. 1978a; Singer & Donlan, 1982; R. Yopp. 1987). We explain the phase-out/phase-in procedure in greater detail in our chapter on "An Instructional Blueprint."

We have found that students can learn active comprehension in relatively few lessons because they have known how to generate questions from age 4 or earlier and acquired knowledge of story grammar as early as Grade 1. We provide further examples of active comprehension instruction in chap. 6.

Question-Answering Instruction

Pearson and Johnson (1978) have defined three types of questions. Textually explicit questions refer to literal statements in the text, textually implicit questions can be answered by making inferences based on information provided in the text in two or more places, and scriptally implicit questions can only be answered by combining a generalization drawn from background experience with information in the text and then making an inference; for example, the text says that "Columbus left his nine-year-old son, Diego, behind on the dock when he set sail for the new world." To answer the scriptally implicit question, "How did Diego feel?" you have to generalize from your knowledge of how boys feel when their fathers go off on exciting adventures and leave them behind. Then you can combine this generalization with the text's statement that Columbus left his son behind. This combination of information enables you to make the inference necessary for answering the question.

Raphael (1986) has taught students to answer teacher-posed questions by recognizing they are (a) *textually explicit* and answers to them can be found "right there" on the page, or (b) *textually implicit* and consequently require students to "think and search" for information from two or more parts of the text and then make an inference, or (c) *scriptally implicit* and therefore they are "on their own" and have to combine the generalization from their heads with the information given in the text. She has found that such instruction, which she refers to as *question and answer relationships* (QAR), enhances students' ability to answer questions and therefore improves their comprehension. But R. Yopp (1987) noted that students taught active comprehension for narrative material did not improve in comprehension when they were also taught how to answer questions. Perhaps Raphael's instruction in question answering is necessary for enhancing comprehension to teacher-posed questions on expository material; evidently such instruction is unnecessary for self-generated questions on narrative material.

Exemplary Reading Programs

Although teachers can make a difference in students' reading during the year, what makes for a cumulative difference in students' reading achievement is the program of instruction conducted by the entire faculty. An analysis of school programs which contrasted schools that obtained high achievement with those schools whose students made less than expected attainment has revealed several characteristics that appear to explain why the difference occurs and what an exemplary program entails.

An exemplary reading program should be comprehensive. But it can still vary considerably. One school emphasized basal reader oral instruction in the morning and individual reading and report writing in the afternoon. In contrast to this two-periods-per-day plan, another school emphasized a skill development program that was carefully monitored for each child and taught by teachers who believed that they could teach children who were "at risk," that is, they were minority students from poverty homes. Another metropolitan school system emphasized a basal reader program with everyone from student teachers to consultants trained in teaching the same basal reader.

What did these programs have in common? They were all comprehensive, consistent, coherent, and cumulative, taught by teachers who were competent and committed to their school's program, and had school principals who had confidence in the teachers and capably administered their programs. The principal also inducted new teachers into the program and made sure that the program was carried out at each grade level. Because the program did not vary, teachers were able to develop confidence in it and the materials used for teaching reading. In all of these schools, achievement was at grade level and above.

Although a teacher can make a difference for individual students in any one year, cumulative differences from grade to grade are made by a stable faculty under leadership of a competent principal who develops a consistent and coherent program that teachers learn and use for some time so that they can develop confidence in their ability to teach it (Singer, 1977a).

Individual Factors Related to Reading Achievement

More research has been conducted on reading than on any other school instruction. In the following sections, we review some research that has made, should have made, and should make for a difference in reading instruction (Russell, 1961; Singer, 1970, 1978c).

Eye-Movement Behavior During Reading

When and how does reading occur? What determines and limits speed of reading?

To answer these questions, scientific research on reading first focused on eye-movement behavior in reading. Javal (1879) showed that in reading, the eyes move across the printed page in jumps, which he called saccades. These are very rapid, ballistic-like movements that last about 20 milliseconds and bring the print into the visual area of greatest discriminating power, the fovea centralis. The eyes then fixate on the print for about 600 milliseconds (six tenths of a second) for beginning readers and 250 milliseconds (a quarter of a second) for college readers. At the end of each line, a sweep movement, lasting about 40 milliseconds (four tenths of a second), returns the eye to the next line. You can observe these eye-movement behaviors by looking at the eyes of another person while he or she is reading.

Buswell (1922) used the eye-movement camera to record eye-movement behavior of average readers at each grade level from Grade 2 to college while they were reading the same paragraph, written at a second-grade level of difficulty. He also studied the eye-movement behavior of beginning readers. On the average, beginning readers make about two fixations per word whereas college readers have only one fixation for one and one-fourth words. Beginning readers regress or jump backward in their eye movements about once for every two words, but college readers regress about once for every two lines. In general, development toward maturity in eye-movement behavior during reading is very rapid during the first four grades, indicating a rapid rate of learning to read, then slows to a gradual rise from Grade 4 to 6, followed by another small rise between Grades 6 and 8, followed again by a slow, gradual rise through high school.

Thus, from beginning to mature reading, the reader's eyes are fixating upon print during most of the reading time. At the high school level, the average student has about four fixations during each second of reading. Consequently, his eye is in motion only 6% of the time. The rest of the time is devoted to fixation pauses.

The implication for speeding up reading at any grade level is not to get the eyes to move faster, because eye-movement time is a negligible part of the total reading time. Hence, those devices and programs that purport to promote faster eye-movement behavior during reading, such as reading rate controllers and tachistoscopes, are focusing on an aspect of reading that is not only minor but at the high school level may be at its physiological limit. For example, Gilbert (1953) found that functional oculomotor control of the eyes, the ability to move the eyes across printed words and back to the next line in a systematic way, reaches maturity around Grade 9. He also pointed out that development of functional oculomotor control during reading best comes about indirectly from instruction and practice in reading.

Only when the eye is fixated can readers perceive print. About 30 milliseconds (three tenths of a second) are necessary for perceiving print during each fixation. The rest of the fixation pause is devoted to stabilization time, the time required for the eyes to focus again after a saccadic movement, and processing time, the time required for interpreting and integrating information into previous accumulations of meaning (Gilbert, 1959). Consequently, speed of reading is determined more by processing time, getting information from the retina into long-term memory, than it is by movement of the eyes during reading. Processing time involves an interaction between the reader's knowledge sources and information or data in the text. Only improvement in these components and in the efficiency of their interactions will reduce the total fixation time, the time when the eye is actually perceiving print, and result in a significant increase in speed of reading. (This interaction concept of reading is explained in greater detail in the last section of this chapter when we explain the interaction definition of reading.)

The average third grader reads about 60 words per minute, the fifth grader about 100 words per minute (the normal speaking rate), and the college reader about 240 words per minute when reading systematically and sequentially with some degree of understanding that involves literal recall and simple inference. The fastest speed for such reading is about 1,100 words per minute.

Skimming or reading to find answers to specific questions has a much greater rate, but the rate depends on the number of words put into the numerator when computing rate. If only the words actually perceived are put in, then the rate is no more rapid than the rate for systematic, sequential reading.

Unit of Perception

A component related to speed of reading is the size of the unit of perception, the number of letters or words you perceive at a glance when you are reading. Cattell (1886) demonstrated that adult readers could perceive a whole word faster than its individual letters. This research was conducted at a time when synthetic phonics, first teaching children letter-sound correspondences and then having them blend the separate sounds together, was prominent in beginning reading instruction. Opponents of this method were quick to take Cattell's finding that had been based on adult responses and overgeneralize it to children. They used it to justify initiation of reading instruction with whole words. Later, Buswell (1922) demonstrated that beginning readers take two fixations to perceive each word.

In processing print, adults can perceive whole words because they have formed associations among the letters in the words and developed knowledge about words and letters that result in expectations of what letters should occur in words. They develop expectations or schemata, abstract knowledge structures, for printed words that enable them to fill in letters before they perceive them. For example, given "th-t," adults fill in the slot for the missing "a" rapidly and perhaps unconsciously (Adams & Collins, 1977/1985). This whole-word expectancy process works only for familiar words whose structure and interletter associations are well known from experience and prior instruction. It is applicable for most functional words (prepositions and conjunctions) and some contentive words (nouns, adjectives, adverbs, and verbs) that occur with high frequency. But it does not apply to technological words in content area texts until students have perceived them frequently enough to develop interletter associations and schemata for them. Such schemata are built up gradually, first by emphasis on pronunciation, spelling, and knowledge of the references and properties of the technical terms and then by perceiving and responding to the terms frequently in a variety of printed contexts. These word schemata and schemata at higher levels, such as syntactic and semantic schemata, then interact with feature, letter, letter cluster, and word detectors to attain speed and accuracy in word identification. (We explain the concept of schemata in greater detail in the third section of this chapter.)

Eye-movement research in reading is still being conducted. Hochberg and Brooks (1970) formulated the concepts of cognitive search guidance and peripheral search guidance. They explained that the syntax and semantics of print lead readers to construct guesses or hypotheses on what to expect and to sample the print in order to confirm or disconfirm these expectations; thus, cognitive search guidance involves fixating on print that will test hypotheses or expectations. Peripheral search guidance is for the attainment of information from the periphery of vision that informs the reader where to jump his eyes next in order to test his hypotheses. McConkie and Rayner (1976) developed an on-line computer that showed that adult readers perceive three elliptical zones of print as they fixate during reading with the print in the central zone being processed for meaning and the other two zones providing information for moving the eyes. Just and Carpenter (1985) have constructed a model of reading based on eye-movement behavior; they postulate that integration of information of simultaneous processing of print, for example, semantic, syntactic, and word perceptual, occurs in a "working system" where these systems can mutually interact and influence each other. That is why readers can complete the interpretation of sentences by the time they have completed them. Even though you have to change the meaning of some of the terms in this sentence, you will still understand it by the time you have come to the end of it:

The run on the bank tired the joggers.

Automaticity

After the third or fourth grade, good readers are so well practiced in reading materials within their ability levels that they have gone beyond accuracy in word recognition to attainment of automaticity in word recognition. LaBerge and Samuels' (1985) explanation is that automatic readers have developed letter and letter cluster detectors, sounds for these letters and letter clusters, a hook-up between them, and unitizers for organizing the symbol-sound relationships into whole words. These components and processes become overpracticed and operate automatically in response to printed words. Consequently, readers only need to allocate minimal attention to these processes and still be accurate in word identification. Because attention is finite, readers can then concentrate maximal attention on processes of comprehension. Automaticity in reading is analogous to an experienced automobile driver who can minimize attention to the mechanics of driving a car and maximize attention to steering the car and attending to other cars and information on the highway and even engage in conversation with a passenger.

Readers who have not yet developed automaticity in word recognition, that is, they cannot read relatively easy material rapidly and identify printed words in them with minimal attention, have difficulty in comprehension because they have to allocate a large amount of their attentional resources to word identification and consequently cannot attend as much to comprehension. Their process of reading is analogous to a reader of a foreign language who laboriously translates the printed words. By the time the reader reaches the bottom of the page, he cannot remember what was on the top of the page. He must then reread the page, this time to comprehend it.

Although automaticity in general is attained by reading a wide variety of material and particularly material that is relatively easy, readers can become automatic in word identification for a particular passage. They can take a short-cut known as the "method of repeated reading" (Samuels, 1979). In this method, students read the same passage repeatedly under teacher guidance, perhaps imitating the oral reading of the passage taped by the teacher or a student in the class. The students who are doing the repeated reading first identify the words and go over the passage several times until they can identify the printed words rapidly, accurately, and with minimal attention to the process. When they read the passage again, reading it silently, they can allocate maximal attention to the process of comprehending the text. Thus, they can derive the same enjoyment from comprehension of the text that readers with automaticity obtain when they read a text once. Indeed, good readers developed automaticity in reading because they not only did an abundance of reading when they were learning how to read in the primary grades but they also read and reread favorite books many times; in a sense, they were engaging in the "method of repeated reading" on their own.

Although Samuels advocated this method for remedial readers, any reader who has to plow laboriously through a passage in any content area that contains a high density of technical terms and complex ideas could profit from the method of repeated reading.

Different Types of Reading

Using an eye-movement movement camera to study silent reading, Judd and Buswell (1922) found that reading varied according to the type and difficulty of the materials, as well as the purpose of the reader. For example, relatively easy materials are read differently than difficult materials. When the reader is familiar with the content, the process of reading has fewer regressions and therefore is smoother and more rapid. If the purpose of the reader is to be analytical or the material is quite dense, then the process of reading is likely to be slower. In other words, students do not have one reading rate or one level of reading comprehension. Instead, their speed and comprehension may vary with the type and difficulty of the content and with their purpose in reading it. Consequently, teachers need to teach students how to read all types of content for a variety of purposes, sometimes analytically and sometimes just skimming to find the answer to a particular question.

FACTORS RELATED TO COMPREHENSION

Intelligence

Intelligence is related to reading achievement, but in a differential way because the term *reading* has two meanings: (a) learning how to read or reading acquisition and (b) general reading achievement—the ability to gain information from text or simply to learn from text. The difference in these two phases of reading becomes apparent when children are assessed in both phases. In the section below on assessment, we explain how to differentially assess reading acquisition and ability to learn from text.

To determine the relationship between intelligence and the two phases of reading development, reading acquisition and ability to learn from text, first determine intelligence quotients (IQs) as assessed by the *Stanford Binet Test of Intelligence* (SB) or the *Wechsler Intelligence Scales for Children* or *Adolescents* (WISC).

On the Stanford Binet Test, IQ = MA (mental age) divided by CA (chronological age) and multiplied by 100. IQ is an index of *rate of learning*. MA is an index of *level of abstract tasks* an individual can do. These tasks are age-graded on the scale by determining the age when they can first be done by 50% of an age-group. Age scores for tasks successfully accomplished on the SB scale are added up to find a person's MA.

Although IQs can vary over the grades for individual students because mental growth is not uniform from year to year, they are relatively constant for groups of students. Thus, the IQ range (IQ 67 and up) for a group of students will tend to remain constant from grade to grade, but their MA range from grade to grade will increase with their chronological age (MA $=$ IQ $\times$ CA/100).

Variability in reading acquisition *decreases* from grade to grade as a group of students progresses through the grades and learns to read. Reading acquisition can be determined from scores on the same test administered at successive grade levels. Hence the correlation between IQ and reading acquisition will *decrease* from grade to grade for a group of students as they progress through school.

However, variability in ability to learn from text *increases* as a group of students progresses through school (see data in chapter 2 on increases in reading achievement variability from Grades 2 through 8). You can determine ability to learn from text by administering a reading achievement test normed for each particular grade level. This increased variability is a result of the increase in difficulty on the reading achievement tests and the increased mental ages of the students. Indeed, reading achievement tests begin to overlap more and more with intelligence tests from grade to grade. Consequently, there is an increasing relationship between IQ and reading achievement as a group of students progresses through school (Durkin, 1964). Thus, IQ has a *decreasing* relationship with reading acquisition and an *increasing* relationship with ability to learn from text.

The decreasing relationship occurs because all children in the normal range of mental development, which goes to about IQ 65 to 70, the level where pathology begins (Zigler, 1967), can learn to read provided they are given adequate time and instruction to learn (Bloom, 1971; Carroll, 1964). Indeed, all but 5% of students have attained the "rudiments" of reading achievement by the time they reach the sixth grade (NAEP, 1985).

However, variability in students' ability to learn from text, as indexed by reading age equivalents on reading achievement tests standardized for each grade level, will increase from grade to grade. These increments in reading age equivalents reflect the students' increasing individual differences in mental age as they progress through school. Indeed, we expect each individual's reading achievement at best to equal his or her mental age. Therefore, we expect schools to (a) teach all students in the normal range of mental ability *how to read* and (b) develop *reading achievement* (ability to learn from text) in all students up to their mental age levels (Singer, 1977b).

Although Americans have an egalitarian ideal in which they expect that all individuals with effort and perseverance can attain any objective, we have to recognize that there are individual differences in mental ability, just as there are individual differences in height. Schools can be held accountable for *decreasing* individual differences in reading acquisition from grade to grade. Thus, the egalitarian ideal can be realized in teaching students how to read. But in ability to learn from text, the schools can only be held accountable for *increasing* the range of individual differences in reading achievement to equal the range of individual differences in mental age among a group of students as they progress through school.

Vocabulary

Vocabulary is the single largest predictor of reading achievement throughout the grades (Singer, 1964). Three factors may account for this relationship (R. Anderson & Freebody, 1985): (a) Vocabulary may represent the meanings individuals have stored in memory that they can mobilize for association with printed words; the larger an individual's vocabulary, the more likely the individual will have within his repertoire the necessary word meanings for comprehending printed materials. (b) Vocabulary is the single best predictor of general intelligence. Hence, vocabulary ability may be an index to brightness and therefore an indication of the mental abilities individuals can mobilize in reading and learning from text. (c) Vocabulary indicates the knowledge structures individuals have for responding to texts, that is, the information, examples, and related concepts that can be activated in response to printed words. All of these factors may be operating to make vocabulary so highly related to reading comprehension.

Morphemic Ability

If individuals do not know the meaning of individual words, they might be able to derive or construct their meanings through analysis of their roots and affixes (prefixes and suffixes). Hence, morphemic ability is related to, but separate from, vocabulary ability. It is a predictor of reading achievement from the intermediate grades (Singer, 1965) through the college level (Holmes, 1954).

Word Recognition

"Word recognition is the foundation for reading" (Gough, 1984). In order to read at all, individuals must first identify printed words. But individuals tend to become alike in this finite ability as they progress through the grades. Unless speed of word recognition is computed, word recognition tends to drop out as a predictor of reading achievement after the sixth grade because individual differences have decreased toward zero in this ability (Singer, 1965). However, at least minimal amounts remain to account for individual differences in reading achievement up through the high school level (R. Anderson & Freebody, 1985; Holmes & Singer, 1966).

Attitudes Toward Reading and Learning from Text

The affective domain is related to reading achievement. Athey (1985) and Athey and Holmes (1969) have demonstrated that personality factors such as drive toward independence, confidence, and criticalness are related to reading achievement in adolescence. Singer and Bean (1982a, 1982b) have shown that desire to know and understand for its own sake is a predictor, along with indices of background knowledge (high school grade point average) and ability to learn from text, of achievement at the college level. It is also a predictor of reading achievement at the college level, over and above the predictions made by verbal factors (Dreher & Singer, 1986). As H. Carter (1957) who constructed the test on attitudes toward learning pointed out, most important for learning and retention are students' attitudes and feelings about what they are learning at the time they are learning it.

Individual Differences in Reading Achievement

Another set of factors also accounts for individual differences in reading achievement, particularly at the elementary level. Students who learn to read early, learn in environments where their peers are also engaged in reading, have parents who foster and promote reading, and are likely to devote a large part of their time during their elementary school years to reading books. These readers are likely to read more than 100 more books per year than students who are low in reading achievement (Stanovich, 1986). This extensive reading promotes fluency in word identification, develops vocabulary ability, and results in a greater range and depth of knowledge, which in turn enhances reading ability and leads to greater enjoyment in reading.

In the United States, at the elementary level, boys achieve in reading below girls, on the average (Preston, 1962), because of identification with traditional attitudes toward male and female roles (DePillis & Singer, 1985). However, under conditions where boys and girls are given equal instruction, their rates are of learning to read do not differ significantly. But in normal classroom settings, girls get more reading instruction and boys get more behavioral control (McNeil & Keislar, 1964). Likewise, high-achieving groups get more reading instruction than low-achieving groups (McDermott, 1985). Thus, differences in conditions of learning in these known groups contribute to individual differences in reading achievement.

An implication for instruction from research on individual differences is to foster early reading acquisition in all students. Those students who have difficulty with a faster pace (Barr, 1973-1974) may need supplementary instruction, particularly in first grade (Ellson, Barker, Engle, & Kampwerth, 1965), instead of a decreased pace that is typically provided for low students. Indeed, when supplementary instruction is given to low-achieving students in first grade, the correlation between their reading readiness tests and their reading achievement, which is usually above .70, drops to .25 (Gates, Bond, & Russell, 1939). In short, early intervention to provide more instruction for low-achieving students pays off, probably not only for achievement at the end of first grade, but also for longer range achievement in reading.

These are the implications of learning to read early. Develop students' fluency in reading by providing them with time to read a wide variety of interesting, but relatively easy, material. They are likely to accumulate vocabulary, information, and concepts as they read. These products of reading will also increase their potential for learning from texts. Thus, a positive and cumulative process will occur that will enhance their ability to learn from text, which in turn will enable them to enjoy reading more, which will result in even more reading.

Teach all the factors that are related to comprehension, including word recognition, word meaning (vocabulary and morphemics), and reasoning factors. Develop a desire to know and learn from text by appealing to students' curiosity and drive toward independence. These nonintellectual factors are important in developing active readers.

For low-reading achievers, have books available that are relatively easy for them to read during their recreational reading time. Use the method of repeated reading on them so that they can gain the experience of comprehending and enjoying learning from text as much as high-achieving readers do.

Teach students to be active in reading by having them formulate and read to answer their own questions from the very beginning of reading instruction. At the first-grade level, students already know how to ask questions; they have been able to do so since age 4. They also are familiar with stories at the first-grade level. Consequently, they can learn to use their knowledge to generate questions as they read. Thus, from first grade on, they can learn a process of comprehending or learning from text.

Have students read different materials for different purposes. They should read some materials by skimming them for answers to particular questions; other materials should be read analytically for answers to more detailed questions. In short, students should learn to vary their reading according to their purposes and the difficulty and types of materials they are reading. Thus, they will have the opportunity to develop flexibility in reading.

Many parents ask schools for homework for their children. The homework can take the form of having parents take their children to public libraries to select books for reading at home. This activity will enable all readers to do the kind of reading that children who become very good readers have been doing since they learned to read and were doing indirectly as their parents read to them at the preschool level. It is the easiest homework assignment to give and the best way of improving reading achievement and fluency, provided, of course, that parents and students cooperate to carry out this assignment.

ASSESSMENT

Speed and Power of Reading

Gates (1921) was among the first to construct a test of reading as reasoning. Its pioneering features are useful to know because most tests today are still based on his early work. His speed-of-reading test consisted of passages and questions on these passages that the average third grader could answer if given adequate time. But Gates limited time on the test to 6 minutes for fourth and fifth graders and to 4 minutes for sixth graders and above. Hence, his speed-of-reading test involved limited time to read and answer simple questions on relatively easy material. However, he did require readers to do some reasoning on it. For example, an item on the test stated: "Snow was on the ground." The reader then had to make a simple inference to answer the test question: "The time of year was: summer fall winter spring." All the items on the test were about equal in difficulty.

In contrast, Gates's comprehension subtest of the *Gates Reading Survey* had test passages that increased in difficulty. The passages had from one to three key words omitted. The reader's task was to determine which of the choices belonged in the passage. Although the test was timed, the time allocation was liberal; consequently, most readers were able to complete the most difficult passage they could comprehend on the test. Hence, it was a *power* test of reading achievement. In current practice, schools do not assess speed of reading, only comprehension.

Types of Comprehension

Two types of comprehension are usually assessed by reading achievement tests: literal and implicit inferential comprehension. Literal comprehension only requires recall or recognition of information directly stated in the text. Implicit inferential comprehension requires the reader to make a deduction from major and minor premises stated in the text. For example, a text might state that "All men are mortal. Socrates is a man." The reader would then infer that Socrates is mortal.

However, readers also make a variety of other responses to text, such as affective and critical evaluations and personal interpretations. For example, a passage might state: "When Columbus set sail for the New World, he left his son, Diego, behind on the dock." To answer the question, "How did Diego feel at being left behind?" a reader would have to construct a major premise about how young boys feel when their fathers go off on an adventure and leave them behind. Then the reader would have to combine this major premise with the minor one given in the text and draw an inference that would answer the question. Note that the major premise represents the reader's generalization, not one that is stated in the text. These kind of inferences and other personal responses to text have been defined by Pearson and Johnson (1978) as "scriptal responses." Because these responses are personal, they cannot be scored objectively. Consequently, standardized tests do not usually include them in assessing comprehension.

Relationships Among Comprehension Tests

Intercorrelations among comprehension tests in the primary grades tend to be low. McCullough (1957) found that comprehension scores for tests of main ideas, details, sequence, and creative reading at the second-grade level range from .26 to .50 with a median of .45. Because scores on comprehension tests in primary grades tend to reflect the specific instruction students receive, teachers should make sure that comprehension tests in these grades have curricular and instructional validity. That is, they should assess what teachers in these grades were supposed to teach and what in fact they did teach. After the third grade, convergence in curricula and integration in students' abilities occur (Guthrie,

1973); then the intercorrelations among various comprehension tests tend to be much higher, in the .70s and .80s.

Since teachers tend to teach what is assessed and prefer to have tests that assess what they teach, they are likely to restrict the scope of their instruction and avoid novel instruction and assessment (Singer, Ruddell, McNeil, & Wittrock, 1983). Consequently, instruction in affective and critical evaluations and personal perspectives and interpretations of text are not likely to be emphasized in classroom instruction.

Other objective ways of assessing silent reading comprehension are (a) reading to follow directions ("Place an X on the ball"), (b) answering literal and inferential questions on information given in a passage, usually with multiple-choice answers provided, (c) paraphrasing a text, that is, restating the information by using synonyms and varying the syntax or recognizing a paraphrase of a text in a multiple-choice situation, (d) deleting absurd words in a text; for example, "Mary's mother sent her to the store to get a loaf of bread. When she got home with the thimble, her mother thanked her."

Assessment of Reading Acquisition and Learning from Text

Schools usually do not report information on changes in students' reading acquisition. They only provide information on students' reading achievement from grade to grade relative to other students' reading achievement on tests constructed and normed for each grade level. Consequently, schools do not obtain the necessary information nor report to pupils, parents, professionals, and the public on students' reading acquisition.

We do not have a particular test of reading acquisition because reading acquisition and learning from text overlap. We do not even have a consensus on the level of reading achievement that would indicate a student had learned how to read and was now using that ability to learn from text. Indeed, as you will see, reading acquisition continues to develop at a decreasing rate whereas ability to learn from text continues to develop throughout a person's lifetime.

However, we can develop a consensus definition on when students have learned how to read. For example, after a group of high school principals read and answered questions on the paragraph shown in Box 4.4, they agreed that a student who could comprehend this paragraph had learned how to read.

We can best represent the relationship between the two phases of reading, reading acquisition and learning from text, by pointing out that most of the instructional time in Grade 1 is devoted to reading acquisition, and some time is spent on instruction in learning from text. The time devoted to these two instructional phases are inversely related as students progress through the grades. The time spent on reading acquisition decreases rapidly from Grades 1 to 4 and begins to approach a small percentage of the time. This curve reflects the fact that reading acquisition involves a finite number of rules that are rapidly acquired. In the meantime, the time spent on learning from text increases and continues to increase throughout the grades because of the fact that the factors

---

BOX 4.4. A Paragraph for Obtaining a Consensus Definition on Attainment of Reading Acquisition

We used a paragraph from the Stanford Reading Achievement Test, Form 1A (1973), to establish that a reading achievement score of grade 5.5 or higher indicates that a student has essentially learned how to read (Singer & Balow, 1987). The passage was an explanation of the Greek myth Pegasus. Correct answers to its range of comprehension questions enable a student's score to change from grade equivalent 5.0 to 6.0. A group of high school principals agreed that students who could read the passage and answer its comprehension questions knew how to read. We took the midpoint of reading scores for the range of questions for the paragraph as the criterion for attainment of reading acquisition. A more stringent criterion would have been reading grade equivalent 6.0. We used the more lenient criterion because we think that the previous passage, which has an average grade equivalent of 4.5 might also have been acceptable. This passage was about mining iron ore in South Africa.

---

involved, such as vocabulary, information, and conceptual ability, are not finite; they increase throughout a person's lifetime. These two curves are depicted in Figure 4.6. However, we can infer that progress in reading acquisition has occurred from assessment on a standardized reading achievement test normed for a particular grade level. The procedure involves two steps. First, administer the *same* reading achievement test to a group of students, probably after intervals of a year, until the students have demonstrated a "mastery" level. The mastery level is an arbitrary score; teachers often consider that the 85th percentile level indicates mastery of a test's objectives. The second step is to use the *same* norms. For example, readminister the reading achievement test given at the end of first grade to students at the end of the second grade who had not yet attained the 85th percentile on the test. Use the same norms at the end of second grade that you used at the end of first grade. Students' scores would thus be compared with the scores they had earned a year earlier. The percentile difference would then indicate the change that had occurred in their reading acquisition (Singer, 1973a).

To assess ability to learn from text, administer a reading achievement test that is constructed and normed for each grade level. If you compare standardized tests at successive grade levels, you will find that test authors make a reading achievement test more difficult by making the vocabulary more abstract, the syntax more complex, the background knowledge required for the test more extensive, and the inferences for answering questions more difficult because they involve more than one step. The reading achievement test compares students at each grade level with each other on norms constructed for the grade level. The percentile rank scores for the test indicate students' reading achievement or ability to learn from text relative to their peer group, the other members of the class.

FIGURE 4.6. *Percent Instructional Time for Reading Acquisition and Learning from Text in Grades 1 through 4. Note: tests are usually administered in the eighth month of the school year.*

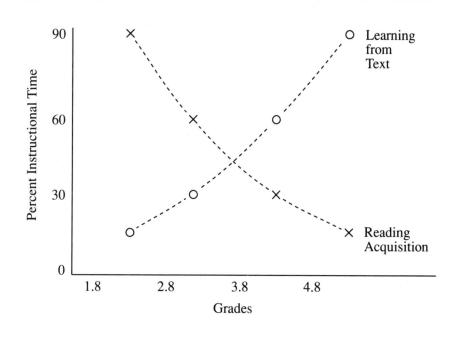

We can use a racetrack analogy to explain the differences that occur in these two types of test results. The reading acquisition test results inform us how far students have progressed around the track while the learning from text test results tell us the relative ranks of the students each time they are assessed. Both types of comparisons are shown in Figure 4.7.

The information in Figure 4.7 shows that the student, a girl, was reading at the 33rd percentile at Grade 1.8. When retested a year later on the *same* test and compared with the *same* norm group, she had increased in reading acquisition to the 93rd percentile. Clearly she had improved in reading acquisition. When she was given the test that was standardized and normed for Grade 2.8, and compared with this norm group, her percentile rank was 33, the same percentile ranking at the end of Grade 1.8. To the untutored eye, it appears she did not improve in ability to learn from text. However, she has also increased in her ability to learn from text because the second-grade test was not the same test given at Grade 1.8; it was a more difficult test. To keep her relative percentile

FIGURE 4.7. Test information on reading acquisition and ability to learn from text for a second-grade student.

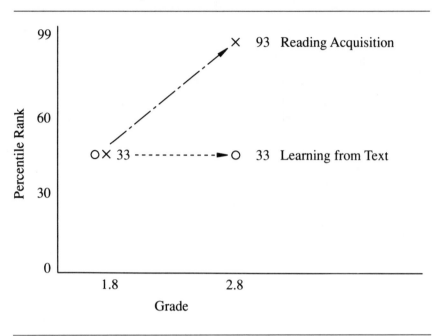

rank, she had to improve in order to maintain her position on the more difficult test. But her improvement in ability to learn from text did not increase any more rapidly than her peer group's ability had increased. So her percentile rank remained the same.

In reporting information to parents, show them the most difficult paragraph the student could read at each testing time. If they do not understand the numerical information, they will readily see from the content and questions that the paragraphs the student can correctly read a year later are more difficult. Thus, you will provide parents with both ''numerical'' and ''meaningful'' information (Dreher & Singer, 1984).

Students learn how to read at a relatively fast rate. Many students have learned how to read by the fourth-grade level. That is, they can communicate as well through the printed medium as they can do orally. If we had a consensus that the ability to read and answer questions on a paragraph that involved material beyond a student's direct experience indicated the student had learned how to read, then we could administer this test repeatedly until students could answer 85% of the questions on the paragraph. For example, read the paragraph in Box 4.4 and then answer the questions on it. Would a student who could answer these questions know how to read? A student who could answer all the questions on this standardized test up to and including the questions in Box 4.4 would have a reading grade equivalent of 4.5.

If we had this consensus, then we could administer a standardized reading achievement test from its beginning and up to and including the one shown in Box 4.4 to students in Grades 1 to 4 until they could answer 85% of the questions on it. We would find that not many first graders would reach the criterion, but more would do so when they were second graders, even more when they were third graders. Probably 50% of them could do so at the end of the fourth grade, and about 95% would have reached this criterion by the end of the sixth grade. Thus, if we keep the task constant, we would find that as students progress through the grades, they become more alike on reading acquisition. Consequently differential assessment would terminate prior to Grade 4 for some of them and almost all of them between Grades 6 and 7 because they had already reached the criterion in reading acquisition. In short, we would be using a criterion of grade equivalent 4.5 on a standardized test as an index that a student had learned how to read.

Thus, research on silent reading led to knowledge of methods, materials, and measurement. It also set the stage for the next development, the formulation of explicit and comprehensive theories of reading.

INTERACTIVE THEORIES OF READING

Prior to the formulation of the substrata factor theory of reading, research in reading was atheoretical. During this period, researchers had discovered a multitude of variables related to reading comprehension. The theory sought to account for these variables and found that they could be organized into several levels or substrates. Hence, the theory is known as the substrata-factor theory of reading (Holmes, 1954; Holmes & Singer, 1966; Singer, 1985).

Subsequently Gough (1976) constructed an information processing model of reading that traced a linear sequence from perception of the printed words to comprehension and oral output of the phrase, "one second of reading." Next, LaBerge and Samuels (1976) developed an automaticity theory of reading that explained how skilled readers focus little or no attention on perception of printed words; therefore, they can allocate a maximum amount of their limited attentional capacity to processes of comprehension. Both the information processing and the automaticity theories were critically reviewed by Rumelhart (1976) when he presented a more adequate explanation, his interactive theory and model of reading. This model was subsequently labeled a "schema-theoretic view of reading" (Adams & Collins, 1977) and expanded with research and theory on metacognition (Brown, 1980) and the affective domain (Athey, 1985).

Since the schema-interactive theory of reading is conceptually similar to the substrata-factor theory of reading (Singer, 1983), we will start this section with a brief summary of the substrata-factor theory. Then we will explain the schema-interactive theory of reading.

SUBSTRATA-FACTOR THEORY OF READING

The theory postulates that general reading ability consists of two major components, speed and power of reading. Underlying each of these components is a multiplicity of interrelated factors, such as reasoning in reading (ability to make inferences, interpretations, and evaluations, and conceptualize information), morphemics (ability to divide words into their constituent meanings of prefix, root, and suffix), semantics (ability to select appropriate meanings for printed words), and graphophonemics (ability to sound out words). The desire to know and understand was also postulated as a factor underlying comprehension.

The theory explains the way these factors operate in the process of reading. The factors can be organized into momentary working systems according to the purposes of the reader and the demands of the reading task. At one moment, a set of factors may be organized to solve a problem on reasoning in reading, at another to determine the meaning of a word, and at still another to identify a printed word. If one working system will not solve a problem, then another working system may be organized, if a reader has appropriate factors in his mental repertoire to solve the problem in another way. For example, if a word cannot be identified at a glance by use of a working system that involved graphophonemics, then a more analytical system might be organized at a lower substrata level that would enable the reader to sound out the parts of the word and blend the parts together. Thus, the theory explains that the process of reading consists of the mobilization of factors into momentary working systems according to the changing purposes of the reader and the demands of the task in order to attain speed and power of reading.

Because the substrata factor theory of reading is conceptually similar to and the predecessor of the interactive theory of reading, the third and most recent definition of reading (Singer, 1983c), we do not present the models of reading that have been constructed at the elementary (Katz & Singer, 1982, 1984; Singer, 1962, 1965), high school (Holmes & Singer, 1966) and college levels (Holmes, 1954). Instead, in the next section, we explain the interactive model of reading and the factors related to it.

SCHEMA INTERACTIVE THEORY
OF READING

The schema interactive theory of reading traces its origin back to the work of Bartlett (1932). He observed that an Indian story, "The War of the Ghosts," that was understandable to the Indians appeared to be misinterpreted when nonnatives read the story. Bartlett noted that the nonnatives interpreted the story according to their own schemata, the abstract knowledge structures they had constructed out of their own culturally determined experiences. We explain here how schemata are used to interpret information.

Because schemata, also known as natural concepts, are the cornerstone of the schema interactive theory of reading, we start this section with an explanation of the formation of natural concepts.

FORMATION OF NATURAL CONCEPTS

Individuals learn to perceive the world by abstracting and generalizing from their experiences to form concepts. These concepts are then used to assimilate further experiences. For example, a child may form a concept that a dog has four legs and a tail. Any creature that fits this concept will then be perceived as another instance of the concept. When an animal with four legs and other properties does not fit the concept, the child may accommodate this deviation by forming another concept to fit the animal.

Concepts are organized into a hierarchy. For example, children initially form concepts of appleness and orangeness. Later they acquire a more abstract concept of *fruit* that consists of the common properties of the two previous concepts and subsumes them, as shown in Figure 4.8.

FIGURE 4.8. *Two Levels in the Hierarchical Organization of a Natural Concept (Schema)*

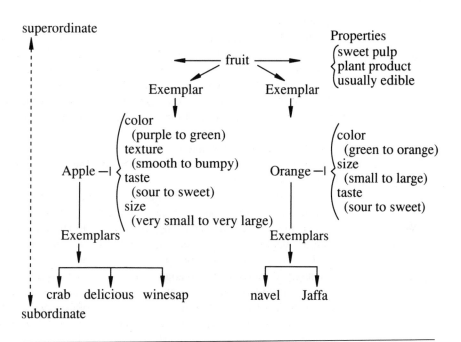

In general, as an individual matures and acquires a greater range and variety of experiences, his concepts become better organized internally and can be formed into a hierarchy, from the concrete to more abstract levels. They also become more communicable; that is, they have elements that are more in common with other individuals' concepts in their language community.

Another term for natural concepts is *schemata* (singular, schema). Schemata are abstract knowledge structures or organizations of characteristic information about a particular topic that has been abstracted from experience. For example, a schema for an object, such as an orange or an apple, will include its properties, exemplars, and relationships to other concepts, including those more abstract ones that subsume it, such as fruit in relationship to orange and apple. There are also schemata for events (relationships between objects) and situations (sequences of events). We provide examples of these schemata below.

Schemata are neither right nor wrong; they are the way individuals represent objects, events, and situations in the world to themselves. Two individuals will communicate effectively with each other, either orally or in print, to the extent that their concepts are congruent.

This introduction provides some background knowledge for understanding the schema-interactive theory of reading.

EXPLANATION OF THE SCHEMA-INTERACTIVE THEORY OF READING

Reading comprehension consists of the construction of meaning that results from an interaction between the characteristics of the text and the resources of the reader. This explanation is depicted in the model shown in Figure 4.9. Figure 4.9 shows that text data interact with visual processes, a feature extraction device and reader resources. The central limited capacity processor (Perfetti, 1975) or pattern synthesizer integrates these resources and selects the most probable interpretation or construction of meaning (Rumelhart, 1976). Text data consists of letters, words, paragraphs and longer units, plus the conjunctions, prepositions, and other grammatical elements that tie them together. (See chap. 4 for information on text data or text features and also see Figure 4.2 for explanation of a feature extraction device.)

Reader resources can act simultaneously with each other and with the text. This simultaneous processing explains why a sentence can be understood as soon as the reader reaches the end of the sentence. Information can also be propagated from the bottom, up, from features to letter formation, grouping of letters into words, syntactic organization of words into phrases, tentative assignment of meaning and subsequent instantiation of terms according to the constraints of the sentence, cognitive and metacognitive manipulation, and affective reactions; the reverse path is from the top, down (Adams & Collins, 1977, 1985). A feedback loop from construction of meaning to reader resources indicates that the reader's knowledge resources are increasing as he reads and becoming available for

FIGURE 4.9. *Schema Interactive Model of Reading (Modified from Rumelhart, 1976; Adams & Collins, 1977; Singer, 1987).*

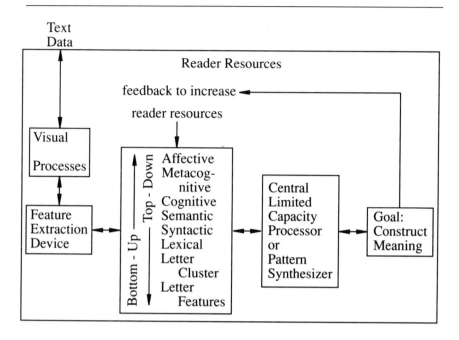

background or prior knowledge for subsequent reading of a text. In the rest of this section, we explain these terms and interactions among the components in the model.

Text and Reader Interactions

The relationship between the printed words in the text and the reader's resources (concepts or schemata) is that the print activates schemata in the reader's resources that result in the construction of meaning (see chap. 5 for text features). For example, the printed word *dog* will activate the reader's concept for dog. The meaning of dog is not in the printed word, but in the reader's concept of dog.

Another example: If a reader has a schema for a flower, then reading that a rhododendron is a flower activates the reader's schema for flower. The characteristic properties of a flower then apply to a rhododendron. Thus, the reader has constructed a meaning for a rhododendron and the rhododendron has become another exemplar in the reader's flower schema.

Individuals develop schemata for objects (man, apple), relationships between objects (The man ate an apple), and situations (two or more related events or sequences of events, such as the sequence of events in a story or in a script for making an apple pie). We explain and exemplify each of these types of semantic schemata.

SEMANTIC SCHEMATA
Objects

An example of a schema for the object, *dog,* appears in Figure 4.10.

The figure shows that the dog has properties, such as a tail, four legs, and a bark, and is exemplified by concrete objects, known as "Fido," "Spot," "Wolfles," and so forth. Moreover, a dog is related to other concepts, such as a *cat.* Dog is subsumed by class membership in *canine* and cat in *feline.* Both of these classes are included in the more abstract concept, *animal.* The schema for *animal* has properties that are common to canines, felines, and other exemplars of animals. Thus, going up in the diagram leads to higher superordinates and more abstract levels, whereas going down results in more subordinates and moves toward the more concrete level.

Schemata and their relationships can be organized hierarchically within memory as shown in the schema for a dog in Figure 4.10. This depiction of a schema is known as a semantic map. Evidence that memory for objects is hierarchically organized as early as age 6 has been experimentally demonstrated by Steinberg and Anderson (1975).

However, semantic maps can be modified by the context or situation. For example, *dog* and *sheep* become semantically closer when an individual experiences them directly or vicariously in a story about a farm where a dog works as a sheepdog (Anderson & Ortony, 1975).

Information stored in memory is not fixed into a particular organization; it can be selected and reorganized according to the purposes of the reader or the demands of the text. For example, you can organize information about automobiles according to their colors and then reorganize them according to their models (Fords, Chevrolets, etc.) or types (two-door, four-door, etc.).

Note that schemata for objects can be stated in abstract terms linked together by a stative verb, such as *has* and *is.* For example, *The dog has a tail* can be represented as *X has Y.* Similarly, sentences of the type *X is Y* can indicate a subordinate-superordinate relationship. For example, *Spot is a dog.* As we see later, similar abstractions can be used for events and even stories. Although these abstract structures are relatively few in number, they subsume an infinite number of sentences.

Some sentences cannot be understood unless the schema that subsumes them is activated. In short, comprehension occurs when an appropriate schema has been located that can subsume the information in a text. For example, the

FIGURE 4.10. *Schema for the Object, dog*

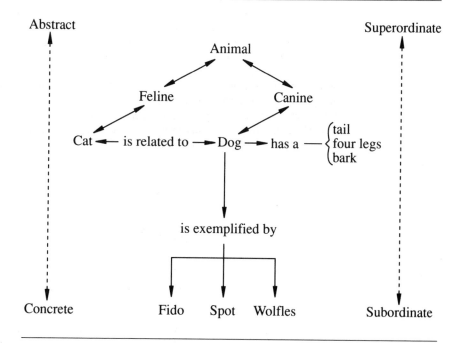

sentence *The split seams made the notes sound sour* is incomprehensible until an appropriate schema for it is activated by the term *bagpipes* (Bransford & Johnson, 1972). Even entire paragraphs cannot be comprehended unless their organizing schemata have been activated. For example, the paragraph shown in Figure 4.11 cannot be comprehended without looking at the picture below it of the "Modern Day Romeo" (Bransford & Johnson, 1972).

The range and variety of schemata individuals possess may be indexed by their vocabulary ability. Vocabulary instruction that consists of learning a word and a synonym (matched pairs) or a word and its dictionary definition is inadequate for development of vocabulary that is related to comprehension. For example, a vocabulary exercise that informs students that a dog is a quadruped canine only provides students with a subordinate-superordinate relationship (dog-canine) and one property of a dog (quadruped). An encyclopedia explanation would include many more properties of dogs, provide exemplars, and show relationships with other objects. From this greater input, students are likely to develop a more adequate schema for dogs. In other words, the reason traditional

FIGURE 4.11. A Modern Day Romeo, after Bransford and Johnson (1972, p. 719)

If the balloon popped, the sound wouldn't be able to carry since everything would be too far away from the correct floor. A closed window would also prevent the sound from carrying, since most buildings tend to be well insulated. Because the whole operation depends upon a steady flow of electricity, a break in the middle of the wire would also cause problems. Of course, the fellow could shout, but the human voice is not loud enough to carry that far. An additional problem is that a string could break on the instrument. Then there could be no accompaniment to the message. It is clear that the best situation would involve less distance. Then there would be fewer potential problems. With face-to-face contact, the least number of things could go wrong.

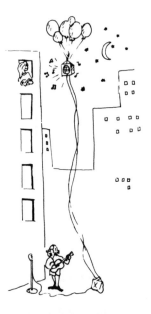

vocabulary exercises do not add to students' text comprehension is that they do not enable students to construct rich schemata.

However, vocabulary that has been developed as natural concepts is most predictive of comprehension throughout the grades and is the best single predictor of general intelligence. Whether vocabulary is an index of general intelligence, which in turn is causally related to comprehension, whether vocabulary is a way of getting appropriate meanings for terms, or whether vocabulary is an index of schemata that students can activate to attain comprehension are three current hypotheses on the role of vocabulary in text comprehension. No evidence has been adduced to support one of these hypotheses over the others (Anderson & Freebody, 1985).

Students progress from about a 5,000-word vocabulary when they enter first grade to about a 50,000-word vocabulary when they graduate from the 12th grade. The rate of acquisition is so steep that it cannot be accounted for solely by time in school (Anderson & Freebody, 1985). Consequently, vocabulary development is a function of experiences in and out of school. Since concepts or schemata represent abstractions from experience, then the more broadly based experiences in and out of school are likely to contribute to greater development of students' vocabulary. Conversely, a narrow curriculum in and out of school is likely to restrict vocabulary development. That may be why schools in one district that narrowed its curriculum in elementary school to instruction in basic skills did not yield inferential comprehension scores as high as comparable schools that maintained a broadly based curriculum that included not only basic skills, but also social studies, science, literature, and fine arts (Singer, McNeil, & Furse, 1983).

Events

Events are represented by sentences that contain an action verb, such as *John hit Bill,* or a process verb, *The wood dried.* In simple, active sentences, noun phrases usually precede the verb, which may be followed by another noun phrase. For example, *The man bit the dog.*

Noun phrases have certain relationships to the verb; these relationships, known as case relationships (Fillmore, 1968), are listed and defined in Box 4.5. For example, the sentence *The dog bit the man* involves the case relationship of "an agent acting on an object." Case relationship theory assumes that when a text has a sentence that contains an event it activates the schema for its case relationship. The particular action and the abstract roles of *agent* and *object* subsume the subject and object noun phrases, respectively, in the particular sentence. In other words, the meaning of sentences is obtained by activating the case relationships implicit in the sentence. Thus, relatively few case relationships can subsume an infinite number of sentences.

Chafe (1970) points out that "the conceptual universe," the world of ideas, is dichomotized into (a) states and events that are implied by verbs and (b) things and abstractions that are made into things that are communicated by nouns. In contrast to Fillmore's case relationships that are dominated by nouns (Box 4.5a), Chafe believes that verbs are central while nouns are peripheral to the organization of meaning. In other words, meaning begins with a verb which usually take one or more nouns. A sentence can then be (a) a verb alone, (b) a verb and one or more nouns and (c) a combination of (b) plus a coordinate or subordinate verb.

There are three types of verbs: (a) stative, (b) process, and (c) action. They take two types of nouns: (a) patient nouns, nouns which accompany stative and process verbs; they indicate what thing is in the particular state or what thing was changed by the process, and (b) agent nouns, which are the N in the question,

---

BOX 4.5a. Case Relationships Within a Proposition

Agentive	The animate doer or instigator of the action. (Who did it?)
	Debbie threw the ball.
Instrumental	Inanimate force or object causally involved in the action or state identified by the verb. (What was done with it?)
	Abie hit the ball *with a bat.*
Verb	Action or state identified by a verb that affects the direct object (object) or indirect object (dative) or recipient of the action. (What is being done?)
Objective	Things directly affected by the verb. (What was changed?)
	Mac opened the *door.*
Dative or Recipient	Person or animal being affected by the verb. (Whom did it affect?)
	Paul threw *Jim* the ball.
Locative	Location or spatial orientation. (Where is it? Where did it occur?)
	The car is *in the garage.*
	John got hit *in the foot.*
Time	Time that action or state identified by the verb occurred. (When did something exist or take place?)
	The story took place *in the Biblical period.*

"What did N do." A type of sentence is called "ambient," the term for environment, because it indicates the state of the environment, "It's hot," or the process occurring in the state of the environment, "It's raining." Together these verbs and their accompanying nouns make up the six patterns of meaning (semantic structures) shown in Box 4.5b.

Some words have multiple meanings, each with its semantic relationships. High-frequency words have more multiple meanings than do low-frequency words (Paivio, Yuille, & Madigan, 1968) and are more susceptible to contextual shifts in meaning (Reder, Anderson, & Bjork, 1974). For example, the word *run* varies in meaning when the context shifts from *stockings* to *notes, banks,* and *cars.* The particular meaning that is appropriate for multiple-meaning terms is determined by the context. For example, the meaning of the word *run* in the noun phrase *The run on the bank* may have a particular meaning in the reader's mind

---

BOX 4.5b. *Patterns of Meaning Organized by Verbs and Accompanying Nouns*

Verb	Test Questions for Type of Verb
1. Stative.	What is the condition of the noun (patient)? Ans.: (be) dry (patient noun) (stative verb) Example: The paint is dry.
2. Process.	What happened to the noun (patient)? Ans.: Process changed it to dry. (patient noun) (process verb) Example: The paint dried.
3. Action.	What did N (noun agent) do? Answer: ran (agent noun) (action verb) Example: Debbie ran.
4. Process and action.	What did N do and what happened? Ans.: hit the ball; (change in condition): hit ball (process and (agent noun) action verb) (patient noun) Example: Debbie hit the ball.
5. State ambient.	What is the environment's condition? Ans.: cold (state ambient) Example: It's cold.
6. Action ambient.	What is happening in the environment? Ans.: snowing (action ambient) Example: It's snowing.

---

that may be changed dramatically when the verb phrase that completes the sentence is added. Then the sentence reads, *The run on the bank tired the joggers.* In other words, the instance or particular meaning that was determined or constrained by the sentence was selected from memory and inserted into the sentence to make the meaning of *run* consistent with *joggers.* This process of selecting particular meanings for sentence-constrained terms is known as *instantiation* (R. Anderson et al., 1976); it occurs spontaneously from the elementary through the college level (Dreher, 1985).

Another general relationship in sentences is between "given" and "new" information. For example, in the sentence, *John is driving the car,* the given information is *John* and what is new about him is that he is *driving the car.* The reader's task is to link up and store the new information with the given or known information (H. Clark, 1977; H. Clark & E. Clark, 1977).

Situations

Situations consist of two or more related sentences. The relationship may be implicit, as in the sentences, *The girl went to the store. She bought a loaf of bread.* Or the relationship may be explicit: *The girl went to the store because she wanted to buy a loaf of bread.* Other interrelationships, explicated by conjunctions, are shown in Box 4.6.

BOX 4.6. Relationships Between Propositions or Events Consisting of Explicit or Implicit Conjunctions

Cause (implicit): Proposition A has an effect upon Proposition B.

	A B
Implicit	Samson cut his hair. He lost his strength.
	or
Explicit	Samson lost his strength because he cut his hair.

Concession: Proposition A grants or concedes a point in Proposition B.

               A   B
Although he was late, he ran to school.

Conditional: Proposition A identifies the purpose of Proposition B.

     A   B
If it rains, I'll take an umbrella.

Intention: Proposition A identifies the purpose of Proposition B.

Implicit	The girl went to the store. She bought some candy.
	or
Explicit	The girl went to the store to buy some candy.

Modifier: An adjective is a Proposition B that describes a quality of another Proposition A.

The man came to dinner. He has a beard.
or
             B   A
The bearded man came to dinner.

Negative:	Insertion of the word "not" negates the sentence.
	The bearded man did *not* come to dinner.
Therefore:	This conjunction states a conclusion in Proposition B based on one or more preceding Propositions A.

A   B

He was late. Therefore, he missed the bus.

Thus:	A Proposition B summarizes one or more preceding Propositions A.

A   A

He rode an airplane. Then he took a train.

A   B

Finally, he hailed a cab. Thus, he got home.

Meanwhile:	Proposition B consists of action or state occurring at the same time as another event B.

A   B

Peter was busy. Meanwhile, Jean slept.

Other cohesive ties, the grammatical elements that link sentences together, such as relative pronouns, and features of text that activate schemata and facilitate comprehension are presented in the chapter on text features, chapter 5.

World Knowledge and Scripts

Two types of situations are *world knowledge* and *scripts*. World knowledge is the general information that individuals have acquired in a given culture. A particular type of world knowledge is called *scriptal*. Scripts are mental representations of commonly occurring sequences of events in the world that causally link together persons, props, and events, such as a script for the sequence of events in a fast food restaurant versus a fancy French restaurant (Bower, Black, & Turner, 1979; Galambos, Abelson, & Black, 1986; Schank & Abelson, 1977).

Readers activate their world and scriptal knowledge to augment and subsume texts (Winograd, 1972). For example, readers have a script that enables them to understand the simple sentence, "The cigarette caused the forest fire." If asked, they can draw upon the script to explain the progressive sequence of events involved in a cigarette causing a forest fire. Readers who do not have such information stored in memory, such as a person from another planet who has never seen a cigarette being smoked, thrown into dry tinder, followed by predictable consequences, would have difficulty in comprehending the sentence. Since writers assume that readers have this world knowledge, they omit it from their texts. If the assumption of this prior knowledge is not valid for a particular reader or the reader does not activate it, the text is not likely to be understood.

Story Schemata.   A situation can also be an entire story. Story schemata are used in the comprehension of narratives. The knowledge structures in story schemata are based on rules for story grammar. These rules state that a story consists of a setting (time and place), characters, theme or problem with initiating events that lead to a goal, plot with episodes or attempt(s) to solve the problem or reach the goal, and finally a resolution or solution to the problem, success in reaching the goal, or giving up and accepting defeat (Adams & Collins, 1985; Mandler, 1984). Readers acquire these knowledge structures as early as Grade 1 (Mandler & Johnson, 1977). Figure 4.12 is a representation of a structured story schema. Each structure subsumes relevant information from a story. As individuals read, they fill in the abstract knowledge structures with particular information from the text. For example, the abstract structure of set-

FIGURE 4.12.   *Representation of a Structured Story Schema*

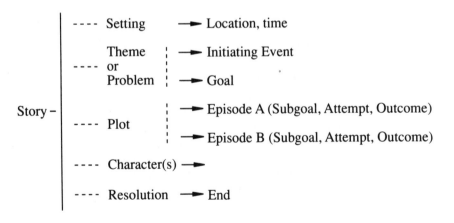

ting subsumes particular time and place information from the text. When all the relevant structures contain information from the text, the story is understood.

Simple fables illustrate story grammar structures with great clarity. You can discern these structures in operation in the fable contained in Box 4.7

BOX 4.7. *Fable of the Thirsty Bird*

A thirsty bird was flying over a desert when it spotted a pitcher on the ground. The bird flew down to the pitcher. First, the bird put his beak in the pitcher but could not reach the water. Then the bird tried to tip the pitcher over but it was too heavy. Finally, the bird saw some pebbles nearby, picked them up and dropped them into the pitcher, drank the water, and flew away.

(Character: bird. Setting: flying over desert. Problem: how to quench thirst. Initiating event: spotted pitcher on ground. Goal: get water. Plot—Episodes A and B: attempts to solve problem of how to get water from pitcher; outcomes are unsuccessful. Resolution: third attempt is successful. Goal achieved: drank water. End: bird flew away. Theme: If at first you don't succeed, try, try, and try again.)

However, students acquire additional, more abstract knowledge structures at higher grade levels. For example, they might learn that a story can be a satire or subsumed by a particular theme or have a symbolic meaning.

Readers' responses to stories, even to fables, include not only application of story grammar structures, but also emotional reactions and detection of symbolic meanings (Guthrie, 1978a). In other words, readers respond to stories in a variety of ways that they learn as they progress through the grades. Thus, a reader of *Huckleberry Finn* may read it as a simple narrative at the elementary level. When the reader rereads it at the college level, the Mississippi River in the story can be viewed as a symbol of purity as depicted by the relationships between the characters, Huck and his black friend, Jim, when they are on their raft on the river. Civilization can be perceived as a corrupting influence on their relationship whenever they go ashore to the towns along the river (Potok, 1968). The story can be categorized as an example of Rousseau's philosophy that man is inherently good, but is corrupted by society.

Readers can read texts at more than one level of interpretation. For example, schemata drawn from Freudian psychology can be applied to an interpretation of fairy tales. Bettelheim and Zelan (1982) have argued that although children may not give a Freudian interpretation to fairy tales, the tales emotionally condition the children for similar events that may occur in their lives. Although emotional reactions to fairy tales can be obtained, they cannot be evaluated as right or wrong. They can, however, be used in discussions about literature.

Readers can also render philosophical, psychological, ethical, or moral judgments about a story. To do so, they have to activate a schema that is a superordinate for the story. For example, in the fable of the thirsty bird, Box 4.7, a moral exhortation was used to subsume the story. But a psychological one on "brains win out over brawn" could also have been involved. The theme that a reader constructs to subsume a story is a function of the reader's knowledge, experience, and level of thinking. Sargent, Huus, and Andresen (1971) have formulated a scale to indicate the profoundness of the thought that the author is communicating or the reader constructs in reading a story. The scale, shown in Box 4.8, has five levels or *planes*. We see how they apply to the "Fable of the Thirsty Bird" in Box 4.7.

BOX 4.8.   *Levels of Profoundness in Conceptualizing Literature*

1. Physical: the reader is aware only of the physical actions of the characters. (Bird tries various ways to get water out of pitcher.)
2. Mental: reader is aware of physical actions and thoughts of the characters. (Story does not reveal bird's thoughts).
3. Moral: reader employs an ethical code for evaluating actions of characters. (Story exemplifies moral: If at first you don't succeed, then try, try, and try again.)
4. Psychological: reader is aware of psychological influences on character's thinking and behavior. (Frustration did not interfere with Bird's problem-solving ability).
5. Philosophical: reader employs philosophical truths to subsume story. (Necessity is the mother of invention.)

Students can benefit from instruction in learning to apply their knowledge structures to complex stories by restating the abstract story structures into story specific forms. For example, instead of asking, "What were the characters doing?" readers can learn to use the actual names of the characters in the story when they ask questions of the text as they are reading it. Thus, they can relate the abstract knowledge structures of story grammar into story specific forms that will enable them to relate the abstract structures to specific words, phrases, or longer units in the printed text (Singer & Donlan, 1982).

Expository Texts

These texts contain explanations of objects, events, situations, or procedures for carrying out activities. A variety of knowledge structures are necessary for subsuming expository texts. The main ones are known as *rhetorical structures*, such as *problem-solution, cause and effect, question and answer, compare and contrast,* and simple *enumeration*. Of course, whenever narratives are embedded

in expository text, story schemata can be applied to them. (See c[...]
more detailed explanation of expository texts.)

Thus, each level of the text, from individual words to whole chap[...], can be
subsumed under appropriate knowledge structures and relationships among these
structures. In short, an infinite amount of materials can be comprehended
through the use of semantic schemata for objects, events, and situations.

SYNTACTIC STRUCTURES

Although texts are written in grammatical form, the reader imposes on texts
knowledge of syntactic structures. Simple sentences can be perceptually grouped
into noun phrases and verb phrases. For example, *The dog (noun phrase) bit the
man* (verb phrase consisting of verb plus noun phrase). Adjectives and adverbs
are embedded sentences. For example, *the large dog* implies two sentences:
There is a dog. The dog is large. Prepositional phrases consist of a preposition
and a noun phrase: *in* (preposition) *the house* (noun phrase, consisting of definite
noun determiner and noun). Adverbial phrases contain an adverb and one or
more noun phrases: during (adverb) the speech (noun determiner and noun).

PERCEPTION OF PRINT: WORD, LETTER,
AND FEATURE SCHEMATA

Readers form schemata for words, letters, and features (Adams & Collins, 1985;
McClelland & Rumelhart, 1985). They acquire knowledge or expectations that
certain combinations of letters form words. For example, readers can readily fill
in the missing letter in the word "th_t." They also learn to perceive letters as a
pattern of features. (See first section of this chapter for instruction on developing
wholistic views of letters.)

Features of letters can be organized into concepts. A conjunctive concept
consists of two or more features always present; for example, a vertical line with
a bar across the top is a *t*. A disjunctive concept consists of two or more features
with at least one feature that can alternate; for example, a vertical line followed
by a circle is a *b* if it is above the horizontal line or a *p* if it is below the horizontal
line. (See Fig. 4.2 for a model for perceiving letters and words.)

PROCESSING PRINTED INPUT
Top-Down, Bottom-Up, and Parallel Processing

Readers have schemata for letter features, letters, whole words, syntax, and
semantics. In bottom-up processing, they may first perceive the features,
organize them into letters, group the letters into words, organize the words into
syntactic structures, and subsume them by schemata for objects, events, and
situations. Thus, information can be propagated upward. Processing can also
operate in a downward fashion. That is, higher order schemata can form expectations for lower order schemata. For example, a top-down direction can start with
a schema for flowers and lead to selection of instances of a flower, such as a
rhododendron.

These processes go on simultaneously and in parallel in response to the printed input. (Rumelhart et al., 1986) The various processes are integrated in a pattern synthesizer that selects the most plausible interpretation of the sentence. This simultaneous and parallel processing and operation of a pattern synthesizer explains why a reader can understand a sentence by the time he or she has reached the end of the sentence. In other words, the processes do not act in an additive fashion. That is, readers do not first identify words, then select meanings for them, and finally combine the meanings into sentences. If they did, they would only comprehend a sentence some time after they got to the end of it.

Readers arrive at plausible interpretations according to the data already processed. For example, an individual may read this sentence at the beginning of a story: "They went up to the window and put $10 down." One plausible interpretation is that they were buying tickets for a movie. An equally plausible interpretation is that they are at a gas station, prepaying for gasoline. As more data from the text enter into the reader's processing, interpretations are rejected or modified. In short, an appropriate schema is finally activated that takes all the data into account. Rumelhart (1982) found that most readers converged on an appropriate schema within a few introductory lines of an initially ambiguous text. This evidence indicates that readers adopt, evaluate, and modify their interpretations with successive interactions between the text data and their resources. In short, they construct closer approximations to meaning as they progress through the text.

However, some texts can activate alternate schemata that represent differences in perspectives that readers can have for a text. For example, Pichert and Anderson (1976, 1977) found that a story about two boys going through a house could be interpreted as "house buyers" or "burglars," depending on the title given the story. If the text was labeled "burglars," readers tended to observe and recall information about the location of silverware and jewels; but if the same passage was labeled "housebuyer," the readers were more inclined to attend to and recall information about architectural features of the house. In short, readers tend to construct meanings that are consistent with their activated schemata. In other words, readers do not derive or extract meaning from the text. The meaning is not inherent in the text. Instead, they construct meaning using their own schemata that were activated in interaction with the text. If the reader's activated schemata are congruent with the author's and with the perspective adopted by the author, then the reader is likely to construct the meaning that guided the author when he wrote the text.

Schematic structures are activated not only by titles and main ideas in printed materials, but also by the reader's metacognitive and cognitive processes.

Metacognitive and Cognitive Processes
Metacognition is knowledge of one's own cognition and the ability to direct and monitor cognitive processes and provide fix-up strategies when necessary

(Brown, 1980). Cognitive processes consist of recall, inference, interpretation, and evaluation. (See previous section for clarification of these processes.)

For critical reading, readers activate standards or schemata for detecting lexical errors, logically inconsistent text-based inferences, and inferences inconsistent with prior knowledge (Baker, 1984; Baker & Brown, 1984; Brown, 1980; Simonsen & Singer, 1985). In short, readers apply evaluation standards not only to their own cognitive processes but also to the text.

Readers invoke cognitive standards (correct or incorrect), affective criteria (like or dislike) and moral standards (consistent or inconsistent with one's values and morals) in their evaluation of what they read. Athey (1985) found that affective characteristics, such as confidence, were related to higher reading achievement. Affective reactions occur not only in remedial readers (P. Johnston, 1985), but in all readers, varying from positive, if the reader is not having difficulty in processing the text, to negative if the reader is frustrated in obtaining answers to questions (Dreher & Singer, 1986). Affective responses, such as liking what one is reading, is likely to add to the prediction of reading achievement, whereas negative responses such as self-derogation type of responses, "I'm not good at reading this kind of material," are likely to subtract from the prediction (Singer & Bean, 1986).

MEASUREMENT OF THE READER'S GOAL

The goal of text-reader interactions is the construction of meaning. If the reader's purpose is to comprehend the author's meaning, and the reader is successful, the constructed meaning should be congruent with the author's meaning. This congruency can occur if the reader's and the author's schemata are identical (Goodman, 1966). However, we do not have measuring instruments that will assess the degree of congruence between the author's meaning and the reader's constructed meaning. These responses can vary within a range of acceptable meanings (Tierney & LaZansky, 1980) and, of course, beyond this range, but the range of acceptable meanings has not been defined and is perhaps undefinable.

Reader responses can be divided into three categories: literal recall or recognition, implicit inferences, and scriptal inferences (Pearson & Johnson, 1978). The first two are assessed on standardized tests because answers to literal recall or recognition and implicit inferences can be objectively derived from the text. That is, readers can point to passages in the text that contain the same information as in their literal recall or recognition. Also, two or more readers can point to major and minor premises in the text from which they made their inferences. But, scriptal responses are a function of a reader's unique or culturally different perspective and knowledge in interaction with text data that do not lend themselves to objective scoring. Often scriptal inferences involve adding a major premise to a minor premise stated in the text and then using inference to reach a conclusion. For example, a text states that "Columbus left his nine-year-old son, Diego, on the dock when he sailed for the New World." To answer the scriptal question "How did Diego feel when he was left behind?" readers have to generate out of their background experience a major premise, such as ''When a father goes on a great adventure and leaves his son behind, the son is unhappy.'' If readers differ on the major premise they construct, then their scriptal inferences will also be different.

Even without directions to do so, readers make scriptal responses to texts, including attitudinal and evaluative responses. They also make scriptal responses that reflect understanding of the text. For example, when Hispanics and Anglos read a text about Mexican customs, the Hispanics made scriptal inferences based on their cultural experiences that the Anglos could not make because they lacked the necessary background knowledge. The Anglos did not know why people carried baskets of food to the cemetery on a certain day of the year. However, both groups made the same scriptal responses to a text that contained American customs (Rogers-Zegarra & Singer, 1981). Standardized tests on the two texts would not have shown these differences because they would have assessed only the literal and implicit inferences. They avoid scriptal questions because the responses cannot be inferred from text data alone, but depend on the knowledge and experiences that readers bring to the text.

IMPLICATIONS FOR INSTRUCTION: AN INTERACTIVE READING AND LEARNING FROM TEXT INSTRUCTIONAL MODEL

The schema interactive model has to be expanded to incorporate the instructor as an explanatory variable when reading occurs in a classroom situation. The expanded model, shown in Figure 4.13, is called an interactive reading and learning-from-text instructional model (Singer, 1985; H. Yopp, 1987; H. Yopp & Singer, 1985; Singer, 1987). The model shows that the instructor influences and is influenced by each component in the model: text features (for selection, modification, clarification, or enhancement of text features, see chapter 5), reader resources (for development of resources within the reader or adding the teacher's resources to the reader's resources to enable the reader to interact with the text or the goal more effectively or more appropriately, see chapters 6–9, 11, 12–16, and 18), and the goal (for selecting or establishing the goal, constructing ways of assessing the results of the text and reader interactions, and acting on

FIGURE 4.13. *Interactive Reading and Learning from Text Instructional Model*

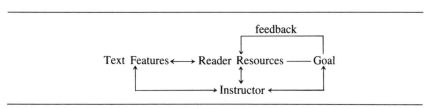

knowledge of the results, see suggestions throughout the text, particularly test-writing objectives in chapter 9, and curricular objectives in chapters 13–16 and 19). In the instructor category are these general implications for instruction:

1. Develop students' schemata for objects, events, and situations by providing them with breadth and variety of direct and vicarious experiences. For example, make sure that school and classroom libraries contain multiethnic literature.

2. Use classroom strategies, such as Quest (see chap. 15), to teach individuals to abstract and generalize from their direct and vicarious experiences.

3. Instruct students on ways of using text information to activate their schemata as they read a text. For example, when students read that ''a rhododendron is a flower,'' ask them about their schema of a flower and point out how it gives meaning to their knowledge of a rhododendron.

4. Teach students to make use of relationships among terms in a sentence (case relationships) by having them find different sentences that fit under the same case relationships. Do the same for relationships between clauses to teach the meaning of conjunctions. Have the students categorize the elements of stories into story schemata. Do the same for rhetorical structures.

5. Have students categorize responses to texts into literal, inferential, and scriptal categories.

6. Teach students to map stories, using story schemata, case relationships, conjunctions, and cohesive ties. (See example of story mapping in chapter 6.)

7. Have students categorize expository texts according to the various types of rhetorical structures. (See chapter 5 for explanation of these structures and other features of text.)

8. Compare vocabulary terms according to their dictionary and encyclopedic entries.

9. Teach students metacognitive strategies for learning from text. Metacognition consists of the ability to regulate, monitor, and evaluate one's own cognitive processes and use fix-up strategies when necessary. The strategies are ways of obtaining the reader's goal(s) in reading. These strategies include establishing purposes in reading, generating questions and reading to answer them, and other strategies that we will present and exemplify in chapter 6.

10. Although schools may be limited to objective assessment for purposes of grading students' comprehension of texts, teachers should nevertheless strive to develop scriptal comprehension and other reactions to text, such as affective responses. (See chapter 13, ''The English Language Arts,'' for a list of reader responses to text.) For example, teachers can ask how students feel about a given story and whether the action taken at a certain

point is morally justifiable. The answers cannot be graded, but they can be discussed and even debated by a class.

11. Develop student independence in acquisition and activation of schemata by phasing out the teacher and phasing in the student (See chapter 12, "An Instructional Blueprint" for detailed instructions on this procedure).

SUMMARY

Explanations of reading have progressed through three major changes. However, instruction under all three still occurs in schools. Teachers today develop oral reading, teach students to obtain meanings from the text (literal and inferential comprehension), and provide students with strategies for activating their resources to interact with and construct meaning for text. They also teach students to direct, monitor, and, when necessary, provide fix-up strategies. Readers also learn to evaluate their responses to text, including cognitive, affective and moral evaluations.

There are tests for oral and silent reading comprehension (literal and inferential), but no tests for assessing scriptal or evaluative responses to texts. However, lack of tests should not preclude instruction in developing subjective responses to texts.

In general, the schema theory explanation of reading indicates that we need to teach students knowledge of text characteristics, develop resources within the reader that are necessary for constructing meaning for texts, and provide instruction and practice in students' use of text data to activate appropriate schemata for interpreting texts. We should also teach students to use their metacognitive abilities for being active in the process of reading by formulating and reading to answer their own questions and directing and regulating their cognitive processes in responding to texts.

5 Text Features

CHAPTER OVERVIEW

Text features vary according to function and type of text. In this chapter, we concentrate on the features of expository text that communicate information. Features that facilitate comprehension of this information are called "friendly text features." They are categorized according to whether they are intra-text or extra-text determinants of friendly texts. At the end of the chapter, the features that occur within these categories are listed in an inventory for evaluating texts. We also have an inventory of a text-friendly teacher that will enable you to evaluate whether the teacher modifies text, reader, and goal components so that students at varying reading ability levels can make successful progress in learning from text.

GRAPHIC ORGANIZER

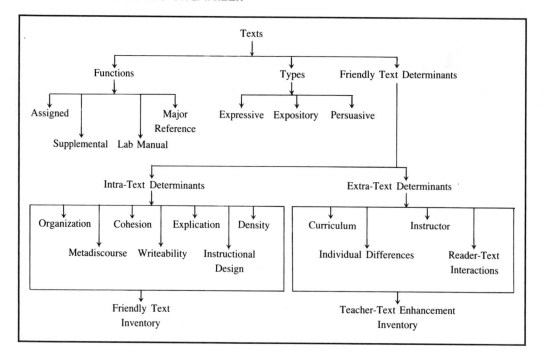

PREPOSED QUESTIONS

1. How do features of texts vary according to functions of texts?
2. What are the different types of texts?
3. What are the determinants within texts that facilitate comprehension?
4. What are the determinants outside of texts that affect comprehension?
5. In what ways can teachers interact with texts, students, and goals to enable all students to progress in learning from text?
6. What will an inventory reveal about the friendliness of texts used in your class?
7. If you evaluate yourself or other teachers on a text-friendly inventory, what will the results reveal about the use of texts?

TEACHER VARIATION IN TEXT USE

To find out about the use of texts in a high school, visit several classes, interview the teacher and students, examine the texts, observe how the teacher interacts with the students and the texts. You will find that teachers vary considerably in use of texts. Some may base their lectures and class discussions entirely on the text, following its organization and content faithfully; others may assign the text but not really use it; some may not have a text at all and rely entirely on lectures and class projects. You are also not likely to find many teachers teaching students how to learn from their texts. Students are likely to tell you that they get the information needed for examinations from the lectures and perhaps from selective reading of the text based on cues from teachers on the information they consider important for students to know (Smith & Feathers, 1983). You will notice that the texts are voluminous, heavy, encyclopedic, and conceptually dense. They do not encourage students to carry them back and forth from school to home.

Teachers have a variety of reasons for not using texts. They know that the texts are too difficult for many students and so some resort to the use of lectures to replace the text, a procedure that teachers had to use prior to the invention of the Gutenberg press! They know that the text is voluminous because state framework committees want texts to be comprehensive and that the knowledge explosion has increased the knowledge available at an exponential rate. They realize that history and civics texts tend to avoid controversial issues, particularly applications to current life; consequently, students do not find them relevant. Teachers frequently provide their own science and lab materials that are written at an easy enough level so that most students in the class can use them. Thus, in general, students are primarily learning from listening. Consequently, they are less likely to learn how to learn from texts, which will adversely affect them when they have to do library research or when they have to achieve in subsequent classes where teachers do expect students to learn from texts.

Even though the attitudes of teachers and students toward texts tend to be valid, texts are still a necessary tool for independent learning. We believe that if teachers know how to teach students to learn from text, they are likely to make more use of texts and teach students how to learn from them, and then students are more likely to improve in their ability to read and learn from text. This belief constitutes the basic purpose of this text. Moreover, we anticipate that the knowledge presented in this chapter will lead teachers to demand texts that have features in them that will facilitate students' learning from them. It will also enable them to answer complaints about "dumbing down books" and calls for "improving the quality of texts," which often mean making texts even more difficult and therefore less likely to be used.

Can a text be readable, understandable, and interesting? Teachers and researchers have been trying to answer this question ever since Gray and Leary's (1935) pioneering study. This knowledge would enable authors to write, select and/or modify books or adopt instructional strategies that would make texts more comprehensible and more engaging to students (Clewell & Cliffton, 1983). Teachers could also use such knowledge to teach students how to learn from texts and determine whether their instruction facilitates students' comprehension.

Although considerable research has been conducted on the readability of texts over the last 50 years, most of this research has been done on formulas to predict readability (Klare, 1984). The most widely used formulas are explained in chapter 10. In general, the formulas are successful in placing a text at a particular grade level, but that does not mean the text has features that will facilitate comprehension for all students at that grade level.

Recently researchers have begun to focus on features of texts and study their effects on the processes of reading and the attainment of meaning. So far they have conducted only a paucity of research on these features. For example, we still do not know how much these features contribute to individual differences in comprehension (Pearson & Camperell, 1985). However, evidence indicates that some features contribute to speed of reading, but not to comprehension (Kintsch & Keenan, 1973); we also know that use of personal pronouns tends to make a text more interesting (Flesch, 1949). Furthermore, we realize that comprehensibility and interest are not a function of text alone, but they are both a consequence of extra-text determinants, such as an interaction between the text and the reader (Adams & Collins, 1985). Although we cite the research that has been conducted on text features, most of the text features that we think facilitate comprehension are only plausible hypotheses on what makes a text readable, comprehensible, and interesting.

TEXT FUNCTIONS AND TYPES

Text Functions

Text features vary according to the functions of a text. Guthrie (1981) has defined five functions for texts used in a course: the course-assigned text is the

---

BOX 5.1. Features Emphasized According to Text Functions

Text Functions   *Features Emphasized*

1. Assigned text. Readable text: vocabulary readily learnable, coherence among sentences so that new information is easily connected with prior knowledge, appropriate questions and review to maintain attention, content presented in the form of principles with examples and illustrations, and length limited to student time available.

2. Major reference (Encyclopedia). Comprehensive information base, no length constraints, concise definitions, cross referencing, abundance of factual detail for principles or concepts, and aids to maximize access to knowledge, such as text headings, section numbers, indexes, content lists, and study guides.

---

primary source of knowledge, a supplemental text is an extension of information provided by a lecturer or another text, a major reference may be the text for a laboratory-based course, a minor reference is one among many reference sources, and a laboratory guide is not a text but mostly directions on how to conduct, analyze, and report on experiments. Two of these functions and their required text features appear in Box 5.1. You can use his criteria for an assigned text to evaluate your classroom text.

Text Types

Defining different modes or forms of writing as "superstructures," Hoskins (1986) has drawn upon Kinneavy's work to categorize a wide variety of texts into three types, depending on whether they emphasize exposition of a subject, a writer's means of expression, or appeals made to a reader. These types are listed here:

1. Subject or expository texts: news articles, reports, summaries, and textbooks.
2. Writer or expressive texts: journals, diaries, personal narratives, manifestos.
3. Reader or persuasive texts: advertising, political documents, legal opinions, editorials, propaganda.

Each of these text types has specific features that fit its purposes. In this chapter, we concentrate essentially on expository texts and features that make them friendly. Although expository texts frequently have narrative passages in them, we do not include narrative features in this section, but we explain narrative structure in the form of story schema in chapter 4.

INTRA-TEXT DETERMINANTS OF FRIENDLY TEXTS: FRIENDLY TEXT FEATURES

Friendly texts contain features that facilitate comprehension (Singer, 1983a, 1986). Compare the two expository texts in Box 5.2. Which one is friendly, that is, helps you understand the explanation?

We assume you will find Text B is friendlier. The only difference between Text A and Text B is that Text B has an analogy: "like bubbles in a pot simmering on a stove." This analogy helps you relate the movement within the earth to your prior knowledge, which you can use to help you comprehend the cause of earthquakes. Thus, texts facilitate comprehension when they use analogies to bridge the gap between prior and new knowledge (Hayes & Tierney, 1982) or supply the necessary information for the student to refine preexisting knowledge or construct new knowledge categories (Bransford, 1984). In short, an appropriate text should start at the level of a student's knowledge framework and build upon it.

BOX 5.2. Comparison of Two Expository Texts

Text A
Explanation of Earthquakes
The earth is made up of three layers: The surface is a crust. The continents lie on the surface surrounded by water. Next comes a layer called a mantle. Below it is a core of hot liquid iron. The hot liquid rises up toward the surface. As it does, it moves the continents. This movement is the cause of earthquakes.

Text B
Explanation of Earthquakes
The earth is made up of three layers: The surface is a crust. The continents lie on the surface surrounded by water. Next comes a layer called a mantle. Below it is a core of hot liquid iron. The hot liquid rises up toward the surface like bubbles in a pot simmering on a stove. As it does, it moves the continents. This movement is the cause of earthquakes.

In the remainder of this section, we present features of texts that make them friendly. In a subsequent section, we present information on extratext determinants that facilitate comprehension. We then summarize the text and extratext determinants in a ''Friendly Text Inventory'' that you can use for evaluating texts. We conclude the chapter with two inventories, one for evaluating expository texts and the other for rating teachers on use of an instructional model for teaching students to learn from texts. (See chapters 4 and 6 for an explanation of this model.)

We have organized friendly text features into seven categories: (1) text organization, (2) cohesion, (3) explication, (4) conceptual density, (5) metadiscourse, (6) writeability, and (7) instructional design. We also explain extratext determinants of comprehensibility, characteristics outside of texts, such as the influence of an instructor, the reader's background knowledge and abilities, and the curriculum, that determine whether a text will be comprehensible to a particular student. This list of text and extratext determinants subsumes the criteria proposed by other researchers (T. H. Anderson & Armbruster, 1981, 1986; Irwin & Davis, 1980; Langer, 1983; Tierney, Mosenthal, & Kantor, 1984).

Text Organization

Text organization refers to the purpose and arrangement of information in a text (Meyer & Rice, 1984). In general, a text that is better organized places less of a demand upon a reader, such as having to recall background information, perceive relationships among ideas in a text, make inferences or draw conclusions, and take time to process the text (Birkmire, 1985; Kintsch, Mandel & Kozminsky, 1977; Kintsch & Yarbrough, 1982). It also influences a reader's comprehension and recall of information (Meyer, 1975; Meyer & Freedle, 1984), particularly if readers make use of its organizing features (Bartlett, 1979; Meyer, Brandt, & Bluth, 1980).

Grimes (1975) divides the organization of a text into three parts:

1. Content that can be divided into events (participants and what happens to them) and nonevents (setting, background, collateral information, and evaluation).

    Example: Late in the evening (setting), the farm door opened and Hank stepped outside to gaze at the stars (event). They were beautiful (evaluative). At this time of the year, during the dry season, the sky was usually clear (collateral information).

2. Staging, ways of featuring information, for example, by its location in a passage or by use of writing patterns, such as problem-solution in which the statement of the problem and its solution stage or focus attention on particular information.

3. Cohesion is use of a grammatical element to tie the same information together in a text, such as pronouns that refer back to nouns.

In other chapters, we deal with the content of textbooks. Later in this section, we present information on staging and cohesion.

One feature of text organization that affects its comprehensibility is discourse consistency, a uniform style of writing and presenting information (Anderson, Armbruster, & Kantor, 1980). For example, a text may attain discourse consistency by using the same rhetorical pattern or combination of rhetorical patterns throughout the text. A rhetorical pattern is a writing pattern that specifies the structural relations of ideas that make up a text. There are five types of rhetorical patterns:

1. Response type, such as a question followed by an answer; statement of a problem and presentation of a solution.

2. Covariance type: cause and effect.

3. Temporal order: sequence of events, stated in their order of occurrence.

4. Adversative type: comparison and contrast pattern in which the similarities and differences between two objects or ideas are stated. An argument is a particular adversative: Evidence is presented for and against a point of view, followed by a summary or a conclusion.

5. Attribution type: list of attributes or characteristics of objects or ideas.

These types of writing patterns can be found in school textbooks at the sentence, paragraph, and larger units of writing, such as an entire chapter (Horowitz, 1985a). The patterns are shown in Box 5.3 along with the texts that prominently use them, signal words that introduce them, and strategies for teaching them. Also, see information on paragraph types in the chapter on writing (Table 9.4) for other types of patterns.

Although a particular pattern may dominate a textbook, analysis of texts indicates that they actually use multiple patterns (Horowitz, 1985b). You can

---

BOX 5.3. Textbook Patterns

Type of Rhetorical Pattern	Text Occurrence	Signal Words	Teaching Strategy
Temporal Order (Sequence)	History texts	First, second, third	Make a timeline
Example: The American revolution came first, then the French revolution, and last, the Russian revolution.			
Attribution (List)	Narratives	First, in addition	Make a list
Example: He bought the car because it has exemplary features. First, it has four valves per cylinder. In addition, it has split rear seats. Last, but of greatest importance to his wife, it has maroon upholstery to match the exterior color.			
Adversative (Compare-Contrast)	Science, math, social studies, history	However, nevertheless	Construct similarities and differences
Example: Computers can only carry out the activities for which they have been programmed. However, the latest generation of computers can modify their own programs according to interactive information they receive from computer users. They are therefore becoming similar to man's ability to learn from his experience.			
Covariance (Cause and Effect)	Science, history	because, as a result, consequently	State cause and effect
Example: The tectonic plate theory explains the cause of earthquakes. They are the result of the movement of plates on which the continents rest.			
Response (Problem-solution Question-answer)	Social Sciences	problem is, solution is, question is, answer is	Identify problem and solution
Example: The question asked repeatedly by Senator Baker at the Watergate investigation was, "What did the President know and when did he know it?" The answer to the question led to President Nixon's threatened impeachment and resignation.			

have your class analyze the course text to determine whether it has discourse consistency and whether it follows a particular multiple pattern. The exercise may enable students in the class to acquire the rhetorical structure of a text and consequently enhance their ability to organize, store, and retrieve information gleaned from the text. For example, the next paragraph is a question–answer type of paragraph with the answer in the form of a list that is in a developmental time-order sequence.

Do students make use of text patterns and does it enhance their performance? Developmental changes occur in awareness of patterns and this awareness determines when they can make use of text patterns. Time order and list structure occur early in development (Meyer & Rice, 1984); fifth-grade good readers are more aware of text structure and recall more high-level ideas, such as main ideas, than fifth-grade poor or third-grade good readers (McGee, 1982); sixth graders recognize different text patterns but do not consistently use them (Elliot, 1980); fifth and sixth graders who were aware of text structure recalled more of a normal than a scrambled passage, which indicated they were relying more on their knowledge of text structure than just on memory alone (Taylor & Samuels, 1983); ninth graders who use text structure have better recall for what they read (Meyer, Brandt, & Bluth, 1980); college students recall more ideas from compare and contrast than from list patterns; and their awareness of text structures is related to successful comprehension and writing patterns that matched text topics and structures (Hiebert, Englert, & Brennan, 1983). This research suggests that training in patterns is more likely to succeed when students are ready to learn a particular pattern. Although research, particularly training studies, is necessary to determine readiness ages for text structure, apparently students are not ready to learn the more complex patterns of problem-solution, cause-effect, and compare-contrast prior to the fifth or sixth grade.

Does training in text patterns enhance performance? Bartlett (1979) trained ninth graders to detect patterns in social studies by directly explaining to the students the parts of a pattern, such as ''this is a problem'' and ''this is the solution,'' and found that the training increased their use of patterns in their written recalls of text-based information. Horowitz (1985b) reported that training community college students to detect cause-and-effect patterns in a variety of ways, including explanations of cause and effect in everyday situations, in passages from history texts underlining cause with two lines and effects with one line, and circling related signal words, plus training in writing cause-and-effect essays significantly increased use of cause-and-effect patterns and elaboration upon history ideas in subsequent writing. Only training students to read and mark these patterns was not any more effective than routine reading instruction. However, the experimenters did not test the effects of only training in writing these patterns. Horowitz's study apparently demonstrates that instruction in knowledge of text patterns is not enough; students also have to be trained in the mode in which they are expected to manifest their knowledge of text patterns.

Does placement of information affect acquisition and retention of information? Meyer (1975) has demonstrated that high-level information, that is a general idea, presented at the beginning of a passage, is remembered better than lower level information, such as clarifying statements, details, and examples, presented later in the passage. Superordinate or more general information is better remembered than subordinate (intermediate and lower level) information regardless of its position in a passage (Brown, 1980). Facts are better remembered when they are close to the main ideas or topics they support. When objects are grouped with their properties rather than separated into categorized lists, such as a particular automobile with its features (type of lights, shock absorbers, etc.) versus separate lists of features and all the cars that have them, students tend to acquire and retain the information better (Frase, 1969a) probably because the related grouping of information facilitates organization of an object schema.

Cohesion

Cohesion is the way information is tied together from sentence to sentence, paragraph to paragraph, and chapter to chapter (Grimes, 1975). It is attained by grammatical elements that interrelate information in a text (Halliday & Hasan, 1976). These elements are the verbal glue that makes a text stick together. Any grammatical element can serve as a cohesive tie. Cohesive elements are technically known as *cataphora,* if the element points to a later referent in the text, and *anaphora,* if the element refers to a prior referent. Mostly, we use anaphora. There are five types of cohesive elements:

1. *Reference:* A word's interpretation depends upon a previous word; for example, interpretation of a pronoun depends upon a previous noun.
2. *Lexical cohesion:* The repetition of words, using the same word, synonym, near synonym, or superordinate term; for example, after using three names, such as Jean, Nancy, and Patricia, in one sentence, referring to them in another sentence by a superordinate, *the women.*
3. *Ellipsis:* Deletion of previous stated words or ideas, such as *Stephen raised his hand and so did Beverly* (raise her hand).
4. *Substitution:* Replacement of one or more words by another element. For example, in the paragraph below, "goal" substitutes for "they wanted to be the best teachers possible."
5. *Conjunctions:* Words that signal how two adjacent segments of a text are related.

The paragraph in Box 5.4 contains examples of all five types of cohesion. As an exercise, try to identify their types.

BOX 5.4. *Narrative with Examples of Five Types of Cohesion*

Hallie and Ruth are identical twins. *Both* are elementary teachers. Two years ago Hallie won the outstanding teaching award for *her* school. This year Ruth won (it). *They* are *both* working towards PhD degrees *so that they* can become the best teachers possible. *Their* mother, also a teacher, inspired *them* to achieve this *goal*. *Their* father is proud of *their* accomplishments.

Conjunctions not only interrelate sentences but also larger units of discourse, such as paragraphs. Unlike anaphora, they provide ideational cues or specify relationships for the reader. There are four types of relationships: additive (also, moreover), adversative (however, conversely), causal (consequently, so that, as a result), and temporal (next, finally). For example, *and* indicates the *addition* of another idea or object. *But* implies subtraction, as in the sentence, "All *but* Douglas had a turn." *Therefore* implies a logical consequence to a sequence of events or signals the reader that a conclusion to an argument is about to be presented. (See chapter 4 for other examples of conjunctions.)

Another form of cohesion is a summary of previous sections of text, frequently occurring at the end of a chapter or the beginning of the next chapter. It is a type of repetition that ties the sections of a text together.

TEACHING AWARENESS OF COHESION.

Perhaps an interesting way to teach students to detect and make use of cohesive elements is to have students identify them in their texts, search for referents, determine lexical equivalencies between terms, add deleted items, substitute original terms, and explicate the meaning of conjunctions. In other words, the students would be constructing a new text without cohesive elements. Or, you can go in the opposite direction by giving them a text without cohesive elements and have them put them in. For example, they could put them in the paragraph in Box 5.5, which contains a modified version of the one presented in Box 5.4.

BOX 5.5. *Text Without Cohesive Elements*

Hallie and Ruth are identical twins. Hallie and Ruth are elementary teachers. Two years ago Hallie won the outstanding award for Hallie's school. This year Ruth won the award. Hallie and Ruth are both working towards PhD degrees. Hallie and Ruth can become the best teachers possible. Hallie and Ruth's mother, also a teacher, inspired Hallie and Ruth to want to become the best teachers possible. Hallie and Ruth's father is proud of Hallie and Ruth's accomplishments.

You can also advise students to examine a new text by reading through all the chapter summaries. Thus, they will get an overview of the text and perhaps be able to develop an ideational framework they can use for storing information as they come to it in a detailed reading of the text.

RESEARCH ON COHESION.

Although cohesive elements make the reading of text interesting and their absence makes it boring, research evidence has not been found that they consistently influence rate of reading, comprehension, and free recall of information (R. Anderson & Freebody, 1983; Roen, 1984; Roen & Grunloh, 1984; Yekovich & Walker, 1978), unless they add interesting material that makes the text read more like a popular magazine (Redd-Boyd, 1984). Perhaps these elements, like syntax in general, play a role in getting information into a form for cognitive processing, but once processing begins, then ability to use the information to construct, store, and retrieve meaning for the text becomes dominant. For example, Bransford and Franks (1974) found that although readers processed text information sequentially, their comprehension and recall of the information in the text indicated they had "chunked" it across sentence boundaries. In short, they integrated and remembered only the meaning relationships.

Explication

To explicate means to state directly, instead of requiring the reader to infer, organize, or construct relationships. For example, a high school history text described the French, English, Russian, and American revolutions, but did not state what they had in common or give any explanation of causal conditions for the occurrence of revolutions. In short, the text provided only descriptions of the four revolutions, but did not explicate any general characteristics for revolutions. When the text was modified by inserting an essay on the causes of revolutions

FIGURE 5.1. Graphic Organizer for an Essay on the Causes of Revolutions (Bean et al., 1986, p. 741).

Revolution—transfer of power			
Social conditions before revolution			Stages of Revolution
Upgrading economically	Intellectuals transfer loyalty from existing regime to discontented.	Government machinery inefficient. Ruling class unable to rule well.	Crisis Stage Rioting in the streets
Prosperous people discontent.			First Recovery Stage Strong man assumes power

(Brinton, 1977) and students were taught to construct graphic organizers, such as the one shown in Figure 5.1, plus use an option guide, Box 5.6, that permitted them to make and defend decisions about events in each revolution, their performance on comprehension of explicit information was equal to that of a group that used outlining or whole-group lecture-discussion, but on an essay test they were better able to predict events in a revolution, the Cuban Revolution, that they had not studied (Bean, Sorter, Singer, & Frazee. 1986).

BOX 5.6. Options Guide for Participating Actively in Decision-Making Process (Bean et al., 1986, p. 741).

Options Guide

Directions: Choose the most plausible option and be prepared to defend your choice.

Richelieu's options for making the king supreme in France

1. Build an army to coerce nobles into disbanding personal armies. Use armies not only against noncomplying nobles but against all non-Catholics.
2. Promise Huguenots personal freedom if they agree to tear down fortified cities granted by the Edict of Nantes.
3. Ask nobles to give up their forces by giving bribes of land (taken from Protestants) and arrest all Protestants. Destroy all fortified towns and distribute land to nobles.

Thus, making the text explicit on causes of a revolution, teaching students to organize the information graphically, and having them be active in responding to information in the text enabled them to transfer and apply their knowledge to a novel situation. According to schema theory, the theory of how knowledge is acquired, organized, and stored in memory (see chapter 4), the students had developed a hierarchical knowledge structure by use of the graphic organizer and had learned to activate their knowledge via the options guide. This combination made it relatively easy for them to predict the causes of the Cuban revolution.

A further implication we draw from this research is that text explication is necessary, but not sufficient for applying the explicated knowledge to new situations. Students also have to be taught how to select, organize, and actively interact with the explicated information in order to apply it to new situations.

Another example is a biology text that states the difference between arteries and veins, but does not explain why they differ (Bransford, 1984).

Do textbooks explicate information? A systematic examination of sixth-grade social studies texts indicates that they do explicate information (Dreher, Singer, & Letteer, 1987). The same is true of elementary science texts (Letteer & Singer, 1985). However, high school texts may not be explicit, particularly on causal conditions in social science, because experts do not agree on the causal factors

(Fitzgerald, 1979). An alternative to no explanation is to provide all competing explanations. In general, adequate explanations enable students to organize and better remember knowledge gleaned from texts than if they had learned it simply as lists of arbitrary information, which is the most difficult information to learn and has a rapid forgetting rate (Stein, Bransford, & Morris, 1978). However, teachers can instruct students on how to make texts explicit and therefore more sensible, but teachers who are expert in their subject fields may not recognize that a text is implicit because they can explicate the text so readily when they read it (Franks et al., 1982). Teachers should therefore consciously examine texts to find out whether the text is not only factually correct but also explains why the facts occur.

VOCABULARY.

The usual rule in textbook writing is to define new terms as they occur. They should, of course, be defined by words that are familiar to the students. The definition can then serve as a bridge between the new knowledge and the reader's prior knowledge. The familiar terms activate appropriate knowledge structures and thus improve comprehension. For example, when Marks, Doctorow, and Wittrock (1974) substituted familiar for unfamiliar words in a junior high school text, they obtained a significant improvement in comprehension. If the new terms are also listed in a glossary, students will find it easy to access them. If they also appear in the index, students can look up all the references to the terms and thus enhance their schema for them.

BACKGROUND KNOWLEDGE.

Texts can be more comprehensible if they provide necessary background knowledge or show students how new ideas in the text are related to knowledge students already have. Some texts achieve this purpose by introductions that contain familiar examples. Another way to relate new knowledge to prior knowledge is through the use of analogies or figurative language. If background knowledge is missing from texts, you can supply it through the use of marginal glosses (See chapter 6) or through a lecture when you introduce the text.

ORGANIZING IDEAS.

Underlying many texts is some organizing theory or explanation. For example, high school chemistry texts can take one of three approaches to chemistry: descriptive, based on principles, or theoretical. College texts may also have a particular viewpoint. For example, Samuelson's leading textbook is based on Keynesian economics, and Bijou and Baer's text on child development is based on Skinner's reinforcement theory of learning, which emphasizes shaping an individual's behavior by rewarding only responses that are consistent with a desired goal. If a theory-based text explicates its underlying theory, readers would be able to use the theory to organize and retain better the multitude of applications and interpretations presented in the text.

Whether students should read and remember a text at a theoretical or only at a descriptive level is a decision the instructor of the course should make. Some authors help their readers by pointing out that you can approach their text from either or both levels of comprehension.

Conceptual Density

The number of new ideas and vocabulary contained in a text determine its conceptual density. Some high school texts may have more than 400 technical words in their glossaries. In an effort to be comprehensive, perhaps to satisfy content guidelines and economic criteria for adoption of texts, and because of the knowledge explosion, particularly in technical fields, high school texts have become burdensome.

Writers can help readers comprehend otherwise dense texts by spacing out the presentation of information. They can do so by following the rules of good paragraph writing: introduce a main idea, clarify it, and give several examples. Texts written this way will be clearer, but longer than terse texts that in essence may state only one main idea or generalization after another, as you would ordinarily find in a summary of a text. Such texts may be understood by instructors who can generate their own clarifications and examples, but not by students. The students need the wordier text to bridge the gap between their own knowledge and experience and the new knowledge in the text (Pepper, 1981).

Another remedy for voluminous and dense texts would be the adoption of a sequence of several texts, instead of one voluminous text for a year-long course.

Metadiscourse

When the author of a text talks directly to the reader about the information in the text, this segment of the text is known as metadiscourse. It is like a conversation between an author and a reader about the text (Crismore, 1983). It may take the form of an I-You dialogue. On an informational level, Crismore (1984) points out, it may be about *goals* of the text, *previews* of its content and structure, *reviews* about the contents and structure, or shifts in the topic, called *topicalizers*. On an attitudinal level, the author may stress the importance of an idea (*salience*), degree of certainty of a statement (*emphatic*), degree of uncertainty (*hedge*), attitude toward a fact or idea (*evaluative*). Although experimental studies at the high school and elementary levels have not shown general effects of metadiscourse on recall of textual information, research on this topic is only in its infancy (Crismore, 1984).

Friendly authors often state in the introduction to a text their purpose in writing it, their logic for the organization of chapters or major parts of the text, background and clarifying information, how readers should read and learn from the text, and how they can apply information gained from the text to other situations (R. Anderson, Osborn, & Tierney, 1984; Rothkopf, 1966; Singer,

1983a). This information also can occur throughout the text. For example, see the Preface to this book. Also see the end of the first chapter where we pose 11 questions and then explain, "The purpose of this book is to show teachers and administrators how to find answers to these questions. . . . In the book, we focus on explaining to teachers how to provide for equality of educational opportunity without stigmatizing students and how to encourage and educate secondary school students to become independent learners."

We think that the trend in texts is toward more metadiscourse, more interaction between the author and reader. Even scientific reports are getting away from the third person, passive tense that omits the agent for the action. Instead of saying, "It was found that something occurred," you are more likely to read, "I found that . . ." or "Stephen discovered that. . . ." This personal approach makes a text more interesting (Flesch, 1949), perhaps because it is more like a narrative and enables a reader to use story schema, knowledge of general characteristics of stories, for organizing, comprehending, and recalling its information. Furthermore, it tends to make the communication more concrete and hence more imageable. The imageable information can then be stored in episodic memory, the memory for particular times, places, and their accompanying objects, events, or situations.

Writeability

Can application of readability criteria of sentence length and word frequency make texts more readable? Some textbook writers and publishers, particularly of basal readers, have adopted the strategy of using these readability criteria as *causal factors* of comprehensibility. They attempt to make texts more readable by reducing sentence length and using more high-frequency words, particularly words that are vivid or more imageable and consequently may be more memorable (Montague & Carter, 1973; Paivio, 1969). However, you should observe several cautions in using readability criteria for writing or judging the friendliness of texts. Shorter sentences still have to be long enough to explicate ideas and causal relationships (Marshall & Glock, 1978-1979; Pearson, 1974-1975), instead of putting the burden upon the reader to make causal inferences. For example, "Mary went to the store to buy a loaf of bread" is explicit, but when separated into two sentences, "Mary went to the store. She bought a loaf of bread," the burden is placed upon the reader to infer the purpose of her going to the store.

More frequently occurring words may be satisfactory substitutes for less frequently occurring words, provided, of course, they are synonyms, such as "boy" for "lad." Under this condition, they can increase text comprehension (Marks et al., 1974). The more frequently occurring word makes the text friendlier because it enables more readers to retrieve or construct a meaning for the word. But a text may have to use a less frequent word in a sentence, particularly if it wants students to understand new words, such as technical terms. Then, the friendlier text will define the new term when it first occurs, divide it into syllables, indicate its pronunciation, and use it in context and subsequently throughout the text.

With these qualifications in mind, we have incorporated into our evaluation of texts the concept of "writeability" that Fry (1983, 1988) has formulated, to promote the application of readability criteria to writing texts. His writeability criteria pertain to (a) words, (b) sentences, (c) paragraphs, and (d) larger units of organization.

WORDS.

Readers are likely to know words that occur more frequently because they have seen these words in print more often, use them in everyday life, and perhaps learned them through direct instruction. For example, some 220 words, mostly functional words, such as noun determiners (a, the, some), conjunctions (and, but, unless), and prepositions (to, from, around) and pronouns (he, she, it) account for 75% of all words read in Grades 1 to 3 and 50% of all adult reading; about 95% of third graders can correctly identify these words in their reading. The words are among Sakiey and Fry's (1979) easier 300 words.

SENTENCE COMPLEXITY.

Kernel sentences are short and active. They frequently consist of only a subject, verb, and object. "John hit Bill." They are easier to comprehend than their negative, "John did not hit Bill," or passive transformation, "Bill was hit by John."

Kernel sentences become more complex with the addition of clauses. If the clause occurs within the kernel sentence, it makes the sentence more difficult to comprehend because it requires the reader to remember part of the kernel sentence while processing the intervening clause (Fry, 1983, 1988) For example, "John, because he stepped back from the plate, hit Bill." The sentence can communicate the same ideas by putting the clause at the end of the sentence, "John hit Bill because he stepped back from home plate." The second version of the sentence enables the reader to process the kernel sentence, store it in long-term memory, because that is the place where sentences go when they are understood (Gough, 1985b), and then the reader can process the additional clause. In short, friendly texts have fewer embedded clauses that intervene in kernel sentences.

RELATIONSHIPS AMONG SENTENCES.

Anaphora, grammatical elements that interrelate ideas within and between sentences, make a text cohesive. But, if their referents are not clear, they can make a text ambiguous and therefore interfere with comprehension of it. For example, the referent for the pronoun in "John hit Bill because he stepped back from home plate" is ambiguous. We do not know for sure the referent for "he." John or

Bill could have taken the step. One way to reduce the ambiguity is to repeat the name, instead of using a pronoun. The implication is that texts are friendlier if the referents for pronouns and other anaphora in the text are clear.

PUNCTUATION.

Although punctuation can make a text more comprehensible, it can also adversely affect a text's friendliness. For example, a long series of items, separated by commas, may be difficult to remember. The more friendly text would list the series of items in outline form. It would also break complex sentences into two or more simple sentences if the sentences do not have to be complex for purposes of explication.

PARAGRAPHS.

A paragraph consists of one or more sentences related to the same idea. A single sentence can express an idea, but usually it takes two or more sentences to communicate a novel idea well enough for a reader to understand it. One sentence can express the idea, another clarify it, a third and perhaps a fourth provide further clarification with examples, and finally a summary sentence or a restatement of the idea and perhaps a transitional sentence conclude the paragraph. Of course, variation in paragraph organization (stating the main idea first, last, or in the middle of the paragraph, and sometimes not making it explicit at all, accompanied by clarification and accompanying examples) provides more interesting text than uniform paragraph organization. The particular type of paragraph organization depends upon the purpose of the author, which can vary from being direct (main idea first), leading up to an idea (main idea last), or allowing the reader to infer the idea (main idea implicit), a useful technique in persuasion.

LARGER UNITS OF TEXT.

Breaking a text into smaller units via chapter headings and subheadings facilitates comprehension because it reveals the text's units of thought to the reader. The chapter headings and subheadings also enable the reader who skims the table of contents and even the text to perceive its main ideas and their relationships prior to reading the text systematically. In short, the chapter headings and subheadings enable the reader to begin to construct a hierarchically organized semantic framework, with more concrete concepts toward the bottom and more abstract concepts toward the top of the framework. This mental map enables the reader to organize information in the text under its appropriate concepts. If the text also provides its own graphic organizers for the organization of the text, it may further facilitate comprehension. However, division of texts into units of thought may facilitate, but do not necessarily improve, comprehension (Duin & Furniss, 1984).

Instructional Devices

Textbooks contain instructional devices that aid the reader's comprehension of the text. A table of contents provides an overview and indicates its sequence of ideas. Other organizational aids are headings and subheadings. A glossary facilitates access to vocabulary knowledge, the most important predictor of comprehension. An index groups related ideas in the text. Some authors provide an overview of a chapter or entire text in verbal or graphic terms. Use of questions at the beginning of chapters arouses students' curiosity and focuses attention on essential information. Diagrams, tables, and graphs enable readers to perceive relationships among ideas, objects, or numerical data. Authors may annotate their own text, sometimes printing information in the margins, usually background knowledge, but more often they write this information into the text. Summaries and conclusions indicate the essential ideas in the text. Problems and questions at the end of each chapter help students test their understanding. Since transfer, ability to apply knowledge gained to new situations, is a major purpose in learning, friendly texts will facilitate it by providing suggestions for application of the text's knowledge to new situations.

The features of a friendly text are restated in Box 5.7 in the form of an inventory with rating scales. The purpose of the inventory is to enable teachers to rate and select texts for their friendliness. Since we have no basis for differential weighting of the items, we have given them all equal weights. Nor do we have any criterion for determining when a text shifts in balance from the unfriendly to the friendly end of the continuum. We can only say that a text with more of these features is more likely to facilitate comprehension than a text with fewer features.

What we do know is that facilitation of comprehension depends not only on determinants within a text but also on determinents outside the text.

EXTRA-TEXT DETERMINANTS OF FRIENDLY TEXTS

Extra-text determinants that facilitate comprehension of texts consist of several factors. One is the position of the text within a curriculum. Another is the role the teacher plays in using the text, particularly how the teacher adapts the text to the individual differences among students in a class (Flood et al., 1985). Comprehension of a text also results from an interaction between the information in the text, the resources a reader can mobilize in response to the task-demands of the text, and the reader's purpose in reading the text (Singer & Bean, 1983a). Finally we have to determine the appropriateness of a text for a particular class of students. We shall clarify each of these extratext determinants of comprehension.

Curriculum

Determine whether the text is consistent with a sequence of instruction and fits into the next step in the student's knowledge development. In short, a text should start at a knowledge level the student has already attained and take the student systematically on to a higher and more abstract level in the acquisition of knowledge, including knowledge of objects, events, and situations (see chapter 4 for information on these knowledge structures). Moreover, we presuppose that the prior curriculum has a sequential and hierarchical organization. We also assume that students have progressed through this curriculum and acquired its contents, processes, and procedures. Consequently their acquisition of background knowledge and ability to learn from the previous texts have prepared them adequately for the next text in the sequence. If so, then we can say that students have the necessary cognitive resources and are therefore ready to go on to a higher level of development. If these conditions are met, then the friendliness of the next text in the sequence is more likely to have a beneficial effect on students' comprehension of the text. Whether the effect is realized also depends upon the classroom teacher.

Classroom Teacher's Role

A teacher plays a role in all aspects of learning in a classroom setting: showing students how to learn in the particular content area and how to glean information from the text, such as the relationship between ideas in the text (MacGinitie, 1984), designing material, such as reading guides, to aid students' ability to learn from text (Herber, 1978; see chapter 5 for examples of this guide), motivating students by explaining the relevance of the course to their knowledge development and to applications in everyday life, explicating and clarifying the text, relating text information to the students' prior knowledge, providing a context for comprehending the text, assigning tasks that help students use and therefore retain information presented in lectures and in the text, providing relevant tests at appropriate points in the course so that students can have knowledge of their progress and information on their strengths and weaknesses. In general, teachers can influence students' interactions with a text by (a) selecting or modifying the text itself, such as inserting supplementary information or questions (Frase 1967, 1968a, 1968b; Rothkopf & Bisbicos, 1967), (b) developing the resources and strategies of the reader by providing background information and teaching students ways of learning from the text, including use of active comprehension (see chap. 4) and how to make sense of arbitrary or inexplicit texts (Franks et al., 1982), (c) establishing appropriate goals, and (d) promoting feedback of knowledge into students' resources; for example, by having students summarize what they have learned from the text and explicating how this knowledge extends what they already know and could do. Indeed, a teacher can make friendly and unfriendly texts more comprehensible to students (Baumann, 1986). For example, when we divided a large class of college students into four groups, gave two of the groups a friendly text and the other two groups a degraded version of the text that was significantly less friendly, and provided a lecture to two of the groups that had each kind of text, we found that students who had the lecture had significantly greater comprehension than students without the lecture, regardless of the friendliness of their texts (Flood et al., 1985). In general, students learn better from texts when teachers are involved in modifying and implementing their own texts (Wade, 1983), probably because they know what to emphasize in their instruction.

Briefly summarized, coherence among all four components of a classroom situation (students, text, test, and teacher) enhances achievement (Singer, 1982). Ecological factors, conditions inside and outside the classroom, including social and economic conditions that students are experiencing, also affect students' performance in the classroom (Singer & Bean, 1982a, 1982c). (See chapter 4, Section 3, interactive model for learning from text in a classroom situation.)

Individual Differences

Although a text may be appropriate and friendly to a particular reader, it is not likely to fit an entire class of students. Any heterogeneous class varies greatly in its ability to learn from text, whether the class is at the first grade or at the college level. As we pointed out in chapter 2, the range in reading achievement at the first grade is 4 years; it gradually expands until at the 12th grade it is 12 years, with half the class between grade equivalent 6 and 12 and the other half between 12 and college graduate. Hence, a friendly text can at best fit only students who have attained a particular level of development. For example, an unfriendly text adversely affected average and poor but not better second-grade readers' comprehension (Zack & Osako, 1986); an inexplicit text (omission of causal and relational connectives) was detrimental to the comprehension of community college students, but did not influence the comprehension of the more fluent Cornell University students (Marshall & Glock, 1978-1979), perhaps because the Cornell students could draw the necessary information from their own resources to explicate the text. The teacher's task is to adopt instructional strategies that will enable all students within the class to interact successfully with and learn from a text. The single- and multiple-text strategies described throughout this text, beginning with chapter 6, will enable teachers to make a text more appropriate for students who make up this wide range of reading achievement within a regular classroom.

Interaction between Text Information and Reader Resources

Even if a text is friendly, comprehension does not depend upon its features or content alone. Comprehension is the construction of meaning that results from an interaction between the text's features and the reader's resources (Rumelhart, 1976; Singer, 1983c), in accordance with the perspective and purposes of the reader (Holmes & Singer, 1966; Pichert & Anderson, 1977), and the demands placed upon the reader by the text and the teacher (Rothkopf, 1982; Singer, 1985; H. Yopp & Singer, 1985). The features of the text activate the relevant resources a reader can command for constructing meaning for the text. A text's metadiscourse can lead a reader to select a particular goal and adopt a particular perspective and purpose for responding to the text. Reader resources are the reader's prior knowledge, abilities, purposes, perspectives, interests, attitudes, values, and feelings. (See chapter 4, schema interactive definition of reading, for a more adequate explanation of the interaction between the reader's resources and text characteristics that result in the construction of meaning.) However, high prior knowledge under certain conditions may interfere with acquisition of new information (Spilich, Versonder, Chiesi, & Voss, 1979; Thorndyke & Hayes-Roth, 1979); for example, students may know the meanings of terms in one discipline, such as *field* in agriculture and consequently have difficulty with the meaning of *field* in electronics, or *bias* in sewing and social studies, and so on. In short, the text may activate inappropriate schemata that can interfere with comprehension; therefore, instructors have to be aware of such interference and teach students new meanings for the familiar words. (See chapter 15 on Science and chapter 16 on Mathematics in this text for additional examples.)

Instructional Appropriateness

Extratext determinants of comprehension are also features of a text's instructional appropriateness. Other instructionally appropriate features are its up-to-dateness and correctness of information, suitable level of difficulty, objectivity, congruence between its contents and course requirements, continuity and adequacy of knowledge development, anticipated appeal to students, and a methodological emphasis consistent with instructional objectives and current explanations of learning processes. It should also have a coherent testing program with provision for knowledge of results and an accompanying teacher's manual that suggests ways of enhancing instruction and adapting the text to a class's wide range of reading achievement. Indeed, only if a text is relatively difficult for students are they likely to learn something new (Herber, 1984). They are also likely to remember a text better if they have to expend more effort in processing it (Kolers, 1975, 1979). Indeed, a trend toward easier texts may account for a general decrease in achievement on such tests as the Scholastic Aptitude Test (Chall, Conard, & Harris, 1977). But a text can be relativey difficult for students and still be a friendly text.

DETERMINING A TEXT'S FRIENDLINESS IN A CLASSROOM SETTING

Although we do not yet have means of assessing all the determinants of a text's friendliness, we have ways of assessing some aspects of its potential friendliness in a classroom setting. We can take three steps in this direction. The first step is to use one of the formulas, such as the Fry Graph, which you will find in the next section, to compute its readability level. The second step is to apply the Friendly Text Evaluation Inventory, shown in Box 5.8, to the text. The third step is to assess the text-friendliness of the instructor by using the "Text-Friendly Instructor Inventory," shown in Box 5.9. You can use it to evaluate your own text friendliness or as an interview schedule to assess another teacher's text-friendliness.

The quality of instruction in a classroom and the effectiveness of learning from text depend, in part, on the friendliness of a text and the way an instructor uses the text. The combination of a friendly text and a text-friendly instructor should greatly enhance students' ability to learn from a text and should lead to higher student achievement in a course.

READABILITY

Teachers can obtain better comprehension results from their students if they select texts that are at appropriate difficulty levels for their students. Readability formulas help in the selection of texts, but the formulas are not infallible. Readability formulas usually consist of two factors: sentence length and word difficulty. Sentence length is an index of syntactic complexity whereas word difficulty is an estimate of the semantic level of a text. But shorter sentences and words do not always make texts easier to understand (Davison & Kantor, 1982; Irwin & Davis, 1980). Some longer sentences are comprehended and remembered better because they explicate causal relationships and make their facts significant (Pearson, 1974-1975; Stein & Bransford, 1979). Although readability criteria subsume some friendly text features, they do not include the features of explication, metadiscourse, and instructional devices, nor extratext determinants of text-reader interactions and the teacher's role in compensating for unfriendly text features, developing or enhancing reader resources for learning from a particular text, and facilitating text-reader interactions in general.

Readability estimates are useful for placing texts at a given point in a graded curriculum. However, the standard error of any readability formula is plus or minus about 1.5 grade levels. For example, a readability level of Grade 4.7 is a midpoint on a readability *range* that can vary from Grade 3.2 to Grade 6.2. In short, a readability level is only a gross indicator of its position in a curriculum and its difficulty level. Formulas for determining readability are in chapter 10.

TEXT FRIENDLINESS

Determination of a text's readability level is only the first step in estimating a text's friendliness. The next step is to evaluate the friendliness of the specific features of a text. Use the criteria in Box 5.7. You can use your evaluation of a text to determine whether to adopt it or to discover where you need to enhance it to make its use in your class more effective.

The inventory is quite long. After some practice with it, you will be able to use a shortened version, shown in Box 5.8, that contains only the major categories. In using either inventory, use the entire text for making overall judgments and no less than an entire chapter for finer analysis. Also, remember that a text is not homogeneous; it may be friendly in one part and unfriendly in another as well as vary in friendliness from other texts on the same subject (Graesser, 1983).

EXTRA-TEXT DETERMINANTS OF COMPREHENSION

Finally, if you want to make a prediction on how well students in a classroom situation are likely to comprehend a text, then the third step is to use criteria that determine how a particular teacher is likely to enhance the friendliness of a text, readers' resources, and interactions between the text and the reader, and provide for individual differences in ability of students to learn from the text. These criteria are in the ''Teacher-Text Enhancement Inventory,'' Box 5.9. Teachers who enhance a text in these ways can be called ''Text-Friendly Teachers.'' For example, we enhanced a text by inserting an essay on causes of revolutions; it enabled students to organize the text's chapters on revolutions as exemplars (See example, Figure 5.1). Teaching students a strategy of active comprehension enhanced their resources. (See chapter 4 for information on teaching active comprehension. Strategies for satisfying individual differences in the classroom appear in chapter 6.)

We have stated throughout this chapter and in other places in the text procedures for selecting and teaching text features. We summarize these procedures in Box 5.10.

SUMMARY

We have presented criteria for determining the friendliness of a text. Selection of a text is a crucial initial step in teaching students how to comprehend and learn from a text. The text should be well organized, consistent, and coherent. It should have examples that activate and make contact with students' prior knowledge and experience, have an appropriate level of conceptual density, and define terms as they appear. It should explain to readers how they can learn from the text, use analogies and other figurative language to explain new concepts, provide information necessary for constructing new knowledge categories, and explicate causal relationships. It should be written in a style and at a level of abstraction that can be related to and build upon a class's knowledge framework. Appropriate, adequate, and well-organized texts facilitate comprehension by enabling readers to mobilize their resources so that they can construct meaning for the text.

We have also pointed out that a friendly text's comprehensibility presupposes a reader with the necessary resources for interacting with and constructing meaning for the text, a curriculum that has adequately developed these resources, a teacher who can favorably influence interactions among readers, text, and the reading goal, and whose tests are appropriate and provide timely feedback on the results of this interaction, and an environment that is conducive to learning from text.

BOX 5.7. *Friendly Text Inventory*

Directions: Read each criterion and judge the degree of agreement or disagreement between it and the text. Then circle the number to the right of the criterion that indicates your judgment.

$$1 \quad SD = \text{Strongly Disagree}$$
$$2 \quad D = \text{Disagree}$$
$$3 \quad U = \text{Uncertain}$$
$$4 \quad A = \text{Agree}$$
$$5 \quad SA = \text{Strongly Agree}$$

I. *Organization*	SD	D	U	A	SA
1. The introduction to the book and each chapter explain their purposes.	1	2	3	4	5
2. The introduction provides information on the sequence of the text's contents.	1	2	3	4	5
3. The introduction communicates how the reader should learn from the text.	1	2	3	4	5
4. The ideas presented in the text follow a uni-directional sequence. One idea leads to the next.	1	2	3	4	5
5. The type of paragraph structure organizes information to facilitate memory. For example, objects and their properties are grouped together so as to emphasize relationships.	1	2	3	4	5
6. Ideas are hierarchically structured either verbally or graphically.	1	2	3	4	5
7. The author provides cues to the way information will be presented. For example the author states: "There are five points to consider."	1	2	3	4	5
8. Signal words (conjunctions, adverbs) and rhetorical devices (problem-solution, question-answer, cause-effect, comparison and contrast, argument-proof) interrelate sentences, paragraphs, and larger units of discourse.	1	2	3	4	5

Discourse consistency	SD	D	U	A	SA
9. The style of writing is consistent and coherent. For example the paragraphs, sections, and chapters build to a conclusion. Or they begin with a general statement and then present sup-					

BOX 5.7. *(Continued)*

	SD	D	U	A	SA
porting ideas. Or the text has a combination of these patterns. Any one of these patterns would fit this consistency criterion.	1	2	3	4	5

Cohesiveness   SD   D   U   A   SA

	SD	D	U	A	SA
10. The text is cohesive. That is, the author ties ideas together from sentence to sentence, paragraph to paragraph, chapter to chapter.	1	2	3	4	5

II. *Explication*   SD   D   U   A   SA

	SD	D	U	A	SA
11. Some texts may be read at more than one level, e.g., descriptive versus theoretical. The text orients students to a level that is appropriate for the students.	1	2	3	4	5
12. The text provides reasons for functions or events. For example, the text, if it is a biology text, not only lists the differences between arteries and veins, but also explains why they are different.	1	2	3	4	5
13. The text highlights or italicizes and defines new terms as they are introduced at a level that is familiar to the student.	1	2	3	4	5
14. The text provides necessary background knowledge. For example, the text introduces new ideas by reviewing or reminding readers of previously acquired knowledge or concepts.	1	2	3	4	5
15. The author uses examples, analogies, metaphors, similies, personifications, or allusions that clarify new ideas and makes them vivid.	1	2	3	4	5
16. The author explains ideas in relatively short sentences.	1	2	3	4	5
17. The author explicates theory on which the text is based. For example; Skinner's theory of learning and especially its concept of *shaping behavior* is the basis for Bijou and Baer's text on *Child Development*.	1	2	3	4	5

III. *Conceptual Density*   SD   D   U   A   SA

18. The author introduces, defines or clarifies, and integrates ideas with semantically related ideas

BOX 5.7. *(Continued)*

		SD	D	U	A	SA
	previously presented in the text, and gives examples before presenting additional ideas.	1	2	3	4	5
19.	The vocabulary load is appropriate. For example, usually only one new vocabulary item per paragraph occurs throughout the text.	1	2	3	4	5

IV. Metadiscourse

		SD	D	U	A	SA
20.	The author talks directly to the reader to explain how to learn from the text. For example, the author states that some information in the text is more important than other information.	1	2	3	4	5
21.	The author establishes a purpose or goal for the text.	1	2	3	4	5
22.	The text supplies collateral information for putting events into context.	1	2	3	4	5
23.	The text points out relationships to ideas previously presented in the text or to the reader's prior knowledge.	1	2	3	4	5

V. Writeability

		SD	D	U	A	SA
24.	Text uses active sentences. For example, "He returned the gift," instead of, "The gift was returned."	1	2	3	4	5
25.	Sentences are short, but still communicate effectively.	1	2	3	4	5
26.	Paragraphs vary in length ranging from one sentence to about a third to a half a page.	1	2	3	4	5
27.	The author uses personal pronouns and sentences that make the text more interesting to the reader.	1	2	3	4	5
28.	The text contains headings and subheadings that divide the text into categories that enable readers to perceive the major ideas.	1	2	3	4	5
29.	Text uses simpler, high-frequency words whenever it is appropriate to do so. For example, instead of "He *proceeded* on his way," the author simply states, "He went."	1	2	3	4	5

BOX 5.7. *(Continued)*

		SD	D	U	A	SA
30.	Embedded sentences or phrases do not split kernel sentences (subject-verb-object). For example, a split kernel would be, "John, if he were responsible, would have phoned." An unsplit kernel would be, "John would have phoned, if he were responsible" or "If he were responsible, John would have phoned."	1	2	3	4	5
31.	Referents for pronouns or other anaphora are not ambiguous. For example, an ambiguous referent occurs in these sentences: "Irv and Dan were supposed to walk together but he was ahead."	1	2	3	4	5
32.	Punctuation helps make the text clear, but does not overburden the reader with too many commas, semicolons, colons, or parentheses.	1	2	3	4	5

VI. *Instructional Devices*

		SD	D	U	A	SA
33.	The text contains a logically organized table of contents.	1	2	3	4	5
34.	The text has a glossary that defines technical terms in understandable language.	1	2	3	4	5
35.	The index integrates concepts dispersed throughout the text.	1	2	3	4	5
36.	There are overviews, preposed questions, or graphic devices, such as diagrams, tables, and graphs throughout the text, that emphasize what a reader should learn in the chapters or sections.	1	2	3	4	5
37.	The text includes marginal annotations or footnotes that instruct the reader.	1	2	3	4	5
38.	The text contains chapter summaries that reflect its main points.	1	2	3	4	5
39.	The text has problems or questions at the literal, interpretive, applied, and evaluative levels at the end of each chapter that help the reader understand knowledge presented in the text.	1	2	3	4	5
40.	The author provides information in the text or at the end of the chapters or the text that enable the reader to apply the knowledge in the text to new situations.	1	2	3	4	5

BOX 5.7. *(Continued)*

VII. *Instructional Appropriateness*   SD D   U   A SA

41. The information in the text is up-to-date. For example, the copyright date is recent and the text's contents reflect current knowledge.   1   2   3   4   5

42. The information and ideas in the text reflect current knowledge and thinking. For example, the author(s) has valid credentials, evidence in the foreword or introduction enhances confidence in the credibility of the text, and inspections of the text's contents provide supporting evidence for this feature.   1   2   3   4   5

43. The text fits into the curriculum at the grade level it will be used. That is, the text builds upon knowledge taught in previous grades.   1   2   3   4   5

44. The content of the text fits the requirements of the course.   1   2   3   4   5

45. The level of difficulty of the text is appropriate for the class.   1   2   3   4   5

46. The text relates its new knowledge to knowledge taught earlier in the curriculum.   1   2   3   4   5

47. The text presents knowledge cumulatively.   1   2   3   4   5

48. New concepts are introduced with adequate examples, properties, and relationships to associated concepts.   1   2   3   4   5

49. Generalizations are adequately developed. The text provides directions to form the concepts in the generalizations by abstracting them from common examples and to perceive relationship between the concepts. Then the text contains the applications of the generalization to new situations.   1   2   3   4   5

50. Information and ideas are communicated objectively with appropriate qualifications or alternate views whenever necessary.   1   2   3   4   5

51. Features in the text, such as its graphics, writing style, approach problems, or suggested activities, make the text appealing to students.   1   2   3   4   5

52. The text's method of instruction is consistent with instructional objectives.   1   2   3   4   5

53. The text has self-tests at appropriate intervals.   1   2   3   4   5

BOX 5.7. *(Continued)*

		SD	D	U	A	SA
54.	The text provides for knowledge of self-test results either listing answers to its tests in the text itself or in an accompanying manual.	1	2	3	4	5
55.	The text has a teacher's manual or teacher's edition with suggestions for enhancing instruction.	1	2	3	4	5
56.	The text, the teacher's edition, or a manual accompanying the text provides for or suggests ways of making the text appropriate for a class's wide range in reading achievement.	1	2	3	4	5
57.	Accompanying the text is a reliable and valid test(s) for the teacher to use to assess student achievement of substantive or procedural knowledge taught by the text.	1	2	3	4	5

Total _____

SCORE
Add the numbers circled.
Score range: 57 to 285 points
Interpretation of scores
A score closer to 285 implies the text is friendly; scores closer to 57 suggest the text is unfriendly.

BOX 5.8. Friendly Text Inventory (Brief Form)

Directions: Circle the number that indicates whether the text is friendly on the criterion listed.

SA = Strongly Agree   D = Disagree
 A = Agree   SD = Strongly Disagree
 U = Uncertain

			Friendly			
		SD	D	U	A	SA
1.	Organization	1	2	3	4	5
	The text is well organized.					
2.	Discourse consistency	1	2	3	4	5
	Style of writing is consistent and coherent					

BOX 5.8. *(Continued)*

		SD	D	U	A	SA
3.	Explication	1	2	3	4	5
	Relationships among ideas are explicit					
4.	Conceptual Density	1	2	3	4	5
	Conceptual density is appropriate for the class					
5.	Metadiscourse	1	2	3	4	5
	Metadiscourse provides appropriate directions for comprehending the text					
6.	Writeability	1	2	3	4	5
	Writing style makes text readable					
7.	Instructional Devices	1	2	3	4	5
	Instructional devices in the text facilitate learning					

Interpretation: A score closer to 7 implies an unfriendly text; a score closer to 35 suggests the text is friendly.

BOX 5.9. *Teacher-Text Enhancement Inventory*

Directions: Read the criterion on the left and indicate your degree of agreement by circling the appropriate number on the right.

SD = Strongly Disagree   A = Agree
 D = Disagree   SA = Strongly Agree
 U = Uncertain

		SD	D	U	A	SA
1.	Curriculum	1	2	3	4	5
	Text is appropriate for use at this grade level because previous grades provided necessary background knowledge for it.					
2.	Reader	1	2	3	4	5
	Readers of this text have the necessary resources for learning from it.					
3.	Goal, the kind of comprehension required at this grade, often defined by a test, is appropriate for text and reader. For example, at the first grade, readers would only learn the story components of a fable. At a	1	2	3	4	5

BOX 5.9. *(Continued)*

	SD	D	U	A	SA

higher grade level it would be more appropriate to have students understand its symbolic meaning.

4. Instructor   1 2 3 4 5

The teacher modifies the text to make it more appropriate for the reader and/or the goal of instruction.

5. The teacher enhances reader resources to enable students to comprehend the text and/or achieve the goal of instruction.   1 2 3 4 5

6. The teacher varies the goal to enable students to attain it.   1 2 3 4 5

7. Feedback   1 2 3 4 5

The teacher feeds information from the test back to the reader to enhance the readers' resources and/or uses text information to make appropriate modifications in enhancing students' resources and/or uses knowledge of test results to modify the goal of instruction.

8. Individual Differences   1 2 3 4 5

Provision is made for individual differences through use of single-text or multiple-text strategies or through variation in time allocation or some other means that enables all students to learn the content without stigmatizing any student.

9. Classroom Environment   1 2 3 4 5

Atmosphere of the classroom is conducive to learning from texts. Classroom library is well stocked, students are attentive and task oriented, and teacher is efficient and effective in teaching students to learn from texts.

10. Text Appropriateness   1 2 3 4 5

Teacher has selected a text that is appropriate for the class.

Interpretation: A score closer to 10 indicates that the teacher is not enhancing the friendliness of a text; a score closer to 50 indicates that the teacher does enhance the friendliness of a text and is therefore a "Text-Friendly Instructor."

BOX 5.10. *Procedures for Selecting a Text and Teaching Its Features*

A. Selecting a text

1. Is the readibility level appropriate for the average student in your class? Use the Fry graph in chapter 10 for a quick estimate of readibility.

2. Is the text consistent with the students' prior curriculum? Examine the school's graded scope and sequence chart of objectives and textbooks used in previous grades to answer this question.

3. Is the text friendly? Use the "Friendly Text Inventory" in Box 5.7 to evaluate the text.

4. Does the text suit its function as a main text? See Guthrie's criteria in Box 5.1.

B. Rate yourself as a text friendly instructor.

Use the Teacher-Text Enhancement Inventory in Box 5.9 for this purpose. In using this inventory, ask yourself whether you will make the necessary modifications in the text or reader resources or goal of instruction to make the text appropriate for all the students in your class. For example, will you use the single- and multiple-text strategies and other instructional procedures described in this text, such as teaching note-taking, listening, discussion, writing, and use of graphs, maps, and charts, when you teach your students? (Also, see section on "extratext determinants" in this chapter.)

C. Teaching the text.

1. Model out loud how you would inspect a text, including its instructional features, and how you would read a section in the text. Students follow along, reading silently in their own texts, your read-aloud procedures

2. Use a directed reading activity (DRA) or other single-text strategy for teaching students how to learn from a chapter in a text. (See chapters 6 and 7 for information on single-text strategies and how to teach them in teaching students to learn from text.)

3. Explain rhetorical patterns and have students identify them in a chapter. (See section in this chapter on rhetorical patterns.) Use a self-test procedure: have students write down patterns for a chapter or a section of a text, if a chapter is too long, and then supply the answers.

4. Explain paragraph structures. (See this chapter and chapter 9, "Letting the Students do the Writing," for explanation and teaching procedures for paragraph structures.) Have students identify paragraph structures and rhetorical terms used in a section of the text.

5. Explain cohesion and have students search for examples in a section of the text. Perhaps use the contrasting strategy outlined in this chapter: furnish students with a paragraph with cohesive elements omitted and have students modify paragraph by reinserting cohesive elements. (See this chapter for cohesive elements and chapter 4 for examples of conjunctions.)

6. Have students analyze a section of text for examples of case relationships explained in chapter 4. Try to discover one sentence for each type of relationship.

7. What syntactic structures are most frequently used in a particular paragraph? In chapter 18, see Singer Sentence Generator, for examples of syntactic structures.

BOX 5.10. *(Continued)*

8. What schemata (objects, events, situations, as explained in chapter 4) predominate in a section of the text?

9. Are narratives used in a chapter of the text? Do they fit story schema structures? (See chapter 4 for story schema structures.) Or, does Grimes's analysis of text content, explained in the beginning of this chapter, provide a more comprehensive way of analyzing the content?

D. Processes of Reading

1. Model the kinds of questions that are appropriate to ask for a particular chapter. (See chapter 4, section on "directed comprehension.)

2. Active comprehension: Teach students in a phase-out/phase-in procedure, as explained in "An Instructional Blueprint," chapter 12, to formulate and read to answer their own questions throughout the text. (See chapter 4, section on "active comprehension" and chapter 6, section on the SQ3R strategy, for explanations of how to teach active comprehension.)

3. Critical reading (See chap. 4 in the section on "Interactive Theories of Reading" for information on critical reading and chap. 11, "Multiple-Text Strategies," for specific propaganda techniques). Are there statements in the chapter that can be distinguished as fact versus opinion? Is the information in the text internally consistent? Does the text's information agree with prior knowledge and other sources of information? Does the author have an objective or a biased interest in the information. For example, compare advertisements, campaign literature, editorials, and encyclopedic information on the same topic. Are word choices appropriate; for example, compare the terms *Russians, communists, reds,* and *Bolsheviks* for various degrees of bias.

E. Use of the text

1. Will students really have to learn from the text?

2. Will you assign chapters to be read in the text and will students be expected to discuss the material read and answer examination questions over the assigned material?

3. Will some questions on the examination cover content assigned and only read, not also presented in lectures or discussed in class?

6 | Single-Text Strategies

CHAPTER OVERVIEW

Most elementary and secondary school teachers instruct students in classes with widely ranging individual differences in ability and achievement. A 4th-grade teacher, for instance, may have a class with an expected 6-year range of differences. A 7th-grade teacher may expect an 8-year range of differences. A 10th-grade teacher might have to deal with a 10-year range of ability or achievement. Despite these student differences, teachers are often expected to reach all students with only one textbook. After you read this chapter, you will understand and be able to apply a variety of strategies to help your students learn from their textbooks. You will thus provide for equality of educational opportunity at the classroom level (Coleman, 1968).

GRAPHIC ORGANIZER

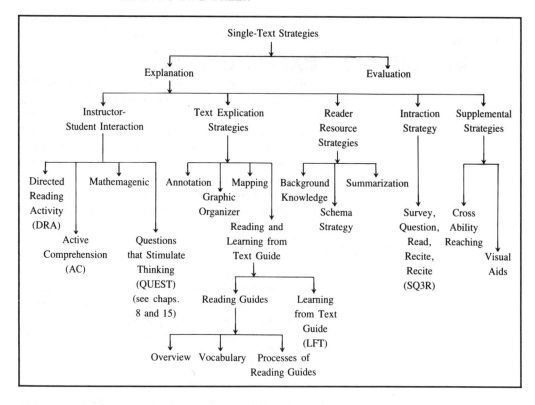

PREPOSED QUESTIONS

1. Examine the graphic organizer that introduces this chapter. Relate the graphic organizer to the model of reading presented in chapter 4.
2. You can use the single-text strategies interchangeably. As you read this chapter, determine whether you agree or disagree with this statement and be ready to defend your decision.
3. Select three single-text strategies and describe how you would use them in your content area classroom.

MISMATCH BETWEEN LEVELS OF STUDENT ABILITY AND TEXT ABILITY

If you recall Mr. Wallace's ill-fated discussion of Carl Sandburg's poetry in chapter 2, you will remember that most of the students were having a problem reading and understanding the text. Although some high school students suffer from a defect, deficiency, or disruption that interferes with their ability to read and learn from text, the major problem at the high school level is the difference between content area texts and the wide range of reading achievement. Even if a text fits the average reader in a class, a mismatch occurs between the text and at least half of the students in the class.

To prevent this mismatch, or at least reduce its interference with student achievement, teachers can effectively employ *single-text strategies* that are suitable for the normal range of 10 to 12 years in reading achievement levels that exists in high school classes. A single-text strategy consists of modifying or supplementing a text or teaching students ways of processing information that will enable them to read and learn from a particular textbook. Although some teachers are fortunate to have multiple texts at their disposal (multiple-text strategies are discussed in chapter 11), most teachers face the problem of making one text appropriate for students with wide-ranging abilities.

STRATEGIES FOR DEVELOPING A MODEL OF READING AND LEARNING FROM TEXT

We can view single text strategies as ways to develop components in our instructional model for reading and learning from text in a classroom situation. On page 156, we show which strategies develop each component.

As students learn the strategies, instructors begin to phase out and students phase in. That is, students begin to use the strategy independently. With further practice, they internalize the strategy. Then instructor-reader interactions, for example, become reader resources that readers can draw upon for interacting with the text. In short, category 1 shifts to category 4. A similar shift occurs for reading and learning from text guides; from category 2 to category 3.

Explanations of how to sequence strategies for learning from text occur in chap. 7, "Teaching Students to Learn from a Chapter," and chap. 12, "A Blueprint for Instruction." Also chap. 12 explains how to phase out the teacher and phase in the students.

In general, strategies for reading and learning from text fit into a category of mental processes. Metacognition consists of knowledge of strategies for directing and monitoring cognitive processes. The cognitive processes are recall and recognition, inference, interpretation, and evaluation. (See chap. 4 for further explanation of metacognition and cognition and their operations on a model of reading and learning from text.)

INSTRUCTOR-READER INTERACTION STRATEGIES

Interactive strategies for teaching students to learn from text focus on all three stages of reading: preparation before the students read, direction while the students are reading, and provision for speaking and writing activities after the students read. Two such strategies are discussed in this section: the directed reading activity (DRA) and mathemagenic behavior. In a later section, we explain a discussion procedure, Questions that Stimulate Thinking (QUEST); it teaches students to progress from facts to concepts, and finally to generalizations in learning from text.

Directed Reading Activity

The directed reading activity (DRA) is a five-stage teaching strategy that teaches students to learn from text in a sequence of activities that guides students before they read, while they are reading, and after they read (Betts, 1955; Burmeister, 1974; Herber, 1970a).

STEPS IN THE DIRECTED READING ACTIVITY

Step 1: Determining Background. Students frequently have experiences they can relate to the chapter. The teacher can elicit these experiences and have them communicated during vocabulary instruction. This information will augment the meaning of the vocabulary and provide the basis for formulations of questions.

Step 2: Building Background. The teacher explains the technical terms in the chapter. To identify them, the teacher either skims through the chapter or searches the index to find them. If the teacher has reordered the entire index by page number, then the technical terms could be organized and grouped by chapters. Thus, they would be readily available for vocabulary instruction.

Teachers frequently assume students, particularly bright students, do not need vocabulary development. Although it is true that brighter students are further advanced in vocabulary than average or less-than-average students, they still need to develop their vocabulary, especially their technical vocabulary. Indeed, all students need to learn technical vocabulary in each content area. If they do, their comprehension in content areas is likely to improve. In fact, research evidence indicates that vocabulary is the single best predictor of reading comprehension at all grade levels (Holmes & Singer, 1966; Singer, 1964).

Step 3: Reading. A. If the text is a story, start with the title. If the text is expository, survey the title and the main headings of the material.

EXAMPLE:
TEACHER: (To the students) What do you think this story (or material) will be about?
STUDENTS: (Make predictions)
TEACHER: Why do you think your predictions are correct?

B. Ask the students to read the first part of the text to test their predictions.

EXAMPLE:
TEACHER: Have any of your found what you predicted to be true?
STUDENTS: (Students respond to question.)
TEACHER: Why do you think so? What clues from the text did you use to make your predictions?

Continue this question and prediction with verification process until the end of the material.

NOTE: For narrative material, insert the teacher questioning process at the crisis points in the story: e.g., after the introduction of a problem, after each attempt to solve the problem, and after the resolution of the problem (see "Story Schema," in chap. 4). For expository text, guide the students through material by stopping intermittently to ask questions about student predictions and whether the text supports predictions.

Following is an example of a Directed Reading Activity planned by Henry Wyatt for his seventh-grade social studies class:

Example: Text: Chapter 3, "Urban Problems"

1. *Exploring Background.*
   a. Ask the students the following questions:
      1. How many of you have heard the expression *urban blight?*
      2. How many of you have lived in or visited a big city?
      3. What examples of *blight* have you seen?
   b. Direct the students to describe in a brief paragraph or list their impressions of the big city they either lived in or visited.
2. *Building Background*
   a. Give the students an overview of Chapter 3.
   b. Review the following vocabulary: enigma, sprawl, hydrocarbons, pollution, sacrosanct
3. *Reading*
   a. Have the students look at the chapter title and make predictions about what they think the chapter will be about.
   b. Have them read the first two pages quietly to see whether their predictions were accurate.
   c. Have the students discuss what passages in the text confirmed or denied their predictions?
   d. Have the students read the rest of the chapter for homework. They are to continue the process of intermittently making predictions, reading, and validating their predictions.

4. *Discussion*

Go through the chapter with the students asking them to review their various predictions and the text passages that validated or invalidated their predictions.

5. *Extension*

a. Have the students write a paragraph in which they take one of the predictions they had made about the chapter and describe how the chapter information either validated or invalidated the prediction.

b. Have the students review current magazines and newspapers for stories about urban blight. Have each student bring one such story to class for discussion in small groups.

Active Comprehension Strategy (AC)

Teacher-formulated questions can stimulate and direct student thinking and serve as a model of the kinds of questions that are appropriate for the content and processes involved in a particular content area.

As students learn to ask appropriate questions in a given content area, teachers can gradually stop asking questions and begin eliciting student-formulated questions. Students can then read to answer their own questions. Teachers will thus be taking students from dependent and teacher-directed thinking to independent and self-directed thinking in reading. This process, which we refer to as *active comprehension,* consists of asking questions throughout the chapter or text, not only at the beginning. In general, it is a kind of dialogue between the student and the text, with the student asking questions and the text "answering" them.

One way to get students to formulate their own questions is to ask a question that gets a question in return. After students have read the title and first paragraph of a chapter, the teacher can ask, "What would you like to know about this chapter?" As the class progresses through the chapter, the teacher can ask such questions as, "What would you like to know next?" Or the teacher can call attention to subheadings and ask students to formulate questions about these subheadings. Then students can read *actively* to answer their own questions. In this way, students will learn a *process of reading* as they progress through the chapter.

Example of Active Comprehension

A highly structured example for teaching active comprehension is presented in Box 6.1. In using this strategy the teacher might do this: Ask students to read the title. Then ask what they would like to know about the story just from reading the title. Next, have them read the story and ask if they have any questions. Usually they ask for the pronunciation of *Malekula* and *New Hebrides*. The teacher pronounces the names. The teacher can then invite anyone who knows anything about the island to present the information to the class.

BOX 6.1. Filming a Cannibal Chief

My husband and I wanted to make a moving picture of savages, and Martin finally decided on Malekula, second largest of the New Hebrides Islands in the Southwest Pacific. We started from Sydney, Australia on a small ship. Soon a storm of warning broke around us.[1]

The teacher-student dialogue continues, as shown below. Note that the teacher asks questions that get student *questions*, not answers, as responses. However, the teacher could switch to a question that gets an answer as a response. We have shown this switch in the dialogue below as a *teacher response* that reflects questions back to the group. Thus, the teacher can lead students to ask and answer their own questions.

> *Teacher question:* What does the size of the ship make you wonder?
> *Student questions:* Why were they going in a small ship? How small was the small ship? Why didn't the author describe the ship?
> *Teacher response:* Who wants to give an answer to this question?
> *(Teacher calls on several students, in turn, to answer.)*
> *Teacher question:* Look at the last sentence. What questions pop into your mind as you read that sentence?
> *Student questions:* What is a storm of warning? What kind of danger are they about to encounter? Will they survive? What was the warning? Did they still go ahead with the trip?
> *Teacher response:* Read the rest of the story to get answers to your own questions.

Motivated by their own questions, students could go ahead on their own, rapidly reading the story to answer their own questions. In the process, they also answer other questions. As they reach answers to their questions, they have a positive feeling, tantamount to saying, "That's an answer to my question!"

When the class finishes reading the entire story from which the example was taken, the teacher has the students review their questions and answers. The teacher repeats this strategy until students can spontaneously generate their own questions. Thus, students can learn to be active readers. They can then apply the process to all of their reading and read to satisfy their curiosity. (See chap. 4 for further explanation of active comprehension and how it differs from directed comprehension.)

---

[1]Osa Johnson, "Filming a Cannibal Chief." In *Reading Skill Building, Level VI, Part I*, edited by Guy Wagner, Gladys Person, and Lillian Wilcox. Pleasantville, NY: Readers' Digest, 1950.

Mathemagenic Behavior

Activities that cause students to learn or to want to learn are called mathemagenic behaviors (Rothkopf, 1982). These kinds of activities can take a variety of forms, directions, questions, clarification of purposes for reading, pointing out passages in the text that will help students read with purpose, and assessment activities, specifically, speaking or writing activities or projects. The following detailed teacher lesson plan for E. B. White's *Charlotte's Web* is a good example of mathemagenic behavior:

LESSON. INTRODUCTION TO *CHARLOTTE'S WEB*

1. Review with students the field trip to Melinda's family's farm. Ask these questions:
   a. How was the farm different from your own neighborhood?
   b. What kinds of animals did you see?
   c. What kind of work does it take to keep the animals clean and healthy?
   d. What are some sad things that farmers have to do to the animals when they get sick or injure themselves seriously?

2. Explain to the students that they will be reading *Charlotte's Web*. Point out that the story is set in a farmyard and that it is about animals who talk and think like people. Prepare them for the opening problem, that is, that Wilbur, the runt pig, is about to be done away with.

3. Begin reading the first part of the first chapter aloud to the students as they follow in their individual paperback copies. After several pages, instruct the students to finish the first chapter silently. Before they begin reading, give them these questions to think about:
   a. When you first meet Wilbur, what do you think of him?
   b. What does he say or do that you like or dislike?

4. To account for the difference in reading speed, have the students who finish early write out the answers to the two questions given under *3*.

5. When the students are through reading, give a short dictated quiz to test their comprehension of the chapter.

6. When the students have finished, have them construct a character sketch of Wilbur with the things the students like about Wilbur on one side of a sheet of paper and the things they don't like about Wilbur on the other side of the paper.

7. After the character sketches are completed, have the students write a short paragraph on "Two Reasons Why I Like Wilbur" or "Two Reasons Why I Don't Like Wilbur." For each reason, the students should supply an example of what Wilbur said or did to make himself likable or unlikable.

TEXT EXPLICATION STRATEGIES

Single-text strategies that are focused on the way in which the text is organized and presented are called text explication strategies. The teacher can plan and use these strategies, in addition to showing students how to use these strategies independently.

Text Annotation

Text annotation, or glossing, is an old technique. Although it had ceased to be used for quite a long while, it is gaining renewed popularity, particularly in social studies and science textbooks. *Glosses* are notes written in the margins of texts. The notes may serve any content or process purpose. In teaching students to learn from texts, marginal glosses can be used to explain technical terms, to prepose questions that will direct reader attention to certain material, to rewrite a passage of text so that it is more readily understood, or just to emphasize a point in the text. The teacher must anticipate what students will need to now as they read their texts. But in writing glosses, teachers will have to be careful to use simpler definitions and explanations than the text uses and to be terse lest students avoid the glosses because they are burdensome and provide more information than is needed or wanted (Richgels & Mateja, 1984). To use marginal glosses, teachers can take the following steps:

1. Read through the text, identifying vocabulary or other material to emphasize or clarify.
2. Write marginal glosses on ditto master with page numbers and line numbers indicated on the left-hand side of the ditto master.
3. Give dittoed glosses to students who insert them in their texts and refer to them as they read. (Examples in this text are glosses written directly on the text.)

CONSTRUCTING ANNOTATIONS

A series of examples illustrates the glossing strategies. Example 1, below, is a passage without the gloss; Box 6.2 is the same passage with a gloss. Note the difference in your reading and learning from the two examples.

Example 1. Imagine that you are an ninth-grade English student. Your teacher has assigned Edgar Allan Poe's "The Tell-Tale Heart" to read for homework. About 9 o'clock in the evening you settle in a chair to begin your reading. You are immediately confronted with the opening paragraph from the story:

> True!—nervous—very, very dreadfully nervous I had been and am; but why *will* you say that I am mad? The disease had sharpened my senses—not destroyed—not dulled them. Above all was the sense of hearing acute. I heard all things in the heaven and in the earth. I heard many things in hell. How, then, am I mad? Harken! and observe how healthily—how calmly I can tell you the whole story.

As a typical ninth-grade student you might have some problems getting into this story, perhaps because of vocabulary, perhaps because of inverted sentence structure; the first-person narration may also have caused you difficulty.

Example 2. If the text you brought home looked like the one in Box 6.2, what problems might have been eliminated? The glossing technique in Example 2 was used to facilitate reading the Poe story. Notice that several kinds of notes were used: definitions of difficult words, clarification of difficult sentence structure, and guiding questions concerning the paragraph's internal organization. This first paragraph from "The Tell-Tale Heart" is important because it establishes the insanity of the narrator. If the student-reader fails to understand that the storyteller's credibility is suspect, the power of the suspense in this classic will be lost. (Note: A good dramatic oral reading of this Poe story can dispel an amazing number of reading problems.)

BOX 6.2.   *Glossed Passage from "The Tell-Tale Heart"*

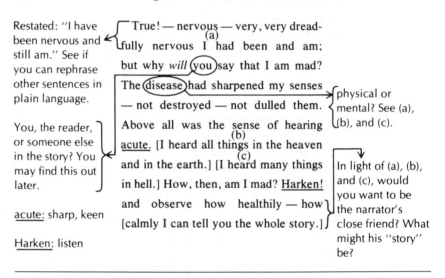

Example 3. Here is another paragraph from "The Tell-Tale Heart." Try your hand at glossing it:

But even yet I refrained and kept still. I scarcely breathed. I held the lantern motionless. I tried how steadily I could maintain the ray upon the eye. Meantime the hellish tattoo of the heart increased. It grew quicker and quicker and louder and louder every instant. The old man's terror *must* have been extreme! It grew louder, I say, louder every moment!—do you mark me well? I have told you that I am nervous; so I am. And now at the dread hour of the night, amid the dreadful silence of that old house, so strange a noise as this excited me to uncontrollable terror. Yet, for some minutes longer I refrained and stood still. But the beating grew louder, louder! I thought the heart must burst. And now a new anxiety seized me—the sound would be heard by a neighbor! The old man's hour had come! With a loud yell, I threw open the lantern and leaped into the room. . . .

Example 4.   As you glossed, you took into consideration vocabulary, sentence structure, and the writer's organization. Your gloss might look something like Box 6.3.

BOX 6.3.   *Glossed Passage from "The Tell-Tale Heart"*

refrained: held back

But even yet I <u>refrained</u> and kept still. I scarcely breathed. I held the lantern motionless. I tried how steadily I could maintain the ray upon the eye. } "I tried to see how . . ."

tattoo: beat

Meantime the hellish <u>tattoo</u> of the heart increased. It grew quicker and quicker and louder and louder every instant. The old man's terror *must* have been extreme! It grew louder, I say, louder } As the beat gets faster and louder, what is happening to "I"? To the victim?

every moment! — do you mark me well? I have told you that I am nervous; so I am. And now at the dread hour of the night, amid the dreadful silence of that old house, so strange a noise as this excited me to uncontrollable terror. Yet, for some minutes longer I refrained and stood still. [But the beating grew louder, louder! I thought the heart

anxiety: worry, uneasiness

must burst. And now a new <u>anxiety</u> seized me — the sound would be heard by a neighbor!] The old man's hour had } What does this tell you about the narrator's state of mind?

come! [With a loud yell, I threw open the lantern and leaped into the room. . . .] } Why did "I" leap at this moment? Read the previous two sentences.

Graphic Organizers

The purpose of graphic organizers is to show the relationships among concepts in a chapter. Using branched diagrams, you represent graphically the coordinate, subordinate, and superordinate relationships of the concepts within a chapter. Here is a simple hierarchical graphic organizer for a science chapter:

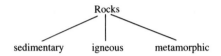

Here is a somewhat more complex graphic organizer for a history chapter:

Here is a complex graphic organizer for a section from a literature anthology:

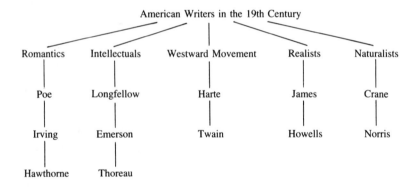

Teacher-made graphic organizers provide students with useful chapter overviews prior to reading. Student-made graphic organizers are discussed in chapter 9, "Letting the Students Do the Writing and Listening."

Mapping

Like graphic organizers, mapping is a pictorial way of showing how ideas in a text relate to one another. Unlike graphic organizers, mapping is more subjective, individualized, and creative. There may be a limited number of ways to design a graphic organizer of, say, color terms, but a teacher could produce a map of a story in an almost limitless variety of ways. Here is one for the story of Solomon: Map of biblical story of "Solomon's Wise Decision." Map depicts agents (doers of the action), actions (verbs), causal connections, objects and recipients of action.

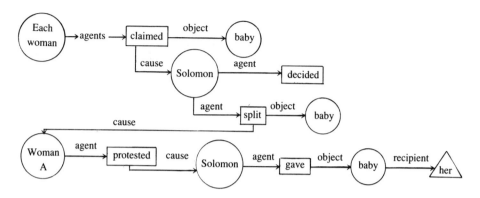

Reading and Learning-from-Text Guides

Textbooks can be made appropriate for a heterogeneous group of readers, by using *guides*. Guides generally take the form of duplicated sheets that engage the students in identifying and classifying information in the text, and in discussion or writing activities aimed at helping them comprehend the textbook. Two basic types of guides are *reading guides,* which focus on reading skills, and *learning-from-text guides,* which focus on thinking processes. We look first at several types of reading guides: *overview guides, vocabulary guides,* and *processes-of-reading guides.* Then we examine learning-from-text guides.

READING GUIDES
Overview Guides

Overview of the content may take the form of a précis (a brief summary of the content) as in the overviews that precede each of the chapters in this text. The example below is an overview guide for a physics text section on Boyle's Laws.

This section explains the relationships among the variables of pressure, temperature, and volume of a gas. To understand the relationships among them, keep one variable constant, vary a second, and observe its effect on a third. More specifically, (a) with temperature constant, increase pressure and observe volume decrease, (b) with pressure constant, as temperature increases, volume increases. These relationships occur in the cylinders of an automobile engine. As shown in Figure 6.1 the piston goes up, decreasing through compression the volume of gas, as in Example A. Then, as shown in B, an increase in temperature through a firing of the spark-plug ignites gas, increases the volume, and pushes the piston down, making the automobile engine revolve.

An overview guide can also be constructed from technical vocabulary used in a chapter. To determine technical vocabulary, a book's index can be reorganized

FIGURE 6.1. Automobile Engine Cylinder Exemplifying Boyle's Laws.

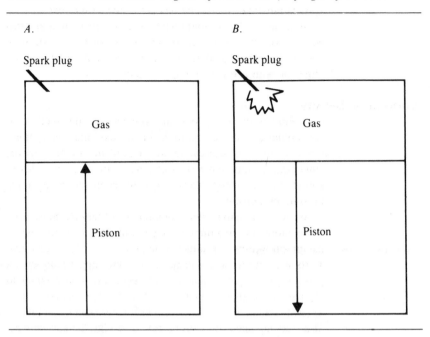

numerically according to page numbers where the vocabulary is introduced. This reorganization can be accomplished by putting each concept and its page number on a file card, then arranging the file cards by page number.

An example of an overview guide, depicting the concepts and interrelationships of a mathematic text, appears in Figure 6.2. This overview guides

FIGURE 6.2. Overview Guide of a Mathematics Text.

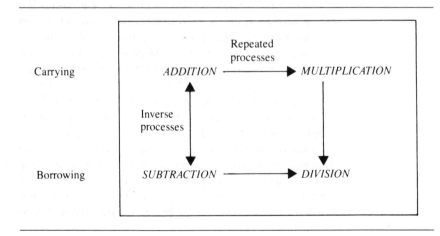

shows interrelationships among addition, multiplication, subtraction, and division. Multiplication and division are repeated processes of addition and subtraction, respectively. Carrying is used in addition and multiplication, and borrowing is used in subtraction and division. Addition and subtraction are inverse processes of each other, as are multiplication and division.

Effectiveness of Overview Guides

Overview guides are more effective than other organizational techniques for previewing, providing advanced organizers, and developing background knowledge for a reading assignment. Estes, Mills, and Barron (1969) compared structured overviews with advance organizers and preposed questions. The overview they used was a diagram showing the relationships among technical terms in a biology lesson. Advance organizers are generalizations or technical terms under which information in a text can be grouped. For example, under the term *nutrition,* we would place information on *food, vitamins, fruit, vegetables, oranges, apples,* and so forth. Preposed questions are both general and specific questions given to students before they read a passage. In contrast to advance organizers and preposed questions, the investigators argued that their overview diagram not only provided the technical terms but also showed their interrelationships. They thought the overview diagram would be superior to both advance organizers and preposed questions for enhancing learning and retention of the passage. However on a multiple-choice biology posttest, the group that used the structured overview did no better than the group that used the advance organizers but scored significantly higher than the group using preposed questions.

Earle (1969a, 1969b) also found that a group that had a structured overview on mathematical relationships learned the mathematical relationships better than a control group. Both groups, of course, read texts containing the technical terms.

The results of both these experiments indicate that either structured overviews or advance organizers to teach technical terms and the relationships among these terms lead to superior comprehension. Moreover, both strategies are better than not giving students any previous instruction or just giving them questions before they read.

Two additional studies showed the effectiveness of structured overviews in improving students' abilities to learn from text. Alvermann (1982) tested the effects of graphic organizers as text overviews versus normal prereading and postreading activities upon thirty 10th-grade students randomly assigned to the two treatments. She found that the students using the structured overviews performed significantly better on recall tests than did the group not using structured overviews. Slater (1985), in a study involving 224 ninth graders, reported that students exposed to structured overviews, regardless of comprehension level, recalled significantly more detail from text passages than did comparable students exposed to note-taking or no technique.

Vocabulary Guides

Students often need help with understanding new and difficult words, especially technical terms. A vocabulary guide can provide this help. To construct this kind of guide, go through a text or chapter or select technical terms and any difficult general terms. Or, if the text's index has been reorganized numerically according to page number, select technical terms from the chapter from the reorganized index. (Students in the class may be given the task of reorganizing the index. Give each student a pack of 3″ × 5″ cards with instructions to copy a column of terms in the index, putting each term on a card along with its page number. Then organize the cards by page number.)

Technical vocabulary can be taught directly, employing the approach used in dictionary entries. Each entry should contain the following information:

> word (syllabified and marked for pronunciation or unmarked with the understanding that the teacher will pronounce it for the students); the meaning(s) of the word; and the location of the word in the text or its context.

After they have been given these specifications, students can complete a vocabulary guide.

An example of a vocabulary guide is shown in Box 6.4. The purpose of the directions is to have students apply meanings of the technical terms in their reading and to learn the terms' meanings as determined by context.

BOX 6.4.   Vocabulary as Part of a Reading Guide

Directions: Some difficult words may give you problems. Read the following words, their syllabication, and definitions. I will pronounce the words for you. Page numbers where these words occur in this anthology selection have been included. Your task is to locate the word in the passage on the page indicated and write in the space provided the sentence in which the word occurs.

Word	Definition	Word occurs on page	Locate and write the sentence in which the word occurs.
scan-dal-ous	offending the sense of what is right and wrong; causing offense or shame	577	_____ _____
com-mis-er-at-ing	feeling or expressing sympathy or pity	578	_____ _____
so-lil-o-quize	to talk to oneself; to deliver a monologue	578	_____ _____

op-por-tune	well-timed; reasonable; suitable	580	_____
			_____
tart-ly	sharply; severely	582	_____
			_____
ex-on-er-at-ed	freed from blame, as of a charge or accusation	584	_____
			_____

This guide was prepared as part of a unit by Karen Skoog in our course "Reading in the Content Areas."

Processes-of-Reading Guides

Processes of reading can also be taught by a reading guide (McClain, 1981; Olson & Longnion, 1982). For example, paragraph structure can be taught as a means of showing students how to locate main ideas. In a *processes-of-reading guide,* students would be given the information shown in Box 6.5.

BOX 6.5. Reading Guide for Paragraph Structure

A paragraph is a group of sentences, all related to a main idea. Usually the main idea is explicit, stated as a sentence. Occasionally, the main idea is implicit, not stated as a sentence. Then the reader has to infer the main idea from the information given in the sentences in the paragraph. Five types of paragraph structure can be identified according to location of the main idea, indicated below as a longer line in the diagram of paragraph structure.

Location of Main Idea	*Diagram of Paragraph Structure*
1. Beginning of the paragraph.	1. _____
	_____
	_____
	_____
	_____
2. Middle of the paragraph.	2. _____
	_____
	_____
	_____
	_____
3. End of the paragraph.	3. _____
	_____
	_____
	_____
	_____

4. No main idea: inferential
type.

4. _____
_____
_____
_____
_____

5. Split type: main idea is
divided into two parts;
each part is clarified by
other sentences in the paragraph.

5. _____   or   or
_____   ____   _____
_____   ____   ___
_____   ____   ___
_____   _____
_____   ____
_____

Examples of each of the five types of paragraph structure listed in Box 6.5 can be given with a note of humor. The teacher can illustrate all three types of paragraph structure simply by reorganizing the sentence in the following paragraph:

John wanted a raise in salary. So he went to see his boss. He told his boss he had not had a raise in years. All during this time the company had high profits. Inflation was on the increase. His wife was going to have a sixth child.

The main idea, stated in the first sentence, can be shifted to the end of the paragraph. Start the paragraph then with the sentence, "John went to see his boss." Keep the rest of the sentences in order and end with the first sentence. Notice that some sentences will be changed slightly.

John went to see his boss. He told him he had not had a raise in years. All during this time the company had high profits. Inflation was on the increase. His wife was going to have a baby. John wanted a raise in salary.

To put the main idea in the middle of the paragraph, start with the sentence, "John went to see his boss." Keep the next three sentences in order. Then state the main idea ("So John wanted a raise in salary"). Finally, add the last sentence, "Moreover, his wife was going to have a sixth child."

John went to see his boss. He told him he had not had a raise in years. All during this time the company had high profits. Inflation was on the increase. So John wanted a raise in salary. Moreover, his wife was going to have a baby.

To provide an example of a paragraph in which the main idea must be inferred, completely omit the second-last sentence in the above paragraph. Start the paragraph with the sentence, "John went to see his boss." Then give the remaining sentences. Finally, add this sentence, "John waited for his boss to reply."

> John went to see his boss. He told him he had not had a raise in years. All during this time the company had high profits. Inflation was on the increase. His wife was going to have a baby. Then John waited for his boss to reply.

For a paragraph of the split type, add another element to the main idea: "John wanted a raise in salary *and a more responsible position.*" Then state the main idea in two sentences. The first would be, "John wanted a raise in salary." Sentences 2 to 6 then support this idea. The second part of the split idea can be stated at the end of the paragraph with or without additional sentences supporting it, as shown below. The structure of this paragraph would be a split main idea, with a sentence stating the first part at the beginning and a sentence stating the second part at the end of the paragraph.[2]

> John wanted a raise in salary. So he went to see his boss. He told him he had not had a raise in years. All during this time the company had high profits. Inflation was on the increase. His wife was going to have a sixth child. Moreover, John asserted that he could handle a more responsible position in the company.

After this explanation of the main idea and the structure of paragraphs, students use a guide on reading for main ideas, as shown in Box 6.6.

BOx 6.6. *Reading Guide for Main Ideas*

STUDENT GUIDE FIVE

Introduction to the Medieval Romances of Charlemagne
  Reading Skills: Reading for Main Ideas
                   Active Comprehension

Before You Read

In reading for main ideas, you must read the whole of each paragraph in the article or story. The main idea of the paragraph is the *meaning* of the paragraph — its heart and core. Without it there is no point to the paragraph at all.

The main idea of a paragraph is usually located in one sentence. This is the sentence to which all the other sentences are related. Most often, this key or topic sentence can be found at the beginning of the paragraph. It may also appear at the end or somewhere in the middle. Sometimes, a paragraph may contain no *direct* statement of main idea although it may be implied. However, more often than not, one topic sentence occurs in a paragraph.

---

[2]Additional reading processes and skills are discussed in chapter 18, "The Future: A Schoolwide Program."

Use these guidelines when reading for main ideas:
1. Read each paragraph carefully.
2. Look for the sentence in each paragraph that expresses the meaning of the *whole* paragraph. This will be the topic sentence which contains the main idea.
3. Be sure that the other sentences of the paragraph relate to this key sentence. An example:

> *Malory speaks of the Round Table in two senses.* First, he refers to it when he means the fellowship that bound King Arthur and his knights. Secondly, he refers to the Round Table when he means the actual table, seating one hundred and fifty knights, that could be transported from Camelot to another of Arthur's courts.

The main idea of the above paragraph is: The Round Table has two meanings. It occurs in the first sentence — the topic sentence. The other two sentences relate directly to this key sentence.

While You Read

Read the introduction to "Charlemagne and Elegast." Do the following:
1. Determine the main idea of each paragraph and write it down in the space provided below. There are three of them. (Skip paragraph one as it is only one sentence long.)
2. Determine which sentence is the topic sentence. Write it down in the space provided below.

Introduction to "Charlemagne and Elegast"
Translated by Lubertus Bakker

The medieval romances that were written about Charlemagne during the height of the Middle Ages were inspired by the historical figure who actually had ruled most of western Europe in his lifetime.

Charlemagne, or Charles the Great (742?–814 A.D.), became King of the Franks in 768. The Franks were a Germanic people who originally lived near the North Sea in the valley of the Rhine River. They invaded France in the fifth century. By the time Charlemagne inherited the throne, the Frankish kingdom was the most powerful in western Europe. Its territories included France, Belgium, and most of Germany. Charlemagne brought even greater glory to the Frankish kingdom. He expanded his territories through military conquest, subdued his pagan enemies and did his utmost to spread the teachings of Christianity. He became a close ally of Pope Leo III, who crowned him Emperor of the Romans in 800. According to many historians, Charlemagne's coronation marks the beginning of the Holy Roman Empire.

It was not surprising that a king and emperor of such power and prestige would soon be exalted in story and song. As his life was embroidered with fiction, Charlemagne passed into legend. He acquired a legendary birth and a group of twelve chivalric knights, or paladins, to share his legendary adventures. He became, moreover, the man chosen by God to defend the Christian faith.

In about the eleventh century, French minstrels claimed Charlemagne as their national hero and sang many *chansons de geste* ("songs of heroic deeds") about him and his paladins. The most famous of these is the *Song of Roland,* which is based upon one of Charlemagne's campaigns in Spain. The Frankish kingdom had long been threatened by the Moors, who conquered Spain early in the eighth century. In 778 Charlemagne led his army across the Pyrenees to establish a neutral zone between France and Spain. While returning to French territory, the rear guard of his army was attacked by natives of the mountains. The *Song of Roland* describes this disastrous attack upon the rear guard, which is commanded by Roland, one of Charlemagne's legendary paladins. Roland, facing certain annihilation, can summon Charlemagne's help if he will sound his horn. He repeatedly refuses to do so. When he finally relents, it is too late for Charlemagne to reach him. French verse epics, like the *Song of Roland,* were the major source of the many medieval romances about Charlemagne and his paladins.

Remember, the main idea of a paragraph is the *central point* of the paragraph. It may appear in the first sentence, the last sentence, or somewhere in the middle (or it may be implicit). It may also be stated more than once. Follow the guidelines given in the *Before You Read* portion of the guide and you should have no trouble.

Paragraph 1: Skip
Paragraph 2: Main idea _____
                 Topic sentence_____
                 _____
                 _____

Paragraph 3: Main idea _____
                 Topic sentence_____
                 _____
                 _____

Paragraph 4: Main idea _____
                 Topic sentence_____
                 _____
                 _____

Key: Topic sentences — last sentence in paragraph 2 and first sentence in paragraphs 3 and 4. Selection is from *Exploring Life Through Literature,* by Robert C. Pooley, et al. Copyright 1951, © 1957, 1964, 1968 by Scott, Foresman and Company. Reprinted by permission.

Following one or more reading guides, students can read a chapter with greater ease and understanding. They can also be helped through the chapter with a learning-from-text guide. To explain this type of guide, we begin by reviewing a taxonomy (or classification) of reading objectives.

LEARNING-FROM-TEXT GUIDES
Objectives
A modified organization of reading comprehension objectives based on the taxonomy formulated by Bloom et al. (1956), as applied to reading by Barrett

(1968), is shown in Figure 6.3. An assumption underlying this taxonomy is that mastery of an objective at a level lower in the taxonomy is a prerequisite for mastering an objective at a higher level. Inspection of the objectives indicates that this assumption is logical.

The objectives are divided into two dimensions. The cognitive dimension precedes the affective dimension. In the cognitive dimension, students recognize (read) literal statements and store them in memory. They can use the information they recognize (or recall from memory) for inferential comprehension and for reorganization of information. In the affective dimension, students can make judgments about the information based on external criteria or standards that the individual brings to reading. The standards can be either intellectual or valuational. Students can also respond emotionally to content through reactions to language (connotative and denotative properties of words); to imagery evoked by content; to characters in the story (identification); or to the structure, style, and form used. These judgments and emotional responses make up the affective dimension of reading comprehension.

The reading comprehension objectives can be put into learning-from-text guides and used to teach students to comprehend their texts. The next section explains how to construct this type of guide. Statement-based guides can be superior to questions because they foster inquiry and open discussion (Riley, 1980).

Constructing a Learning-from-Text Guide

To make a learning-from-text guide, follow this procedure.

Step 1.   Read through a chapter of assigned reading material to determine which is relevant. The assumption in this step is that students do not need to learn all the content in a chapter. Some chapter content may be irrelevant to the teacher's objectives.

Step 2.   Analyze relevant content and categorize it as follows for use in the three levels of the guide:

1. *Information, explicit or directly stated* (for use in the informational level): This information is given in the words of the text; for example, a detail, inference, interpretation, or evaluation given by the author.
2. *Relationships, inferences, or interpretations* (for use in the inferential and interpretive level): A *relationship* consists of an integration or synthesis of facts or information stated in the text. Inferences are deductions from major and minor premises stated in the text. Interpretations are inferred by constructing a major generalization and using a stated detail as a minor premise.
3. *Generalizations and evaluations* (for use in the generalized and evaluative levels): The teacher selects a generalization from the text: All great civilizations rise and fall. Students can then debate whether the information in

FIGURE 6.3. Cognitive and Affective Dimensions of Reading Comprehension

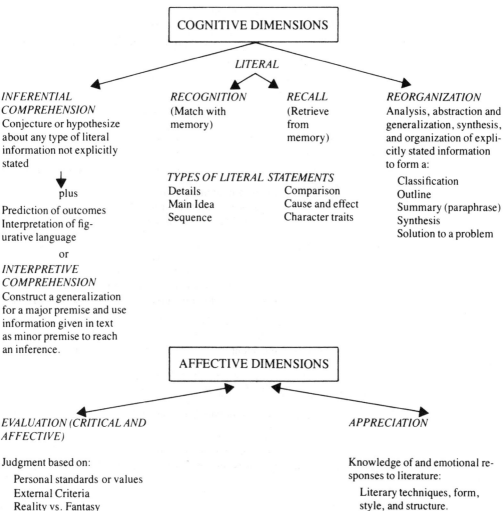

Thomas E. Barrett, "The Barrett Taxonomy: Cognitive and Affective Dimensions of Reading Comprehension," in H. M. Robinson (ed.), *Sixty-Seventh Yearbook of the National Society for the Study of Education,* Part II. Chicago, Ill.: University of Chicago Press, 1968, pp. 19–23. Adapted with permission.

the text supports this generalization. Or the teacher may construct a generalization that goes beyond, but assumes, information and generalizations contained in the text; that is the central ideas of the text can be grouped under the extended generalization. For example, this quotation from Robert Browning's poem "Andrea del Sarto" can be debated by members of a group as being applicable or not applicable to Einstein's life as presented in a given biography:

> Ah, but a man's reach should exceed
> his grasp,
> Or what's a heaven for?

The teacher can also select or formulate evaluative statements. These statements may refer to the truth or validity of information or conclusions in the text or to the desirability or worth of the information or conclusions. An example of an evaluation statement is given in Box 6.7.

In constructing the guide, work backwards: Start with the generalized or evaluative statements; then select the inferences and interpretations that support them; and finally list the factual level of information that supports the inferences, interpretations, and generalizations.

Step 3. Construct the factual, informational, or explicit level of the guide by listing significant statements made in the text and interspersing among them statements not made in the text. The students' task is to read these statements and determine which statements were made in the text and which were not. Students may justify their identification by locating and writing down, next to the statement, the page in the text where the informational or explicit statement was made.

The purpose of the informational or explicit level of the guide is twofold: (a) to indicate which information in the text is important for students to know and (b) to form the basis for inferences, interpretations, generalizations, and evaluations. All students who are striving to do well and who are beyond the reading acquisition stage can usually get all the informational items correct. Some students who have not gotten many items correct on previous class exercises or on standardized tests are delighted to get so many explicit items correct on learning-from-text guides. Since informational statements are more numerous than the other types of statements in the guide, the score of items correct can be quite high for all the members of the class. Note: included in the informational level are all statements explicitly made in the text, even though some of them are inferences, generalizations, and evaluations *made by the author*.

Step 4. Construct the inferential and interpretive level of the guide. This level goes beyond recognition or recall of explicitly stated information. The processes of thinking required at this level of the guides are (a) inference and (b) construction of generalizations that can be used along with factual or explicitly stated information for making interpretations. The classic example of an inference is shown in Figure 6.4. The missing word in the conclusion is, of course, *mortal*.

FIGURE 6.4. *Classic Example of an Inference Shown in Two Forms.*

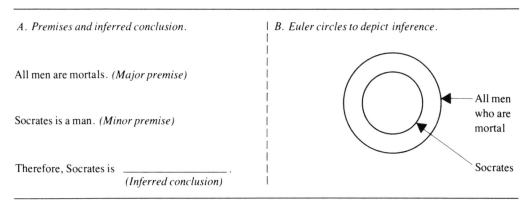

A. Premises and inferred conclusion.

All men are mortals. *(Major premise)*

Socrates is a man. *(Minor premise)*

Therefore, Socrates is _____ .
  (Inferred conclusion)

B. Euler circles to depict inference.

All men who are mortal

Socrates

Socrates is in the class *all men,* and what is true of all men is therefore true of Socrates.

This inference is also shown in the Euler circles in Figure 6.4. Euler circles are used to represent sets (collections of objects) and their relationships. The larger circle represents the set *all men who are mortal.* The smaller circle represents Socrates, a man, and consequently a member of the set *all men who are mortal.* Therefore, the conclusion must be that Socrates is mortal because the smaller circle is entirely within the larger circle and what is true for what the larger circle represents is also true for what the smaller circle represents.

In a story, the major and minor premises are usually not stated or not stated succinctly. The reader has to perceive the relationships among sentences and infer or interpret in order to arrive at a conclusion. For example, this sentence occurs in a short story:

> My husband and I wanted to make a moving picture of savages, and Martin finally decided on Malekula. . . .

Perception of relationships in the sentence will provide a reasonable inference of an answer to the question, "Who is Martin?" The answer is "the writer's husband." How do you know? To explain, you would point to the proximity of the phrase "my husband and I" to the name "Martin," which suggests that Martin is the husband. But you would have to add that this inference is only a plausible hypothesis, to be confirmed or refuted by subsequent passages in the story. This process of hypothesizing and confirming is fundamental to the ability to learn from text.

Another example of constructing a generalization and using explicitly stated details to arrive at an inference occurs in answer to this question about the sentences below.—How did the son feel?

An explorer, about to sail off on a voyage, says goodbye to his 9-year-old son at the dock, boards his ship, and sails off. His son, waving goodbye, remains on the dock until the ship is out of sight.

The passage itself does not answer this question. A major premise, such as the following, has to be constructed:

When fathers go off on exciting adventures and leave their sons at home, their sons are unhappy.

With this major premise and a minor premise that states the son was left at home, the reader can infer that the son was unhappy.

Step 5. Construct the generalized and evaluative levels of the guide. A generalization or application consists of statements that encompass literal or interpretive information, but go beyond the passage. In the passage about the father leaving his son behind, the generalization might be:

Adventurous jobs make for unhappy family life.
or
Absence makes the heart grow fonder.

These generalizations can be debated. To conduct a debate, set a time limit. Divide the class into pairs or small groups so that students can express their opinions to each other and become aware of their own systems of values. This grouping also permits many students to talk at the same time. Thus, maximum participation is attained with minimal use of class time.

The truth or falseness of a generalization can also be debated, perhaps leading to reference reading to buttress a position. After reading about the history of Egypt, Greece, Rome, or Great Britain, a generalization that may be made is, *All great civilizations rise and fall*. This statement can be debated. In an advanced history class, students might do supplementary reading to get evidence on the applicability of the generalization. Or, they might draw upon their previous reading to gather evidence for a debate.

An example of a learning-from-text guide is shown in Box 6.7. After reading ''Seagull Story,'' individual students can complete the guide on their own or under the teacher's direction; or the students can be grouped to (a) complete the guide, (b) compare their answers and try to resolve discrepancies, and (c) discuss their justification for selection of the statement that *best* represents ideas in the passage read. Later, questions on these three levels can replace statements (see the questions used in the guide in Box 7.15.

After completing the three levels of the guide, the students' affective and critical responses to a selection can be elicited by *evaluation activities*. Critical and affective responses should be based upon external criteria or personal standards and values (Russell & Fea, 1963). The kinds of questions that will elicit evaluative responses follow: How did you feel about . . . ? Was it right or wrong for the main character to . . . ? Is the author's statement true? After writing brief sentences to crystallize their affective reactions, students can form groups and communicate and discuss their reactions with each other.

BOX 6.7. A Learning-from-Text Guide

Directions: Read the story below. Then respond to the items in the informational and inferential sections by checking "yes" or "no." If the response is "yes," indicate the line or lines in the story on which you base your response. You can also respond to the Generalized and Evaluative Level items with a "yes" or "no." It would be helpful to explain, discuss, and justify your responses, especially those for the last level, in a class or group discussion.

SEAGULL STORY

For years millions of hungry seagulls have flown inland and seriously damaged Swedish crops and gardens. Experts at first tried to reduce the number of gulls by destroying their eggs but found that the gulls merely laid more eggs.

Now armed with saucepans and cooking stoves, the experts boil the eggs and carefully replace them in the nests. The gulls, not knowing the eggs will never hatch, sit on them hopefully until it is too late to try again.

READING GUIDE

Informational Level (What the Author Said)	Yes	No	Line
1. Seagulls are seriously damaging Swedish crops and gardens so attempts are being made to reduce the number of gulls.	——	——	——
2. A way to keep seagulls from multiplying is to make it impossible for their eggs to hatch.	——	——	——
3. Seagulls actually help farmers.	——	——	——

Inferential Level (What the Author Means; Relationships Among Statements)

	Yes	No	Line
4. Seagulls outwitted the experts.	——	——	——
5. Seagulls don't recognize hard-boiled eggs even when they are sitting on them.	——	——	——
6. The Swedes have found a way to control the seagull plague.	——	——	——

Generalized and Evaluative Levels
(Broader Idea; Discussion: Explicate Values)

	Yes	No	Line
7. Man's ingenuity insures his survival.	——	——	——
8. If at first you don't succeed, try, try, and try again.	——	——	——

Harold L. Herber, *Teaching Reading in Content Areas,* © 1970, p. 63. Reprinted by permission of Prentice-Hall, Inc., Englewood Cliffs, New Jersey.

An example of an evaluation activity is shown in Box 6.8. This one, designed for a unit on ecology, presents the pros and cons of an issue. Students can use this guide by selecting a position on the issue and debating their views in groups.

BOX 6.8. *An Evaluation Activity in Ecology*

Students first read a selection which gives the following information:

> The Colorado River was dammed up to create Glen Canyon Dam. The river's water backed up behind the dam to form Lake Powell. Hundreds of miles of scenic canyons now lie buried beneath the lake; while water released from the dam runs down to turn turbines and drive generators producing millions of watts of electricity. Swiftly and quietly the electricity is transported to distant cities to provide energy for people and machines who are unaware of changes wrought in nature to create their power.

The evaluation guide consists of the following statements:
1. Man's need for electrical power is more important than protection of scenic areas.
2. Scenic areas are legacies for our children. We should protect and preserve these areas at all costs.

To enhance the process of debating their views on the issue presented in Box 6.8, students can use the *Reader's Guide to Periodical Literature* to locate magazine articles written before, during, and after Glen Canyon Dam was built. The students would then have more information to buttress their points of view. Although the issues may not be resolved, students participating in the debate would, in the process, tend to achieve the objective of using external criteria explicitly or formulating and stating their own standards and values for evaluating this and similar social issues. Reading and learning from text guides explicate the text. They also contribute to the development of reader resource strategies.

READER RESOURCE STRATEGIES

Single-text strategies that are organized toward the thought processes of individual readers are called reader resource strategies. Unlike text explication strategies that help the students to understand the structure and style an author uses in writing a particular text, reader resource strategies concentrate on how the students process the information that they read from texts. In teaching sixth graders to comprehend a chapter from a world history text, a teacher can preview technical vocabulary and show the students how to read difficult sentences and paragraphs using one or more explication strategies. However, determining whether the students have enough world knowledge to understand distant and seemingly abstract civilizations would involve the use of reader resource strategies. To determine students' prior knowledge and to develop further knowledge for a text, the teacher can use a Background Knowledge Guide.

Background Knowledge Guide

In this single text strategy the teacher matches what the students already know about a topic with what they need to know in order to understand new text material. The information can be plotted in the form of a chart, graphic organizer, or map representing the relationship between prior knowledge and new requisite knowledge. What follows is a brief classroom dialogue that shows how the advance organizer works:

Scene: *Hedy Davis is about to introduce her fifth-grade students to a social studies chapter on maps. In using the Background Knowledge Guide, Ms. Davis uses yellow chalk to write down on the blackboard students' responses. When she has exhausted their background knowledge, she fills in the diagram with white chalk the information that students need to learn in order to understand the chapter.*

Davis: How many of you have taken long car trips, either across the country or across the state? (*A number of students raise their hands.*) Good. Now think back to these trips? How did you know where you were going and how to get there?

Josie: My mother knew where she was going because we've been there many times before.

Raul: My dad stopped at a lot of gas stations and asked.

Rosanne: My brother drove and he had a lot of information written down on the back of an envelope.

Cassie: My dad used a map.

Tom: So did mine.

Others: Yes, so did mine.

Davis: Well, if you don't know where you're going, maps can be useful. We're going to study about maps. But before we do, I want to know everything you know about maps.

Sondra: They're on big sheets of paper.

Tom: Sometimes they're in books.

Rosanne: They are in bright colors.

Cassie: They have a lot of lines on them that tell you where the roads are.

Jim: Some maps show mountains and rivers.

By this time, Ms. Davis has constructed the GRAPHIC ORGANIZER based on the Students' contributions, shown in Box 6.9. Ms. Davis now tells the students what they will learn from the chapter on maps that they are about to read.

Davis: All of the things that you mentioned are in the chapter on maps that you are about to read. The chapter will tell you the kinds of materials that maps are written on and how colorful they are. Most of the chapter deals with the lines that are used on maps and the kinds of information that the lines can give you. A map is made up of lines that go across the map, up and down and side to side. When these lines come together they form big squares. This is called a grid. Each grid has a number or letter on it so that you can tell one grid from another. For example, if you wanted to find where the town of Tooterville is you would look on a list or *Index* that is on the back or side of the map. The Index might

BOX 6.9. Graphic Organizer of Students' Background Knowledge

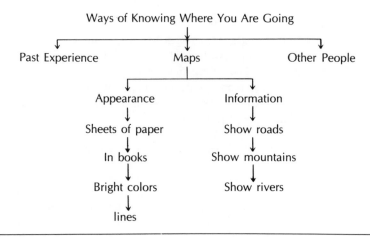

say G-7. The town of Tooterville would be found by seeing where the G line and the 7 line come together.

As Ms. Davis was talking to her students she finished the GRAPHIC ORGANIZER by adding the new words and concepts. The new organizer looked like the one shown in Box 6.10. Ms. David directs the students to copy the graphic organizer from the board and use it as a guide to reading the chapter on maps.

Box 6.10. Graphic Organizer for Students' Background Knowledge Augmented by the Teacher

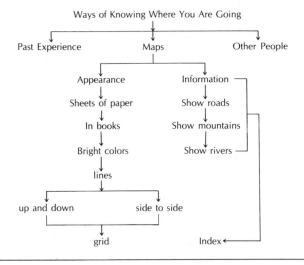

SCHEMA STRATEGIES

A schema is a knowledge structure organized from experience that a person has about an object, an event, or a situation. Situations or sequences of commonly recurring events are known as scripts. A schema of an object is activated when the phrase ''ice cream'' is read or heard. For example, a sixth-grade student would think ''cold, sweet, soft, treat, dessert,'' all associations from past experiences with ''ice cream.'' However, when that sixth grader encounters Ray Bradbury's short story, ''The Man in the Ice Cream Suit,'' the student must learn to make new associations with the word *ice cream,* specifically that with *suit* the term *ice cream* refers to color and style of a suit. Consequently, the more limited world knowledge a particular student has, the fewer schemata the student will have developed. As a result, the student may be continually frustrated in learning from text because of having to learn new concepts and make new associations with already learned concepts (Singer, 1986).

Given the wide range of differences that can exist in a 6th-grade, a 9th-grade or a 12th-grade class, the teacher must ensure that students encounter new text with a common frame of reference, by referring to existing schemata and building new ones. For example, assume that you were about to teach a class of 8th-grade social studies students a unit on ancient China. One of the concepts you might want to introduce the students to is *Ruling Families* or *Dynasties.* Students may already be familiar with ''dynasty'' through the popular television show of the same name. A profitable discussion would begin with having the students list everything they know about the television show as it relates to the title ''Dynasty.'' The teacher would then select those items from the students' list that related to the dynasties of China and teach these learned concepts as they apply to the new situation, ancient China.

Elementary and secondary school curricula are replete with new concepts that students must learn and already learned concepts with new associations. Here are just a few examples:

CONTENT AREA	NEW CONCEPT	REASSOCIATED CONCEPT
English	vorticism	romantic
	stanza	criticism
Social Studies	ballot	party
	insurgent	platform
Science	photosynthesis	volatile
	testtube	experiment
Mathematics	surd	interest
	cosine	principal
Language	paradigm	subject
	pluperfect	clause

One of the terms in Engish is *criticism.* Box 6.11 contains an example of the schema strategy used by Mr. Wallace in his eleventh-grade honors English class to develop his students knowledge of this term. The result of his lesson is that students have acquired a schema for *criticism*.

Box 6.11. Development of a Schema for the term *criticism*

Wallace: Today, I am going to introduce a new concept to you. First of all what does the word *criticism* mean to you?

Students: (Make various contributions to the discussion. As the students talk, Mr. Wallace makes a list of their comments on the blackboard.)

Wallace: All right, now, let's look at the list that we have assembled on the front board. What I would like to do is reconstruct this into a graphic organizer. Where do I start? (The students have already studied graphic organizers and, through discussion, they assist Mr. Wallace in constructing the following diagram:)

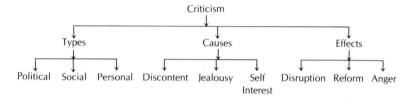

Wallace: The reason I had you discuss the concept of *criticism* is that we are going to begin a new unit, not on literature, but on essays written about literature. These essays are called "literary crticisim." The people who write them are called "literary critics." (At this point, Mr. Wallace refers to the blackboard diagram and checks off those student contributions which apply to literary criticism. As he checks them off he explains why the general terms the students have associated with *criticism* apply to *literary criticism*. He then adds new terms to the diagram and explains them. This revised diagram follows:)

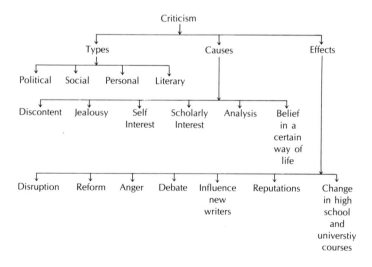

> *Wallace:* As you can see, five of the items you mentioned about criticism are also true of literary crticisim. But there are a number of new ideas you will need to learn. You will notice that I have placed these in capital letters. In this new unit, we will discuss each of these new aspects about literary criticism that you do not already understand.

In effect, Mr. Wallace used the following steps in applying a schema strategy to the concept of *literary criticism,* steps you can use in introducing a new concept to your students:

Step 1. Introduce a new concept at a higher level of abstraction. Notice that Wallace used *criticism* to introduce the concept of *literary criticism.* Ask students to tell you all that they know about the more abstract concept. As the students provide answers, list them on the front board or on an overhead projector transparency.

Step 2. Reconstruct the list into a graphic organizer.

Step 3. Add the new concept to the appropriate part of the graphic organizer and place check marks by the existing terms that apply to the new concept. Clearly explain the relationship between the checked items and the new concept.

Step 4. Add new terms associated with the new concept to appropriate parts of the graphic organizer. Indicate how these new terms will apply to the new material.

Summarization

The old cliché ''The best way to learn anything is to write it down'' may possess a great deal of truth. Summarization, the process of writing down from memory what you have just read, aids the recall and comprehension of text (Bean, Singer, Frazee, & Sorter, 1983; King, Biggs, & Lipsky, 1984; Singer, 1986; van Dijk & Kintsch, 1977). For summarization to be effective in the classroom setting, the process must be taught to the students. Summarization has five rules:

1. Delete nonessential information.
2. Identify or construct topic sentences.
3. Construct superordinate terms.
4. Integrate superordinate terms into generalizations.

STEPS IN CONSTRUCTING A SUMMARY
Delete Nonessential Information.
In learning to write good summaries, students must first learn to delete the unimportant information. Consider the following brief text passage:

> Living in a tropical rain forest climate one is faced, paradoxically, with rapid change and yet no change. On a given day, the morning features intense, continual

rain. In the afternoon, the sun comes out and it is unbearably hot and steamy. Could you get used to wearing a raincoat in the morning and having to strip down to short sleeves in the afternoon? And this happens every day, Sunday through Saturday, without relief.

If one were to delete the nonessential information from the above paragraph, it might look something like this:

tropical rain forest climate

paradox   rapid change

yet no change.   a given day   morning

intense, continual rain

afternoon   sun   out   unbearably

hot   steamy.   get used to

A student summary, given this deletion of nonessential detail, might look something like this:

Climate in the tropical rainforest is a paradox. The weather can change rapidly from heavy rain in the morning to hot, steamy rain in the afternoon. Yet the weather is like this every day.

Identify or Construct Topic Sentences.

Since topic sentences contain the main ideas of paragraphs, students need to include them in summaries or create them if they are absent in the text. Consider this text example that omits the topic sentence:

By 1929, stocks continued to surge upward along with spiraling rates. Countless investors bought stocks on margin, that is, paying only a small percentage down and owing the balance. The market was flooded with new convenience items. Everyone seemed to own a refrigerator, a radio, and an automobile. Yet, farmers were losing money on crops. The unemployment rate was growing.

The author of this particular text obviously believed that the reader could make the proper inference: Despite apparent prosperity, economic conditions in the late 1920s were not healthy. In order for students to make sense out of the paragraph, they would have to supply the topic sentence that ties the details in the paragraph together. A student summary of this text passage might look like this:

Things were in bad shape by 1929, even though the stock prices were higher than ever. People bought these stocks with small down payments. There was unemployment and crop failure. Stores were full of items people did not want to buy.

Construct Superordinate Terms

Sometimes when recalling text, students need to construct their own superordinate terms when these are not supplied by the author of the text. For instance, read the following passage from a literature text:

> He watched the clerk looking feverishly through the weathered record book. He enjoyed watching people scurry at his commands. He liked snapping his fingers at the housekeeper. A raised eyebrow signaled his wife to pour more coffee into his cup. He even brandished dollar bills before his barber to insure the prefect haircut. Pointing at piles of toys was all Mark had to do to initiate room clean-up.

As with most fiction, authors seldom make direct statements about character; rather, they show the reader through action and dialogue. The reader must supply the generalization, as in this student's summary of the passage just given:

> Mark was kind of a bully. He picked on those who depended on him. He made the people who waited on him feel small. He mistreated members of his own family.

Although the author did not use the words "bully," "made feel small," or "mistreated," the student created these superordinate expressions to categorize the kind of behavior Mark engaged in. These constructed terms provided the student with increased comprehension of the story, causing the reader to read not only the lines but also between the lines.

Integrate Superordinate Terms
into Generalizations

Given the constructed superordinate terms *bully, made feel small,* and *mistreated,* the student might have carried the summary farther into a generalization:

> Mark was kind of a bully. He picked on those who depended on him. He made the people who waited on him feel small. He mistreated members of his own family. MARK MUST HAVE BEEN UNHAPPY WITH HIMSELF BECAUSE MOST BULLIES HAVE INFERIORITY COMPLEXES.

An advanced organizer is an introductory verbal framework at an abstract level that can subsume information in the text (Ausubel, 1960; Earle & Barron, 1973). A summary or abstract placed at the beginning of a text can serve as an advanced organizer. Then a Background Knowledge Guide can graphically depict the knowledge students already have for the text. By knowing what knowledge the text-writer has presumed students already have in their background when he wrote the text, the instructor can infer the additional knowledge that must be taught to the students or insert as annotations in their texts.

INTERACTION STRATEGIES

Interaction strategies are those learning from text strategies that a student uses when interacting with the text, generally without a teacher's assistance or without adjunct materials or guides. The instructor-student interaction strategies described at the beginning of this chapter gradually shift to become internalized in the students. In other words, when students become so proficient in using these strategies that they can apply them automatically as they read, they have become independent in their ability to read and learn from texts.

Survey, Question, Read, Recite, Review (SQ3R)

The last of the single-text strategies to be discussed is SQ3R—survey, question, read, recite, and review. Consider a chapter from a sewing textbook. First, the students *survey* the contents of the chapter, focusing on such parts as (a) an overview, (b) a summary, (c) pictures of sewing patterns or products, (d) marginal gloss, (e) headings and subheadings, (f) highlighted vocabulary. Second, since this survey suggests to the students what the chapter is about, the students pose *questions* that they will try to answer by reading the text (Nist, Kirby, & Ritter, 1983). "What kinds of clothing will this chapter teach me to make?" "What materials will I learn to use?" "How can I make certain kinds of stitches?" Third, having posed these questions, students then actively *read* to find answers to their questions. Fourth, having read, students can *recite* the material, by putting the chapter contents into their own words, either in writing or in discussion. Last, students could *review* the information, perhaps by making a garment according to the guidelines set down in the chapter. Once the students learn to use SQ3R, they are on the road to becoming independent readers.

SQ3R, formulated by F. Robinson (1961), is the oldest strategy for developing independent learners (Johns & McNamara, 1980). He based the strategy on implications drawn from basic research in human learning. However, to be effective in using it, students have to learn what questions are appropriate to each content area. We demonstrate how SQ3R can be applied to each content area in chapters 11–14.

SUPPLEMENTARY STRATEGIES

Two techniques that can be used to supplement the preceding strategies are (a) cross-ability teaching and (b) using visual aids. These techniques can also be used by themselves to make texts more intelligible to students with a wide range of abilities.

Cross-Ability Teaching

Cross-ability teaching involves an able person teaching a less able one. According to this definition, cross-ability teaching is what teachers have been doing all along. However, in its technical meaning, the term is more restricted. *Cross-ability teaching* usually refers to more able *students* teaching less able *students*.

Within a class, cross-ability teaching occurs naturally in group situations when members of the group are discussing controversial issues or trying to solve problems or answer questions through reference reading. In this group situation, cross-ability teaching consists of one member of the group explaining something or trying to convince another member of the group. Frequently, cross-ability teaching means pairing two individuals from the same class or from two different classes. To avoid resentment in both tutor and tutee, pairing is best done on a voluntary basis.

Frequently tutors benefit more than tutees, particularly when tutors need further practice in what is being taught. If instruction consists of content or processes the tutor has already mastered, the tutor will experience no gain. However, the tutee may still benefit considerably from the instruction. At the other extreme, if the tutor does not understand what is being taught, neither tutor nor tutee is likely to benefit. The optimum condition is somewhere in the middle, a situation in which the tutor is more advanced than the tutee in knowledge or ability, but has not yet mastered the content or processes involved. The tutor, for example, may know the Bill of Rights, but not without some hesitation; after teaching it to another student, the tutor is likely to have progressed toward mastery of it.

Is cross-age tutoring effective? Cross-age tutoring has been found frequently to help tutors more than tutees. However, this benefit does not necessarily occur when tutors are not very capable. For example, high school seniors in a low-ability class volunteered to teach low-ability seventh and eighth graders for a year. They attended weekly seminars on tutoring before and after 1-hour weekly tutoring sessions. Despite weekly training and teaching sessions, these tutors did not gain significantly over a control group (Dillner, 1971).

Tutoring can have a significant effect on tutees, especially when the tutors are competent. For example, students in Grades 4, 7, and 10 were randomly assigned to adult tutors, ages 21 to 55, who were recruited by newspaper advertisement. The tutors passed *Sequential Test of Educational Progress*[3] and an interview. The results showed that, with intelligence controlled on the *California Test of Mental Maturity*,[4] students tutored by these adults were significantly higher than a control group in reading achievement and received better grade point averages in math, social studies, and English.

From these research studies, we can draw conclusions about what kind of tutor is likely to be effective. Tutors may benefit from the instruction they give if they need to practice processes already acquired in the content area and if they have the capabilities and the maturity for doing so. If they already have some knowledge and some skill in processes of reading and learning from texts in a content area, they may use their skills to acquire additional content in that area as they tutor. In doing so, tutors can demonstrate and teach tutees processes of

---

[3]Educational Testing Service, Princeton, New Jersey, 1969.

[4]California Test Bureau, Division of McGraw-Hill Book Co., Del Monte Research Park, Monterey, California.

reading and learning from text. Tutors must know either content or processes of reading and learning from texts in a content area and know how to communicate them effectively if the tutees, or the tutors themselves, are to benefit from the instruction.

Visual Aids

Visual aids can be used in all the preceding strategies. Use of such aids is, in itself, a strategy for handling individual differences in modes of processing stimuli: Some students can learn and recall relationships better in pictured form than they can in verbal form. Hence, whenever possible, teachers should use visual aids and teach students to transform verbal statements into pictorial relationships. (See chapter 16, ''Mathematics,'' Box 16.10, for examples of this type of transformation.)

EVALUATION OF SINGLE-TEXT STRATEGIES

In this chapter we have presented four single-text strategies. Although we have reviewed research that supports the effectiveness of some of them for handling individual differences in the classroom, teachers should also make their own evaluations of the effectiveness of these strategies in their own classrooms with their own students. In this section of the chapter we present several ways in which teachers can evaluate use of single-text strategies in their own classrooms.

To evaluate any of the single-text strategies, divide a class into two groups. A simple way to do this is rank the class according to students' reading ability. Then begin to assign students alternately to Group 1 and Group 2. This procedure is likely to produce two groups of equal ability in reading. Then have one group use one of the four strategies to accompany its reading of a passage while the other group simply reads the same passage. Both groups should be told that their comprehension will be tested at the end of the passage. After administering the comprehension test, find the average scores of both groups. Did the group that used the strategy have a higher average score than the other group?

Also obtain the affective reactions of the two groups. At the end of the comprehension test, ask both groups the following questions:

1. How do you rate the difficulty of this passage? Indicate your responses by circling one of the following choices: 1. Very easy, 2. Easy, 3. Average, 4. Difficult, 5. Very difficult.
2. How interesting was this assignment? 1. Very interesting, 2. Interesting, 3. Average, 4. Uninteresting, 5. Very uninteresting.

Average the choices circled for each group and compare. See if the group that used one of the strategies in this chapter found that the passage was easier and/or more interesting.

You can compare the effectiveness of the strategy for the low-reading achievers (lower half of the class) and high-reading achievers (upper half of

FIGURE 6.5. *Comparison of average comprehension test scores of high- and low-reading achievers who used a strategy versus those who did not*

		Teaching technique		
		Did not use strategy	Used strategy	Sum
Reading achievers	High (upper half of class)	A. Nine students Avg. = 85	B. Nine students Avg. = 87	172
	Low (lower half of class)	C. Nine students Avg. = 68	D. Nine students Avg. = 73	141
	Sum	153	160	313

class) in each group by writing the average, first on the comprehension test and then on the affective questions, for each group in each box in Figure 6.5. For example, the average comprehension test score earned by the high-reading achievers who did not employ the strategy goes in Box A of Figure 6.5.

Figure 6.5 will help you determine whether the strategy was effective, regardless of general reading achievement, by adding B + D, then A + C. By comparing the two sums, you can determine whether the strategy made a difference. If B + D is much greater than A + C, the strategy probably was effective.[5] Since Figure 6.5 shows that those who used the strategy scored 160 compared with 153 for those who did not use the strategy, we can conclude that the strategy, in this class, was probably effective in raising the comprehension test scores. You can also determine whether high-reading achievers still attained more than low-reading achievers, regardless of the strategy, by comparing the sum A + B with the sum of C + D. Since the sum of A + B (172) is much greater than the sum of C + D (141), then high-reading achievers probably attained more.

You can also find out whether there is an interaction between level of reading achievement and use of the strategy by determining whether the differences between B and D are less than the differences between A and C. Here B − D (87 − 73 = 14) is less than A − C (85 − 68 = 17). Any interaction can be perceived by plotting the results as shown in Figure 6.6. The converging lines in the figure indicate one kind of interaction between strategy and level of reading achievement: the low group benefits from the strategy more than the high group.

The following are additional ways to evaluate the effectiveness of the strategies:

---

[5]For a statistical test of significance of differences such as analysis of variance, see an introductory statistics text.

FIGURE 6.6. Average scores of group who used a strategy versus those who did not

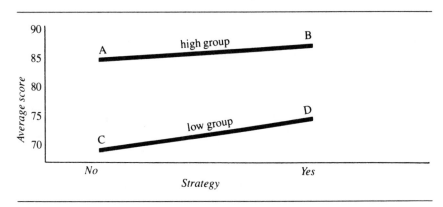

1. Observe whether students are more attentive to reading and learning from text with a strategy than without one.
2. After students have participated in one of the strategies, rate whether they concentrate on the assignment more, whether they are more independent of the teacher, whether they participate more in class discussion, or whether their reports are more germane and contain more technical vocabulary and higher level responses. In Figure 6.7, fill out the two by two tally table for each of your students. Rate each one's reaction as either high or low and classify the rating according to whether the student has used a strategy or not and was in a high or low reading-achievement group.
3. Observe whether students of high- and low-ability levels are able to learn

FIGURE 6.7. Tally table for rating each student's reaction to an assignment

		Strategy			
		No		Yes	
		High	Low	High	Low
Concentration or independence or participation or quality of reports	Upper half of group				
	Lower half of group				

from the assignment. If so, you would expect an equal number of high- and low-ability members in each No and Yes column in the above figure.

4. Interview a sample of your students and use their reactions to put them into one or another category in your table. Ask, for instance, ''How did you like this assignment?'' ''Did this assignment help you?'' ''Would you like more assignments like this one?''

The evaluation procedures can be applied not only to the single-text strategies but also the multiple-text strategies to be presented in chapter 11 of the text.

SUMMARY

Single-text strategies that enable students varying widely in ability to read and learn from a text without stigmatizing any of them were defined in this chapter. Although a teacher may use a textbook that fits the average reading level of a class, she or he needs to employ one or more strategies to make the text more appropriate to the class's range of ability to read and learn from the textbook. All of the single-text strategies are also useful in so-called homogeneous classes and in college preparatory classes because even these classes include students with varying ability.

Although the single-text strategies were described separately in this chapter, they can be used in varying combinations. In the next chapter, we demonstrate how the single-text strategies can be combined to teach students how to read and learn from a textbook currently being used in a junior high school social studies class and a senior high school woodshop class.

Of course, single-text strategies, such as guides for reading and learning from text, require preparation time. Mostly the materials can be perceived as part of a teacher's plans for teaching lessons or for helping students with their reading assignments. However, resourceful teachers who have mastered the strategies will think of ways of having students, teaching aides, or community volunteers assist with preparation of materials under their direction. Some suggestions for doing this are given in subsequent chapters.

ACTIVITIES

1. Select a poem by Carl Sandburg, or any poet. Develop a single-text strategy for teaching high school students to read that poem. Suggestions: (a) Follow the steps in DRA. (b) Develop a reading process that focuses on the reading of poetry. (c) Develop a learning-from-text guide that takes the students through the four levels of comprehension.

2. Select a chapter in any content area textbook of your choice and prepare a lesson on it, using the five steps of the DRA.

3. Explain in detail how you would attempt to teach students to use SQ3R in comprehending a science text.

4. Explain how you would test the *relative* effectiveness of two different types of reading guides used in a hypothetical class (Berget, 1973; Herber, 1978).

7 | Teaching Students to Learn from a Chapter

CHAPTER OVERVIEW

In the last chapter, you learned about strategies for teaching students to learn from a single text. In this chapter, you will learn how to apply some of these strategies to specific textbook chapters: (a) a junior high school social studies text, (b) a high school woodshop text, (c) a high school biology text, (d) a high school government text, and (e) a high school American history text.

GRAPHIC ORGANIZER

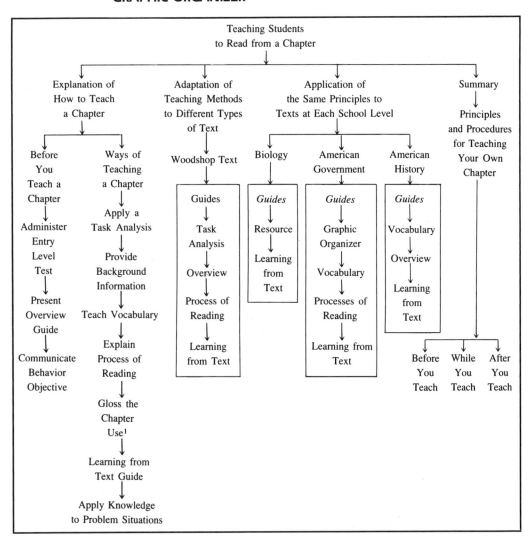

PREPOSED QUESTIONS

1. What is the purpose of a task analysis? How does it relate to behavioral objectives and to reading and learning from text guides?

2. The purpose of the processes of reading guide is to teach the students a method of learning. As such, it must be broken into a sequence of learning steps so that the students can move smoothly from one concept to another. How would you develop a processes of reading guide for teaching the students to read and understand comparison and contrast.

3. How could the strategies presented in this chapter help you to evaluate your effectiveness as a teacher?

USE OF A COMBINATION OF STRATEGIES
TO TEACH A CHAPTER

Even if improved textbook organization occurs, teachers will have to continue to teach students how to learn from texts. In the last chapter, you learned that there are numerous strategies for helping students to learn from a single text. In this chapter, we combine some of these strategies to show you how to teach a complete chapter from a junior high school social studies text.[1]

In demonstrating the strategies, we introduce you to several supporting techniques as we go along. In the second part of this chapter, you will examine some reading and learning-from-text guides for teaching a chapter from a woodshop textbook. Thus, we demonstrate that single-text strategies are equally applicable to both academic and vocational texts.

In the third part of the chapter we demonstrate how various guides can be used in such classes as biology, American government, and high school American history.

Finally, we will summarize the chapter and present principles you can use for teaching chapters in your own texts.

EXPLANATION OF HOW TO TEACH
A CHAPTER

Before You Teach a Chapter

ADMINISTER ENTRY LEVEL TEST

Before you present a chapter for class study, you should make sure the students have the background to read it. One way of doing this is to administer an *entry level test*. An entry level test assesses what information the students have retained from prior reading that will be useful in forthcoming reading. Examine Box 7.1. Notice that the entry level test contains test items on vocabulary, factual recall, inferences, and generalizations from the previous chapter. The teacher who prepared this test selected information from *Quest for Liberty*, chapter 2, that students would need to know to understand chapter 3. The objective nature of the test makes it easy to score, thus less time-consuming. Simply going over the answer in class might be enough to prepare the students for chapter 3.

Not only is the entry level test easy for the teacher to score, it is also easy for the student to take. All the student has to do is read each item and respond to it, either with an *X* or with no mark. If the items were written so as to demand short answers, the student would have to rely on expressive language, which for some students would be difficult. Chapter 9 shows you how to teach students to write answers to study questions.

---

[1]Throughout this chapter, the social studies text chapter referred to is Chapter 3, "The Colonies Fight for Independence" in *Quest for Liberty* by Chapin, McHugh, and Gross (San Francisco: Field Educational Publications, 1971.

BOX 7.1. Entry Level Test

CHAPTER 3: "THE COLONIES FIGHT
FOR INDEPENDENCE"

Part 1. Vocabulary. Match the terms on the left with their meanings on the right.

_____ 1. colony
_____ 2. dissent
_____ 3. indenture
_____ 4. mercantilism
_____ 5. representation
_____ 6. resource
_____ 7. conformity

A. a labor contract
B. doing what the group does
C. mother country getting raw
   materials from colony
D. a source of supply
E. to disagree with a majority
F. democracy
G. people choose others to act for them
H. totalitarianism
I. a territory ruled by people in
   another land

Part 2. Put an X by all factual statements about the colonial period that are true.

_____ 1. Prior to 1790, English, Irish, and Negroes made up the largest proportion of
        immigrants.
_____ 2. The Southern colonies, unlike New England and the Middle colonies, were
        primarily agricultural.
_____ 3. Catholicism was the main religion in the New England colonies.
_____ 4. Puritans, unlike other colonists, tended to be sober and serious people who
        wore dark clothing.

Part 3. Put an X by all conclusions that you can make about colonial life.

_____ 1. Opposition to slavery in the colonies was based on good business rather
        than on high ideals.
_____ 2. Religious intolerance was transplanted from England and Europe to the
        colonies.
_____ 3. Religion influenced the economic and cultural lives of the colonists.
_____ 4. The colonies, from the start, lacked unity; to form them into a United States
        would be an almost impossible task.

Part 4. Put an X by all general sentences that apply to life today.

_____ 1. The present conflicts between the North and the South developed right
        before the Civil War in the 1850s.
_____ 2. Religion still has an influence on political life in the United States.

PRESENT OVERVIEW GUIDE

In introducing the chapter to the students, a teacher might want to give the
students an *overview guide* of the chapter. In Box 7.2 you can see that one social
studies teacher prepared an overview guide by dividing the chapter into three

BOX 7.2. Overview Guide

CHAPTER 3: "THE COLONIES FIGHT
FOR INDEPENDENCE"

Part 1. Background of the
American Revolution (pp. 75–84).
a. What is a revolution? (p. 76)
b. What happened when the colonies ⎤ Events *1* (b–e)
   started to govern themselves? (pp. ⎟ caused the
   76–77) ⎟ Declaration of
c. What happened when England ⎟ Independence
   started to crack down? (pp. 78–79) ⎬ to be developed.
d. How did the colonies react to ⎟
   England's crackdown? (pp. 79–81) ⎟
e. How did England go too far? (pp. ⎟
   82–84) ⎦

Part 2. The Declaration of
Independence (pp. 84–88). ←

2 (a–b)
resulted in war. ⎰ a. How is the *Declaration* organized?
⎱   (pp. 84–87)
     b. What can we tell about the people
        who signed the *Declaration*? (pp.
        87–88)
     c. Why was it dangerous to sign the
        Declaration of Independence?

→ *Part 3.* The Revolutionary War
  (pp. 88–103).
  a. Who fought in the war? (pp. 88–89)
  b. What was it like to fight in the war?
     (pp. 89–94)
  c. How were the Americans able to
     win the war? (pp. 94–101)
  d. What happened when peace finally
     came? (pp. 102–103)

Parts 1–3. Overview (pp. 75–103).
a. It would have been impossible for
   the British to have won the War for
   American independence. Attack and
   defend that statement in one
   paragraph.
b. In what ways were the colonists
   ready to handle independence?

Pages referred to are from *Quest for Liberty.*

logical sections, asking major questions, and indicating where the students could find answers to those questions.

COMMUNICATE BEHAVIORAL OBJECTIVES

Accompanying the overview guide is a list of *behavioral objectives* (goals written in terms of student activity) which are subdivided by step-by-step enabling activities. Notice the detail that one social studies teacher used in preparing the objectives list in Box 7.3.

BOX 7.3. Behavioral Objectives

CHAPTER 3: "THE COLONIES FIGHT
FOR INDEPENDENCE"

Goal. After reading chapter 3, "The Colonies Fight for Independence," you will understand the causes for and the effects of the American Revolution.

Objective. In studying the background for the American Revolution, you will be able to explain how freedom in the colonies caused England to create controls which, in turn, caused the colonists to rebel.

Enabling Objectives:
a. You will look over *Part 1* of the *Overview Guide* to see what kinds of questions the text material on pp. 75–84 will answer.
b. You will write the exercises in the *Process Guide* (see box 5.6) on cause and effect.
c. You will read pp. 75–84 and answer questions 1:a–e in the *Overview Guide.*

Objective. In studying the *Declaration of Independence* you will be able to describe its organization and draw conclusions about the signers.

Enabling Objectives:
a. You will look over *Part 2* of the *Overview Guide,* which covers pp. 84–88 of the text.
b. You will read pp. 84–88 of the text and answer questions 2:a–c of the *Overview Guide.*

Objective. In studying the American Revolutionary War, you will be able (1) to list and identify the participants, (2) to describe battle conditions, and (3) to demonstrate how the Americans were able to win.

Enabling Objectives:
a. You will look over *Part 3* of the *Overview Guide,* which covers pp. 88–103 of the text.
b. You will read pp. 88–103 of the text and answer questions 3:a–d of the *Overview Guide.*

Ways of Teaching a Chapter

The techniques discussed so far—the entry level test, the overview guide, and the behavioral objectives—have been preteaching activities. Now, a number of ways in which a teacher actually teaches students to learn from a textbook chapter are discussed.

DO A TASK ANALYSIS

A chapter can be taught in various ways. For instance, the teacher can expand the list of behavioral objectives into a teacher *task analysis*. If you look at Box 7.4, you can see one social studies teacher's task analysis for chapter 3 of *Quest for Liberty*. Notice how this teacher has, for each objective, listed (a) the content the student must know to fulfill the objective and (b) the reading and thinking processes the student must have to master the content. In order for a student to describe the organization of *The Declaration of Independence* and draw conclusions about the signers, the student must know the relationship of main idea to subordinate idea and be able to draw inferences from facts. This task analysis focuses the teacher's attention on important areas of instruction and provides guidance for developing techniques and strategies. For instance, it looks like some teaching of the cause and effect thinking process is in order.

BOX 7.4. Teacher's Task Analysis

CHAPTER 3: "THE COLONIES FIGHT
FOR INDEPENDENCE"

Goal and Objectives	Content	Process
Students will understand causes and effects of the American Revolution by —		
1. explaining how freedom in the colonies caused England to create controls which, in turn, caused the colonists to rebel	definition of term *revolution* colonies' self-government England's pressure colonists' reaction to pressure	cause and effect
2. describing the organization of *The Declaration of Independence* and drawing conclusions about the signers	the main idea of the Declaration supporting ideas backgrounds of the signers	main idea/ subordinate idea drawing inferences from facts

3. listing and identifying the war's participants, describing battle conditions, and demonstrating how the Americans were able to win	who fought in the war
	  Colonists
	  Indians
	  British
	  French
	the battles
	  sequence
	  outcomes
	  conditions
	superior strategy of colonists
	  use of surprise
	  guerrilla warfare
	conditions of peace
		reading for details
		reading for chronological order
		drawing inferences from facts

PROVIDE BACKGROUND INFORMATION

After preparing the task analysis, the teacher might decide to teach a chapter with the direct reading activity (DRA) approach first by providing background information. See chap. 5 for example on how to develop background information.

TEACH VOCABULARY

After providing this background, the teacher would introduce the chapter vocabulary, possibly through use of a reading guide that focuses on vocabulary. In Box 7.5 you can see how one social studies teacher prepared a vocabulary guide for chapter 3, *Quest for Liberty*.

BOX 7.5. Vocabulary Guide

CHAPTER 3: "THE COLONIES FIGHT
FOR INDEPENDENCE"

Hard Words. Below are some difficult words you will run across in this chapter. I will pronounce them for you. Study the meaning of the word and the sentences from the chapter that use the word. Some of this information can be found in the textbook glossary (pp. 660–663).

Word	Meaning	Sentence from Text
compromise	the process of settling a conflict in which each side gives in on some points	The two sides were unable to *compromise*. (p. 83)
nationalism	love of your country to the point that you support it at the expense of other countries	Demands for independence are usually related to a growth in *nationalism*. (p. 104)

Word	Meaning	Sentence from Text
neutral	not a part of either side of a conflict	Historians used to think that about only one-third of the colonists actively supported the war, and that another third were *neutral* . . . (p. 88)
patriots	those who are extremely loyal to their country	The British soldiers met the American *patriots* on the village green . . . and shooting broke out. (p. 83)
rebellion	organized opposition to and defiance of a government or someone in authority	The *rebellion* against England became a practical possibility because the British had allowed some free institutions to flourish in the colonies. (p. 76)
revolution	a rapid and far-reaching change, especially the overthrow and replacement of a government	The desire for independence often leads to a *revolution.* (p. 76)
treason	an attempt to overthrow one's government	Some in the middle colonies were reluctant to commit "*treason*" and break permanently with England. (p. 84)

Having reviewed the vocabulary, the students could profitably reexamine the overview guide (Box 7.2) for questions to guide their reading. Perhaps, the students could even add questions of their own.

EXPLAIN PROCESSES OF READING

At this point, the teacher might want to insert a *processes-of-reading guide*. As you see in Box 7.6, the teacher, concerned that students might have difficulty with cause and effect, prepared a processes-of-reading guide that took the students step-by-step into the text material. Good practice suggests that the teacher do the first half of the guide orally with the class as a whole and gradually ease the students into working on their own as they read the chapter.

BOX 7.6. *Processes-of-Reading Guide: Cause and Effect*

CHAPTER 3: "THE COLONIES FIGHT
FOR INDEPENDENCE"

Cause and Effect

Just knowing the order in which events happen is not enough. In reading and understanding history it is important to know the CAUSES and the EFFECTS of the events. Below are some everyday events. Try to figure out what caused these events to happen, and what the effects of the events were:

Example:

Event: The milk in the refrigerator is sour and lumpy looking.
Cause: It was either bad when it was bought or it was left too long in the refrigerator.
Effect: Someone will have to go to the store for more milk or go without.

Event	*Cause*	*Effect*
1. All the lights at home suddenly go out.		
2. You reach into your pocket for money to pay for a Coke; the pocket is empty.		
3. Your younger brother hits you with a toy truck.		
4. War protesters refuse to fight in Viet Nam.		

Now, relate cause and effect to history.

Pages 85–104. As you read, jot down the *causes* for the following events:
1. The Continental Congress was moved and stirred to demand official independence from England.
2. Not all colonists supported the Revolution.
3. Colonists massed for attack at Breed's Hill and Bunker Hill.

Pages 90–104. As you read, jot down the *effects* of the following events.
1. General Gage won the battle at Bunker Hill and Breed's Hill.
2. Washington surprises the Hessian troops on Christmas Eve at Trenton.
3. Fighting conditions were unhealthful and unsanitary.
4. American colonists employ guerrilla warfare.

GLOSS THE CHAPTER

In addition to a processes-of-reading guide, the teacher might also wish to *gloss* some sections of the chapter. Look at Box 7.7 to see how one teacher, who felt The Declaration of Independence was hard reading, glossed it for the students.

BOX 7.7. Gloss

CHAPTER 3: "THE COLONIES FIGHT
FOR INDEPENDENCE"

Instructions: The main ideas are underlined. Read those first, then read the entire selection. The words in italics are technical terms for which synonyms appear in the margins.

The Declaration of Independence

Even when the war with England had been going on for more than a year, many colonists still hoped for a peaceful settlement. Some in the middle colonies were reluctant to commit "treason" and break permanently from England. On the other hand, in the Continental Congress the delegates from Virginia and New England (*favored*) an official declaration of independence.   wanted

Then, in January, 1776, Thomas Paine, a newly arrived immigrant from England, published his famous article *Common Sense,* in favor of independence. Within several months, 120,000 copies were printed. The piece was widely discussed by the colonists. Paine's brilliant arguments pointed out for the first time the disadvantages of living under a king and the ability of Americans to rule themselves better. This article helped (*stir*) the Continental   move

Congress to demand official independence from England.

In June, 1776, the Continental Congress *proposed* that independence be considered for the colonies and that the ties with England be finally cut. The Continental Congress chose a committee of five to write a statement of the official reasons for the separation of the colonies from England. Young Thomas Jefferson was the principal author of this Declaration of Independence. The other committee members were Benjamin Franklin, John Adams, Roger Sherman, and Robert R. Livingston.

strongly urged

changed

The Congress *modified* some of the documents prepared by the committee. One part, blaming the king for promoting the slave trade, was *omitted* because of objections from slaveholders as well as New England delegates. Why would *the latter group* have objected? On July 4, 1776, Congress formally adopted the Declaration of Independence.

left out

the New England delegates

Analysis of the Declaration

The document is divided into three main parts: (1) the first two paragraphs, outlining the basic rights of man; (2) a very long, detailed list of *grievances* that were directed against King George III, although Parliament had officially passed the laws; and (3) additional reasons that forced the colonists to separate from England.

strong complaints

The Declaration of Independence
was truly a (*revolutionary*) document. In   It contained
an age when most European nations   shockingly new
were ruled by kings, the idea of rebel-   ideas.
ling against the king was considered
dangerous and radical. Certainly, if the
independence movement failed, its
leaders and the signers of the Declaration of Independence would be risking
their lives, their fortunes, and their sa-
cred honor. Benjamin Franklin was
right when he told the signers, "We
must indeed all hang together, or, most
(*assuredly,*) we shall hang separately."   definitely

Passage from *Quest for Liberty* by June R. Chapin, Raymond J. McHugh, Richard E. Gross. Copyright © 1971, 1974 Field Educational Publications, Inc. Reprinted by permission of Addison-Wesley Publishing Company, Inc.

USE LEARNING FROM TEXT GUIDE

Having read the chapter, the students are now ready for discussion and writing. The teacher could construct this discussion around a learning-from-text guide, aimed at assessing four levels of comprehension: (a) directly stated or informational, (b) inferential, (c) generalized, and (d) evaluative. Box 7.8 presents such a learning-from-text guide based on chapter 3, *Quest for Liberty*.

BOX 7.8.   *Learning-from-Text Guide*

CHAPTER 3: "THE COLONIES FIGHT
FOR INDEPENDENCE"

Part 1: Informational Level

Instructions: Answer the following questions while you are reading chapter 3, "The Colonies Fight for Independence." The page and paragraph numbers will help you find the answers.

1. Name three things the colonists did to show they were capable of governing themselves. (page 77)

   a. (page 77, paragraph 3) _____
   _____
   _____

   b. (page 77, paragraph 4) _____
   _____
   _____

   c. (page 77, paragraph 5) _____
   _____
   _____

2. What did England do to regain control? (page 79, paragraph 2)
   _____
   _____

3. In what ways did the colonists protest? (pages 79–81 or chart on top of page 79)
   a. England did: _____
      The Colonists did:_____
   b. England did: _____
      The Colonists did:_____
   c. England did: _____
      The Colonists did:_____

4. What act by parliament was "the last straw," as far as the colonists were concerned? (page 82, paragraph 3)
   _____
   _____

5. What are the three main divisions of *The Declaration of Independence*? (page 84, paragraph 6–page 85, paragraph 1)
   _____
   _____

6. What battle gives you the clearest picture of what it was like to fight in the Revolutionary War? (page 85, paragraph 2)
   _____
   _____

7. Name three things the Americans did to win the war. (pages 94–101)

a. (94) _____

_____

b. (97) _____

_____

c. (99) _____

_____

Part 2: Inferential Level

Instructions: Match *the historic fact,* on the left, with the *conclusion you could draw,* on the right.

_____ 1. Fifty to seventy-five percent of white colonial males could vote for their own representatives.

_____ 2. New England and the Middle colonies start to manufacture their own products.

_____ 3. British troops fight French and Indians on American soil.

_____ 4. The British tax tea.

_____ 5. American soldiers use guerrilla warfare.

A. England could easily be frightened by competition.

B. England is in sore need for money.

C. People do what is natural to them.

D. Democracy was flourishing before the Revolutionary War.

E. The British want to "control the action."

Part 3: Generalized and Evaluative Level

Instructions: Reread "Bringing issues up to the present" (page 104 of the text) and answer the following questions. Then, in small groups, compare your answers and try to resolve your disagreements.

1. Do you feel that America feels the same today as it did in 1776 about these issues:
   a. colonialism
   b. mercantilism
   c. slavery
   d. taxation
   e. freedom

2. If there have been changes in attitude since 1776, have these changes been good or bad? Give reasons for your opinions.

3. Is it good or bad that today conflicts exist between states, specifically, the North and the South? In answering this question, cite current events that will support your beliefs.

APPLY KNOWLEDGE TO PROBLEM
SITUATIONS

Having discussed and written about the chapter, the students can extend their learning to another situation. Box 7.9 contains a list of problems that junior high school students might enjoy working on after they have read chapter 3, "The Colonies Fight for Independence."

BOX 7.9. Problems

CHAPTER 3: "THE COLONIES FIGHT
FOR INDEPENDENCE"

Instructions: Select one of the following problems to write up. Use classroom sources and/or go to the library.

1. You are a movie director who is working on a high-budget movie about the Revolutionary War. For your producer, the man who gives you the money, prepare a list of what you'll need for one scene: *The Battle of Bunker Hill.* What would you need in the way of (1) scenery, (2) equipment and props, (3) actors, (4) animals, (5) cameramen to shoot from different angles? Since your producer will prepare a budget, be specific as to how many of each item you want.
2. Assume you are a British subject visiting the colonies. One night you take a stroll down to the harbor and find that you are an eyewitness to the Boston Tea Party. Write home to a friend, describing in detail what you saw.
3. Assume you are a British General in the midst of the Revolutionary War. Draw a battle map of Boston, showing how you would surround the city and force the colonists to surrender.
4. Pretend you are a judge. Get one person to be trial lawyer for the crown and another to be trial lawyer for the colonies. What would the judge want to know about the following:
   a. Who started the war?
   b. What were the claims on each side?
   c. Were the claims justified?
   d. What other questions would be asked?
   Have the trial lawyers argue the merits of the case. Let the class be the jury.

ADAPTATION OF TEACHING METHODS TO DIFFERENT TYPES OF TEXT

Woodshop Text

You have learned in detail how to teach a social studies chapter. This section will describe, in much less detail, how to help woodshop students understand the text *Wood Materials and Processes.*[2] Boxes 7.10–15 show you a teacher task analysis, sample reading guides, and learning-from-text guides.

---

[2]John L. Feirer, *Wood Materials and Processes* (Peoria, IL: Charles A. Bennet, 1975).

Our purpose in showing you how to teach from the social studies and the woodshop text is to demonstrate that (a) the reading and learning-from-text guides can be applied to all content areas and that (b) the specific characteristics of each content area result in variations in the guides. For example, social studies has verbal and pictorial materials (charts, maps, and graphs), whereas woodworking has verbal and pictorial materials (blueprints), *plus* measurement, computational, and motor activities. These additional activities in woodshop overlap with mathematical and science content where measurement and computation are the main activities. Hence, woodshop students require separate sections on measurement and computation in their reading and learning-from-text guides. (See chapters 15 and 16 for science and math guides.)

BOX 7.10. Teacher Task Analysis

SECTION IV
"Making Pieces of Curved or Irregular Designs," pp. 164–180

Unit	Content	Process

18
 	
 D R A W
	Identification and description of tools
	   a divider
	   a pencil compass
	   trammel points
	 Procedures for laying out and transferring designs
	   circles
	   rounded corners
	   octagons
	   hexagons
	   ellipse
	 Procedures for enlarging designs
		Relating verbal description to diagram and picture
		
		 Reading definitions
		
		 Following directions
		   a. verbally
		   b. from diagrams and pictures

19
 	
 C U T
	Identification and description of tools
	   coping saw
	   saw bracket
	   vise
	   compass saw
	 Procedures for cutting curves
	   adjusting blades
	   turning handles
		ditto

20
 	
 S M O O T H
	Identification and description of tools
	   spokeshave
	   drawknife
	   file
	   rasp
	   surform tool
	   solid-router
	     drills
	 Procedures for forming and smoothing curves
		ditto

BOX 7.11. Overview Guides

SECTION IV

"Making Pieces of Curved or Irregular Designs," pp. 164–180

When you finish reading Section IV, you should know how to do the following things:

Draw Designs *(Unit 18, pp. 165–170)*	*Cut Designs (Unit 19,* *pp. 170–174)*	*Smooth Designs* *(Unit 20, pp. 175–180)*

You will learn how to put curves and irregular designs on wood before you cut it.
I. Tools you will need
  a. a divider
  b. a pencil compass
  c. trammel points
II. Designs you can make with these tools
  a. circles
  b. rounded corners
  c. an octagon
  d. a hexagon
  e. an ellipse
III. Enlargements of irregular designs that you can make
	You will learn how to cut curved patterns.
	I. Tools you will need
	  a. a coping saw
	  b. a compass saw
	II. Methods of cutting with these tools
	  a. with the work supported on a saw bracket
	  b. with the work held in a vise
	  c. proper turning of the handle by sawing
		You will learn how to form and smooth the curves you have cut.
		I. Tools you will need
		  a. spokeshave
		  b. drawknife
		  c. file and rasp
		  d. surform tool
		  e. solid-router drills
		II. Things you can do
		  a. cut concave and convex edges
		  b. Remove large amounts of stock quickly
		  c. scrape wood
		  d. smooth and form wood

1 **DRAW** ⟶	**2** **CUT** ⟶	**3** **SMOOTH**

BOX 7.12. Vocabulary Guide

SECTION IV

"Making Pieces of Curved
or Irregular Designs," pp. 164–180

Instructions: Below are some of the hard words you will find in Unit 20. Look over
the definitions and the sentences from the textbook that contain them.

Word	Page	Definition	Sentence from Text
convex	175	a curve that bends outward	A spokeshave is used to plane *convex* (dome-shaped) and *concave* (cup-shaped) edges.
concave	175	a curve that bends inward	
exposed	176	open, in plain sight, not hidden	The long, *exposed* blade can be dangerous.
bevel	176	slant	Hold the tool in both hands, with the blade firmly against the wood and the *bevel* side down.

Pages referred to are from *Wood Materials and Processes.*

BOX 7.13. Processes-of-Reading Guide
FOLLOWING PRINTED INSTRUCTIONS

Activity 1. Look at each one of the houses below. What is wrong with each house?

  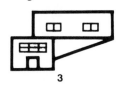

1   2   3

Activity 2. Each of those houses was built poorly because instructions were not
followed. What sorts of instructions were not followed in each case?

Case 1: _____

_____

Case 2: _____

_____

Case 3: _____

_____

Activity 3. Test your own ability at following written instructions by drawing pictures as you are directed to do.

1. Draw six parallel lines.

2. Draw circle with a one-inch diameter.

3. Draw a circle with a one-inch radius.

4. Draw a three-inch line. Divide it into three equal parts. Starting on your left, erase the first part. Darken the second part. Draw an X through the third part.

Activity 4. Read these instructions before you begin. Write your name in the top right hand corner of the paper. Draw a line connecting "Activity 4" with your name. On this line list the names of three tools you have used in woodshop this past week. After you write your name, don't do anything else.

BOX 7.14. Learning-from-Text Guide

SECTION IV: UNIT 18

Instructions: Read each of the following statements. If the statement is true put an *X* in the space provided.

Informational Comprehension

_____ 1. A divider, like sandpaper, is useful for smoothing out a piece of wood you have cut.
_____ 2. Trammel points come in handy when you are drawing circles.
_____ 3. When laying out a rounded corner, a try square and a divider are more useful than trammel points and a ruler.
_____ 4. Unlike an ellipse, you can draw a hexagon without a pencil compass or divider.

Inferential Comprehension

_____ 1. When drawing a circle, if your lines don't meet the problem might be with the thumbscrew.
_____ 2. John and Mark are both making table tops — one a hexagon, one an octagon. If they start drawing plans at the same time, Mark will be finished before John.

Generalized Comprehension

____ 1. George has found some plans in a magazine for building an American Eagle wall plaque. However, the plans are ½₆ the size of the actual plaque when built. The drawing is 8″ by 8″. George cannot hang his finished eagle over the fireplace.

Evaluative Level

____ 1. The chapter was well written and the pictures and diagrams were clear to me.

____ 2. The information in this chapter got me more interested in woodworking than I was before.

BOX 7.15.   *Learning-from-Text Guide*

SECTION IV: UNIT 19

Questions for Informational (or Directly Stated) Comprehension

1. What does the frame of a coping saw look like? (page 170, column 1, paragraph 4)
2. If you are going to cut a hole in the middle of a piece of wood, what would you need to do to your coping saw? (page 171, column 1, paragraph 1)
3. If cutting with the coping saw gets hard, what can you put on the blade to help? (page 171, cclumn 2, paragraph 1)
4. Describe the shape of the compass saw. (page 173, column 1, paragraph 2)
5. How do you handle the compass saw in such a way so as to allow you to cut curves? (page 173, column 1, paragraph 4)

Questions for Inferential Comprehension

1. Contrast the designs of the coping and the compass saw. What sorts of tasks would be better done with a coping saw rather than a compass saw?
2. Why is the direction of the saw's teeth, with respect to the handle, important when using a saw bracket?

Question for Generalized Comprehension

Explain how you would go about cutting the letters of your first name.

Questions for Evaluative Comprehension

1. What items in this unit were particularly well presented?
2. What items were not clearly presented? How might the unit have been better presented?

Pages referred to are from *Wood Materials and Processes*.

APPLICATIONS OF THE SAME PRINCIPLES
TO TEXTS AT EACH SCHOOL LEVEL

In the following section, you will see guides and related materials teachers can develop for helping students to learn from biology and American government. Since the first section of this text dealt with learning from a junior high school American history text, we will contrast this with a series of materials used in teaching high school students to learn from American history text. Although these materials were developed for actual textbooks, the texts themselves may not be in current edition or be available within the school districts with which you are currently associated. However, regardless of specific text, the principles of preparing the materials are constant and the examples used should be considered only as examples.

Biology

High school biology presents students with many problems in learning from text. In Box 7.16 you will see a strategy for helping the students become familiar with the various resources in their textbook. The guide is constructed to take the students quickly through the book's preface, table of contents, art work, appendix, glossary, and index. The activities that the students are requested to perform are all literal level, thus easily corrected. Also, notice that the activities do not require prior knowledge of biology. Some teachers use this kind of guide at the beginning of the school year when they are dispensing new biology texts to students. Box 7.17 contains a learning-from-text guide for a biology chapter dealing with viruses. As indicated on the guide, 10 items are at the literal level, 5 at the interpretative level, and 2 at the generalized/applied level.

BOX 7.16. Overview Guide for a Biology Text

Otto and Towle. *Modern Biology.*
  New York: Holt, Rinehart and Winston, 1977

Getting to Know the Biology Textbook

Instructions: Before you begin reading your biology textbook, please answer the following text questions. They will help you learn more about your book and how to use it.

  1. *Preface,* pp. v–vi. Who is Truman J. Moon and why are the authors of your textbook grateful to him?

   Truman J. Moon——————————————————————————.
   The authors are grateful to him because——————————————————.

2. *Table of Contents*, pp. vii–ix. What units are the following topics to be found in?

	Topic	Unit
EXAMPLE	viruses	3
	habitat	_____
	tobacco	_____
	insects	_____
	birds	_____
	*backboned animals	_____
	*glossary	_____

3. *Art Work*, pp. 2–12. Which of the following kinds of art work does not appear in chapter 1?

    1. color photographs
    2. diagrams in black and white and one other color
    3. black and white photographs
    4. drawings
    5. cartoons

4. On pages 98 and 107, the same two colors are used. What topic does this chapter deal with that causes the publishers to use these two colors?_____

5. On page 217, what disease is pictured and described?_____

6. On page 233, there are two pictures. Under these two pictures are the numbers 19-17. The 19 refers to_____. The 17 refers to_____.

7. *Appendix*, pp. 713–714. How many quarts are in three liters?_____.

8. *Appendix*, pp. 715–721. On what pages would you find these terms:

Term	Page
phylum molluska	_____
order carnivora	_____
class arachnida	_____

9. *Glossary*, pp. 723–41. What is dura mater?_____

10. *Index*, pp. 743–757. Which word is introduced first in the textbook: apoda, fatty acid, ecology, or theory?

BOX 7.17. Learning-from-Text Guide for a Biology Text Chapter Otto and Towle. *Modern Biology.*

Chapter 15: *The Viruses*
Learning from Text Guide

Instructions: Put an X before each of the following statements that is true.

_____ 1. Scientists have known about viruses for a long time.
_____ 2. Viruses have qualities of both living and non-living things.

_____ 3. Viruses are single-celled organisms.

_____ 4. Viruses were able to be studied with the invention of the light microscope.

_____ 5. Cores of viruses tend to be filled with an acid substance.

_____ 6. Viruses depend upon attaching themselves to living cells.

_____ 7. Any cell can be invaded by a virus.

_____ 8. A bacteriophage is a bacterium that eats viruses.

_____ 9. A temperate phage does no immediate damage, so it causes scientists no concern.

_____10. Viruses can cause cancer.

_____11. Scientists have had for the last 50 years the technology to locate and describe viruses; they lacked only the knowledge to do it.

_____12. It is inaccurate to describe a virus as a chemical.

_____13. The debate about whether viruses are living or non-living things can be settled through chemical analysis.

_____14. Viruses are parasites.

_____15. If there were such a word as a brainphage, it would be defined as a virus that could eat brain tissue.

_____16. A bacteriophage is more destructive to human beings than is a prophage.

_____17. Our ignorance about the nature of viruses makes them man's most deadly enemy.

American Government

Like biology, American government can present students with problems in learning from text. One of the principal problems inherent in American government is the proliferation of technical terms and the complex nature in which these terms relate to one another. What follows are three guides that are designed to help students learn more effectively from one particular government text. In Box 7.18 is a graphic organizer for vocabulary used in the first chapter of an American government textbook. The terms are arranged hierarchically and the graphic representation shows the coordinate, subordinate, and superordinate relationships that exist among the chapter's technical terms. In Box 7.19 is a process-of-reading guide that directs the students through a series of activities that is aimed at teaching the students how to read a bar graph. The items, carefully sequenced, are written in the form of questions and cloze patterns that direct the students, step by step, to an understanding of how to read a particular bar graph. Box 7.20 is a learning-from-text guide that attempts to teach the students the same concepts as the processes-of-reading guide, except that it is phrased as statements, not questions and clozes. Six items are at the literal level, three at the interpretive level, and two at the generalized/applied level.

BOX 7.18. Overview Guide for an American Government Text Chapter

Turner et al. *American Government: Principles and Practices.*
Columbus: Merrill, 1983.

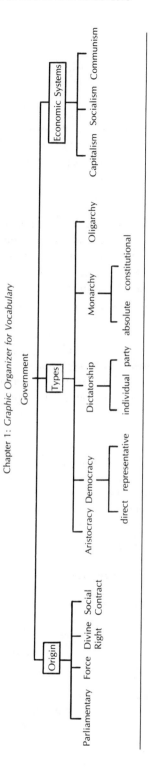

Chapter 1: *Graphic Organizer for Vocabulary*

BOX 7.19. Processes-of-Reading Guide for an American Government Text Chapter

Turner et al. *American Government*

Chapter 21: Government and the Economy
How to Read a Graph

Instructions: Turn to page 507 in your textbook. Look at the graph that is printed on that page. Now answer the following questions on that graph.

1. A bar graph usually gives you two kinds of information. One kind of information goes on a line from left to right. Look at the line right above the colored boxes at the bottom of the graph.

    What kind of information does that line give you?_____

    A second kind of information is located on a line or column that goes from top to bottom. Look at the column of numbers at the left-hand side of the bar graph.

    What kind of information does the left-hand column give you?_____

2. Notice that the bars have three colors.

    A *blue* bar will tell you how much money was _____ by the government in a particular year.

    A *yellow* bar will tell you how much money was _____ by the government that particular year.

    A *red* bar tells you how much money the government _____ that particular year.

3. To get the amount of money shown on any red bar you subtract the money in the _____ bar from the amount of money in the _____ bar.

4. The reason the red bars appear below the blue and yellow bars is that they _____.

5. Now in your own words, describe how the federal government ended up 1.6 million "in the hole" in 1965.

BOX 7.20. Learning-from-Text Guide for an American Government Chapter Turner et al. *American Government*

Learning from Text: The Bar Graph

Instructions: Look at the bar graph on page 507 of your textbook. Put an X by the following statements that are true.

1. If you read the graph from left to right, you will find out what happened between 1940 and 1980 with respect to how much money the federal government lost in those years.
2. The number 150 in the left-hand column really means 150 million dollars.

3. Red bars were placed below the lines because there was no room above the lines.
4. If you subtract the numbers on the yellow bars from the numbers on the blue bars you get the numbers below the red bars.
5. In 1945 the deficit was less than in 1970.
6. The greatest revenue was reported in 1980, but the greatest deficit was reported in 1945.
7. Since 1940, revenues have tended to grow larger in the same pattern as have expenditures.
8. The United States was involved in wars between 1940 and 1945, 1950 and 1955, and 1965 and 1970. It is safe to say that war tended to increase the deficits without increasing the revenues.
9. The statement that the federal government has continued since 1940 to spend more money in one year than in previous years is not backed by information on this graph.
10. The only period when this country has not undergone inflation is between 1955 and 1960.
11. Since 1940, presidents have claimed that they want to balance the federal budget. Only Nixon succeeded.

High School American History

What follows is a description of five guides to help students learn from high school American history text. Box 7.21 contains a vocabulary guide that introduces students to eight technical and difficult words from a particular chapter that are thematically related: They all concern tolerance. In this guide, each term is introduced with a colloquial definition, a page reference, and the verbatim context from the chapter. An accompanying 10-item exercise can be used to determine whether the students can use the words in the proper context. Boxes 7.22, 7.23, and 7.24 are examples of overview guides that present the basic concepts to be introduced in the chapter but arranged in a meaningful context. These overview guides can be used in a variety of ways. Presented to the students before they read, they can direct the students to read for main ideas. Presented while the students are reading, they can form checklists to ensure that the students are covering all of the important information while they are reading. Presented after the students read, the guides can be useful departures for class discussions, study guides for tests, and the bases for short essays or summaries.

BOX 7.21. Vocabulary Guide for a High School American History Text Chapter

Todd and Curti. *Rise of the American Nation.*

Chapter 5: *Vocabulary Guide*

Instructions: Here are some hard words from the chapter you are about to read. Read the definitions and notice which pages in your textbook the words appear on. Notice also the sentence from the textbook that contains the word.

WORD	MEANING	PAGE	SENTENCE FROM TEXT
tolerance	acceptance of an idea or an opinion different from your own	71	"The growth of religious *tolerance* in colonial America."
intolerance	prejudice; rejection of an idea or opinion different from your own	71	"Roger Williams, as you have read, was one colonist who dared to fight against *intolerance*."
tolerate	accept another person's point of view or way of life	*	*Gradually, different groups began to *tolerate* one another's differences.
toleration	the act of accepting another person's point of view or way of life	72	"In both Maryland and Pennsylvania the principle of religious *tolerance* became part of the basic law."
tolerant	unprejudiced; fair-minded	72	". . . all of the colonies eventually grew more *tolerant* in matters of religion."
persecuted	punished because of one's ideas or way of life	71	"Even within the colonies the various religious groups often *persecuted* one another."
exiled	driven out of a place because of one's ideas or way of life	71	"Once *exiled*, they might be put to death if they returned."
discrimination	unfairness of treatment as a result of being different	73	"Angered by this *discrimination* . . . "

*This form not used in the textbook

Vocabulary Guide

Instructions: Now that you have been introduced to the vocabulary for Chapter 5, see if you can use the words in sentences.

1. The Puritans showed their_____when they_____ a certain family from their town because they were Quakers.

2. I try to_____my brother's stereo music, but it's so loud I think my ears will break.

3. The Act of_____set down certain guaranteed freedoms for colonists.

4. They made George sit at the back of the auditorium; he considered this pure_____.

5. In colonial days there was a kind of_____against women in the sense that many of them had no role in determining their own lives.

6. The old man was_____for his Judaic beliefs and later _____to a faraway land.

7. I'm not so_____that I will allow you to stick tar in your sister's hair.

8. _____toward minority groups is less frequent now than it was 30 years ago.

9. His_____of my cracked voice as I gave my speech was a kind and thoughtful act, even for a speech teacher.

10. The_____against women in sports can still be found in many areas.

BOX 7.22. *Overview Guide for a High School American History Text Chapter*

Todd and Curti. *Rise of the American Nation*.
  New York: Harcourt, 1977

Chapter 5, Democratic Ideas in Colonial America

	RELIGION	CIVIL RIGHTS EDUCATION	SELF-GOVERNMENT
PEOPLE	Roger Williams Lord Baltimore Anthony Benezet	Phyllis Wheatly John Peter Zenger	Governor Berkeley Nathaniel Bacon
TERMS	Catholic Protestant Anglican Separatist Puritans Separation of Church and State	public school tuition elementary school navigation accounting commercial law primer	colony royal colony proprietary colonies self-governing colonies constitution assembly qualifications property qualification religious qualifications
EVENTS	Rhode Island Charter (1663) The Maryland Toleration Act (1649) Pennsylvania Charter of Privileges (1701)	Massachusetts Public School Law (1647)	Fundamental Orders of Connecticut (1639) Bacon's Rebellion

BOX 7.23. Overview Guide for a High School American History Chapter

Todd and Curti. *Rise of the American Nation.*

Chapter 5
Religion: Old World to New World
Structured Overview

ENGLAND   NEW ENGLAND COLONIES

                                                             Main
                                                             New Hampshire
                                                             Massachusetts
                                                             Rhode Island
HOLLAND   Connecticut

FRANCE   MIDDLE COLONIES

                                                             New Jersey
                                                             New York
                                                             Delaware
SPAIN   Pennsylvania
                                                             Maryland

PORTUGAL   SOUTHERN COLONIES

Suggested Questions: Virginia
                                                             North Carolina
1. Where did the Roman Catholic Church tend to   South Carolina
   have its strongest influence?   Georgia
                                                             Spanish Florida
2. What country provided the greatest variety of
   religions for the New World?

3. What colony provides the best setting for religious intolerance?

BOX 7.24. Overview Guide for a High School American History Chapter

Todd and Curti. *Rise of the American Nation.*

Chapter 5
Types of English Colonies
Structured Overview

	ROYAL	PROPRIETARY	SELF-GOVERNING
MEMBERSHIP	Maine Massachusetts New Hampshire New York New Jersey	Virginia N. Carolina S. Carolina	Maryland Pennsylvania Delaware	Rhode Island Connecticut
AUTHORITY	King		Proprietor appointed by King, usually living in England	People
GOVERNOR	Appointed by King	Appointed by proprietor	Elected by the voters
UPPER HOUSE	Appointed by King. Councilors worked closely with governor; also served as high court	Appointed by proprietor. Councilors (Maryland only)	Elected by the voters
LOWER HOUSE	Elected by qualified	Elected by voters Pennsylvania had only one house—the Assembly	Elected by the voters

BOX 7.25. Learning from Text Guide from a High School American History Text Chapter

Todd and Curti. *Rise of the American Nation.*

Chapter 5. *Learning from Text Guide*

Instructions: Put an X by each of the following statements that are true.

_____ 1. The first settlers to the New World brought their religions with them. (p. 71)

_____ 2. The religious groups in the colonies tended to get along with one another.

_____ 3. The first colony to grant religious freedom was Rhode Island.

_____ 4. The Toleration Act of 1649 granted total religious freedom to individuals living in Maryland.

_____ 5. Colonists did not encourage the education of Black people, slaves or free, because they feared it would hurt the economy.

_____ 6. Some colonists were exiled for their beliefs but they were never put to death.

_____ 7. The Rhode Island Charter of 1663 granted political but not religious freedom.

_____ 8. Quakers were more tolerant of Blacks than were other religious groups.

_____ 9. Education in the New England Colonies before 1647 was harder to get than was education in Virginia before 1647.

_____10. The Massachusetts Public School Law of 1647 was the start of public schools in this country.

_____11. New York was a proprietary colony, but Virginia was not.

_____12. Bacon's rebellion was the first successful revolt in the colonies.

_____13. The Pennsylvania Charter granted more religious freedom than did the Maryland Toleration Act.

_____14. Philadelphia was a place where Blacks could be educated and practice religion without intolerance.

_____15. Prior to 1647, education had to do more with economics than with geography.

_____16. Women's literacy was higher than men's because they had a bit more leisure time to read and study.

_____17. Considering all the colonies as a group, the process of getting a lower house legislature was more democratic than the process of getting an upper house legislature.

_____18. If you wanted to practice Judaism in colonial times, you would probably try to settle in Connecticut.

_____19. If you were young and Black and wanted to learn to read, you probably would have had an easier time in Philadelphia than you would in New York.

_____20. If you were a radical and were looking for injustice so that you could start a rebellion, you would probably settle in Maryland rather than Massachusetts.

Thus they are not only an aid to reading but also to writing. Finally, Box 7.25 contains a learning-from-text guide of 20 items, 12 on the literal level, 5 on the interpretive level, and 3 on the applied level.

SUMMARY

You have studied many techniques for teaching a chapter. We provided you with examples from social studies, industrial education, and science. Using a chapter in social studies, we showed you how to construct such preteaching devices as (a) an entry level test, (b) an overview guide, (c) behavioral objectives, and (d) a teacher's task analysis. These techniques would help prepare your students for reading. Techniques to help your students while they are in the process of reading and learning from text are (a) a vocabulary guide, (b) a processes-of-reading guide, (c) a gloss, and (d) a learning-from-text guide. After students have read, you can present them with problems related to the chapter. We also showed you a variety of techniques that could be used in teaching a chapter from a woodshop text, a biology text, an American government text, and a high school American history text.

As you can see, teaching students to read and learn from a textbook chapter requires a large amount of your time and effort. Since you do not have the time to use *all* the strategies on *all* the chapters you teach, select a few, try them, reuse them, select others. Over a few years, you will have a fine collection of instructional materials. You will also have become experienced in the use of these strategies.

Principles and Procedures
for Teaching a Chapter

BEFORE YOU TEACH

1. Know what you want to teach. Construct behavioral objectives. Give the students duplicated copies of the objectives so they can understand what you are planning to teach them. What follows is only one of many suggested procedures for writing behavioral objectives.

Procedure for Formulating Objectives

a. A behavioral objective must have a clear statement of what the student is expected to know: e.g., "The student will demonstrate his understanding of the causes and effects of the Revolutionary War. . . ."

b. A behavioral objective must have a clear description of how the student will demonstrate having gained this knowledge: e.g., ". . . by writing an essay that includes at least two causes and two effects . . ."

c. A behavioral objective must state the conditions under which the student will demonstrate his knowledge: ". . . as part of a closed book examination of one-hour duration."

2. Know what you want to teach. Do a *task analysis* of the chapter to clarify its facts, concepts, and generalizations.

Procedure for a Task Analysis

    a. Review the behavioral objectives.

    b. For each behavioral objective, list the content from the chapter the students will have to know in order to achieve the objective. The content in the chapter could be organized according to (a) technical vocabulary, (b) main ideas, and (c) facts supporting the main ideas.

    c. For each behavioral objective, list the reading processes the students will have to use in order to understand the required content.

3. Use an *entry level test* to assess students' background knowledge of the chapter. The test should contain previously learned information that will be used in the new material.

Procedure for Constructing Entry Level Test

    a. Examine the *task analysis* for the chapter you are about to teach. Determine knowledge from previous chapters that will need to be reviewed before the students learn from the new chapter.

    b. Organize this prerequisite knowledge into four categories: vocabulary, factual statements, inferences, and generalizations.

    c. Prepare a series of test items on each of these four categories of knowledge.

    d. Reteach items missed by students on the *entry level test.*

WHILE YOU TEACH

1. Do whatever is necessary to clarify the text. Use *text explication strategies* such as *overview guides.*

Procedure for Making a Graphic Organizer

    a. Examine the way in which the chapter is organized, paying particular attention to the headings.

    b. Using the headings, prepare either an outline of the chapter or a graphic organizer for the chapter.

    c. Duplicate the overview guide for discussion with your students.

2. Develop student resources for comprehending a text, such as *reading guides,* (vocabulary and processing guides). Use *learning from text guides* to make students aware of the facts (literal, explicit information), inferences and interpretations (implicit information), and generalizations made by the text emanating from students' background knowledge (schemata) that can subsume information in the text. For PROCEDURES for constructing vocabulary guides and learning from text guides, see Chap. 6.

Procedure for Constructing Processes of Reading Guides

  a. Examine the *task analysis* you prepared for the chapter. Select one reading process listed in the task analysis. You will develop a processes of reading guide for this reading process.

  b. Decide what you want the students to know how to do when they finish the guide: e.g., understand cause and effect relationships in a social studies chapter, locate main ideas in a science chapter, make inferences about character and mood from a short story.

  c. In a series of sequential exercises, show the students how to develop the reading process, step by step. You can find examples of processes of reading guides in Chaps. 13 and 14.

 3. Conduct a discussion with the class to lead them to comprehend the facts, concepts, and generalizations. Use QUEST method to achieve this purpose.

Suggested Procedure for Conducting Quest (See explanations for Quest in chaps, 8 and 15)

  a. Begin the discussion bv soliciting factual information from the students with such questions as, ''What was this chapter about?'' (focus) and ''What else was in this chapter?'' (extension).

  b. Once the factual information has been provided, *lift* the level of discussion by having the students make inferences and interpretations. Use such questions as, ''What is the relationship between this idea and that idea?'' or ''What is the importance of this idea?''

  c. After students have made a number of inferences *lift* the level of discussion again by having the student make *generalizations* about what they have read. Use such questions as, ''What does the author want you to learn about how society operates?'' or ''Why is this chapter in the book?''

 4. Develop the students' strategies for interacting with the text. Use DAR method for teaching students to make predictions, confirm their predictions with evidence, and support their confirmations. (See Chap. 6 for the specific steps in using DAR.) Teach students to be active comprehenders by arousing their own curiosity and generating questions that they will strive to answer as they read the text. Have the students use SQ3R to get an overview survey (S), generate questions (Q), read the text to find answers to their questions (R), discuss their findings or otherwise recite (R) and reconstruct the text (R) by summarizing it or use the text information in a short essay or other project.

 5. Teach students to be independent in use of the strategies by *phasing out*

the teacher and *phasing in* the student. Have the students use the strategies until they internalize the processes, using them automatically. *Cross-ability teaching* may facilitate this phase-in/phase-out procedure.

AFTER YOU TEACH

After you teach the chapter have the students apply what they have learned in discussions (see chap. 8), writing activities (see chap. 9), and other projects (see chap. 11).

ACTIVITIES

1. Select a section of text from your own content area and prepare instructional materials for three parts of a lesson: one to be used by students before reading, one to be used while they are reading, one to be used after they have finished reading. If you have two sections of students taking the same course, use all three sets of instructional materials with one group but use none with the other. Simply assign the second group the chapter to read. Give the two groups a comprehension test based on the chapter. Is there a significant difference in the scores of the two groups?
2. Teach one of the strategies in this chapter, such as the use of a learning-from-text guide, to a group made up of your classmates (preservice teachers). Select content for your guide from any textbook. Tape the lesson for analysis and evaluation of your teaching.

8 Letting the Students Do the Talking

CHAPTER OVERVIEW

As you recall from reading the last two chapters, teaching students to learn from textbooks involves planning discussion activities so that you can see what they know. Unfortunately, not all students come to class willing and/or able to participate in classroom discussions. This chapter focuses on three concepts: (a) teacher and student behaviors and attitudes that ensure a successful classroom discussion, (b) the types of discussion that stimulate student interaction, and (c) procedures for grouping students for discussion and related work.

GRAPHIC ORGANIZER

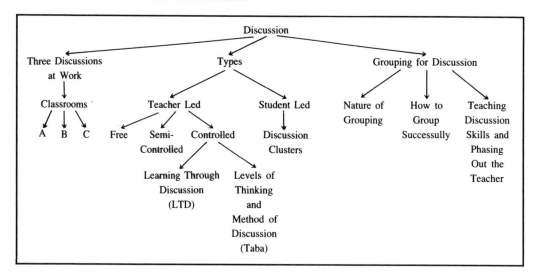

PREPOSED QUESTIONS

1. What are the crucial characteristics of a good discussion?
2. At what point should the teacher turn the responsibility of leading discussion over to the students?
3. What are the characteristics of a good discussion leader? How can a teacher model these effectively?
4. What are the various forms of discussion that would work effectively for you in your own classroom?

DISCUSSION TO EVALUATE READING AND
LEARNING FROM TEXT

To evaluate a student's ability at swimming, a coach usually has the student swim. To evaluate a student's ability at painting, a teacher has the student paint. The same is true of music, writing, and speaking. It is ironic that teachers usually evaluate a student's ability at reading and learning from text by asking the student to speak or write. Perhaps the most common classroom devices used to evaluate student ability at reading and learning from text are (a) classroom discussions and (b) written assignments. This chapter focuses on discussion; the next chapter, on writing.

THREE "DISCUSSIONS" AT WORK

Suppose that you, the reader, could be transported immediately to Monroe High where, at this moment, three science teachers are carrying on "discussions" with their students. Standing outside their respective rooms, you might hear the conversations that follow.

Classroom A

Mr. Phelps: All right, class, as you know, you were asked to read chapter 2 last night. As you recall, the chapter dealt with freshwater communities. Certain plants and animals can get along in some types of freshwater environments and some cannot. For instance—I hope you plan to take notes on this, especially in light of the test we're having next Friday—in sluggish water, such as that which you find in ponds, you will find algae, perhaps even fungi, that couldn't survive in the more rapid streams of the mountains. Ducks live beautifully on ponds, but I doubt that you'd find them paddling around the treacherous rapids of the Merced River, for example. Examine the long sleek appearance of the trout, and I dare any of you to find a better environment for the trout other than the swiftly running stream. How long do you think a goldfish could survive in a tank of chemically softened water? Not very long I tell you. It's nature's way to have the environment interact with the life forms that exist in it. Are there any questions you have on your discussion? Yes, Jim?

Jim: What does the word *environment* mean?

Mr. Phelps: Look it up in the dictionary! Any other questions for discussion? Good. Now for tonight, read the next chapter and we'll discuss it tomorrow.

Classroom B

Ms. Carley: Class, last night for homework you read chapter 2. Would you open your books to page 41? And let's talk about the chapter. First of all, what is an alga? (*No response.*) You might be familiar with it by its plural form, *algae.* Yes, Eric.

Eric: Isn't it a plant that grows in the water?

Ms. Carley: Lots of plants grow in the water! Could you be more specific? Yes, Debbie.

Debbie: It's a scum?

Ms. Carley: What do you mean by *scum?*

Debbie: Slimy?

Ms. Carley: We're still not making it. Refer to the glossary at the back of your book. Would anyone care to read the definition for *alga* out loud? Yes, Abe?

Abe: "One of the group called *algae.*"

Ms. Carley: That does us a lot of good. What are algae?

Abe: Do you want me to read that definition?

Ms. Carley: Please.

Abe: "A group of water plants that produce their own food. They often take the form of scum on rocks."

Debbie: That's what I said.

Eric: Me too.

Ms. Carley: Yes, that's true, but your definition was not as precise as it might have been. Now, let's take that definition and look at the pictures on page 45. How does the definition fit the pictures? Yes, Tom?

Tom: Can I sharpen my pencil?

Classroom C

Mr. Spont: Open your books to page 43. I want you to study the picture there. Now how many of you want to go swimming in that body of water? I don't see any hands. Don't you like to swim?

Mike: I like to swim, but not in that junk!

Mr. Spont: What do you mean "junk"?

Kathy: Look at all that slimy stuff that's on the water. Look at the ducks.

Paul: What if you swallowed some of that stuff?

Mr. Spont: Where would you rather swim?

Dave: In a pool.

Kathy: A lake.

Dan: A river, the ocean. But not in that stuff. It's like a swamp.

Mr. Spont: Why do you think the ducks like it?

Kathy: They're probably used to it. They get their food from the pond.

Mr. Spont: What do they eat?

Mike: Little bugs and worms, maybe. Plants.

Mr. Spont: What do the plants eat?

Kathy: They get their food from the water.

Mr. Spont: What does this all mean?

Paul: That animals and plants depend upon each other.

Mr. Spont: Can you think of any other situations in which plants and animals depend upon each other?

WHAT IS DISCUSSION?

You can see, from the three examples above (and any experience you may have had in the classroom), discussion is not the easiest strategy to develop. If you asked all three teachers what they were doing they would probably all say they were attempting to carry on a discussion. Nevertheless, even a casual observer would note the dramatic differences in the three teaching styles.

In Classroom A, Mr. Phelps is lecturing—that is, imparting to the students information that they are to assimilate. Even though the teacher asks for questions, it soon becomes clear to the students that he would consider any contribution they might make to be at best minor.

In Classroom B, Ms. Carley is making some attempt at interaction, that is, asking questions about the text material that, it is hoped, the students can answer. However, students perceive that the teacher wants specific, almost preconceived answers, and after a minute or so, the casual observer is aware that this "discussion" will be short-lived, collapsing from lack of interest.

In Classroom C, Mr. Spont is stimulating students' response to text by posing an offbeat question or problem that the students solve by using text material. Unlike Mr. Phelps and Ms. Carley, Mr. Spont neither transmits information nor asks narrow questions, but rather encourages active responding by refusing to pass value judgments on the responses and by giving shape to students' responses in the form of new questions. Even in Classroom C, however, discussion is not functioning at the optimum level because only four students are participating. What are the other 20 or 30 students doing? Listening? Taking notes? Daydreaming? Doodling?

This chapter focuses on ways to stimulate total participation as students respond to text material. The first parts of the chapter are concerned with the nature of discussion and the relationship between discussion and critical thinking. The second part of the chapter deals with grouping strategies that can be used to help a teacher ensure better discussion.

A popular school dictionary (Thorndike & Barnhart, 1971) defines *discussion* as the process of "considering [an issue] from different points of view . . . talk." Discussion can range from perfunctory chatter about the weather to the awesome deliberations of the United Nations. Somewhere between these two extremes is classroom discussion—more formal than over-the-fence gossip, less formal than summit conferences. If one accepts that a classroom of students is a social structure, the importance of that discussion is obvious. Discussion fosters the *exchange* of information rather than the *search* for information (Charles, 1983).

TYPES OF DISCUSSION

Teacher Led

Effective classroom discussion varies with the instructional purpose. Four general types of discussion, however, make differing demands on teachers: *free discussion, semicontrolled discussion, controlled discussion* (Hill, 1969; Taba, 1965, 1967), and *discussion clusters*.

FREE DISCUSSION

Free discussion is relatively unstructured and demands a minimum of teacher control. It allows students to (a) react emotionally to a text selection, (b) speak randomly on an issue, (c) let off steam, (d) raise an issue for future consideration or (e) discuss classroom roles (Emmer, Everston, Sanford, Clements, & Worsham, 1984). Read the following excerpt from a free discussion in Ms. Jones's 10th-grade world history class.

> *Ms. Jones:* What did you learn about the ancient Egyptians last night?
> *Joe:* I didn't like them.
> *Mary:* I didn't either.
> *Ms. Jones:* Why not?
> *Joe:* They were mean—the way they made their slaves do everything.
> *Carlo:* I couldn't see why they're so important.
> *Mark:* I couldn't pronounce half the names.
> *Jo-Anne:* The book shows you how to pronounce them.
> *Chris:* The chapter was too long.
> *Gloria:* Too many facts.
> *Ms. Jones:* Didn't any of you like anything about the Egyptians?
> *Sally:* They built pyramids.
> *Sam:* What's so good about that?
> *George:* Hey, man, that's great architecture.

Notice that in the preceding discussion, the teacher's focusing question was general, open-ended, allowing students to expound freely on what they liked or didn't like about content in their world history chapter. Discussion, then, is a way of learning more about students' values and needs (Fraenkel, 1980).

Although free discussions are occasionally beneficial, even therapeutic, they should be balanced with discussions that get somewhere, that reach a conclusion, such as the semicontrolled and the controlled discussions.

SEMICONTROLLED DISCUSSION

Semicontrolled discussion occurs when students exchange and integrate information for some future instructional purpose. Generally, this strategy is used when students have different, but related, textbook assignments. In Mr. Wallace's 12th-grade literature class one group had been assigned the poetry and prose of John Milton; another group the Cavalier poets; another group selected readings from John Dryden, Izaak Walton, and Samuel Butler; and a fourth group of the plays of William Congreve. After the class had done most of the reading, Mr. Wallace brought them together to discuss social problems in 17th-century England as reflected in the literature, in preparation for a research paper assignment. An excerpt from that discussion follows:

> *Mr. Wallace:* What social problems did the seventeenth-century British writers write about, either directly or indirectly?
> *Jose:* Religion was one.
> *Margo:* There was so much religious confusion.
> *Mr. Wallace:* Who wrote about that?
> *Margo:* Milton. I don't think Roman Catholics or Anglicans cared too much for his view of God in Paradise Lost.
> *Mr. Wallace:* Before we get into that, what other problems were there?

> *George:* Milton also wrote about censorship, in *Areopagitica.*
> *Jo-Ann:* Some writers didn't deal with social problems.
> *Jim:* Izaak Walton—fishing.
> *Mary:* What about all those poets?
> *Marcella:* They *were* a social problem.
> *Jim:* Now watch that stuff, Marcy.
> *Marcella:* You know what I meant.
> *Mr. Wallace:* We'll need to list a few more. Then we'll go back one by one, starting with religion, and see what research paper topics we can come up with.

Like free discussion, semicontrolled discussion begins with a fairly broad focusing question: What social problems did the 17th-century British writers write about, either directly or indirectly? Also, students are encouraged to contribute with little control from the teacher. Note, however, that students are contributing information that will be used later in the discussion—they are not merely talking freely—and that the teacher is starting to shape the direction the discussion will follow.

CONTROLLED DISCUSSION

Controlled discussion occurs when students contribute to a carefully planned, articulated, and sequenced hierarchy of questions, generally starting with those meant to elicit lower order cognitive processes and going on to those calling for higher order reasoning. Unlike free discussion, the teacher controls the flow of discussion to ensure the maintenance of sequence (Roe, Ross, & Burns, 1984). Two models of controlled discussion provide direction for teaching discussion of text: the Learning Through Discussion (LTD) method (Hill, 1969) and Hilda Taba's levels of thinking and method of discussion (Taba, 1965, 1967).

Learning Through Discussion (LTD)

Mr. Spont teaches an ecology course. One chapter in the textbook focused on how industry has altered the physical environment. One student remarked that the book's treatment was unfair to industry. Another student claimed the book was objective. To settle the argument to the class's satisfaction, Mr. Spont decided to use the *learning through discussion method* (LTD), which is a method for effective problem solving. The topic the class discussed was whether the chapter was biased or objective. Mr. Spont led them through the nine steps of LTD in sequence. See Box 8.1. Whereas LTD may be too formal and academic for many teachers' tastes, *Taba's levels of thinking* is more acceptable.

BOX 8.1. *The Learning-Through-Discussion Method*

1. Definition of terms to be used in solving the problem the readings pose is first rendered by the participating students.

2. One or more students state in general terms the author's message.
3. The principal themes are established.
4. Time is allocated for the discussion and its sub-parts.
5. Major themes of the text are discussed.
6. Ideas are integrated.
7. Ideas are applied to another situation.
8. The author's message is evaluated.
9. The discussion process itself is evaluated.

Levels of Thinking and Method of Discussion

This method of controlled discussion, developed by Taba (1965, 1967), proceeds in nine sequential levels grouped in three major divisions, as shown in Box 8.2.

BOX 8.2. Taba's Levels of Thinking and Method of Discussion

Note: The levels are arranged from the beginning of the discussion at the bottom of the table and proceed upwards.

Level	Activity	Major Divisions
9	Verifying Predictions	III. Application
8	Explaining/Supporting Predictions	of Principles
7	Predicting Consequences	
6	Making Inferences	II. Interpreting
5	Explaining Identified Points	Inferring
4	Identifying Points	Generalizing
3	Labeling/Categorizing	I. Concept
2	Grouping	Formation
1	Enumerating and Listing	

To direct a discussion that gets somewhere, that is, leads to a conclusion, the teacher will have to pose a series of questions that will move the discussion sequentially from recall of factual information to construction of a generalization. As discussion proceeds the teacher must be in control to prevent students from moving too quickly to higher levels of thinking or staying too long at one level.

In the role of discussion leader, the teacher must be able to (a) set the focus for discussion; (b) refocus on the discussion topic as student contributions wander from the topic; (c) change the focus of discussion when such a shift is needed; (d) clarify confusing points; (e) offer support (broaden patterns of thinking); (f) initiate exploration of new dimensions; (g) recap and summarize; and (h) lift the discussion to higher levels by having students abstract from literal levels and then asking them to generalize and/or evaluate a conclusion.

In Box 8.3 are excerpts from a high school class discussion that follows the Taba method. Left marginal glosses indicate the roles the teacher is assuming in the discussion. Right marginal glosses indicate the levels of thinking being used.

BOX 8.3. *Excerpt from a Taba Levels-of-Thinking Discussion in a High School English Class*

Focus ⟶   *Mr. Inglish:* What would the plots of Shakespeare's tragedies be like if Shakespeare were writing today?

Mary: They'd be about today's problems.

George: No, they would be about the past. Shakespeare didn't write about his own times.

Mr. Inglish: Now before we go off in all directions, it's important that we think this topic through carefully. What sort of things do we know about Shakespeare? As you say these items, I will list them on the board.   I. Concept Formation

Refocus ⟶

Jo-Anne: He wrote plays and poems.

Sam: He was popular. Everyone liked his stuff.   A. Enumerating and Listing (Level 1)

Margo: He wrote quickly and much.

Sally: He said things that are still quoted today.

Mary: He wrote different types of plays: comedies, tragedies, and histories.

Refocus ⟶   *Mr. Inglish:* We may want to use that information later, but right now we want to concentrate on the tragedies.

Phil: This may also be off the track, but weren't very few of his plays original? Didn't he borrow his plots from other sources?

Support ⟶   *Mr. Inglish:* Yes he did, and we'll use that.

George: He wrote in verse.

Mary: And, as you pointed out, the same lines could mean different things to different people. For instance, with *Macbeth* some of the audience actually believed in witches, so the weird sisters were truly frightening to them. To other people in the audience, witches were only symbols.

José: You can never tell what Shakespeare's true feelings are.

David: You don't know which character to side with. There don't seem to be villains — I mean there are villains but you tend to like them.

Clarification ⟶ *Mr. Inglish:* Shakespeare makes all his characters human — is that what you're saying?

David: Yes, they are all complicated people.

Martha: I couldn't stand *Hamlet.*

Initiating a new dimension ⟶ *Mr. Inglish:* Maybe we should take a look at our list now and see where we are. Do any of the items on the board group themselves with other items?   B. Grouping (Level 2)

George: "Plays and poems" seems to go with "he wrote in verse."

Phil: "Popular" goes with "lines with different meanings for different people."

Margo: "Wrote quickly and much" goes with "borrowing plots." That's probably why he wrote so fast.

Initiating a new dimension ⟶ *Mr. Inglish:* Do these groups have titles — that is, can we give names to these groups?   C. Labeling/ Categorizing (Level 3)

Dan: We seem to have two categories up there: items about plays themselves and items that deal with the way people react to reading or seeing the plays.

Clarification and recap ⟶ *Mr. Inglish:* In other words, you are saying the items group themselves like this: (*Teacher puts the following chart on board*).

The Plays Themselves
1. He wrote plays and poems.
2. He wrote in verse.
3. He wrote quickly and much.

4. He borrowed his plots.
5. His characters were three-dimensional, complicated.

How People Reacted to Plays
1. The plays were popular.
2. They had something for everyone.
3. You can't figure out Shakespeare's attitudes and beliefs.
4. People today still quote lines from Shakespeare.

Mr. Inglish: Is there anything else that could be added in either category?

Tom: If people quote lines from Shakespeare, doesn't that mean they would have to read or see the plays more than once.

Broadening patterns of thinking ⟶

Mr. Inglish: We'll add that point. What bothers me about this list is that these statements could hold for all plays. Is there anything we could say about tragedies?

Dan: I thought we had said the villains were likeable. That would be a specific comment about tragedies.

Mr. Inglish: We could list that, I guess.

Refocus, clarification ⟶

But there were villains in comedies, too.

Mary: Evil always tends to be punished.

Margo: The leading characters usually destroy themselves through some sort of weakness in their personalities.

Phil: A lot of times they get caught up in their own plots.

José: Another thing I have noticed is that, even though they lose out in the end, you sort of feel that they could have made it if they'd tried harder.

Mr. Inglish: I think we've got enough to start with here. Let's see, we've

Recap ⟶

listed some characteristics about the plays themselves and another group of items that deal with how people have reacted to the tragedies. Now

Initiating a new
dimension ——————>

{ our next concern is to see how this information can help us see what Shakespeare's tragedies would be like today. Let's start with the category of facts under people's reactions. Were the people in Shakespeare's time different in tastes than the people today?

II. Interpreting, inferring, and generalizing

José: It depended on the social class you were from, but generally, as far as our book said, the chief competition for the theater was bear-baiting. That's bloody. So the people wanted something sensational, exciting.

Identifying point #1

Mr. Inglish: Is that different from people today?

Mary: No, look at the attendance at football games, basketball games, boxing matches. People like the sight of blood.

Explaining point #1

José: Yes, but are Shakespeare's tragedies as bloody as a boxing match?

Mary: Bloodier. The blood's real, not make-believe.

Clarification ——————>

Mr. Inglish: What you seem to be saying, is that Elizabethan audiences liked real blood and make-believe blood about the same, but that you're not sure about modern audiences.

David: Modern audiences like make-believe blood more. More people watch crime shows on television than go to boxing matches — or even better, more people watch sporting events on TV than in person.

Refocus ——————>

Mr. Inglish: Hold the discussion of TV for later. So we've identified violence as one common characteristic of today's and Elizabethan audi-

Broadening
patterns of
thinking ——————>

{ ence. What other common characteristics are there? (*Waits, but there are no other contributions.*) Well, are there points of contrast?

Jack: Behavior at plays was different then than it is today. People sat all over the place, ate food, even yelled

Identifying point #2

back to the players. It was more like being at a sporting event. Theaters today are more stuffy and who can afford them. My Dad paid twenty-five dollars for two tickets to a play.

<u>Explaining point</u> #2

Clarification ⟶ *Mr. Inglish:* What you seem to be saying is that the theater has become more middle-class and upper-middle-class.

Margo: People today like television and movies more. That's where the entertainment is focused. TV and movies have something for everyone; theater doesn't.

José: Just as we said people saw Shakespeare plays over and over, today we see movies over and over. My aunt claims she saw *Gone With the Wind* twelve times.

Mary: And everyone knows lines from *Casablanca.*

George: In fact, I think if Shakespeare were living today, he'd be writing not for the theater, but for television or the movies.

<u>Inference drawn from discussing points #1 and #2</u>

Initiating a new ⟶ dimension *Mr. Inglish:* How do the rest of you react to that? *(General agreement.)* All right, let's say that Shakespeare would be a television or movie writer. Would he be able to write tragedies that have the characteristics we've talked about?

Margo: I don't think people would dig verse, even if it were in modern language.

<u>Identifying point</u> #3

John: There have been some modern plays in verse, like some of Maxwell Anderson's.

<u>Explaining point</u> #3

Clarification ⟶ *Mr. Inglish:* But, remember, John, we're talking about movies and television.

John: I saw the movie *Winterset,* but I can't remember if that was in verse.

David: I saw something on television several years ago — a story about men in space, and it was in blank verse.

Clarification ⟶ *Mr. Inglish:* But was it popularly received?

Margo: How many in here heard of it? (*No hands.*)

Mr. Inglish: It seems, then, that Shakespeare's tragedies could not be in verse, if he were to write for movies and television and be popular.

Recap ———→   Inference drawn from point #3

John: Television writers write a lot — and fast too. So do movie writers. Shakespeare would fit in well here.

Identifying/explaining point #4

Mr. Inglish: No disagreement here, John. What about borrowing plots? Would that go on television?

Support ———→
Broadening
patterns of
thinking

Identifying point #5

Jim: There are only so many plot lines. Practically everything you see on television is a rehash of something else.

Explaining point #5

Mr. Inglish: That may be true, but Shakespeare's borrowings were more than a rehash. He got the ideas from other literary works or historical sources and then modeled successful literary works from them.

Clarification ———→

Now the question is what comparable sources would be available to today's Shakespeare?

Refocus ———→

Mary: Newspaper stories, magazine articles.

Phil: Novels. That's done all the time.

George: Television writers even rewrite old Broadway plays or even older movie scripts.

Mr. Inglish: So today's Shakespeare could still borrow and convert satisfactorily. What about complicated characters?

Recap ———→
Broadening
patterns of ———→
thinking

Inference drawn from point #5
Identifying point #6
Explaining point #6

Sally: That's hard to deal with. Most people like heroes and villains and don't want to think.

José: But Shakespeare, I think we said, entertained on all levels. He could have complicated characters but present them in such a way that people who were simple could still enjoy the play.

Jo-Anne: How could that be done?

José: By making the plot interesting, having lots of action, humor, even slapstick. Look at some of those funny scenes in *Hamlet*.

Mr. Inglish: So, then, you feel that

Clarification and recap →	today's Bard could have complicated characters without alienating the audience. *(General agreement.)*	Inference drawn from point #6

(The discussion proceeds through other characteristics of Shakespearean tragedy.)

Recap	*Mr. Inglish:* So far we have determined that Shakespeare today would probably be writing for movies or television, that he could successfully portray complicated characters, in borrowed plots, and that these plots could have downbeat, or unhappy, endings without alienating the audi-	III. Application of principles
Initiating a new dimension →	ence. Now, can we predict some specific plot lines that Shakespeare might write successfully?	

José: How about a love story set in the midst of the Civil War, in which a young Yankee soldier falls in love with a Southern Belle — and all the problems they get into.

> A. Prediction of consequences

Margo: What about a ruthless businessman whose ambition drives him to commit murder and later pay the consequences with a guilty conscience.

Sally: How about a young college student returning home from a year of study, only to find his widowed mother remarried to his uncle, who he thinks killed his father.

Mr. Inglish: What makes you think that these would be Shakespeare's plots,

Initiating a new dimension →	other than the fact that you borrowed these ideas from his plays? Let's start with José's plot.	B. Explaining/ supporting predictions

George: Stories about the Civil War make good viewing. Look at *Gone With the Wind, The Red Badge of Courage, Raintree County* — all movie scripts borrowed from other sources.

Judy: Plus the fact that many people were killed in the Civil War. We think of it a lot. It makes us sad.

Mary: And the characters could seem modern. The boy could look and act like a high school senior today. The girl could act like a cheerleader or something like that. Shakespeare's characters were all Elizabethan, regardless of where the play was supposed to take place.

(The class moves through the other two plot lines.)

Initiating a new dimension →

Mr. Inglish: Now that we have established three probable plot lines for today's Shakespeare, how can we verify that our predictions are correct?

C. Verifying predictions

Jim: One way is to get the television ratings and box office statistics for movies and programs that have comparable plot lines. We could see what the popular appeal will be.

Mary: Well, you know right now that crime, violence, and sex are the entertainment world's staple products.

Jerry: Another way is to research the lives of prominent movie and television writers to see how they write, what attitudes about human beings they have, and where they got their ideas.

Support →

Mr. Inglish: These are all good ideas. Since time is running out, I would like to summarize what we've done. By examining the nature of Shakespeare's tragedies and the people who attended them, we felt that today's Shakespeare would write for television and/or the movies. His tragedies would have lots of action,

Recap →

be based on novels, plays, magazine articles, or any other available source; they would also have complicated characters and unhappy endings. We predicted the content of three such tragedies, supported our predictions by comparisons to Shakespeare's existing works as projected into a twentieth-century medium, and were able, potentially, to verify our plot predictions by television ratings and box office sta-

Support →

tistics. I'd say you did a good day's work today. Class dismissed.

So far you have seen examples of teacher-led discussion. In teaching your students to be independent learners you should instruct them to apply LTD and Taba's levels of thinking to their own student-conducted discussions. The best device for applying these two is the discussion cluster, which can be led by students.

Student Led Discussion

DISCUSSION CLUSTERS

Discussion clusters, or groups, can best be used with staged panel discussions. The teacher may pose a specific problem and divide the class into five or six clusters to discuss the problem and come up with solutions. Under ideal circumstances, the chairperson of each cluster then forms a staged panel discussion to deal with the various solutions. Ms. McCubbin's music theory class became involved in a heated discussion about whether synthesizers could ever replace human musicians in a symphony orchestra. During the discussion Ms. McCubbin listed these five points on the board:

1. Individuality of style
2. Art versus science
3. Limitations of computers
4. Seen versus heard performance
5. Reforming the music curriculum.

Because time didn't permit a detailed discussion of each one of these points, the teacher divided the class into five clusters, and assigned one problem to each. Every cluster was to (a) select a leader to moderate discussion and a recorder to take notes, (b) determine how serious the problem was, (c) pose solutions to the problem, and (d) have the recorder write down the cluster's findings. The students were given 5 minutes to discuss the question and each cluster leader was given 1 minute to report to the rest of the class. From the first to the last shuffling of chairs, the entire discussion took less than 15 minutes, but Ms. McCubbin felt it covered an amazing amount of material.

When first using clusters, the teacher should keep the tasks simple. When the clusters return to the total class setting, the teacher should have the students discuss how they performed as cluster members. According to Moffett and Wagner (1983) successful discussion is based on attention, participation, and interaction.

GROUPING STUDENTS FOR DISCUSSION

So far in this chapter, you have read examples of successful and unsuccessful classroom discussions. You have noted that, although free discussion has its place in the classroom, controlled discussion that gets somewhere requires students to develop and use multiple thought processes. In teaching students to discuss what they've read from text, you must be a model discussion leader, and you must transmit discussion skills to the students so they can function independently in small-group discussions. Consequently, you will need to understand (a) the nature of grouping, (b) how to group successfully, and (c) how to teach discussion skills to students.

The Nature of a Group

Several definitions of *group* provide insights into the nature of clustering students for discussion of text or related work. Lee (1968) defines a group as "those children who at that time have common specific concerns, needs, interests, or plans" (p. 198). K. M. Evans (1966) gives a definition that is psychologically oriented. It differentiates between *group* and *togetherness*. The group is goal-directed. Togetherness implies no particular goal other than social interaction. Another definition of group (Barrington & Rogers, 1968) stresses student self-selection and self-direction. All these definitions include (a) united effort and (b) orientation toward a task.

How to Group Successfully

According to Flanders (1954), successful grouping procedures are difficult to achieve for five reasons:

1. Some teachers have misguided notions about grouping.
2. Some teachers have not developed the skills necessary to handle small groups.
3. Successful groups cannot be formed randomly or haphazardly.
4. Developing leadership in each group is a challenge to any teacher.
5. Students must be indoctrinated as to their roles as group members.

Suggestions on how to avoid each of these difficulties are given as prerequisites 1–5.

PREREQUISITE 1. AVOID ACCEPTING MYTHS ABOUT GROUP WORK

Teachers hear many myths about small-group work. The first myth is that a group can learn. In reality, only individuals within a group can learn (Allen, 1968). As a result, a teacher cannot assume that success in a group project necessarily means that all group members participated equally and learned the same amount. A second myth is that group success occurs automatically when students of similar achievement and intelligence levels are bound together in a united effort. It is wrong to assume that achievement and intelligence are the only bases for grouping; it is equally wrong to assume that students will automatically be self-directed once they are placed in groups. A third myth is that grouping requires the teacher to prepare an endless number of questions for the group to answer. Although a teacher-prepared discussion guide containing questions is useful, students in a group need to generate their own questions and problems. (See chapter 6 for procedure on teaching students to ask their own questions.)

PREREQUISITE 2. ACQUIRE THE SKILLS
NECESSARY TO HANDLE SMALL GROUPS

Success in handling small groups requires certain qualities in the teacher. Flanders (1954) suggests nine teacher qualities necessary for successful small group procedures. These qualities are:

1. Alertness and readiness to share responsibility of selecting particular students to be in a group
2. Knowledge of the subject matter used in groups
3. Sensitivity to pupil readiness for group work
4. Evaluative skill
5. Tolerance of noise and confusion
6. Calmness
7. Willingness to foster independence in students
8. Sensitivity toward differences in group pace
9. Willingness to share ideas with the principal and the rest of the faculty

Now, turn to the three discussions on pages 235–236 of this chapter. Which of the above qualities did the teachers in Classrooms A, B, and C exhibit? Which of the above qualities might the teachers in Classrooms A, B, and C have the potential to exhibit, given the appropriate classroom circumstances?

PREREQUISITE 3. KNOW HOW GROUPS ARE
BEST FORMED

Knowing how to form a group is, in a sense, the most difficult problem for a classroom teacher. Teachers can group students geographically, that is, by where they sit in the classroom. In just a few seconds, students can move their chairs around to form small clusters. One teacher staged practice drills in which students were timed to see how quickly they could move into groups. Teachers can also group students randomly by assigning numbers (1, 2, 3, 4, 5, 6) to six students and repeating for another six students, and so forth. (If the division is not even, assign any leftover students to the groups being formed.) Then all the 1s will form one group, the 2s will form another group, and so forth.

Another way to form a group is by interest. The teacher circulates a list of discussion topics. Students sign up for the topics that interest them. Then they form groups with others who signed up for the same topics.

No matter which group technique is used, teachers should pay attention to group size and balance of topics. One recommendation for group size is a minimum of *three* and a maximum of *eight* (Barrington & Rogers, 1968). With less than three, group process is impossible. With more than eight, it is improbable. Also crucial is the list of topics: all topics should be equally attractive. Avoid situations in which there is oversubscription to one topic on the one hand and universal rejection of another topic on the other hand.

We illustrate successful grouping by means of the case study presented in Box 8.4. In this case study a teacher employed group discussion techniques and experienced several problems.

BOX 8.4. Case Study: Reading of a Short Story Followed by Group Discussion

Introduction: Stephen Crane's short story, "The Open Boat," can be difficult reading, even for seniors enrolled in "Modern Literature," a course designed for students planning to attend community colleges. The students, generally speaking, didn't do their homework; as a result, the teacher scheduled time in class for quiet reading. After introducing the story, reviewing reading and language problems the students might have with it, the teacher allowed thirty minutes of class time for the students to read "The Open Boat"; they were asked to finish the story for homework.

By the next day, the teacher had prepared a small group discussion guide to facilitate understanding of the story. At the beginning of the period, she had the students count off by 4 and had them form groups based on their numbers. Each group was asked to select (1) a chairperson who would direct discussion, (2) a recorder to take notes and report the group's findings to the rest of the class in a symposium with the other recorders, and (3) a topic from the discussion guide — topic I, II, III, or IV. What follows is a copy of the discussion guide. The parenthetical comments were made by the teacher observing the discussions.

"THE OPEN BOAT"

A Discussion Guide with Parenthetical Comments
by the Teacher on Students' Discussion

    I. *Characterization. (This was a popular topic that three of the four groups selected. It seemed to be easier than the other three. Problems arose in the symposium because three of the four recorders said about the same thing. It would have been better if I had advised two of the three groups to change topics.)*
      A. The cook
        1. What impressions does Crane give us about the cook in the second paragraph of the story? *(Students found the word* impressions *difficult to deal with. I had to explain to each of the three groups what I meant.)*
        2. How do his manner of speech and his appearance fit together?
        3. What verbs in this paragraph are particularly effective in describing the cook?
        4. What additional character traits does the cook reveal as the story progresses?

B. The oiler
1. In what ways is the oiler prepared for his struggle with the sea?
2. How does he differ from the cook? List several specific ways.
C. The correspondent
1. How does the correspondent differ from the cook and the oiler? *(Students complained that these questions were repetitive and uninteresting.)*
2. Crane says that the correspondent "wondered why he was there." What is the significance of that line? *(I should have written* importance *rather than* significance.) In other words, what does the line reveal about the correspondent's character and personality? *(I'm glad I added this enabling rephrasing of the previous question.)*
D. The injured captain
1. What is the author's general attitude toward the captain? *(Students copied sentences from the book, I feel, without understanding what they meant. Recorders tended to read the copied sentences rather than paraphrase them.)*

II. Plot *(One group picked this topic.)*
A. Conflict
1. What are the two forces pitted one against another, creating a vital conflict situation? *(I had to rephrase this question for the group.)*
2. Are the forces evenly matched? Explain. *(There occurred much giggling in the group because students started talking about matches and cigarettes.)*
3. Does the conflict of the men in the boat bring out the strengths and weaknesses of their characters? Explain, using specific examples and direct quotations from the story. *(I overheard the chairperson ask a conscientious student to get the right answers, write them out, and give them to him to read. The student obliged.)*
B. Artistic Structure *(I should have written "Plot Structure.")*
1. At what point in the story does the suspense reach the highest point — the turning point in the story? *(The students couldn't agree on the turning point; they insisted on finding the "right" answer.)*
2. This turning point is called the climax or crisis. What are the events preceding the crisis that would make up the rising action? *(Students wanted to know what I wanted from them.)*
3. What events following the crisis would make up the falling action?

III. Theme *(No group took this section.)*
A. Is "The Open Boat" merely a story about a group of men who battle the sea or is there a deeper significance to the story? Explain.
B. What are the attitudes of the characters toward the sea? Indicate their specific actions that reveal these attitudes.
C. What do you think is the author's attitude toward nature? What poignant phrases does he use to reveal this attitude?
D. Of what significance is the fact that the oiler, the most fit to survive, is the one to drown?
E. Why hasn't Crane given his characters specific names?
F. Do the four occupants of the boat make up a cross section of society? Explain.

Look up the word *microcosm* in the dictionary. How does that word apply to the story "The Open Boat"?

IV. Style *(No group took this section.)*

A. How would you characterize Crane's use of language: simple or complicated? Take into consideration such factors as the words he uses, the formality or informality of his sentences. Why does he use this particular style of language?

B. One critic has said that Crane has caught the rhythm of the sea by varying his sentence length so that, in a given paragraph, a short sentence is followed by a longer sentence and then by a still longer sentence, then a shorter sentence, then a short sentence. Select several paragraphs, and by counting the number of *syllables* in each of the paragraphs, determine if the critic was correct.

C. Crane is a master at mood. He can prejudice the reader by the words he uses. How does Crane prejudice the reader against the forces of nature? Select several of his most vivid passages for examples.

Now that you have reviewed the discussion guide with the teacher's parenthetical comments, ask yourself these questions:

1. Was the teacher unduly critical of the discussion guide or was she justified?

2. Refer to Flanders's nine teacher qualities on page 251. How many of these qualities were presented in the preparation of the discussion guide?

3. How might the grouping of the students, the distribution of topics, and the questions themselves have been handled more thoughtfully? Refer to the discussion of LTD and Taba's levels of thinking on pages 239–249.

PREREQUISITE 4. TRAIN STUDENTS TO BE LEADERS

The concept of group leadership is complex. To be effective, each small group should function with a student leader, selected either by the group (internal authority) or by the teacher (external authority). K. M. Evans (1966) sees the type of leadership role as dependent on (a) the source of the leader's authority and (b) the source of the task, whether an external source (the teacher), the leader of the group, or the group itself. His chart on the possible leadership situations is in Table 8.1.

Barrington and Rogers (1968) describe, in more general terms, three types of leadership. The *authoritarian* leader maps out a plan of action that the group members accept and follow. This type of leadership is desirable when the goal is a high-quality *product* or result. However, when the goal does not emphasize the product, nor the process, nor the means to a goal, then *democratic* leadership,

TABLE 8.1. Possible Leadership Situations

Leader	Source of Authority	Source of Task
I. outsider	external	external
outsider	external	leader
outsider	external	group
II. outsider	internal	external
outsider	internal	leader
outsider	internal	group
III. group member	external	external
group member	external	leader
group member	external	group
IV. group member	internal	external
group member	internal	leader
group member	internal	group
V. no leader		external
		group
		no task

Source: K. M. Evans, "Group Methods," *Education Research* 9 (1966): 44–50. Reprinted by permission.

where there is group agreement on division of labor through preliminary discussion, is best. *Laissez faire* leadership, where each member marks out a particular aspect of work for himself or herself and then proceeds with it, can end in chaos.

Since many students lack knowledge and skill in leading a group, training for leadership skills should become an important part of the curriculum. Have training sessions for your discussion leaders in which you communicate to them the LTD and Taba methods. The leaders could function as a small group with rotating leaders. See the Quest procedure in Chapter 15 and review the sections on LTD and Taba in this chapter for discussion procedures.

PREREQUISITE 5. TEACH STUDENTS TO ASSUME ROLES IN GROUPS

In training students to become leaders, a broader consideration of the possible roles a student can assume in a discussion group is helpful. As shown in Box 8.5, there can be as many as 18. Students can learn to assume maintenance and task roles. They can also learn to avoid self-serving roles by frequently evaluating themselves and others in group situations.

BOX 8.5. Student Roles in a Discussion Group

I. Maintenance roles
  A. Encouraging
  B. Expressing group feelings
  C. Harmonizing
  D. Compromising
  E. Gatekeeping (keeping communications channels open)
  F. Setting standards

II. Task roles
  A. Initiating
  B. Information or opinion seeking
  C. Information or opinion giving
  D. Clarifying or elaborating
  E. Summarizing
  F. Consensus taking

III. Self-serving Roles
  A. Dominating
  B. Blocking
  C. Deserting
  D. Quarreling
  E. Recognition seeking
  F. Goofing off

David M. Litsey, "Small-Group Training and the English Classroom," *English Journal* 58 (1969): 920–27. Copyright © 1969 by the National Council of Teachers of English. Reprinted by permission of the publisher and the author.

Teaching Discussion Skills and Phasing Out the Teacher

By teaching students discussion techniques, group process, and leadership, a teacher can train students to be independent in discussions. This training occurs in phases:

Phase 1: the teacher is a model discussion leader, exhibiting in classroom discourse ideal leadership traits.

Phase 2: students become aware of these traits on a gradual trial and error basis, with teacher evaluation, attempt to model them in small-group discussions.

Phase 3: students gain so much facility in discussion that they rely on teacher direction less and less. Gradually the teacher is phased out and the students are phased in. (See chap. 12 for explanation on phasing out the teacher and phasing in the students.)

SUMMARY

Discussion can be a rewarding way for a student to respond to text. However, the discussion process must be taught actively and learned. This instructional activity means that the teacher must know how to lead a discussion that reaches a conclusion. In turn, students must learn to be discussion leaders and develop skills as participants in a discussion group. Some types of discussion a teacher can use include free, semicontrolled, and controlled. Procedures for conducting these types of discussion are Learning through Discussion (LTD) and the Taba methods. Through imitation and a phase-out strategy, students can eventually learn to function independently in small discussion groups.

In addition to discussion, another way to respond to text is through writing. Our next chapter presents types and ways to teach writing.

ACTIVITIES

1. Review the three discussions presented on pages 235–236 of this chapter. Select a discussion conducted by one teacher—Mr. Phelps, Ms. Carley, or Mr. Spont—and write a critique of the discussion, using the five prerequisites of good discussion as a basis for your critique. See how your critique agrees or disagrees with another student's critique. Discuss the reasons for the differences. Are your perspectives and values on education different from that student's in any way?

2. Plan a discussion activity in your content area that requires discussion clusters. Remember to pose a general problem that is to be solved by dividing it into subproblems for small-group discussions. Try your plan out in two classes. In one class, give the groups only the main problem. In the other class, give the groups each a subproblem. Note which class discusses the problem at greater length and depth. Why?

9 Letting the Students
Do the Writing
and Listening

CHAPTER OVERVIEW

In the last chapter, you learned how students can be taught to discuss what they read. In this chapter, you will see how students can learn to write clearly about what they have read. Although the teaching of writing is primarily the responsibility of the English teacher, other teachers who give writing assignments need to help their students learn how to do them. This chapter demonstrates how to teach such writing techniques as paraphrasing, reporting procedures, exposition, narration, argumentation, and answering essay questions. In addition, you will learn how to prepare model papers for students to emulate, how to evaluate papers, and how to grade them. Not all writing needs to be evaluated or graded. We describe four "writing-to-learn" activities that help students learn from text and that require little or no teacher time to implement. At the conclusion of this chapter, you are taken, step by step, through a specific writing assignment involving reference reading.

GRAPHIC ORGANIZER

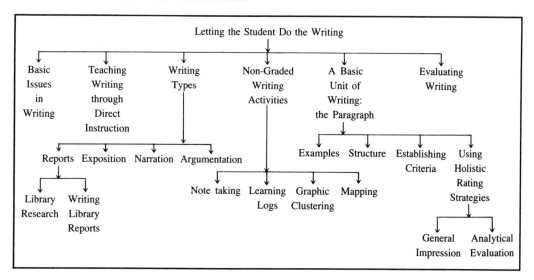

PREPOSED QUESTIONS

1. How can students be made to feel less apprehensive about their classroom writing?
2. How can writing help students learn from text more effectively?
3. What kinds of formal and informal writing activities can you implement in your classroom?

DIFFICULTIES IN WRITING CLEARLY

Like discussion, writing in the classroom is an important means for student response to text. Like discussion, writing can take many forms. Like discussion, writing is often taken for granted: it is assigned but not taught. As a consequence, student writing can result in bitter disappointment for teacher and student alike. Ms. Jones gave this essay question to her history class: "Who do you think was the most important figure in the Revolutionary War?" Consider her chagrin when she read the answer below.

> I think the Gorge Washington the most impartat figure in the Revaltionary War. He new how to get long well with is men and the respect him. Tack for insense, the surprise attack at Vally forge. The British wernt expect him, so he cam down on knight and suprized them his men follow him the hole way. Thats why Washington most importat of alother peopel in this war.

Then consider how the chagrin deepened when Ms. Jones subsequently received this library report, done at home, by the same student:

> WASHINGTON, GEORGE (1732–1799), won a lasting place in American history as the "Father of his country." For nearly 20 years, he guided his country much as a father cares for a growing child.
>
> In three important ways, Washington helped shape the beginning of the United States. First, he commanded the Continental Army that won American independence from Great Britain in the Revolutionary War. . . .[1]

Student writing does have its lighter moments. Examine the following samples from Mr. Wallace's literature class:

1. "Bewick Finzer" was indeed a sadist; he was always going around feeling sorry for himself.
2. The bus pulled to the curb, stopped, and got off.
3. The dark figure crept up behind her and stabbed her between the nose.

The extreme difficulties of students' learning to write clearly can be vividly seen in the H*Y*M*A*N* K*A*P*L*A*N stories by Leonard Q. Ross (Leo Rosten). Hyman Kaplan is an exuberant, undaunted immigrant who is taking nightschool English to gain citizenship. He is not unlike the students at Monroe High for whom English is a second language. In one of the stories, Hyman Kaplan writes on the front board the composition below for class analysis:

> My Job A Cotter in Dress Faktory
> Comp. by H*Y*M*A*N K*A*P*L*A*N
> Shakspere is saying what fulls man is and i am feeling just the same way when I am thinking about mine job a cotter in Dress Faktory on 38 st. by 7 av. For why shold

---

[1] *The World Book Encyclopedia*, 1972, s.v. "Washington."

we slafing in dark place by laktric lights and all kinds hot fo $30 or maybe $36 with overtime, for Boss who is fat and driving in fency automobil? I ask! Because we are the deprassed workers of world. And are being exployted. By Bosses. In mine shop is no difference. Oh how bad is laktric light, o how is all kinds hot. And when I am telling Foreman shold be better conditions he hollers. Kaplan you radical!! . . . So I keep still and work by bad light and always hot. But somday will workers making Bosses to work! And then Kaplan will give to them bad laktric and positively no windows for the air should come in! So they can know what it means to slafe! Kaplan will make Foreman a cotter like he is. And give the most bad dezigns to cot out. Justice.

Mine job is cotting Dress dezigns.

T-H-E- E-N-D

You may not have a Hyman Kaplan in your classroom, but you will have a range of individual differences in writing as evident as the range in reading. In one class, you might have students who have severe spelling problems and who can barely form complete, coherent sentences. In the same class, you might have students who write maturely with ease and fluency. Although this chapter describes in depth techniques for improving the writing of students who vary widely in ability, a few general techniques might be mentioned now. To improve spelling, have students keep individual lists of words they have misspelled and supply them with a list of ''spelling demons'' in your content area. To improve sentence accuracy and coherence, have students read their papers aloud either to themselves or to other students, to catch errors.

Students can learn to write. In this chapter we present ways of solving the problem of how to get students to write clearly and effectively in response to text material. The first section explains basic issues with respect to teaching writing. The second section discusses teaching writing through direct instruction. The third section examines writing and describes different types of writing as a reflection of thinking in various content areas. A fourth section deals with the paragraph, a basic unit of writing. The last section suggests methods for evaluating writing.

BASIC ISSUES IN WRITING

Fear of Having to Write
versus Ease of Writing

One of the most pervasive instructional problems is writing apprehension. This occurs when the level of anxiety toward writing is so high that students either avoid writing or undertake it with resistance. Research has indicated that students with writing apprehension do not write as well as those who do not have it (Faigley, Daly, & Witte, 1981), avoid situations that demand speaking or writing (Daly & Shamo, 1978), and eventually seek occupations that do not require speaking or writing as job demands. Daly and Hailey (1984) suggest that five classroom situations contribute to students' writing apprehension. First, and perhaps the most powerful, is prior experience. Students who have had continually unsatisfactory experiences in writing, say, essay examinations and reports, may develop cumulative apprehension to the point that achievement in school is severely hampered. Second, students tend to be apprehensive when their names are clearly associated with writing that other people read. This attribute is called conspicuousness. Teachers can reduce the threat of conspicuousness by having students submit papers for others to read using code names or numbers. Third, assignments that are ambiguous or unclear provoke high levels of apprehension. Teachers need to specify exactly what students are expected to do on an assignment. Later in this chapter, we describe a number of strategies for eliminating ambiguity in writing assignments. Fourth, students frequently become apprehensive over innovations or first-time assignments. For example, a 4th-grader's first library report or the 11th grader's first term paper produces, by the very novelty of the assignment, anxiety. To avoid the effect of novelty, teachers should relate each new assignment to previous assignments. Later, in this chapter, we show you ways of teaching writing in sequential steps that build carefully on students' prior experience. Fifth, students become extremely apprehensive if their writing is to be thoroughly evaluated by the teacher. To avoid this condition, you should vary evaluation strategies. For instance, you evaluate some writing thoroughly, some writing only selectively, and some writing with a mere check mark. By consciously attempting to reduce students' fears of writing, you will be able to improve achievement of the widely varying students in your classroom.

English Teacher versus All-School Responsibility

In many ways reading and writing are beset with the same pedagogical problems. Almost everyone agrees that teaching students to read and write is important, but few teachers seem to perceive teaching them as their individual responsibility. Consider the secondary school situation. The reading teacher has the primary responsibility for teaching students *how to read*. But the reading teacher cannot ensure that students will make appropriate application of skills to reading in every content area. Application and instruction in how to learn from the particular textbook or textbooks used in the classroom are the responsibility of the content area teacher. Likewise, the English teacher has the primary responsibility for teaching students *how to write*. However, because the English teacher teaches a content of literature and language and subsequently asks students to write about that content, the English teacher cannot ensure that students will make appropriate transfer of skills to writing in every other content area. In effect, just as teaching students to read is an all-faculty responsibility, so is teaching students to write.

Composing versus Copying

Having read the answer to the essay question and the library report on George Washington earlier in this chapter, you probably noted the startling differences that can exist between composing and copying. Composing is a creative act; copying is not. Composing demands that the writer translate his or her thoughts into special, idiosyncratic language; copying does not. In effect, composing at its best can be an exhilarating experience; copying at its best is only degrading. Consider the joy of a second-grader after writing a first poem, the pride of a student on a short story just finished, the glory of a valedictorian's graduation speech. No doubt these young writers feel as stimulated as did the great novelist Virginia Woolf when she wrote in her diary:

> Determination not to give in, and the sense of an impending shape keep one at [writing] more than anything. I'm a little anxious. How am I to bring off this conception? Directly one gets to work one is like a person walking, who has seen the country stretching out before. I want to write nothing in this book that I don't enjoy writing. Yet writing is always difficult.[2]

Each teacher is responsible for teaching students the difference between composing and copying, especially when assigning library reports. Three techniques can be invaluable in assigning library reports. First, base the assignment on more than one source so that the student will have to assimilate the material. Second, control the sources; that is, limit the references to only a few that every student has access to. If necessary, duplicate the sources for the entire class. Third, conduct brief *paraphrasing* exercises in class in which students synthesize two sentences relating identical or similar content into one original sentence.

Ms. Jones might teach students to paraphrase by following the three steps in Box 9.1. Instructing students in paraphrasing is only one aspect in the teaching of writing.

BOX 9.1. Steps in Teaching Paraphrasing

Step 1: Present the student with a textual passage together with its paraphrase. Ask the student to discuss differences in language.

Text	Paraphrase
After teen-aged George Washington gave up hopes of becoming a sailor, he became interested in exploring the frontier. Becoming a surveyor and marking out new farms in the wilderness would give him a chance to leave home to seek adventure.	When George Washington was a teenager, he realized he would rather be a surveyor than a sailor. Surveying would permit him to lead a more adventuresome life away from home.

---

[2]Janet Emig, *The Composing Processes of Twelfth Graders*. Urbana, IL: National Council of Teachers of English, 1971, p. 11.

Step 2: Have the student paraphrase short passages from text, supplying guide ques-tions as hints.

Text	Hints for Paraphrasing
Braddock assembled his forces at Fort Cumberland, Md., about 90 miles south-east of Fort Duquesne.	1. What phrase would sound less book-ish than "assembled his forces"? 2. Locate Fort Cumberland on a map and see if you can write an alterna-tive location, other than 90 miles southeast of Fort Duquesne. 3. Can the 15 word passage be rewritten in fewer words?

Step 3: Provide the students with a longer piece of text to paraphrase. Eliminate or reduce the number of hints.

Text

At the age of 26, Washington turned to seek happiness as a country gentleman and to build a fortune. During the next 16 years, he became known as a skilled farmer, an intelligent businessman, a popular legislator, a conscientious war-den of a Church of England and a wise county court judge.

All *Text* copy is from *The World Book Encyclopedia*, 1972, s.v. "Washington."

Teaching versus Assigning Writing

The maxim "Most writing is assigned, not taught" is all too true. The 500-word composition or the 10-page library report, assigned on Monday and collected on Friday without any intervening instruction in how to write a composition or prepare a library report, has unfortunately secured a fast place in American education. The by-products of such a system include confused students, blatant plagiarism, unimaginative writing, and disappointed teachers. Fortunately, some educators have devised methods of teaching writing.

TEACHING WRITING THROUGH DIRECT INSTRUCTION

Composition as Transaction

James Moffett (1968) isolated and described types of writing he referred to as "Writing up," "Writing down," "Writing out." These include stories, jokes, riddles, puns, sensory recording, dialogue recording, memory writing, fiction, idea writing, dramatic dialogue, Socratic dialogue, journals, diaries, reportage, research, and reflection. Writing of any type, Moffett believes, should flow naturally from classroom discussion and from reading literature. Students should meet frequently in small groups to react to and critique each other's writing. Moffett believes that students learn best by learning from each other's critiques. Box 9.2 contains a lesson outline inspired by Moffett's philosophy. In the example in Box 9.2, students respond to text while writing about their own feelings, beliefs, and ideas. Notice that their responses to the ideas presented in the text may change as they react to each other's drafts. This change in ideas is referred to as *transaction*.

BOX 9.2. Lesson Outline for Writing

A CHILD'S CHRISTMAS IN WALES

by Dylan Thomas

[*Synopsis:* The great Welsh poet recalls fondly, with rich sensory detail, how Christmas was celebrated in his home town when he was a child.]

1. *Before Reading*
   a. *Writing:* Students are asked to recall a favorite Christmas or comparable holiday and write down random memories as they come to mind.
   b. *Discussion:* Students talk together in small groups about what they have written.
2. *While reading* "A Child's Christmas in Wales" students add more details to their lists.
3. *After Reading*
   a. *Discussion:* Students in small groups discuss their personal reactions to "A Child's Christmas in Wales," using their own experiences as a basis.
   b. *Writing:* Students compose their own memory writings, based upon previous discussion and writing.
   c. *Discussion:* Students meet in small groups to react to each other's first drafts.
   d. *Writing:* Students compose second drafts based upon comments from fellow students. The second drafts are submitted to the teacher.

Now that you have some information on direct instruction in writing, you might be able to answer this question. How would the students have responded if Ms. Jones, the history teacher, had given the following writing assignment without any writing instruction? "Now that you've read the chapter on the Revolutionary War, assume that you are George Washington. Write a letter home to your wife Martha recounting the hardships of Valley Forge yet show your determination to overcome the enemy."

Composition as Personal Growth

Emig (1971) has suggested that students put more effort into *reflexive* writing than *extensive* writing. Motivation to write is stronger when it comes from a personal desire to communicate than from a determination to meet the demands of the teacher's assignment. For example, a 14-year-old girl will spend twice as much time and precision composing a letter to her best friend than writing answers to end-of-chapter study questions. Because most students easily engage in some form of personal writing, teachers should try to make effective use of personal writing in their classrooms.

One of the best vehicles for personal writing is the journal, or what Kirby and Liner (1981) refer to as "the J." Kirby and Liner believe journal writing increases students' fluency and self-awareness. First, the journal is private; so students feel free to explore, with their own language, their feelings and ideas. Second, journal writing is fairly unstructured and thus inviting. Third, since the journal is private and unstructured, students tend to express themselves more honestly and powerfully. Fourth, since students write journals to themselves, they may be more critical of what they write. Contrast, for instance, these two passages written by 13-year-old Ellen Mary. The first is a response to a teacher's assignment; the second is an entry in her personal journal:

> The poetry of Walt Whitman was patently revolutionary for its time. Critics entertained it with hostility and derision. One reason for this deluge of criticism was Whitman's employment of free verse, a form then considered barbaric.

> The street is quiet. Too quiet. To the people who live on the street the silence is deafening. No birds singing, no dogs barking, no radio playing, and no cars rumbling. No one speaks or even breathes too loudly. Through the silence a baby screams. No one goes to it and it soon quiets.

The first passage, written in response to an end-of-chapter question, is bookish, perhaps copied. The second passage, an unassigned journal entry, shows the student's use of personal, and powerful, language. Though appearing extreme, these two examples dramatize the differences between assigned and personal writing.

Kirby and Liner suggest four types of journals that students can keep: (a) the writer's notebook, (b) the class journal, (c) the project journal, and (d) the diary. The *writer's notebook* is a type of journal in which students systematically make personal notes about their observations. The notebook may contain interesting words and phrases the student has collected, as well as ideas, insights, and reactions. These data may become the basis for a writing assignment. Some teachers encourage students to observe human and speech patterns before composing short narratives. Students, keeping these observations in writer's notebooks, may use or adapt them for the short story assignment.

The *class journal* is used for in-class personal writing. Teachers use class journals in various ways. Some teachers allow students 5 or 10 minutes each period to make free or spontaneous entries. Other teachers supply a focus for the entries, for instance, a film, guest speaker, class discussions, or textbook reading assignments. Teachers find the class journals useful in determining how students are responding to class activities.

Students use *project journals* for keeping track of their progress while preparing a long-term individual or small-group project, such as a research or library paper, a dramatic presentation, or a demonstration. Entries could consist of notes on pertinent readings, lists of possible sources, minutes of group planning sessions, deadlines, or lists of things to do. Project journals help students plan their time on long-term assignments, precluding the "night before rush job."

The *diary* functions as an emotional outlet for students. Students frequently use diaries to record intimate feelings and beliefs. Some teachers choose never to read these; other teachers collect them, read them, and, on occasion, respond with personal notes to the student. Most sensitive teachers avoid responses that are preachy and moralizing. Many teachers, however, feel uncomfortable with the diary, and never use it.

Journal writing is widely practiced in English language arts classrooms. Teachers in other content areas, too, might find journals useful classroom ac-

TABLE 9.1. Overview of Suggested Journal Uses, by Type and by Content Area

JOURNAL TYPE	English	Social Studies	Science	Math	Industrial & Home Arts
Writer's Notebook	Recording observations of people in preparation for a short story	Personal reaction to propaganda on television and radio	Logs of growing plants; record of climatic changes	Record of humorous experiences with counting of money or change	Personal opinions of new fashions in clothing and automobiles
Class Journal	Writing short stories or poems to music as it is playing	Reacting to a teacher-selected or student-selected current event	Recording of observations during a demonstration or experiment	Recounting problems experienced in completing math homework	Log of successful and unsuccessful experiences in operating equipment
Project Journal	Plans and procedures for preparing an 8mm film on poetry of nature	Progress on research paper sources, notes on readings, rough drafts, outlines	Progress notes on a science fair project: experiments, observations	Materials, measurements, procedures for building a geodesic dome	Daily progress entries on problems and procedures in building a chest of drawers
Diary	Student records personal and intimate ideas, beliefs, attitudes, and values.				

Source: Dan Kirby and Tom Liner, *Inside Out: Developmental Strategies for Teaching Writing.* Rochelle Park, N.J.: Hayden, 1980.

tivities. Table 9.1 shows how the four types of journals can be used in various content areas.

Composition as Language Structure

In reviewing over 50 years of research in composition, Richard Braddock and others (Braddock, Lloyd-Jones, & Schoer 1963) came to the conclusion that the formal study of grammar had little or no effect upon writing proficiency. This conclusion came as a blow to staunch supporters who had consistently defended the applicability of grammar to speech and writing.

Subsequent to Braddock's review, a series of studies attempted to show that practice with sentence building effected maturity in student writing. Perhaps the best known of these studies is that of O'Hare (1972) who improved seventh graders' writing by having them perform exercises in sentence combining. Although students manipulated many different grammatical structures, they did so without being exposed to the complex terminology of grammar. A sentence-combining exercise might proceed in the sequence shown in Box 9.3.

BOX 9.3. Sentence-Combining Exercise

Instructions: Combine each of the following groups of sentences into one sentence, using THAT or THE FACT THAT.

1. Julio should admit SOMETHING. He was there.
   Answer: Julio should admit *that* he was there.
2. Peter notices SOMETHING. There were nine golf balls in the river.
   Answer: (You supply.)
3. SOMETHING is certain. Human beings will survive.
   Answer: (You supply.)

These are only simple exercises. Try your hand at combining the following series of sentences in one short sentence:

The gas station attendant stumbled out of his shack.
He was *an emaciated looking fellow.*
He had *white hair and skin the color of an old saddle.* (WITH)
He *stood scowling at us.* (AND)
His chin was *thrust forward.* (WITH)
His eyes were *blazing.*

Here is what you might have come up with:

The gas station attendant, an emaciated looking fellow with white hair and skin the color of an old saddle, stumbled out of his shack and stood scowling at us, with his chin thrust forward, his eyes blazing.

Ms. Jones might have helped her students with their writing assignment by having them do the exercises in sentence combining similar to the two which follow.

1. George Washington was a general in the Revolutionary War.
2. He suffered many hardships at Valley Forge.
3. He was a courageous soldier.

Combine these three sentences into one:

1. American colonists were clever soldiers.
2. They acted like today's guerrillas.
3. They always outsmarted the British.

Composition as Process

More and more is becoming known about the processes students use in writing. In a seminal study, Emig (1971), observing how eight 12th-grade students wrote, found that they spent more time composing and revising in response to their own thoughts and feelings (reflexive writing) than in response to classroom experiences (extensive writing). Echoing Emig's findings, Britton, Burgess, Martin, McLeod, & Rosen (1975), in an assessment of thousands of papers written by British school children, found that when they were writing for the teacher, children produced stilted, uncreative language. In effect, when a writing assignment demands that a student report facts, the teacher assumes the role of *examiner*. According to Britton, this role makes student writers uncomfortable and constrained. Nevertheless, content area teachers, assessing what students have learned from text, are functioning as examiners. If they occasionally modify their role of "examiner" to "helper" (or as Britton puts it, "trusted adult") students might feel freer to express their thoughts and feelings at greater depth. Ms. Jones might have had better luck with her students had she asked them to write on this topic: "Which of your closest friends is most like George Washington (or any other figure in the Revolutionary War) and why?" On giving the assignment, Ms. Jones could make it clear that she would read and respond to it in writing, but would not grade or discuss it in class.

Subsequent to the pioneering research of Emig and Britton, researchers have continued to explore how children, adolescents, and adults write. For example, Graves (1979), Calkins (1980), and Dyson (1987) have observed how children in primary grades attempt writing tasks. Kantor (1984) observed how classroom environment can affect the writing habits of high school children. Bridwell's (1980) study of over 100 high school students showed that good writers revised their writing differently from poor writers. Perl (1979) discovered that unskilled college writers have problems revising their papers that their skilled counterparts do not share.

Summary of Writing Through Direct Instruction

In stressing direct instruction of writing, not merely assigning it, five specialists in English language education have aided English teachers and their students. Their ideas for direct instruction can also be used by teachers in other content areas. Box 9.4 summarizes these ideas.

BOX 9.4. Summary of Ideas for Direct Instruction of Writing

Specialist	Contribution
1. Moffett	1. *Classroom organization* a. Small groups for reading, discussing, and writing. b. Writing as a natural outgrowth of classroom reading and discussion. c. Student reacting to the writing of their peers. d. Prewriting activities and revision techniques.
2. Kirby and Liner	2. *Composition as data about the writer* a. Use of student journals and diaries. b. Drawing inferences about students based upon what they write. c. Planning additional reading and writing based on cues from student writing.
3. O'Hare	3. *Improving student writing style* a. Sentence-combining exercises. b. Drawing sentences from individual content areas: e.g., George Washington led his country in war and peace. He was called the father of his country.
4. Emig and Britton	4. *Composition as Process* How students act when they are in the process of writing — in class and at home — both for the teacher as examiner and as trusted adult.

It is primarily the English teacher's responsibility to teach students how to write, using the ideas of specialists prominent in the field of composition. Because teachers in other content areas assign writing, they too should know the ideas of these specialists. In addition, all teachers should be familiar with the four basic types of writing that can be assigned.

TYPES OF WRITING APPLIED TO CONTENT AREAS

On the following pages four types of writing are defined and specific examples of them are supplied: reporting, exposition, narration, and argumentation.

Reporting

Written reporting can be defined as the relaying of information in response to a question or an assignment. Frequently, the teacher gives the student a set of *study questions* for which the student is to supply answers; the answers may vary in length from one sentence to several paragraphs. In this activity, a teacher assumes the role of *helper*. In addition to study questions, teachers give written examinations, in which students relay information ranging from answers of one sentence or phrase to whole paragraphs. In this role, a teacher functions as an *examiner* and *evaluator*. As an evaluator, the teacher's task is to apply explicit criteria to students' writing. Another form of reporting is the library report in which students demonstrate that they have retrieved and organized relevant information on a given topic. Here the teacher may function as an interested adult reader, an evaluator, or both.

Reporting and other forms of writing can be differentiated by the creative demands they make on the student. Reporting is simply information retrieval and relay; it requires factual recall and paraphrasing. Consider this assignment: ''Report on the contributions of Pythagoras to modern geometry.'' It merely asks the student to tell what the contributions are, not apply them, analyze them, synthesize them, or evaluate them.

Study Questions

Generally, as students use reading and learning-from-text guides, they are directed to write answers to questions that facilitate the reading of the chapter. In devising study questions, the teacher must make it clear to students whether they are to write a sentence or phrase, a short paragraph, or a more extended answer. In Boxes 9.5, 9.6, and 9.7 are guide questions and these different types of answers by students. Sometimes study questions demand more response than a sentence or sentence fragment. Read the question and answer in Box 9.6.

BOX 9.5. *Guide Questions and Short Answers (Phrases or Sentences)*

SCIENCE

What causes the green color you see on a pond? (page 4, column 1, paragraph 2)

pond scum or algae

The green color you see on a pond is caused by *pond scum* or *algae*. (Some teachers believe students should answer questions in complete sentences.)

SOCIAL STUDIES

What was the purpose of the Boston Tea Party?

to protest the tax on tea

ENGLISH

Why did "I" in Edgar Allan Poe's "Tell-Tale Heart" want to kill the old man?

"I" wanted to get rid of the old man's eye.

BOX 9.6. *Guide Questions and Paragraph Answers*

SCIENCE

Briefly describe the environment of a pond.

A pond's water is slow moving or still. Because of this, a scummy growth called algae can be seen on the top and under the water. Ducks and other waterbirds like ponds because of the gentle water and the bugs that live there.

BOX 9.7. *Study Questions for Report-Type Answers*

MATHEMATICS

Explain the meaning of this equation: $3 \sqrt{56} < 15 \times 4$.

SOCIAL STUDIES

Why were the Hessians surprised at Valley Forge?

ENGLISH

What preparations had Pepe made for his trip to the mountains in Steinbeck's "Flight"?

SCIENCE

Describe the environment of a mountain lake.

INDUSTRIAL EDUCATION

What equipment would be necessary for you to repair a Model-T Ford?

Box 9.7 contains study questions that require short answers, paragraphs, and more extended answers. Decide what kind of answer each question calls for.

Written Examinations

Just as study questions demand report-type responses ranging in length from a single sentence or sentence fragment to one paragraph or more, so do written examinations. In fact, some teachers use study questions to "dry run" written examinations. Consequently, much of what was said on the preceding pages about study questions holds for written examinations.

Many students have difficulty writing longer examinations—essay examinations—principally because they do not understand what is expected of them. It is possible that a high school history student might answer each of the four questions below in the same way:

1. What were the causes and effects of the Spanish-American War?
2. What was the principal significance of Spanish-American War?
3. What were the principal events in the Spanish-American War?
4. Describe the principal outcomes of the Spanish-American War?

Question 1 asks for two sets of data: What phenomena led to the war and what changes in American society resulted after the war's conclusion. Some students may not understand the difference in the definitions of *cause* and *effect* and, as a result, may merely summarize the war without differentiating between the two sets of data. In addition, the term *what* does not clearly indicate how much the student is to say about each cause and each effect. Specifically, is the student to list, to describe, to evaluate—or WHAT?

Question 2 does not request specific information about the war. It asks the student to recall what the textbook mentioned was the long-range, retrospect importance of the Spanish-American War. But the question is not specific because it doesn't say "significance to what." Significance to American foreign policy? Significance to American culture? Significance to America's economy?

Question 3 merely asks the student to recall the major happenings of the war. Again the student might not know the meaning of *events*. Does *events* refer to battles, legislation, political strategies, speeches?

Question 4 may appear to be similar to part of Question 1; however, *outcomes* suggests more immediate results than does *effects*. Whereas *effects* might concern changes in foreign alliance, legislative acts, changes in attitudes, *outcomes* might concern deaths and casualties, victories and defeats, fiscal gains and deficits.

As a result of analyzing these four essay questions on the Spanish-American War, it becomes apparent that teachers must learn to write clear essay questions and teach the students to read them carefully and analyze them.

Writing Effective Essay Questions

A well-written essay question contains three elements: (a) a *performance verb*, that is, a verb that tells the student how to answer the question; (b) an indication of the *content* of the response; and (c) *enabling suggestions* for how to proceed in organizing the answer. Box 9.8 contrasts a set of poorly written essay questions with the same essay questions in well-written form.

BOX 9.8. *Poorly Written and Well-Written Essay Questions*

1. What were the causes and effects of the Spanish-American War?

performance verb — (List) the [causes and effects of the   content
Spanish-American War.] Include the
causes in one paragraph and the effects   } enabling
in a second paragraph. Then write a   suggestions
third paragraph describing your own
feelings about whether the war was
worth the effort.

2. What is a pond's environment like?

performance verb — (Describe) [what a pond looks like, including such information as (1) the ap-
pearance of the water, (2) the types of   } content
plant and animal life in the pond, and
(3) how the plants and animals depend
on one another.] Devote several sen-   } enabling
tences to each of the three points listed.   suggestions

3. How would you repair a Model-T Ford?

How would you [repair a Model-T
Ford's transmission after the gears had   } content
been stripped?] (1) (List) each piece of
performance verbs   equipment you would use and why you   enabling
would use it. (2) (List) the steps you   } suggestions
would take in fixing the transmission.
Write one paragraph for (1) and one
paragraph for (2).

Writing essay questions in this way facilitates evaluation by establishing the following criteria for a good answer: *a mode of response* (list, compare, contrast, describe), *content of response* (causes, effects, outcomes, important features), and *organization of response* (three sentences, two paragraphs). But it is not enough to write good essay questions. You have to teach students to comprehend those questions.

TEACHING STUDENTS TO COMPREHEND ESSAY QUESTIONS

The first step in teaching students to comprehend essay questions is to explain the various performance verbs and the modes of response they suggest. Table 9.2 contains some of the most commonly used performance verbs in well-written essay questions, their definitions, and the modes of response they evoke.

The second step in teaching students to comprehend essay exam questions is to have them articulate what is expected of them in given essay questions. A class discussion on a given essay question might focus on questions like those in Box 9.9.

BOX 9.9. *Class Discussion of Essay Questions*

What difficulties would you have answering this essay question:

List the causes and effects of the Stamp Act.

1. What would you be expected to do in a list?
   a. What form would the list take?
   b. How much detail would you have to supply for each cause and effect?
2. What are causes and effects?
   a. Are causes the same as effects — or different?
   b. Is there an effect for every cause?
3. Which of the following pieces of information would not be appropriate in writing the essay?
   a. Principal politicians responsible for the Stamp Act.
   b. The history of taxation patterns in the colonies.
   c. Armed resistance to the British army.
   d. The Boston Massacre.
   e. The Boston Tea Party.

In addition to understanding the meaning of the performance verbs, deciding what mode of response is appropriate, and discussing the meaning of given essay questions, students must follow the enabling suggestions on organization. When the enabling suggestions in an essay question say "write one paragraph on *causes* and one paragraph on *effects*," the student ought to check the answer to

TABLE 9.2. Performance Verbs Commonly Used in Well-written
Essay Questions and Modes of Response to Them

Verb	Definition	Suggested Mode of Response
1. to list	to compile a series of related items	Student enumerates the requested items *with little or no further explanation*. List may be in outline, numbered sequence, or sentence form.
2. to identify	to describe the most significant features	Using one or more sentences, the student describes *only the most important* aspects of a person (what he or she did that was noteworthy), a place (what happened there, why it is unique), an idea (what makes this idea different from all others), and an event (What happened? Why is it important?).
3. to describe	to write about major and minor features	Using one or more paragraphs, the student will write about all of the features of a person, place, idea, or event—not merely the most important ones.
4. to compare	to show the similarities and dissimilarities of two or more phenomena	The student will show how two phenomena are alike in one paragraph and different in a second paragraph.
5. to contrast	to show only the dissimilarities of two or more phenomena	The student will show how two phenomena are different by selecting several key aspects and devoting a paragraph to each aspect.
6. to illustrate or amplify	to give examples	The student will supply examples to clarify a point, devoting a sentence or two for each example.
7. to justify	to give reasons for	The students will supply reasons to defend or argue a point, devoting a sentence or two for each reason.
8. to discuss	to talk over	Students consider a topic from various points of view.
9. to define	to make clear the meaning of a term or concept	Students explain what is meant by a term, supplying an example.
10. to explain	to define or otherwise make clear	Students clarify an idea, process, concept, event.
11. to outline	to list major points and minor subpoints	Using letters and numbers, students arrange a sequence of major and minor ideas.

be sure it contains information on the *causes* and *effects* in order to satisfy the requirements of the question.

SAMPLES OF WELL-WRITTEN ANSWERS TO ESSAY QUESTIONS

Boxes 9.10–9.12 show three samples of student writing in response to essay questions from three content areas: social studies, science, and English. Each of the samples contains the topic, the teacher's enabling suggestions, and marginal glosses explaining what the student did to meet the criteria of the assignment.

BOX 9.10. Social Studies

1. Topic: *What were the causes and effects of the Spanish-American War?*

List the causes and effects of the Spanish-American War. Put the causes in one paragraph and the effects in a second paragraph. Then write a third paragraph describing your own feelings about whether the war was worth the effort. — Teacher's enabling suggestions

Was It Worth It? ← — Catchy title

Introduction
It seems as if the United States has always found it difficult to stay out of armed conflicts. The Spanish-American War is no exception. The Spanish-American War was caused by several — Topic sentence

Enumeration transition
factors. (First,) the Americans were displeased over Spanish tyranny in Cuba. Uprisings against the Spanish were powerful enough to unsettle Spanish

Transition
rule but not overthrow it. (Second,) William Randolph Hearst and other journalists exaggerated the conditions in Cuba and got the Americans interested — Three causes

Transition
in intervening. (Third,) the battleship *Maine*, sent to Cuba to protect Ameri-

cans from pro-Spanish rioters, mysteriously exploded, killing 260 people on board. The situation was ripe for war.

Clincher statement

Topic sentence
As with most wars, there was disagreement as to the positive value of the effects. *Transition* (In the first place,) Cuba was granted freedom, and the United States acquired Guam, Puerto Rico, and the Philippines. *Contrast transition* (In addition, however,) strong anti-imperialist feelings grew in the United States, questioning the goodness of foreign policy. *Contrast transition* (Nevertheless,) the urge, now, to connect the Caribbean Sea and the Pacific Ocean led to the building of the Panama Canal.

Three effects

I have mixed feelings about the Spanish-American War. *Transition* (On the positive side,) America became less isolationist and began to grow as a world power. Our commerce and industry grew as a result of our expanded international interests. *Contrast transition* (On the negative side,) our territorial claims outside the continental United States have made us targets of criticism. How much we help the territories and how much we exploit them has been a never-ending discussion. Eventually, we will be forced to choose between granting total freedom to our territories or continually justifying what appears to be an imperialist foreign policy.

Topic sentence

Positive and negative reactions

BOX 9.11. *Science*

2. Topic: *What is a pond's environment like?*

Describe what a pond looks like, including such information as (1) the appearance of the water, (2) the types of plant and animal life in the pond, and (3) how the plants and animals depend on one another. Devote several sentences to each of the three points listed. Confine your writing to one paragraph.

Teacher's enabling suggestions

The Pond

Topic sentence

A pond is fairly easy to recognize. (First of all,) unlike rivers and streams, the water has a still surface. Unlike a lake's, the pond's surface is spotted with plant life. (Second,) much of this plant life consists of algae and scum. These and other forms of pond growth, such as rushes, stimulate an active insect community. The stillness of the water, which fosters the growth of these plants, also makes for attractive living quarters for water birds, particularly ducks. (Third,) water, plants, and animals live together effectively. As small fish and insects feed on plants, larger fish and birds feed on the insects. Animals give CO_2 to the plants. You can always find nature's balance at work in a pond.

Appearance of water

Plant and animal life

Dependence

Enumeration transition

Enumeration transition

Enumeration transition

Clincher sentence

BOX 9.12. English

3. Topic: *Compare and constrast the ways in which Holden Caulfield and Gene Forrester coped with the world around them.*

> Define "coping" in an introductory paragraph that gives an overview of your composition. In a second paragraph, point out similarities that exist between Holden and Gene. In a third paragraph, point out dissimilarities between the two boys. Illustrate general statements with specific information from the novels *A Catcher in the Rye* and *A Separate Peace*. In a concluding paragraph, attempt to judge which boy "copes" better.

Enabling suggestions

To Cope: An Adolescent Problem

Offbeat opening

> A recent successful Broadway musical has focused on the increasing inabilities people have in learning to cope with life around them. "To cope"

Main idea for composition

> means to adjust to life's pressures and "make the best of it." Two adolescent fictional heroes — Holden Caulfield from *A Catcher in the Rye* and Gene Forrester from *A Separate Peace* — try to cope with life, but with varying degrees of success.

Two points of similarity

> Both Holden and Gene have the brains to deal with life, if they want to. Both boys are incisive about human nature, particularly the ability to see through sham. For instance, just as Holden detects the detachment and lack of interest shown by his teachers

Example transition

at Pency, so does Gene sense the irrelevance of the teachers at Devon. (However,) despite this incisiveness, both boys escape when life makes demands. (For example,) Holden runs away from school, and home, before his parents are notified of his expulsion. In a more subtle way, Gene escapes learning about himself by submitting to Devon's many questionable rituals. (In effect,) opposing forces — intelligence versus fear — in both boys make ''coping'' a difficult task.

Contrast transition

Example transition

Conclusion transition

Topic sentence

Holden and Gene have marked contrasts in personality that affect their respective abilities to cope. Holden takes a light-hearted, almost glib, look at the world's shortcomings, criticizes them, and consciously sets himself apart. In reality, Holden is guilty of the same types of sham he lampoons in others. His patronizing attitude toward the nun and his pseudo-sophistication with the prostitute are only two examples of his lack of self-awareness. Gene, (on the other hand,) less glib, less willing to attack or lampoon, makes a more conscious attempt to act consistently with his values. He recognizes the seriousness of what he has done to Finny and broods over it. (In addition) to being more self-aware, Gene is more willing to accept society's norms and live within them — to compromise; Holden cannot compromise.

Topic sentence

Two points of dissimilarity

Contrast transition

Extension transition

In conclusion, <u>one can argue that Gene copes with life better than Holden</u>. The reader is allowed to see Gene, a mature man, having come to peace with himself. Although we are not allowed to see Holden as a mature man, <u>the final chapter of the book suggests that he may always have problems dealing with those aspects of life he can't accept.</u>	Topic sentence Clincher sentence

TYPES OF WRITING

Reports

LIBRARY RESEARCH

Students frequently engage in reference reading for their English, social science, and science classes. In reference reading, they have to find the answer to a question by locating and reading relevant materials in the library. This presumes that the students know how to locate information in the library and judge its relevance. These skills are taken up in chapter 18, "Future Scene: A Schoolwide Program."

Let's suppose for now the student has located the references needed to answer the question. The student still has to judge which parts of the references are relevant. To teach the student to judge relevancy, the teacher can take the entire class through the two exercises below. In the first, a question is stated, discussed, and broken up into its implicit subquestions. References should be available to answer each subquestion.

> *Main Question:* How do mass media attempt to control the ways in which people act?
> *Subquestions:* How are people influenced by advertising? How can newspapers try to control how people think? What devices do politicians use to influence people?

Then the teacher takes the class through an exercise like that in Box 9.13 for judging the relevancy of a reference passage for answering a question or subquestion.

BOX 9.13. *Exercise for Judging Relevancy*

Question: How are people influenced by advertising?
Passage: Generally speaking, color photographs, rather than black and white, appeal
to slick magazine readers. The sight of a freckled child grinning over a bowl of
steaming tomato soup can stir the gastric juices.
Teacher: Does this passage contain any information for answering our question?

The teacher takes the class through a reference a passage at a time, asking the
students to judge whether or not each passage is relevant to a given question. If
so, the essential information is put on cards.

To teach the students to get the most relevant material, start with the broadest
relevant topics and proceed to the narrower topics. Looking under the broad topic
''government,'' students could eventually find the steps in the passage of a bill
through the legislature; but the process would be slow. It would be better to teach
students, first, to use an index to search for the specific category. If this search
fails, they can switch to the broad-to-narrow search strategy.

Research on reference reading (Gans, 1940) suggests that (a) if students are
frustrated in their search, they modify the question to such an extent that the
answer obtained is the answer to an entirely different question; (b) students do
not appear to improve from fourth grade to college in reference reading; and (c)
reference reading results in more achievement than reading a single textbook,
perhaps because students can select books they can comprehend (Barrilleaux,
1967).

The probable reason for lack of development in reference reading is that it is
not taught systematically through the grades. Teachers tend to assume students
know how to read reference literature in each content area. Not until students get
to the college level do they have courses, such as historiography, in which they
learn how to do library research.

To teach reference reading, teachers should admonish students to keep their
questions in mind; use an index; search from broad to narrow categories; judge
relevancy; and, as a follow up, they should check to make sure students answered the questions as they were posed, not as they may have modified them.

WRITING LIBRARY REPORTS

After the information has been collected, the next step is to organize it to use in a
written report. The teacher asks the class to organize cards into groups that
contain similar information. These groups are then placed under their related
subquestions. Now the information can be organized in paragraphs for a report.

The first step in writing paragraphs is to decide on a writing pattern for a
particular group of cards. See Table 9.3 for types of writing patterns. Of course,

the same information can be written into different types of paragraphs as shown in Box 9.14. After paragraphs have been written for each groups of cards, decide on the type of organization for the entire report—expository, chronological, problem-solution, question-answer—and arrange the paragraphs to fit this organization. Then write an introductory paragraph and transitional sentences. The result is a completed report. Essentially, the process is the reverse of reading and then outlining a passage.

BOX 9.14. The Same Information in Two Writing Patterns

1. People tend to be influenced by the colors they see in magazine advertisements. Red makes them excited. Blue and green are soothing. Yellow produces a warming sensation.
2. The fiery red of a lipstick ad would not be appropriate for use in a coffee ad. Yellow would be ineffective in selling cigarettes. People are affected by the colors they see in magazines.

After teaching the whole class to write reports, the next step is to give the same set of information to different groups and have each group organize and write a report. The last step is to assign each individual to organize and write a report based on given information on a question. Through this sequence, the teacher phases out from maximum to minimum direction. Each member of the class should now be ready to engage in reference reading and writing. To evaluate their ability, the teacher might give each student a question to research in the library. Every student does the library work (locates and abstracts relevant material) and writes a report with the resulting information. (Preferably the library assignment and the report will be short.) Students then read their reports in groups for initial critical evaluation, editing and polishing, and final group evaluation. With successful completion of this assignment, the teacher will know the members of the class are ready for reference reading and report writing.

Reporting is only one of the four types of writing. The second type of writing is called *exposition*.

Exposition

Exposition is the type of writing that deals with explanation—explanation of a process, explanation of a point of view, explanation of a work of literature, explanation of an idea, explanation of a philosophy, and so forth. This type of writing is more demanding than reporting because, rather than merely recalling and relating information, the writer interprets the information, analyzes the information, or reacts to the information. In Box 9.15 are some writing topics that demand exposition, not mere reporting. These topics can be used for in-class or out-of-class writing assignments.

BOX 9.15. Topics for Expository Writing

SCIENCE

1. Which one of the following scientists made the most significant contribution to physical science: Lavoisier, Newton, Priestley, Galileo? Explain the significance of this contribution. (Contrast this topic with "Report on the contributions of Lavoisier, Newton, Priestley, and Galileo to physical science.")
2. What erroneous assumptions about the universe did Copernicus make? Why did he make them? (Contrast this topic with "Describe Copernicus' view of the universe.")

SOCIAL STUDIES

3. Do you think that Benedict Arnold was truly a traitor? Explain your thinking.

ENGLISH

4. How does the horror in Nathaniel Hawthorne's "Dr. Heideggar's Experiment" differ from the horror in Poe's "The Cask of Amontillado"?
5. Do you think Holden Caulfield acts immaturely? Explain your answer.

MATHEMATICS

6. Explain why the intersection of two planes makes a *straight* line and why the intersection of a plane and a sphere forms a *curved* line.

HOMEMAKING

7. Explain what you would have to do differently in preparing a dinner for two and a dinner for eight hundred that would be equally satisfying to all the diners.

As with reporting, students find it difficult to organize their ideas for expository writing. For writing exposition, there is no better advice than "Tell 'em what you're gonna tell 'em; tell 'em; and tell 'em you told 'em." In other words, you need a beginning, a middle, and an end. In the technical vocabulary of the writer, you need an introduction, a body, and a conclusion.

An *introduction* can do several things. First, it can contain eye-catching, highly motivating material that arouses the reader's interest. Second, it can pose a provocative question. Third, it can state the main idea of the composition. Fourth, it can provide information on what will appear in subsequent paragraphs. Here is the opening paragraph of a student composition entitled "How to Conduct a Scientific Experiment":

It wasn't a large explosion—merely a hiss as the piece of magnesium I had dipped in bromide water flew away after I lighted it on the Bunsen burner. Had I done wrong by experimenting? Wasn't this how all great discoveries were made— through trial and error? I have now learned that scientific experimentation is more than mere trial and error. In the following paragraphs, I will (a) review the basic steps in conducting any sceintific experiment, (b) describe an experiment, using the basic steps, and (c) contrast this experiment with one in which I had used trial and error.

Certainly, every introductory paragraph doesn't need to be so elaborate. In fact, many teachers might prefer a simpler, more direct introduction:

> In this paper, I am going to contrast trial-and-error experimentation with the scientific method.

or

> That scientific method and trial-and-error experimentation are in sharp contrast will be demonstrated in this paper in three stages. First, I will review the basic steps in scientific inquiry. Second, I will describe an experiment, using the basic steps. Third, I will contrast this experiment with one using trial and error.

The *body* of a piece of expository writing usually contains two or more paragraphs, each focusing on one aspect of the paper's main idea. In a paper with the topic above, one paragraph might focus on reviewing the steps of scientific inquiry. A second paragraph would focus on the properly conducted experiment. A third paragraph would contrast the scientific experiment with another experiment using the trial-and-error method.

A *conclusion* summarizes the paper briefly and leaves the reader with a sense of completeness:

> In this paper I have attempted to demonstrate the differences between scientific method and trial-and-error experimentation. By citing actual experiments, I hope I have made the contrasts more vivid.

A sequence of brief activities that will help you to *teach* expository writing is given in Box 9.16.

BOX 9.16. Sequence of Activities for Teaching Expository Writing

Select one of the seven topics listed in box 7.15. Briefly describe how you would help students to organize a four or five paragraph composition focusing on the topic. Be sure to:

1. help the student plan a main idea (indicate what this main idea might be).
2. offer suggestions for body paragraphs that would function as subpoints to the main idea.
3. offer suggestions for writing an introduction.
4. offer suggestions for writing a conclusion.

After students gain experience at writing library reports and expository compositions (preferably using resources that you can control), they may be ready to begin elementary forms of research. Systems that can help in the teaching of term paper and research paper writing are available to teachers. Such systems generally include methods for writing bibliography cards and note cards, outlining, writing footnotes and bibliographies, and so forth.[3] With the ubiquitous nature of such materials, it would be repetitious to dwell on research writing, other than to say that it is frequently assigned.

The values of the long research paper for high school students has often been debated. Many teachers maintain that the experience of writing a term paper will assist students who plan to attend college. Other teachers maintain that the time demanded to teach the term paper is excessive in relation to the quality of work that high school students are capable of doing. Still other teachers have their students do the research but write a short paper or abstract.

Most teachers require students to give credit for ideas that are not original. This crediting of sources is called *documentation*. There are two types of documentation, formal and informal. Formal documentation requires footnotes for direct quotations, indirect quotations, and any other references to ideas that are not original to the writer of the research paper. Box 9.17 contains an example of formal documentation.

BOX 9.17. *Example of Formal Documentation*

. . . . That Washington was the greatest military leader in American history has been disputed by prominent historians.[4] One in particular wrote, ''The fact of the matter is that whereas George Washington was a brilliant strategist, there were many of his colleagues equally qualified.''[5] Indeed, Jon Best believes that Benedict Arnold had superior qualities of military leadership.[6]

[4] Philip Bowson, ''What Leading Historians Say about George Washington.'' *History Journal,* vol. 34 (April 1956), p. 36.

[5] Beaudreau McDorf, *George Washington: Leader of Men.* (New York: Bragwick Publishing, 1965), p. 467.

[6] Jon Best, ''Not Now, Traitor,'' *Timely History,* vol. 76 (June 1948), pp. 33–45.

With informal documentation the writer merely cites the author and work within the context of a paragraph as shown below.

---

[3] For examples of these methods see the following: Dorothea M. Berry and Gordon P. Martin, *Guide to Writing Research Papers.* New York: McGraw-Hill, 1971; Kate L. Turabian, *A Manual for Writers of Term Papers, Theses, and Dissertations,* 4th ed. Chicago: University of Chicago Press, 1973; The University of Chicago Press, *Chicago Manual of Style,* 13th ed., rev. Chicago: University of Chicago Press, 1983.

That Washington was the greatest military leader in American history has been disputed by prominent historians. In his article, "What Historians Say about George Washington," appearing in the April 1956 issue of *History Journal*, Philip Bowson refers to at least twenty historians who cite Washington as being of lesser military ability than contemporary American generals. . . .

Whether teachers assign short research papers or long ones, students, particularly those in upper grades, should be taught methods of careful documentation. If students cannot discriminate their own ideas from those of other writers, the experience of research writing will be hollow for them.

Narration

Simply stated, *narration* is storytelling. It usually involves a series of events (often chronologically arranged) and sometimes dialogue. Some of the more common forms of narration assigned to students are jokes, anecdotes, tall tales, vignettes, short short stories, and short stories. One of the most difficult problems in narration is writing dialogue. In Box 9.18 is an example of correctly written story dialogue, glossed so you can see the number of conventions in form.

BOX 9.18. *Story Dialogue Illustrating Conventions in Form*

The two men faced each other unbelievingly.

The taller man spoke. "Don't I know you from somewhere?" — Note sequence of punctuation

Explainer — "Yes," the shorter man said. "Your bank refused my loan application."

No explainer needed — "Yes, I remember now. You didn't have enough collateral."

"Now I have less." He stared intently at the taller man with almost frightening ferocity. — Explainer continues thread of story

---

Argumentation

The last type of writing to be discussed is *argumentation*. Unlike exposition, which explains an idea from an *objective* viewpoint, argumentation is *subjective*. The writer's purpose is to persuade the reader to accept a point of view. Among several types of argumentation are these:

1. defending a social, political, religious, or cultural ideology
2. taking a stand on a current event
3. attacking or defending an individual

The following paragraph is an excerpt from a high school composition, an argument, entitled, "What School Rule Needs Changing Most"? The intended audience was a group of the school's administrators and counselors.

> Another reason the campus should close is student morale. As it is now, students are allowed to come and go as they please. Sometimes there's more going than coming—with a harmful result: students feel teachers don't care if they come to class or not. We used to think freedom on campus was a good thing. But kids can't handle too much freedom—they mistake freedom for indifference.

Summary of Writing Types

The basic types of writing are (a) reporting, (b) exposition, (c) narration, and (d) argumentation. As you have read, these types have basic differences. Table 9.3 summarizes these differences.

Although students may use four different types of formal writing in responding to text, they can also use informal kinds of writing which you do not need to collect or evaluate.

TABLE 9.3. *Characteristics of Four Basic Writing Types*

Writing Type	Purpose	What Is Required of the Student	Sample Assignment
Reporting	Organize and relay information	Gather information and organize it according to questions or other directions	1. Answers to study questions 2. Answers to essay questions 3. Library research
Exposition	Explain	Interpret, analyze, and react to information	1. Solve a problem 2. Tell how to do something
Narration	Entertain	Retell fictional events in chronological order; use dialogue	1. Anecdotes 2. Vignettes 3. Short stories
Argumentation	Persuade	Defend a point of view by supplying only the evidence that supports it	1. Taking a stand on a current event 2. Attacking an individual 3. Defending a political belief

WRITING ACTIVITIES YOU DON'T NEED
TO COLLECT AND GRADE

In the previous section, we described several kinds of traditional writing assignments that teachers collect, grade, and return to the students—for example, study guides, essay examinations, library reports, and term papers. These are sometimes referred to as *writing products*. Other kinds of classroom writing do not have to be submitted for evaluation. In other words, students can write in class as a means of helping themselves learn from text more efficiently. These kinds of processes are called "writing-to-learn" activities (Gere, 1985). Although there are many writing-to-learn activities, five will be treated here in detail: note-taking, learning logs, graphic organizers, clustering, and mapping.

Note-taking

One of the most common forms of writing to learn is note-taking. As students read text, listen to lectures or class discussions, they make notes so that they can remember information for examinations. If note-taking is a product of careful reading and listening, it can become a powerful means for learning.

NOTE-TAKING AS A REFLECTION
OF READING SKILL

As students begin to read independently, for example, as they prepare library reports, note-taking is a valuable technique for retrieving information from a large number of sources not available to students at home. In order to take effective reading notes, students must generate questions, read to find answers to the questions, and record the answers in their own words in note form, to be retrieved later as they prepare reports. Further discussion of this note-taking for reports appears in chapter 6 (SQ3R) and earlier in this chapter, under "paraphrasing."

NOTE-TAKING AS A REFLECTON
OF LISTENING SKILLS

Just as effective notetaking is an indication of good reading and study skills, it is also a reflection of good listening skills. Although various kinds of note-taking strategies exist (Askov & Dupuis, 1982; Readance, Bean, & Baldwin, 1981) all of them require students to listen to information critically and record it for later use. If students listen accurately, they will generally make accurate notes to help them recall information for a test. Low scores on tests that focus on recalling lectures and discussions may suggest poor listening habits. Here is a general procedure that Mildred Montgomery uses in her ninth-grade social studies class:

STEP 1.   Listening while following a complete outline:

For the first lecture of the year, Ms. Montgomery prepares a detailed outline that the students read as she lectures. The students supply no further information. After the students study the outline, she gives the students a short quiz on the material. After the quiz is corrected, Ms. Montgomery shows the students where in the outline the answers to the quiz questions are found.

STEP 2.   Listening for specific examples:

After repeating STEP 1 several times, Ms. Montgomery prepares a less detailed outline of a lecture. As before, the students follow the outline as she lectures. However, at designated points in the lecture, students are directed to supply missing examples on the outline form. As before, Montgomery gives students a quiz immediately after the lecture. The score on the quiz indicates how well the students followed the outline, listening for the missing examples, and writing them down on the outline page.

STEP 3.   Listening for details and specific examples:

After repeating STEP 2 several times, Ms. Montgomery continues to give students outlines of her lectures, gradually eliminating detail for the students to supply. Again, after each lecture, she gives the students a quiz. The quiz score, as she points out, is an indication of how well the students listen for information that is omitted from the lecture outlines.

STEP 4.   Listening for major ideas, details, and examples:

Eventually, Ms. Montgomery is able to lecture effectively to her students without providing them with either lecture outlines or quizzes that assess short-term memory. However, Ms. Montgomery admits that every class is different. Some move more quickly to independent note-taking than others. For example, in one ninth-grade social studies class, she found she was still using STEP 2 in February, almost 6 months after introducing STEP 1.

So far, we have discussed general note-taking. What follows is a specific writing strategy for teaching students to become independent learners.

Learning Logs

Learning logs can be an effective way of note-taking to retain information read in the text or obtained in class lectures and discussions (Barr, D'Arcy, & Healy, 1982). In fact, research conducted by Tierney (1981) and Wotring (1981) shows that students can learn the content of even the most difficult courses such as chemistry and biology by using learning logs. Although there are a number of ways students can maintain a learning log, the method described here is typical.

The learning log is maintained in a notebook containing split page columns. Stenographer pads are particularly useful for this kind of note-taking. As students read text, listen to lectures, or participate in discussions, they make notes in the right-hand column. Notes would include technical vocabulary with definitions, examples, explanations, and data charts, demonstration problems. The notes, each day, are reviewed by the students (some teachers allow class time for reviewing learning logs). As the students review notes, they make notations in the left-hand column in the form of questions, comments, explanations, drawings, or symbols. The notations are made directly left of the classnotes in question. For example, a page from a 12th-grade student's science learning log might look something like this:

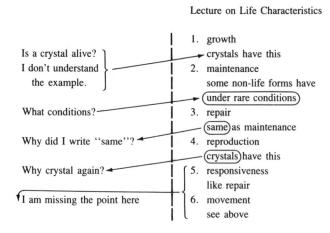

Lecture on Life Characteristics

In the learning log, the student has taken somewhat sketchy lecture notes which, upon reviewing, he doesn't seem to understand. The cause may be inadequate listening skills, as well as comprehension. However, the process of writing in the learning log clarifies what it is he doesn't understand so that he can ask intelligent questions in class. For example, ''Mr. Phelps, why did you keep referring to crystals when you were talking about life forms? Is the crystal a life form? Are you saying that there is no sure way to differentiate between life and nonlife forms?'' Standard note-taking procedures do not allow the students the opportunity to review their notes and interact with them. Knowing what it is you do not understand is the first step in learning. Analyzing and improving note-taking skills may improve listening skills.

Graphic Organizers

In chapter 6, ''Single-Text Strategies,'' we discussed graphic organizers as a text feature strategy you could use with students in helping them to learn more effectively from text. If you have demonstrated graphic organizers to your students, they can learn to make their own graphic organizers as study aids for organizing text's idea structure.

When students first begin to make graphic organizers, you can present them with a partially completed graphic structure, such as the example below:
Instructions: Now that you have read chapter 5 on drugs, review the chapter and complete the following graphic organizer.

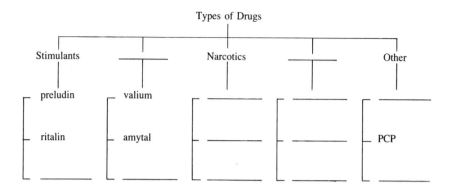

When students complete their graphic organizers, you can review the organizer on the front board or with an overhead projector. Students can also share their organizers in small groups with these focusing directions:

1. Share your graphic organizer with other members in your group.
2. If you disagree on the placement of any item, return to the textbook for the correct answer.
3. Be prepared to share your group's agreed-upon graphic organizer with the rest of the class.

As students continue to work with partially completed graphic organizers, they gradually learn to make their own. Students can use graphic organizers as effective summaries of text chapters to be used in subsequent classroom discussions. In addition, students can use graphic organizers in lieu of the traditional outline, as they prepare to write essay examination questions and library reports (Donlan, 1985).

Clustering

Clustering, like graphic organizers, is a writing activity intended to help students learn more effectively from their textbooks. Clustering can be used both as a prereading and as a postreading activity. As a prereading activity, clustering helps students understand and organize information they already know about a given topic they will soon encounter in the textbook. As a postreading activity, clustering provides students with a method for recalling information from a text passage and putting it into some sort of logical framework. Whether used as a prereading or a postreading activity, clustering has three distinct stages. First, students list in random, almost stream-of-consciousness form words and phrases they associate with a given topic. Second, students group these words and phrases together into categories by connecting them with lines, numbers, or circles; arrows are used to connect these newly formed clusters (Southwest Regional Educational Laboratory, 1982). Third, the students use the clusters as the basis for writing a brief summary of the topic. What follows is an example of a cluster prepared by a fifth-grade student on the topic ''My Community'':

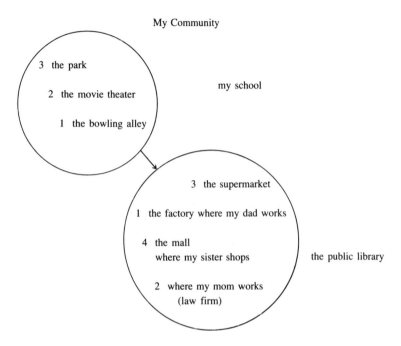

This clustering exercise helped the student write the following short essay about his community:

> The community I live in means a lot to me and my family. I like my town because I can have a lot of fun in it. I can go bowling at Verity Lanes. If I don't want to bowl, I can always go to a movie at The Palace, or go skateboarding in the park. My family likes the community because they work there or shop there. My father works as a foreman at Sheila Foods. My mother is a lawyer at Willbanks, Breckner, and Totah. We all to to the store at Fill the Kart. And then there's my sister, who spends her life at Bergener's Mall. I really like my town.

Rather than writing an essay based on disorganized and random facts, the clustering activity helped this student organize his thoughts so that he could describe his community in a somewhat logical way. Having written this essay, he can now begin to read the social studies chapter, ''Life in the Community,'' from his social studies text.

Mapping

Like graphic organizers and clustering, mapping is a visual means of organizing ideas into structure in preparation for reading or writing or as a summarization strategy. Whereas graphic organizers and clustering must adhere to certain structural procedures, a map can take any form the student wishes to give it. Like clustering, mapping proceeds in a series of three steps. First, the teacher directs students in a brainstorming activity—eliciting words and phrases from students on a given topic. Second, the items in the list are grouped together for similarities and then categorized with labels (see the Taba method described in chapter 8, ''Letting the Students Do the Talking''). When the students are finished they place all of the items and category labels on a map that clearly shows the relationships among the items (Buckley & Boyle, 1983). What follows is a map the same fifth-grade social studies student made about his community:

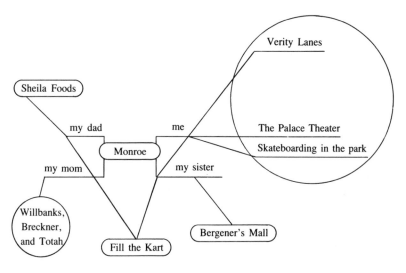

The map could also have looked like this:

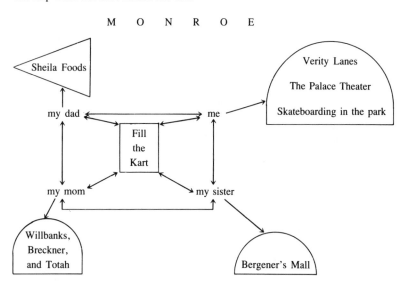

or like this:

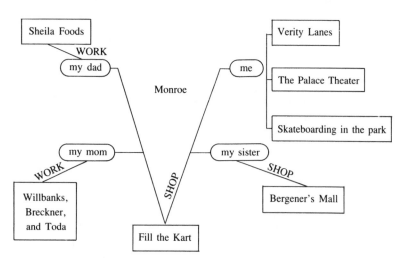

A BASIC UNIT OF WRITING:
THE PARAGRAPH

Writing and reading are intimately related. What an author writes, someone is likely to read. When an author writes in simple, straightforward language, the reader has few problems comprehending the text. When an author writes in difficult, convoluted language, the reader has many problems comprehending the text. For example, which of the two passages below is harder to read?

Examples

HIGH SCHOOL LEADERS FLUNK OUT!

You'll find it is hard to lead an active extracurricular life and keep up your grades. Last year, for example, four cheerleaders failed English. Next, five varsity players had only C averages. Then, twelve members of the marching band had to drop math or science classes because they couldn't keep up. So, you can see that extracurricular activity and study don't mix too well.

—Sammy Smith, Grade 10 for *Monroe High Currier*

FAILURE AMONG HIGH-POTENTIAL
STUDENTS

Involvement in extracurricular activity frequently precludes effective scholarship. Last year's grade average statistics verify the above assertion. Students directly and indirectly affiliated with varsity sports were frequently unable to make high grades or to carry appropriate academic course loads. That scholarship and peripheral school-sponsored activities do not mix is patently obvious.

—George Phelps, in response to
Monroe High School Accreditation Inquiry

Both passages say approximately the same thing. Sammy, a tenth grader, wrote in his own straightforward style for the school newspaper. Those who read Sammy's article should have few problems comprehending it. George Phelps, a science teacher, wrote in his own technical style for a school accreditation team. Those team members who read Phelps's article should have few problems comprehending it. The problem arises when Sammy tries to write like Mr. Phelps or when Monroe High students try to comprehend what Mr. Phelps has written. However, with instruction, you can teach students to read paragraphs such as that written by Mr. Phelps, and later to write such paragraphs. In other words, instruction in learning from text and instruction in writing are closely connected. Therefore, content area teachers might profitably spend some time showing students how to read and write paragraphs, since the paragraph is the basic organizational unit of writing.

Table 9.4 contains a list of paragraph types and the purposes they serve in communication (H. A. Robinson, 1975; Shepherd, 1978). Each type has some signal words that indicate the writer's intent and prepare the reader for what is coming. Students should become knowledgeable about the paragraph types and the signal words to help them in writing and in reading. In the last column of the table are listed teaching strategies to help the student become familiar with paragraph types through writing or reading exercises. A general strategy, not listed in the box, is to have students do a paragraph-by-paragraph analysis of a text: Students are likely to discern that the text follows a pattern of writing, as a sequence of paragraph types begins to repeat itself on successive topics in the text. This knowledge will help the students understand writing style and facilitate their reading and learning from text as well as their own writing in response to text.

The Structure of a Paragraph

The paragraph is supposed to be a series of carefully sequenced sentences tied together by a main idea, or topic sentence, which is located at the beginning of a paragraph. At least, this definition is accepted by most teachers of reading or writing. In actual practice, unfortunately, the "rule" is broken more frequently than adhered to. According to Braddock (1974), who examined the paragraph structure of numerous prose passages found in popularly read magazines, the topic sentence is located at the start of a paragraph only 14% of the time. The rest of the time it is either at the end, in the middle, or missing completely. The challenge for teachers is to show students how to write good paragraphs by the "rules," while at the same time teaching them how to read text paragraphs that violate the rules. It is in the study of paragraph structure that students as readers and students as writers come closest together.

TABLE 9.4. Paragraph Types

Paragraph Type and Purpose	Example	Signal or Transition Words	Teaching Strategy
1. *Introductory* overview, establish purpose (sometimes written in narrative style)	"In this chapter we shall explain three ideas."	this chapter describes; let's examine; here we will study . . . (questions)	State major points of section or chapter
2. *Narrative* (who, what, where, when, how) tell a story, integrate ideas and feelings in concrete situations, form visual image	"John is going through three steps now."	the scene is	Answer *wh* questions
3. *Descriptive* set the scene, visualize	"Picture this scene . . ."	describe; imagine; picture	Draw a picture or diagram
4. *Definitional* (may overlap with expository) clarifies meaning of word, phrase, or clause	"Rubella is a virus."	called; for example; means; that is (aids: parentheses, comparison or contrast, synonym, appositional phrase)	1. Tell what something is or means. 2. What is something like? 3. What is another word for?
5. *Expository or Explanatory* explain and inform	steps in process; chronology; directions; relate cause-effect; problem-solution; question-answer	first, next, after, then, to make, to do, since, because	1. Outline steps or events. 2. Answer question on cause for effect or solution for problem or answer to question.
6. *Summary and Conclusion* restate essential ideas	To summarize the two main points covered: (1)____ and (2)____.	thus: to briefly review; consequently; hence; you can see; in summary; to conclude we found . . . ; from the evidence; therefore; as a result . . .	State major points of section or chapter.

7. *Transitional*

(hybrids, mixture of two or more types) relate what proceeded to what follows (may be in question form)	"Now that we have covered our first two points, let's go on to our third point."	Now we shall consider . . . ; What do these reports tell us? however; on the other hand; yet; meanwhile; although; conversely; nevertheless; otherwise	Separate preceding from forward pointing ideas

FOUR BASIC STRUCTURES

Paragraphs can be written in any number of ways. However, there are four basic structures that students will encounter as they read text. What follows are brief examples of these four structures, along with explanations of the structures. Later in this chapter, we show you how to teach students to recognize paragraph structures and apply these structures in their own writing.

We begin with a simple three-sentence paragraph about differences among siblings:

> My two brothers are different from one another. John, the older of the two, studies continually and is planning to be a doctor. Phil, the youngest, constantly works on cars and plans to be a professional racer.

The same paragraph can be written by placing the topic sentence at the end of the paragraph:

> John, the older of my two brothers, studies continually and is planning to be a doctor. Phil, the youngest, constantly works on cars and plans to be a professional racer. My two brothers are different from one another.

Even though the information in both paragraphs is identical, it is presented in markedly different ways. In the first paragraph, the main idea is presented at the beginning, with the supporting details following it. This type of organization is referred to as *Deduction*. In the second paragraph, the main idea follows the supporting details. This kind of organization is called *Induction*.

Although many paragraphs are written either inductively or deductively, many other paragraphs are presented with the topic sentence in the middle or absent. Here is the previous paragraph written with the topic sentence in the middle of the supportive details:

> John, the older of my two brothers, studies continually and is planning to be a doctor. To show you how different brothers can be, let me contrast John with Phil, my younger brother. Phil constantly works on cars and plans to be a professional racer.

This paragraph can also be written without a topic sentence:

> John, the older of the two, studies continually and is planning to be a doctor. Phil, the youngest, constantly works on cars and plans to be a professional racer.

With this paragraph, the reader must make an inference as to the main idea, since the author does not supply it.

Teaching Students to Recognize Basic Paragraph Structures

If students recognize and understand the basic paragraph structures, they can more readily learn from text. One way to understand paragraph structure is to diagram paragraphs by assigning number values to each sentence within the paragraph (Christensen, 1967; Donlan, 1980; Horn, 1973). The number 1 is assigned to the main idea or topic sentence. A number 2 is assigned to any sentence that supports the topic sentence. A 3 is assigned to any sentence that supports a number 2 sentence. And so forth. Here is how this method could be applied to the paragraph about John and Phil:

> (1) My two brothers are different from one another. (2) John, the older of the two, studies continually and is planning to be a doctor. (2) Phil, the youngest, constantly works on cars and plans to be a professional racer.

The first sentence is labeled 1 because it is a topic sentence. The other two sentences are labeled 2 because they directly support the topic sentence. The diagram for this paragraph would look like this:

1. My two brothers . . . another.
   2. John . . . doctor.
   2. Phil . . . racer.

Had the paragraph been written inductively, the diagram would look like this:

   2. John . . . doctor.
   2. Phil . . . racer.
1. My two brothers . . . another.

Had the topic sentence appeared in the middle, the diagram would look like this:

   2. John . . . doctor.
1. My two brothers . . . another.
   2. Phil . . . racer.

Had the paragraph been written without a topic sentence, the diagram would look like this:

    2. John . . . doctor
    2. Phil . . . racer.

or like this:

    1. John . . . doctor.
    1. Phil . . . racer.

Students can learn to diagram simple content area focused paragraphs such as these:

> There are basically three kinds of rocks. Sedimentary rocks are made from sand and gravel particles. Igneous rocks were formed by fire, such as lava. Other rocks, like marble, are called metamorphic rock because over time they changed their form because of chemical or climatic conditions.

This paragraph can be described as a 1-2-2-2 paragraph which would be diagramed like this:

    1. There are . . . rocks.
      2. Sedimentary . . . particles.
      2. Igneous . . . lava.
      2. Other rocks . . . conditions.

Here is an example of a simple inductively written paragraph from a social studies text:

> Most of the soldiers were either asleep or recovering from drunkenness. The sentries could be found only in a couple of lookout positions. Much of the heavy artillery was locked in sheds or covered in canvas. Four of the commanding officers were absent from the post. The army was totally unprepared for the guerilla attack.

This inductively written paragraph has the topic sentence, or main idea, at the end of the paragraph, as evidenced by this diagram:

      2. Most of the soldiers . . . drunkenness.
      2. Sentries . . . positions.
      2. Much of the . . . canvas.
      2. Four of the . . . post.
    1. The army . . . attack.

Students can be taught later to diagram more complicated deductively and inductively organized paragraphs:

> It should have been no surprise to the community when Gudmunsen Motors went bankrupt. For five years, the company had been involved in a major lawsuit. A

customer who had purchased a new car claimed in court that the car had an inadequate braking system. The customer also claimed that the company's failure to make good on the warranty by repairing the breaks was the direct cause of a serious automobile accident in which three children were seriously injured. Mr. Gudmunsen had become somewhat of a scandal in town when auditors determined that he had misused four hundred thousand dollars in investors' money to buy common stock on margin. When the stock declined in value, rather than increase as Gudmunsen had thought, he was unable to replace the funds. Competition also reduced Gudmunsen's profit margins. In 1954, Gudmunsen was the only major new car dealer in town. Now, there were twelve other dealerships.

Now reread the same paragraph with the appropriate numbers before each of the sentences:

(1) It should have been no surprise to the community when Gudmunsen Motors went bankrupt. (2) For five years, the company had been involved in a major lawsuit. (3) A customer who had purchased a new car claimed in court that the car had an inadequate braking system. (3) The customer also claimed that the company's failure to make good on the warranty by repairing the brakes was the direct cause of a serious automobile accident in which three children were seriously injured. (2) Mr. Gudmunsen had become somewhat of a scandal in town when auditors determined that he had misused four hundred thousand dollars in investors' money to buy common stock on margin. (3) When the stock declined in value, rather than increase as Gudmunsen had thought, he was unable to replace the funds. (2) Competition also reduced Gudmunsen's profit margins. (3) In 1954, Gudmunsen was the only major new car dealer in town. (3) Now, there were twelve other dealerships.

As you can see, the topic sentence, labeled 1, is at the beginning of the paragraph. It is the most general sentence in the paragraph. It asserts that the community should not have been surprised at the bankruptcy. The rest of the paragraph supports that assertion by providing background information on the three factors leading to the bankruptcy: the lawsuit, the misuse of money, and competition. Sentences that introduce these factors are labeled with 2s. The remaining sentences are labeled 3s because they provide additional information concerning the factors. The paragraph's diagramed structure would look like this:

1._____
  2._____
    3._____
    3._____
  2._____
    3._____
  2._____
    3._____
    3._____

By identifying sentences in paragraphs by numbers and diagramming the paragraphs, students learn not only how sentences relate to one another in paragraphs but also, and more important, how ideas within those sentences relate. Continual analyses of paragraph structures will improve students' abilities to learn from even difficult and ambiguous text.

EVALUATING WRITING

The concept of evaluating writing is simple: you make a judgment on how well the student has met the criteria of the assignment. If you haven't established the criteria or goals for the student to attain, you have no basis for evaluation. If you ask students to write a 10-page report on rocks, you have expressed only two criteria: length and subject. Whereas many student would have no problem meeting your requirements, some students might mistakenly believe they were meeting the assignment by copying the entire report from reference books.

Establishing Criteria

The first step in establishing criteria is to decide upon the *manuscript form* you wish the student to use and distribute a copy of it at the beginning of the course; thus, you will avoid having to repeat the conventions each time you give the assignment. !n Box 9.19 are directions for manuscript form that you may want a student to follow throughout the course. The second step in establishing criteria is to decide *how much spelling, punctuation, capitalization, and usage will count, if at all*. Students in English classes are used to being evaluated in terms of the ''correctness'' of their writing, but they seldom expect it in other classes unless the teacher announces it ahead of time.

The third step in establishing criteria is to *decide what the paper's content is to be and how the student should organize the content*.

BOX 9.19.   Directions for Manuscript Form

Please follow these directions for each manuscript you turn in during this course.
1. Write on one side of each page. Use pen or typewriter (double space).
2. Number all pages in the right-hand corner beginning with the second page.
3. Fold paper in half lengthwise and endorse on the outside flap in the following way:

LAST NAME, First name
Class name, period
Date
Assignment Title

Using Holistic Rating Strategies

English teachers spend many hours evaluating student papers—writing in margins; supplying introductory and terminal comments; correcting spelling, punctuation, and usage; and perhaps even rewriting passages. Although this has proved to be most useful in helping students to improve their writing, other content area teachers shy away from such an onerous task, and perhaps they should. To avoid lengthy and time-consuming evaluation of student papers, teachers may use two rating techniques that are not only quick but also *holistic*, that is, they evaluate all aspects of a paper (Braddock & others, 1963; Cooper & Odell, 1977). The first of these holistic *evaluation* techniques is the *general impression method*. The teacher reviews each paper quickly and assigns a grade based on a general impression. The general impression is formed by the criteria that the teacher has established for the assignment. Box 9.20 contains an example.

GENERAL IMPRESSION METHOD

BOX 9.20. Assignment with Enabling Suggestions and Holistic Criteria for Evaluating Written Responses

ASSIGNMENT

Student Instructions: Select a Civil War battle that you feel accomplished little or nothing for either the North or the South. In an introductory paragraph describe the battle briefly. In a second paragraph explain how the battle accomplished nothing for the North. In a third paragraph explain how the battle accomplished nothing for the South. Remember to use specific names of people, places, and events; in other words, give good, clear examples. Attach a brief summary paragraph.

CRITERIA

Rating	Description
6	A **6** paper will be *outstanding* in all aspects. The selected battle will be summarized *briefly, yet fully.* The writer will *clearly* show, by concrete example, how both the North and South gained little or nothing from the battle. The four-paragraph structure will be *strictly maintained as required by the assignment.* The paper will show *excellent style* and be *accurately written* with regard to spelling, punctuation, usage, sentence structure.
5	A **5** paper will be *strong* in all aspects. The selected battle will be summarized *briefly, yet fairly completely.* The writer will *tend to show* by concrete example, how both the North and South gained little or nothing from the battle. The four-paragraph structure will be *reasonably maintained as required by the assignment.* The paper will show a *sense of style* and be, *for the most part,* accurately written with regard to spelling, punctuation, usage, sentence structure.
4	A **4** paper will be *adequate* in all aspects. The selected battle will be summarized *briefly,* but the *writer may forget one or two important events*

in the battle. The writer will *occasionally* show, by concrete example, how both the North and South gained little or nothing from the battle. The four-paragraph structure will *occasionally be disregarded.* A sense of style *may be absent.* The paper will show *occasional* errors in spelling, punctuation, usage, sentence structure.

3　A **3** paper will be *flawed* in one or two aspects. The selected battle will be summarized in *unneeded length* or the writer may *forget many important events.* The writer will *tend to avoid* concrete examples, although he or she may include one or two. The essay will either be in *one complete paragraph or in many small paragraphs. No attempt at style will be made.* The paper has *frequent* errors in spelling, punctuation, usage, sentence structure.

2　A **2** paper will be *seriously* flawed. The selected battle will be badly and inaccurately summarized. There will be *no concrete examples.* The paragraph structure will be random and chaotic, totally disorganized. The paper has *so many errors that it is virtually unreadable.*

1　A **1** paper fails to respond to the assignment.

ANALYTICAL EVALUATION

Another holistic rating strategy is the *analytical evaluation,* whereby a reader assigns points to various aspects of the writing, adds up the points, and arrives at a final score. In Box 9.21 is a writing assignment, together with the rating scale for its analytical evaluation.

BOX 9.21. *Writing Assignment with Analytical Rating Scale for Evaluating Responses*

ASSIGNMENT

Using three library sources, write a report describing the Mojave desert environment. Include such information as (1) the appearance of the desert, (2) the types of plant and animal life that coexist in the desert, and (3) the damage modern technological society is doing to the desert environment. The report should be written in five paragraphs: an introduction, one paragraph each for (1), (2), (3), above, and a conclusion. Attach a bibliography at the back of the report. Synthesize the information; do not copy. Concentrate on correct usage, variety in sentence length and structure, and accurate use of technical vocabulary.

RATING SCALE

Organization	40 points
introduction	5 points
paragraph on appearance	10 points
paragraph on life	10 points
paragraph on damage	10 points
conclusion	5 points

Documentation	30 points
synthesis of information	10 points
use of three sources	10 points
bibliography	10 points
Style	30 points
correctness of language and convention	10 points
sentence variety: length and structure	10 points
appropriate use of vocabulary	5 points
manuscript appearance	5 points

SUMMARY

This chapter has focused on the teaching of writing, not just assigning it. In doing so, it has emphasized that the general characteristics of writing can be taught in English classes, but that content teachers have to supplement this instruction by teaching students the writing requirements emphasized in their content areas, including spelling of technical words, correct word choice, and ways of organizing information in written responses. Four types of writing were explained: reporting, exposition, narration, and argumentation. The special case of essay writing, particularly on examinations, was discussed with emphasis on well-written questions as a prerequisite for well-written answers. The seven types of paragraphs were defined and illustrated. Throughout we gave suggestions for teaching students to write, including how to write a report on reference reading. We concluded with a section on two holistic ways of evaluating writing: general impression and analytical.

When students can respond to texts with fairly fluent discussions and writing, they are ready to move into multiple-text situations. But, first you will have to know ways of determining reading and readability levels. Then you will be able to select an appropriate range of textbooks. We explain how to determine reading and readability levels in the next chapter.

ACTIVITIES

1. Select a textbook in a content area you want to teach. Develop two writing assignments you would give in (a) narration and (b) argumentation that would show what the students learned from the text. Compare the results, noting how different types of writing led to different emphases of information in the text.
2. Compose directions for a writing assignment in your content area. Include all the criteria you wish to evaluate. Then develop both a general impression and

an analytical rating scale for evaluating it. Which one is more useful for diagnosis? Which is easier to construct and score?

3. Examine two textbooks in your content area. Do they suggest writing assignments, other than particular study questions? Do they give the students enough help in writing these assignments? Are the criteria for evaluation clearly stated?

4. Rewrite the following vague essay questions. In rewriting, (a) supply performance verbs that suggest the mode of student response; (b) limit the content of the response; and (c) make enabling suggestions as to the organization of the response.

   a. Discuss the differences between tropical and subtropical climates.

   b. How is Billy Buck a friend to Jody in *The Red Pony?*

   c. How do the "new mathematics" and the "old mathematics" differ?

   d. Discuss Priestley's experiment using mercurous oxide.

   e. Describe a well-equipped auto shop.

   f. Why are soufflés difficult to make?

10 Readability: A Text Selection Strategy

CHAPTER OVERVIEW

If you teach a ninth-grade science class, a strong possibility exists that half of your students will not be able to comprehend the textbook, even if the book has a ninth-grade readability level. This important chapter focuses on the readability of textbooks. First, you will learn several methods for computing or otherwise determining the reading difficulty of the textbooks you use. Second, you will be shown strategies for predicting how well your students will be able to comprehend their textbooks. Finally, you will see results from surveys and research studies that indicate how well people have to read to survive in school, to function well on the job, and to engage in pleasure reading.

GRAPHIC ORGANIZER

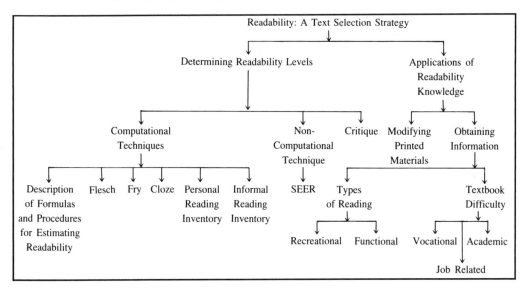

1. What is the difference between computational and noncomputational ways of determining readability levels?
2. What are the differences among the Flesch, Fry, and cloze techniques for assessing readability levels?
3. How do you construct a personal or informal reading inventory?
4. What is the difference between an informal reading inventory and a standardized test? (See information on a standardized test in chapter 3.)
5. What cautions should be observed in using readability formulas?
6. What information has been gleaned by use of readability formulas about levels of difficulty of recreational, job-related, vocational, and academic texts?
7. What do adults read? How much time per day do they spend in reading? Where do they do their reading? How well do they comprehend functional reading tasks?
8. What are the functional reading requirements for college students?

TEXT SELECTION STRATEGY

Teachers make a single textbook appropriate to the range of individual differences in a class by using the single-text strategies, described in chapter 6, in two ways: (1) they use directed reading activities (DRA), reading and learning-from-text guides, and the SQ3R method to adapt the text to individual differences among students; and (2) they teach students to use strategies for reading and learning from text on their own (see chapter 12, "A Blueprint for Instruction," for procedures on developing students toward independence in reading and learning from text).

Another way the teacher makes the single text fit the needs of all students is to use some procedure for determining the *readability* of the text for a group of students. If the teacher can select a textbook that is about average in difficulty for the class, the text will be easier to adapt to the entire range of abilities in the class than a text that is closer to the low or high achievers.

If textbook selection is made during the summer when students are not present, the teacher has to rely only upon the characteristics of the text itself and personal judgment to determine whether the text would be appropriate for the class. For this purpose, the teacher can use either a *readability formula* or a technique for estimating readability. The formulas that we explain in some detail in this chapter are the Flesch Reading Ease Formula and the Fry Readability Graph. The technique for estimating readability is the SEER technique.

However, if the students are available, then the teacher does not have to use a formula that *predicts* reading difficulty or a procedure for *estimating* readability. Instead, the teacher can actually try the material out with the students and find out how difficult *in fact* the text is for them. The "try out" types of readability testing are the cloze technique and the personal or informal reading inventories. These ways of determining readability require considerable student and teacher time but provide the best way of determining readability for a particular group of students.

DETERMINING READABILITY LEVEL TECHNIQUES

Determination of readability and reading difficulty fits into two categories: (a) computational and (b) noncomputational techniques. We first briefly describe each of these techniques and then explain in greater detail how to use or construct them.

Computational Techniques

DESCRIPTION OF FORMULAS AND
PROCEDURES FOR ESTIMATING REDABILITY

Readability formulas of the computational type have been available for the past 40 years (Klare, 1984; Singer, 1975). All of them use some variation of sentence complexity and word difficulty (Klare, 1974–1975). Three of the standard formulas in wide use are appropriate for somewhat different segments of the grade-level continuum. The Spache formula (1953) was designed for Grades 1–3, the Dale-Chall (1948) for Grades 4–8, and the Flesch (1949) formula for Grades 4 to college graduation. Although readability formulas have helped determine what makes reading easy or difficult, much is still unknown about reading difficulty (Bormuth, 1966; Klare, 1974–1975).

The computational formulas are time-consuming and tedious to use. They require the user to count syllables, words, or sentences. Consequently, some researchers have developed procedures for reducing the time and tedium in computing readability levels of materials (Fry, 1968; McLaughlin, 1969). A noncomputational procedure has achieved the greatest reduction in time for estimating readability level. This procedure consists of matching unknown material to a standard scale. Although this third approach to determining readability level is somewhat subjective, it is nevertheless as accurate as some computational procedures (Singer, 1975).

The *cloze technique* uses a totally different way of determining reading difficulty level. To employ this technique in the original way, as defined by its inventor, Taylor (1953), simply delete or omit every fifth word from a passage of approximately 250 words. Leave a sentence before and after each passage intact. A total of 50 words will be deleted from the passage. The reader's task is to infer from the remaining context what the missing words are, retrieve the exact words from vocabulary stored in his or her memory, and insert them into the passage. When you score only the exact original word as correct, you prevent disputes from arising on whether a word is a synonym for the missing word or not. The cloze technique places a premium upon the reader's ability to infer the missing words from the semantics and syntax of the remaining words in the passage and upon the reader's vocabulary repertoire and ability to retrieve words from storage in memory. Since the reader also has to identify printed words in order to infer the missing words, the reader performing on the cloze test has to use semantics, syntax, graphophonemics, graphomorphemics (Goodman, 1976; Ruddell, 1976), and reasoning processes (Davis, 1968; Fredericksen, 1972). Look at this sentence: *After locating his flock, the shepherd gathered the sh_____*. The *semantics,* or accumulated meanings of the sentence, suggest what the shepherd gathered. The *syntax,* or the order in which words in English must occur, signals the type of word that should be coming next or at least soon in a sentence. In the sentence above, the noun determiner *the* indicates a noun belongs in the next slot in the sentence, the slot for the missing word. *Graphophonemics* is the ability to give sounds to individual letters or to letter groups which function as single units, such as *sh*. *Graphomorphemics* is a two-part process. In one process, the student recognizes boundaries between meaningful units in words, such as *shep-herd*. Knowledge of words and word structures in English enables the reader to recognize and correctly segment words at their structural boundaries. Then the reader can apply graphophonemics to relate the units of print to sounds. The reader also has to use *reasoning processes,* such as inference, to try to determine the word that has been deleted. Hence the cloze technique is a way of assessing all of these systems and their operation in the process of reading (Singer, 1975). Of course, other factors also enter into replacing missing words, such as knowledge of an author's style.

A fourth way of estimating readability of content area materials is through a reading inventory based upon graded material drawn from a specific content area. In this procedure, an individual reads and answers questions on successively more difficult, graded paragraphs. As the reader progresses through the paragraphs, more errors in answering comprehension questions occur, provided the questions that the teacher constructs are relevant and appropriately difficult for the grade level of the paragraphs. Later in this chapter we present information on how to construct these questions. The resulting score determines the reader's fluency, instructional, and frustration levels. These levels use arbitrary criteria that teachers find useful. The *fluency level* is the grade level of a passage at which the reader can correctly answer 90% or more of the comprehension questions. The *instructional level* is the grade level of a passage at which the reader attains 70% to 90% comprehension. The *frustration level* is the grade level of a passage at which the reader's comprehension drops below 70%.[1] How readers respond to their difficulties in reading is also dependent on other factors, especially their interest in the material and their desire to read it.

Now that we have had an overview of the various ways of determining readability and reading difficulty, we go into each way in greater detail.

THE FLESCH READING EASE FORMULA

The Flesch Reading Ease Formula for computing readability level uses two criteria: number of syllables per hundred words and average number of words per sentence in a 100-word sample. The number of syllables in a word is an index of the difficulty of the word because longer words are usually more difficult. The words per sentence are an index of sentence complexity. Usually longer sentences are syntactically more complex and hence more difficult.

To use the Reading Ease Formula you will need to make two computations: (a) count the syllables in a passage that has approximately 100 words. Remember that a word has as many syllables as it has vowels or vowel-like sounds. Simply say each word and count the number of vowel sounds you hear. Examples of common syllables are shown in table 10.1. (b) For words per sentence, count the number of words in the passage and then divide by the number of sentences in the passage.

---

[1]In an arbitrary set of criteria devised by Betts (1947), in widespread use at the elementary school level, word recognition errors are also counted in determining reading levels: five or more errors per hundred words with less than 70% comprehension define the frustration level; more than 90% comprehension and one or few word recognition errors indicate a fluency level. The instructional level lies in between the frustration and the fluency levels. However, other factors, such as motivation and interest, may also determine whether a student is likely to read and comprehend reading material despite a high degree of word recognition difficulty.

See Powell (1971) for a critique and modification of the formula, but note that the Powell formula is also arbitrary.

TABLE 10.1. Basic Syllables and Combinations of Basic Syllables

Word(Basic Syllables)	Number of Syllables
oak	1
bet-ter	2
on-ly	2
a-ble	2
nick-el	2
ea-gle	2
work-er	2

Word (Combinations of Basic Syllables)	Number of Syllables
un-a-ble	3
ad-van-tage	3
au-to-mo-bile	4
op-por-tu-ni-ty	5
un-a-li-en-a-ble	6

The division of syllables follows *Webster's Third New International Dictionary*, which, unlike the *Second*, switched from phonetic division to printer's division of syllables. For example, *i-de-a* is divided in the latest edition as two syllables, *i-dea*, because a printer would not put a hyphen after *e* and carry a syllable over to the next line if *idea* came at the end of a line and space allowed for only two syllables on the line.

The scales in Figure 10.1 allow you to determine the Reading Ease Score. Just locate the words per sentence on the left scale and syllables per hundred words on the right scale. Then connect the points on the two scales with a ruler. The point where the ruler intersects the middle scale indicates the Reading Ease Score of the Passage.

Example:
Words per sentence = 15
Syllables per 100 words = 160
Intersection point = 57.
The score of 57 is the Reading Ease Score for the passage.

Now look at Table 10.2 to see the difficulty level and the grade level of the passage and the kind of publication that usually contains passages this difficult. Table 10.2 indicates that a Reading Ease Score of 57 is fairly difficult and is equivalent to passages found in such magazines as *Harper's* and *Atlantic*. Also, the grade level of the passage is equivalent to the difficulty of printed materials in Grades 10–12 (high school).

FIGURE 10.1. "How Easy?" Chart

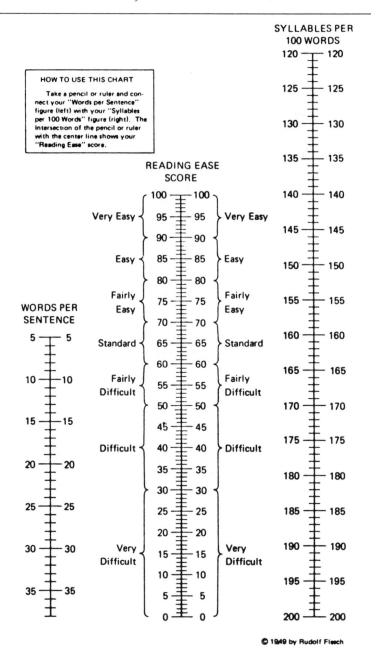

© 1949 by Rudolf Flesch

From *The Art of Readable Writing*, rev. ed. by Rudolph Flesch. Copyright 1949, © 1974 by Rudolph Flesch. Reprinted by permission of Harper & Row, Publishers, Inc.

TABLE 10.2. Meaning of Reading Ease Scores

Reading Ease Score	Style	Grade	Typical Magazine
90 to 100	Very Easy	5	Comic books
80 to 89	Easy	6	Pulp fiction, such as *Western Magazine*
70 to 79	Fairly Easy	7	Slick fiction, such as *True Stories; California Driver's Handbook*
60 to 69	Standard	8–9	*Reader's Digest, Time* magazine
50 to 59	Fairly Difficult	10–12 (high school)	Some high school texts; journals, such as *Language Arts;* magazines, such as *Harper's* and *Atlantic*
30 to 49	Difficult	13–16 (college)	Academic—college texts
0 to 29	Very Difficult	17+ (graduate school)	Scientific, such as *American Medical Association Journal;* graduate school texts, such as *Theoretical Models and Processes of Reading*

Source: Adaptation of pp. 177 and 178 from *The Art of Readable Writing*, rev. ed. by Rudolph Flesch. Copyright 1949, © 1974 by Rudolph Flesch. Reprinted by permission of Harper & Row, Publishers, Inc.

BOX 10.1. Computing the Reading Ease Score of a Passage

Find the Reading Ease Score of the passage in box 8.1. If you follow steps 1–6 correctly, you should obtain the results shown in box 8.2.

THE NEGATIVE IMAGE OF WOMEN
IN CHILDREN'S LITERATURE

   In considering select nursery rhymes and folk tales, one can see that women are portrayed somewhat negatively, either as ineffectual creatures who need to be dominated by men or as aggressive monsters who must be destroyed by men. One can assume that these folk materials were born in and perpetuated by societies that maintained the "natural inferiority of women." However, today, when women are seeking liberation and equality, a young child's image of what is read to him may be in sharp contrast to what he sees. On the other hand, liberated women may unwittingly be perpetuating the "monster" image; after all, one of the liberation organizations was called W.I.T.C.H.

1. Number of words _____
2. Number of sentences _____
3. Number of words per sentence (divide 2 into 1) _____
4. Number of syllables per 100 words _____
5. To obtain the Reading Ease Score on figure 8.1, use a ruler or pencil to connect the words per sentence figure and the syllables per hundred words figure. Read the score where the pencil or ruler intersects the middle scale and enter it here: _____
6. Find the Reading Ease Score on table 8.2 and write the grade equivalent here: _____

Quoted passage is from Dan Donlan, "The Negative Image of Women in Children's Literature," *Elementary English* (April 1972): 604–11.

BOX 10.2. *Sample Computation of a Reading Ease Score*

In considering select nursery rhymes and folk tales, one can see that women are portrayed somewhat negatively, either as ineffectual creatures who need to be dominated by men or as aggressive monsters who must be destroyed by men. One can assume that these folk materials were born in and perpetuated by societies that maintained the "natural inferiority of women." However, today, when women are seeking liberation and equality, a young child's image of what is read to him may be in sharp contrast to what he sees. On the other hand, liberated women may unwittingly be perpetuating the "monster" image (100 words in passage to this point); after all, one of the liberation organizations was called W.I.T.C.H. (110 words in total passage)

1. Number of words __110__
2. Number of sentences __4__
3. Number of words per sentence (divide 2 into 1) __27.5__
4. Number of syllables per 100 words __171__ (Note: Syllables are marked in the passage.)
5. Reading Ease Score at intersection of straight line formed by placing pencil or ruler between words per sentence of __27.5__ and syllables per 100 words of __171__ is: __34__.

6. Table 10.2 indicates that a Reading Ease Score of *34* is equivalent to passages usually found in *academic and scholarly* magazines or in reading material used at grade levels 13–16 (college).

If the answer you computed in Box 10.1 agrees with the answer in Box 10.2, then you have learned how to use the Flesch Reading Ease Formula. However, the Reading Ease Formula does not provide grade-equivalent scores. Another formula, which does, and is also easy to use is the Fry Readability Graph.

THE FRY READABILITY GRAPH

The Fry Readability Graph appears in Figure 10.2. This figure also contains directions on how to compute readability with an example. In the Fry technique, you find the average number of syllables and the number of sentences in three samples of 100 words. Then you use these figures as coordinates and determine where they intersect on the graph in Figure 10.2. The large number between the lines on the graph which is closest to the point of intersection indicates the approximate grade level of the passage.

The example in Figure 10.2 is for three 100-word samples from a text with an average of 141 syllables and an average sentence length of 6.3. To use the graph to determine readability level, locate 141 on the top of the graph and put the finger of your right hand at this point. Then locate 6.3 on the left side of the graph and put a finger on your left hand on this number. Now move your right finger down and your left finger across the graph. Where they intersect you'll find a dot between two lines. The number between these two lines stands for Grade 7. Since the dot is close to, but not on line 7, you then estimate the readability of the passage is about grade level 6.9.

A procedure that does not compute readability, but simply judges it by comparison with a standard, is the SEER technique.

Unlike the Flesch and Fry formulas, the cloze technique requires that a sample of the printed material must be *tried out* on the individual or group of students who are actually going to read the material. Thus, the cloze technique determines the difficulty of the material relative to the reading ability of the students who are actually going to read the material.

THE CLOZE TECHNIQUE

In the cloze technique every 5th word from a 250-word passage is deleted, but the sentence before and after the passage is left intact. A modification calls for the deletion of every 10th word from a 500-word passage. The technique implicitly requires the reader to rely upon the syntax and semantics of the passage plus such aspects as writing style to infer what the missing words are and then to retrieve these words from his or her vocabulary repertoire. In scoring, only the

FIGURE 10.2. Graph for Computing Readability

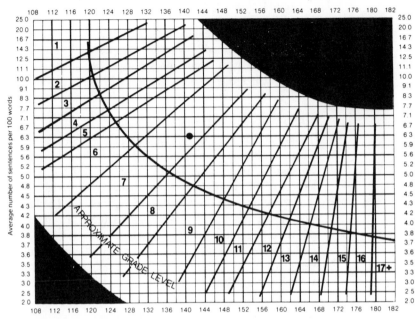

GRAPH FOR ESTIMATING READABILITY —EXTENDED

Average number of syllables per 100 words

DIRECTIONS: Randomly select 3 one hundred word passages from a book or an article. Plot average number of syllables and average number of sentences per 100 words on graph to determine the grade level of the material. Choose more passages per book if great variability is observed and conclude that the book has uneven readability. Few books will fall in gray area but when they do grade level scores are invalid.

Count proper nouns, numerals and initializations as words. Count a syllable for each symbol. For example, 1945 is 1 word and 4 syllables and 'IRA' is 1 word and 3 syllables.

EXAMPLE	SYLLABLES	SENTENCES
1st Hundred Words	124	6.6
2nd Hundred Words	141	5.5
3rd Hundred Words	158	6.8
AVERAGE	141	6.3

READABILITY 7th GRADE (see dot plotted on graph)

For further information and validity data, see Edward Fry, ''Fry's Readability Graph: Clarifications, Validity, and Extension to Level 17,'' *Journal of Reading* (December 1977).

exact, original word is counted as correct. The original technique did not score synonyms as correct. Such a scoring procedure is not practical because it is difficult to determine the boundary lines for synonyms, that is, where a word stops being a synonym for another word and becomes a word whose meaning is different for the passage.

To use the cloze procedure, simply select graded material from a content area. Lists of these graded materials can be found in library catalogs for the three school levels. (See chapter 11, Box. 11.3, ''Multiple-Text Strategies,'' for glossed directions on how to read the library catalogs.) Once suitable materials have been found, follow the steps below:

1. After selecting a book at each grade level from a particular content area, take a passage of about 125 words from each book. Then delete every 5th word from each passage, but leave the first and last sentences intact. (If you want to make this task less difficult, take 250-word passages and delete every 10th word.) You can then combine results on successive passages to obtain the required 250-word passage length.

2. Have the students read the passages, starting at the lowest level, and ask them to insert the missing words. Count the number of exactly correct inserted words. The formula for determining the percentage of correct words is:

$$\text{percent correct} = \frac{\text{words correct} \times 100}{\substack{\text{total words deleted} \\ \text{from passage}}}$$

3. The instructional level is the level at which the student begins to obtain a score of 44% correct insertions in the passage. A score below 44% means the material is frustrating for the student; a score above 58% means the material is too easy or at an ''independent study'' level for the student (Bormuth, 1968). The ''supervised'' instructional level is between 44% and 57%.

4. The cloze test results will indicate the range of reading achievement of the class in the content area books selected. The teacher can use this knowledge to select an appropriate range of reading materials for the class.

Box 10.3 contains an example of a series of graded passages in the content area of general science. A teacher selected these passages from books in the school library catalogs, and made them into a cloze test by simply deleting every fifth word.

You can use the cloze technique in other ways. You can assess knowledge of technical vocabulary in a content area text by simply deleting the technical words in a passage. You can also provide students with multiple choices for the deleted words, just as the Gates-MacGinitie Survey Test does (see chapter 3 for examples of the Gates-MacGinitie Test). Unlike the traditional way of using the cloze technique, these other ways have no rules for determining what scores mean. However, the information can be useful in making teaching plans: the test on technical words can provide information on how familiar the technical terms are and which terms need to be stressed.

You can administer a cloze test before and after instruction. If the scores on the pretest are low and those on the posttest are high, a teacher can reasonably infer that students have learned the content during the course.

A limitation of the cloze technique is that it tends to work best only when the passages are near the reader's difficulty level. If the passages are too easy for students, the students are likely to insert many synonyms. These synonyms are then scored as errors. Consequently, easy passages lead to an underestimation of students' actual reading levels (Smith, 1972–1973). At the other extreme, if the passages selected are too difficult, readers also obtain a low score for different reasons: they do not have the missing word in their vocabulary, cannot retrieve it from their memory, cannot use syntax or semantics from which to infer the missing word, lack motivation to search for it, or some combination of these reasons. Hence, the cloze technique should be used cautiously. If reader's scores are low, get higher, and then become lower as they progress through graded passages, the passages which yielded the higher scores should be used for obtaining students' readability levels.

Counting only exact words correct simplifies the task of scoring the cloze test because it eliminates pondering over what is a synonym and what is not. If you do decide to accept synonyms in scoring, allow students to judge which synonyms are acceptable; this will save you a classroom hassle. However, the meanings of the scores given in Box 10.3 are not appropriate when synonyms are accepted. Indeed, researchers have not devised any scoring method applicable to the use of synonyms.

The cloze technique has advantages over other readability techniques because teachers can construct test passages easily and do not have to write comprehension questions, as they do when using the personal or informal reading inventory technique that is discussed next.

BOX 10.3. Applying the Cloze Technique to Science Passages

Directions: In the following passages, we have deleted every fifth word. Your task is to insert the missing words. Then compare your answer with the key provided at the end of the box. The point where your cumulative score drops below 44 percent, indicates when the material has reached your frustration level of reading. Above 44 percent you are at the instructional level and above 57 percent at the fluency level in this type of reading material.

PASSAGE 1

Grades 1–3

Passage length: 122 words

What Things Will Stick __1__ Magnets?
　　Touch a tack __2__ the end of your __3__.
　　What happens?
　　The tack __4__ to the magnet!

Now __5__ a nail and a __6__ and see if they __7__ to the magnet.
Touch __8__ toothpick, a penny, a __9__ band with the magnet.
__10__ happens now?
They do __11__ stick to the magnet.
__12__ around your house and __13__ a pencil, a book, __14__ bobby pin, a glass, __15__ eraser, a nail, a __16__ of scissors, a toy.
__17__ you think any of __18__ will stick to your __19__?
Try each one.
If __20__ things you touch have __21__ in them, they will __22__.
If they do not __23__ iron in them, they __24__ not stick.

PASSAGE 2

Grades 2–4

Passage length: 132 words

Look around you. You __1__ see many things made __2__ metal. Perhaps you see __3__ metal doorknob, a key, __4__ pair of scissors, or __5__ shiny band around one __6__ of your pencil. All __7__ things are made of __8__. Any of them made __9__ iron will be pulled __10__ by a magnet. In __11__, you can use a __12__ to help you find __13__ that are made with __14__.

The space around a __15__ where its pulling power __16__ found is called a __17__ field. A magnetic field __18__ away from a magnet __19__ all directions.

You cannot __20__ a magnetic field, but __21__ can outline its shape. __22__ a heavy piece of __23__ on top of a __24__. Sprinkle some iron filings __25__ the paper. Tap the __26__ edge gently.

PASSAGE 3

Grade 5

Passage length: 134 words

The first kind of __1__ known to man was __2__ natural magnet. Natural magnets __3__ found in the ground. __4__ look like dark-colored rocks __5__ stones and are rough __6__ irregular rather than round __7__ smooth. These natural magnets __8__ made up of an __9__ ore called magnetite and __10__ called lodestones.

Sailors learned __11__ ago that when they __12__ a thin piece of __13__ on a string and __14__ the magnetite to swing __15__ it would point to __16__ north. This helped the __17__ to find their way __18__ night when they could __19__ see land. It helped __20__ to find their way __21__ it was cloudy and __22__ could not see the __23__. The magnetite would always __24__ them on the right __25__. The sailors called the __26__ of magnetite "leading stones."

PASSAGE 4

Grade 7

Passage length: 139 words

Long before the birth __1__ Christ, Chinese philosophers found __2__ second magnetical quality in __3__ magnet-stone. They placed it __4__ a wooden raft floating _5_ a bowl of water. _6_ stone on its raft _7_ turned slowly until it _8_ pointing north-and-south.

The Chinese _9_ it showed where south _10_. Their floating magnet-stone was _11_ tchi-nan, the chariot of _12_ south. This was apparently _13_ first compass, and it _14_ said to have guided _15_ caravans across the endless _16_ of Tatary in Asia.

_17_ hundreds of years passed _18_ men on the opposite _19_ of the world also _20_ that the magnet-stone could _21_ more than "drawe yron _22_ it selfe." They chose _23_ think of the magnet-stone _24_ pointing north. They sometimes _25_ the stone, and sometimes _26_ suspended it by a _27_. The stone spun slowly.

PASSAGE 5

Grade 9

Passage length: 126 words

Magnetism in the Atom. _1_ things are made of _2_ units called molecules (MOLL-uh-kyouls). Each _3_ is made up of _4_ units called atoms. Scientists _5_ formed a picture of _6_ atom that explains how _7_ behave. The picture of _8_ atom shows that every _9_ is a small magnet. _10_ is the reason why:

_11_ atom is made of _12_ small lump called a _13_ (NEW-klee-uhs) surrounded by electrons. The _14_ has an electrical charge _15_ the kind called positive. _16_ electron has an electrical _17_ of the kind called _18_.

The electrons in an _19_ are moving in two _20_ ways: 1) The electrons revolve in _21_ around the nucleus the _22_ the earth revolves around _23_ sun; 2) each electron spins _24_ an axis like a _25_.

PASSAGE 6

Grade 11

Passage length: 153 words

There is yet another _1_ source of understanding about _2_ nature and phenomena of _3_ upper atmosphere and the _4_ beyond. This is the _5_ of the variations of _6_ earth's magnetic field. The _7_ may at first seem _8_, because the earth's magnetism _9_ a property of the _10_ earth. Its cause is _11_ yet fully understood, but _12_ believed to be a _13_ of electrical currents flowing _14_ the inner liquid core _15_ the earth. Unless continuously _16_, such currents would die _17_, owing to electrical resistance. _18_ period of decay might _19_ reckoned in many thousands _20_ years, but is certainly _21_ brief compared with the _22_ of the earth (a _23_ billion years). Hence the _24_ currents are believed to _25_ maintained by a process _26_ similar to that of _27_ self-exciting dynamo: the dynamo _28_ electric currents by motion _29_ some of its parts _30_ the magnetic field generated _31_ these same currents.

KEY

Passage (Grade Level)	Deleted Words
1 (1–3)	1. to, 2. with, 3. magnet, 4. sticks, 5. touch, 6. clip, 7. stick, 8. a, 9. rubber, 10. what, 11. not, 12. look, 13. find, 14. a, 15. an, 16. pair, 17. do, 18, these, 19. magnet, 20. the, 21. iron, 22. stick, 23. have, 24. will.
2 (2–4)	1. can, 2. of, 3. a, 4. a, 5. the, 6. end, 7. these, 8. metal, 9. with, 10. on, 11. fact, 12. magnet, 13. things, 14. iron, 15. magnet, 16. is, 17. magnetic, 18. stretches, 19. in, 20. see, 21. you, 22. place, 23. paper, 24. magnet, 25. on, 26. paper.
3 (5)	1. magnet, 2. a, 3. were, 4. they, 5. or, 6. and, 7. and, 8. are, 9. iron, 10. are, 11. long, 12. hung, 13. magnetite, 14. allowed, 15. freely, 16. the, 17. sailors, 18. at, 19. not, 20. them, 21. when, 22. they, 23. stars, 24. keep, 25. course, 26. pieces.
4 (7)	1. of, 2. a, 3. the, 4. on, 5. in, 6. the, 7. always, 8. was, 9. said, 10. is, 11. called, 12. the, 13. man's, 14. is, 15. great, 16. grasslands, 17. many, 18. before, 19. side, 20. discovered, 21. do, 22. to, 24. as, 25. floated, 26. they, 27. thread.
5 (9)	1. all, 2. tiny, 3. molecule, 4. smaller, 5. have, 6. the, 7. atoms, 8. the, 9. atom, 10. here, 11. every, 12. a, 13. nucleus, 14. nucleus, 15. of, 16. each, 17. charge, 18. negative, 19. atom, 20. different, 21. orbits, 22. way, 23. the, 24. around, 25. top.
6 (11)	1. important, 2. the, 3. the, 4. space, 5. study, 6. the, 7. fact, 8. surprising, 9. is, 10. massive, 11. not, 12. is, 13. system, 14. in, 15. of, 16. maintained, 17. away, 18. their, 19. be, 20. of, 21. very, 22. age, 23. few, 24. electrical, 25. be, 26. essentially, 27. a, 28. produces, 29. of, 30. through, 31. by.

Passage 1 from Tillie S. Pine and Joseph Levine, *Magnets and How to Use Them* (New York: McGraw-Hill, 1958), pp. 10–11. Passage 2 from Raymond Sacks, *Magnets* (New York:

Coward-McCann, 1967), pp. 18–21. Passage 3 from Edward Victor, *Exploring and Understanding Magnets and Electromagnets* (Westchester, Ill.: Benefic Press, 1967), p. 8. Passage 4 from E. G. Valens, *Magnet* (New York: World Publishing Co., 1964), pp. 4–5. Passage 5 from Irving and Ruth Adler, *Magnets* (New York: John Day, 1966), pp. 25–26. Passage 6 from Sydney Chapman, *I.G.Y.: Year of Discovery* (Ann Arbor: University of Michigan Press, 1959), p. 76.

THE PERSONAL READING INVENTORY (PRI)
OR INFORMAL READING INVENTORY (IRI)

The Personal Reading Inventory or Informal Reading Inventory—both names appear in journals—are tests that teachers construct. The inventory uses graded passages and comprehension questions after each passage to assess reading level. To use this technique, follow the steps below.

1. Simply take a set of graded passages in a content area. See the graded passages in Box 10.3. The passages should be at least 100 words long.

2. As a rule of thumb, write three or four comprehension questions for each passage. In general, ask one or two questions at the literal level (what the passage stated explicitly, including technical vocabulary defined in context), one or two at the interpretive or inferential levels (what the passage means), and one or two at the generalization level. (See the headings "Directed Reading Activities" and "Reading and Learning-from-Text Guides" in chapters 13–16 for questions in four content areas; chapter 15.1, Table 15.1, for information on constructing a table of specifications and using it for diagnostic purposes; chapter 15, Box 15.5 for seven types of questions.)

3. Have a student start at a level about one grade below your estimate of his or her reading level. After each passage, students try to answer the questions on the passage they have just read. Multiple-choice answers will make the scoring objective and easy.

4. Determine student's reading level according to the following rule-of-thumb criteria:
   Fluency Level: 90% or higher comprehension
   Instruction Level: 70%–89% comprehension
   Frustration Level: 69% and lower in comprehension

As students progress upwards, from easy to more difficult passages, their comprehension scores should decrease. If the drop is not progressive, then you will have to modify the comprehension questions. Note that the type of questions in Box 10.4 appear in parentheses next to each question. The types form a gradient in difficulty. The questions in the lower grades are literal and shift to paraphrase in the middle grades, and end up in the upper grades as inferential, interpretive, and generalization types of questions.

BOX 10.4. Reading Inventory on General Science Content

The teacher has a student begin the inventory at a passage that is at least one grade level below the student's estimated reading level and lets him or her continue until the comprehension level drops below 70%. In this inventory, we have only two or three questions per paragraph. We therefore use this rule-of-thumb: stop when a student answers two successive questions incorrectly.

Directions: Read each passage, starting with a passage that is easy for you. Then answer the questions for the passage. The key for checking your answers is at the end of the reading inventory. Continue on to more difficult passages. Stop when you miss two successive questions. Your reading level is the grade level just before these two questions.

PASSAGE 1

Grades 1–3

Passage length: 162 words

A bird seems to float like a feather and be blown like a leaf; climb up on the wind; slide down on a breeze; play tag through the trees.

Why can't you?

A bird can fly because its wings are big compared to its small, light body. Even a tiny bird has wings enough to move the air, big enough to hold it up. Air moves under and over a bird's wings.

You have no wings. You have arms. Your arms are smaller than your body. Your arms can't catch the air and move it under and over you. That's why you can't fly.

BUT a bird has no hands on its wings! Think of all the things you can do with your hands. You can catch a ball and write your name, hold a book, pick a flower, and button your coat. Wouldn't you rather have hands than wings? You can always fly in airplanes and in dreams.

Comprehension Questions (and Types)

1. What can birds do that you can't do? (Contrast)
    (a) fly
    (b) eat
    (c) play
    (d) climb
2. A bird can fly because (Literal)
    (a) the wind blows it
    (b) it has wings bigger than its body
    (c) it has feathers all over
    (d) it wanted to and learned how to fly
3. A bird has no (Literal)
    (a) wings
    (b) feathers
    (c) hands
    (d) feet

PASSAGE 2

Grade 5

Passage length: 150 words

From Reservoir to You. People can get a drink of water in lots of ways. They can scoop water up from a brook, a handful at a time; they can haul it up from the well, a bucketful at a time; they can pump it up, a splash at a time.

But in your wonderful house, all you need to do is turn a faucet. The water will keep coming, as long as you want it to. It won't stop until you shut it off. You don't have to scoop it up, or haul it up, or pump it up. What makes the water keep coming up from the cellar, through the pipes into your faucet?

All the water that's not in pipes goes down. Rain falls down, rivers and brooks flow down. But the water in your house flows up from the cellar, no matter how high up you live.

Comprehension Questions (and Types)
1. All a person has to do to get water in a modern house is   (Literal)
   (a) pump it up
   (b) scoop it up from a brook
   (c) turn on a faucet
   (d) haul it from a well
2. Water in rivers and brooks   (Literal)
   (a) flows down only
   (b) flows up only
   (c) flows up and down
   (d) flows only down in pipes

PASSAGE 3

Grade 7

Passage length: 169 words

No matter where or when you walk you are always completely surrounded by a great variety of noises. Strangely enough, most of the time you do not hear them unless you make a definite attempt to do so.

You have trained yourself from childhood not to listen to most of the customary sounds. But now, in order to make your scientific walking jaunts more exciting, you should try to analyze or track down some of these sounds. It can be fun to find the origin of a strange sound by making it into a game or treasure hunt. Call it a "sound-hunt."

If you stop for a few minutes and listen carefully to every sound, you will be surprised to find that in the "silence" around you there are many noises indeed. First and foremost today are the sounds of automobiles starting, stopping, popping, squealing, or hissing. Then there are airplane noises, bird calls, church bells chiming, and electric tools whining, You may even hear the rustling of leaves!

Comprehension Questions (and Types)
1. Wherever you walk you can always hear   (Inference)
   (a) trees

(b) autos
(c) noises
(d) people
2. The reason you do not hear many noises most of the time
   is because you   (Paraphrase)
   (a) learned not to hear them
   (b) are more interested in looking
   (c) do not have good hearing ability
   (d) do not listen to unusual sounds
3. The noises you usually do not listen to occur   (Paraphrase)
   (a) rarely
   (b) only at night
   (c) frequently
   (d) only when you are walking

PASSAGE 4

Grade 9

Passage length: 137 words

There are three most prominent kinds of "citizens" in the world within the atom. They are the protons, the neutrons, and the electrons. The number of these particles within the atom determines the weight and chemical character of the atom. Two of the particles, the protons and neutrons, are found only in the nucleus, the very tiny, very heavy central core of the atom. They both have about the same weight. To determine the relative weight of different atoms, which are much too light to be actually weighed, the protons and neutrons are considered one unit of atomic weight each. Thus the oxygen atom, with eight protons and eight neutrons in its nucleus, has an atomic weight of sixteen. And the uranium atom, with 92 protons and 146 neutrons, has an atomic weight of 238.

Comprehension Questions (and Types)
1. Electrons are   (Inference)
   (a) found in the nucleus of atoms
   (b) without any weight
   (c) determiners of atomic weight
   (d) not part of an atom's nucleus
2. In determining the weight of an atom, scientists   (Paraphrase)
   (a) weigh its particles
   (b) add together its protons and neutrons
   (c) do not attempt to do so
   (d) use oxygen atoms as a unit of atomic measurement
3. The particles outside the central core of the atom are   (Inference)
   (a) heavy protons
   (b) light electrons
   (c) light protons
   (d) heavy electrons

PASSAGE 5

Grade 11

Passage length: 157 words

Almost in the beginning was curiosity.

Curiosity, the overwhelming desire to know, is not characteristic of some forms of living organism, which, for that very reason, we can scarcely bring ourselves to consider alive.

A tree does not display curiosity about its environment in any way we can recognize; nor does a sponge or an oyster. The wind, the rain, the ocean currents bring them what is needful, and from it they take what they can. If the chance of events is such as to bring them fire, poison, predators, or parasites, they die as stoically and as undemonstratively as they lived.

Early in the scheme of life, however, independent motion was developed by some organisms. It meant a tremendous advance in their control of the environment. A moving organism no longer had to wait in stolid rigidity for food to come its way; it went out after it.

Comprehension Questions (and Types)
1. Curiosity is a characteristic of   (Generalization)
    (a) all things that live
    (b) the beginning of living things
    (c) all organisms with locomotion
    (d) all organisms that ingest food
2. Trees and other organisms such as sponges and oysters   (Interpretation)
    (a) control their own environment
    (b) like all living creatures, are curious, but only in unusual ways
    (c) search constantly for water and nourishment
    (d) are victims of noxious environmental elements

Key: Passage 1 (1–3) 1a, 2b, 3c. Passage 2 (5) 1c, 2a. Passage 3 (7) 1c, 2a, 3c. Passage 4 (9) 1d, 2b, 3b. Passage 5 (11) 1c, 2d. Passage 1 from Jeanne Bendick, *Why Can't I?* (New York: McGraw-Hill, 1969), pp. 12–17. Passage 2 from Herman Schneider and Nina Schneider, *Let's Look Inside Your House* (New York: William R. Scott, Inc., 1948), p. 5. Passage 3 from George Barr, *Young Scientist Takes a Walk* (New York: McGraw-Hill, 1959), pp. 22–23. Passage 4 from Melvin Berger, *Triumphs of Modern Science* (New York: McGraw-Hill, 1964), pp. 110–111. Passage 5 from Isaac Asimov, *The New Intelligent Man's Guide to Science* (New York: Basic Books, 1965), p. 1.

You can test out the passages and questions on students who are at grade level for a passage. For example, give the passage and questions at Grade 7 level to seventh graders, the passage and questions at Grade 8 level to eighth graders, and so on. If the students at each level on the average get about 50% of the questions on a passage correct, you know you have a well-graded set of questions. Using this criterion, we would probably have to modify the questions in Box 10.4, which we constructed only as a classroom exercise.

A variation on the PRI is the "Open Textbook Reading Assessment" (Shepherd, 1973). In this variation, the instructor writes comprehension questions at all three levels (literal, inferential, and generalized) on three sample passages taken from the textbook that is to be used in the class. Those students scoring below 70% get further, individual testing. First, they read the passages orally so that the teacher can determine whether their relatively low comprehension scores reflect word recognition difficulties. If not, they take a test on the technical vocabulary terms from the specific text passages to determine whether low vocabulary ability is the causal factor for their low comprehension scores.

Non-Computational Technique

THE SEER TECHNIQUE FOR ESTIMATING READABILITY LEVEL

SEER is an acronym for ''Singer Eyeball Estimate of Readability'' (Singer, 1975). It is a judgmental technique that involves taking a passage, usually a paragraph of about 100 words from materials of unknown readability level, and matching it to a paragraph in a set of scaled paragraphs whose reading levels have been computed and are indicated next to the paragraphs. The directions for using the SEER Scale tell the teacher to take a paragraph whose readability is to be estimated, move the paragraph up and down the scaled paragraphs until a judgment is made that the unknown paragraph is about equal in difficulty to a paragraph on the scale. In making a judgment, the teacher is likely to use such criteria as sentence length, word difficulty, writing style, and concept level. Then the teacher notes the readability level of the paragraph on the scale that matches the paragraph whose readability level is being judged. If the difficulty of the unknown paragraph lies between two of the scaled paragraphs, assign the grade-level readability between the two paragraphs. The graded paragraphs on science content in Table 10.3 can be used in the SEER technique, particularly for estimating the difficulty of science content.

The SEER technique is more accurate when the textual material for matching and the scaled paragraphs are in the same content area. The estimated reading level of a matching paragraph will be accurate, plus or minus one grade level, in two out of three cases. This technique of estimating readability is easier than the Fry technique's tedious and Time-consuming computations (Singer, 1975). If the content of the scaled paragraphs and the paragraphs for matching do differ, the reading level estimation is likely to be off by about plus or minus 1.5 grade levels for two out of three comparisons (Carver, 1974). That means that the readability of a passage estimated to be at a Grade 10 level of difficulty might be somewhere between Grades 8.5 and 11.5. This measurement variability applies to all computational formulas. However, this degree of accuracy is still useful for practical purposes.

To select passages for constructing a set of scaled paragraphs in a particular content area, such as history, biology, mathematics, literature, use the school library catalogs. Note that only the elementary school catalogs (chapter 11, Box 11.3) provide readability grade levels. Readability grade levels of 7–9 are implied by listing books in the junior high catalog, and readability grade levels of 10–12 are implicit in books listed in the high school catalog. If a book is not listed in the catalogs, the teacher can use the SEER technique.

Another estimation formula determines the probable range of reading ability of a heterogeneous group of students. Although we have already presented this formula in chapter 3, we simply repeat it here, and refer you to chapter 3 for further discussion of it:

Expected range of reading level = $\frac{2}{3}$ × average chronological age of the group.

Thus, a 10th grade class with an average age of 15 will have a 10-year reading range, from grade equivalent 5 to grade equivalent 15.

The Flesch Reading Ease Formula and the Fry Readability Graph compute and predict the grade level of reading material from characteristics of the printed material alone. The SEER technique *estimates* grade-level difficulty.

Critique of Reading Difficulty Formulas

The reading difficulty of a text can be determined apart from any particular reader, as the Fry and Flesch formulas do. In addition to the criteria these formulas use for arriving at readability levels, we may also consider other features of the text. For example, a text may be relatively difficult because it has a high density of ideas and a high degree of interrelatedness or coherence among the ideas. But, whether these characteristics of a text are difficult or not also depends upon the reader's prior knowledge, vocabulary ability, reasoning processes, purposes, and goals in reading the text. For example, if a text is densely packed with ideas but the reader's purpose is only to get the general idea of the text, the reader is likely to find the text easier than if his or her purpose was to comprehend the text fully. Hence, we recognize that the difficulty level of a text as computed by the Fry and Flesch formulas and as estimated by the SEER technique is only the *average* or *general* level of difficulty of a text.

To determine the difficulty of a text for a particular reader, for example, a student who was having difficulty in reading and learning from a text, we would examine factors not only within that text but also within the reader. In short, *reading difficulty for a particular individual depends upon an interaction between the text and the individual.*[2]

APPLICATIONS OF KNOWLEDGE ABOUT READABILITY

Modifying Printed Materials: Making Reading Materials Easier or More Difficult

Although teachers do not usually have time to modify teaching materials or write them, they sometimes find themselves working on summer projects to prepare materials for teaching. Sometimes a school district may even provide time for

---

[2]The cloze technique and the informal reading inventory come closest to a practical procedure for assessing this interaction between text and reader. Kintsch and Vipond (1979) have devised a more complex formula for assessing this interaction, but their formula is more appropriate for researchers than for practitioners. A more practical interaction assessment of readability has been constructed by Zakaluk and Samuels (1988).

preparation of materials. Occasionally teachers take a course or participate in a workshop where they write materials for teaching. Then they can use their knowledge of readability criteria to modify or construct reading materials so as to make them easier or more difficult. Two variables that can be manipulated for this purpose are sentence length and word difficulty.

Longer sentences are usually more syntactically complex and may have one or more embedded sentences, or subordinate clauses. (See chapter 9, Box 9.3 for sentence-combining exercises.) Hence, combining sentences, especially where subordination results, is likely to increase the difficulty of the sentence, but not always (Pearson, 1974–1975). Although it may at first appear more difficult, the longer sentence in 2, below, is easier than the three shorter ones in 1 because the reader does not have to infer the intersentence relationships:

1. In the lab, Kimber mixed oxygen and hydrogen. He got water. (He also got an explosion.)
2. In the lab, Kimber mixed oxygen and hydrogen to get water (plus an explosion).

Researchers have not discovered much about intersentence syntax and intersentence difficulties (Bormuth, Carr, Manning, & Pearson, 1970) or about syntactic difficulties in different types of sentences and paragraphs. However, they have found out that students are more likely to comprehend written passages in which the syntax is the same as the syntax they use in their own oral language (Ruddell, 1965).

Word difficulty is another variable to use for manipulating the difficulty of reading material. You can substitute synonyms of higher frequency to make the material easier and, conversely, synonyms of lower frequency to make the material more difficult. Armed with a Thesaurus and Carroll, Davies and Richman's (1971) word frequency book, a teacher or writer can modify the difficulty level of textual materials. But the teacher has to exercise judgment because word frequency counts do not encompass all indices of word difficulty. They do not account for difficulty of word identification in context or for the difficulty of the contextual meaning of words. Students might understand *run* as a verb form but have more difficulty in comprehending it as a noun form, or as part of an idiom (a *run* on a bank or a *run* in a stocking).

Although materials that the teacher has simplified may enable more students to comprehend the content of the materials, such simplification represents downward adaptation of the curriculum. Another tack to take is to *stimulate* the development of students by teaching them to comprehend more complex material. For example, teach students to analyze complex sentences and make them simpler. Also teach them to comprehend the meaning of affixes (prefixes and suffixes) and roots so that they can analyze the meanings of complex words by breaking them into their constituent parts. Wolfe (1974) has reported considerable success in improving high school students' reading by having them learn affixes and roots and then using them in analyzing content area technical terms.

To help students develop toward greater maturity in reading and learning from text, follow a sequence like this: simplify material at first; then teach students to comprehend more complex words and syntactical relationships within and between sentences (McCullough, 1971). Table 9.4 in chapter 9 contains a list of sentence and paragraph cues that will help. For this sequential instruction, use textbooks you have selected from school catalogs that are graded in difficulty. (See an example of such graded materials in Box 10.3.)

Obtaining Information

How well do students have to read? To answer this question, we would have to respond rhetorically by asking another question: how well do students have to read *for what purpose?* How well do students have to be able to do recreational reading at various levels of difficulty, or to do the practical reading required in everyday life (newspapers, job applications, receipts, recipes, directions, and so forth), or to comprehend job-required reading materials, or to learn from texts in various content areas? Researchers have used reading difficulty formulas to determine reading levels in each of these areas.

TYPES OF READING
Recreational Reading Levels

Flesch (1949) applied his Reading Ease Formula to various types of *recreational reading material.* As shown in Table 10.2, a fifth-grade level of reading ability is necessary for comprehending print in comic books. *Time* magazine has an 8th- to 9th-grade level of reading difficulty and *Atlantic* magazine a 10th- to 12th-grade level of reading difficulty.

Functional Reading

Definition. The army coined the term *functional reading* in World War II. Then, the term meant "the ability to understand written instructions for carrying out basic military tasks." A serviceman was functionally literate if he could read at least at the fifth-grade level (Sharon, 1973–1974).

Today, a higher reading level would probably be necessary for the attainment of functional literacy. (See Table 10.4, "Readability Levels of Texts in Vocational Courses," and the information under the heading "What Are Job-Related Reading Requirements?" on page 334). However, neither university researchers nor public school officials have reached any agreement on a definition of functional literacy. Perhaps we can define functional literacy only in relation to a person's purpose, the requirements of the situation (reading government forms, textbooks, and so forth), and the school's expectation for successful accomplishment in reading and learning from text. For a cook in the army it would be one level; for a college student, another level; and so on. Hence, we could not state

TABLE 10.3. *Time per Day That Adults Spend Reading*

	Percent of adults	*Time spent on reading (in minutes)*
1. Traveling and commuting	70	3
2. Recreation	54	7
3. Working around house	46	7
4. Meals	42	3
5. Shopping	33	7
6. Work	33	61
7. Club or church work	10	16
8. School	5	68
9. Theater, other events	4	7

that functional literacy is at a fifth-grade, ninth-grade, or any specific grade level.

One way to determine *functional reading level* is to determine what adults actually read and how much time they spend on reading. Sharon (1973–1974) conducted a cross-sectional survey of a national sample of 5,067 adults. The results indicated that the average adult reads for about 2 hours on a typical day, frequently while pursuing such daily activities as working, shopping, attending school or church or theater, traveling or commuting, as well as during free time.

The survey indicated that adults read the materials listed below.

1. Newspapers: 70% of adults read newspapers for an average of 35 minutes a day.
2. Mail: 53% read mail for 5 minutes a day, but 96% receive mail every day.
3. Magazines: 40% read magazines for 35 minutes a day.
4. Books: 33% read books about 47 minutes a day.

When do adults do their reading? The answer is in Table 10.3. According to the survey, the higher an individual's socioeconomic status, the more reading he or she did. But 5% of all adults interviewed were unable to read (define as unable to read newspaper headlines) including 2.3% who were visually handicapped, 1.6% who were foreign language readers, and 1.1% who were illiterates (those adults who never learned to read in any language and did not have visual difficulties). The members of this nonreading group were also members of an extremely low socioeconomic group. They had to depend on others to read to them.

How Well Do Adults Comprehend Functional Reading Tasks?   The National Reading Council, appointed by President Nixon, commissioned Louis Harris and

Associates (1970) to measure the literacy rate in the nation, using a representative sample of 1,685 persons, ages 16 and up. The study measured the "survival" literacy rate for functional, or practical, reading skills. These reading skills consist of the ability to read such application forms as required for obtaining a Social Security number, a personal bank loan, public assistance, medicaid, and a driver's license. Those who answered three questions incorrectly (30% of the items on the forms) were considered illiterate. The percentage ranged from 3% (public assistance form) to 34% (medicaid form). On the average, 1 out of 8 adults (or, at that time, 18.5 million Americans) would have had difficulty in obtaining government assistance because they could not read well enough to fill out the application forms.

The lowest age group in the Harris survey (age 16–24) had the lowest illiteracy rate (range 1% to 9%). The lowest illiteracy rate in the nation was found in the West and the highest was in the South.

The remedy for inability to read application forms and other functional reading tasks is twofold: (a) simplify the language used in the forms, use larger print accompanied by pictured directions, and provide cassette tapes for auditory explanations; (b) seek to improve literacy, starting with high school students still in the functionally illiterate category, and reducing the relatively low rate of this group even further; then go on to older illiterates.

TEXTBOOK DIFFICULTY
What are the Reading Demands of Texts in Vocational Courses?

Using a modified Dale-Chall readability formula, Sticht and McFann (1975) found that the texts used in secondary school and community college vocational programs had the readability levels shown in Table 10.4. The two researchers then gave a general reading test to students enrolled in these courses. They found that the average reading ability of students was *below* the average difficulty of the texts they used—about 0.6 of a year below in food services, 1.0 years below in auto mechanics, 1.7 years below in building trades, 3.5 years below in welding, and 4.0 years below in radio and TV repair! The instructors of these courses corroborated the findings. They reported that over half the students in their courses could not comprehend their texts without the instructor's help.

What are Job-Related Reading Requirements?

Sticht and McFann (1975) used a specially constructed set of tasks based on *actual* reading done in various army occupations. As a criterion they used the percentage in comprehension scored by enlisted men with various levels of reading ability. Cooks, mechanics, and supply clerks whose general reading level was about 6.5 scored only 50% in comprehension, and students reading at grade level 12.8 got 90%. With a 70% comprehension score as the criterion, the reading level required to be a successful cook would be the 7th-grade level, for mechanics the 9th-grade level, and for supply clerks the 10-grade level. Addi-

TABLE 10.4. Readability Levels of Texts in Vocational Courses

Course	Readability Grade Level of Text
Radio and TV Repair	14.0
Welding	12.0
Appliance Repair	12.0
Medical Office	11.2
Clothing Services	10.5
Building Trades	10.2
Auto Mechanics	10.0
Food Services	9.2

tional data on reading, listening, and arithmetic requirements of military occupations that have civilian counterparts can be found in Sticht, Caylor, and Kern (1970).

"Literacy in the workplace" has become the title for a new field of research. Mickulecky and Strange (1986, pp. 320–321) report on several studies that indicate work-type reading differs considerably from school text reading. Middle-level workers and professionals spend an equal amount of their reading time in reading for application, assessment, and acquisition of new information. Workers' reading includes directions, diagrams, manuals, forms, flyers, computer print-outs and textbooks. The difficulty levels of these materials average 11th-grade level, but range from 9th grade to college level. They read to make applications, solve problems, relate information in the text to known information and form judgments. They compare textual information against the actual equipment described. The reading often occurs in the context of a group, and workmen ask each other questions about their reading more than twice as often as high school students do. They average about 2 hours per days in reading, usually in short blocks of about 5 minutes per reading episode, whereas high school students spend about 98 minutes per day in reading. Since 95% of high school reading is from textbooks, mostly to learn factual information, Mickulecky and Strange conclude "there is little in the school experience to prepare new workers for the range of literacy strategies called for in the workplace."

In general, workers tend to read better than high school students. Blue-collar workers average between 10th and 11th grades in reading ability. Only 5% of blue-collar workers but 16% of high school juniors experienced extreme difficulty with a 9th-grade newspaper passage. Mickulecky and Strange think that "many individuals with low literacy abilities are not being allowed to enter or remain in the work force."

Even those with relatively high literacy abilities, but still below the expectations attained by those of equal intelligence and backgrounds, are not as likely to qualify for professional occupations that emphasize scientific knowledge. They are more likely to go into sales jobs where nonacademic skills are more important (Guthrie, 1984). In short, the required literacy level is relative to the reading demands of the occupation. In other words, inadequate literacy levels are not only likely to affect the job opportunities of blue-collar workers but also white-collar professionals.

The assumption that training in general literacy would transfer to the specific reading demands of the workplace does not appear to be warranted (Mickulecky & Strange, 1986). However, high schools cannot go the other extreme to train students for all the specific types of reading in the workplace. What they can do is teach students general reading ability, how to read some specific job-related materials, probably in conjunction with occupational courses for the purposes and in the way workers read on the job, perhaps enable them to learn how to learn job-related materials, and develop in students the expectation that they will have to learn how to read the specific materials in each particular job they enter. Employers will also have to learn that they will have to provide reading instruction on the job in specific job-related materials to high school graduates, whether they are blue- or white-collar workers. They will have to emphasize the specific types of reading, technical vocabulary, information, and procedures required for the job. The army has already accepted this requirement. Instead of general literacy training, the army provides for specific job literacy training in each of its 120 major military jobs.

What Are the Reading Demands of Texts in Academic Courses?

High school texts vary considerably in difficulty level even in the same content areas. Belden and Lee (1961) found that four of five biology texts had average readability levels higher than the average reading levels of students in six Oklahoma high schools; only one text had a readability level suitable for 50% of the students who used it.

Mallinson, Sturm, and Mallinson (1952), using the Flesch formula, found that 11 of 16 high school physics texts had 9th-grade readability levels; these texts were suitable for all students enrolled in physics classes. Three texts scored between 9th- and 10th-grade reading levels; they were appropriate only for average and better physics students. But, two texts were too difficult even for superior students!

These studies indicate that the teacher of content area classes should be aware that there is a range of texts from which to choose for content area instruction. If limited to one text, the teacher can probably select a text that is appropriate for at least half the class. But if more than one text is available, knowledge of the readability levels of texts and reading abilities of students would enable the teacher to select texts appropriate to the entire class.

To give the reader a concrete idea of the difficulty level of content area reading materials, we selected some texts used in some high schools in southern California. We took samples from them and computed their Flesch Reading Ease scores. See the results in Box 10.5.

BOX 10.5. *Flesch Reading Ease Scores for Sample High School Textbooks*

CHEMISTRY

One of the activities of science is the search for regularity. Regularities that directly correlate experimental results are generally called rules or laws. A more abstract regularity, expressing a hidden likeness, is generally called a model, theory, or principle. Thus, the behavior of oxygen gas summarized in the equation $P \times V = a\ constant$ is called a law. The explanation of this same regular gas behavior in terms of the motion of particles is called a theory. It is a greater abstraction to connect the PV product with the mathematical equations that describe rebounding billiard balls. Nevertheless, rules, laws, models, theories, and principles all have a common air — they all systematize our experimental knowledge. They all state regularities among known facts.

Words in sample = 118
Average sentence length = 15
Syllables per 100 words = 198
Reading Ease score = 26
Evaluation = very difficult: college level material

PHYSICS

Radiation damage can be prevented. Radioactive isotopes, x-ray machines, and nuclear reactors must be shielded so that dangerous radiation does not reach the people who operate them. Alpha and beta rays can be stopped by thin shields, but x-rays, gamma rays, and neutrons are more penetrating. Neutrons from a reactor are controlled by reflecting them back into the reactor, often by a layer of graphite. The ability of a shield to stop x-rays and gamma rays depends on its thickness and its density. The more mass there is between a person and a reactor, the better he is protected.

Words in sample = 98
Average sentence length = 16
Syllables per 100 words = 162
Reading Ease score = 56
Evaluation = fairly difficult: high school grades 10–12.

HISTORY

American relations with the nations of the Western Hemisphere have undergone a noticeable change in recent decades. A spirit of cooperation and partnership has gradually supplanted an attitude of paternalism. Whereas in the past this nation's sister republics in Latin America both envied and feared American political power and economic wealth, they no longer seem so frustrated by the "Colossus of the North" in their search for national identity and importance.

Past American policy regarding hemispheric problems had caused conflict and resentment. Much of this can perhaps be attributed to the fact that Americans have attempted to understand very different cultures on the basis of American values and beliefs.

Words in sample = 108
Average sentence length = 20
Syllables per 100 words = 190
Reading Ease score = 27
Evaluation = very difficult: college-level material

ALGEBRA

The set of all points associated with ordered pairs of numbers in the solution set of an open sentence in two variables is called the graph of the solution set, or simply, the graph of the open sentence. The graph of every equation equivalent to one of the form $Ax + By = C$, where A, B, and C are constants such that not both A and B equal 0, is a straight line. Notice that in any linear equation, $Ax + By = C$, each term is either a constant or a monomial of degree 1. Hence, $2x + 3y = 27$ is a linear equation; but $y = x^2$ and $xy = 5$ are not, and their graphs are not straight lines.
Words in sample = 124
Average sentence length = 31
Syllables per 100 words = 150
Reading Ease score = 47
Evaluation = fairly difficult: material for high school grades 10–12

ENGLISH

The novel is a comparatively new form of writing in the English language. About three hundred years old, it came into being after a major political and social revolution that took place in England in the seventeenth century. During that revolution the English monarchy in the person of King Charles I was overthrown by the followers of Oliver Cromwell, who sought a more democratic form of government than that offered by the crown. As a result of this revolution, a new social class — the middle class of merchants, bankers, and shopkeepers — started its rise to power, firmly establishing itself by the eighteenth century.
Words in sample = 102
Average sentence length = 25
Syllables per 100 words = 166
Reading Ease score = 42
Evaluation = Fairly difficult: material for high school grades 10–12

Chemistry passage from George E. Pimentel, ed., *Chemistry: An Experimental Science* (San Francisco: W. H. Freeman, 1963), p. 17. Physics passage from Robert Stallberg and Faith Fitch Hall, *Physics: Fundamentals and Frontiers* (Boston: Houghton Mifflin, 1965), p. 140. History passage from Robert F. Madgic, et al., *The American Experience* (Menlo Park, Calif.: Addison-Wesley, 1971), p. 335. Algebra passage from Mary P. Dolciani, Simon L. Berman, and William Wooton, *Modern Algebra and Trigonometry: Structure and Method, Book Two* (Boston: Houghton Mifflin, 1965), p. 82. English passage from V. S. Pritchett, "The Novel," in *Adventures in Appreciation* (New York: Harcourt, Brace and World, 1968), p. 585.

These texts ranged from fairly difficult (requiring some high school grades completed) to difficult (high school and some college work completed) to very difficult (college completed). Only the fairly difficult levels would be appropriate for even advanced high school students!

Of course, the passages in these texts do not represent the range of difficulty within each text. More difficult and easier passages could be found in each text. That is why an average based on at least three samples from three different parts of a text is necessary in establishing the reading level of the text.

Readability formulas have other limitations. They do not take into account the conceptual level nor the information density of the material. The algebra sample is equal in difficulty to the English sample, but the algebra vocabulary appears to be much more difficult than the English vocabulary. Hence, in addition to using a formula for assessing readability, teachers should analyze the content of a text to determine its semantic difficulty, information density, conceptual level, and style of writing. Unfortunately, scales for assessing semantic difficulty, or for conceptual levels, or for density of concepts or information, or for relating writing styles to difficulty of reading are not available. Consequently, teachers can make only subjective appraisals of these aspects of reading difficulty.

How Well Do College Students Have to Read? At the college level (as well as at any other level) the question has to be: how well should a student have to read what kind of material and for what degree of comprehension? As Sticht and McFann (1975) pointed out, above, readers can have varying degrees of comprehension. Furthermore, required reading materials in college (as in other levels of education) vary in readability level; and the average and range of readability ability of college students also vary. The University of California, which has nine campuses (Berkeley, UCLA, Riverside, and so forth), by law can accept only the top 12.5% of high school graduates who have taken a particular program of academic courses. Hence, freshman clases consist of students from the upper 12.5% of their high school classes. To complete effectively in this freshman environment, a student should have reading comprehension abilities at least equal to those of the top 12.5% of high school seniors. However, the California State University and College System (San Francisco, San Diego, Fullerton, Humboldt. San Bernardino), which is a separate system from the University of California, can accept the top one third of high school graduates. Students with reading abilities at least within the range of the 67th to the 99th percentile of high school seniors are likely to be able to compete with varying degrees of success in the State University and College System. The community colleges in California can accept any high school graduate. Consequently, a wider range of reading abilities occurs among the junior college population. Similar variation exists among institutions of higher education throughout the country.

Since teachers tend to normalize instruction, that is, teach toward the average student, the reading demands and criteria for successful academic accomplishment are likely to reflect the capacities and skills of the average student. In short, to decide what level of reading achievement a student needs to be successful at the college level, teachers have to know (a) a student's capacities (particularly the skills of reading and learning from text) and aspirations for achievement as well as (b) the demands of the institution and the average level of ability of students in the institution.

Speed of reading, a factor that is important at any level, becomes increasingly significant as students progress through the grades and becomes crucial at the college level because of the heavy load of reading.

To determine why speed of reading is crucial at the college level, let's look at the reading requirements at college and compute the time required to do the assigned reading and complete the texts. D. W. Gilbert (1955) estimates that a college student at the University of California has 16,000 pages of reference reading to do each semester. The average college freshman reads relatively easy (sixth-grade level) material at a rate of 250 words per minute. Van Wagenen (1953) determined this speed in his rate-of-comprehension test. (See Box 10.6 for speed-of-reading data.)

We recognize that an individual has different rates of reading that vary with his or her purpose and the demands of the material (Holmes & Singer, 1966); by

---

BOX 10.6. Description and Norms for Rate of Comprehension

TYPICAL RATE OF COMPREHENSION PARAGRAPH

Directions: Cross out the word that does not fit in with the meaning of the rest of the paragraph.

Jane needed a spool of silk thread to finish her new dress. But when she went to the store for her mother she forgot to get the buttons she needed.

Reading Ease Score: Fairly easy, sixth-grade level

Answer: You should have crossed out the word "buttons."

The scale has 56 paragraphs similar in difficulty to the sample paragraph. In grades 4 to 9, only 5 minutes, and in grades 10–12, only 4 minutes are allowed for working on the scale. In this type of reading task and with these time limitations, the following norms or average scores are attained:

Words per minute	Grade Level	Age Level
237	13.0	18-2
220	12.0	17-2
207	11.0	16-2
188	10.0	15-2
170	9.0	14-2
157	8.0	13-2
134	7.0	12-2
117	6.0	11-2
93	5.0	10-2
63	4.0	9-2
50	3.0	8-2

Quoted passage is from *Rate of Comprehension Scale, Form A.* Minneapolis, Minn.: M. J. Van Wagenen, 1953.

thinking of 250 words per minute as a kind of average rate of reading, estimating 500 words per page, and assuming a 44-hour week of reading, we can compute the number of weeks required to read through 16,000 pages as follows:

$$\frac{16,000 \text{ pages} \times 500 \text{ words per page}}{250 \text{ words per minute}}$$

Computation gives, 32,000 minutes or 533 hours—about 13.5 forty-hour weeks![3] Since a semester is usually 18 weeks long, the students who reads at this average rate has to spend most of the semester reading assigned material in order to survive academically. Hence, students have to learn to be extremely efficient in reading and to develop effective strategies for reading and learning from text.

Instead of waiting until students reach high school or college, we need to start at earlier levels to teach them efficient and effective strategies they can acquire cumulatively as they progress through school. In chapters 15 and 16 we explain roles content area teachers and reading specialists can play in working towards the goal of improving the ability of all students to read and learn from texts efficiently and effectively.

Prior to this chapter, we provided knowledge, strategies, techniques, and tools for teaching students with a wide range of individual differences to read and learn from a *single* text. We are now ready to explain ways of handling individual differences through strategies for reading and learning from multiple texts.

SUMMARY

We can determine readability of written materials and reading levels of students in several ways. Two types of techniques for arriving at the readability or reading difficulty-level of materials are (1) computational procedures: the Flesch Reading Ease Formula and the Fry Readability Graph; and (2) a noncomputational, estimation procedure: the SEER technique. We can use standardized tests to measure the reading levels of students. (For a description of standardized tests, see chapter 3.) Or we can compute student reading levels on samples of materials that are to be read in class by using the cloze technique and the personal reading inventory (PRI) or the formal reading inventory (IRI). Because the cloze technique and the inventory assess students on samples of actual classroom materials, these procedures have content and curricular validity; they also assess more closely the difficulty level of the interaction between the text and the reader.

---

[3]When reading and learning from more difficult texts, particularly when the purpose is to prepare for an examination, the rate is, of course, likely to be much slower. Consequently, 250 words per minute is probably an overestimate of a high school or college student's reading rate for typical textbook material. Therefore, at a lower speed of reading, a student will take longer than the 13.5 weeks to read 16,000 pages of material.

Comparison of reading levels of students with readability of materials demonstrates the usefulness of these procedures in revealing the reading demands that various types of written material (recreational and functional materials, vocational texts, job-related materials, and academic texts) place upon the reader.

Recreational reading of magazines demands reading levels varying from a fifth-grade level for comic books to advanced high school level for the *Atlantic* magazine. The average American adult reads newspapers, magazines, mail, and books for a total of about two hours per day, doing most reading at work or at school. But five percent of the population cannot read at all in English. However, only 1.1% of American adults are illiterate; that is, they cannot read in any language. These adults speak English, and they are not visually handicapped. Yet, 12.5% of the adults in this nation have difficulty in reading and filling out various application forms.

Vocational texts can vary in difficulty from a 9th-grade level for food services to the 14th-grade level for radio and television repair manuals. Students in these vocational courses have reading abilities that, on the average, are below the readability levels of the texts: from 0.6 of a year in food services to 4.0 years in radio and television repair courses. To read materials needed on the job with a 70% level of comprehension, an army cook would have to read at a 7th-grade level, mechanics at a 9th-grade level, and supply clerks at a 10th-grade level.

Academic texts also vary in difficulty. Although high school texts in any academic subject can be below or at the average level of reading ability of the students who use them, most texts are appropriate only for advanced high school students or for college students. The implication is that teachers can adopt single texts appropriate to the average reading ability of their students or they can select multiple texts to suit the entire range of reading abilities in their classes.

College students have to be effective *and* efficient readers because of the difficulty of their texts and the abundance of reading required each semester. Many beginning college students read at least at the 13th-grade level and with a speed of 250 words per minute when reading fairly easy (6th-grade level) material. However, the average reading ability of college students varies from one college or university to another as a function of student selection and institutional admission policies. Since college and university professors, as well as classroom teachers, tend to normalize instructional demands, that is, teach toward the average student and use texts appropriate to this level, competition for a student with a particular level of reading ability can be less in one institution and greater in another. Of course, successful achievement is also dependent on a student's level of aspiration. For example, a B average may mean success to one student and failure to another, even though both may have the same reading ability.

Although procedures for determining student reading levels and text readability levels have their limitations, they are nevertheless useful for estimating difficulty of reading tasks, for selecting material appropriate to the range of a class's reading abilities, and for understanding problems in teaching and reading and learning from text. We can conclude from information on these problems that ability to read and learn from texts is not only dependent upon a student's reading level and motivation but also upon the difficulty of a text and the instructional demands that are made by the teacher.

ACTIVITIES

1. Select a passage from this text or from a content area textbook. Determine its readability using the Flesch, Fry, and SEER techniques. Compare the results. How do you account for differences? Compare your explanation with that of another student.
2. Administer a cloze test on a passage from a content area textbook to (a) one or more of your colleagues in your content area and (b) one or more colleagues out of your content area. Compare the results and explain differences, if any.

11 | Multiple-Text Strategies

CHAPTER OVERVIEW

In the last four chapters, you have learned (a) how to teach students to learn from a single text, (b) how to teach discussion and writing, and (c) how to determine the readability of textbooks. This information can now be applied to multiple-text strategies as students start to become more independent readers. Three multiple-text strategies are discussed in this chapter. Because these strategies frequently require group work, the chapter also covers various ways in which groups can report to the rest of the class.

GRAPHIC ORGANIZER

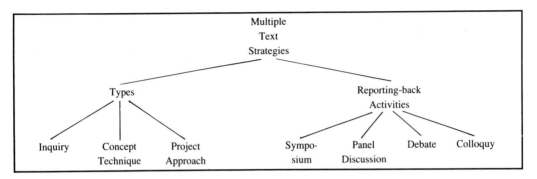

PREPOSED QUESTIONS

1. Chapter 8 focused on using discussion methods in your classroom. How can that information help you to employ multiple-text strategies effectively?

TEACHING FROM MULTIPLE TEXTS

In chapter 6, you read about strategies to use when teaching a single textbook to an entire class. These strategies are crucial to teaching all students to learn from text, without holding some students back and stigmatizing other students as slow. The single-text strategies accomplish this goal because they take a text that has a particular level of reading difficulty and make it fit better the wide range of ability to read and learn from text that is present in a class. In other words, single-text strategies enable more students to read and learn at their own levels from the class's single textbook.

Moreover, single-text strategies develop some skills that are required for use with multiple-text strategies. The Directed Reading Activity emphasizes prediction and verification; Active Comprehension and SQ3R strategies teach students to formulate their own questions. The reading and learning-from-text guides give students opportunities to learn to conduct and participate in group discussion and to report to the class. Discussion and writing are necessary skills for multiple-text strategies. We devoted separate chapters to each of these skills so that teachers can demonstrate and teach them to their students. On the assumption that teachers have done so while using the single-text strategies, we are now ready to go on to multiple-text strategies. The first is the inquiry method. To introduce this technique, we start with a scenario that dramatizes the need for inquiry.

TYPES OF MULTIPLE TEXT STRATEGIES

Inquiry

SCENARIO

One day after school, Ms. Jones was chatting with one of her students, Iris Carrington. Iris was angry because she felt she'd been "ripped off" by a cosmetics company that sold her a preparation "guaranteed to free the buyer of any complexion problems." Iris had sent the company a money order for $10 and had received back a small bottle of what looked and smelled like ocean water. When she applied it to her face, her skin became increasingly irritated. In consoling her, Ms. Jones pointed out that she was an innocent victim of propaganda. Iris stared at her blankly as if to ask, "What's *propaganda?*"

Ms. Jones reflected on the hundreds of pre-teens and teens who are victims of false and misleading advertising, or the thousands of adults who are prey to political speeches, inflammatory editorials, and malicious gossip. Ms. Jones thought of how many people react to things they read and hear emotionally rather than analytically: Why did Iris think that a cosmetics company, unknown to her and hundreds of miles away, could solve her complexion problem?

It was then that Ms. Jones decided to teach her students inquiry—the technique of solving problems by careful examination, interpretation, and evaluation of evidence. The students, have been instructed in single-text strategies, were developing good critical reading habits. It might, she felt, be a good opportunity to see if they could apply what they had learned to multiple-text situations.

TYPES OF INQUIRY

Ms. Jones was aware that there are different types of inquiry, so she tried to decide which one would be the best for the purposes of students in her classroom. Three types of inquiry she studied about were (a) open inquiry, (b) guided inquiry, and (c) text-based inquiry.

Open Inquiry

In open inquiry, a teacher poses a problem and the students have to solve it, using any means they have. One time, Mr. Wallace had given his class a series of ethnic jokes that had been generated by one culture about another culture. The jokes had been edited to eliminate specific references that might cue the students to the true identity of either culture; what remained was humor. The problem was to determine the characteristics of (a) the culture that produced the creator of the jokes and (b) the culture that the jokes were about. In solving the problem, the students used material in the jokes, their own experience, other examples of ethnic humor, and materials they had read inside and outside of class. Mr. Wallace's objective was to see if the students could apply critical reading skills to solve a problem. Mr. Wallace consulted with students upon request but didn't direct them through a series of problem-solving steps.

Guided Inquiry

In guided inquiry, a teacher poses a problem and the students have to solve it using a specified sequence of steps (Joyce & Weil, 1986). These steps usually include (a) identifying and gathering data, (b) interpreting data, (c) analyzing data, (d) judging data, (e) hypothesizing from data, and (f) testing hypotheses. Examples of this type of inquiry are discussed in chapters 12 and 13.

Text-Based Inquiry

In light of what had happened to Iris, Ms. Jones felt that text-based inquiry might be valuable for her students. Text-based inquiry ia a process of determining whether a so-called factual statement in a text is true. Ryan and Ellis (1974) point out that information presented as fact in a textbook, or for that matter in any written material, may not be true. Their example is taken from a social science text that stated that Admiral Byrd was the first person to fly over the North Pole. They raised this question: "How do we know this statement is true?" Their next question was, "How can we find out whether it's true?"

If the class is not familiar with inquiry procedures, the teacher must first instruct the students in means for obtaining evidence, including newspaper stories and especially reports by observers at the events the news reports describe. The class Ryan and Ellis worked with was led by the *Readers' Guide to Periodical Literature*[1] away from a single text toward other texts, including

---

[1]*Readers' Guide to Periodical Literature*. New York: H. W. Wilson, 1900–.

newspaper reports written at the time of Byrd's flight by reporters located at Byrd's base camp. The class discovered one newspaper report that charged Admiral Byrd merely faked a flight over the Pole. The class got additional information from other sources. The students then had to weigh the evidence pro and con. They selected a jury to hear the evidence presented by students who were for as well as those who were against Byrd. The jury concluded that the evidence presented by the former students supported the claim that Admiral Byrd was the first person to fly over the North Pole.

Information in any text may be disputed. In challenging information in a text, students can learn to be critical, to search for evidence, and to arrive at their own conclusions. In doing so, they can learn to ask two basic questions of any content area: (a) What does the author mean? and (b) How does the author know?

In answering these questions, students will engage in library activities similar to those suggested for use in the project approach discussed later in this chapter. If the library has a variety of references at different levels of difficulty, then students can select materials appropriate to their levels and contribute whatever information they have located. If students are working in groups or teams, they can help each other locate information and evaluate it.

The teacher's task is to help students formulate standards or determine criteria for evaluating any controversial material they might read. Ms. Jones did just that.

Iris Carrington had, in effect, believed the statement ''guaranteed to free the buyer of any complexion problems'' to be a fact when it obviously wasn't. Ms. Jones collected a series of statements from advertising and political campaigns and built a lesson around teaching the students to detect the difference between fact and opinion. Her lesson sheet appears in Box. 11.1

BOX 11.1. *Ms. Jones's Lesson Sheet for Teaching Fact Versus Opinion*

Activity A. Below are seven statements. If the statement is a fact, put a *check mark* in the box provided. If the statement is not a fact, put a *zero* in the box.
- ☐ 1. All Democrats believe in heavy taxation.
- ☐ 2. Presweetened cereals are most harmful to your digestive system.
- ☐ 3. Most human hands contain five fingers.
- ☐ 4. Ninety-nine percent of people dying of cancer each year have eaten a pickle at least once in their lifetime.
- ☐ 5. Labor unions keep the economy rolling.
- ☐ 6. Compact cars are the wave of the future.
- ☐ 7. Bankers are stingy people.

Comment: Only one item in activity A is a *fact,* that is, a statement that you can verify by observation. The rest of the items may read like facts but actually are not; they are statements that try to persuade you to think a certain way. These statements are called *opinions.* In other words, your past experience verifies that most human hands have five fingers, but you would have a hard time verifying that all Democrats believe in heavy taxation. Yet many people would accept both statements as being equally true. To prove that Democrats believe in heavy taxation you would have to survey a representative sample of the Democrats in the United States. Do you think they would all believe the same way?

Activity B. Explain what you would have to do to prove statements 2, 4, 5, 6, and 7 in activity A are true.

Comment: As you probably discovered in activity B, to prove whether a statement is fact or opinion requires a lot of effort. The library might help you determine fact from opinion since it has many sources of information.

Activity C. Read each of the following statements. What sources of information in the library would help you determine whether these are statements of *fact* or *opinion?*
1. Babe Ruth was the greatest hitter in baseball history.
2. Cigarette smoke causes lung cancer.
3. Classical music is greater than pop rock.
4. Big cities breed crime.
5. Senior citizens are healthier today than they were twenty years ago, but less happy.

Comment: As you continue to use the library you will probably add more sources to your list.

After the students had completed Activity C, Ms. Jones gave them a problem, taken from D. W. Gilbert's *Manual* (1956), that needed to be solved by checking sources of information in the library. The problem is stated in Box 11.2.

BOX 11.2. *Inquiry Problem for Ms. Jones's Students to Solve at the Library*

Instructions: Read the following three news releases concerning the Operator's Union Strike at the Rapid Transit Company. When you are through, answer the questions at the end of the lesson by using library sources.

NEWS RELEASES

News Report (Factual)

The strike between the Operator's Union and the Rapid Transit Company is now entering its 30th day. The operators are demanding a 25-cent-per-hour wage increase and the company has countered with an offer of a 10-cent-an-hour increase. No settlement is in progress.

The Same Report Slanted Toward the Operators (Opinion)

The good citizen interested in fair play is watching the dispute between the Operator's Union and the Rapid Transit Company with a mixture of admiration and alarm. He knows the average operator is trying to maintain a decent home for his wife and children, and that living costs have skyrocketed to the highest point in history. Even when the operator is working (to make management richer) he can scarcely make ends meet. While the Company officials sit out the strike complacently in plush offices and smoke 50-cent cigars to pass the time, the carman is worrying about shoes to carry his children back to school and milk for their lunch pails. The solid citizen takes off his hat to the patient courage of the operator, but he, too, is wondering what will happen to the innocent youngsters.

The Same Report Slanted Toward the Company (Opinion)

In some circles, the sympathy in any strike goes to the worker. But what are the facts in the current hold-up by the Operator's Union for wage increases? Despite miracles of economy in operation, rising costs have forced R. T. Co. to operate at a loss for the past two years. In the interest of public service, no dividends have been declared and top management agreed to sharp cuts in personal salaries. Meantime the workers have asked and received three separate wage boosts, so that they are now better paid than the police and the teachers. But still they can't live on their wages. Caviar and Cadillacs come high this year.

Fortunately the Company does not need to be concerned about the public reaction. The people are too smart to be duped by gangster tactics. With the facts on the table it becomes entirely clear that the operators are not striking for groceries but for glory. Labor has its eye on the national scene.

QUESTIONS FOR LIBRARY INQUIRY

1. The "news report" came from the November 15, 1977 issue of the *Monroe Herald*. Check similar news reports in the *Monroe Eagle* and the *Monroe Times*. Do the three newspapers agree on (a) the duration of the strike, (b) the amount of the wage increase and (c) the amount of the counter offer? If they don't agree, how would you determine what the truth is?
2. What opinions expressed in the report favoring the operators would the operators accept as fact? Select one opinion and try to check it against library resources to see if it is true, e.g.: "Even when the operator is working (to make management richer) he can scarcely make ends meet."
3. What opinions expressed in the company report would management accept as fact? Select one opinion and try to check it against library resources to see if it is true.
4. Below are descriptions of seven propaganda techniques. See how these techniques are used in the two slanted reports.
   a. *Card stacking*. In this technique, facts are provided, but not *all* the facts, only those favorable to one side of the argument. Beware when the trial lawyer says, "Ladies and gentlemen of the jury, I shall now summarize the facts of this case. Since you are intelligent people, I know you will use these facts to

arrive at correct conclusions." The lawyer then provides only facts favorable to one side of the case, omitting those that are unfavorable. The lawyer has also used flattery to get the audience to arrive at conclusions favorable to his or her side of the case.

b. *Authority.* An expert may testify. The idea is to have the expert's testimony be accepted because of his or her reputation as an expert. The assumption is that experts really know, but that assumption is not always true. The expert may have a conflict of interest and therefore be biased, or the expert may not be as expert as someone else who comes to a different conclusion. Hence, experts are cross-examined carefully by trial lawyers, or other experts are brought in to dispute their testimony. Internal consistency in presentation of a viewpoint and ability to resolve discrepancies are two criteria for determining which person is more objective and more expert.

c. *Transfer.* A well-known, popular, or admired person is associated with something or someone. The characteristics of the admired figure are carried over to the new object or person. For example, advertisers use sports figures in their commercials so that the viewing public can associate the admired sports figures with shaving lotion or shaving cream. The idea is that if you use it, you will also be admired.

d. *Name calling.* Name calling may be used to discredit someone or something. The process may be blatant or subtle. For example, a union may be striking for higher wages. Management then reports how much *some* workers are being paid per hour, what kind of cars they drive, what kind of homes they own (card stacking). The implication is that the workers are well paid, but they are still not satisfied. They want more, more than their share. The implication is that workers are hogs.

The workers' propaganda retaliates by describing the "cigar-smoking, Cadillac-driving, coupon-clipping officers of the company who are getting rich off workers' labor." They are really Simon Legrees, whipping the poor workers and benefitting from the workers' hard labor.

e. *Bandwagon.* The idea of this technique is that the trend of events is going in a particular direction, and if you want to be on the side of a winner, you should jump aboard the wagon. At one time bandwagons were actually used in political campaigns. People who sided with particular candidates jumped upon their bandwagons.

If opinion polls are favorable to them, political candidates will cite the results. If the polls are not favorable, they'll try to ignore or discredit them, sometimes using name calling and implying that the pollsters are dishonest.

Stock market reports that stocks are going up create a bandwagon effect. The propaganda is that if you want to make money, you should buy stocks now and make money as you see the price of the stock go up. Of course, if stock prices go down, it is rationalized or explained away as "only an adjustment," or "profit-taking," or some *temporary* downward turn. The desired effect of propaganda from the viewpoint of the companies involved is that you should not get on the downward bandwagon and sell. Instead, you should, "Wait, the stocks will go up again."

f. *American values.* Motherhood, family, God, and patriotism are some things Americans value highly. These values are being used when political candidates introduce their mothers, display their wives and children, hire bands to play patriotic music, and let everybody know they attend church regularly. For example, reports are regularly issued about the president's churchgoing activities, whether he is in the White House, on vacation, or on a ship out at sea.

g. *Glittering generalities.* Sweeping phrases that sound good, but do not specify what is meant, may appeal to you. For example, the president said, "What this country needs is solid progress." But he did not specify what solid progress is nor what he would do to bring it about.

5. Apply these propaganda techniques to the speeches of two candidates for public office who are debating an issue.

News releases are from Doris Wilcox Gilbert, *Power and Speed in Reading.* Englewood Cliffs, N.J.: Prentice-Hall, Inc., 1956, p. 150. Reprinted by permission of D. W. Gilbert and Prentice-Hall, Inc.

Concept Technique

After using inquiry, students can function more independently in the concept technique. The *concept technique* consists of using a group of materials all related to one particular concept. By definition, a *concept* is an "idea of something formed by mentally combining all its characteristics and particulars" (J. Stein, 1973).

In literature, the idea might be *courage;* in social studies, *revolution;* in science, *power,* and in mathematics, *calculators and computers.* Another unique feature of the technique is a three-stage process that allows students to have greater self-selection, independence, and responsibility. The first stage consists of teacher-conducted lessons that explain the various facets of the idea. The second stage allows those students interested in a particular facet to form a group for further investigation of it. The third stage permits individual self-selection of a facet and materials to pursue an independent investigation.

Teachers could choose their own concepts and select materials to develop them by using the *Children's Catalog* (Shor & Fidel, 1972), the *Junior High School Library Catalog* (Fidel & Bogart, 1970), and the *Senior High School Library Catalog* (Fidel & Berger, 1972). Glossed examples from these catalogs are shown in Box 11.3. Teachers could select books on a particular concept from these three catalogs. The annotation for each book in the catalogs would help in the selection.

BOX 11.3. *Glossed Directions for Reading Three Catalogs*

CHILDREN'S CATALOG

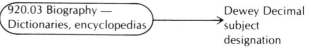

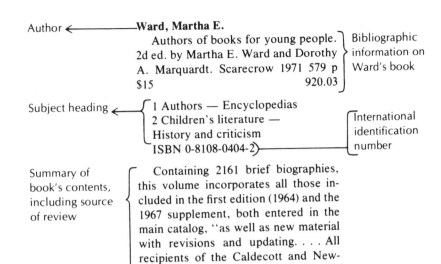

Author ← **Ward, Martha E.**
Authors of books for young people. ⎫ Bibliographic
2d ed. by Martha E. Ward and Dorothy ⎬ information on
A. Marquardt. Scarecrow 1971 579 p ⎪ Ward's book
$15   920.03 ⎭

Subject heading ← ⎧ 1 Authors — Encyclopedias
⎨ 2 Children's literature —
⎩ History and criticism   ⎤ International
ISBN 0-8108-0404-2)   ⎥ identification
                            ⎦ number

Summary of ⎡   Containing 2161 brief biographies,
book's contents, ⎥ this volume incorporates all those in-
including source ⎨ cluded in the first edition (1964) and the
of review   ⎥ 1967 supplement, both entered in the
                  main catalog, "as well as new material
                  with revisions and updating. . . . All
                  recipients of the Caldecott and New-
                  bery medals through 1970 are included.
                  . . . The new edition also identifies
                  publisher and year of publication for
                  each title listed, and provides cross ref-
                  erences for pseudonyms." Publisher's
                  ⎣ note

JUNIOR HIGH SCHOOL CATALOG

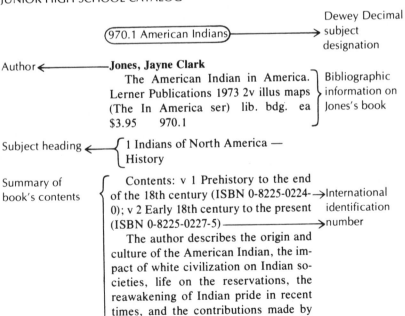

                                              Dewey Decimal
(970.1 American Indians) ────────────→ subject
                                              designation

Author ← **Jones, Jayne Clark**
The American Indian in America. ⎫ Bibliographic
Lerner Publications 1973 2v illus maps ⎬ information on
(The In America ser) lib. bdg. ea ⎪ Jones's book
$3.95   970.1 ⎭

Subject heading ← ⎧ 1 Indians of North America —
⎩ History

Summary of ⎡   Contents: v 1 Prehistory to the end
book's contents ⎥ of the 18th century (ISBN 0-8225-0224- →International
                ⎨ 0); v 2 Early 18th century to the present identification
                ⎥ (ISBN 0-8225-0227-5) ──────────→number
                    The author describes the origin and
                  culture of the American Indian, the im-
                  pact of white civilization on Indian so-
                  cieties, life on the reservations, the
                  reawakening of Indian pride in recent
                  times, and the contributions made by
                  ⎣ American Indians in various fields

''Ms. Jones has attempted to write a corrective to the numerous tales of daring-do depicting heroic cavalry charges and sly savage natives that dominate juvenile histories of the American Indians. . . . Rather than a history, the two volumes are more a bill of particulars in an indictment against white treatment of the American Indian.'' Science Bks } Direct quotation from book review, with source.

SENIOR HIGH SCHOOL CATALOG

812 American drama → Dewey Decimal subject designation

Author ← **Baldwin, James**
One day, when I was lost; a scenario based on Alex Haley's ''The autobiography of Malcom X.'' Dial Press 1973 (c1972) 280p illus $7.50   812 } Bibliographic information

Subject heading ← 1 Malcolm X — Drama

Background on ← First published 1972 in England
book   ''This film script outlines the facts of Malcolm's life. The first part, using flashbacks, describes his early life. Part two, beginning with his conversion to Islam traces his career and closes with his assassination in 1956.'' Book Rev Digest
          ''An extremely moving reading experience recommended for mature young adults, whether they have read the original or not.'' Booklist } Direct quotations from book reviews, with sources

Author ← **Simon, Neil**
The comedy of Neil Simon; with an introduction by Neil Simon. Random House 1971 657p $12.95   812 } Bibliographical information

International ← ISBN 0-391-47364-7
identification
number
          ''A bright wit warmed with honest compassion and a clear understanding of the foibles of men and women characterize Simon's plays brought together here. . . . Simon adds a humorous biographical introduction titled Portrait of the writer as a schizophrenic.'' Booklist } Direct quotation from book review, with source.

SCHOLASTIC LITERATURE UNITS

Eleven Scholastic Literature Units, for Grades 6 to 10, were an excellent example of the concept technique. Unfortunately, they are no longer in print. However, the ideas in them are still very useful. Indeed, literature units are coming back into vogue. For example, the state of California has adopted a reading framework based on literature. Therefore, teachers may want to use the ideas from the Scholastic Literature Units to construct their own literature units. All the units are listed in Table 11.1.

Each unit is divided into three phases: (a) an anthology for classwide reading, (b) books for group reading, and (c) books for individual reading. Each student receives a Student Log containing directions for required and optional activities for independent work. A Teacher's Notebook consists of lesson plans for teaching and writing, reproductions of the Student Log activities, procedures for managing the program, guides and quizzes for each book, and a final test. Also, posters depicting the theme accompany the unit.

TABLE 11.1. Scholastic Literature Units Series 5100: Themes in Literature

Grade Range	Unit Title	Literary Focus
6-7-8	*Animals*	Short story
	Adventure and Suspense	
	Small World	
	Family	Family biography
7-8-9	*Courage*	Novel
	Decisions	Biography, Vocational literature
	Frontiers	Novel, Personal narrative
8-9-10	*Mirrors*	Drama
	Survival	Novel of adventure, Personal narrative
	Personal Values	Autobiography
9-10	*Tomorrow: Science Fiction and the Future*	

Source: Dwight L. Burton, Stephen Dunning, and Terrence D. Mosher, *Scholastic Literature Units: Courage.* Copyright © 1972 by Scholastic Magazines, Inc. Reprinted by permission of Scholastic Book Services, a division of Scholastic Magazines, Inc.

TABLE 11.2. Phase II Books

Least Difficult	Average Readers	Sophisticated Students
A Man Called Horse, Dorothy Johnson *The Contender,* Robert Lipsyte	*The Endless Steppe,* Esther Hautzig *No Easy Answers,* C. G. Hart	*Fahrenheit 451,* Ray Bradbury *The Old Man and the Sea,* Ernest Hemingway

Source: Dwight L. Burton, Stephen Dunning, and Terrence D. Mosher, *Scholastic Literature Units: Courage.* Copyright © 1972 by Scholastic Magazines, Inc. Reprinted by permission of Scholastic Book Services, a division of Scholastic Magazines, Inc.

A Teacher's Guide accompanies each story in the unit. An example of the guide for *The Red Badge of Courage* is shown in Box 11.4. The guide consists of a synopsis, a critical discussion, incidents illustrative of the central concept, and a list of difficult vocabulary in the story. At the end of the guide is a Check Quiz.

Designed to cover 6 weeks of instruction, the unit is divided into three 2-week phases. Because the units are identical in organization, we explain the three phases in more detail for only one of them, Burton, Dunning, and Mosher's unit, *Courage:*

Phase I: Class Reading, Discussion, and Written Work.   Students read the anthology *Courage*. Lesson plans contain procedures for discussing articles in the anthology.

Phase II: Group Reading, Discussion, and Oral Presentation.   After reading and reporting as a class, students group themselves through self-selection of Phase II books (Table 11.2). Students who select the same book form a group. Each

TABLE 11.3. Phase III Books

The Red Badge of Courage, Stephen Crane
My Enemy, My Brother, James Forman
Love of Life, Jack London
Split Bamboo, Leon Phillips
The Soul Brothers and Sister Lou, Kristin Hunter
Patton, Ira Peck
Profiles in Courage, John F. Kennedy
Megan, Iris Noble

Source: Dwight L. Burton, Stephen Dunning, and Terrence D. Mosher, *Scholastic Literature Units: Courage.* Copyright © 1972 by Scholastic Magazines, Inc. Reprinted by permission of Scholastic Book Services, a division of Scholastic Magazines, Inc.

group reads its Phase II book, uses Group Discussion and Program Suggestion Sheets for guidance in sharing ideas, and completes activities in the Student Log. Finally, each group prepares and presents group programs.

Phase III: Individual Reading and Reporting. Eight titles related to the theme of the unit *Courage* are used in this phase. The books range in difficulty and conceptual sophistication from Stephen Crane's *Red Badge of Courage* to easier books such as Leon Phillips's *Split Bamboo*. The titles for this phase are shown in Table 11.3.

BOX 11.4. Teacher's Guide

THE RED BADGE OF COURAGE

by Stephen Crane

Synopsis: Farm boy Henry Fleming enlists in the Union Army to take part in the Civil War. After weeks of monotonous drilling and fatiguing marching — a far cry from the excitement he had expected — Fleming comes finally to the scene of battle. The vast confusion of commanding, shooting, and shouting horrifies him, and when the enemy charges his regiment, Henry drops his rifle and runs. He wanders about the rear area in a lonely nightmare of confusion and conscience, and finally returns to his regiment at night. Ironically, he is welcomed as a semihero, for his companions mistake the wound on his head, which he received from the gun butt of a fleeing Union soldier, for a graze by a Confederate bullet. His problem now is to live up to his "red badge of courage," which he does in a succession of battles and brief respites. In the purposeless horror of war, "he had been to touch the great death and found that, after all, it was but the great death. He was a man. . . . He had rid himself of the red sickness of battle. The sultry nightmare was in the past. . . . He turned now with a lover's thirst to images of tranquil skies, fresh meadows, cool brooks — an existence of soft and eternal peace."

Point at Which Conflict or Problem Appears in Story: Henry enlists in the Union Army, p. 5.

Critique: This short novel has been hailed as one of the masterpieces of American fiction, and it furnishes an appropriate challenge to the superior reader. Its greatness lies in its power of style and its insight into the psychology of men in battle. Crane's mastery of words and description makes this a compelling story in which the reader moves through the nightmarish confusion of battle with a young Everyman, referred to in the novel as "the youth." It does not matter that this war is the Civil War. This is a universal situation of men in battle and of callow youth's inevitable rendezvous with evil, a painful initiation that is nevertheless essential to growth and maturity. This is a tribute to the courage demanded by circumstance; that is, the courage through which men who are suddenly faced with nightmarish conditions of violence and horror somehow find it possible to remain rational and perform their duties. It is through this courage of circumstance that Henry earns his red badge.

Courage Focus: A badly wounded soldier is bearing up unbelievably, making conversation with Henry, and praising the courage and fighting ability of his comrades (pp. 60–61); Henry's badly wounded friend finds the strength to go on his own; he seems ashamed to accept help even at this time (p. 64); in the midst of battle, Henry and another soldier rescue the colors from the hands of the dying Color Sergeant (pp. 125–126).

About the Author: Stephen Crane was born in 1871, the son of a New Jersey minister. He attended Claverack College, Lafayette College, and Syracuse University, although he graduated from none of them. For four years after he left school, he struggled to support himself, occasionally reporting for New York and New Jersey newspapers. In the last years of his life, he traveled as a correspondent to Mexico, Greece, and Cuba. He didn't see actual combat until his visit to Greece in 1897 — although *The Red Badge of Courage* was published three years before. Stephen Crane died in 1900. (See also pages iii–vi of *The Red Badge of Courage*.)

Vocabulary

word	page	word	page
purled	1	annihilated	44
twoscore	2	pommeling	47
oblique	3	resplendent	53
prowess	4	redoubtable	54
effaced	4	abject	54
impregnable	5	maniacal	57
clangoring	5	trepidation	62
adieu	7	doggerel	68
vivacious	8	spectral	72
martial	8	reiterated	73
secular	8	ague	77
dexterously	11	philippic	78
altercation	13	contortion	78
unscrupulous	16	sinuous	84
ominous	18	malediction	85
orbs	18	altercation	95
vindication	20	gamin	90
felicitating	20	audacity	110
blithe	20	lugubrious	114
pilfer	20	fracas	119
satanic	21	temerity	125
pontoon	26	accouterments	139
extricate	26	stoic	141
ponderous	27	gyrated	144
aggregations	27	epithets	149
perambulating	27	tableau	153
harangue	31	portals	155
demeanor	32	perturbation	155
reconnoitering	34	portentous	165

viands	34	expletives	165
crescendo	35	paroxysm	168
prophetic	36	catapultian	170
facetious	39	ghouls	172

Check Quiz

1. _____ Before he enlisted in the army, Henry lived (a) in the South; (b) on a farm; (c) in a large city; (d) in the Far West.

2. _____ Before his first battle, Henry was most worried that he would (a) be killed; (b) be wounded; (c) run from battle; (d) not be able to fire his gun.

3. _____ During his flight through the forest after the second battle, Henry came upon (a) a wounded enemy soldier; (b) a young girl; (c) a dead soldier; (d) a dying horse.

4. _____ Henry fled from the tattered soldier (a) because he wanted to know where Henry had been wounded; (b) because he threatened to report Henry as a deserter; (c) because he was a Confederate; (d) for no reason at all.

5. _____ The title *The Red Badge of Courage* refers to (a) a flag; (b) a medal; (c) an armband; (d) a wound.

6. _____ Henry was wounded by (a) an enemy bullet; (b) a blow from a retreating Union soldier's rifle; (c) his best friend Wilson; (d) a bad fall.

7. _____ Henry overheard an officer say his regiment, the 304th, fought like (a) lions; (b) heroes; (c) children; (d) mule drivers.

8. _____ Henry and his friend first earned the respect of their fellow soldiers and their commanders by (a) rescuing the Union flag when its bearer was shot; (b) holding the enemy off singlehanded; (c) discovering the enemy's hiding place; (d) taking a very important message to the President.

9. _____ During the final battle, Henry and his friend captured (a) the enemy's flag; (b) an enemy soldier; (c) an enemy tank; (d) enemy ammunition.

10. _____ At the end of the story, Henry Fleming felt that he was (a) a farmer; (b) a man; (c) a true Confederate; (d) still a boy.

From *Scholastic Literature Units: Courage* by Dwight L. Burton, Stephen Dunning, and Terrence D. Mosher. Copyright © 1972 by Scholastic Magazines, Inc. Reprinted by permission of Scholastic Book Services, a division of Scholastic Magazines, Inc.

In Phase III, as in Phase II, students select their own books. Since all books are related to the theme of the unit, all students can enter into a discussion, contributing examples and critical incidents on the concept of courage from their own books. As a consequence, students develop a rich and differentiated conception of courage. Thus, the thematic or concept technique provides a way of solving the problem of individual differences in reading ability without stigmatizing students.

FIGURE 11.1. Strategy for Teaching a Class with Varying Reading Levels

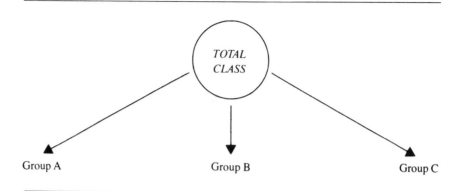

PREPARING YOUR OWN UNIT

An advantage of the Scholastic Units for teaching is their completeness. They come with lesson plans, tests, titles organized around a theme, a management system, and paperbacks of each title for the entire class. However, teachers can prepare their own units, provided they have a library with materials already on hand or a fund for purchasing paperbacks, and, of course, the necessary time.

Using the *Children's Catalog* (Shor and Fidel, 1972), *Junior High School Catalog* (Fidel & Bogart, 1970), the *Senior High School Library Catalog* (Fidel and Berger, 1972), examples of which are shown in Box 11.3, and the *Reader's Guide to Periodical Literature,* a group of teachers participating in a master's degree program constructed units and reading guides to accompany them.[2] Students selected a concept, such as the American Dream, conflict, courage greatness, human evolution, pollution, power. Essays, short stories, incidents from novels, and newspaper articles of different levels of reading difficulty were selected, all related to the same concept. The chosen materials were then reproduced and stapled in booklet form. The class read some materials together and then subgroups were formed, based on self-selections of materials students chose to read. Each subgroup read and discussed the selection and completed the reading guide accompanying the selection. Class discussions were conducted in which all members participated by adding information to the discussion gleaned from materials they had selected. All individual differences in reading were accommodated by this self-selection strategy, and no group could dominate the discussion because each group read materials on the same concept at a suitable reading level. A schematic design of this organization is shown in Figure 11.1.

---

[2]Teachers enrolled in a master's degree program at the University of California, Riverside, constructed these units under the direction of Dr. Robin McKeown. The teachers were Sylvia Andreatta, Anthony Bechtold, Jane Davenport, Chris Gutierrez, Vaughn Hudson, David Kahl, Dale Johnson, Jean Fruehan, Patsy Miller, Margaret Minor, Bonnie Parmenter, and Richard Zimmerman, and the supervisor was Elizabeth Arnold.

Note that the entire class reads some materials as a class. Then the class is subdivided into discussion groups A, B, C according to materials selected. Each group contributes ideas gleaned from the material read in a general class discussion on the same concept. A condensation of the unit on the American Dream is presented in Box 11.5.

BOX 11.5. Teacher-constructed Unit on Multi-ethnic Literature

THE AMERICAN DREAM — A DREAM DEFERRED?

by Anthony Bechtold and Dale Johnson

Focus: Racial and ethnic intolerance in contemporary America

Central Questions: Why is there racial and ethnic intolerance? How is it expressed? What are the apparent reasons for it? What are unique aspects of intolerance experienced by some group? What is integration? Separation? Pluralism?

Level: Junior and Senior High; reading range: grades 4–8.

Objectives of the American Dream: Liberty and justice for all. More specifically: What is most important is the drawing out of students' personal responses to the readings. The unit assumes that fear, ignorance, or threat to one's established security leads to inequality of liberty and justice. It assumes further that (1) the expression of one's own fears, (2) the confrontation of one's own ignorance, and (3) the discussion of the threat to one's own security will lead to a recognition of the essential humanity of others, regardless of racial or ethnic background. Although it is hoped that the unit will increase student sensitivity to the consequences of intolerance, the unit cannot guarantee that students will become more tolerant as a matter of fact. It must be recognized that increased polarization of student emotion may be the result.

Procedure
1. Unit is taught in ten 50 minute class periods.
2. Period 1. Orientation: taped recording of Langston Hughes's "One Friday Morning." Discussion topic: Why racial intolerance? Explain unit: self-selection of readings grouped within a topic, followed by discussion within groups, and then between groups in class discussion on how tolerance is expressed in each selection and its probable causes.
3. Period 2. Focus on definition of issue and terms. Students get reading lists, make selections from the lists, form into groups to complete guide.
4. Periods 3–6. Complete reading guides based on students' reading selections and then discuss each section of the guides.
5. Period 7. Present hypotheses on causes of intolerance.
6. Periods 8–9. Test hypotheses again, new selections.
7. Period 10. Complete unit by selecting a way of expressing conclusions: writing, art, music, and so forth.

Annotated Topic for the Unit

Reading #5. "After You, My Dear Alphonse" by Shirley Jackson. In *Small World,* edited by R. Smith, J. Sprague, and J. Dunning. (New York: Scholastic Book Services, 1964), pp. 136–141. Short story, 4½ pages, Dale-Chall score 4.5.

This story was chosen because it reveals, in a very subtle manner, some of the stereotyped ideas about Blacks that are still widely accepted in American society. It is the story of Mrs. Wilson's patronizing attitude toward a Black friend of her son, and her injured sensibilities as she slowly learns the reality of his average, middle-class background. As the boys are in their early teens, many of her prejudicial comments are lost on them because of their innocence. Although the story is very easy to read in the decoding sense, these subtleties may have to be drawn out in the discussion. One question which might prove fruitful in this respect is: "How are prejudices passed on from one generation to another?"

Direction to Teacher: This is the reading guide for the selection. Students are to complete the guide by finding the page and the paragraph on which the True-False statements occur. They are to discuss Section B. The passages on which Section B is based are shown on the key. Section C goes beyond the selection to generalizations which students can discuss and articulate their own beliefs.

Anthony Bechtold and Dale Johnson earned their M.A. degrees in Education at the University of California, Riverside. Mr. Bechtold is a reading consultant in Poway, California, Unified School District and Mr. Johnson is a high school teacher in the Oceanside, California, Unified School District. This unit is reprinted with their permission.

In case you want to teach this unit on multi-ethnic literature, the selections are listed in Box 11.6. They should be available in almost any large library. Read and annotate them and prepare your own reading and learning-from-text guides.

After they have used a few guides you have prepared, some students in your class may become so sophisticated with guides that they can construct their own and thus help you prepare guides for the entire unit. (See the sections on reading and learning-from-text guides in chapter 4, and the boxes in chapter 5.)

Remember that students are to be given a choice of titles within a group of selections, regardless of the reading level of the student or the selection. Students who choose the same selection read the selection and meet to complete the guide based on the selection. The size of the group may be limited by the number of copies available. Indeed, the size of the group should be limited so that all students in a group can have an opportunity to participate in discussion.

BOX 11.6. Readings for the Unit
"The American Dream—A Dream Deferred"

ASIAN-AMERICAN

"An American-Born Japanese in America" in *Orientals and Their Cultural Adjustment,* Social Science Source Documents #4 (Nashville, TN: Social Science

Institute, 1964), pp. 95–100. Autobiographical account, 5 pages, Dale-Chall score 8.4.

"A High School Japanese Student's Opinion on the Race Problem" in *Orientals and Their Cultural Adjustment,* Social Science Source Documents #4 (Nasville, Tennessee: Social Science Institute, 1964), pp. 105–106. Autobiographical account, 2 pages, Dale-Chall score 8.3.

"Born in Los Angeles—Reared in Oriental Fashion" in *Orientals and Their Cultural Adjustment,* Social Science Source Documents #4 (Nashville, Tennessee: Social Science Institute, 1946), pp. 24–26. Autobiographical account, 2 ½ pages, Dale–Chall score 8.3.

BLACK AMERICAN

"One Friday Morning" by Langston Hughes in *American Negro Short Stories,* John Henrik Clarke, ed. (New York: Hill & Wang, 1968), pp. 114–123. Short story, 9 pages, Dale-Chall score 8.0.

From *Native Son* by Richard Wright (New York: Harper & Row, 1968), pp. 18–25. Conversation from a novel, 7 pages, Dale-Chall score 7.6.

"The Revolt of the Evil Fairies" by Ted Posten in *The Best Short Stories by Negro Writers,* Langston Hughes, ed. (Boston: Little, Brown, 1967), pp. 86–90. Short story, 4 pages, Dale-Chall score 7.5.

From *Soul on Ice* by Eldridge Cleaver (New York: Dell, 1968), pp. 173–175. Conservation from chapter, 2 pages, Dale-Chall score 5.8.

"After You, My Dear Alphonse" by Shirley Jackson in *Small World,* Smith, Sprague, and Dunning, eds. (New York: Scholastic, 1969), pp. 136–141. Short story, 4 ½ pages, Dale-Chall score 4.5.

MEXICAN-AMERICAN

"Ramon Lopez—Between Two Worlds" by Ramon Lopez in *Scholastic Scope,* 10:10 (April 11, 1969), pp. 4–9. Autobiography, 2 ½ pages, Dale-Chall Score 4.9.

"Court Vindicates Farm Workers' Dead Hero," by Gene Blake, Los Angeles Times Morning Edition (February 3, 1970), pp. 1,22. Newspaper report, 1 page, Dale-Chall score 8.7.

From "Enemy Territory" by William M. Kelly in *Sight Lines,* Charlotte Brooks, general editor (New York: Holt, Rinehart & Winston, 1969), pp. 197–202. Narrative, 5 pages, Dale-Chall score 6.0.

From "The Land of Room Enough" by E. P. Maxwell in *Search for America,* Charlotte Brooks, general editor (New York: Holt, Rinehart & Winston, 1969), pp. 169–171. Incident from a short story, 3 pages, Dale-Chall score 6.0.

NATIVE AMERICAN

"To Catch a Never Dream" by Bruce King in *Scholastic Scope,* 11:2 (September 22, 1969), pp. 10–13, 25, 28, 30. Play, 5 pages, Dale-Chall score 4.5.

"The Returning" by Daniel de Paola in *Conflict,* Charlotte Brooks, general editor (New York: Holt, Rinehart & Winston, 1969), pp. 72–85. Short story, 12 pages, Dale-Chall score 6.4.

"Fire" by Lawrence E. Stoltz in *Small World,* Smith, Sprague & Dunning, eds. (New York: Scholastic, 1964), pp. 17–21. Short story, 4 ½ pages, Dale-Chall score 8.5.

WHITE

"Tracke" in *Manhattan Transfer* by John Dos Passos (Boston: Houghton Mifflin 1953), pp. 101–103. Incident from section of a novel, 3 pages, Dale-Chall score 5.5

"Yes, Your Honesty" by George and Helen Papashvily in *Small World,* Smith, Sprague, & Dunning, eds. (New York: Scholastic, 1969), pp. 39–47. Autobiographical account, 8 pages, Dale- Chall score 5.4.

"Strong Contrast Between Elsinore Today and City of Hate" by Will Thorne, Riverside *Press-Enterprise* (February 15, 1970), Section B, p. 5. Newspaper article, 3 pages, Dale-Chall score 11.5

From "Prelude" by Albert Halper in *Search of America,* Charlotte Brooks, general editor (New York: Holt, Rinehart, & Winston, 1969), pp. 120, 121, 130–133. Short story, 5 pages, Dale-Chall score 4.4.

"Konnichi Wa" by Barbara L. Reynolds in *Small World,* Smith, Sprague, and Dunning, eds. (New York: Scholastic, 1969), pp. 10–16. An incident from a short story, 2 pages, Dale-Chall score 6.7.

"A Man Called Horse" by Dorothy M. Johnson in *Sight Lines,* Charlotte Brooks, general editor (New York: Holt, Rinehart & Winston, 1969), pp. 161–182. Biographical account, 17 ½ pages, Dale-Chall score 8.0.

CONCLUDING READINGS

"A Word of Warning" by Tom Galt in *Small World,* Smith, Sprague, & Dunning, eds. (New York: Scholastic, 1969), pp. 1–2. Short story, 2 pages, Dale-Chall score 5.6.

"Which Way Toward 'Liberty and Justice for ALL'?" in *Scholastic Scope,* 10:8 (March 21, 1969), pp. 6–14. Essay, 9 pages, Dale-Chall score 7.7.

Project Method—Independent Formulation of Questions

The *project approach* is the most complex of the strategies because it gives students a greater range of choices in questions, places the most responsibility upon students, and gives them the greatest independence in reading and learning from text. Unlike the inquiry strategy that focuses on a narrow range of questions or the concept strategy that is organized about a single idea, the project approach covers an entire unit of study, such as the Westward Movement, and allows students to formulate and investigate any question on the unit that interests them. However, the inquiry strategy is like the project approach in that it allows students to select their own materials to answer their questions; also, as in both the inquiry and concept strategies, students using the project approach discuss issues in groups and report as a group of the entire class. But the reports are complementary and eventually form a complete unit as the information gathered by the various groups is combined. After the group process, students work on individual units and report to the class. Because the project approach utilizes all the features of the other strategies—including formulation of questions, selection of library materials for reference reading, participation in discussion groups, writing reports, and communicating results to the class—the project approach is the most complex and therefore the last of our strategies. All the rest of the strategies lead up to it. Yet, this approach has some steps that are unique.

The project approach starts not with a text but with (a) arousing student curiosity, (b) encouraging student formulation of questions, (c) grouping of students who have questions in common, (d) providing for student self-selection of books or reference reading to get information for answering their own questions, and (e) advising students on novel and creative ways of reporting answers to their questions.

STEPS IN THE PROJECT METHOD

1. Create an atmosphere for arousing student curiosity by using posters, newspaper clippings, dramatizations, movies, prominent speakers, or discussions of local events. Any one or a combination of these ways of introducing a topic could arouse students' curiosity; of course, the introduction has to be relevant to the subject. For example, a unit on United States history might begin with discussion of a local building or geographic site related to the particular era in the history unit.

2. Conduct discussions of curiosity-arousing episodes. (See chapter 6 on discussion strategies and techniques.) Perhaps you could impanel a board of inquiry. To end this step, have students formulate their own questions to pursue in studying the unit. In a curiosity-arousing environment, students are likely to formulate their own questions eagerly, unless they have little rapport with the teacher or are completely jaded by previous negative experience in school. The teacher may simply ask students what they would like to know about the topic in such an environment. Try to obtain at least one question about the topic from each student. Use your imagination for eliciting questions. A ninth-grade English teacher injected competition into question-formulation by pitting one side of the room against the other side. Students wrote questions formulated by their side on the board. Each side tried to list more questions than the other side.

3. Group students. First lead students to group questions in categories. Simply ask students to group together the questions that have something in common. In a history unit, all the questions on government would form one category, military events another, economics a third, and so on. Then students whose questions are in the same category should form a group to search out answers to their questions. Since all members of the group have responsibility for answering all questions in the category, members of the group can help each other. Consequently, cross-ability tutoring is likely to occur and an atmosphere of cooperation is fostered within the group.

4. To answer their questions, the group must have access to books containing information to answer the questions asked by the group. For each question or topic, the books should also vary in reading difficulty so that all students can locate materials on their own level. Some students may choose books at a

relatively easy level, whereas other students may select books above their reading levels. The criterion is to get a book that will help to answer a question or question. The teacher may aid students in selecting books, but should refrain from assigning them so that no stigma is likely to be attached to students for using easy books.

5. Allow time for students to engage in reading references. The key to success in reference reading is (a) to formulate and keep a question or questions in mind, (b) to judge whether the reading material is relevant while searching for information, and (c) to select only the relevant material. Relevancy is, of course, a matter of degree. (See further discussion on library or reference reading.)

6. Encourage all members of a group to discuss answers to their questions. This verbalization will enable students to perform well in the next step, writing answers to their questions.

7. Use procedures similar to those suggested in chapter 8 for teaching students to write answers to their questions.

8. Act as a consultant to the groups; encourage members of a group to cooperate; get them to agree on a chairperson and a recorder; help the group locate materials; make sure the group tests whether questions are being maintained and relevancy judgments are made; and help the group decide on an interesting way to report findings to the class.

9. Suggest methods for reporting. Findings can be reported in writing, or in novel, more creative ways. For example, groups can give dramatized reports, weaving information into the drama or they can turn out a newspaper, reporting answers to questions as though they were current events.

10. Leave time for evaluation. The class can evaluate each report to determine whether the questions have been answered. Then the class can relate answers to each other and perhaps formulate higher order generalizations. (See chapter 7 for discussion procedures and for techniques to elicit generalizations from a group discussion.)

Example of the Project Method

After Hedy Davis's fifth graders had studied the American Revolution, she thought the children would enjoy doing some related projects. After reviewing the textbook material that the children had just read, she presented them with a duplicated list of projects:

PROJECTS ON THE AMERICAN REVOLUTION

1. Pretend you are a motion picture director planning to film a scene about the Boston Tea Party. Before the producer okays the scene, she wants to know what it will cost. Prepare a budget for the producer listing the total costs you expect to have while filming the scene.

2. Prepare a puppet show that portrays General George Washington's surprise attack on the Hessians.
3. Design the first American flag as you think it might look had two more colonies joined the original 13. Which two colonies do you think those might be?
4. Present a skit that takes place in England. King George III's advisors are giving their opinions of what should be done about the American colonists.
5. Decorate a wall with graffiti that might have been painted by gangs of colonial rebels to show their dislike of the British.

Next, Ms. Davis passed around a sign-up sheet and her students divided themselves into project work groups. First, they made group lists of questions they would have to find answers for, either in their textbooks or in the library. While they were preparing the lists, Ms. Davis circulated throughout the room, offering help and suggestions. After checking their questions, Ms. Davis had each group prepare a "to do" or task list, dividing responsibility equally among group members. In the next 3 weeks, Ms. Davis's students spent an hour working on the projects, either in the classroom or in the library. At the conclusion of the 3 weeks, the groups, one by one, presented their projects to the rest of the class.

REPORTING BACK ACTIVITIES

Because multiple-textbook strategies involve the use of small groups of students (Donlan, 1976), you should teach your students techniques of reporting information back to the entire class. However, junior and senior high school students might know how to give individual oral reports to the class. These reports may take the form of informal talks, book reviews, or some other kind of *individual* student oral account. Reports of this kind are common. What is not common is having *groups* of students report. We present four types of group reporting that you can teach to your students.

The Symposium: A Staged Series of Reports

A *symposium* involves a group of two or more students reporting together, each on separate aspects of a problem or topic. Often mislabeled a *panel discussion,* a symposium has limited, or no, interaction among the participating members (Donlan, 1974). For this reason, the symposium is the easiest group-reporting technique for students to learn. It is usually staged before the class and, for the most part, operates free of questions from the teacher. Generally, the symposium chairperson introduces each speaker separately and makes transition statements between speakers. A symposium on famous mathematicians and their contributions would have each group member either (a) reporting on a different mathematician, or (b) reporting on a different concept and incidentally discussing how various mathematicians contributed to the concept. Following the symposium, the students or the teacher may decide to have a *forum,* or question period, during which members of the class ask questions of the participating members of the symposium. The following paragraph describes how a symposium can develop.

Assume that you are teaching a unit on the Revolutionary War. You notice that several students have shown more than average interest in the topic, as evidenced by their willingness to participate in class discussions, and that the same students appear to read the text material with little difficulty. You might encourage these students to form a group that would present a symposium on "Heroes of the American Revolution: The Human Interest Angle" or some other topic that either you or the group select. You could free these students time for library research and planning sessions. In the presentation (an enrichment experience for the rest of the class) the chairperson of the symposium has a dominant role from start to finish. The chairperson introduces the topic and presents an overview of what each participant will be talking about. Then the chairperson introduces each speaker. Their topics might be, (a) George Washington's medical problems; (b) the strange disappearance of Thomas Paine's remains, and (c) the many talents of Thomas Jefferson. After each speaker, the chairperson makes a transition statement to the next speaker. At the end, the chairperson summarizes and concludes, then solicits questions from the audience and directs them to the appropriate speakers.

Panel Discussion

Very similar to the symposium is the *panel discussion.* It consists of a group of three or more students staging a problem-solving situation before the class. The group members, working from a common outline of main points, interact with one another under the guidance of a strong chairperson who regulates the discussion so that each member participates. All members of a panel, unlike members of a *symposium,* are equally conversant with all aspects of the problem.

Teaching students to stage discussions may be difficult. One successful teacher would randomly select five or six students to sit at the front of the room and "talk about" a highly charged emotional issue: *Should students be allowed to smoke on compus? Should juvenile crime be punished more severely than it is now? Should the minimum driving and drinking age be the same?* After several sessions, the students realized they could stage lively discussions that were as engrossing as informal out-of-school discussions.

With the principal obstacle to staged discussion eliminated—stage-fright—students could be taught more controlled staged discussion. Such discussion demands that students (a) realize the various roles discussants can assume (chapter 6); (b) work together in cooperative problem solving; (c) explore the ramifications of a problem; and (d) pose alternative solutions.

Consider the topic *Should juvenile crime be punished more severely than it is now?* The group might decide to rephrase the topic as a problem: *How should juvenile crime be punished in a fair and equitable manner?* Next, the group might prepare a discussion outline like the one that is given below.

    I. Problem: How should juvenile crime be punished in a fair and equitable manner?

    II. Background

        A. Statistics on recent juvenile crime

        B. Notorious news stories involving juvenile crime

        C. Published pleas for reform in juvenile justice

    III. Should juvenile justice be reviewed and revised?

        A. Arguments in favor

        B. Arguments opposed

    IV. What specific changes in juvenile justice should be made?

        A. Proposed change #1

        B. Proposed change #2

        C. Proposed change #3

    V. If changes are made, what might be the effects of these changes?

    VI. Conclusion

After planning the outline, the members of the group would do outside reading on one or more of the subtopics and meet frequently to pool notes. The staged discussion would, then, involve all of the members talking about their combined information under the direction of a chairperson who moderates.

Debate: A Staged Argument

A more difficult form of group report is the *debate*. Debate involves the presentation of two opposing views. Rules for formal debating require affirmative and negative deliveries followed by rebuttal and cross-examination. Informal debates may be carried on in a variety of ways. Unlike a panel discussion, there is no attempt in a debate at compromise or problem solving. Speakers hold firmly to their positions, and the class may vote on which side made the most convincing presentation. Cross-examination may take the form of a forum, or questions from the students.

The first prerequisite for a successful debate is an issue (preferably controversial) to whet the divided opinions of the students: *single* versus *multiple interpretations of a poem; biblical* versus *scientific theories of the origin of humanity; new mathematics* versus *old mathematics; states' rights* versus *federal control;* and so forth.

After the issue is established, you should present it in the form of a question:

1. Does a poem have only one meaning?
2. Is the biblical interpretation of the origin of humanity the most valid?
3. Is the new mathematics superior to the old mathematics?
4. Do states' rights have precedence over federal control?

Unless you present the issue in question form, it will not be clear what the affirmative and negative sides will be.

Next, select students (preferably verbal, resourceful students) to debate the two sides. Some teachers ask students to debate the side they agree with; other teachers feel emotional involvement with an issue precludes effective argumentation. At any rate, debaters should be able to present their points of view articulately. Articulateness can occur only if the students (a) organize their points in an outline and (b) document their statements with authoritative sources—newspapers, magazines, books, editorial writers, news commentators. Unless students are well organized and prepared, debate is rather pointless. Consequently, debate is not for all students.

After the student debaters have been given time to prepare their points of view, speaking order and time allotments should be determined. Debate teams usually consist of two speakers per side, but one or three per team can be used. More than three on a side produces repetition and decreases sharpness of presentation. Normally, the affirmative speaker is first. Here are some possible speaking orders:

A. Initial Argument
    1. Affirmative Speaker 1
    2. Negative Speaker 1
    3. Affirmative Speaker 2
    4. Negative Speaker 2
B. Rebuttal
    1. Negative Speaker 2
    2. Affirmative Speaker 2
    3. Negative Speaker 1
    4. Affirmative Speaker 1
C. Cross-examination
    1. Affirmative Speaker 1
    2. Cross-Examination from Negative Speakers
    3. Negative Speaker 1
    4. Cross-Examination from Affirmative Speakers
    5. Affirmative Speaker 2
    6. Cross-Examination from Negative Speakers
    7. Negative Speaker
    8. Cross-Examination from Affirmative Speakers

After the speaking order has been determined, it is vital to set time limits, for the entire debate as well as for each speaker. Consider, first, the length of the class period; do not hold the debate on a day when a school assembly shortens the class period. In some formal debates, speakers are allowed 8 minutes each for an initial argument and 4 minutes each for a rebuttal or cross-examination—a 48-minute presentation. A teacher may wish to scale down the time allotments—with equity. Members of the class (the audience) should refrain from participating with questions or comments until the debate is concluded.

The audience may vote on which team gave a better presentation, but the voting should be based on debating skill, not on the merits of one or the other side of the issue.

Colloquy: A Panel of Experts

Colloquy occurs when a "panel of experts" is available for further information, clarification, or settlement of dilemmas. For instance, if a group of high school students is presenting a symposium or debate, perhaps even a panel discussion, on the works of John Steinbeck, the colloquy might include English professors from neighboring colleges. Ideally, the colloquy makes no formal presentation but merely serves to advise.

Summary of Reporting Back Activities

As you use multiple-text strategies with your students, you will need to show them how to report back. Some techniques of reporting back are more difficult than others, so you should teach the techniques sequentially. Begin with the *symposium*. Although it is *staged,* members of a symposium do not have to interact, merely report. After the students have gained experience reporting in a staged situation, introduce the *panel discussion*. Students will feel easier if you suggest that a panel discussion is like a staged discussion cluster. Because of the argumentative nature of *debate,* students will participate in debate more readily if they've had experience participating in symposiums and panel discussions where weighing of evidence and problem solving are practiced. Last, and most difficult, is the *colloquy*. Students have to make arrangements for bringing outside experts to the classroom. They have to make sure that these experts function only in a consultant capacity. In other words, students must integrate the contributions of experts into their own well-organized and staged symposium, panel discussion, or debate.[3]

SUMMARY

In this chapter you have learned three ways to teach through multiple-text strategies. With *inquiry,* the students investigate assertions made in their textbooks by doing additional reading. When *concept technique* is used, students selected books on varying levels of difficulty but related to the same *concept,* such as "survival" or "courage." The *project approach* focuses on students formulating their own questions and engaging in reference reading to answer these questions. In addition to multiple-text strategies, you have studied four ways in which

---

[3]Other reporting activities are role playing, improvisational dramatics, new broadcasts, murals or collages, class newspapers or magazines, and slide-tape presentations.

groups of students can report back to the class on what they have learned: the symposium, the panel discussion, the debate, and the colloquy. Having learned about single- and multiple-text strategies, you will discover in chapter 12 how to put these strategies into an instructional blueprint.

ACTIVITY

Drawing upon a topic from your own content area, develop a multiple-text strategy, using either inquiry or the concept technique.

12 | An Instructional Blueprint

CHAPTER OVERVIEW

Many well-seasoned, experienced teachers are able to plan learning experiences for their students that extend from September to June. So far this text has provided you with numerous strategies for teaching students how to read and learn from content area textbooks. Now, you may ask, how does it all fit together? Chapter 12 presents you with a blueprint for combining these strategies in an instructional framework. While you are reading this chapter, keep this question in mind: Should a teacher instruct a class the same way in June as in September?

GRAPHIC ORGANIZER

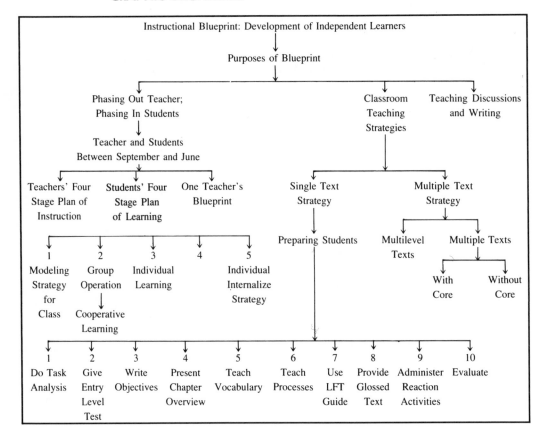

Instructional Blueprint: Development of Independent Learners

Purposes of Blueprint

Phasing Out Teacher; Phasing In Students

Classroom Teaching Strategies

Teaching Discussions and Writing

Teacher and Students Between September and June

Teachers' Four Stage Plan of Instruction

Students' Four Stage Plan of Learning

One Teacher's Blueprint

Single Text Strategy

Multiple Text Strategy

Preparing Students

Multilevel Texts

Multiple Texts

With Core

Without Core

1 — Modeling Strategy for Class

2 — Group Operation — Cooperative Learning

3 — Individual Learning

4

5 — Individual Internalize Strategy

1 — Do Task Analysis

2 — Give Entry Level Test

3 — Write Objectives

4 — Present Chapter Overview

5 — Teach Vocabulary

6 — Teach Processes

7 — Use LFT Guide

8 — Provide Glossed Text

9 — Administer Reaction Activities

10 — Evaluate

PREPOSED QUESTIONS

1. Why is it important that a teacher's instructional procedures evolve as the school year progresses?
2. What is the best sequence for employing single-text strategies?
3. At what point in the school year should multiple-text strategies be introduced?
4. What role does cooperative learning play in an instructional blueprint for reading and learning from text?
5. How do you know when a student has become an independent learner in your classroom?

SUCCESSFUL TEACHERS DEVELOP
INDEPENDENT LEARNERS

Successful teachers tend to build a repertoire of classroom activities that work. This repertoire is the result of continual experimentation and revision. Occasionally, teachers discover that sound educational theory and research support what they've been doing instinctively in the classroom. Both authors of this book have had considerable teaching experience. In both cases, their repertoire included the phase-in/phase-out technique as part of their teaching style long before they wrote this book. The primary assumptions of the phase-in/phase-out technique are (a) that the purpose of education is to produce independent learners, that is, they have learned how to learn, and (b) that teaching means showing students how to teach themselves. However, the class usually starts with activities done under close teacher-direction and may gradually lead to independent learning. One of the authors recalls, for instance, the trauma of facing 40 hostile seniors in an English class that was required for graduation. For self-preservation, he had to plan each class period tightly, with four or five activities, to provide the necessary structure for gaining control of a class. Subsequently, as his discipline problems began to dissolve, he needed fewer teacher-directed activities and found that the class could progress to student-centered activities—discussion clusters, panel discussions, trips to the library, projects, even improvisational dramatics. Without the structure at the start of the school year, students might never have been able to function in the more independent situations.

As you read this chapter, keep in mind that the instructional blueprint we advocate in this chapter isn't a pipe-dream; the philosophy of progressing from a teacher-centered to a student-centered classroom and from dependent to independent learners is in reality just good sense.

PURPOSES OF THE BLUEPRINT

So far in this book, you have learned that today's schools have evolved in the last century from selective institutions with a narrow curriculum to all-inclusive institutions with seemingly unlimited educational offerings. Concurrent with growth, increasing problems of students have complicated the teacher's job. For instance, in a given "average" 10th-grade class, a 10-year range of student achievement precludes much success if the teacher chooses to move all students from instructional level A to level Z at the same time with *identical* instruction. At the other extreme, *individual instruction* is unmanageable. With wide-ranging differences in reading achievement in a class, you must teach *some* students how to read and *all* of the students how to learn from text, specifically how to get meaning from interacting with the text and how to talk and write about what they have read. Our single- and multiple-text teaching strategies facilitate students' learning how to learn from text. Yet, the random and unsystematized use of these strategies will not be effective in teaching students how to learn. What is needed is a blueprint for instruction in which all the strategies are integrated.

An instructional blueprint ensures purposive teaching and learning. Such a blueprint has three dimensions: (a) teachers should plan instructional time in such a way that students progress from dependent to independent learning; (b) the teacher has to use a variety of teaching techniques to prepare the students for learning from text, to guide them while they are reading, to assess their responses to what they have read, and to decide upon the next teaching step; (c) the teacher should teach students discussion and writing strategies so that they can express their responses to text in varied and articulate ways. We have organized these three dimensions into an instructional blueprint.

DIMENSION ONE: PHASING OUT THE TEACHER AND PHASING IN THE STUDENTS

A psychological definition of *learning* would point out that learning involes initiation of behavior or change in a learner that is relatively permanent and that occurs as a result of reacting to a situation and obtaining knowledge of results (Hilgard & Bower, 1975). Teaching is one way to produce such an initiation of behavior or change in the learner. The change is from dependent to independent learners. The teacher's goal is to guide learners toward independence (Herber, 1970a). Parents ''teach'' their children to talk and walk with the hope that independent communication and movement will result. Swimming instructors teach children to survive in water on their own. Primary school teachers want their students to read books at home and to solve day-to-day arithmetic problems in their lives. In effect, good teachers phase themselves out by teaching their students how to perform alone. If students and teachers realize this objective, students will be more capable of directing their own learning at the end of a course than they were at the beginning of the course. However, if students are still dependent upon the teacher to provide ''the right answers'' at the end of the course, they will not have become independent learners. The teacher and the students will have failed to attain a basic objective of education.

Teachers, then, need to be teaching differently in May and June than they were teaching in September and October. Specifically, in September, the teacher will initiate and independently carry out similar activities. In September a teacher would direct class discussion of a text chapter by posing questions and problems; by June, the students should be directing discussion around question and problems they have posed for themselves. If this happens, the teacher will have trained students to become more independent learners (Rosenthal, Zimmerman, & Durning, 1970).

What the Teacher Does Between September and June

Many teachers who assign reading, discussion, and writing complain about the low level of student performance without realizing that it is the continued dependence of students on the teachers that contributes to this low-level performance. Such teachers continue to give assignments without instructing students in how to read and learn from text and how to express themselves through discussion or writing. A swimming instructor who taught this way would support students in deep water until the end of the course. Then, when the student went on to another course where the water was even deeper, the students would have to learn to swim alone or sink. Although some students learn to survive this kind of instruction, learning can occur more readily with the proper kind of teaching. Even though many students might prefer to take the path of least effort and remain dependent, the job of teachers is to have students overcome this inertia and become independent.

A teacher who wants to phase out by June plans a careful and gradual turnover of learning to the students who accept reasonability for their own learning. The teacher phase-out process can occur through use of a specific teaching plan.

TEACHER'S FOUR STAGE PLAN OF INSTRUCTION

A four-stage teaching plan will take students from dependence to independence as they learn how to use a particular strategy. It will phase in the students as the teacher phases out.

FIRST STAGE: Modeling Strategy

The teacher introduces a strategy to students and directs the entire class through all steps in the strategy. Suppose, for example, that a teacher initiates the use of a reading and learning-from text guide. (See an example of this type of guide in chapter 6.) Under teacher direction, students read the text and then as a group complete the guide, perhaps volunteering information on facts and main ideas, interpretations and inferences, and then discussing generalizations, central ideas, or evaluating the material (the section, chapter, or story) covered. This stage of the teaching plan may cover more than one class period, perhaps an entire week.

SECOND STAGE: Group Operation

The teacher, serving as leader of a group made up of the entire class, demonstrates how to operate as a group. All students learn the roles of members of the group and, at least some, learn through imitation to serve as leaders of a group. The teacher then divides the class into groups of about six students each, including a chairperson and a reporter. The task of every group might be, for example, to complete a reading and learning-from-text guide.

At this stage, the teacher has to establish ''ground rules'' for group chairpersons and members and for giving reports (Evans, 1966). The chairperson will keep members of the group on task (Donlan, 1973), have each member participate in completing the guide, allow members to justify their responses, and make sure individuals listen to each other, particularly when the group discusses controversial issues or makes evaluations. The chairperson should realize, particularly when the group is making *affective* evaluations, that various values can emerge from a group; consequently, the chairperson, at this second stage, has to decide whether the group members can converge to a consensus or whether the group will end up with a plurality of affective evaluations. Each member's role is to participate, contribute, listen to others, and help the others to think through their own ideas. The reporter's task is to take notes on what the group has done, to record information, and when the class reconvenes, to relate what the group accomplished. Thus, in Stage 2, the group applies not only skills in gaining information from text but also skills in discussion and writing.

An advantage of the group process is that more students are likely to formulate and express their ideas than would have done so in a whole-class situation. Since the act of expression requires people to create ideas and to organize and direct their thinking processes, more individuals whould have the opportunity to do so in a small group than in a large class situation. Through the give-and-take process in small groups, students teach each other and learn through experience the validity of the frequently made observation: "If you want to learn something, teach it."

Cooperative Learning Techniques for Stage 2. In implementing Stage 2 in your classroom, you may want to use one or more cooperative learning strategies (Kagan, 1985; Slavin, 1980).

For example, STAD (Student Teams-Achievement Division) involves the teacher's forming equal, cross-ability teams of students. Team members are trained to work cooperatively to achieve maximum points on frequent quizzes and course content. The teams compete with one another for points.

In Jigsaw II, another cooperative learning technique, the teacher divides the class into equal, cross-ability teams. Each student on a given team is assigned to an expert group. The expert groups study specific areas of content and become experts. They return to their teams to relay their newly acquired expert information. Here is how Hedy Davis used Jigsaw II in her fifth-grade class for social studies:

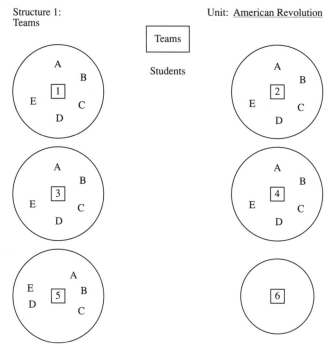

Structure 1:
Teams

Unit: American Revolution

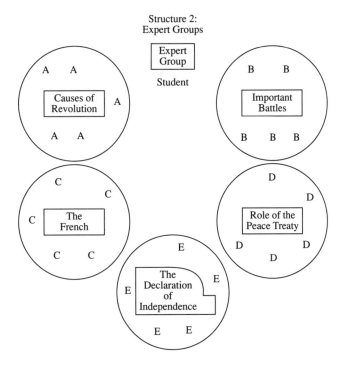

Structure 2:
Expert Groups

As you can see by the diagrams, Ms. Davis first grouped her 25 students in two ways. First, she formed 3 five 5-member teams of equal mixed ability. Each member of the team was to be responsible for a specific area of content. For instance, Student *C* in each group was to focus on "the role of the French in the Revolution." Later, she regrouped students into "expert groups" to exchange information and increase expertise. The students next returned to their teams to share newly acquired information in preparation for a quiz. She pooled individuals' quiz scores for team scores and awarded prizes to each team according to rank.

A third technique for cooperative learning is *Co-op Co-op*. In *Co-op Co-op*, equally matched teams of students study cooperatively and share their findings with the rest of the class. *Co-op Co-op,* then, eliminates the competitive aspects of STAD and Jigsaw II.

In conclusion, in the second stage there are similarities to the various forms of "cooperative learning." However, rather than a finite instructional system, Stage 2 is an intermediate step between teacher-directed and student-initiated learning.

THIRD STAGE: Individual Learning

Having learned from teacher guidance of the whole class and from group interaction, students are now able to complete assignments individually. At least they fully understand what they are to do. The work the students complete on their own can be used as a means of evaluating their skills and abilities in applying reading, thinking, and learning processes to the content areas. Eventually they develop their own study guides.

FOURTH STAGE: Internalization

Having learned to complete tasks successfully and independently by using a given strategy, the student internalizes the strategy. Thus, the strategy becomes "second nature."

What the Students Do Between September and June

STUDENTS' FOUR STAGE PLAN OF LEARNING

Figure 12.1 shows in schematic form, the four stages in learning a strategy.

Stage 1

Whole Class: students function as members of class. The teacher is the leader of the class. In this stage, the teacher teaches the class as a whole, and therefore each student in the class, and models what the chairperson of a group does and what is expected of each member of the group. The teacher can also appoint a reporter at this stage and have a member of the class demonstrate this role.

FIGURE 12.1. Scheme of three stages in teaching a strategy

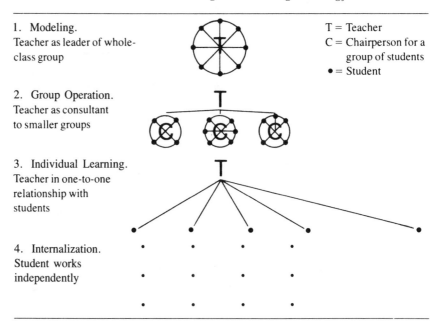

1. Modeling. Teacher as leader of whole-class group		T = Teacher C = Chairperson for a group of students ● = Student
2. Group Operation. Teacher as consultant to smaller groups		
3. Individual Learning. Teacher in one-to-one relationship with students		
4. Internalization. Student works independently		

Stage 2

Smaller Groups: the students function as members of smaller groups. The teacher relates to each group as a consultant and moves from group to group. At each group, the teacher-as-consultant observes, defines, and receives problems, and helps the group develop its group processes and solve its problems.

The *C* at the center of each group represents the chairperson. The role of this person is similar to the role modeled by the teacher in Stage 1. Presumably the chairperson's role is learned by imitation and by experience in the role.

For the first attempts, the teacher can appoint chairpersons, reporters, and group members. Ideally, each group ought to be heterogeneous in ability and knowledge in the particular subject area so that cross-ability teaching can occur. Although the more knowledgeable students will probably benefit more from this relationship, all students will have to learn the strategy, if not in Stage 2, then in Stage 3. The chairpersons at first may be highly respected members of the class, but subsequently the position ought to rotate. Likewise for the reporter.

At first, the task of the group should be relatively short, perhaps covering only a section or a page, and accomplishable in less than a class period. After 20 to 30 minutes of group activity, the teacher can call for reports and have each group evaluate its understanding of the strategy and how it functioned as a group. Subsequently, as groups demonstrate their knowledge of the learning strategy and their ability to function as groups, they should be given longer assignments and required to report periodically.

Stage 3

Individual Learning and Conferring: individuals complete their own assignments and, through them, communicate directly with the teacher. The teacher can use the individually completed guides to evaluate student progress and to diagnose reading, learning, and thinking skills and processes. For this purpose, the teacher should confer with individual students and obtain explanations of how and why they gave the responses they did.

The next step in guiding students toward independence is to teach them to *construct* their own guides. The teacher can do this in the same three stages used in teaching the class to *use* a guide. The aim for both single- and multiple-text strategies is to have students eventually internalize a process of thinking while learning from text. The mean for attaining this goal of learning how to learn and inquire in each content area is to have the class first learn to *use* a particular strategy in three stages. Then the class members should learn now to construct and self-administer the strategy. Finally, the students should know the strategy so well that they can apply it automatically to gaining and communicating information in each content area. In all strategies used in any content area, students are to learn to formulate and answer their own questions, at first by observing and answering the kinds of questions formulated by teachers and then, by imitation, formulating their own questions (Rosenthal et al., 1970).

The teacher's objective, then, is to get students to the point where they can pose their own questions and use this ability not only before reading in content areas but throughout the entire study of the content (Singer, 1978a, 1979). The process is analogous to a question-and-answer dialogue with single texts or with multiple texts. Hence, successful teaching means that students begin to think like content area specialists who know not only the content of their subject area but also its mode of inquiry, whether the content be industrial arts, English, science, or social science. Thus, evaluation of students is also a self-evaluation for teachers. The question is whether students have become independent learners in a particular content area. If so, the teacher has been successful.

Stage 4
Independent Learning and Internalization: the students are independent learners for the strategy taught in Stages 1–3. The teacher is available for an occasional consultation, but students have learned how to learn from text on their own. They are now able to automatically use strategies developed in Stages 1, 2, and 3. For example, as they read a text, they can mentally apply a reading and learning from text strategy by noting text-defined vocabulary, categorizing text data as literal, or explicit inferences, interpretations, and generalizations, and drawing upon their background knowledge to make inferences, interpretations, and generalizations.

ONE TEACHER'S BLUEPRINT
One teacher's blueprint for developing student independence in using reading and learning-from-text guides over the academic year appears in Table 12.1.

TABLE 12.1. One Teacher's Blueprint for Developing Student Independence

Month	Instructional Goal
September October	Teacher leads the class through chapters 1–4 with guides; conducts class discussion.
November December	Teacher groups students for chapters 5–8; students work with guides and learn independent small group discussion.
January February	Students select guides they need for chapters 9–12. They form their own groups for discussion.
March April	Teacher shows students how to make guides for chapters 13–16 for their own use.
May	Students prepare their own guides for chapters 17–18.
June	Students learn from chapters 19–20 without preparing guides.

FIGURE 12.2. Teacher phase out, student phase in for two strategies

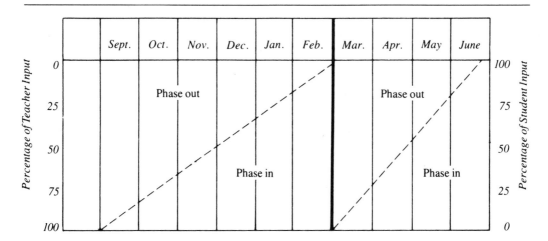

Notice that teacher input is heavy in September-October but light in January–February when students have learned to *use* a strategy. In March–April teacher input is again heavy as a new process begins: teaching students to make guides. Notice also that the reverse is true for student input. The planned phase out of the teacher might be diagramed, as shown in Figure 12.2.

DIMENSION TWO: CLASSROOM TEACHING STRATEGIES

The best way to guide students to become independent learners, then, is to teach them to do for themselves what many teachers ordinarily do for them. Before you can do this, you have to know what the strategies are and how to use them.

Single-Textbook Strategy

In the traditional high school learning situation, the entire class works from a single textbook (Herber, 1970a). Because the students represent a wide range of achievement, many will not learn from one text readily, but fortunately a variety of teaching strategies and techniques can be used for meeting the wide range of individual differences in reading and learning from single texts. What follows is a discussion of some single-text strategies that teachers can combine to teach students to learn from text.

HOW SHOULD YOU PREPARE STUDENTS TO LEARN FROM A SINGLE TEXT?

Before students begin to read the text you can provide certain classroom activities to facilitate their learning.

Do a Task Analysis

Before assigning a chapter from a textbook, make a brief outline of the main concepts you want to stress and a companion outline of the processes the students will need to know to master the content. In chapter 7 (Box 7.4), you saw an example of a task analysis for a chapter in a history text. Notice that it stressed ''main concepts'' rather than an accumulation of more or less related facts. Ineffective learners tend to approach all ideas with little differentiation. As a result, you will have to identify the essential main ideas (or the main ideas you want to teach) and relate the rest of the detail to these ideas. In addition, you will have to teach the students the thought processes the textbook authors used. Notice that the task analysis for the American history chapter includes *cause and effect* as a thought process students would need to know before reading the chapter. Table 12.2 gives an overview of concepts and processes in specific content areas. Table 12.3 gives a detailed task analysis for a series of related concepts in science. *Once you make a task analysis, show it to your students and tell them how you prepared it.* Later in the school year, you may want them to compose their own task analysis.

TABLE 12.2. General task Analyses for Specific Content Areas

	Concept	*Prerequisite Process*
English/ Language Arts	Poetry	Understanding figurative language
		Reading with rhyme/meter
		Drawing inferences
	Reading nonfiction	Main idea/supporting details
		Chronological order
Social Studies	The American Revolution	Cause and effect
		Chronological order
		Reading maps
	Declaration of Independence	Main idea/supporting details
		Using context clues
Science	The ecology of water	Drawing inferences from pictures and charts
		Cause and effect
	Conducting lab experiments	Following printed directions
		Using formulas
		Interpreting diagrams
		Drawing inferences
Mathematics	Percentage/interest	Reading word problems
		Translating symbols
	Solving algebraic equations	Reading math ''sentences''
		Interpreting symbols
		Moving numbers

TABLE 12.3. Task Analysis for a Science Unit on the Ecology of Water

Concept	Prerequisite Process
Water environments affect plant and animal life	Drawing inferences from pictures Cause and effect
Fresh water communities differ from salt water communities	Comparison/contrast Reading diagrams
Life in ponds, lakes, and rivers varies as a result of the water conditions	Cause and effect Technical terminology Context clues
Water changes as chemicals are added	Following directions Drawing inferences from visual data Understanding sequence

Give Your Students an Entry Level Test

To ascertain what your students need in order to read a chapter, plan a test to evaluate how adequate the students' backgrounds actually are for learning the chapter (Glaser, 1962). The test could be no more than a brief quiz, containing true-false, multiple-choice, short-answer, or matching items. Prerequisite content might be found in the previous chapter of the text you are using; thus, a final examination for chapter D might be used as an entry level test for chapter E. Prerequisite processes could be evaluated by simple classroom exercises. One test item, for instance, might be a scrambled list of events that is to be unscrambled. This test item might assess a student's knowledge of events and ability to perceive chronological order. *Show your students how to make entry level tests and let them participate with you in composing these tests.*

Write Classroom Objectives

A task analysis and entry level test can help you to write classroom objectives or revise existing objectives (Gagne, 1962). After the task analysis, you might write objectives on how you want students to perform after they've read the chapter. These objectives would be *ideal* performances. Results from the entry level test might cause you to revise, scale down, or expand your original objectives. Differentiated performance on the entry level test might suggest individualization of objectives; that is, the entry level test might determine what individual students need to know to benefit from the next chapter. Individual "contracts" indicate what objective(s) each student agrees that he or she must achieve. Consider Figure 12.3. Sarah DeJong agrees that she needs to accomplish objectives 1, 2, and 3; but Margaret Amato sees that she needs to accomplish all 14 objectives. Figure 12.3 also shows that Joseph Adams, who contracted for all 14 objectives, completed only 6. Mike Borjus, on the other hand, has to date completed 3 out of the 4 objectives he contracted to achieve.

FIGURE 12.3. Teacher's Record of Contracted and Completed Objectives

Key
✱ = contracted objectives
✔ = completed objectives

STUDENT	1. Knows water affects life	2. Drew inferences from pictures	3. Explained cause/effect	4. Fresh water/salt water differ	5. Made comparison/contrast	6. Read/understood diagrams	7. Ponds, lakes, rivers differ	8. Showed cause/effect	9. Knew technical terms	10. Used context clues	11. Conducted lab experiment	12. Followed directions	13. Inferred from visual data	14. Understood sequence
Adams, Joseph	✱✔	✱✔	✱✔	✱✔	✱✔	✱✔	✱	✱	✱	✱	✱	✱	✱	✱
Amato, Margaret	✱✔	✱✔	✱✔	✱✔	✱✔	✱✔	✱✔	✱✔	✱✔	✱✔	✱	✱	✱	✱
Blake, Sam	✱✔	✱✔	✱✔	✱✔	✱✔	✱✔	✱✔	✱	✱	✱				
Borjus, Mike											✱✔	✱✔	✱✔	✱
Carter, Louise	✱✔	✱✔	✱✔	✱	✱	✱								
Donato, Manuel	✱✔	✱✔	✱✔	✱✔	✱✔	✱✔	✱✔	✱✔	✱✔	✱✔	✱✔	✱✔	✱✔	✱
DeJong, Sarah	✱✔	✱✔	✱											

Show your students how to write performance objectives and give them practice at composing their own (Mager, 1962). Box 12.1 shows several types of performance objectives, glossed with explanation.

BOX 12.1. Types of Performance Objectives

content ——

1. The student will demonstrate his/ her understanding of Poe's use of single effect by composing an original short story of at least 500 words that focuses

—— task

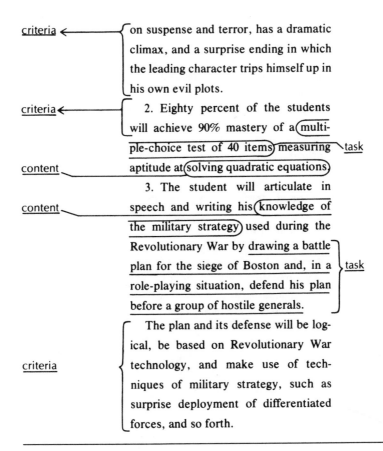

criteria	on suspense and terror, has a dramatic climax, and a surprise ending in which the leading character trips himself up in his own evil plots.	
criteria	2. Eighty percent of the students will achieve 90% mastery of a	
	multiple-choice test of 40 items measuring	task
content	aptitude at solving quadratic equations.	
	3. The student will articulate in	
content	speech and writing his knowledge of the military strategy used during the	
	Revolutionary War by drawing a battle plan for the siege of Boston and, in a role-playing situation, defend his plan before a group of hostile generals.	task
criteria	The plan and its defense will be logical, be based on Revolutionary War technology, and make use of techniques of military strategy, such as surprise deployment of differentiated forces, and so forth.	

Give the Class a Chapter Overview

Before students read a chapter, tell them what they should expect to find (Ausubel, 1964). An overview activity might consist of reviewing the items on your task analysis. It could also be an outline of the chapter's content, based on the author's organizational principles. It could be a series of page references with a brief statement about what the student will find on each page. You can give the overview orally, offering explanations as the students thumb through the chapter; or you can use a dittoed handout that you could take the class through. *Show the students various methods of preparing overview activities and, later in the year, have them prepare their own overviews.*

Review Difficult Vocabulary

In addition to understanding the author's thought processes, students need help with vocabulary, technical terms, and other difficult words. By going over vocabulary before the students read, you can facilitate their learning the concepts of the chapter. First, present the students with a list of words, pronounce them for the students, give the page numbers where the words occur, define the words in simple language, and provide a context for each word in a sentence from the textbook. Second, you can present merely the context sentence and work with the students in trying to infer meaning. Third, you can present the vocabulary in a demonstration apart from the text. Many shop teachers label tools and shop areas with signs and take the students on a tour prior to reading a chapter of text. *Teach your students the various means of learning the definitions of words and have them construct their own vocabulary lists.*

Teach the Students Needed Thought Processes

Your task analysis indicated certain thought processes the students would need to develop in order to comprehend the content of a chapter. You will have to teach the students how to engage in these processes; you will have to help them develop their thought processes. In chapters 6 and 7 (specifically, in Box 7.6), you saw an outline for a process of reading guide that attempts to teach students how to engage in cause and effect thinking. The best way to teach a thought process is to begin with a practical, everyday problem and then have the students explain how they would solve the problem. Consider teaching students the logical order of directions. First, supply the students with a list of *scrambled* steps one must take to make something—for instance, a peanut butter and jelly sandwich. Second, as the students unscramble these steps, have them take note of the clues they are using to obtain the proper order. Third, see if they can apply what they have learned to another situation, for instance, unscrambling the events in a recent film. Fourth, see if they can now apply what they have learned to a textbook situation—unscrambling events in a chapter. *Teach your students to teach themselves to think by having them prepare their own processes-of-reading guides. (See chapters 6 and 7.)*

HOW SHOULD YOU GUIDE THE STUDENTS WHILE THEY ARE READING?

So far you have been concerned with preparing students for reading by using task analysis, entry level tests, writing and revising objectives; by leading overview activities, learning-to-read activities, processes-of-thinking activities; and, most of all, by showing them how you teach. Preparation, however, is not enough by itself. You have to provide guidance while the students are reading and, more important, show them how to guide themselves.

Provide them with Learning-From-Text Guides

You can provide the student with a set of preposed questions for which they will find answers while they are reading. You might even supply the page numbers where the student may find the basis for answers. If the students review the questions prior to reading, they will search for answers as they read. The questions will lead them to focus on what your preposed questions have, in effect, emphasized. Later in the year, you can have the students pose their own questions. *Show students how to write questions* that ask for information, that ask for inferences, and that ask for evaluation and application of what they have learned. In Box 12.2 is an example of a learning-from-text guide.

BOX 12.2. *Learning-from-Text Guide*

LIFE: ITS FORMS AND CHANGES

Chapter 1, pp. 4–23

A. *Factual Level*
   1. What causes the green color that you see on a pond? (page 4, column 1, paragraph 2)
   2. What are *algae* and how do they help out in a pond? (pages 4, 2, 1)
   3. List the names of two algae that have similar shapes. (pages 5 and 6)
   4. List two other types of plants that live in the pond. (page 7)
   5. List four types of animals that eat the plants of the pond. (pages 10 and 11)
   6. Who are the producers of the pond and who are the consumers? (pages 18, 19, 23)
B. *Inferential and Interpretive Level*
   1. If there were no producers in the pond what would happen to the consumers?
   2. Of what use is the microscope to people who want to study life in a pond?
   3. Are producers always plants and are the consumers always animals?
C. *Generalization and Evaluative Level*
   1. If you wanted to build a giant glass aquarium for people to examine pond life, what would you have to fill it with to keep everything from dying?
   2. What problems do managers of public aquariums face every day?

Although early in the year it is important for you to pose the questions in a learning-from-text guide, you can gradually teach students to write questions on different levels, and eventually they will be able to ask their own questions and direct their own learning (Rosenthal et al., 1970).

If Possible, Gloss a Chapter

Glossing is a helpful learning device. As you recall, glossing is the use of marginal notes to facilitate learning. Glossing may take the form of word definitions, paraphrasing, and the posing of questions. Many textbooks use glossing, but even if you use such textbooks you may wish to add your own touches. Because you cannot collect the students' textbooks every night and write marginal notes for all your students, you'll have to resort to expedient measures. First, you can dictate glosses to the students for them to write in the margins of their own books (or in their notebooks if writing in books is not allowed). Second, if your "textbook" consists of dittoed handouts, you can write the gloss directly on the ditto masters. Third (a fairly complicated measure), you can duplicate glosses aligned with the textbook margins on facing ditto pages that can be slipped between the textbook pages. *Eventually, you can educate students to write their own glosses, based on what they perceive as their own learning problems.*

HOW DO YOU ASSESS STUDENTS' LEARNING AFTER READING?

After students have read, you will want to assess what they have read by getting them to *react* to the text and *evaluate* it.

Plan Reaction Activities

You will want to plan activities that allow students to react to what they've read. At a simple level, one such activity could be a discussion of answers to the questions posed in the learning-from-text guide. At a more complex level, students could engage in individual and group projects in which they apply what they have learned. Science students, after reading a chapter on osmosis, might devise an experiment showing the process of osmosis, demonstrate the experiment before class, and relate the experiment to content in the text chapter. Reaction activities can involve symposia, panel discussions, debates, dramatic improvisations, student-written plays and stories, demonstration or research projects, as well as answering questions that show the students' abilities at making inferences, analyzing ideas in a text, and problem solving. *As with other strategies, you can show students how to plan reaction activities and later get them to plan, implement, and evaluate their own activities.*

Plan Evaluative Experiences

Too often students are not given the opportunity to evaluate the textbooks they are reading or the ideas within the textbooks. Students have ideas and feelings that are well worth exploring. Permit them the opportunity to pass judgment on a textbook, but require that they substantiate their judgments. Evaluation activities could include a range of experiences from direct responses to cognitive judgments (Is the material correct? How do you know?) to subjective questions (What did you like least about this chapter? Why?) to role-playing situations. (A group of students could function as an editorial board in a publishing house responding to the content and style of the class text.)

Multiple-Text Strategy

A popular learning approach in elementary high school is the use of multiple texts within the same classroom. Three multiple-text approaches indicate the need for deft planning: the use of multilevel texts, the use of multiple textbooks with core readings, and the use of multiple textbooks without core readings.

MULTILEVEL TEXTBOOKS

As the name suggests, in a multilevel textbook approach, two or more textbooks at varying levels of readability and parallel organization serve as the basis for grouping students for instruction. Consider a 10th-grade science class with a 10-year range of reading achievement. The entire class could be studying photosynthesis, but each student could select one of three texts best suited to her or his ability and use it to search for answers to questions. All three texts would include content on photosynthesis. Consequently, all the students could participate in discussion and other class activities even though they had used different texts that varied in difficulty level. Because students could select their own texts, no stigmatization is likely to occur. In a situation like this, you would use single-text strategies where needed for each of the three books. You would assume that high-achieving 10th-graders would experience problems with a text they selected just as low-achieving students would have problems with a text. In effect, the type of teaching you would be doing in a single-text situation would not be very different from the type you would be doing in a multilevel text situation. You would just be doing it several times. For example, in a situation where you had three levels of text and were using a Directed Reading Activity (DRA) strategy, you would construct lesson plans for each text. In the same way, if you had a marginal gloss strategy, you would prepare a gloss for each text. You would also prepare three learning-from-text guides.

MULTIPLE TEXT WITH CORE READINGS

More common than the approach involving multilevel texts is the multiple-text approach that involves supplementary core readings (Ryan, 1963). Using this approach, you would employ single-text teaching strategies to have the entire class engage in the common reading of a single anthology or a science text. Following the reading of the one text, you would allow students to choose, individually or in groups, additional readings on their own and report back to the class. Independent and group projects, generated from core readings, can provide you with additional opportunities to assess student learning. In addition, these projects allow students opportunities to try their wings in independent work. If you plan ingeniously by continually alternating core reading experiences with group and individual projects, students can learn, developmentally, to learn on their own.

MULTIPLE TEXTBOOKS WITHOUT CORE READINGS

In using this approach, in which students share no common reading experience, you will have to build other classroom activities to bring students together, particularly overview activities. In such activities, you and the students define and pose problems and schedule reporting sessions in which students can share what they have learned.

DIMENSION THREE: TEACHING
DISCUSSION AND WRITING

In order for you to evaluate how well your students are learning from text, they must respond in ways that can be assessed. A student in sewing class demonstrates proficiency by sewing. A swimmer demonstrates proficiency by swimming, a pianist, by playing music. A reader cannot demonstrate proficiency by reading only. The reader must make his or her reading and learning from text audible or visible if you are to assess it. Therefore, to demonstrate what he or she has learned, a reader must speak or write for a teacher or student audience. Discussion and writing are vital activities in assessing reading and learning from text. However, if you expect students to speak and write effectively, you must teach them how to do so. To meet this challenge, teachers should devote time, especially at the beginning of the school year, to showing students how to participate in a discussion and how to prepare writing assignments. For specific suggestions on teaching discussion and writing, see chapters 8 and 9.

SUMMARY

Teachers in today's classroom must provide for a wide range of individual differences in ability to read and learn from text. Single- and multiple-text strategies for teaching students to read and learn from text are effective in dealing with this range of individual differences; and they are even more effective when organized into a blueprint for instruction.

A blueprint for instruction has three dimensions. First, it provides for phasing out the teacher and phasing in the student in a three-stage process:

1. The teacher introduces a strategy and directs the entire class through it.
2. The teacher has the students work through the strategy in small groups. In this stage, the teacher functions as a consultant.
3. The students can learn to apply the strategy independently.

Second, the instructional blueprint provides for a sequence of classroom teaching strategies, beginning with single-text strategies and shifting to multiple-text strategies. Third, the instructional blueprint ensures that the teacher will teach students various ways of discussing and writing about the text. The teaching goal implicit in the instructional blueprint is to change students from dependent to independent learners.

ACTIVITIES

1. Review the three stages of the phase-out/phase-in procedure. Develop three separate lesson plans that incorporate discussion, using topics from your own content area. The first discussion should be teacher directed, with the entire

class participating. The second discussion should be planned for small groups of students, using topics generated by you. The third discussion should be planned for either the entire class or for small groups of students, where students generate their own topics for discussion.

2. Explain by example how, in May, you would teach technical vocabulary to students in your content area differently than you did in October. If you wish, use the form suggested for vocabulary guides in chapter 5.

13 | English Language Arts

English language arts is one of the most complex subjects in the curriculum. Not only does it integrate three intellectual disciplines—literature, linguistics, and rhetoric—but it also includes the basic communicative processes—reading, writing, speaking, and listening. This chapter focuses upon teaching students to learn from literature texts. The beginning sections of the chapter deal with the structure of the study of literature and the processes students use in responding to literary text. The bulk of the chapter, however, presents a series of single- and multiple-text strategies teachers can use to help their students learn from reading literature.

GRAPHIC ORGANIZER

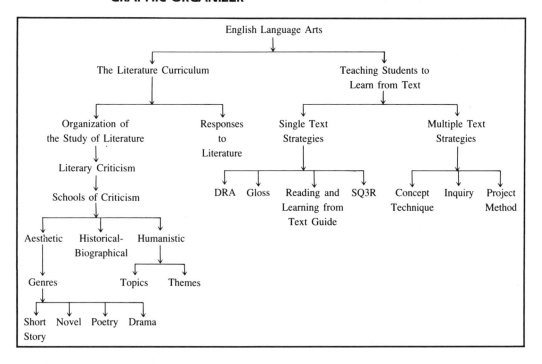

PREPOSED QUESTIONS

1. Why is English, or language arts, a difficult subject to teach?
2. What are the various types of text that English language arts teachers are expected to teach? What are the instructional problems inherent in getting students to learn from literary text?
3. How would you develop a unit in literature that would contain both single- and multiple-text strategies?

INTEGRATION OF ENGLISH LANGUAGE ARTS IN CONTENT AREAS AT ELEMENTARY AND HIGH SCHOOL

You could argue that English language arts is the most important subject in the curriculum because it includes instruction in basic communicative processes - reading, writing, speaking, and listening. Students use these skills in most of the other content fields.

Elementary school teachers can easily relate the language arts processes to science, mathematics, social studies, art, and music because they teach all of these subjects to the same students. For example, Ms. Davis developed a unit on E. B. White's *Charlotte's Web* that included instruction on how to read a novel, how to write a character sketch, and how to give an oral report based on a character sketch. In addition, Ms. Davis related the novel's content to science (the study of spiders, pigs, rats, geese, etc.) and to social studies (problems of operating a small farm). The unit culminated in a field trip to a local farm. For enrichment, students prepared a "rural arts fair." In secondary schools, English teachers generally teach students only one hour a day and are unable to see that language arts processes are transferred to other content areas. (Chapters 8 and 9 illustrate ways that content area teachers can reinforce speaking, listening, and writing processes in their own classrooms.)

Like elementary school language arts teachers, English teachers teach literature, language, and composition. However, the opportunities to relate this content to science, social studies, mathematics, arts, and music are somewhat limited, although English teachers occasionally cooperate with teachers in other content areas in team teaching.

Although some teachers may use three texts—a literature text, a language text, and a composition text—and achieve some degree of integration of these texts, this chapter focuses on how teachers can enable students to comprehend literature.

To gain a consensus on a definition of *literature* is difficult. Nineteenth-century critic Matthew Arnold referred to literature as the best that has been thought and said in the world. A high school student once defined it as "anything you read." We define *literature* as "those writings of a country or from a period of time that are known for their beauty and universal appeal." G. Robert Carlsen (1967) attempted to bridge the two viewpoints by separating literature from what he termed *subliterature:* comic books, juvenile and adult romance, westerns, and other adventure yarns. Subliterature tends to use formula plots and stereotyped characters, and it tends to present a false picture of life. Although many teachers shun subliterature, other teachers use it in the classroom to motivate students to read serious literature. Regardless of definition, selection of literature for any program is the reflection of teacher taste, student need, instructional purpose, and school or district guidelines.

THE LITERATURE CURRICULUM

How Is the Study of Literature Organized?

Literary criticism, written by scholars who analyze and evaluate works of literature, has influenced the teaching of literature to generations of students. When critics agree about the salient aspects of literature, their views form ways of thinking, or *schools of criticism.*

Some critics in the school of *aesthetic criticism* see the greatness of a poem, whether it be written by T. S. Eliot or Dr. Seuss, as emerging from the poet's skill at blending elements of meter, sound, imagery, and message. Aesthetic critics have influenced teachers to use the *literary genre,* or type, approach to teaching literature. Consequently, we find that units, courses, and minicourses in today's classrooms focus on genres such as the short story, the novel, poetry, and drama. The advantage to the students of studying literature by type is that they can learn more readily the form and style inherent in a genre. Frequently, the genre approach includes a collateral creative writing element, allowing students the opportunity to apply literary principles to their own writing.

Some critics stress authors' lives and times. These critics attempt to gain insight into literature by studying how an author's personality and environment affected his or her writing. Some critics, for example, have examined the impact of Edgar Allan Poe's personality on the content and quality of his writing. Other critics have focused on how history shaped the writing of given authors. They have examined the works of Mark Twain and Bret Harte, for example, as products of the Westward Movement. Their views form the school of *historical/biographical criticism* and have influenced teachers to use the historical approach to teaching literature. Consider high school courses you may have taken in American literature (Washington Irving to Ray Bradbury), British literature (*Beowulf* to Harold Pinter), or more recently, ethnic literature—Black literature, native American literature, Hispanic-American literature, Jewish-American literature and so forth. Your teachers tended to organize these courses historically or biographically. The advantage to students of studying literature historically and biographically is that they can view literature not only as art but also as a result of interacting social, economic, and political forces.

Critics in the school of *humanistic criticism* tend to stress the human values implicit in literature. They become concerned with how well women and men in literature meet the challenges of life. They believe that human beings should be portrayed as having the potential for nobility, greatness. Young children can sense this greatness in *Charlotte's Web* just as older students observe it in *Hamlet.* Humanistic critics have influenced teachers to use topical or thematic approaches to teaching literature.

In a topical approach, literary selections of various types and from various historical periods are clustered in *topics: survival, courage, man and nature, self-fulfillment.* Thematic units, like topical units, cluster literary selections around ideas, rather than around genres or historical periods. Unlike topics, *themes* are propositional statements:

Topics	*Themes*
1. Survival	1. The survival of the human race depends upon its knowledge of scientific laws.
2. Courage	2. Courage is born from stubbornness.
3. Man and Nature	3. Man eventually loses his struggle against nature.
4. Self-fulfillment	4. Self-fulfillment is a by-product of hard work and frustration.

Themes are narrower than topics. The principal difficulty, and disadvantage, to topical and thematic teaching of literature are the artificiality of "pigeon-holing" diverse selections and perhaps imposing relationships among selections that might not exist; we could classify *The Catcher in the Rye, Don Quixote,* and *The Diary of Anne Frank* under each of the above topics or themes, but the classification would not be appropriate. The principal advantage of a thematic and topical approach, and perhaps the reasons for its immense popularity, is that it deemphasizes traditional aesthetic and historical academic approaches in favor of issues and ideas.

In effect, an English language arts teacher's mode of organization tends to reflect a set of values. It is hoped that the teacher will base these values upon reasonable assumptions about how students learn effectively.

Responses to Literature

In addition to being aware of the various schools of literary criticism, teachers of literature are concerned about how students *respond* to literature (Richards, 1929; Rosenblatt, 1976).

How a student responds to a piece of literature depends upon a number of factors—the nature of the literary text, the background experience the student brings to the text, and how the teacher has presented the text to the student. Ms. Willbanks, for example, has a classroom library that she encourages students to use before, during, and after class. The library contains hundreds of paperbacks, ranging from Lois Duncan's *Killing Mr. Griffin* to Rostand's *Cyrano de Bergerac.* After students complete books, they write their impressions on small file cards, making sure their names and book titles appear also on the cards. One student wrote, "I liked this book a lot because the characters reminded me of my family. They got into funny situations like my family does. I think the book showed me how to deal with my younger brother who is a pest." Another student wrote, "I felt very sad when he died at the end. I really like him. He was like a friend so when he died it was like losing a friend." A less enthusiastic student wrote, ''I hated the book. The characters were dumb and the story was boring.'' What Ms. Willbanks found interesting was that all three students were commenting on the same book. The three students came from different backgrounds. The first student came from an extended family situation. Her mother, a widow, was raising her and her younger brother with the help of two aunts, a grandmother, and the grandmother's close friend. The second student was in a foster home, the third in a succession of unhappy placements. The third student was a gifted, but underachieving boy who reacted negatively to any school activity. The dramatic range of comments is a result of Ms. Willbanks's philosophy about reading literature: ''Students should read what they want to and should react freely to what they read.''

TEACHING STUDENTS TO LEARN FROM LITERATURE TEXT

In teaching students to understand literature, Mr. Wallace, the English teacher at Monroe High School, faced a wide range of individual student differences. Some of his students came to class never having read a book voluntarily in their entire lives. Other students were voracious readers. Under the headings below are descriptions of Mr. Wallace's classroom strategies designed for effective teaching of literature to mixed-ability classes. The activities are in a developmental sequence; that is, they are arranged in the order in which Mr. Wallace used them during a school year. Toward the beginning of the year he made heavier use of *Directed Reading Activities* (DRAs) and *glosses;* toward the end of the year he made heavier use of *inquiry* and the *project method.*

To present the strategies in a unified and coherent way, we demonstrate their use in a hypothetical topical unit, *Moments of Choice,* that Mr. Wallace devised. As the unit develops, Mr. Wallace moves through the unit, progressing from single-text strategies—DRA, glossing, reading and learning-from-text guides, and SQ3R—to multiple-text strategies—concept, inquiry, and project methods. In this hypothetical unit, Mr. Wallace goes through the seven strategies in 4 to 8 weeks. In reality, a teacher would take a school year to go through this sequence. Some of the strategies given in boxes are glossed with literary terms you might want to teach directly or indirectly to your students.

Single-Text Strategies

It is probably wise to begin the school year by having all of the students read the same text assignment. First of all, it facilitates planning. Second, it provides an opportunity to observe individual differences in ability to read and learn from text.

DIRECTED READING ACTIVITY

In teaching students to comprehend literature, you will want, at first, to provide them with much guidance (Donlan, 1985b). Before they read a selection, you will want to *prepare* them for what they are about to read. This involves (a) exploring their background to see what personal experiences they are approaching the selection with and (b) building any background you feel they will need to comprehend the selection. While the students are reading, you may want to guide them with preposed questions. After the students read, you will want to engage the students in discussion and other follow-up activities that will *extend* their understanding of the literature.

In Box 13.1 is a DRA lesson on Nelson Algren's fast-moving story "He Swung and He Missed" (1965). If you were teaching the unit *Moments of Choice,* you might want to make "He Swung and He Missed" one of the opening selections, just as Mr. Wallace did. As you read through the lesson, try to imagine yourself teaching these activities to a high school English class.

Box 13.1. Unit: Moments of Choice (DRA)

"HE SWUNG AND HE MISSED"

by Nelson Algren

Synopsis: Rocco grew up the hard way, by fighting. Unfortunately, he was never a winner. When offered money to throw a fight he refused, lost the fight anyway, but found himself.

I. Mr. Wallace explores his students' background.
    A. Mr. Wallace asks the students if they have read the books *Rocky* or *Sylvester Stallone's Official Rocky Scrapbook,* and if so, what they liked about the books. Other questions might be:
        1. What was there about Rocky, the man, that you particularly liked or disliked?
        2. Was Rocky a winner or a loser?
    B. Mr. Wallace asks students to place items 1–6 on a values continuum:
        1. Watching prize fighting on TV
        2. Watching boxing in person
        3. Watching movies about boxing
        4. Collecting autographs of boxers
        5. Boxing
        6. Teaching boxing

Values Continuum

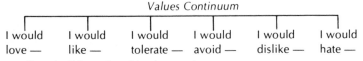

| I would love — | I would like — | I would tolerate — | I would avoid — | I would dislike — | I would hate — |

II. Mr. Wallace builds students' background.
    A. Mr. Wallace explains difficult words from "He Swung and He Missed":
        1. nurtured
        2. languidly
        3. impassive
        4. feinted
        5. decapitated

B. Mr. Wallace reviews boxing jargon used in "He Swung and He Missed":

1. catch weight
2. purse
3. middleweights
4. light-heavies
5. took a dive
6. set up
7. soft touch
8. comer
9. duke
10. put down for ten

C. Mr. Wallace gives the students a few preposed questions to guide their reading:
   1. What sort of person is Rocco?
   2. What important decision does he make?
   3. Would you want Rocco as a friend?

III. The students read the selection in class or for homework.

IV. Mr. Wallace has the students discuss the selection:
   A. Informational, or Directly Stated, Level
      1. How did Rocco's earlier matches turn out?
      2. What people did Rocco particularly like?
      3. Before his "moment of choice" what deal did he make?
      4. After he married, what was his career like?
      5. Did he live up to his bargain?
      6. What was the surprise ending?
   B. Inferential Level
      1. What do you learn about Rocco's character from the following lines?
         a. "Friends came, friends left, money came in, was lost, was saved. . . ."
         b. "He gave Lili every dime of that [prize] money."
         c. "He'd end like he started, as a fighting man."
         d. "Miss Donahue would have been proud."

         } Making inferences about characterization through dialogue

      2. In what ways had Algren prepared you, the reader, to accept Rocco's quick switch in the ring?

         → (1) Foreshadowing
         (2) Motivation

   C. Generalized Level
      1. Does Rocco fit a stereotyped image of prize fighters? Explain.
      2. We are all "tested" sometime during our lives, usually by having to make crucial decisions. How was Rocco tested? Did he "pass the test"? Explain.

V. Mr. Wallace has the students participate in activities that extend their understanding of "He Swung and He Missed."
   A. Dramatics
      1. Suppose Rocco had won the fight. Reenact the final scene between Rocco and Lili.
      2. Enact a spontaneous scene in which Rocco is being interviewed by a well-known sports writer prior to the fight. In the dialogue make use of prize-fight jargon.
   B. Writing
      1. Describe a tense moment during an athletic event. Create tension by using powerful verbs that denote action.

2. Rewrite from memory the fight between Rocco and Kid Class. Compare your version with the original.
3. Describe situation that "tested" you because you had to make an important decision. Why did you make the decision you did?

"He Swung and He Missed" first appeared in Algren's collection, *Neon Wilderness* (New York: Hill & Wang, 1960). It has been widely anthologized, and appears in Robert C. Pooley et al., eds., *Accent USA* (New York: Scott, Foresman, 1965). Both Julia Sorel's *Rocky* (1977) and *Sylvester Stallone's Official Rocky Scrapbook* (also 1977) are available in paperback, *Rocky* from Ballantine and the *Scrapbook* from Ace Books.

GLOSS

In addition to using the Directed Reading Activity, you might also gloss several reading selections to help your students learn to understand literature. The process of *glossing,* you remember, includes providing *marginal aids* to comprehension, such as defining difficult words, clarifying difficult concepts, asking thought questions. Glossing poetry is often necessary because the intensity of meaning contained in terse and concise language can make comprehension of poetry very difficult. Fortunately, poems tend to be short and therefore require little time to gloss. When students have poems or other difficult materials to read as homework assignments, the gloss becomes the "guardian angel," the "teacher" away from school. To determine what you want to gloss, ask yourself what questions students might have to ask you as they read at home or quietly in your classroom; answer those questions with the gloss.

In Box 13.2 is Mr. Wallace's gloss of a fairly difficult poem "We Wear the Mask," by Paul Laurence Dunbar. Read through the poem and see if the gloss helps you understand its meaning:

BOX 13.2. Moments of Choice (Gloss)

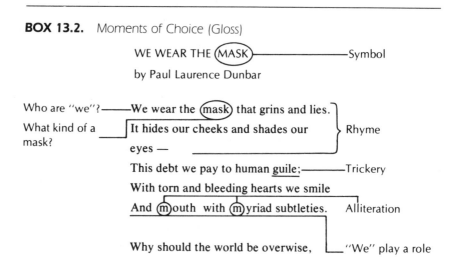

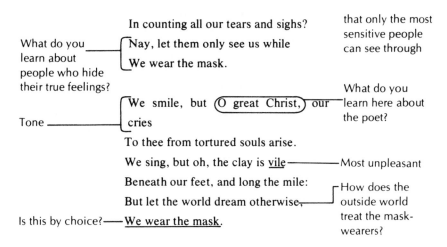

In counting all our tears and sighs?

What do you learn about people who hide their true feelings? — Nay, let them only see us while / We wear the mask.

that only the most sensitive people can see through

Tone — We smile, but (O great Christ,) our cries

What do you learn here about the poet?

To thee from tortured souls arise.

We sing, but oh, the clay is vile — Most unpleasant

Beneath our feet, and long the mile:

But let the world dream otherwise, — How does the outside world treat the mask-wearers?

Is this by choice? — We wear the mask.

The poet is Black. Does that change the meaning of the poem? Could "we" be of any color?

"We Wear the Mask" reprinted by permission of Dodd, Mead from *The Complete Poems of Paul Laurence Dunbar.*

READING AND LEARNING-FROM-TEXT GUIDES

The strategies used thus far (DRA and glossing) progress from teacher dependence toward student independence. The next step in this progression is the use of reading and learning-from-text guides. We shall see how these guides apply to teaching a novel.

Fahrenheit 451, by Ray Bradbury, a novel that Mr. Wallace taught in the unit *Moments of Choice,* contains difficult language and difficult concepts. Even some independent readers have problems interpreting what Bradbury is trying to say. To deal with the difficult language, you might want to prepare a processes-of-reading guide. in Box 13.3 is a processes-of-reading guide for *Fahrenheit 451.*

BOX 13.3. *Processes-of-Reading Guide*

FAHRENHEIT 451

by Ray Bradbury

MAKING INFERENCES ABOUT CHARACTER

Instructions: It is human nature to make judgments about other people on the basis of what these people say and do. If you see a small child lying on the floor of a supermarket crying and kicking, you might conclude that the child is *spoiled.* If you see a young woman pick up a package that an elderly man has dropped, you assume that this woman is *thoughtful*. These judgments that you make about people's character are called *inferences*. Generally, people reveal their character through what they say and through what they do.

Activity I. Below are statements that people have made. What inferences about their character can you make?
A. Young man, don't you dare talk to me like that again!
B. If I were you, I'd wear something a little nicer and more expensive looking.
C. Now, as your best friend, I think you should know that people are talking about you behind your back.

Activity II. Below are descriptions of what people have done. What inferences about their character can you make?
A. A fourth grader sticks his tongue out at his teacher when the teacher's back is turned.
B. An elderly woman fills her purse with food she hasn't eaten at a restaurant.
C. A man fixing a clock seizes the clock and throws it against the wall.

Activity III. The book you are about to read, *Fahrenheit 451*, contains interesting and complicated characters. It is important for you to know how to make inferences about their character by judging what they say and do. Below are statements by and about characters from *Fahrenheit 451*. Even though you haven't started to read the book, see if you can make inferences about the characters:
A. Clarisse
   1. "I like to watch people. Sometimes I ride the subway all day and look at them and listen to them."
   2. Clarisse attends amusement parks and likes to ride in the jet cars.
   3. Clarisse eavesdrops on conversations in soda fountains.
B. Beatty
   1. "You must understand that our civilization is so vast that we can't have our minorities upset and stirred."
   2. "That's what we live for, isn't it? For pleasure, for titillation?"
   3. Beatty believes that books should be burned in order to keep people happy with life.
C. Montag
   1. "You ever seen a burned house? It smolders for days. Well, this fire'll last me the rest of my life."
   2. Though a fireman, Montag doesn't like the idea of burning books.

Passages quoted in this box are taken from Ray Bradbury, *Fahrenheit 451* (New York: Ballantine, 1953).

SQ3R

The purpose of sequencing DRA, glosses, and reading and learning-from-text guides is to change the students from dependent learners to independent learners. SQ3R is another step toward the goal of student independence in learning. It teaches by having students formulate and find answers to their own questions.

SQ3R is not an effective technique for reading fiction. It works much better for nonfiction essays or articles. In Box 13.4 is Mr. Wallace's lesson on the essay "Sport's Worst Tragedy," by Joseph P. Blank, an illustration of how to teach students the SQ3R technique.

BOX 13.4. Unit: Moments of Choice (SQ3R)

"SPORT'S WORST TRAGEDY"

by Joseph P. Blank ──────────────────────────────→ nonfiction

Synopsis: This(essay)is a terrifying account of a riot during a soccer match in Lima, Peru. The essay shows how people react in the face of panic.

I. Mr. Wallace has the students *survey* the essay by asking questions like these:
   a. When you see the title "Sport's Worst Tragedy," what do you think about? In other words, what sort of tragedy might it be?
   b. Read the first paragraph of the essay. Notice that Maria Rodriguez wonders how it was possible for her son to be killed at a *futbol* game. Examine these passages:
      1. "The crowd carried me halfway down the tunnel without my feet touching the concrete floor."
      2. "My wife and five children are dead. All dead! My God!"
      3. "Only spectators like St. Dongo in the North section witnessed the horror that seethed in the stands and erupted in the tunnels."

II. Mr. Wallace has the students ask themselves *questions* they want to find answers for. These questions could emerge from their survey of the essay:
   a. What caused the crowd to react in horror, to seethe?
   b. Did eyewitnesses shed any light on how the tragedy occurred?
   c. What caused people to be killed during a *futbol* game?
   d. Could this sort of tragedy happen in the United States today?

III. Mr. Wallace instructs the students to *read* the essay to find answers to their questions. (If the teacher wishes, students can write the answers to the questions when they finish reading.)

IV. Mr. Wallace then has the students *recite* their answers to questions in a variety of ways. Students can submit written answers or share differing questions and answers with classmates in total class or small-group discussion.

V. The students might engage in "review-by-doing" projects such as these:
   a. Doing outside reading in popular psychology magazines on the subject of mass hysteria and crowd behavior.
   b. Researching another disaster involving group panic: the *Hindenburg* explosion, the sinking of the *Andrea Doria*.
   c. Rereading the essay to come up with further insights.

Passages quoted in this box are from Joseph P. Blank, "Sport's Worst Tragedy," *Kiwanis Magazine* 30:3 (March 1965), pp. 34–36, 45–47. This article is reprinted in its entirety in Jay Cline, Ken Williams, and Dan Donlan, eds., *Voices in Literature, Language, and Composition 2* (Boston: Ginn and Company, 1969).

Multiple-Text Strategies

So far, you have been teaching your students to comprehend literature independently. For this purpose, you have used DRA, glosses, guides, and SQ3R in *single-text situations*. Now you are ready to have your students try out multiple-text situations. We will explain and apply three multiple-text strategies: the concept method, inquiry, and the project method.

CONCEPT TECHNIQUE

Despite continuing attention to training independent learners, you may still find wide differences in your students' ability to learn from text on their own. You want to use a strategy that will allow students to read and learn from texts that are appropriate to their abilities, but you do not want to stigmatize any student. You also want your students to read texts on the same topic or theme so that they can all engage in a class discussion and enrich their understanding by learning from each other. One of the best ways to provide for individual differences without stigmatizing students is to have the students self-select what they will read and, more or less, group themselves. You might, for instance, choose five or so reading selections that vary in difficulty, introduce the selections to the class as a whole, and permit the students to make the choices (Ryan, 1963). This technique should be introduced with short selections and later followed with longer ones. Accordingly, we will describe two of Mr. Wallace's self-selection activities in Box 13.5, one for short stories, the other for novels.

BOX 13.5. Unit: Moments of Choice
(Concept Technique)

SHORT STORIES

Mr. Wallace: So far the entire class has been reading the same literature. Now you are going to select one particular story from a group of five that deal with the unit's theme *Moments of Choice*. Before you decide which story you want to read, you will probably want to have a "teaser" on each story. Textbook page references are on the blackboard. Copy them down for your handout in case you want to glance through the story before making your choice. You will receive a handout that lists the story "teasers." Later, a sign-up sheet will be passed around; indicate your choice of story on this sheet by signing your name in the appropriate section. You will later participate in a group of students who chose the story you selected. Your group will discuss and plan a presentation for the rest of the class.

Handout: Story "Teasers"

1. "Flowers for Algernon," by Daniel Keyes: Is it possible for a mentally retarded adult suddenly to become a genius? Do scientists have the right to decide whom they will experiment upon? Charly, a retarded adult, and Algernon, a rat, share common experiences.
2. "An Occurrence at Owl Creek Bridge," by Ambrose Bierce: A man is about to be executed. He suddenly discovers he has an opportunity to escape. What should he do? What will be the consequences of his decision?
3. "The Most Dangerous Game," by Richard Connell: Rainsford finds himself staying in the luxurious home of a strange retired army officer. Suddenly, the comfortable experience becomes a nightmare and Rainsford finds he has to choose a method of survival.
4. "Four Eyes," by Joseph Petracca: Joseph Esposito finds out he can't read the blackboard at school. His teacher wants him to get glasses, but Joey's father won't allow it. Some hysterically funny situations arise as Joey finds himself caught in the middle.
5. "Beauty Is Truth," by Anna Guest: Jeanie is told by her creative writing teacher to write about real-life experiences. Poignantly, she describes her life in Harlem. Her classmates find it a memorable experience.

Sign-Up Sheet

Instructions: After you have selected one of the five stories, sign your name under its title below. You and other classmates who select the story will (1) discuss the story in small groups; the discussion will be on answers to questions your group has preposed; (2) plan a discussion, debate, dramatization, or media presentation; and (3) present your project to the rest of the class.

1. "Flowers for Algernon"
   a. _____
   b. _____
   c. _____
   d. _____
   e. _____
   f. _____
2. "An Occurrence at Owl Creek Bridge"
   a. _____
   b. _____
   c. _____
   d. _____
   e. _____
   f. _____
3. "The Most Dangerous Game"
   a. _____
   b. _____
   c. _____
   d. _____
   e. _____
   f. _____

4. "Four Eyes"
    a. _____
    b. _____
    c. _____
    d. _____
    e. _____
    f. _____
5. "Beauty Is Truth"
    a. _____
    b. _____
    c. _____
    d. _____
    e. _____
    f. _____

NOVELS

Mr. Wallace: Now that you have had experience working in small-group projects on a fairly short-term basis, you are about to embark on small-group projects that may take 3 or 4 weeks to complete. Although you will have class time for the project, you will have to do most of this work on your own time. Some groups may find they will have to meet outside of class after school or on weekends to complete the work. For this project, you will select a novel from a group of five that deal with the unit's theme *Moments of Choice*. As I did before, I will give you a handout that provides an overview of each of the five novels. Later, you will sign up for a particular novel and be responsible for a series of group activities related to it.

Handout: Novel Overviews

1. *Killing Mr. Griffin,* by Lois Duncan. A group of high school students kidnap their unpopular English teacher to scare him. Unfortunately, the teacher dies of heart failure during the kidnapping. The students are faced with a serious problem.
2. *The Catcher in the Rye,* by J. D. Salinger. Holden Caulfield decides to quit school and have a fling in New York City. He learns a lot about himself, almost too late.
3. *A Separate Peace,* by John Knowles. Gene and Finny are close friends; nevertheless Gene feels a sense of rivalry, an uneasiness about their friendship. Perhaps unconsciously, he triggers an unfortunate chain of events that bring near tragedy to himself.
4. *Native Son,* by Richard Wright. The setting is Chicago during the depression of the 1930s. Bigger Thomas, a Black chauffeur for a wealthy White family, is confused by the contradictions in the White world that he feels shapes his life. He strikes out, with tragic consequences.
5. *Cress Delahanty,* by Jessamyn West. A teenage girl discovers the excitement of life, growing up in Orange County, Califronia, as it was 25 years ago. Her family doesn't always approve of her antics, but you will find many of the book's situations funny, enjoyable.

Sign-up Sheet: Novels

1. *Killing Mr. Griffin*

   a. _____
   b. _____
   c. _____
   d. _____
   e. _____
   f. _____

2. *The Catcher in the Rye*

   a. _____
   b. _____
   c. _____
   d. _____
   e. _____
   f. _____

3. *A Separate Peace*

   a. _____
   b. _____
   c. _____
   d. _____
   e. _____
   f. _____

4. *Native Son*

   a. _____
   b. _____
   c. _____
   d. _____
   e. _____
   f. _____

5. *Cress Delahanty*

   a. _____
   b. _____
   c. _____
   d. _____
   e. _____
   f. _____

Group Instructions

1. *Meet in class in small groups to survey the novel and pose questions to which you want answers. Allow one week to complete the book. (You will have some class time each day for reading.) Plan to devote 3 half-hour meetings to organize the oral presentation based on your reading of the novel; these three meetings will be during class time. The remainder of the meeting time will be on your own time.*
2. *Decide the form your class presentation will take: symposium, panel discussion, debate, role playing, improvisational dramatics, media.*

3. Assign individual responsibilities with specific deadlines for task completion. Some deadlines could coincide with each of your three scheduled meetings.
4. In planning your group project, try to deal with these questions:
   a. How does your novel relate to the unit topic *Moments of Choice?* ⎤
   b. How is your novel like or unlike other selections read in this unit? ⎦———Theme
   c. Keep logs of your feelings and reactions to your novel. The entries in your log may provide you with ideas for the group project: How was I affected by the book?

The short stories discussed in this box are widely anthologized. Many of them can be found in the series, *Voices in Literature, Language, and Composition* (Boston: Ginn and Company, 1969). The Keyes and Bierce stories can be found in volume 4, edited by Jay Cline, Ken Williams, Barbara Mahoney, and Kay Dzuik. The Petracca story appears in volume 1, edited by Jay Cline, Ken Williams, and Dan Donlan. The Guest story appears in volume 3, edited by Jay Cline and Ken Williams. Richard Connell's story can be found in *Adventures in American Literature,* edited by Rawley Bell Inglis et al. (New York: Harcourt Brace & World, 1953). All of the novels discussed are available in inexpensive paperback editions: *Killing Mr. Griffin* (first published in 1978) from Dell, *The Catcher in the Rye* (1951) and *A Separate Peace* (1960) from Bantam, *Native Son* (1940) from Harper & Row, and *Cress Delahanty* (1954) from Avon.

INQUIRY

Inquiry, unlike expository teaching, engages the students actively in problem solving (Clark & Starr, 1976, pp. 224–225). Recognition of a problem occurs after a certain amount of exploration. Students define the problem, state a hypothesis, test the hypothesis, and come to some sort of conclusion. Inquiry is more commonly used in social studies and science, but we can adapt it to the study of literature.

In the unit *Moments of Choice,* students have read literature selections where characters have had to make important decisions. What isn't always clear is the *why* or the *what* of the decisions. In this particular lesson (Box 13.6), Mr. Wallace uses Kohlberg's (1968) stages in moral reasoning from which to draw hypotheses and asks students to determine whether these hypotheses explain why characters in the literature selections made the decisions they did. The teacher (a) reviews the problem posed in the literature selections the students have read; (b) introduces the Kohlberg stages; (c) tests the stages by having the students collect data from the literature selections; (d) has the students form a hypothesis about a character's level of moral reasoning; and (e) has the students test the hypothesis with more examples from the character's moral reasoning. In addition, students can interview people they know and test their levels of moral reasoning. Such an activity is appropriate as the culmination of a unit on decision making.

BOX 13.6. Unit: Moments of Choice
(Inquiry)

Mr. Wallace: The characters in the literature we have been reading so far in this unit have all been tested; that is, they have
had to make important choices. It has been hard to determine specifically what made them choose as they did; their ⎤———— Motivation
reasons are not always clear. ⎦

Lawrence Kohlberg, a psychologist, believes that people make important
moral decisions for a variety of reasons: (1) they act out of fear of punishment, or
out of anticipation of reward; (2) they act to help someone with the idea that they
will be helped in return; (3) they want to be known as "good boys" or "nice
girls"; (4) they act out of respect for law and order; (5) they act out of respect for
their fellow human beings; (6) they act out of a noble and high sense of what is
right. Kohlberg claims that these six reasons are levels or stages that people move
through as they get older. For instance, a small child would tend to act more out
of fear of punishment than out of respect for fellow human beings. Imagine a 5-
year-old boy who decides not to pull his sister's hair because he suddenly discovers his mother watching, not because such a physical assault will hurt his
sister. An adult, on the other hand, would tend to act out of respect for fellow
human beings rather than out of fear and punishment; one would hope that a
husband brings his wife candy and flowers to make her happy, not to atone for
staying out late the night before.

We are going to examine the leading characters of the literature we've been
reading in this unit to see if there is a correlation between age and level of moral
choice.

(At this point the teacher takes the class through filling out the data collection
sheet in Table 13.1).

Mr. Wallace: We've now documented the age (or approximate age) of each of the
leading characters of the literature we've read in this unit. We also have the levels
of moral choice they were operating from. Now can we hypothesize that there is
a correlation between the age of the person and a higher level of moral choice
being used?

(Suggestion: Arrange the characters chronologically by age, from young to
old. Next to their names list their ages and levels of choice. Divide the list in half
at the middle. You now have two populations: younger and older. Determine the
average level of choice with the younger group and compare it with that of the
older group. If the score is higher in the older group, then the hypothesis is
correct. If the score is lower in the older group then the hypothesis is incorrect.)

Mr. Wallace: We began with the idea that as people get older the reasons for making
moral choices tend to be on a higher level. Now the result of our examination of
literature shows some older people are more able to reason at higher moral levels
than younger people, but the evidence isn't conclusive. On the basis of this, do
we wish to form a new hypothesis? If so what would it be? (Writes on blackboard:
New Hypothesis: _____.) Now, how would we go about testing this
hypothesis?

(Suggestions: (1) Students could compile a revised data chart based on the

TABLE 13.1. Data Sheet

Selection	Character	Age	Docu-mentation (page)	Moment of choice (describe)	Docu-mentation (page)	Choice (describe)	Level of choice: 1,2,3,4,5,6 (explain)
"He Swung and He Missed"	Rocco						
"We Wear the Mask"	(unnamed)						
Fahrenheit 451	Montag						
"Sport's Worst Tragedy"	any character						
"Flowers for Algernon"	Dr. Strauss						
"An Occurrence at Owl Creek Bridge"	Peyton Farquahr						
"The Most Dangerous Game"	Rainsford						
"Four Eyes"	Joseph						
"Beauty Is Truth"	Jeanie						
Killing Mr. Griffin	Susan						
The Catcher in the Rye	Holden						
A Separate Peace	Gene						
Native Son	Bigger						
Cress Delahanty	Cress						

new hypothesis and examine 5 or 10 additional selections of literature, filling in the sheets as they go. Perhaps the selections could be ones read prior to the unit. (2) Students could compose a moral dilemma with six possible solutions. They could then field-test the situation by asking 25 or 30 people of various ages to select one of the choices. Students could then correlate the level of choice with the age of the respondent.)

Suggested Moral Dilemma

You are a member of a poor family. Your mother has a high fever and may die if she doesn't get more of a drug prescribed by the family doctor. It is two in the morning. The drug stores are closed and the doctor cannot be reached. No one can help. The corner drugstore contains the needed drug and you know exactly where it's kept. Would you break into the drugstore to get the medicine? Why? Why not?

Suggested Data Collection Sheet

	Respondent	Decision	Reason for Decision	Implied Level of Decision
(Ages 10–12)	1.			
	2.			
	3.			
	4.			
	5.			
(Ages 12–15)	1.			
	2.			
	3.			
	4.			
	5.			
(Ages 16–18)	1.			
	2.			
	3.			
	4.			
	5.			
(Ages 19–25)	1.			
	2.			
	3.			
	4.			
	5.			
(Ages 26–40)	1.			
	2.			
	3.			
	4.			
	5.			

PROJECT METHOD

Once students have learned inquiry techniques they are ready to branch out into more independent learning. The project method stimulates students to perform independent reading to answer a question or solve a problem. Box 13.7 has a project activity, drawn from the unit *Moments of Choice*, that shows how students can actively engage in reading to find answers to questions and solve a teacher-posed problem.

BOX 13.7. Unit: Moments of Choice
(Project Method)

Background: Assume that you are the chairperson of a board of directors of a major manufacturing company. The president of the corporation has just died of a sudden heart attack. The board has decided to hire *outside* the firm. Five finalists have been selected for the position:

Holden, from *The Catcher in the Rye*
Joseph, from "Four Eyes"
Miss Kinnian, from "Flowers for Algernon"
Montag, from *Fahrenheit 451*
Jeanie, from "Beauty Is Truth"

Your Assignment: Select a new president for your corporation.

Assume:
1. All five candidates are 35 years of age.
2. All five candidates have had successful corporate training and experience.
3. You are bound by fair decision-making procedures, including the consideration of Affirmative Action guidelines—that is, equal treatment for women and members of ethnic minorities.

Your president must have:
1. High intelligence
2. Adaptability
3. Rationality when acting under pressure
4. Ability to make competent decisions

You must:
1. Compose a series of questions you would ask in an interview to all five characters above.
2. Compose an imaginary interview with each of the five, indicating how each would respond to your questions. Be sure the characters act consistently with the way they act in the literature you have read about them.
3. On the basis of the interviews and your job criteria, make a choice of a president and defend it.

SUMMARY

Although English integrates the studies of language composition and literature, this chapter focused only on literature. Teachers organize the content of literature by literary type, literary period, or literary theme. The processes of comprehending literature are both cognitive (interpreting, evaluating) and affective (valuing, creating). In illustrating how students learn from literary text, we selected a topical unit—*Moments of Choice*—around which we built single-text strategies (DRA, glosses, reading and learning-from-text guides, and SQ3R) and multiple-text stragegies (concept technique, inquiry, and project method). In the next two chapters, you will see how these seven strategies apply to social studies and science. Since students in literature classes read much nonfiction and technical writing, English teachers might want to read chapters 14 and 15.

ACTIVITIES

1. Using the DRA lesson in this chapter as a model, construct a directed reading activity for a short story that might be added to the unit *Moments of Choice*. Teach the lesson to a small group of English students or to an entire class. List the ways in which you perceive the lesson helps the students.
2. Would SQ3R work if you were teaching students to comprehend detective stories? Give reasons for your answer.
3. Select a poem that you feel would be hard for students to comprehend, and gloss it. To determine the effectiveness of the gloss, have two groups of students read the poem, but only one group use the gloss. Then administer a brief comprehension test for both groups and compare the results.

14 | Social Studies

CHAPTER OVERVIEW

Like English, social studies is an integrated subject. The individual academic disciplines comprising social studies range from history, which can be considered part of the humanities, to psychology, which is a behavioral science. Two conflicting theories on teaching social studies maintain that the content should be taught (a) in integrated fashion, using the "problem" approach, or (b) as a series of discrete academic disciplines. Both theories may be operating even within the same high school department. This disparity of approach, combined with the incredible range of textual materials used in social studies classes, makes teaching the subject a challenge. By reading this chapter, you will get a clearer understanding of how the subject social studies is organized. In addition, you will learn various single-text and multiple-text strategies that will help you teach your students to become independent learners in the social studies.

GRAPHIC ORGANIZER

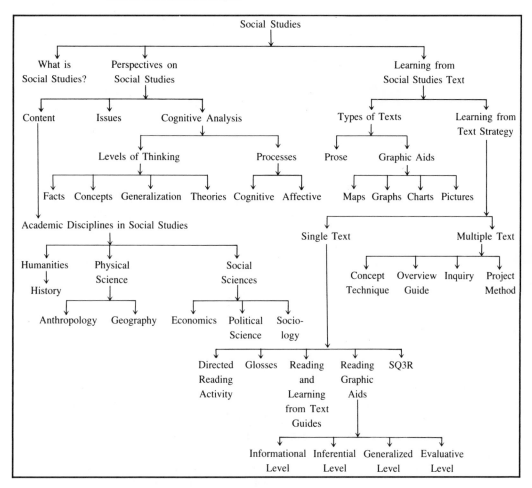

PREPOSED QUESTIONS

1. What are the two theories concerning how social studies should be taught? Which theory do you favor?
2. Social studies students are expected to learn from a wide variety of text forms. What are these various forms?
3. How would you use and sequence single- and multiple-text strategies in teaching your students social studies content?

WHAT IS SOCIAL STUDIES?

> A social studies student is sitting in a classroom, listening to a discussion of the "Teapot Dome scandal." The day has been long, and he is tired. Looking out the window he notices that the steel plant a block away is belching smoke. He has thought about the benefits of having many factories in his home town—he is the son of a foundry worker—but the disadvantages of heavy industry are obvious to him, too. He begins asking himself questions about industry's relationship to the environment, its use of human and natural resources, and its demands on society for governmental services. It occurs to him that he isn't sure how much and what kinds of industry are good for society. (Shive, 1973, p. xi)

Shive dramatizes, in the previous passage, the natural curiosity young people have concerning social problems. Occasionally, curiosity leads to taking sides, and arguments highlight the complexity of the problems. Social studies is that area of the curriculum where students are taught to deal with complex social problems. According to Kenworthy, social studies "is wide as the world and as long as the history of man, yet it can be defined with one word. That word is *people*" (Kenworthy, 1973, p. 5). And since, to paraphrase the words of poet Alexander Pope, the proper study of people is people, what other area of the curriculum deals more directly with the reality of life!

PERSPECTIVES IN SOCIAL STUDIES

If you were to walk into Hedy Davis's fifth-grade class during social studies time, you would probably see the students seated in small groups around tables, sharing newspaper clippings, magazine articles, library books, maps, and charts. The room would be lively, with all students productively engaged in discussion and problem solving. Ms. Davis has divided her students into equal, cross-ability cooperative groups. Each group has been given a "sack of data." Each sack contains information about a particular current event. Newspaper and magazine articles provide recent developments whereas the charts and library books provide the background. Each group is to prepare a panel discussion on the current event data in the sack. To make things livelier, Ms. Davis has offered prizes to each group on the successful completion of the panel discussion. If you were to ask Ms. Davis what her students were doing, she would probably reply that they were learning social studies through critical thinking and cooperative group process. However, Ms. Davis would add that each teacher at her school approaches the teaching of social studies from a different perspective. She would be the first one to admit that social studies is a difficult concept to define. To answer the question "What is social studies?" you must determine, first, the content of the social studies curriculum and, second, the processes students use to deal with the content.

Social Studies as Content

Ehman, Mehlinger, and Patrick (1974) have compiled data that dramatize the lack of consensus regarding the nature of social studies content. They interviewed students who saw social studies as the study of revolutions, wars, and depressions, and felt the focus should be on issues. Kenworthy (1973) notes that teachers often disagree on the content of social studies. On one end of the continuum, he suggests, is the teacher who isolates history from geography, teaching them as separate disciplines. On the other end of the continuum is the teacher who believes "that anything which helps children to become wholesome, worthwhile, contributing members of various groups is a part of the social studies" (p. 3). Ehman and others (1974) quote six leading authorities on social studies education, each with varying definitions of content.

Social Studies and Academic Disciplines

Social studies encompasses many *academic disciplines*. Fraenkel (1973, 1980), for instance, includes under social studies history and social science disciplines—anthropology, geography, economics, political science, psychology, and sociology.

HISTORY

According to Clark (1973), history is the study of facts seen through the eyes of a historian, a "humanistic study of things past" (p. 177). Since, as Wesley and Wronski (1973) point out, the past cannot be observed directly, the historian relies upon "those observations, clues, or traces that are left behind" (p. 153). These historical sources include *records* and *remains*. Clark includes under *records,* three types of tradition—written, oral and pictorial. Written tradition includes documents and reports. Oral traditions are in national and local legends and folk tales. Pictorial traditions are in maps, diagrams, sculptures, and pictures. Unlike records, which purposively are intentional, *remains* such as artifacts and relics tend to be, in Clark's (1973) words, "accidental survivals of the past (p. 178). By critically examining these sources, the historian can reconstruct the story of human life.

Fraenkel (1973, 1980) suggests that the teaching of history can be organized according to generalizations, or major ideas. One such idea is, *Historical events can rarely, if ever, be explained in terms of a single cause.* Using this idea, the teacher trains students to examine historical text as a complex framework of cause and effect. Wesley and Wronski (1973) suggest another major idea: *The past can help us to deal with the present and the future.* Using this idea, the teacher trains students to examine historical text as a data source to solve present problems. Crucial to this approach is student skill at comparison and contrast. For instance, to determine whether Washington's advice to stay out of entangling alliances would work today, students would need to compare the social, economic, and political situation today with that in 18th-century America.

ANTHROPOLOGY

"Anthropology has one foot in the field of science and the other in the domain of the social sciences" (Kenworthy, 1973, p. 20). As a science, anthropology focuses on the physical features of human beings. As a social science, anthropology is concerned with culture, that is, how societies live. Anthropologists gather data from fieldwork, personal observation, surveys, censuses, and psychological tests. Experts in social studies (Clark, 1973; Fraenkel, 1973) agree that anthropology deals with certain major ideas, such as *man has needs; man's needs are satisfied within a social structure; the social structure itself has needs that must be satisfied if it is to persist.*

GEOGRAPHY

Like anthropology, geography is not exclusively a social science. Clark (1973) notes that geography contains elements from natural and biological science as well as from social science. Geography is concerned with *spatial relationships.* Fraenkel (1973) lists certain major ideas shaping the teaching of geography, such as: "The similarities among different areas have been brought about through different combinations of physical, biotic, and societal forces" and "Uniform and modal regions are often related to each other through gravitation to the same central place" (p. 117). Wesley and Wronski (1973) stress two major concepts in teaching geography—*accessibility* (how easy it is to get from one place to another) and *centrality* (how far away in terms of time and distance one place is from another). Village A may be only 3 miles away from village B (centrality) but a treacherous river and an impassable mountain separate the two (accessibility).

For students to understand geography, they must be able to read maps, charts, and graphs. Environmental issues related to geography demand that students engage in critical thinking so they can answer questions such as these:

1. How is population related to the standard of living?
2. Should governments exercise population control?
3. How does overcrowding affect the personality of individuals?
4. What relation exists between population pressures and war? (Wesley & Wronski, 1973, p. 188).

ECONOMICS

Economics is the study of "the ways in which we manage our productive human and natural resources and the goods that result from the employment and use of those resources (Clark, 1973, p. 229). Basically, economics is concerned with supply and demand, or,

1. What shall we produce with our limited resources?
2. How much can we produce and how fast can our economy grow?
3. Who shall get the goods and services produced? (Kenworthy, 1973, p. 22).

Wesley and Wronski (1973) claim that the economist's tools are statistical data, models, and logic. *Statistics* comprises much of the raw data that students deal

FIGURE 14.1. A Circular Flow Model of the American Economy

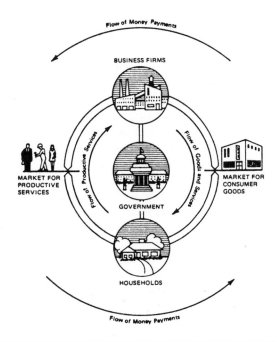

Reprinted by permission of the publisher, from Edgar B. Wesley and Stanley P. Wronski: Teaching Secondary Social Studies in a World Society (Lexington, MA: D.C. Heath, 1973).

with. Students must understand and interpret the data. Pictorial and diagrammatic *models* can sometimes explain complicated economic concepts. In Figure 14.1 is one such model.

Since most students have limited backgrounds in economics, they may often engage in fallacious thinking: One such fallacy "leads many to look upon government fiscal operations as being subject to the same conditions that govern finance, (Wesley & Wronski, 1973, p. 222). For example, we have the fallacious statement that "if the federal government spends more than it takes in, it will go bankrupt."

POLITICAL SCIENCE

According to Wesley and Wronski, political science is concerned with "the institutionalized and informal patterns of power functions in the polity and the behavior of people with respect to these formal and informal patterns, (p. 197). Political science consists of nine fundamental ideas: for example, "As the people's wants enter the political system for satisfaction, they become demands. These demands are screened," (Fraenkel, 1973, p. 112). Clark (1973) maintains that students of political science need to learn (a) how to gather data, (b) how to use political science methods, and (c) how to think critically about political issues. Students of political science gather data from a continuum of sources, from civic documents to novels that deal with political behavior (Wesley & Wronski, 1973).

PSYCHOLOGY AND SOCIOLOGY CONTRASTED

Psychology and sociology are alike in the sense that they both focus on human behavior. Whereas psychology is concerned with the behavior of individuals *per se,* sociology stresses behavior of individuals as members of groups. Wesley and Wronski (1973), admitting that psychology is a relatively new subject in secondary school curriculum, describe several lessons where students deal with psychology content to analyze the nature of *rebellion.* Students begin by reading a technical article that attempts to relate adolescent behavior to social pressure. They examine two case studies of adolescents and then have to decide, using information in the article, which of the two students is more likely to rebel against the system.

Sociology, like psychology, can deal with problems of great concern to adolescents, especially when you consider how important belonging to groups is to most teenagers. Fraenkel (1973) maintains that sociology deals with three major ideas:

1. Values and norms are the main sources of energy to individuals and society.
2. Society's values and norms shape social institutions, which are embodied in organizations and groups, where people occupy positions and roles.
3. People's positions and roles affect their attitudes toward society's values and norms, and result either in support of the existing values and norms, or in demands for modification of them, and the circle starts again.

Students of sociology study or originate questionnaires, interviews, cases, and experiments in addition to performing logical analysis, historical analysis, and content analysis (Clark, 1973).

In Figure 14.2 is a simple diagram that presents the content of the social studies curriculum. It shows that social studies comprise three areas: humanities, physical science, and social science. Each of these areas has its own subfields. Humanities subsumes history. The physical sciences and social studies overlap in geography and anthropology. The social sciences subsume economics, political science, psychology and sociology.

Social Studies and Issues

Whereas some teachers believe that they should teach the individual academic disciplines of social studies separately, many other teachers believe that they must integrate the disciplines in order to analyze social *issues* and solve problems

FIGURE 14.2. The Subfields in the Social Studies Curriculum.

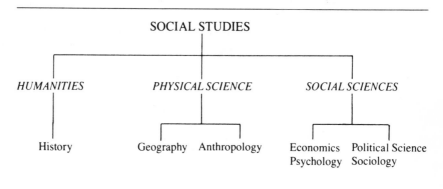

(Sanacore, 1982). Consider the issue we presented at the opening of this chapter: *How much industry is good for society?* Such a complex issue involves more than the *economics* of supply and demand. It also includes knowledge of the effect of industry on the physical environment (geography) and the effects of heavy industry upon the personalities of urban dwellers (psychology). How management and labor view expanding industry is the subject of sociology. How government policy regulating industry is influenced and implemented is a concern of political science. According to Shive (1973), "There are no economic, political, social, or anthropological issues. There are only issues with economic, political, social, and anthropological dimensions (p. 16).

Social Studies and Cognitive Analysis

LEVELS OF THINKING

Social studies content has four levels of knowledge: facts, concepts, generalizations, and theories (Fraenkel, 1973, 1980).

Facts According to Fraenkel (1973):

> . . . are what logicians refer to as contingent statements or testable propositions. Their proof is contingent upon the presence or absence of empirical evidence with which any disinterested or nonpartial observer would agree (p. 93).

Here are some examples of social studies facts:

1. Columbus discovered America in 1492. (history)
2. The distance from Modesto, California to San Francisco is 93 miles. (geography)
3. In 1941, a loaf of bread cost about 12 cents. (economics)

All higher learning in social studies is based on factual knowledge. However, when teachers make students ''learn the facts,'' the teachers should have a clear idea of what the students are expected to do with them.

Factual learning by itself has limited value. Facts have to be organized into some type of framework; otherwise the universe will appear chaotic and random.

Concepts

A *concept* becomes our way of giving the universe some type of organization. More specifically, ''Concepts . . . are mental constructions invented by man to describe the characteristics that are common to a number of experiences, (Fraenkel, 1973, p. 95). Here are social studies concepts that encompass, respectively, the facts in the list above:

1. exploration (history)
2. centrality (geography)
3. prewar prices (economics)

The attention that social studies teachers give to the teaching of technical vocabulary reflects their interest in concept development. In learning about government, students soon realize that *democracy, referendum, congress,* and *propaganda* are basic ideas, not merely hard words to look up in the dictionary.

Generalization

When concepts are in some valid relationship, they form a *generalization.* Even more than concepts do, generalizations provide a structure for data. Consider these generalizations:

1. During the Renaissance, European rulers sought to extend their influence by exploring new continents. (history)
2. Modern highway construction has eliminated many geographical barriers to direct travel. (geography)
3. The expenses of World War II caused much worldwide inflation during the middle and late 1940s. (economics)

Theory

Just as a generalization represents a set of interrelated concepts, a *theory* represents sets of interrelated generalizations. Social studies theories might include:

1. Given social, political, and economic conditions at home are prerequisite for a country's colonial ambitions. (history)
2. As geographical barriers are eliminated, rapid communication among disparate cultures ensues. (geography)

FIGURE 14.3. Relationships Among Four Levels of Thought.

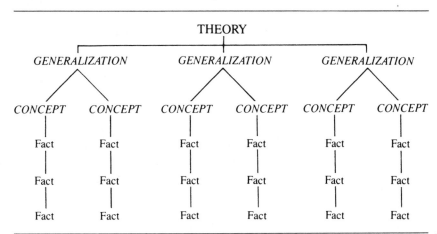

3. When a country engages in war, it begins to destroy its economy. (economics)

In summary, the diagram in Figure 14.3 represents the relationships that exist among the four levels of thought.

SOCIAL STUDIES AS COGNITIVE ANALYSIS

Whether teachers present social studies as separate academic disciplines, as issues, or as levels of ideas, students have to *process* the content, both cognitively and affectively.

Cognitive Processes

Here are some steps in processing social studies content:

1. *Identifying and Gathering Data:* Students first need to get the facts. Facts are in a plethora of sources: newspapers, textbooks, maps, charts, reports, court transcripts, television and radio broadcasts, graphs, films, records, biographies.

2. *Interpreting Data:* Students need to deal with two questions. First: What are the data? Second: What do the data mean? For instance, a graph might indicate that the rate of growth for Company A is higher than that of Company B. But what if Company A is a local corporation, employing 45 and Company B is an international firm, employing 3 million? Data *say* A is faster growing than B. However, the data *mean* that is it is easier for a smaller company to grow at a *faster rate* than it is for a larger company. The data *do not mean* that A is necessarily on sounder economic ground.

3. *Analyzing Data:* After students make inferences about what the data say and mean, they can move to more intense examination. For instance, in a political speech, a senatorial candidate asserts that he is a proponent of Civil Rights. Students wishing to test the truth of the assertion will look for substantial evidence in the text of the candidate's speech and check that evidence against previous speeches the candidate has made, voting record, news stories, and editorials about the candidate. In effect, analyzing data involves collecting evidence to substantiate truth or falsity of the data.

4. *Judging Data:* After students have gathered, interpreted, and analyzed data, they need to judge the worth of them. For instance, assume students are looking for a worthy corporation to invest imaginary money in. Stock market data and company financial reports suggest that Blaylock Automobiles is a fast-rising corporation where investments can double in a short period of time. Two editorials in newspapers mention Blaylock by name. The first, written by a prominent economist, warns the public against speculative automobile investments, especially with government restrictions on fuel consumption. The second, written by a prominent investment broker, claims that the automobile industry is the surest investment for quick return on investments. The answer to the question "Is Blaylock a good investment?" will become evident in time, but a shrewd student-investor will weigh the authority of the economist against that of the broker and make a choice.

5. *Hypothesizing from Data:* After judging data, students can develop informed opinions or generalizations about data:

   a. Companies with less than 5,000 employees tend to grow at a faster rate than do companies with more than 5,000 employees.

   b. Political candidates who emphasize Civil Rights in their speeches sometimes mask their true feelings as documented by prior words and actions.

   c. In times when fuel shortages exist, automobile industries become poor investments for short-term speculators.

6. *Testing Hypotheses:* Perhaps the most exciting aspect of social studies is testing original hypotheses. After students develop informed opinions, they can test their opinions by repeating the process of identifying and gathering, interpreting, analyzing, and judging data, and perhaps even forming new hypotheses.

An Affective Process: Valuing

Social studies is concerned with human behavior. When human beings interact, potential for controversy exists as stated in the old aphorism: *No two human beings are alike.* What makes people differ, primarily, is their value systems—what they like, dislike, stress, ignore, treasure, discard. The study of controversies on *valuing in social studies* can lead to these interesting questions:

1. Were the colonies justified in wanting independence from Britain?
2. In a democratic society, does a monopoly have a right to exist?
3. Does a democracy eventually legislate freedom away from the people?
4. Is public welfare in violation of the democratic spirit?
5. Is foreign investment in American business helpful or distructive to our economy?

To facilitate the controversial handling of values in the classroom, students can engage in values-clarification activities (Simon, Howe, & Kirschenbaum, 1972). Such activities not only help to clarify for students what their own values are but also educate students in how to deal with values different from their own. One such exercise, *values whips,* has the teacher firing rapid, short-answer, values questions at students in the classroom. The questions may put students on the spot, but they make them aware of their values. Here are some examples: What is something you are proud of? What is something you really believe in strongly? What is some issue about which you have taken a public stand recently?

Students should reflect on their own values to see how valuing could affect the way they function in society.

LEARNING FROM SOCIAL STUDIES TEXT

Types of Text

What kinds of text are social studies students likely to use? The answer, of course, rests with the teacher. Some teachers use a single textbook, such as the one used in chapter 6. Other teachers may draw on additional materials such as newspapers, magazines, novels, government reports, court transcripts, even the *Congressional Record.* These book and nonbook texts impart information principally through prose and graphic aids.

PROSE

Most of the material that social studies students encounter is written in prose— descriptions of historic events, case studies, transcripts, explanations, comparisons and contrasts, and examples. Shepherd indicates that social studies students who have learned to read story-type material and acquired literary concepts in the earlier grades will be "faced with factual prose jammed with data when they enter high school social studies class" (Shepherd, 1978, p. 188). The principal problem the students will have with social studies, Shepherd claims, will be their lack of background to understand the concepts. In addition, students will find it difficult to deal with vocabulary, sentence structure, and ideational relationships with paragraphs in social studies texts (Baumann & Serra, 1984; Donlan, 1980).

Vocabulary is a three-level problem. First are those general words which are unfamiliar to the students, such as *constraint, ubiquitous, prerequisite.* Second are those words that have both general meanings and technical meanings, perhaps confusing the students, such as *revolution, principal, initiative.* Third are words that stand for abstract concepts, such as *democracy, propaganda, referendum.*

Sentence structure can present reading problems even to students who understand the vocabulary contained in the sentence. Consider these examples.

1. Not only was the general ill-advised in attacking the fort, he was also ignorant concerning battle conditions, including climate, with which he was excusably unfamiliar, and land forms, with which he was inexcusably unfamiliar.

2. Contrary to public opinion, Senator Clotz, long an opponent of public welfare programs, voted against the Welfare Reform Bill for reasons no one here, at least at the Capitol, can understand.

As you can see, the two sentences given contain no particularly difficult vocabulary, but they do contain difficult grammatical structure. Note especially the internal phrases set off with commas, such as "with which he was excusably unfamiliar" and "at least at the Capitol." Had the two passages been written in simpler sentences, using the same vocabulary, students would no doubt comprehend the meaning more readily. For example, compare these paragraphs with originals.

1. The general was ill-advised in attacking the fort. He was also ignorant of battle conditions. For example, he was excusably unfamiliar with the climate, but he should have been more familiar with the land forms.

2. Senator Clotz has long been an opponent of public welfare programs. However, contrary to public opinion, he voted against the Welfare Reform Bill. No one at the Capitol seems to understand his reasons.

Students also have problems understanding *how ideas relate to one another* in a paragraph. Generally, when students understand the *structure of paragraphs,* they can also understand how ideas within that paragraph relate. Chapter 9 "Letting the Students Do the Writing and Listening" goes into great detail on the organization of paragraphs as well as how transition expressions (*first, second, on the other hand*) clarify for the reader how sentences within a paragraph relate.

Shepherd (1973) indicates that social studies texts have certain, recurring specific patterns of thinking and writing, such as *cause and effect, sequential events with dates, comparison/contrast, detailed statement-of-fact, propaganda, fact/opinion.* To understand these patterns, students need to (a) recognize main ideas, (b) draw inferences, (c) understand relationship of time, place, and events, (d) anticipate outcomes, and (e) make evaluations (Thomas & Robinson, 1972).

GRAPHIC AIDS

In addition to the prose social studies texts, students must use maps, graphs, charts, pictures and pictorial models to get information. According to Edward Fry (1981) students must have "graphical literacy."

Maps

According to Shepherd (1973), students may encounter as many as 13 types of maps, ranging from street maps to weather maps. Each type of map presents a specific kind of information. General map skills students will need include understanding north-south, east-west direction; comprehending longitude and latitude; using scales and keys; locating places; making inferences from symbolic and abstract representations.

Graphs

Graphs generally present information, usually numerical information, along vertical and horizontal axes. Students must be able to translate spatial and symbolic representations into verbal statements and then draw information from these. Later in this chapter, we present a lesson on reading graphs.

Charts

Charts contain pictorial, verbal, and numerical information arranged in such a way that its mere visualization assists the reader in understanding the information. Look at the example in Table 14.1.

Pictures

All too frequently, students skip the pictures in texts, mainly because they assume the pictures are not relevant to the text. Teachers need to prepare students to use the pictures by making sure they understand the objects in the pictures and by asking questions that demand inference.

TABLE 14.1. Rutland Motors Sales Records (In Millions of Dollars)

Year	Tractors	Trailers	Trucks
1930	90	10	70
1940	80	30	40
1950	65	50	20
1960	53	70	10
1970	21	90	0

Learning-from-Text Strategies

Teachers can help students by teaching them how to learn from their social studies textbooks. Suzanne F. Wade (1983) reviewed numerous research studies that focused on how students learned in social studies classes. She discovered that when teachers taught students how to learn from social studies text, both their achievement and reading scores increased.

So far, this chapter has discussed the content of social studies, the learning processes necessary to get students to interact in a meaningful way with social studies texts, and the specific learning skills students need to comprehend a wide variety of social studies text material. Now you will see how we can apply these single- and multiple-text strategies (DRA, glosses, reading guides, SQ3R, the concept technique, inquiry, and the project method) specifically to social studies text.

Chapter 6 has already provided you with an abundance of single-text strategies and multiple-text strategies for teaching social studies material. However, the focus was on teaching only *one chapter* out of *one particular history textbook*. Here the focus is on teaching a wide variety of social studies materials over the school year, using the phase-in/phase-out procedure dealt with in chapter 12.

SINGLE-TEXT STRATEGIES

As we noted in chapter 13 "English Language Arts," a teacher who has a classroom of students with a wide range of learning abilities ought to begin by having the students read from the same text at the same time with the help of single-text strategies. Early in the school year, the DRA and glosses provide specific and direct guidance. A little later in the year, the teacher might introduce reading guides—first for use by the entire class, second for small groups of students, and third for individuals. When the students can work on reading guides individually, they can begin to use SQ3R. We now demonstrate how to use each of these single-text strategies in a sequence for teaching social studies.

Directed Reading Activity

DRA is an effective strategy to use when introducing the class to their first reading assignment in a textbook. As we noted before, students find social studies text material difficult because it is replete with factual data condensed into a few words. An entire battle of the Civil War can be "told" in five or six densely packed sentences. A complete chapter of this type of condensed writing can present many problems to less able students who look on all words, all sentences, all ideas as being of equal importance. With the DRA, the teacher (a) explores the students' backgrounds to see what personal experiences they are approaching the chapter with and (b) builds the background they need. While students are (c) reading the chapter, either in class or at home, the teacher can guide them with preposed questions. After the students have read the chapter, the teacher can engage the students in (d) discussion and (e) other follow-up activities that extend their understanding of the chapter.

In Box 14.1 is Ms. Jones's DRA lesson on "Explorers of the Western Hemisphere," the first chapter in *Quest for Liberty* (Chapin, McHugh, & Gross, 1971). As you read through the lesson, try to imagine yourself teaching activities to a junior high school history clas.

BOX 14.1. *Class: American History (DRA)*

"EXPLORERS OF THE WESTERN HEMISPHERE"

(pp. 10–39)

I. Ms. Jones explores students' backgrounds.
   A. She shows the students a series of pictures or slides depicting strange or exotic, deserted geographical locations (desert scenes, surface shots of the moon or Mars, tropical jungle). She then poses these questions:
      1. What do all of these pictures have in common? (They are out of the way, weird, scary, deserted, strange.)
      2. How would you feel if you, alone, suddenly found yourself in the middle of one of these places? What would you do?
      3. If you moved around in your surroundings, what might you expect to find in the way of (a) people, (b) animals, (c) buildings, (d) plants?
   B. *Ms. Jones:* What you have just described to me is called *exploration* — that is, moving around in strange surroundings trying to find out what's there. Today, there are very few areas on earth that are unexplored. But if you still wanted to be an explorer, where would you most likely go? (the ocean, outer space.) I would now like you to see this movie about the 1969 landing on the moon. As you know, Mr. Armstrong was the first human being, we believe, that put a foot on the moon. As you watch the film, try to put yourself in his place as he walks around in a totally strange atmosphere. What sorts of things might you have expected to find?" (Ms. Jones shows the film and then reposes the questions.)

II. Ms. Jones builds students' background.
   A. Ms. Jones summarizes the previous experience and introduces the chapter: "If you find your exploration of the moon frightening as well as thrilling, you are no different from the early explorers of the Western Hemisphere (pointing to the Western Hemisphere on a map). In olden days, people used to think the world was *flat* and that if you sailed too far you would drop off the edge of the world and into the clutches of monsters. You can imagine what courage it took the early explorers to sail into unknown lands, not knowing what danger awaited them. The chapter you are about to read talks about the early explorers of the Western Hemisphere and what they found.
   B. Ms. Jones next gives the students an overview of the chapter by having them read the summary on page 36 and by showing them the various old maps and pictures that form the chapter's abundant illustrations.
   C. Ms. Jones reviews with the students difficult vocabulary they will encounter—hard general words and the technical vocabulary, which is clearly explained in context on the textbook pages indicated in parentheses below:

| | Technical Vocabulary |
Hard General Words	Explained in Context

<table>
<tr><td>

1. debate (p. 12)
2. encounter (p. 13)
3. influence (p. 15)
4. flourished (p. 17)
5. smelted iron (p. 21)

</td><td>

1. authentic (p. 12)
2. archeologists (p. 13)
3. cultures (p. 15)
4. data (p. 21)
5. primary sources (p. 21)
6. secondary sources (p. 21)
7. standards and values (p. 25)
8. environment (p. 29)
9. technology (p. 30)

</td></tr>
</table>

D. Ms. Jones gives the students a few preposed questions to guide their reading:
  1. How much of the Western Hemisphere was explored between 1450 and 1620?
  2. What types of good information sources do we have today to let us know what these early explorations were like?

III. The students read the chapter in class or at home, using any of the following strategies:
  A. The students can be assigned the entire chapter to read overnight at home.
  B. The teacher can assign the first part of the chapter for in-class reading, with the remainder to be completed for homework.
  C. The entire chapter can be read in class over one or more class periods.
  D. Since the chapter is long, the teacher can break the assignment into smaller units and intersperse discussion sessions.

IV. Ms. Jones has the students discuss the chapter.
  A. Informational Level Questions
    1. What explorations of the Western Hemisphere took place before the time of Christopher Columbus?
    2. What evidence is there to verify these earlier explorations?
    3. What explorations of the Western Hemisphere took place after the time of Christopher Columbus?
    4. What two kinds of sources do historians refer to when they attempt to reconstruct the past?
    5. What are the two kinds of environment that this chapter discusses with respect to the Western Hemisphere?
  B. Inferential Level Questions
    1. Why are historians referred to as detectives?
    2. Suppose that you want to find out why explorers voyaged to the Western Hemisphere. For which group of explorers would you be most likely to find more evidence — pre-Columbus explorers or post-Columbus explorers? Why?
    3. What arguments would you use against the statement: "All secondary sources are worthless?"
    4. If you were an archeologist, would you be more interested in the physical environment or the cultural environment? Why?

C. Generalized Level Questions
  1. The year is A.D. 4000. You, as a historian, are given the task of determining how extensive the exploration of the moon was in the 20th century. What primary sources would you use? What secondary sources?
  2. Describe the physical environment of the town or city where you live. What sorts of things would you include in your description of the cultural environment of your community?

V. Ms. Jones has the students do activities that extend their understanding of the chapter.
  A. Discussion and dramatics
    1. Assume that Leif Ericson and Christopher Columbus had an argument over which of them actually *discovered* America. Dramatize this debate, using information from the textbook to support the claims of either explorer.
    2. Suppose that a time machine has moved you ahead 3,000 years and has dropped you on a strange planet. Enact a skit in which you and several companions explore the unknown planet. Be sure to include elements of both physical and cultural environment that you might encounter.
  B. Writing, drawing, construction
    1. Construct a map of your town as you think it might have been 1000 years ago. Imagine a civilization living there and how their community might be laid out. Construct a diorama of this community using a shoe box.
    2. Create a primary source document that would question Columbus's claim to discovering America and support the claim of Sir Winston Pilgrim, a little-known English explorer of the 13th century.

Glosses

As with the directed reading activity, glosses provide students with guidance, but without teacher-student interaction. *Glossing* gives the students marginal aids to comprehension (defining difficult words, clarifying difficult concepts, asking provocative questions). Some teachers underline main ideas to help students skim or scan the text. The teacher can effectively gloss a chapter in different ways: (a) by having students write in the margins of their books (if the school district permits); (b) by preparing ditto guide sheets aligned with text margins that students can insert between text pages; (c) by listing the glosses on a separate study sheet, with appropriate cross-references to text pages, columns, and paragraphs. It is much easier, though, to gloss shorter text items, such as newspaper clippings. In Box 14.2 is a gloss of a newspaper clipping that (a) guides the student to the main points of the article, (b) provides definitions and clarification, and (c) shows the student the process of reading a newspaper article.

BOX 14.2. Text: News Story (Gloss)

PLANE WITH 156 ——————— Eye-Catcher
HIJACKED IN INDIA

Flight Believed Seized ⎤ Additional eye-
by Japanese Leftists ⎦——————— catching material

From Reuters ——————— News service
agency

Place from which ←— Tokyo — A Japan Air Lines DC-8 was
story was released

hijacked today shortly after takeoff   A four-engine
jetliner.
from Bombay and the airline said (un-

Rumored or ⎤ confirmed) reports indicated it had   Par. 1. *Lead* Who?
unchecked ⎦ What? Where?
been seized by members of the radical   This sentence
contains the key
Japanese Red Army guerrilla group.   information.

How would you The airline said the hijackers had or-
like to be on that dered the aircraft, carrying 142 passen-
plane?
gers and 14 crew members, to head   Par. 2. Further
information but
toward its scheduled destination of   less important
than the lead
A city in Thailand —— Bangkok. The flight originated in Paris
with a final destination of Tokyo.

Why do you think The number of hijackers and their
so much of this demands were not immediately known,
story contains
unconfirmed but the airline quoted an unconfirmed   Par. 3. More
facts? information but
report from a Bombay air traffic con-   less important
than par. 2
troller that they were members of the

ultra-left Red Army. Airline spokes-

For some reason, men said the pilot had sent a signal
he didn't want to about the hijacking, but declined to
go into more
detail. elaborate.

This must have The aircraft at one stage turned back   From here on the
confused the information
passengers. toward Bombay but then changed   becomes less
important.
course again for Bangkok.
Note: News story
The first report of the hijacking   writers are trained
to put the most
came in a brief radio message from the   important
information at the
aircraft's pilot to the Bombay airport   beginning
because editors
control tower.   trim the stories
from the bottom.
Japanese airliners have been hi-

jacked in the past by Red Army guerril-

This is not the first hijacking. Should this type of terrorist activity be dealt with severely? How? What can be done to discourage it?

las, but the most recent such incident was more than seven years ago, in March, 1971.

The extreme-left Red Army, which advocates "world simultaneous revolutions" through armed actions, has carried out several guerrilla operations in different parts of the world.

The most spectacular was the massacre at Israel's Lod airport in May, 1972, when three Red Army guerrillas killed 25 people and wounded more than 80 others. Two of the terrorists were killed.

Other operations included an abortive attack on an oil refinery in Singapore in 1974, an attack on the French Embassy in The Hague, Netherlands, later that year, and a raid on the U.S. Embassy in Kuala Lumpur, Malaysia, in 1975.

News stories must contain facts, not opinions, unless they are quoted from people whose names appear in the story.
Bad Journalism: The Red Army is a pack of gangsters.
Good Journalism: "The Red Army is a pack of gangsters," said Barry Philbein, an airlines ticket agent.

Article reprinted by permission of Reuters, from the *Los Angeles Times* (September 28, 1977), pp. 1, 14.

Reading and Learning-from-Text Guides

After you have used the DRA and glossing techniques, you could begin using reading and learning-from-text guides in the classroom, implementing a phase-in/phase-out procedure. Chapter 7 presents a number of guides which you can use in teaching a chapter from a history text. You might want to review that chapter before reading the remainder of this section.

Since graphic aids are a significant part of social studies text, this chapter presents *processes-of-reading guides* that teach students how to read and learn from graphs. In Box 14.3 is a processes-of-reading guide that Ms. Jones used to teach students graph reading.

BOX 14.3. Subject: Business and Government (Learning guides)

THREE PROCESS GUIDES

for Learning to Read Graphs

Version A: Teacher presents guide to entire class.

Lesson Objective: The purpose of this lesson is to teach you how to read the graph in figure 1. To begin, you will learn to read some simple scales.

FIGURE 1. Comparative Sales Figures for Rutland Motors' Tractors
            and Trailers over the Past 40 Years.

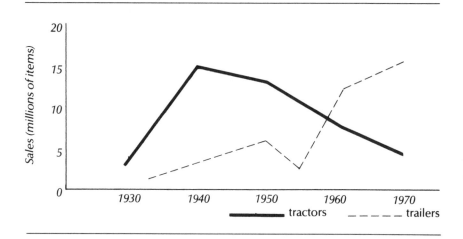

Activity 1: Learning how to read graphs is easy once you learn how to read scales. Look at each of the scales in figures 2 and 3. Then answer the questions that follow.

FIGURE 2. Scale on the Dashboard of an Automobile.

| 0 | 10 | 20 | 30 | 40 | 50 | 60 | 70 | 80 | 90 | 100 | 110 |

1. If you saw the scale in figure 2 on the dashboard of an automobile, what sort of scale do you think it would be?
2. The line that ends at 60 tells you what information?

FIGURE 3. Scale on the Outside of a Building.

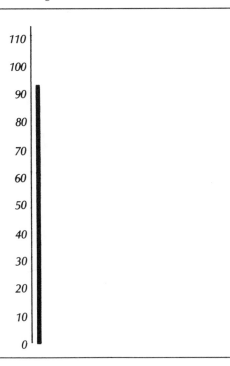

3. If you saw the scale in figure 3 on the outside of a building, what sort of scale would you think it would be?
4. The line that ends at 90 tells you what information?

Activity 2: In Activity 1, you learned that you can read information on scales going across, or *horizontally,* and up-and-down, or *vertically.* Dots, or other marks, on the scale give you specific information about that scale. The horizontal scale, or speedometer, in figure 2, showed you that the driver was going 60 miles an hour. The vertical scale, or thermometer, in figure 3 showed you that it was 90° F. Each of the scales in figure 4 has dots placed on it. See if you can read the information correctly.

Activity 3: So far you have learned to read scales, both horizontal and vertical. But a scale can give you only one type of information. What would happen if you put two scales together — one horizontal scale and one vertical scale?

Result: By putting the two scales together you make a *graph* like the one in figure 5. A *graph* has two lines of information — one horizontal and one vertical. When you put dots on graphs you show the *relationship* that exists between the information on the vertical scale and the information on the horizontal scale. Examine the graph in figure 5 and answer these questions:

FIGURE 4. Three Types of Scales.

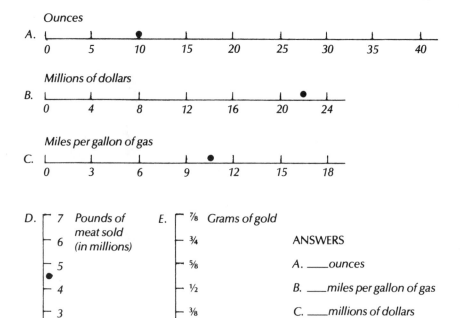

FIGURE 5. Dots, Intersection Points, Alone on a Scale.

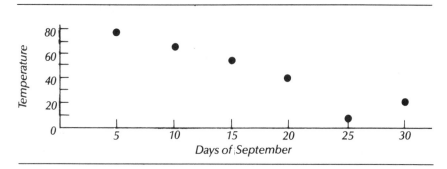

1. How hot was it on the fifth of September?
2. How hot was it on September 30?
3. As the month of September moved along, what was the general tendency of the temperature? What was the one exception to this tendency?

So, the preceding graph told you the relationship between *temperature* and *different days in September*. From this information (dots) you drew the inference that *with one exception, the weather became cooler between September 1 and September 30*. Figure 6 shows the same information in two different forms. Because dots on graphs tend to be hard to read, graphmakers tend to (a) connect the dots with straight lines, as in *A* in figure 6, or (b) highlight the dots with heavy bars, as in *B* in figure 6. *A* is a *line graph* and *B* is a *bar graph*. Sometimes, the dots do not appear on graphs—just the lines or the bars.

FIGURE 6. Two Ways of Graphing the Same Information.

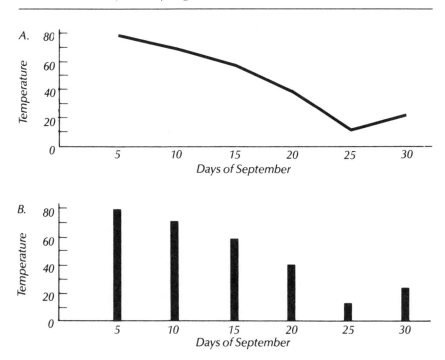

Activity 4: Now return to the graph in figure 1. Examine the graph and answer the following questions:
1. What type of information is on the horizontal scale?
2. What type of information is on the vertical scale?
3. When the two scales come together, as in this graph, you are trying to find out the relationship that exists between _____ and _____.
4. First look at the solid line on the graph that represents *tractors*.
   a. In what year did Rutland Motors make its *best* sales in tractors? How many were sold?
   b. Other than in 1930, in what year did Rutland Motors make its *worst* sales? How many tractors were sold?

    c. Between what years did the sale of Rutland's tractors boom?

    d. What has been the trend in sales since 1940?

5. Now look at the broken line on the graph that represents *trailers*.

    a. In what year did Rutland Motors make its best sales in trailers? How many were sold?

    b. In what year did Rutland Motors make its worst sales in trailers? What could account for those low sales?

    c. Between what years did Rutland's trailers experience a strange sales pattern? What do you think happened then?

6. Suppose you were on the board of directors of Rutland Motors. What recommendations might you make concerning the manufacturing and sales of tractors? About the manufacturing and sales of trailers?

Activity 5: Select either the information about *tractors* or the information about *trailers* and convert it from its present form, a line graph, to a bar graph.

Reading Graphic Aids

Students frequently do not pay attention to graphic aids in textbooks. First, students may not know how to read them and extract information from them. Second, students may think of graphic aids as pictures, rather than as abstractions of complex concepts and their relationships in the form of symbols, numbers, lines. These features of graphic aids need to be stated. Students have to identify the symbols, numbers, lines, and bars and state the information they represent. Next they must interpret and infer relationships, and finally draw whatever general conclusions are appropriate from the data in the graphic aid. After all this, the student can make judgments and evaluations. Teachers frequently do not teach students to get information from graphic aids, perhaps because they assume that students already know how to read and learn from them.

The strategies for teaching a text can be applied to teaching graphs. Box 14.3 shows a processes-of-teaching guide on graph reading. The process of reading graphs and learning from any graphic aids can be taught in other ways. For example, a DRA technique for a learning-from-text guide could show students how to read a specific graphic aid located in the textbook. Regardless of strategy, you want the students to (a) know what the aid says (informational level of understanding), (b) know what the information in the aid means (inferential level of understanding), (c) generalize or apply knowledge about the aid to another situation (generalized level of understanding), and (d) evaluate the information and make judgments based upon the information, interpretation, and generalizations drawn from the aid. For example, let's focus on graphs:

Informational Level. To know what a graph says, students must know how to read the horizontal and the vertical axes and translate this information into words. See how to teach the reading of graph axes and how to identify the information in the graph by examining Box 14.3, *Activities 1 and 2.*

Inferential Level. To know what a graph means, students must understand the relationships that exist between the horizontal and vertical axes and be able to express those relationships in words. See how to teach students to draw inferences from graphs in *Activities 3 and 4.*

Generalized Level. After students learn to read axes and extract meaning from them, students can generalize about what they have learned from them.

Evaluative and Judgmental Levels. Next, students can evaluate the information from the graph and make judgments by applying the information to the solution of a problem. See *Activity 4, Item 6* and *Activity 5.*

Although we have concentrated on graphs, the same procedure of moving from informational level of inferential level to generalized level can be applied to pictures, charts, and maps (Estes, 1973).

SQ3R

The reason for sequencing DRA, glosses, and learning guides is to move the students from dependence to independence in learning. SQ3R requires students to become more independent. It teaches them to find answers to their own questions. In Box 14.4 is Ms. Jones's lesson on ''The Civil War and Reconstruction'' [Chapter 10 of *Quest for Liberty* (Chapin, McHugh, & Gross, 1971)]. It demonstrates how to teach students the SQ3R technique.

BOX 14.4. Course: American History (SQ3R)

''THE CIVIL WAR AND RECONSTRUCTION''

1. Ms. Jones has the students *survey* the chapter, particularly the headings, by asking questions like these:
   A. When you see the chapter title ''The Civil War and Reconstruction,'' what do you think is to be reconstructed? What had been destroyed?
   B. Look through the pictures of the chapter and note their captions. What impressions are you left with? What questions are raised in your mind about the Civil War and the Reconstruction period that followed?
2. Ms. Jones has the students ask themselves questions they want to find answers for. These questions might be some that emerge from their survey of the chapter headings and graphic aids.
   A. What were some of the harmful effects of the Civil War and Reconstruction on the South? On the North?
   B. What was the effect of Lincoln's assassination upon the politics of the South? Of the North?
3. Ms. Jones instructs the students to *read* the chapter to find answers to their questions. (If the teacher wishes, students can write the answers to their questions when they finish reading.)
4. Ms. Jones then has the students *recite* their answers to questions in a variety of ways. Students can submit their written answers or share differing questions and answers with classmates in total class or small group discussion.

5. Ms. Jones invites the students to engage in "review" projects such as these:
   A. Do additional outside reading on topics of particular interest: Lincoln's assassination, the KKK, Mitchell's *Gone With the Wind*, W. E. B. DuBois, Booker T. Washington.
   B. Reread the chapter to come up with further insights.

The chapter under discussion in this box is chapter 10 in Chapin, McHugh, and Gross, *The Quest for Liberty*, pp. 296–327.

MULTIPLE-TEXT STRATEGIES

So far, you have been educating your students in how to comprehend social studies text material independently. DRA, glosses, guides, and SQ3R have been used in single-text situations. Now your students should be ready to work independently in multiple-text situations. We will describe three strategies: the concept technique, inquiry, and the project method.

Concept Technique

Even though you have been teaching students to be independent learners, you may still find that they have wide differences in learning ability. In this case, your job is to allow all of your students the opportunity to engage in independent learning, but at differing levels of difficulty. A good method for providing for individual differences without stigmatizing students is to have each student select what he or she will read. Then all the students who have selected the same book will form discussion groups. You might provide four or more reading selections that vary in difficulty, introduce the four selections to the class as a whole, and permit each student to choose one of the four. In Box 14.5 is Ms. Jones's self-selection/self-grouping strategy for social studies.

BOX 14.5. *Unit: The Faces of War*

Ms. Jones: So far the entire class has been reading the same sources. Now you are going to be asked to select one particular source from a group of four that deal with the unit's theme, *The Faces of War*. Before you decide which source you want to read, you will probably want to know what each one is about. You will receive a guide that gives you an overview of each source. Later, I will pass around a sign-up sheet. You will indicate your choice on this sheet by signing your name. You will later form groups according to the text-source you select. Your group will then plan a presentation for the rest of the class.

OVERVIEW GUIDE

Sources for *Faces of War* (World War II)

1. *Anne Frank: A Portrait in Courage*, by Ernst Schnabel. This is not the diary, but it is a sensitive description of the young girl who wrote the diary, then left it behind on her way from Amsterdam to a Nazi prison camp. Schnabel gives you a keen insight into the personal feelings of the teenage girl who was forced to live in hiding in an attic apartment for 3 years because she was Jewish. Although she died in March, 1945 in the concentration camp at Bergen-Belsen, she lives today in the hearts of all who understand and appreciate courage.
2. *Hiroshima*, by John Hersey. An unforgettable account, nonfictional, of the horrible aftermath of the destruction of the Japanese city of Hiroshima in the closing months of World War II. Descriptions of pain and suffering are graphic. This book is not for the squeamish.
3. *Up Front*, by Bill Mauldin. Strangely enough, war can have its humorous side. Read of the hilarious misadventures of Willie and Joe, two soldiers in World War II who get themselves into ridiculous situations. You may have seen the movie made from this book.
4. *Brave Men*, by Ernie Pyle. Ernie Pyle was a war correspondent during World War II. He was killed before the war ended. However, he managed to set down memorable portraits of fighting men he knew. This book gives you a rare insight into what war is really about.

Sign-Up Sheet for *Faces of War* (World War II)

Instructions: Select one of the four sources below and sign your name under it. You and other classmates who select the source will be asked to (a) discuss the story in small groups, the discussion to be based on answers to questions your group has preposed; (b) plan a discussion, debate, dramatization, or media presentation; and (c) present your project to the rest of the class.

1. *Anne Frank, a Portrait in Courage*
   a. _____
   b. _____
   c. _____
   d. _____
   e. _____
   f. _____
2. *Hiroshima*
   a. _____
   b. _____
   c. _____
   d. _____
   e. _____
   f. _____
3. *Up Front*
   a. _____
   b. _____
   c. _____
   d. _____

e. _____

f. _____

4. *Brave Men*

a. _____

b. _____

c. _____

d. _____

e. _____

f. _____

Of the books discussed in this box, *Anne Frank* (first published in 1958) and *Hiroshima* (1946) are available in inexpensive paperback editions, Schnabel's book from Harcourt Brace Jovanovich and Hersey's from Bantam. *Up Front* (1945) was reissued in hardcover by Norton in 1968. *Brave Men* (1943) is out of print, but should be available in most libraries.

Inquiry

As we noted in chapter 13 "The English Language Arts," inquiry is the direct opposite of expository teaching. With inquiry, students engage actively in problem solving. Recognition of a problem occurs after a certain amount of exploration. Students define the problem, state a hypothesis, test the hypothesis, and come to some sort of conclusion. Look at Ms. Jones's inquiry lesson in Box 14.6.

Project Method

Once students know how to engage in inquiry, they are ready to branch out into more independent learning. The project method motivates students to perform independent reading to solve problems. In Box 14.7 is Ms. Jones's project activity that shows how students can become actively engaged in reading for problem solution.

BOX 14.6. *Unit: The Rights and Privileges of Voting*

INQUIRY

Ms. Jones: So far in this unit we have been reading and talking about what it means to be able to vote, the rights and privileges, one of which is the right to a secret ballot. In line with this last right, here is a clipping from a recent newspaper in which this right has been challenged. Read the clipping and we'll discuss the questions that follow it:

Court may jail citizens who refuse to reveal how they voted

By THEODORE ILIFF

ANN ARBOR, Mich. (UPI) — Who is correct — the defeated mayoral candidate who says he has the right to know whether the 20 votes illegally cast were for him or against him? Or some of the 20 voters, who say they will go to jail rather than give up their right to a secret ballot?

That dilemma comes up in Circuit Court this week, and stands a good chance of winding up in the state Court of Appeals.

For the 20 voters, the dilemma is more than academic, because they are facing contempt of court citations that could put them in jail. One 21-year-old college woman already has spent 90 minutes in handcuffs for refusing to tell her vote.

The candidate, Louis Belcher, a Republican, lost by one vote to Democratic incumbent Albert Wheeler in last April's mayoral race. Belcher immediately went to court alleging voting irregularities.

In July, election officials admitted that 20 residents of unincorporated "township islands" were registered as legal city voters but actually were not entitled to vote. Officials emphasized it was the city's error, not the voters'.

But how can the 20 votes be thrown out if it isn't known what they were?

That's what Belcher is trying to find out in court and last week, Susan VanHattum, a 21-year-old University of Michigan junior, was asked in court how she voted. The question was based on a 1929 state court ruling that illegal voters could not keep their ballots secret.

When VanHattum refused to answer, Visiting Circuit Judge James Kelley cited her for contempt. She was handcuffed and confined in his chambers for 90 minutes. He then freed her, giving her until tomorrow to change her mind.

Diane Lazinsky, a UM research assistant, also balked at the same question. Although spared the handcuffs, she was given the same ultimatum. Three other witnesses revealed their votes.

Belcher, a 38-year-old management consultant, said he had a sinking feeling as VanHattum quietly insisted on her right to secrecy.

"I don't want to see anyone go to jail," Belcher said in an interview. "But now that it's out, I assume the judge will go through with this.

"Once the question was asked and (VanHattum) refused to reply, there was nothing I could do. It became a matter between the witness and the judge, and I felt kind of helpless."

Other than Belcher, few principals want to discuss the case. Kelley, Wheeler, and both of the women are avoiding publicity.

"I've caught a cold, I can't get any sleep and I've fallen behind in my school work," VanHattum said. "I'll do all my talking in court."

The American Civil Liberties Union said it would ask the state Court of Appeals today to take control of the case on grounds Kelley ignored the 1963 state constitution and later laws mandating ballot secrecy.

However, Belcher, while regretting the threat to witnesses, said he would not budge from his contention that the election was invalid.

He said the rights of legitimate city voters also were at stake in the case that already has cost him $13,000 in legal fees.

"The rightful electorate has a right to know how the ballots were cast," he said. "What rights of the 21,000 legal electorate are being violated? Right now there is no way of saying if the people of Ann Arbor have had their say on who is going to be mayor."

Questions

1. Before we consider the problem, let's deal with certain basic facts as presented in this newspaper article:
   a. What election is the focus of this problem?
   b. What was the final result of the election?
   c. Who challenged the results of the election?
   d. On what grounds did he challenge the election?
   e. What court did he go to for satisfaction?
   f. What did Judge Kelley insist that those who testified tell him?
   g. On what legal precedent did Judge Kelley act?
   h. Why did some of those who testified refuse to answer the judge's question?
   i. What happened to those who refused to answer?
   j. What was the reaction of the election officials?
   k. What was the reaction of the American Civil Liberties Union? What was their legal precedent?
2. Now that we understand the facts of the article, we can begin discussing the problem. The problem occurs because a number of individuals and groups are

asserting what they believe to be their rights. Review the article again and finish the incomplete sentences below, in addition to citing any page references from your textbook and supplementary sources that support the individual's rights.

a. *Louis Belcher* claims, "I have a right to know _____

_____ , because _____
(what has he a right to know?)

_____ .
(state what you think are his reasons)

Textbook pp. _____ support Belcher's rights. (Other sources _____.) Textbook pp. _____ do not support Belcher's rights. (Other sources _____.)

b. Judge Kelley claims, "You voted illegally; therefore, you must tell me _____ because _____
(what does he want to know?)

_____ .
(what are the judge's reasons?)

Textbook pp. _____ support the judge's right to information. (Other sources _____.)

Textbook pp. _____ do not support the judge's right to information. (Other sources _____.)

c. Susan VanHattum and Diane Lazinsky claimed, "We don't have to tell you _____ , because _____ ."
(what information?) (give their reasons.)

Textbook pp. _____ support the two women's rights.

(Other sources _____.)

Textbook pp. _____ do not support the two women's rights. (Other sources _____.)

3. You now have (1) the facts of the case, (2) the issues involved, and (3) some legal grounds for making a court case. Suppose the case is moved to the state Court of Appeals. Also suppose that you are the judge that hears the case.

a. Would you defend Judge Kelley's right to obtain ballot information from the unqualified voters? _____ yes _____ no. Why? _____

_____

b. Would you defend VanHattum's and Lazinsky's right to remain silent? _____ yes _____ no. Why? _____

_____

Ms. Jones: Now that each one of you has "judged" the case, let's see how the class as a whole voted. How many of you favored Judge Kelley's right to obtain information? (Ms. Jones tabulates the vote.) How many of you favored the two women's right to keep silent? (Ms. Jones tabulates the vote.) What we have here is a ratio: the number who favor the judge as opposed to the number who favor the two women: (5 to 30 or 12 to 23 or 15 to 20). You are all high school government students who have voted on this case. Do you think other people, for instance, high school students who have not had a course in government, would vote in the same proportion? Why or why not?

(Ms. Jones engages the students in discussing why the other students might or might not vote in the same proportion. The following hypothesis is formed and Ms. Jones writes it on the board: "Given the information in the Belcher case, students not taking government will respond differently than students taking government.") How would we go about proving this? For instance, what does "respond differently" mean and how will we know if they do respond differently or not? Should we form more specific hypotheses? *(The class refines the first hypothesis into the following more workable hypotheses, which Ms. Jones writes on the board.)*

1. Given the information in the Belcher case and asked to support either the judge or the two women, nongovernment students will support the judge in a (greater, lesser) proportion than did government students.
2. Given the information in the Belcher case and asked to support either the judge or the two women, nongovernment students will support the two women in a (greater, lesser) proportion than did government students.
3. When asked to give reasons for their decision, nongovernment students will cite personal feelings and emotions rather than personal knowledge of law and government.

Ms. Jones: Now how shall we go about determining whether our hypotheses are correct? Here is a suggestion: Each student in the class can contact another student who has not had government, ask the other student to read the editorial, and decide either in favor of the judge or the two women, giving reasons. Then we can collect and tabulate the results in class.

Article reprinted by permission of United Press International, from the Riverside (California) *Enterprise* (October 10, 1977), p. A-3.

BOX 14.7. *Unit: Industry and Ecology (Project)*

Instructions: Assume that you are the president of Rutland Motors, a company that manufactures trailers and tractors. Business is going so well that you would like to recommend to the board of directors that a new plant be opened. The board agrees in principle, but requests that you prepare a report on each of three possible sites: Sacramento, California; Mobile, Alabama; and Detroit, Michigan. At the conclusion of the report, you are to rank the three sites according to the following criteria:

1. Potential for business opportunities in the area, particularly the lack of competition from similar industries, that is, other tractor or trailer companies.
2. Favorable environmental impact studies, that is, how civic organizations would react to having your plant in their area, with regard to pollution, noise, and use of the area's human and natural resources.
3. Accessibility to raw materials and effective transportation and shipping systems. Prepare such a report. Use textbooks, encyclopedias, maps, atlases of the area, information you can get from chambers of commerce. The final report should be about five pages that contain the necessary information the board wants to know.

SUMMARY

Social studies, like English, is an integrated subject. Two conflicting theories about teaching social studies advocate respectively (a) presenting the content as separate disciplines and (b) focusing on problems and issues. The processes students use in learning social studies are both cognitive (gathering data and so forth) and affective (valuing and so forth). In learning from social studies text, students encounter prose and graphic aids. Prose text includes textbooks, magazines, newspapers, and government documents. Graphic aids include maps, graphs, charts, and pictures. In teaching students to learn from text, teachers whose students have a single text may use DRA, glosses, guides, and SQ3R. If students have multiple texts, teachers may use the concept technique (self-selection/self-grouping), inquiry, and the project method.

ACTIVITIES

1. Using the DRA lesson in this chapter as a model, construct a directed reading activity for a social studies chapter. Teach the lesson to a small group of social studies students or to an entire class. List the ways in which you perceive the lesson as helpful to the students.
2. Select and gloss a newspaper article or editorial that you feel would be difficult for students to comprehend. To determine the effectiveness of the gloss, have two groups of students read the article, but have only one group use the gloss. Administer a brief comprehension test for both groups and compare the results.
3. Construct a processes-of-reading guide that teaches students to learn from a graphic aid (map, chart, graph). Use the guide with a small group of social studies students and describe the ways in which the guide helps the students learn from the graphic aid.

15 Science

CHAPTER OVERVIEW

Most students have a natural curiosity about scientific principles—What keeps airplanes aloft? What makes trees grow? Why is the sky blue? What keeps the earth from disintegrating? Answers to these universal questions can be found in science texts. Unfortunately, the reading difficulty of most science materials (caused by condensed and technical language) prevents many students from satisfying their curiosity by reading and learning from science texts. This chapter demonstrates how teachers can make science textbooks more understandable to their students. After you read this chapter, you will understand a number of methods for helping your students learn from science texts.

GRAPHIC ORGANIZER

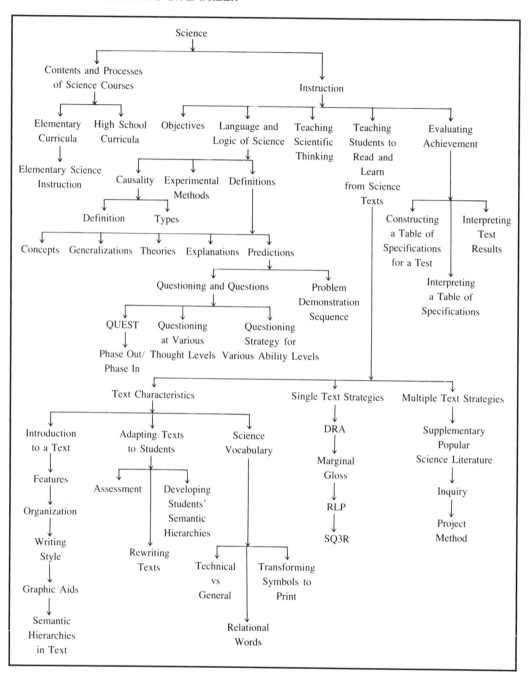

PREPOSED QUESTIONS

1. Does the elementary science curriculum provide the concrete foundation for the high school curriculum?
2. What are the objectives of science instruction? The concept of causality and scientific methods?
3. What are some methods for teaching scientific thinking, that is, for teaching students to form concepts, generalizations, and theories?
4. What are the features of a science text?
5. How would you adapt a text to fit students and vice-versa?
6. What instructional strategies would enable you to teach students with a wide range of reading abilities to read and learn from texts?

Although natural and life sciences are organized into three branches of knowledge—physics, chemistry, and biology—these branches are nevertheless interrelated. The interrelationship occurs in such courses as physical chemistry and biochemistry. Yet, even when divided up, year-long courses in physics, chemistry, and biology are still so broad that instructors and texts have to be selective in the topics they can cover. This selection is apparent in an examination of curricula developed for these subjects.

CONTENTS AND PROCESSES OF SCIENCE COURSES

Elementary Curricula

Elementary schools usually adopt science texts that publishers claim are graduated in difficulty from Grades 1 to 6. The gradation tries to take into account the reading and the conceptual levels of the students. The reading levels are based upon readability formulas that essentially use two indices of reading difficulty: word frequency and sentence length (See chapter 10 for readability formulas). Words that occur frequently tend to be concrete; hence, word frequency is an indication of a word's level of abstraction. Sentence length is an index of complexity of thought because longer sentences frequently involve subordination. Of course, some frequent words may be very abstract and some short sentences may involve a complex thought, such as Shakespeare's famous sentence, "To be or not to be—that is the question."

However, word frequency counts have been based essentially on literary, not on scientific terms. Because scientific words do not appear frequently in the literature sampled for word frequency counts, use of these word frequencies for science materials is inappropriate. When they are used, they often give science materials a higher level of difficulty than they deserve. Consequently, instead of indicating grade level correspondence of their texts, some publishers only indicate their sequential levels.

Science textbook writers also try to take into account conceptual levels of difficulty. Although they strive to write textbooks that progress from concrete to more abstract levels of thought, there is no precise way of measuring conceptual levels of difficulty.

Moreover, levels of thought may be domain-specific and therefore a separate metric would be required for each domain. If we had such separate metrics for each domain, we would probably find that individuals have a profile of conceptual abilities. A profile with high scores in one domain and low scores in another would probably mean that a person may be able to think at an abstract level in one domain or content area, but not in another. We might also find that children's developmental experience repeats the world's development of knowledge. For example, in the domain of science, children might think the world is flat and only gradually learn to think of it as a sphere; they might egocentrically think of the sun as revolving about the earth and later adopt the heliocentric view of the earth. In short, their acquisition of knowledge is a function of their ability to form increasingly more abstract knowledge structures and to restructure or re-organize their hierarchy of knowledge structures as they develop (Vosniadou & Brewer, 1987).

When information on children's development of science knowledge becomes available, we will be better able to relate science texts to students' cognitive developmental levels. In general, elementary science texts begin at a concrete, observational level of thought and introduce concepts from a wide range of science. This range is discernible in the scope and sequence charts for two widely used science textbook series that are shown in Box 15.1. Space permits showing only the beginning level, 1, and the last level, 6, from their scope and sequence charts.

BOX 15.1. *Scope and Sequence Charts for Two Widely Used Elementary Science Textbook Series for Grades 1 through 6*[1]

Textbook Series	*Content*	*Levels*	
		1	6
Harcourt Brace Jovanovich	Life Science		
	Plants and Animals	More Plants More Animals	Living things Interdependence
	The Environment	Earth, Our Home	Earth's Biomes
	The Human Body	Growing up Healthy	Bacteria Viruses Genes
	Earth Science		
	Planet Earth	Rain and Shine	Energy from stars
	Space	Day and Night	Energy—over time
		Earth, Long Ago	
	Physical Science		
	Matter	Matter all around you: solids, liquids, gases	Electrical energy
	Energy		Light-radiant energy
		Push and pull; Friction	
		Down and Up: gravity	
Silver Burdett	Life Science		
	Plants	Many kinds of Plants and Animals	Plant growth and responses
	Animals		Life processes
	Ecology	Learning about our world (the senses)	Climate and life (Biomes)

Textbook Series	Content	Levels	
		1	6
	Physical Science		
	Matter	Describing things	Matter and Atoms
		Living and not living	Chemical changes
	Energy	Moving things	
	Earth Science		
	Earth	Comparing rocks	Earth's resources and crust
	Space	Observing sun and moon	Exploring space
	Weather	Observing weather and seasons	Forecasting weather
	The Human Body	Investigating, and taking care of the body	Body control systems
		Learning through the senses	Growth and development of the new organism

[1]HBJ Science (Levels 1–6). San Diego, CA: Harcourt Brace Jovanovich, 1985.
Silver Burdett Science (Kindergarten through Grade 6). Morristown, NJ: Silver Burdett, 1985.

Comparison of these charts indicates that the topics and their placement are very similar. In both charts, the progress in conceptual levels is also very similar. In general, both curricula begin by developing the observable and tangible evidence and end by introducing more abstract concepts.

Instruction in Elementary Science

Because scientific terms do not occur in the vocabulary used in basal readers for teaching reading, they have to be taught in science classes. Elementary science teachers not only have to teach students to identify scientific terms, but they also have to teach the meaning and interrelationships among these terms. To do so, they will have to use the same procedures for teaching word identification and word meaning that occur in teaching beginning reading (See chapter 4, part I, oral reading instruction; part 2, word meaning, and part 3, concept development for objects). The knowledge acquired from such instruction will tend to increase students' word identification and vocabulary abilities, and also the background knowledge that readers require for making inferences as they read. In short, instruction in science, as well as in other content areas, expands students' potential for reading and learning from texts in general. In fact, when elementary schools were matched with socioeconomically and ethnically similar schools in the Los Angeles Unified School District, the schools that had a broad curriculum that included instruction in basic skills of reading, writing, and arithmetic plus science, social studies, art, and music were significantly higher on inferential comprehension at the end of sixth grade than schools that had increased ''time on task'' to focus on basic skills and therefore had a narrow curriculum that excluded instruction in science, social studies, and the fine arts. (Singer et al., 1983).

Thus, instruction in elementary school science increases the word recognition, word meaning, and informational background that students have to mobilize for reading and learning from texts. It also provides the foundation for the high school curriculum in science.

High School Curricula

Box 15.2 summarizes three courses developed by scientists and teachers working together in a large-scale, federally funded project. These scientists and teachers cooperated to develop courses that would better prepare students at the high school level for future careers as scientists (Heath, 1964). The physics course was organized around the two theories of how light travels. The emphasis in the chemistry and biology courses was on methods of inquiry. All of these courses recognize that the role of scientists is to produce knowledge. Moreover, each of the three courses recognizes that as a result of conducting experiments students are likely to gain a better understanding of current scientific theories, laws, and concepts, and learn how to acquire and modify scientific knowledge. Perhaps the lab activities and the job of discovery, particularly when supplemented by encouragement from an enthusiastic instructor, will help students identify with the role of scientists and foster careers in science. Essentially, these federally funded science courses do not stress mastery of content, but use of content for learning how to learn principles and procedures that will generate knowledge. Although the three courses have unique problems, concepts, procedures, and instruments for laboratory investigations, they do have some features in common: (a) they all contain theories, generalizations, and concepts about ultimately observable events; and (b) they all rely upon the scientific method as a way of determining whether explanations are supportable or not.

BOX 15.2. Outline of Natural and Life Sciences Curriculum Revisions Under the National Defense Education Act

   I. *Physical Sciences Study Committee Curriculum (PSSC)*
      A. *Organizing Concepts*
         1. Two theories on how light travels (the wave and particle theories)
         2. Theory of the atom

    B. *Topics*
        1. Optics
        2. Wave theory
        3. Newton's Laws of Thermodynamics
        4. Electric forces
        5. Atom
    C. *Collateral Reading*
        1. Sound
        2. Electric circuitry
        3. Theory of relativity

II. *Chemical Education Material Study Curriculum (Chem Study)*
    A. *Organizing Concepts*
        1. Experimental approach
            a. Perform experiments prior to reading about them in the text. Purpose: to emphasize discovery approach to learning; to collect and analyze data in order to answer questions to unknown problems; and to formulate data-based generalizations.
            b. Teach students to distinguish between observation and interpretation.
        2. Arrange the series of 44 experiments in hierarchical order with decreasing teacher direction and increasing student mobilization of cumulative knowledge and procedures gleaned from previous experiments. (Phase out teacher/phase in student.)
    B. *Three Phases in the Organization of Text and Related Experiments*
        1. Phase I
            a. Atomic-molecular theory
            b. Chemical reactions
            c. Gas phase
            d. Kinetic theory
            e. Condensation phase
            f. Atom structure
            g. Periodic table
        2. Phase II
            a. Energy
            b. Rates
            c. Equilibrium
            d. Chemical calculations
            e. Atomic theory and structure
            f. Molecular structure
            g. Bonding
        3. Phase III: Application of principles developed in Phases I and II to chemistry of typical elements and their compounds.

III. *Biological Science Study Committee Curriculum (BSSC)*
    A. *Organizing Concepts*
        1. Topics
            a. Organic evolution
            b. Nature of racial and individual differences
            c. Sex and reproduction in the human species
            d. Population growth and control

2. Emphasis on biology as experimental science with methods of inquiry
   a. Controlled experimentation
   b. Confirmable, accurate, and quantifiable observation
   c. Mathematical analysis of data
3. Divided scope of biology into three courses
   a. *"Yellow" Course:* Initially: Genetic and developmental knowledge. After revision: Cellular approaches and integration of biochemical with biological processes.
   b. *"Blue" Course:* Initially: Biochemical and physiological topics. After revision: origin of life and its evolution, and nature of scientific inquiry presented like a detective investigation.
   c. *"Green" Course:* Ecological and evolutionary approaches. (No revision.)
4. Themes included in courses
   a. Interdependence of structure and function
   b. Regulation and homeostasis
   c. Genetic continuity of life
   d. Evolution of life
   e. Diversity of type together with unity of pattern
   f. Biological roots of behavior
   g. Relation of organism to environment
5. Treatment of topics
   a. Levels of organization: molecular to ecosystem
   b. Stages of process: chemical reaction through ontogenetic growth and development to evolutionary changes.
6. Laboratory
   a. Demonstrations
   b. Use of microscope
   c. Dissection of plants and animals
   d. Labeling drawings and learning names
7. Use scientific method to investigate
   a. Growth of microbes
   b. Nutrition
   c. Interaction
   d. Amount of growth and development
   e. Interdependence of structure and function
8. Develop logic of scientific inquiry
   a. Observation, collection of data, hypothesis formulation, design and control experimentation to test hypothesis.
   b. Concepts of causality: factors, multiple causality, time sequences, negative causation, and feedback mechanisms.
   c. Quantitative relationships: linear and experimental, rate and rate of change, limits and constants.
   d. Function in biology: evidence of doubtfulness, argument from design, argument from adaptation.

Descriptions of curricula in this box were taken from Heath (1964). Congress passed the National Defense Education Act in reaction to Russia beating the United States in the race to outer space by launching Sputnik in 1957. The Act aimed to improve the education of future scientists, engineers, and mathematicians, in part by developing better high school courses. The development of these courses was extremely expensive: $6,000,000 to construct the physics course; another $6,000,000 to train teachers in how to teach the course!

In contrast, traditional science courses emphasize content. Some of these courses organize their content in accord with, for example, a definition of physics as a study of matter and energy and the transferability or conversion of energy into heat, electricity, light, sound, and mechanical forces. Topics in such a physics course would be matter, molecules, fluids, solids, gases, heat, sound, light, magnetism, electricity, electronics, and radiation. Texts for courses like this present these topics in a didactic way rather than promoting discovery. See *Elements of Physics* (Boylan, 1962) for an example.

Traditional courses and curriculum in science continued in many high schools during the great curriculum revision of science in the 1960s. Now those schools that tried the new courses have tended to return to traditional courses as funds became unavilable for purchasing lab equipment, films, and in-service training for teachers—all necessary features of the new courses.

INSTRUCTION

Objectives

However, in either type of course or at the elementary and high school levels, even though the emphases may differ, students must (a) learn definitions for technical terms and symbols; (b) become knowledgeable about the concept of causality, scientific methods, measurement devices and units, and how to apply them (See Box 15.3 for steps in an experimental scientific method, the definitions of these steps, and their application to a particular problem); (c) develop familiarity with a selected set of theories, generalizations, and concepts; and (d) learn to use knowledge acquired to analyze, compute, interpret, and generalize from data frequently presented in the form of charts or graphs (See Social Studies, chapter 14, and especially Box 14.3, for procedures on teaching students to read and learn from charts and graphs.)

Language and Logic of Science

CAUSALITY

Definition of Causality

Causality is an action (A) that regularly produces an effect (E). When we say that *A produces E,* we only mean that when A occurs in close temporal contiguity with an object, we can *predict* that E will probably follow; in short, causality means that there is a *predictable* or *functional* relationship between a cause and its effect (Schlick, 1949).

The terms *necessary* and *sufficient* are used to define the type of relationship between a cause and its effect. If A is a necessary condition for an effect, then each time an *A* occurs, an *E* follows. For example, decoding printed words in sequence (*A*) is a necessary condition for reading (*E*).

Although *A* may be necessary, it may not be sufficient to produce an effect. For example, decoding (*A*) is necessary for reading comprehension, but not sufficient. We also have to have other factors, such as vocabulary, syntax, and reasoning processes co-occur.

If two or more actions (*A, B*) could produce the same effect, then we infer that either *A* or *B* is *sufficient* to produce *E* but neither is a *necessary* condition for *E*. For example, phonics (*A*) or making an inference from context (*B*) could result in the decoding of a word (*E*).

But if and only if *A* produces *E*, then *A* is a necessary *and* sufficient cause of *E*. Thus, a temperature below 32 degrees at sea level in close temporal contiguity with a container of fresh water (*A*) constitutes the necessary and sufficient conditions for freezing the container of fresh water (*E*).

Types of Causality

Several types of causal relationships can be identified:

a. *Undirectional:* *A* causes *E*. For example, Boyle's law: If the volume is kept constant, then an increase in temperature (*A*) will increase the pressure (*E*).

b. *Bidirectional* (mutual and reciprocal): *A* causes *E* and *E* in turn has an effect upon *A*. For example, phonemic awareness, the ability to segment words into their constituent sounds (Test item: Say ''sand'' without the *s*), will facilitate acquisition of phonics instruction (learning letter-sound relationships) and phonics instruction, in turn, will improve phonemic awareness.

c. *Multiple factors:* $A + B + C \ldots + N$ cause *E*. Example: reasoning, vocabulary, morphemics, graphophonemics, and desire to know and understand are factors that cause or predict reading comprehension.

d. *Time Sequence:* *A* causes *B, B* causes *C, C* causes *D.....E*. Parents (*A*) read to children, which gets them ready to learn to read (*B*), this readiness enables them to be successful in early instruction in reading (*C*), which leads them to engage in lots of reading (*D*) and as a result they become fluent in reading (*E*-1) and develop a wide range of knowledge (*E*-2) that combine as multiple factors to make them better able to comprehend and learn from text (*F*).

e. *Concomitance*. If two phenomena vary commensurately, then either may be the cause or effect of the other, or both are connected through some fact or causation. Thus, concomitance or correlation between two phenomena does not constitute causation. The only claim that can be made is that two phenomena (*C* and *E*) are *not* causally related, if *C* varies, but *E* does not.

CANONS OR RULES FOR EXPERIMENTAL INQUIRY

The purpose of the canons or methods is to determine for each appropriate factor considered as a possible cause whether the factor is *invariably* related to the effect. Invariability or regularity between cause and effect means that (a) each time a cause occurs, the effect should also occur and (b) if the cause does not occur, neither should the effect. Also, we should not observe (c) the cause occurring, but no effect and (d) the cause not occurring, but the effect appearing. Thus, the methods are useful for eliminating some or all the alternative hypotheses for a given phenomenon. The problem in having the methods be useful for discovery or proof of knowledge is to formulate and include in the alternatives a suitable hypothesis from which the phenomenon can be shown to be a consequence. In other words, for each experimental inquiry we would have to start by stating the proposed causal hypotheses ($H_1, H_2, \ldots H_n$) for explanations of the phenomenon (P).

1. *Method of agreement.* If two or more instances of a phenomenon are all in agreement that they have only one circumstance in common, then the circumstance is a cause (C) or effect (E) of the observed phenomenon. The method requires that the instances be *unlike* in every respect except one. This method is faulty because it assumes that the effect has only one cause. Nevertheless, the method is useful because it can eliminate proposed causes that do not meet the essential condition of invariability, that is, nothing can be a cause for an effect, if the cause does not occur each time there is an effect.

2. *Method of difference.* If two sets of individuals are alike in all respects save one (C), and for each difference we observe an effect (E), the difference is the cause or an indispensable cause of the effect. The way we achieve two groups alike is to *randonmly assign* students to experimental and control groups, provide the treatment (C), and then test both groups for effects (E) of the treatment. We expect that the difference between the treatment and control groups will be greater than chance. The design would be:

Groups	Treatment (C)	Effect (E)
Experimental	Yes	Yes
Control	No	No

Note that the canon allows for the factor to be a *partial* cause, that is, it may be a necessary condition but it may not contain the sufficient conditions for the effect. This method is useful for eliminating proposed causes under the rule that nothing can be the cause of an effect if the effect does not occur when the supposed cause does. It can only be a method of proof or discovery if we have tested for possible elimination all the alternatives including the factor which is in fact the cause. Hence, experimenters use this design to try to eliminate or falsify a causal hypothesis. If it cannot be falsified, then it is "tenable," that is, the experimenter "holds" the hypothesis, which implies that it will be held only until it is falsified.

3. *Method of Concomitance.* When two phenomenon or vairables vary together in some particular way, then one may be the cause or the effect of the

other or they are connected with each other through some causal factor(s). In other words, for each increment in variable A there is a corresponding positive or negative increment in variable B, but the cause(s) for the variation may be due to other factors.

The statistical procedure for this method is correlation. For example, speed and comprehension in reading are correlated. That is, if you rank students in speed of reading, you will find that their rank in comprehension is similar. However, correlation does not necessarily imply causation. That is, increases in speed of reading are not necessarily the cause of increments in comprehension, or vice-versa. They vary together because "they are connected with each other" by factors that are common to both of them, such as general intelligence, vocabulary ability, general knowledge, and automaticity in word recognition (Holmes and Singer, 1966). This method is valuable for eliminating irrelevant circumstances because nothing can be a cause for an effect if one varies but the other does not vary concomitantly. (Consult an introductory statistic text for formulas on computing correlations.)

4. *Method of Residues.* This canon states that you subtract from any phenomenon the part that you know from previous knowledge to be the effect of certain causes, and the part remaining is the effect of the remaining causes. A classic example of this method is that the planet Neptune was discovered by predicting that the perturbation in the orbit of Uranus was caused by a planet of the size and distance from Uranus that Neptune would be. When the astronomers looked at the predicted point, they discovered Neptune. Their reasoning was based on the fact that the Sun (A) and the planets within the orbit of Uranus (B) had a calculated effect on the orbit of Uranus. But the observed effect (X) was greater than predicted. So C (Neptune's gravitational effect on Uranus) was postulated as the cause of the additional effect or perturbation. The magnitude of the effect was calculated as $[C = X - (A + B)]$.

APPLICATIONS OF EXPERIMENTAL METHODS

To test the unidirectional type of causality (A causes E), we can use the classical method of difference, also known as the rule of the single variable (the treatment or instructional difference). In this method, as explained in Box 15.2, all relevant factors or variables that may also be causes for an effect are held constant (equal for both groups), then, if the experimental variable (A) produces an effect (E), the hypothesis is tenable. We can infer that A probably causes E.

However, we have not proven that A causes E. We have only not experimentally eliminated A as a possible cause of E. For example, we can test the unidirectional hypothesis that phonics instruction will improve students' phonemic awareness. We can test this hypothesis by randomly assigning half the beginning readers to instruction in phonics and the other half could have some irrelevant instruction, such as learning numbers. After the experimental group has reached a criterion in learning phonics, then we would test both groups' phonemic awareness. The design for this experiment is:

	Teach	Test
Experimental Group	*A*	*E*
Control Group	—	*E*

For bidirectional causality, we can use the classical design, but we first measure A and then teach E; next we retest A. Thus, we can determine whether phonemic awareness facilitates acquisition of phonics, and whether phonics instruction, in turn, increases phonemic awareness. For example, we assess beginning first graders and find those who have some degree of phonemic awareness. Then we assign them randomly to the experimental and controls groups (A1, A2). We also assign to the experimental group and control group first graders who are not phonemically aware (B1, B2). We then teach phonics (E) to the experimental group for a given number of trials.

We then compare A1 and B1 of the experimental group on phonics achievement to determine whether there is a significant difference. We would expect A1 to be significantly better on phonics achievement than B1. We then retest the phonemic awareness of both the experimental and control groups (A1 vs A2 and B1 vs B2) to determine whether the experimental groups are significantly better on phonemic awareness than the control groups. We would expect A1 to have improved significantly over A2, and B1 over B2.

	Test *PA*	Teach and Test Phonics	Test *PA*
Experimental Group	*A1,B1*	*E*	*A1,B1*
Control Group	*A2,B2*		*A2,B2*

Thus, we can infer whether phonemic awareness facilitates learning phonics, and whether phonics acquisition, in turn, produces an improvement in phonemic awareness.

We use a statistical procedure to test for the significance of a difference; that is, to determine whether the difference is probably due to chance or not. A difference that is statistically significant is defined by convention as one that would have occurred by chance five or fewer times in 100 for the size of the sample.

However, even if we have obtained a statistically significant difference, we have not proved that phonemic awareness is the cause of success in phonics instruction or that phonics instruction is the cause of improvement in phonemic awareness. Another factor, such as greater conceptualization ability (discrimination, abstraction, and generalization), may be causally related to both phonemic awareness and phonics instruction, and this common factor is more closely related to A1s, Es, and A2s. (For experimental and quasi-experimental designs in education and their strengths and limitations, see Campbell and Stanley, 1963).

The method of concomitance asserts that variation in A is functionally related to variation in E. If A increases or decreases, then we expect a commensurate increase or decrease in E. If the hypothesis is tenable, then students with more of A, such as phonemic awareness, should have attained significantly more phonics achievement than those with no phonemic awareness (control group). Statistical procedures of correlation, single and multiple, and their transformation into regression equations for predicting effects are classified under this canon.

However, concomitant variation does not mean that phonemic awareness causes phonics achievement. We have already pointed out that another factor, common to both A and E, may be the causal factor.

In the method of residues, we have factors that we think are additive and each additional factor influences the effect (E). For example, we may randomly assign students to three groups. The random assignment means that the groups are comparable in an infinite number of ways. However, we can check after random assignment to determine that the mean, standard deviation, and shape of the test distributions are identical, that is, not statistically different for the three groups. Then one group is a control, the next group gets word meaning instruction (WM) and the third group gets instruction in both word meaning and a strategy for comprehending (CS). Then we test the reading achievement (Ach.) of the three groups. After transforming raw scores into standard scores, we can substract the achievement of Group I from Group II to find the achievement attributable to CS. Then we subtract the achievement of the control group from Group 1 to find the effect of word meaning instruction on achievement. The experimental design is the following:

	Training	Test
Experimental Group 2	WM and CS	Ach.
Experimental Group 1	WM	Ach.
Control	(None)	Ach.

Thus, scientific inquiry seeks to determine cause and effect relationships. The relationships may be necessary, sufficient, or necessary and sufficient. To determine the relationship, we use experimental methods that are based on rules of experimental inquiry. However, none of the experimental methods proves that *A* causes *E* but only eliminates hypotheses, and those that are not eliminated are only tentative hypotheses until closer approximations can be made. As Einstein said in the introduction to his theory of relativity, let us take Newton's theory of gravity as an approximation to the first degree. He then stated that his theory of relativity was an approximation to the second degree. The implication is obvious: someone, someday, could formulate another theory that would be an approximation to the third degree, and so forth. In short, science involves an infinite series of approximations in pursuit of cause and effect. Its basic assumption is that there is order in the universe and the task of science is to determine the laws involved in this order.

BOX 15.3. *Steps in the Scientific Method*

Observation: A can, without a cap, such as one that had contained duplicating fluid, is placed on a source of heat. After a few minutes, the cap is replaced, screwed down tightly, and the heat is removed from the can. Gradually, the can begins to crumple. Why?

Hypothesis (Explanation that is to be tested): Air pressure causes the can to crumple.

Design to test a hypothesis: The hypothesis or explanation can be tested by arranging conditions so that one variable can be changed (independent variable) while other variables are held constant, or controlled. Under these conditions, variation in the independent or antecedent variable can be related to its consequent, the dependent variable. Under this rule of the single variable, cause and effect can then be logically inferred.

> *Design A:* To test the effect of heat alone, use two identical cans with plastic window on one side, caps off, thermometers attached to their sides, one air pressure gauge inside each can, and one outside the cans; put only one over heat; place balloons over the caps; observe which balloons expand and which can crumples when the balloons are removed; the caps are replaced and the cans are removed from the heat.

> *Design B:* To test effect of heat and prevention of air from being sucked back in can, use two identical cans, place both over sources of heat, place balloons over cans, cap one, and remove both from heat. Observe which can crumples and which does not.

Observed measurements and Interpretation: The temperature in the cans went up, then down as the heat was removed. The air pressure in the heated can went up as the can was heated, then down below 14.7 lb/sq in. as the capped can cooled. The can continued to crumple until the air pressure inside the can equalled the outside air pressure. The cans remained intact when the heat was not applied or when the heat was applied but the cap was removed during the cooling period, but they crumpled when the heat was applied and followed by replacement of the cap. Since it is known that heat causes a gas to expand and that air pressure is 14.7 lb/sq in., we can infer that heat caused the gas to expand and was forced outside the can, but could not return when the cap was replaced; then as the can cooled, the gas contracted, exerting less pressure inside the can. The greater outside air pressure then caused the can to crumple.

Conclusion: Objects, such as tin cans, do not crumple when the pressure inside and outside are equal. But, if the pressure inside is reduced, the atmospheric pressure will crush any such object whose walls cannot resist 14.7 lb of pressure.

Since concepts, generalizations, and theories are such important ideas in science, we define each of them and then explain a strategy for teaching students to formulate them in science classes.

DEFINITIONS OF SCIENCE CONCEPTS, GENERALIZATIONS, THEORIES, EXPLANATION, AND PREDICTION

A concept is a label for an abstraction and organization of properties that an idea or an object has in common with other ideas or objects. A concept may also be related to other concepts. The concept of an apple, for example, consists of such properties as color (which can vary in value from yellow to purple), size (from the size of a crabapple to that of a delicious apple), shape (round to heart-shaped), taste (sweet to sour), and so forth. Of course, *apple* can also refer to a particular apple, such as a Winesap, which consists of variations in these properties: color (purple), size (medium), and shape (round). But when we think of an apple in an abstract way, we have to think of what all apples have in common (their properties and variations in these properties). Likewise, concepts in science, such as *gravity* in physics, *atom* in chemistry, and *cell* in biology are abstractions from observed phenomena. Concepts can be developed by providing students with a range of objects that embody the attributes and variations in the attributes that make up a concept. Then, students can be taught to perceive what properties the objects have in common.

Generalizations are relations between or among concepts. The generalization *The volume of a gas is directly proportional to its temperature, keeping pressure constant* consists of relationships among the concepts of volume, temperature, and pressure. (Of course, the generalization also contains other concepts, such as "proportional" and "constant.") This particular generalization holds up over such a wide range of variations that it qualifies as a *law* (Boyle's law). A generalization can be taught by first developing the concepts involved in the generalization and then guiding students to perceive the relationship among the concepts. In Boyle's Law, for example, gas pressure can be observed to correlate with temperature (when temperature increases, so does pressure, if volume is kept constant).

A *theory* is an explanation that usually involves interrelationships among a set of generalizations. For example, molecular theory that consists, in part, of explanations and conditions that affect molecular movement, can be used to explain Boyle's law.

Explanation consists of determining the cause(s) of an observed phenomenon by searching for the theory or premises from which the observed phenomenon can be deduced. It is analogous to having a deduction for a syllogism and then discovering its premises.

Prediction goes in the opposite direction. You already have the theory or premises. The inference you draw is a prediction. You then test the prediction to determine its empirical validity. If the premises are true and the deduction is valid, then the prediction should be true.

Scientific Thinking

Now, notice that in progressing from concepts to generalizations to theories, we proceed from observation of particular objects or events to abstractions (or concepts), relationships among these abstractions (or generalizations) and on to theories (abstractions and the interrelationships among the generalizations). We can use this progression in teaching science. That is, a science lesson can start with observation or recall of objects or events in everyday life. From these observations, we can construct abstractions and then form these abstractions and the relationships between them into generalizations. A lesson in physics can start with an ordinary household candle. Students can observe that the candle changes from a solid to a liquid state, and from a liquid to a gaseous state as heat is applied. As we use similar examples, we can teach students to abstract from these examples and to form generalizations.

The purpose of using the candle example is to illustrate how a lesson can progress from concrete to abstract levels of thinking (Taba, 1965). This progression is one way that the teacher can try to cover the range of ability among students. Most, if not all, students can grasp the concrete stage of the lesson; some can go on to the more abstract levels; and some students may be able to progress to comprehension of the more abstract theoretical levels of thought, the quantification of relationships, and even express them in mathematical form. By starting with observable concrete objects and events and progressing in steps to more abstract levels, we can accommodate a greater range of individual differences in ability in a science lesson than if the lesson started at an abstract level of thought. Therefore, more students can learn science, at least the concrete aspects of it, if we start a lesson at the concrete level and then proceed to more abstract levels.

QUESTIONING AND QUESTIONS
Question Sequence for Teaching Thinking
(QUEST)

An instructional procedure for taking students from observation to conceptualization and from conceptualization to generalization consists of a question sequence for teaching thinking (Taba, 1965). This *question sequence for teaching thinking* (acronym: *QUEST*) is a way a teacher can direct a discussion that does not meander, but goes somewhere, and through phase out of the teacher and phase in of students can teach them to direct their own thinking processes.

Development of teaching plans for Quest, as for any instructional procedure, begins with the formulation of an objective. In the example given in Box 15.4, the objective is to develop the generalization: *Energy is neither created nor destroyed, only transformed.* Then the teacher works backward to ask what concepts or interpretations or inferences this generalization rests upon (concepts of electrical and mechanical energy). The answer to this question then leads to the question: "What input observations, measurements, or data must these concepts rest upon?" (Measurement of energy input and energy output from such transformations as electrical to mechanical energy, as in an electric clock.) Then the teacher must provide for this input, either through direct experience (a laboratory investigation) or a vicarious experience (the use of films or texts). In short, lesson planning works backward from the teaching goal or objective, while actual instruction, such as the Quest procedure, works forward as demonstrated by the lesson in Box 15.4.

BOX 15.4. Questioning Sequence for Teaching Thinking (QUEST) Applied to a Science Lesson

Type of Question	Purpose	Question
Focusing	Initiate discussion or focus on issue.	What types of energy conversion do we observe in a house? From electrical to mechanical (clock), to heat (broiler), to radiant energy (lamp); from mechanical to electrical (crystal in phonograph).
Controlling	Direct or dominate discussion.	Would you focus now only on the house?
Extending	Obtain more information at a particular level of discussion.	What other examples can we think of? Mechanical to kinetic (door opening); mechanical to potential (coiled door spring); chemical to heat (burning gas).
Ignoring or rejecting	Maintain current trend of discussion.	Would you bring that issue up later?
Raising	Move discussion from factual to interpretive, inferential, or abstraction and generalization level.	In all of these energy conversions, is energy created, destroyed, or only transformed? What can we say about all changes in energy? (Formulate the law of conservation of energy.)

PHASE OUT/PHASE IN FOR QUEST

The teacher can initiate phase out in a lesson by dividing the class into groups, providing them with a Quest guide, and appointing discussion leaders who will take their groups through input, focusing, extending, raising, and higher-order questioning until the groups form a generalization. Eventually almost every student should be able to use a Quest guide alone.

The Quest procedure systematically develops a sequence of thinking. However, the progression from one level to another in this sequence is in marked contrast to what actually occurs in the classroom. Most of the questions teachers ask are at the literal level of comprehension (Guszak, 1967). They are the *how, what, who, where, when* type of questions. They aim at memory, or direct recall, of information. Of course, information at the literal level is necessary before teachers can ask higher level questions, questions that lead to interpretations, inferences, generalizations, and evaluations. But some teachers are prone to stop their question asking at the literal level instead of stimulating students' thinking at higher levels.

Questions at Various Levels of Thought

Spache and Spache (1977) stress seven types of questions. In Box 15.5 we define and apply them to science content.

BOX 15.5. *Questions at Various Levels of Thinking*
Applied to Science Content

1. *Memory:* Recognizing or recalling information.
   a. Who formulated the theory of relativity?
   b. What is meant by the formula $E = mc^2$?
2. *Translation:* Expressing ideas in different forms (words to pictures, pictures to words, numbers to graphs, etc.) or language (paraphrase).
   a. In your own words, explain the laws of genetic inheritance.
   b. Using the data in this temperature table, draw a graph to depict the average daily temperature over the last three months.
3. *Interpretation:* Constructing a generalization that can be used for inferring the meaning of an event.
   (Construction of generalization): After grass has been covered by a log for a week, the grass is yellowish. Why? (Sunlight is necessary for plants to produce chlorophyll which give their leaves green color.)
   (Observation): The log prevented the sun's light from reaching the grass.
   (Inference): Therefore, the grass's chlorophyll content was reduced, resulting in a yellowish color.
4. *Application:* Using a given generalization or concept to solve a problem.
   What use can be made of the knowledge that barium hydroxide (BaOH) combines with hydrochloric acid (HCh) to form an insoluble compound, barium chloride ($BaCl_2$)? (One application: use barium hydroxide to remove chlorine from water.)

5. *Analysis:* Dividing a problem into its several parts or following a procedure to separate a problem into its constituents.
   Which system is malfunctioning in the television set? (Observe first whether the picture, sound, or power system is not functioning. Then isolate the problem further within each of the three major components.
6. *Synthesis:* Combining elements to make a whole which has its own properties.
   How would you make table salt from the basic elements? (Combine sodium and chlorine.)
7. *Evaluation:* Making judgments by applying criteria.
   Which is more efficient, a steam or a gas engine? (Formulate criterion for efficiency: ratio of output/input. Then use this criterion on the two engines.)

The questions in Box 15.5 elicit answers or *products* of thinking. Another set of questions can elicit not only answers but also *processes or procedures for arriving at the answers.* To get at these processes, we can ask students: (a) What steps would you follow in doing an experiment? (b) How would you determine that a child inherits an equal number of chromosomes from each parent? (c) What process converts radio waves into sound?

Questions—whether they are in a sequence as in Quest, or whether they are isolated questions aimed at products of thought or processes—are useful ways of directing students' attention and getting them to think about the content and mode of inquiry within a course, either before or after they read. If we use a phase-out procedure in conjunction with these questioning strategies, then we phase students in to asking their own questions and using their own questions to guide their own thinking as a process of studying and learning from text on their own. The following is a procedure for transferring a strategy to students. (We can use a similar procedure with the other types of questions.)

Questioning Strategy for Various Ability Levels

Questioning strategies help solve the problem of individual differences in ability to learn content in science. Almost all students can make or recall observations and answer *wh*-type questions (those beginning with the words *who, what, when, where, how*). Fewer are able to follow higher levels of questioning. Even fewer can attain the more abstract, generalized levels of thought. But all students can participate to the limits of their capabilities, and the questioning strategies can stimulate the further development of their capabilities. Another way in which to make science understandable to a wider range of students is through use of what we call a Problem Demonstration Sequence.

PROBLEM DEMONSTRATION SEQUENCE

Frequently the authors of science texts present definitions, concepts, measurements, and principles in a chapter, then ask students to apply them to the solution of problems at the end of the chapter. However, they give no demonstration in the chapter of how to solve the problems. Often, the teacher places the burden of integrating and applying the chapter content to the solution of problems upon the student. Of course, we can agree that students who can solve these problems without assistance have passed a difficult test of their understanding of the chapter. But students who cannot do so experience frustration and unnecessary failure. Science texts, like mathematics texts, should demonstrate how to work a problem before students are asked to solve similar problems on their own. If they did, more students would be likely to have successful experiences with science and consequently develop a more favorable attitude toward the subject. If a science text does not demonstrate how to solve problems, the teacher can supply this missing instructional step. The following example is similar to one in a physics text (Boylan, 1962), which contains a "step-by-step" method for solving problems that we have augmented in the demonstration in Box 15.6.

BOX 15.6. Problem Demonstration Sequence

Problem	*Demonstration*
A 300-lb block of granite weighs only 50 lb when completely submerged in water. What is (a) its apparent loss of weight, (b) the weight of fluid displaced, and (c) the volume of the block?	a. The apparent loss of weight of the object is its weight in air minus its weight after submerging in water: 300 − 50 = 250 lb. The apparent loss of weight is equal to the weight of fluid displaced, which is the same as the buoyant force exerted by the fluid on the object. b. The weight of the fluid displaced is also 250 lb, for according to Archimedes' law, an immersed body is buoyed up by a force equal to the weight of the fluid displaced by it. c. The volume of the block is the weight of the fluid displaced (250 lb) divided by the weight of the fluid displaced by a 1-cubic-ft (ft^3) object, which is 62.5 lb. Therefore, 250/62.5 lb = 4 ft^3.

Even if a science text does demonstrate how to solve a problem, it may not provide instruction in (a) how to manipulate a formula to solve for one unknown, given the other variables, (b) how to transform the syntax so that the variables stated in the problem come in the same order as the variables in the formula, (c) means for recognizing synonyms (for example: *buoyancy* and *lifting force,* and

(d) interrelationships among formulas that are necessary for solving multiple-step problems.

After awhile, a class will become familiar with the algebraic and linguistic manipulations in science problems. As they do, the instructor can phase out of doing these manipulations and phase in the students. After this instructional sequence, the instructor would known, not just assume, that the students could do the manipulations.

Box 15.7 presents an outline and an application of Problem Demonstration Sequence. The outline shows algebraic and linguistic manipulations, plus recall of unsupplied information necessary for solving the problems. The formulas used in Box 15.7 are on buoyancy. Notice that we have stated terms of the formulas as variables, which means that each term can vary in value and that the formulas are in a general form. (See chapter 16 for discussion of more abstract formulas.)

BOX 15.7.   Problem Demonstration Sequence

1. List basic formulas

Variable A	Variable B	Variable C
Weight in air	− Weight submerged	= Apparent loss of weight *or* (synonymously) buoyant force exerted on the object.

2. Show how basic formulas can be algebraically manipulated so that given any two variables, the third can be computed:
   a. Given A and B, find C: $A - B = C$
   b. Given A and C, find B: $A - C = B$
   c. Given B and C, find A: $B + C = A$

3. Show how linguistic manipulations can be made, that is, how synonyms and syntactic transformations can vary the way in which problems are stated. Demonstrate the reverse processes students must use so that they know what formula to apply. They can then do the necessary computation, which involves relatively simple arithmetic.

   Example: What is the "force by which an object is buoyed up?" (Recognize that this means the same as "buoyant force exerted on the object.") Then, students know questions can be answered by solving for C (formula 2a, above).

4. Recall the physics principle that is necessary for solving the problem.

   Example: What volume of fluid is displaced? Students are to recall Archimedes' principle: "An immersed body is buoyed up by a force equal to the weight of fluid displaced by it." Consequently, students can recognize that in formula 2a, variable C will give them the weight in pounds of fluid displaced.

But, the question asks for volume. Consequently, students must know how to transform from weight in pounds to cubic feet.

5. Teach transformation of measurement:
   a. Recall that 1 cubic ft of water = 62.5 lb.

   b. Therefore, volume in cubic feet $(D) = \dfrac{\text{pounds of fluid displaced } (C)}{62.5 \text{ lb/ft}^3 \ (E)}$

   c. Recognize algebraic restatement of above formula:

   $$D \times E = C, E = C/D$$

   d. *Now, given* C (pounds of fluid displaced), D (volume in cubic feet) can be found by substituting in above formula.

The Problem Demonstration Sequence may accompany other teaching strategies such as the directed reading activity (DRA), marginal gloss, and reading and learning-from-text guide.

Teaching Students to Read and Learn From Science Text

TEXT CHARACTERISTICS
Introduction to a Science Text

Individual differences also occur in how students orient themselves to a text. Some students may familiarize themselves with a text and adopt appropriate strategies for using it. Other students may read only the assigned pages. To overcome this difference among students, the instructor may derive valuable pay-off by taking some time to introduce the text.

Features of a Text

Introduction to a text is useful for pointing out features students frequently overlook. First, explain the organization of the text. You can glean the organization from noting the sequence of topics in the table of contents and in the chapter headings and subheadings. Also, organizational information may be found in the preface to a text. (Often the preface contains ideas and suggestions on how to use the book.) Second, point out data in the appendices, such as tables that will be helpful in comprehending the text. Third, have students note other information in the appendices, including possibly a glossary of technical terms and an answer key for problems in the text. Fourth, demonstrate the value of the index for obtaining information located in diverse places in the text. To solve a problem in electronics, for example, students might need to get information on the theory from chapter II, on electrical circuits from chapter IX, and on electrical measuring devices from chapter X.

After this overview, the teacher should clarify certain science terms that occur frequently in science texts. We have defined a few such terms in Box 15.8.

BOX 15.8. Some Science Terms and Their Definitions

Term	Definition
1. science	1. Knowledge obtained and tested through use of the scientific method.
2. scientific method	2. Procedures, such as a controlled experiment (see Box 15.3 for confirmation or disconfirmation of a hypothesis whose terms can be operationally defined.
3. operational definition	3. A definition that is based upon identifiable and repeatable operations or observations. For example, electricity can be defined by voltmeter and ohmmeter measurements of an electrical circuit. These measurements then define electrical current as: $$I = \frac{E}{R}$$ *where:* I = current in amperes $\quad\quad E$ = pressure in volts $\quad\quad R$ = resistance in ohms
4. observation	4. A fact or phenomenon recognized directly through the senses or indirectly through measurements. For example, Darwin's observations about coral led him to suggest a hypothesis for the formation of atolls.
5. hypothesis	5. An explanation of some phenomenon, pending further evidence that may confirm, disprove, or modify the hypothesis.
6. theory	6. A theory is an explanation based on several hypotheses. For example, Einstein's famous theory on the relationship between energy and matter: $$E = mc^2$$ *where:* E = energy $\quad\quad m$ = mass $\quad\quad c$ = velocity of light $\quad\quad\quad$ (186,000 mi/sec)
7. controlled experiment	7. A planned test of a hypothesis that involves a change in one factor or

condition at a time. A scientist can then observe the results (effects) and with some degree of certainty relate them to the changed factor or condition. For example, see Box 15.3. Repeated confirmation of this cause-and-effect relationship results in the formation of a scientific law.

8. law

8. An observed regularity of nature; a statement or formula of an order or relationship that so far as is known has been found to be invariable (unchanging) under the same conditions. For example, the law of gravitational pull is the product of the masses of two bodies divided by the square of the distance between them. The formula is:

$$\frac{m_1 \times m_2}{d^2}$$

where: g = gravitational pull
m = mass of each body
d = distance between the bodies

Organization of a Text

Texts usually have a plan for organizing and presenting information within chapters. An analysis of a text will reveal this plan. Pointing out the plan to the students should help them learn the content. One physics text uses this plan: After an introduction consisting of a few concepts drawn from observations or examples in everyday life, a major generalization is stated at the beginning of a chapter. Then the rest of the chapter explains the concepts, the generalization, and measurements that can be made. Thus, in a chapter entitled "Buoyancy" are examples like these: *Your body feels lighter in water. You float near the top of the water. As you lift objects out of water, they feel heavier.* Then the text sums up by stating a generalization: "Fluids buoy up all objects immersed in them" (Boylan, 1962, p. 56). The rest of the chapter explains this generalization by (a) experimental proof of the principle, (b) experiments on flotation, and (c) applications of the law of flotation. These explanations involve the use of appropriate measurements and formulas.

The chapter concludes with a summary, a list of words and laws presented in the chapter, discussion questions, and problems. A similar pattern is repeated in each chapter. (Patterns of textual organization vary, of course, from text to text. Consequently, instructors have to analyze each text and then communicate this organization.)

Style of Writing

Texts differ in the author's style of writing. The style may consist of a similar sequence of paragraph types in each chapter. The types of the paragraphs may be definition, enumeration, classification, comparison and contrast, generalization and proof, hypothesis and evidence, problem and solution, sequence of events (H. B. Smith, 1965b; H. A. Robinson, 1975). (See chap. 9 for further explanation of paragraph types.) In pointing out the style of writing, a teacher can facilitate students' reading and understanding of text.

Graphic Aids

Science writing differs from literary writing not only in use of a high density of technical terms and formulas but also in several other ways. Unlike English texts, which rarely include tabular graphic aids, science texts are replete with them. Students frequently skip over them when reading. We think they do so because they do not know how to read and interpret them. Consequently, we urge science instructors to use instructional procedures on teaching construction and interpretation of graphic aids, like those explained in chapter 14, Social Studies, to help their students read and learn from them as they occur in their texts. Such instruction will also develop students' ability to draw conclusions based on evidence, to evaluate interpretations and conclusions, and other reasoning abilities.

Semantic Hierarchies in Text

Definition. Another type of organization is a semantic hierarchy. In a semantic hierarchy, the technical terms in a content area are arranged in ascending order from the concrete to more abstract levels, as shown in Fig. 15.1.

Adapting Text to Students

Assessment. A cloze pretest can determine whether a text is appropriate for a class. A text is appropriate if the class's average on the cloze test is between 41% and 60% correct insertions (Thelen, 1976). See chap. 10 for a more detailed explanation of the cloze technique and other ways of determining readability.

Rewriting Texts. What if a cloze pretest indicates that the difficulty of a science text exceeds the reading ability of the students? That is, what if the students get less than 40% of the insertions correct? Indeed, this is likely with any text because of the wide range of reading ability that exists in any class. One solution is to rewrite the text. Will rewriting help? Corey (1977) reported on the rewriting of ninth-grade biology materials to simplify the style of writing and vocabulary. The rewritten materials significantly enhanced an experimental group's comprehension on a 100-item test that had high reliability and content validity. Although the materials had been rewritten to benefit students whose reading ability was below grade level, the students who were reading above grade level also comprehended better. Why does it work? We think rewriting passages is effective because it provides a semantic bridge between abstract ideas in the text and the students' knowledge hierarchy. In short, rewriting a text enables students to relate new ideas to concepts already within their repertoire.

We recognize that teachers have little time during the school year for rewriting, but we also know that some school districts are providing release time for preparation of materials and are supporting such activities during the summer time. Consequently, the suggestions in this section may be put to use at these times.

Develop Students Semantic Hierarchies. An alternate to rewriting is to develop students' semantic hierarchies to the point where the semantic level of technical terms in the text is close to the highest level of abstraction in the students' semantic hierarchies. Then, if a student reads a passage which contains technical terms that are new, the teacher can use directed reading activities, marginal glosses and reading and learning-from-text guides to relate these terms to subordinate concepts in the student's semantic hierarchy. A student may have a semantic hierarchy that goes up to *food,* but not to *nutrition.* Since *nutrition* is semantically close in level of abstraction to *food,* the student is likely to make the connection when the relationship is pointed out.

A structured overview (Barron, 1969), which is a visual arrangement of technical terms in a text, depicts the semantic relationships among the technical terms. If students have this overview before reading a text, they can use it to perceive where technical terms fit into a semantic hierarchy as they encounter the terms. Of course, not all the technical terms in a science text could be put into an overview. An overview for technical terms in a particular chapter would be reasonable. As students progress through a text, the highest level terms in one chapter can be related to equally abstract terms in subsequent chapters. Thus, students could accumulate a semantic hierarchy for the entire course as they progress through it.

FIGURE 15.1. Semantic Hierarchy for Nutrition

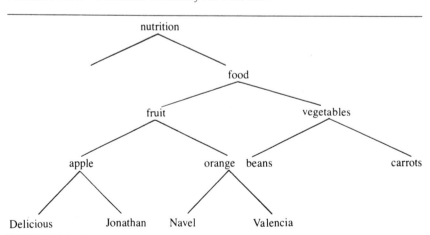

Science Vocabulary

Technical Versus General Vocabulary. In developing students' semantic hierarchies, teachers should be aware that science vocabulary must be differentiated from general vocabulary. The word *field,* for example, is defined as a large, open expanse of land in general vocabulary and, of course, in the technical vocabulary of agriculture. But the technical term *field* in electricity refers to the invisible lines of force that emanate from magnets and electrical circuits. Students must also realize that a technical term in one content area may have a different meaning in another. The word *current* in physics means something different than *current* in social science.

Although the vocabulary load of science is high, the load decreases when you instruct students in the meanings of roots that occur in many words (*therm*al, iso*therm,* and *therm*ometer), and when you teach the meanings of affixes that appear in words in science text (therm*al* and *iso*therm). Fortunately, many scientific terms are constructed from combinations of Latin and Greek roots and affixes. Teaching the meanings of these word parts will facilitate the acquisition of technical science vocabulary. (See chapter 18 for a list of affixes and roots.)

Relational Words. You can also help students by teaching relational words that occur frequently in science texts. Among such words are those that imply cause and effect (*therefore, because*), time (*during, after, before*), comparisons (*like, different, than*), degree of importance (*essential, least*), and evaluation (*best, poorest*) (Shepherd, 1978). See chapter 9 for a list of these and other signal and transitional words.

Translating Symbols and Formulas. Students also have to relate technical terms to the symbols that represent them so they will be able to translate these symbols into words. If the symbols are in an equation, then the translation of symbols into words has to be expressed in sentences. Consider this formula:

$$g = \frac{m_1 m_2}{d^2}$$

where: g = gravitational pull
m = mass of a body
d = distance between the two bodies

Translated into words, the formula reads: *The gravitational pull between two bodies is equal to the product of their masses divided by the square of the distance between them.* This translation takes the abstract formula a step in the direction of a more concrete level of thinking. Students next have to use their semantic hierarchies for these terms in order to relate them to concrete events. These events in science are frequently observations of reactions made visible through the use of measuring devices and other apparatus. For example, the "Bubble Chamber" is a liquid medium for making visible the tracks of high-energy particles passing through it.

Teaching Students to Read and Learn from Text

Skills in science and skills in reading and learning from text overlap. Carter and Simpson (1978) point out that designing investigations, collecting and interpreting data, communicating results, and formulating conclusions are analogous to processes used in general reading and study skills. Consequently, it is not surprising to find that instruction in science enhances reading achievement (Morgan, Rachelson, & Lloyd, 1977) and vice versa.

All of these similarities and differences between the study of science and the general ability to read and learn from text can be taught through the use of single- and multiple-text strategies. We believe that, if the single- and multiple-text strategies presented in this book are applied to any text, more students could successfully learn the content of physics, chemistry, and biology to the limits of their individual abilities. What teachers need to do to achieve this goal is to start with concrete, everyday activities and progress to abstract levels of thought. To do so, they can use (1) single-text strategies such as directed reading activities, marginal glosses, reading and learning-from-text guides (RLTs), SQ3R, and (2) multiple-text strategies, such as the concept technique, the inquiry approach, or the project method. Although these strategies are applicable to teaching any science content, we demonstrate how to apply all of them to reading and learning from text in a physics course.

SINGLE-TEXT STRATEGIES
Directed Reading Activity (DRA)

Science texts are dense with technical terms, examples, concepts, and generalizations. But students do not necessarily have to learn and remember all this content, at least not all the examples. The task of the teacher is to (1) decide which content to stress and point it out to students and (2) explore and build background, then use preposed questions to guide students while they are reading and learning from the chapter and use postposed questions afterwards to make sure students understand and remember the important points. Some texts try to incorporate these DRA components, but no text can carry out an interaction between an instructor and a class as DRA does.

In Box 15.9 is Mr. Phelps's DRA for a chapter from *Elements of Physics* by Boylan.

BOX 15.9. Class: Physics (DRA)

"HOW MATTER BEHAVES,"

I. Mr. Phelps explores the students' background.
   A. Mr. Phelps questions the class about their experiences with concepts to be developed in this chapter (properties of matter: inertia, elasticity, universal gravitation, and impenetrability).

      1. Have you been on a bus when it started or stopped suddenly?
      2. What happens when you squeeze a rubber ball or stretch a rubber band and then let go?
      3. If you jump up, how long do you stay up?
      4. When you get into a bathtub, what happens to the level of water?
  B. Mr. Phelps then explains the relationship between the students' background and the concepts in the chapter: "These questions are related to the four major concepts you are going to learn in this section. Look at the summary on page 22 of your physics text; this summary will give you an overview of this chapter."

II. Mr. Phelps builds the students' background.
  A. Mr. Phelps reviews with the students the technical vocabulary in this chapter.
    Technical Vocabulary
      1. Inertia (p. 13): Matter can neither start nor stop itself.
      2. Elastic (p. 14): Most matter upon which a force has acted, within certain limits, tends to return to its shape.
      3. Universal attraction (p. 15): Each particle of matter attracts every other particle.
      4. Impenetrable (p. 16): Matter cannot occupy space already occupied by other matter.
      5. Length (p. 17): the distance between two points
      6. Time (p. 17): the duration or interval between two events
      7. Mass (p. 17): the quantity of matter in a body
      8. Force (p. 20): a push or pull that tends to change a body's motion or shape (1 lb force = change of velocity of 1 slug or <u>pounds</u> by 1 ft/sec/sec).   32
      9. Density (p. 21): mass per unit of volume of a substance: (space)   (mass/volume)
      10. Weight (p. 17): the force with which a body is attracted towards the earth
  B. Mr. Phelps gives some preposed questions to guide reading:
      1. What properties does matter have?
      2. What measurements in what units are used to measure energy changes?
      3. What is Hooke's law?

III. Students read chapter.

IV. Following the reading, the class engages in a discussion.

  A. Factual level
      1. Questions on definitions
      2. Preposed questions
      3. Process questions (How do you find volume? Mass?)
  B. Interpretation or Inferential level
      1. What property does plastic or glass lack that allows it to be broken when a force is applied?
      2. Why can a nail be driven into wood?
      3. The mass of a body never changes, but its weight does. Why?
  C. Generalized level (These questions require use of principles explained in the chapter. The teacher can demonstrate their application, then divide the class into groups to solve other problems.)

1. If you watched two cars start from rest and wanted to know which had the better engine, what measurements would you take and what computations would you make?
2. How many pounds of force are required to steadily lift a shot put that has a mass of 16 lbs?
3. You want to know whether a crown is made of gold or silver. How would you find out if you know only that the density of gold is 1,200?

V. Mr. Phelps involves students in extending their understanding of how matter behaves.

Discussion: How would matter, such as a 16-lb shot put or a 180-lb man, behave after it had been transported to the moon? Remember: the gravitationl pull of the moon is one-sixth that of earth. Apply your discussion to each of the concepts listed in the technical vocabulary.

Examples in this box are adapted from *Elements of Physics,* revised by Paul J. Boylan, pp. 13–23. © Copyright 1962 by Allyn and Bacon, Inc. Reprinted by permission. Numbers in parentheses identify the pages in the Boylan text where the technical vocabulary is explained in context.

Marginal Gloss

A marginal gloss is analogous to having the instructor accompany the student while he or she is reading a homework assignment. The marginal gloss may consist of paginated, dittoed notes handed out to students when homework is assigned. Students may use these notes as they do their assigned homework.

In the dittoed notes, the instructor may clarify a term in the text; explicate a passage; provide background information that is necessary for comprehension; concretize or relate an abstract idea to students' experiences; indicate what is significant and important to remember (some students may think everything is equally important and hence suffer from an information overload); and, most important, show students how to solve assigned problems (see Problem Demonstration Sequence, Boxes 15.6 and 15.7). In short, the instructor provides whatever marginal notes are necessary for helping students read and learn from text. In some cases, the gloss may contain more words than the original text. In Box 15.10 is a marginal gloss that Mr. Phelps provided for maximum clarification of a section in a chapter of a textbook. Italics have been added.

BOX 15.10. *Gloss Examples*

TEXT: "MOLECULES AND THEIR BEHAVIOR"

Gloss	*Text*
Ancients refers to those thinkers who lived in an early period of history before A.D. 476. Why could they not prove it?	The ancients had the idea that matter was made of small particles, but *they could not prove it.*

Definition of a molecule. Note two important points: (1) smallest particle of matter, (2) retains properties of the substance. For example, the properties of chalk are whiteness, softness, fine-grained, easily rubbed off.

. . . The molecule is the smallest particle of substance (chalk, iron, sugar, etc.) *which has the properties of the substance.*

This passage implies that molecules can only be further divided by chemical, not by physical, means. Chalk consists of the compound C_aCO_3. Divided chemically into atoms, it consists of atoms of calcium, carbon, and oxygen. How different are the properties of these atoms from C_aCO_3? Remember: The only important point in this section to remember is the definition of a molecule.

If you persuaded a chemist to break up the chalk molecule, by chemical, not physical means, you would have smaller units, called atoms, of which the chalk molecule is made, but which are different from the chalk.

Note contrast: *Cohesion* refers to attraction between *like* (same) molecules.

Adhesion refers to attraction between *unlike* (different) molecules.

. . . The name we apply to the attractive force between like molecules is cohesion. . . . *This attractive force between unlike molecules is called* adhesion.

The phrase, "it seems," implies that scientists are not sure, but only think that all molecules are in motion. Molecules exhibit two kinds of motion. Can you "dance" without changing your location?

It seems certain molecules of all substances are in a state of motion . . . real motion in which the molecule gets somewhere . . . or simple vibration in which a molecule dances around and ends up where it started.

Remember the definitions of *cohesion* and *adhesion* and the two types of molecular motion. Molecular motion will help you understand the next section on the three states of matter (solids, liquids, and gases).

In the remainder of the chapter learn the properties of solids, liquids, and gases, and why they have properties.

Text passages in this box are from *Elements of Physics,* revised by Paul J. Boylan, pp. 23–25. © Copyright 1962 by Allyn and Bacon, Inc. Reprinted by permission.

Reading and Learning-From-Text Guide

The reading and learning-from-text guide (RLT) organizes information in a science text so that it progresses from observations or facts to concepts, inferences or interpretations, and then on to generalizations. The basic purpose of an RLT is to facilitate progression from concrete to abstract, and from particular events to generalizations that subsume these events.

The way to construct an RLT is to start with one or more generalizations students are to read, learn, and understand in a section or in an entire chapter of a text. Then work backward to single out the concepts, interpretations, or inferences that support the generalization(s). (The author may have developed some of these concepts in a previous chapter. The concept of molecules and force occurred in the text prior to the passage we used for our RLT guide in Box 15.10. We listed these and other concepts from our passage concepts in a section on definitions.) Next, list the concrete elements, the observations, facts, or literal statements underpinning the entire structure. In science, we also need a section in our RLT on measuring devices and units. These devices represent an application of the scientific principles explained in the passage.

To demonstrate how to construct an RLT, let's take another chapter from the science text we have been using (Boylan, 1962, pp. 39–45). The major generalization in this chapter is Pascal's law, which applies to all fluids, whether they are liquids or gases, and *at rest* (Note the limiting condition: the law applies to fluids at rest): *Pressure applied to an enclosed fluid is transmitted equally in all directions without loss, and acts with equal force on equal surfaces.* A basic concept in this law is *pressure,* which is defined as "force per unit area." Along with this concept, students must learn that pressure is measured in units of lb/in.^{2}, lb/ft^2, g/cm^2, kg/cm^2, dyn/cm^2. They also need to know that fluids transmit pressure in two ways: (1) pressure applied to the liquid from without or (2) gravity pressure from the liquid's own weight. Why do fluids transmit pressure? Because molecules which make up fluids are free to move, and they continue to move against each other and their container until the pressure is the same on each molecule and the wall of the container. Now, these concepts and Pascal's law rest upon observations that can be made in everyday life: (1) When a flat fire hose fills with water, the hose becomes round, indicating that the fluid is pushing at right angles. Puncture the hose and the water squirts out at right angles. (2) A skater on thin ice may break the ice, but the same skater lying down on a board on the ice might not, illustrating that the skater's weight per square inch (or pressure) on the ice is less when the skater is lying down on the board. (3) Press a water gun and you see the water squirt out—your finger transmits pressure to the water, which increases the force per unit area at the narrower area of the nozzle. What are some practical applications of the principles of hydraulic pressure? The major ones are a hydraulic jack or hydraulic brakes.

Mr. Phelps put this information into an RLT (Box. 15.11) in such a way that students became cognizant of the definitions, the relationships between observations and generalizations or principles that explain them, and the applications of these principles to measuring devices and other uses.

BOX 15.11. *Reading and Learning-from-Text Guide*

"PRESSURE IN FLUIDS"

Definitions: Use your text to match these terms with their definitions. (If a term is not defined in this section, use the glossary at the end of the text.)

Terms	Definitions
1. fluid ( )	a. force per unit area
2. pressure ( )	b. stationary
3. static ( )	c. flow
4. force ( )	d. push or pull
5. millibar ( )	e. 1,000 dyn/cm²

Facts or Observations: Indicate which of the following are true (+) or false (−) observations.
1. When a garden hose that is going full blast is punctured, the water at the puncture site dribbles out ( ) or squirts out at a right angle to the hose ( ).
2. Lifting a filled bucket by its handle with your hand is more difficult than with your finger ( ).
3. When you decrease the nozzle opening, the water from your hose squirts farther ( ).
4. A pressure gauge at the waterworks miles away from your home will indicate the same pressure as a gauge on the closed faucet at your home ( ).
5. Water in a pan on a level surface is stationary ( ).

Concepts, Interpretations, or Generalizations: Next to each statement below, fill in the number of the observation above that goes with it.
1. Two equal forces acting in opposite directions on an object result in no movement of the object.   ( )
2. When you *decrease* the area on which a force is being exerted, you *increase* the pressure.   ( )
3. A fluid always pushes at right angles against the wall that holds it.   ( )
4. Pressure is force per unit area.   ( )
5. Pressure applied to an enclosed fluid is (a) applied equally in all directions without loss of force and (b) acts equally on all equal surfaces.   ( )

Measurement: Fill in the missing word or numbers in these sentences from the choices given below.
1. A pressure gauge works because water pressure is exerted _____ and at _____ _____.
2. A 160-lb person standing on the ice exerts a _____ of 160 lbs on his or her shoes.
3. Pressure is force per unit area or Pressure = $\frac{\text{Force}}{\text{Area}}$. If the force is 160 lb and the area is 32 cm², then the pressure is _____ per cm².

4. Pressure can also be measured in metric units of _____ per cm² or
_____ cm² or _____ per cm².

Choices:

5 lbs	dynes
grams	kilograms
force	right angles
equally	

Applications (for group discussion):
1. Explain how a 200-lb person using a hydraulic jack can lift a car to change a tire on a 5,000-lb car.
2. Your car has hydraulic brakes. Why does pressure on one brake pedal exert pressure on four brake surfaces with enough pressure to stop a car? Draw a diagram to illustrate your explanation.

SQ3R

SQ3R is, in a sense, a self-instructional study procedure. The student learns to survey (*S*) the material and formulate questions (*Q*) to be answered while reading the material; then the student reads (R_1) the material, recites (R_2) the answers to the questions, and, finally, reviews (R_3) the material to check the answers.[2]

Preceding SQ3R with the other strategies (DRA, Gloss, and RLT) can help teach the student (through transfer of learning) what to observe in a survey of a section or chapter of a text and what kinds of questions are appropriate and valid to ask about a particular content area text. A phase-out/phase-in strategy applied directly to SQ3R may also directly develop this learning. In the phase-out/phase-in procedure, the instructor first demonstrates with one section or chapter for the entire class, then has groups each do an SQ3R on another section or chapter, and eventually has individual students use SQ3R on their own as a valid procedure for reading and learning from their text.

In using SQ3R, the students might (a) note the headings as they survey the section, and transform them into *wh- questions* (who, where, what, when, how, why); (b) check to see if the text defines technical terms in bold-faced type or italics; (c) put these terms into *wh- questions* form, (d) do likewise with generalizations, (e) observe whether the text provides generalizations in the form of formulas: (f) ask how they apply; (g) look for measuring devices and ask how they work; (h) check for questions at the end of the section: read the questions;

---

[2]A variation on SQ3R is PQRST (Spache, 1963). The letters stand for Preview (skim selection), Question (develop questions to be used as purposes for reading), Read (to answer self-posed questions), Summarize (organize and write summary of information), Test (compare summary with information in passage).

use them as preposed questions for subsequent reading, reciting, and reviewing. See Box. 15.12.

BOX 15.12. *SQ3R*

"GRAVITY PRESSURE"

1. SURVEY AND QUESTION
   Heading: *Gravity Pressure*
   Question: How is gravity pressure different from external pressure?
   Heading: *Pressures due to Gravity*
   Question: What is pressure due to gravity? How great is this pressure?

   Note italics:
   Pressure depends upon vertical height of the liquid above the surface pressed upon and *pressure depends upon the density of the liquid.*

   Question: What does gravity pressure depend upon?
   Note formula: Pressure = height × density, or p = hd.
   Question: What is the formula for determining gravity pressure?
   Heading: *Size and Shape of Container*
   Question: How do the size and shape of the container affect gravity pressure?
   Heading: *Upward and Sideward Forces*
   Question: Are the upward and sideward forces the same as the force on the bottom?
   Heading: *Water Power*
   Question: How is water power developed and used?
   Heading: *Water Supply Systems*
   Question: How are water supply systems designed?
   Heading: *Manometers*
   Question: What is a manometer? How does it work? Why does it work this way?
   Heading: *Calculations of Pressure and Total Force*
   Question: How are pressure and total force computed? What units are used?

   Note at the end of the chapter: questions, summary, words to understand and learn, discussion questions, problems

2. READ AND RECITE: Read a section, using the questions posed for that section. Recite: test yourself on each question.
3. REVIEW: Reread section by section to check on the accuracy of your answers.

Headings in this box are from *Elements of Physics*, revised by Paul J. Boylan, pp. 45–55.
© Copyright 1962 by Allyn and Bacon, Inc. Reprinted by permission.

MULTIPLE-TEXT STRATEGIES

Although a science class usually has only one textbook to use, other science texts at different levels of difficulty are available. You can use these other science texts for group or individual reference projects. Moreover, you can identify books on various science topics in the school catalogs. (See chap. 13, The English Language Arts, for use of these catalogs.) A selection of these can also be useful for group or individual projects.

Supplementary Popular Science Literature Texts

You can also supplement science texts with popular science literature and science-related books. Some of these books, which can also be found in the elementary, junior high, and high school catalogs (See references for Fidel and others), are listed in Box 15.13.

BOX 15.13. *Some popular science and science-related books at the elementary, junior high, and high school levels:*[1]

Elementary
Blood and Guts by Linda Allison. Boston, MA: Little Brown, 1976.
 A funny, fast-reading book packed with neat information and great illustrations of the human body.
It's Going to Sting Me by Ronald Rood. New York: Simon & Schuster, 1976.
 A book about snakes, spiders, and other animals and plants that can harm you, and what you can do about them.
The Book of Think by Marilyn Burns. Boston, MA: Little, Brown, 1976.
 Interesting and easy-to-read book that helps you solve problems.
Beloved Benjamin is Waiting by Jean Karl. New York: Dell, 1978.
 Young girl communicates with aliens from outer space and learns to cope with her problems.
The Phantom Tollbooth by Norton Juster. New York: Random House, 1964.
 Easy-to-read fantasy book about a boy who is bored with life.
Hold Zero by Jean Craighead George. New York: Thomas Y. Crowell, 1966.
 Young boys build a model rocket that woke up the town's adults and the Air Force.
Misty of Chincoteague by Marguerite Henry. Chicago: Rand McNally, 1947.
 Two children who wanted a particular horse and how they got it.

Junior High
A Wrinkle in Time by Madeleine L'Engle. New York: Dell, 1962.
 Science fiction fantasy about kid's who try to find their father on a distant planet.
Never Cry Wolf by Farley Mowat. New York: Dell, 1963.
 Scientist in the Arctic trying to find out how wolves live.
Island of the Blue Dolphins by Scott O'Dell. New York: Dell, 1960.
 Adventure story about a girl left stranded on an island.
A Wind in the Door by Madeleine L'Engle. New York: Farrar, Strauss & Giroux, 1973.
 Fantasy science fiction about kids' encounters with an alien creature.

Life Battles Cold by Jane Kavaler. New York: John Day, 1973.
How plants, animals, and people can survive in Antarctica.

Kon Tiki by Thor Heyerdahl. *Chicago: Rand McNally, 1950.*
Adventure story about a group of scientists who cross the ocean on a raft.

Julie of the Wolves by Jean Craighead George. New York: Harper and Row, 1972.
Award-winning narrative of young girl's adventure in Arctic wilderness.

The Sea Around Us by Rachel Carson. New York: Simon & Schuster, 1958.
Classical book. Narrates mysteries of the ocean.

Woodswoman by Anne LaBastille. New York: E. P. Dutton, 1976.
Autobiography of woman who lives by herself in the mountains.

The Reasons for Seasons by Linda Allison. Boston, MA: Little, Brown, 1975.
Easy-to-read book with lots of illustrations, ideas, experiments, and information about the earth and the solar system.

Science Experiments You Can Eat by Vicki Cobb. Philadelphia, PA: J. B. Lippincott, 1972.
Explain scientific principles through activities with food.

The Flying Circus of Physics with Answers by Jerry Walker. New York: Wiley, 1977.
Question and answer book with lots of pictures that explains how physics affects your everyday life.

Gifts of an Eagle by Ken Durden. New York: Simon & Schuster, 1972.
How to love, train, and then let go of an eagle.

Starship Trooper by Robert Heinlein. New York: G. P. Putnam's Sons, 1960.
Problems we face when we begin traveling in space.

Star Trek Puzzle Manual by James Razzi. New York: Bantam Books, 1976.
Puzzles, games, and activities for Star Trek fans.

High School

Masterpieces of Science Fiction edited by Thomas Durwood. Kansas City, MO: Ariel Books, 1978.
Short, science fiction stories illustrated with Star Wars-type space scenes.

Please Explain by Isaac Azimov. New York: Dell, 1973.
Answers to 100 questions about the sun, black holes, the beginnings of the universe, and other questions you've always had about space.

The Making of a Surgeon by William Nolen. New York: Pocket Books, 1970.
Day-to-day events in a hospital and the life of a doctor.

The Monster of Loch Ness by Ray Machel. Chicago: The Swallow Press, 1976.
Discuss whether or not large monsters live in Loch Ness and what they might look like.

Growing Plants Indoors by J. Lee Taylor. Minneapolis, MN: Burgess Publishing, 1977.
Shows you how to grow plants indoors and ways to decorate your room with plants.

A Partnership of Mind and Body: Biofeedback by Larry Kettlekamp. New York: William Morrow. 1976.
Tells how your mind can control your body.

A Ring of Endless Bright by Madeleine L'Engle. New York: Farrar, Straus & Giroux, 1980.
Weaves a tapestry of life and death, of stars and physics, starfish and dolphins.

Folktales of American Weather by Eric Sloane. New York: Hawthorn Books, 1963.
   Entertaining account of myths and folktales about the weather.
Aku-Aku by Thor Heyerdahl. New York: Pocket Books, 1960.
   Scientific expedition that led to the discovery of a lost civilization.
The History and the Future of Garbage in America by Hatlan Kelly. New York:
   Saturday Review Press, 1973.
   Humorous book about garbage collection and what is done with garbage in
   America.
Sea and Earth: The Life of Rachel Carson by Philip Sterling. New York: Thomas Y.
   Crowell, 1970.
   Biography of a famous biologist and writer.
The Cosmic Connection by Carl Sagan. New York: Dell, 1973.
   About the universe and the possibility of life on another planet,

[1]Reorganization of table by Janice A. Dole and Virginia R. Johnson. Beyond the textbook:
Science literature for young people. *Journal of Reading,* April, 1981, 579–582. Reprinted with
permission of the authors and the International Reading Association.

Inquiry

At the heart of a science course is a mode of inquiry, such as experimental methods. From these methods, science students learn not to accept information on the basis of the text's or the instructor's authority but to question and determine the validity of assertions made in the text or in the class. In short, science students learn to use the assertion as an hypothesis, and then apply the scientific method to test the hypothesis. (See Box 15.3 for the steps in this method.)

Suppose the students' text states: "Water rises to its own level." Is this statement true? How can it be tested experimentally? The class can proceed to investigate this question under teacher direction. If the class has already had some phase-out training in the use of the scientific method, the students can divide into groups. If you have already given students enough training in the experimental method, they can pursue the question on their own.

Project Method

The Project Method consists of the students formulating questions about a chapter and getting answers through library research—first as a class, then as members of groups, and finally as individuals. (See chapter 11 for further explanation of the project method.)

You can investigate almost any topic in a chapter. Some topics, such as conversion of water energy to electricity, may require construction of a miniature hydroelectric system. Students might search the library for information on how to construct their own weather stations, radio receivers, television sets, or telescopes and use the information to actually build these instruments. The results can be displayed at science fairs.

Science fairs have featured projects at all school levels for many years; but, frequently, the projects have not been a part of regular classroom instruction. However, the sequence of strategies from DRA to the project method can take students progressively from dependence towards independence in reading and learning from text and can teach students how to get information to satisfy their own curiosity. The phase-out/phase-in sequence applied to each strategy will contribute to this progression towards independence. Through use of the project method, we think more students would do projects on their own. In doing projects, they would also gain greater understanding of and interest in science and its applications, not just as a school subject, but as an important part of their everyday lives.

Although teachers can observe whether students are learning to read and learn from text through classroom observation, student reports, and construction activities, they should also use a systematic way of evaluating student achievement. For this purpose, in the last section of this chapter, we explain the construction and use of a table of specifications. To illustrate this table we use content and processes from physics, but the table of specifications is a generic concept that works in any content area, with, of course, appropriate modifications in the table's content and processes.

Evaluating Achievement

CONSTRUCTING A TABLE OF SPECIFICATIONS FOR A TEST

Teacher-made tests should start with a *table of specifications* to determine whether evaluation is comprehensive and appropriate for the course. See an example of a table of specifications for an entire physics textbook in Table 15.1. The table consists of content (major concepts) on one dimension, and processes (definitions, observations, concepts, interpretations, generalizations, measurement, and applications) on the other dimension. The cells of the table indicate the particular content for a particular process. The sums for each column and each row of the table show the number of items on the test for a particular content or process. The number of items in cells, rows, or columns thus indicates the emphases within the test. Ideally, the test emphases should match the instructional emphases.

INTERPRETING A TABLE OF SPECIFICATIONS

Let's see how we would interpret a table of specifications. In Table 15.1, the numbers in the cells refer to the items in Box 15.11, which we can also use as an achievement test. Table 15.1 shows that our test was entirely on the content of a chapter section—pressure in fluids—and that we asked 21 questions on five of the seven processes. We did not question students on the processes of interpretation or generalization. We had about equal emphasis on four of the five processes. The least emphasis was on applications. Therefore, this test stressed retention of knowledge more than interpretation and generalization. (A test of a laboratory investigation might have the opposite emphasis.)

TABLE 15.1. Table of Specifications for a Physics Test

PROCESSES

CONTENT	Definition	Facts or Observations	Concepts	Interpre-tations	Generali-zations	Measurement	Applications	Subtotal
Matter								
Molecules								
Fluids	5	5	5			4	2	21
Solids								
Gases								
Heat								
Light								
Magnetism								
Electricity								
Electronics								
Radiation								
Subtotal	5	5	5			4	2	21

Interpreting Test Results

After we administer the test to a class, we can summarize the results on another table of specifications. By inspection, we can then determine the cells in which the class did well or poorly. We can do likewise for an individual's test results. Then we would have to investigate whether the class did poorly on some items because of instructional inadequacies, learning and retention inadequacies, or both.

SUMMARY

Although science courses can vary in emphasis (from science as a body of knowledge to be mastered to science as an application of principles to produce new knowledge), they all contain an abundance of technical words, concepts, generalizations, theories, and, of course, procedures for discovering and verifying new knowledge.

The verbal density, particularly of high-level abstractions, places a heavy burden upon science teachers and students. But, if science lessons can progress from the factual or concrete to the abstract and theoretical aspects of science, more students could successfully learn science. For this purpose we advocate (a) use of a problem-solving sequence that not only demonstrates the steps in solving a problem but also explains the linguistic, algebraic, and recall processes that are necessary for solving a problem, particularly in physics, and (b) a questioning sequence (Quest) that will stimulate students to think in a systematic way from observation to generalization.

Following this emphasis on content versus process and instructional procedures in teaching science, we then move on to teaching students how to use texts and strategies on how to read and learn from texts. The strategies are directed reading activities, glosses, reading and learning-from-text guides, SQ3R, inquiry, and the project method. These strategies help students to progress from dependence toward independence and from teacher-directed to self-directed learning.

In all of these strategies, students must learn technical terms and how to differentiate these terms from everyday vocabulary. The teacher's task is to help students make this differentiation and to be sure that a gap does not arise between the semantic and knowledge hierarchy students bring with them to science, on the one hand, and the level of meanings and technical knowledge required for reading and comprehending science texts on the other. Teachers can either select appropriate texts, rewrite or gloss passages, provide guides, or, in general, develop students' semantic and knowledge hierarchy through single- and multiple-text strategies and problem-solving and Quest sequences so they can comprehend the specialized content and processes of scientific writing.

Scientific writing has some unique aspects to it, including not only technical concepts but also measurements, scientific method, graphic and tabular data, and emphasis upon particular types of paragraph structures (enumeration, classification, comparison and contrast, generalization and proof, problem and solution, question and answer, and sequence of events). Often authors adopt a style of writing in which they use these paragraphs in a sequence in each chapter of a textbook. If teachers point out this style of writing, they can facilitate the students' processing of a text.

Of course, the reading of science materials is similar to reading in other content areas. The skills necessary include detection of main ideas and the use of reasoning abilities—making inferences, interpreting, generalizing, and evaluating conclusions.

A table of specifications for a test of achievement can be used to determine whether the content and processes on the test reflect what the teacher has taught. If the teacher records the class's or an individual's test results in a table of specifications, the teacher can see where the strengths and weaknesses are. This knowledge will be helpful in making subsequent plans for teaching students to read and learn from texts.

ACTIVITIES

1. Analyze the pattern of a physics text by identifying the sequence of paragraph types at the beginnings of successive chapters. (Use the paragraph types in chapter 9 to help you with this activity.) Is the sequence of paragraph types the same in both chapters?
2. Prepare a Problem Demonstration Sequence of a physics problem. (See Box 15.7.) Follow it up with a lesson plan for a Quest sequence to develop observation of factual information, concepts, and relationships among concepts. (See Box 15.4.)
3. Write out your plan for a directed reading activity (DRA) covering one section of a text. Anticipate in your plan student questions and your responses to them.

16 | Mathematics

CHAPTER OVERVIEW

So far in this book you have studied general methods of teaching students to learn from their textbooks. In addition, you have seen how these methods can be applied to the content areas of English, social studies, and science. The chapter you are about to read focuses on mathematics. As you read you will see how two conflicting theories of learning have influenced the teaching of mathematics in today's schools. You will also discover not only that mathematics is a language in itself but also that it shares with English many grammatical features. In addition to learning about four types of mathematics vocabulary, you will learn how to apply DRA, marginal gloss, RLT guides, SQ3R, the project method, and phase in/phase out to mathematics textbooks.

GRAPHIC ORGANIZER

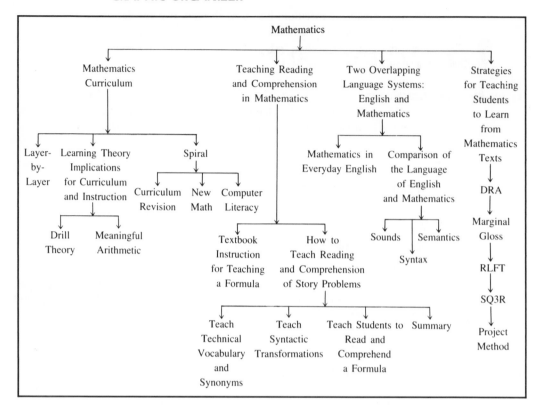

PREPOSED QUESTIONS

1. How do the two conceptions of curriculum differ?
2. What is the drill theory of arithmetic and what is its strength?
3. What is meant by meaningful arithmetic? How is it different from a drill theory?
4. In what ways are reading and math comprehension similar?
5. What is the language of mathematics? How does it relate to prose? What must students do to read and comprehend math problems?
6. What single- and multiple-text strategies can be used for making math texts fit an entire class?

MATHEMATICS CURRICULUM

The mathematics curriculum has gone through two revolutions within the past two generations. The curricula that grew out of both are still in use. To understand the math curriculum today, it is necessary to understand both the old and the new.

Layer-by-Layer Curriculum

The old curriculum could be characterized as a layer-by-layer curriculum. In the *layer curriculum,* topics were presented by grade levels, as shown in Box. 16.1.

BOX 16.1. *Mathematics Topics in the Layer Curriculum*

Primary Grades: arithmetic operations (addition, subtraction, multiplication, division)

Intermediate Grades: fractions, decimals

Junior High School: measurement, percent, introduction to algebra

High School: geometry, advanced algebra, trigonometry, introduction to calculus. (Calculus has moved back and forth from high school to college; it now is taught in some high schools and in all college math programs.)

Learning Theory Implications for Curriculum and Instruction

DRILL THEORY

Instruction in the layer curriculum, particularly in the elementary schools, was based on Thorndike's *drill theory* of arithmetic (Brownell, 1961). This theory of teaching arithmetic stemmed from Thorndike's stimulus-response theory of learning. Thorndike's theory stated that individuals learned when they responded to a stimulus and found the consequences satisfying, as when the teacher said, "Yes, that's a correct answer." According to the theory, a teacher would show a stimulus (3 + 5 =) and identify the correct response, 8, for a student. Then on subsequent trials whenever the student saw the stimulus "3 + 5" and responded with "8" the teacher would say, "Yes" (Stephens, 1956). Moreover, the connection between the stimulus (S) and the response (R) was strengthened through practice that had satisfying consequences. Hence, students not only gave the correct responses, but they also practiced them till they could make the correct response to the basic arithmetic fundamentals accurately and efficiently.

Thorndike assumed that understanding or insight was a consequence of building up a framework of connections. After students had learned the artihmetic fundamentals, they would then begin to perceive the interrelationships within each operation and between the operations—that the columns and rows in an addition table consisted of increments of one; that subtraction is the inverse of addition; that multiplication is successive addition or combining into groups; that division is successive subtraction or separating into groups.

The drill theory was heavily criticized by *gestalt* psychologists because students were not given an opportunity to perceive relationships in arithmetic at the beginning of instruction. Under the drill theory concept, only after the students had learned to add by 1s, then 2s, then 3s, and so on through 10s were they allowed to perceive the complete addition table. The gestalt psychologists thought the sequence should be reversed. They would start learners off with the table, show them the interrelationships, and *then* have them learn the individual combinations.

Mechanical Versus Meaningful Learning

Brownell et al., (1949) was also critical of the drill theory of arithmetic, which he called "mechanical learning." In its place, he advocated what he referred to as *meaningful arithmetic*. In meaningful arithmetic, students were instructed to understand arithmetic concepts, relationships, and generalizations (Brownell and Hendrikson, 1950) rather than learn them on the basis of teacher authority and rote memorization. For example, they were taught to think of 3 + 5 as 3 ones (111) added to 5 ones (11111). Hence, a student could get the answer by counting up the ones. Likewise, they were taught to see 7 × 6 as 7 sixes, which is different from 6 sevens. To determine whether students understood the relationships and the number system in general, Brownell would give a transfer test, that is, he would test the students to see if they could apply their arithmetic understanding to situations in which they had received no training. Students who had been trained to add 3 (ones) + 5 (ones), would be tested, for example, on adding 6 (ones) + 4 (ones). After testing, Brownell would interview students to determine whether they had learned merely by authority (rote memory) or in a meaningful way. He would challenge the validity of their responses and then see whether students had an alternate solution. For example, he would ask a student who had learned the multiplication tables, "What is 7 sixes?" If the students said, "42," Brownell would say the answer was wrong. If the student disagreed, Brownell would say, "Prove it." The student could do so by adding up a series of 7 sixes. Brownell would again challenge the answer, still saying it was wrong. The student would then have to go further and translate each six in the series to a group of six ones and add by ones,[1] as shown in Box 16.2. After this step, Brownell would agree that the student had learned multiplication in a meaningful way by developing a *quantitative hierarchy* of knowledge.

Algebra extends this quantitative hierarchy to a higher level of abstraction; for example, let *a* equal each group of six ones in our arithmetic hierarchy. Then, 7 times $a = 42$, as shown in Box 16.3.

The relationship can be made more abstract and more general: let *b* equal a multiplier that can represent any number, including 7. Then $ba = 42$. To make the equation completely general, let *c* equal the product, then $ba = c$. Thus,

---

[1]This process can, of course, be taken one more step to actual objects, such as apples or oranges.

BOX 16.2. A Quantitative Hierarchy for the Multiplication of Seven Sixes

$$
\begin{array}{cccc}
6 & 6 & 111111 \\
\underline{\times 7} \quad = & 6 & 111111 \\
42 & 6 \quad = & 111111 \\
& 6 & 111111 \\
& 6 & 111111 \\
& 6 & 111111 \\
& \underline{+6} & \underline{+111111} \\
& 42 & 42 \\
\end{array}
$$

BOX 16.3. An Algebraic Equivalent for the Multiplication of Seven Sixes

$$
\begin{array}{rl}
a = & 1111111 \\
a = & 1111111 \\
a = & 1111111 \\
a = & 1111111 \\
a = & 1111111 \\
a = & 1111111 \\
a = & \underline{1111111} \\
7a = & 42 \\
\end{array}
$$

---

algebra makes relationships and equations among numbers abstract and general and takes the quantitative hierarchy to a higher cognitive level. As students progress up the hierarchy, they reorganize their thinking and learning of mathematics (Brownell, 1939).

Through its laws, algebra also makes arithmetic operations abstract and general. In elementary arithmetic, students learn to add, subtract, multiply, and divide. Algebra states general rules for these operations as shown in Box 16.4.

BOX 16.4. Algebraic Rules for Arithmetic Equations

Arithmetic	*Algebra*
$2 + 3 = 5$	$a + b = c$
$5 - 2 = 3$	$c - a = b$
$3 \cdot 4 = 12$	$a \cdot b = c$
$\dfrac{12}{4} = 3$	$\dfrac{c}{b} = a$

In demonstrating the continuity between arithmetic and algebra, a teacher shows that the quantitative hierarchy progresses from the concrete to the abstract level. It is hoped that this demonstration enables students to develop a mental framework without any discontinuity in it. We suspect that some students who do not perceive the relationships between arithmetic and algebra get lost in algebra because they cannot move down the hierarchy whenever it is necessary to substitute numbers for algebraic letters. Hence, they cannot draw upon their arithmetic knowledge for understanding algebra and for solving algebraic problems.

The job of the teacher is to provide the bridges and fill in the gaps between arithmetic and algebra. We suggest that these bridges be built in an inductive fashion, using the Quest technique. (See chapter 15 for an explanation of Quest.) The teacher should thus construct (a) a number hierarchy that spans the range from numbers representing objects to letters for depicting general quantities and relationships and (b) functions of arithmetic that are subsumed by the fundamental laws of algebra—the *commutative law*, the *associative law*, and the *distributive law*. These laws represent arithmetic operations at a more abstract level, as shown in Box 16.5. By building these hierarchies, students will perceive the continuity between arithmetic and algebra at the same time they are developing their mathematical hierarchy to a higher level of abstraction and generalization. They will then have a mental framework that will help them not only read but also comprehend algebra.[2]

BOX 16.5. Algebraic Laws That Represent Arithmetic Operations

1. *Commutative Law*
   a. Addition: $a + b = b + a$, or $2 + 3 = 3 + 2$
   b. Multiplication: $a \cdot b = b \cdot a$, or $2 \cdot 3 = 3 \cdot 2$
2. *Associative Law*
   a. Addition: $x + (y + z) = (x + y) + z$, or
             $2 + (3 + 4) = (2 + 3) + 4$
   b. Multiplication: $x \cdot (y \cdot z) = (x \cdot y) \cdot z$, or
                   $2 \cdot (3 \cdot 4) = (2 \cdot 3) \cdot 4$
3. *Distributive Law of Multiplication over Addition:*
   $x \cdot (y + z) = xy + xz$, or
   $2 \cdot (3 + 4) = 2 \cdot 3 + 2 \cdot 4 = 6 + 8 = 14$
   or $2 \cdot (3 + 4) = 2 \cdot 7 = 14$

Thorndike also used a social criterion for the curriculum. The only arithmetic topics to be included in the curriculum were those that adults actually used in

---

[2]This mental hierarchy should also be extended to geometry, trigonometry, and to more advanced courses in mathematics. See Anderson *et al.* (1977) for a discussion of schema hierarchies in the acquisition of knowledge.

their everyday lives. Hence, after conducting a survey on arithmetic adults used, Thorndike recommended elimination of such arithmetic instruction as finding the cube root of a number. Indeed, elimination of such rarely used algorithms was beneficial to the curriculum.

Spiral Curriculum

CURRICULUM REVISION

The meaningful approach to arithmetic instruction was followed by curriculum revision on a large scale in the 1950s and 1960s (Heath, 1964). One of the major groups involved in this curriculum revision was the School Mathematics Group (SMSG). This group, directed by E. G. Begle, was funded over a 5-year period (1958–1963) for more than $5,000,000 by the National Science Foundation (Wooton, 1964). In this group, mathematicians, high school mathematics teachers, and representatives of science and technology banded together to write sample textbooks—first for Grades 7 to 12 and subsequently for elementary school. They then tested these books in school settings, revised them, and made the revisions available for purchase. The content of the textbooks was not much different from the traditional curriculum, but concepts and mathematical structures were provided that gave meaning to the skills and facts stressed in the texts. Box 16.6 shows the content of SMSG. SMSG also decided to present mathematics for students in Grades 7–12 in less formal fashion, using more concrete illustrations and a slow pace, so that the middle range of students could learn algebra and geometry. Moreover, some, but not all, of the content was related to physical models, such as topics found in physics texts.[3]

BOX 16.6. *Content of School Math Study Group*

Grade 7: numeration, number systems, plane geometry (intuitive); applications

Grade 8: graphs; plane, solid, and nonmetric geometry (intuitive); probability; additional work with number systems; applications

Grade 9: elementary algebra

Grade 10: Euclidean plane and solid geometry

Grade 11: algebra and trigonometry

Grade 12: elementary functions and matrix algebra

NEW MATH

The curriculum was popularly known as "New Math." But mathematicians had known the "new math" for over 200 years.

---

[3]Some mathematicians would emphasize the use of mathematics for the solution of physical problems and would present all mathematical concepts in physical or genometric terms (DeMott, 1964).

The elementary materials included concepts such as commutation ($7 + 2 = 2 + 7$) and some simple geometric ideas (points, lines, plane figures) that provide a bridge (number line) between geometric and numerical ideas. The elementary texts also introduced algebra concepts ($N + 2 = 5$) and taught arithmetic operations in bases other than 10 so that students could gain a better understanding of the number system. In short, elementary mathematics no longer consisted of a layer-by-layer curriculum but was characterized by a *spiral curriculum*. Assuming that any individual could learn anything at any age, provided it was presented in a thought form appropriate to the individual's stage of development (Bruner, 1963), topics from geometry and algebra were introduced in the primary grades at a concrete level of thinking. Later in the spiral curriculum, the same topics were tackled at a more abstract level, just as American history is taught in Grades 5, 8, 11, and again at college at increasingly higher levels of abstraction.

Along with the revision of the curriculum, many teachers took in-service training courses, frequently in summer institutes funded under the National Defense Education Act. Some states, such as California, required all elementary teachers to have a course in mathematics taught by a math department. Many parents also took math courses so they could help their children. The teachers and parents were taught what was called the "new mathematics." Although the new math was new to most elementary teachers and parents, it had been known to mathematicians for hundreds of years.

Teachers placed great emphasis on having students understand the new math. While doing so, they tended to teach students to be accurate and effective, but not efficient, in doing fundamental arithmetic operations. Consequently, although students may have learned to understand math, their performance on tests that stressed computation (particularly when the testing time was short) was not as good as it should have been. As a result, some teachers and school districts dropped the new math and returned to the drill theory of teaching arithmetic. So today, mathematics instruction is a mixture of the old and the new arithmetic.

COMPUTER LITERACY

A more recent development occurred with the advent of inexpensive electronic calculators. They are now in wide use not only in math classes but also in physics classes where they have replaced the slide rule that was once part of every engineering student's basic school equipment. They are also being used in elelmentary schools. Calculators and miniature computers are now serving as cash registers and in almost all monetary operations. Indeed, clerks have hardly any arithmetical operations to perform; they only have to read prices, punch buttons correctly, recognize bills, and count out change.

In the 1980s microcomputers came into widespread use in the schools, mostly for computer-assisted instruction and some use as word processors and computer-managed instruction in classrooms and for accounting procedures in the office (Singer & Phelps, 1983). The National Council of Mathematics (1977) called for the addition of computer literacy as another K–12 developmental strand for the mathematics curriculum. Subsequently a graded curriculum was constructed to develop computer literacy. It progresses from use of computers for instruction in the lower grades to programming for computers for problem solving at the higher grade levels (D. Johnson, Anderson, Hansen, & Klassen, 1980; Singer et al., 1982).

This brief review of curriculum revision provides a background for our approach to teaching students to read and learn from math texts. We agree that accuracy, meaning, and efficiency in arithmetic operations, whether presented in a layer or spinal curriculum, are necessary prerequisites for computing and solving problems (particularly algebra problems) in high school mathematics. But we also believe that many students who know, understand, and can perform the fundamental operations of arithmetic, with or without a calculator, can become more effective in higher level math courses (particularly algebra and trigonometry), if they are taught through strategies that can cope with a wide range of individual differences. These strategies do not assume that students already know what they are to be taught. Nor do they rest upon the discovery method of learning, teacher-posed questions, or text-posed problems given as homework after only a single problem applying a rule has been worked in a text. Our strategies for teaching students to read and learn from text progress from maximum dependence on a teacher to maximum independence for the student through a phase out of the teacher and a phase in of the student. This phase out and phase in is used for each strategy. Thus, as students progress through such strategies as (a) directed reading activities, (b) marginal glosses, (c) reading and learning-from-text guides, (d) SQ3R, (e) the use of multiple texts, and (f) the project method, they become increasingly able to learn how to learn from text on their own. We show how these strategies apply to teaching mathematics after we have set the scene that will enable us to differentiate reading from comprehension in mathematics. The scene consists of a lesson in a junior high school text and a frequently heard complaint about students' inability to read story problems.

TEACHING READING AND COMPREHENSION IN MATHEMATICS

Textbook's Instruction for Teaching a Formula

Let's take a look at the interaction leading up to *story problems*. A typical instructional plan in an algebra text appears in Box 16.7.

BOX 16.7. Plan for Teaching Students to Read a Formula and Substitute Numbers in It

1. Computing interest is introduced with a statement that interest is the amount of money earned by a loan of money at a given rate.

2. Then a formula is stated:

$$\boxed{\text{Interest} = \text{Principal} \times \text{rate} \times \text{time}}$$

3. The third step is to apply this formula to a problem: $500 is loaned at 6% interest for one year. The interest is computed as follows:

$I = Prt$
$I = \$500 \times 6\% \times 1$
$I = \$500 \times .06 \times 1$
$I = \$30 \times 1$
$I = \$30$

4. Then story problems are presented, usually for homework assignments. These problems are stated in various ways:
   a. A man gives a *sum* of money. . . .
   b. Two men make an *investment* in a company. . . .
   c. A person gets a *loan*. . . .

How to Teach Reading and Comprehension of Story Problems

TEACH TECHNICAL VOCABULARY AND SYNONYMS

Notice that in none of these problems is the term *principal* used. Instead, synonyms are used: *sum, investment, loan.* If students do not know that these words are synonyms for *principal*, they have no way of doing the problems. What's the remedy? It is twofold:

1. State the first story problem using the same terms as in the formula. The teacher can then assess whether students understand the problem as presented.

2. Teach students synonyms for the technical terms in the formula. Almost all the other words in story problems are usually within students' reading abilities, particularly those students with reading abilities above the sixth-grade level.

TEACH SYNTACTIC TRANSFORMATION

Another problem students encounter is manipulation of syntax. The formula is presented in a given order, $I = Prt$. But in the story problem students might get the information for this formula in a variety of sequences: *Prt, rPt, trP, tPr.* To use the formula, students have to reorganize the sentence or else substitute information in the correct place in the formula without regard to the order in which the information is given. What can the teacher do? Again, the teacher can do two things:

1. Make sure that information in the first story problem is stated in the same language and order that the formula requires: $I = Prt$. If so, the initial

problem will be relatively easy and will give students confidence that they understand how to do such problems.

2. Prepare students for changes in wording by teaching synonyms, and for changes in syntax either by presenting the information in the formula in various orders, by stating information in the problem in various ways and showing students how to substitute the information in the correct order in the formula, or both.

Assuming that students know the arithmetic involved, the probability is high that the students can then solve the problem. Thus, additional instructional steps will increase the ability of students to read story problems.

TEACH STUDENTS HOW TO READ AND COMPREHEND A FORMULA

A third step the teacher could take would involve showing students not only how to *read* but also how to *comprehend* a formula. Consider the following formula for computing distance:

$$\text{distance} = \text{rate} \times \text{time}$$

To *read* this formula, the student must know how to identify the three words and the two symbols: *distance, rate, time,* and the symbols for equality and multiplication. Most students can read the words by the ninth grade. If not, it would not take much time in a math lesson to teach them how to do so.

Synonyms for the multiplication symbol also have to be taught. These synonyms are parentheses: $(r)(t)$; a dot: $r \cdot t$; the times sign: $D = r \times t$; or nothing at all between rate and time: $D = rt$. If students can identify the terms and symbols they can *read* the formula.

Students must not only know word and symbol synonyms and syntactic manipulation of text, they must also be told that the time has to be measured in the same unit as the rate. If the rate is per annum, then the time must also be expressed in years. If a problem asks how much interest was earned in 6 months and the rate was expressed per annum, the time must be computed as a fraction of a year.

Moreover, the teacher should help students to comprehend a formula by mentally manipulating it or by transforming it. The students might be taught to comprehend $I = Prt$, by asking themselves, "What happens to I when P, r, or t increases?" Also, students must be able to transform the formula to comprehend its relationships. Hence, they should be taught to ask, "What if you know P and t and I but not r? How can you determine what r is?" The answer:

$$r = \frac{I}{Pt}$$

Likewise, if they need to know what t is, given r and I and P:

$$t = \frac{I}{Pr}$$

These ways of thinking about the formula and these types of questions enable students to *comprehend* the formula. In essence, the reason why students do not know how to do story problems is that they are usually taught only how to *read* a formula, that is, only to identify its terms, and then substitute figures for the formula's variables. They also need to learn how to *comprehend* a formula by asking a series of questions about it. These questions concern two aspects of a formula: (1) treating terms as variables by asking what happens when a term increases or decreases and (2) determining relationships among the variables by transforming the formula and solving for each term in the formula. Consequently, when story problems are presented, students will have a greater probability of solving them because they have been taught not only how to *read* but also how to *comprehend* a formula. Eventually students will internalize the comprehension processes for a formula and ask their own comprehension questions. Of course, they might still have some difficulty with story problems, but the difficulties are not likely to be with the reading and comprehension of the formula or with the words and syntax of the story problem. Instead, they are likely to be mathematical difficulties.[4]

SUMMARY

To teach students to read and comprehend a formula, teach them to identify the terms and symbols in the formula and to know their synonyms. Then teach them to manipulate the formula in answer to self-formulated questions. These manipulations should consist of treating the terms as variables and solving for each variable. In practice, the teacher may teach students to comprehend a formula this way by a series of lessons, with each step followed by application to a homogeneous set of problems. Of course, the number of problems necessary and the number of steps that can be covered in a single lesson depend on a particular class's ability and how far along the class is in understanding how to comprehend formulas. By the end of a semester, students should know how, on their own, to read and comprehend new formulas. They will then more likely be able to answer the typical guiding questions for solving a story problem: "What is given?" and "What is asked for?"

If students know their basic arithmetic operations and can read and comprehend formulas, they are ready for instruction in algebra. This instruction can begin by making students aware that, in their everyday speech, they are using

---

[4]Among the difficulties may be lack of realization that a problem involves two or even three steps that must be solved in order. Hence, problems should be organized in order of complexity and students shown how the problems can be solved through multiple-step procedures (Pribnow, 1969).

quantitative language involving the kind of quantitative thinking which occurs in arithmetic and algebra.

TWO OVERLAPPING LANGUAGE SYSTEMS: ENGLISH AND MATH

Mathematics in Everyday English

Quantification and arithmetical processes are implicit in English; indeed, it is almost impossible to construct a sentence in English in which quantification does not occur (Gleason, 1961). For example prearticles (*each one of, every one of, all, none of, any of, some of*) and articles (*the, a*) precede nouns or pronouns in such sentences as "One of the boys . . . ," "None of us . . ." Cardinal and ordinal numbers occur in such a sentence as, "He took the first five volunteers." Comparisons, implying equality between two things, are expressed in such sentences as, "Harry ran as fast as Dan." Inequalities are communicated by such comparisons as, "Irving is taller than Harry," or "Harry is not as strong as Jay." Superlatives identify comparisons of an arrayed series of more than two items, such as "Hal is the tallest of the three men" (Knight & Hargis, 1977).

Arithmetic operations also enter into day-to-day language. For example, "Debbie joined the group" or "Abe left the team" or "Each member of the winning team gets an equal share of the prize money" or "He went to practice each day for the entire month."

Even the commutative, associative, and distributive laws of mathematics occur in everyday language: "Robert and Mary" will be recognized equal to "Mary and Robert"—commutative law: $a + b = b + a$; "Robert and Mary were together with Ann" equals "Ann and Mary were together with Robert"—associative law: $a + (b + c) = (a + b) + c$ (Capps, 1970).

Although children as early as first grade use quantification and arithmetic operations in their natural language, students may have difficulty transforming the meanings of these terms from natural to mathematical language. Consequently, some practice in making these transformations is necessary and may enhance problem-solving ability. Box 16.8 contains some English sentences translated into mathematical language.

BOX 16.8. English Statements and Their Mathematical Equivalents

English Statement	*Mathematical Equivalent*
Each one of the boys writes fast.	$1 + 1 + 1 \ldots$
Harry ran as fast as Dan.	In respect to running, Harry = Dan
Irving is taller than Harry.	In repect to tallness, Irving > Harry

Harry is not as strong as Jay.	In respect to strength, Harry $<$ Jay
Hal is tallest of the three.	In respect to tallness, Hal $>$ x and y; Hal $=$ tallest. tallness
Debbie joined the group.	Group $+$ 1
Abe left the team.	Team $-$ 1
Each member of the winning team gets an equal share of the prize money.	$\dfrac{\text{Prize money}}{\text{number of members}} = \text{Equal share}$
He walked five miles each day, or 155 miles, during July.	5 miles $\times$ 31 days $=$ 155 miles.

Students should realize that (a) although mathematics has its own language, it overlaps with English and (b) quantitative knowledge and processes underlie both languages. However, students also should realize that mathematical language is different from English.

Comparison of the Language of English and Mathematics

Language is a system of organized symbols whose meanings are shared among members of a speech community (Ruddell, 1974). The three major components of a language system are sounds, syntax, and semantics.

SOUNDS

The sound system used for responding to English print and to mathematics is the same. When numbers are spelled out, the principles of English phonology are used; for example, in *seven,* each symbol (letter) corresponds to a sound. However, a *logograph, 7,* can also be used; when it is, it can evoke different phonological responses, for example, *sieben* in German. Thus, the number system in its logographic form can be and is used as a symbol system for the sound systems of various languages. In this sense, the *language of mathematics* is truly international.

SYNTAX

In English, syntax can be transformed in various ways. In Box 16.9 are four story problems that represent four major types of syntactic transformations in English. However, all of these transformations are still read in a left-to-right sequence following English convention. Although syntactic transformations also occur in mathematics (as demonstrated in our section on ''Teaching Reading and Comprehension in Mathematics''), mathematics itself is not limited to a left-to-right sequence but can be read in a variety of directions: horizontally (left to right

---

BOX 16.9. *Syntactic Transformations*
of a Story Problem

1. *Active:* Harry earned 5% interest on the $500 he loaned to Irving for a year.
2. *Active, negative:* Harry did not earn any interest on the $500 he loaned to Irving for a year.
3. *Passive:* Five percent interest was earned by Harry on the $500 he loaned to Irving for a year.
4. *Passive, negative:* Five % interest was not earned by Harry on the $500 he loaned to Irving for a year.

---

or right to left), vertically (top to bottom or bottom to top), diagonally, or a combination of these (Hater, Kane, & Byrne, 1974). The same problem can be read in three directions: "What does 30 divided by 6 equal?" can be written and read as follows:

$$\frac{30}{6}, \ 30 \div 6, \text{ or } 6\overline{)30}.$$

Graphs often require horizontal, vertical, and diagonal eye movements as the student reads the values on the ordinate (y-axis) and abscissa (x-axis) and then follows the graphed line; or the reverse sequence may occur, proceeding from the graphed line to the x or y axis. Because of such syntactic variations in mathematics, it is not surprising that training of seventh graders in the use of syntax in mathematics improved their arithmetic achievement (Sax & Ottina, 1958).

SEMANTICS

Both syntax and vocabulary may be sources of interference in problem solving. When the difficulty level of the syntax and vocabulary of the same problem were varied, and both versions were presented to fourth graders, the problem with the easy syntax and easy vocabulary resulted in the best problem solving (Lindille, 1970).

Although the number of syntactic arrangements are relatively few, the vocabulary load is voluminous. Indeed, dictionaries of mathematical terms are available (Gundlach, 1961; James & James, 1959).[5] Moreover, the terms can be known at various levels of difficulty, including the concrete, the functional, and

---

[5]Structured overviews depicting interrelationships among branches of mathematics and topics within particular branches have also been devised. The claim is that such overviews enable students to perceive relationships among the terms, including those that have been studied, those that are being learned, and those about to be learned. To prepare one, simply arrange the vocabulary in a tree-type diagram that depicts the relationships among the concepts (Earle, 1976).

the abstract levels (Chase, 1960). Addition, for example, can mean any one of these levels of response:

1. Put one box on top of another (concrete)
2. When you see 2 + 1, you say 3 (functional)
3. You combine numbers to get a sum or total (abstract)

Although a graded curriculum may teach the level of abstraction commensurate with the students' mental capabilities, students respond to mathematical terms at various levels of abstraction. Their response levels are moderately correlated with their mental capabilities (Chase, 1960), but perhaps their levels of responding are also related to whether and how they had been taught these terms. In either case, instruction can improve students' mathematical vocabulary ability. The techniques of direct study, including explanation by the teacher, class discussion, and use of a dictionary, improved the general mathematical vocabulary of fifth graders significantly as assessed by the *Iowa Test of Basic Skills* (Vanderlinde, 1964).

Instruction and practice on mathematical vocabulary in isolation through test-like exercises (such as matching symbols with their verbal definitions, which is recommended by Hafner (1977) and which frequently occurs in math laboratory exercises) do not appear to transfer to math problem-solving ability (H. C. Johnson, 1944; Vanderlinde, 1964). Indeed, numerous studies have demonstrated that transfer is more likely to occur if teachers provide for it by having students practice in the actual situations in which teachers want transfer to occur.[6] Hence, we think that vocabulary instruction should occur in context, that is, as an intrinsic part of classroom lessons in mathematics. Accordingly, we have done so in the five strategies we demonstrate in the last half of this chapter.

The vocabulary that has to be taught can be grouped into four categories.[7] One category consists of symbols. A partial list of symbols used in algebra is provided in Table 16.1; the symbols consist of nouns, conjunctions, adjectives, and some verbs. Table 16.2 contains another set of symbols for arithmetic with their verbal representations; these symbols are verbs or action words. Needless to add, students must not only learn the symbols but also their verbal equivalents and their synonyms.

Another set of terms comes from the *metalanguage* of mathematics, the

---

[6]See Lewis Aiken's (1972) comprehensive review of language factors in learning mathematics. When Call and Wiggin (1966) participated in a controlled experiment in which vocabulary as well as other reading skills were taught by an *English teacher* in the context of teaching algebra, the group so taught performed significantly better on problem solving in algebra than the control group taught by an algebra teacher!

[7]Of course, instances of several categories, such as verbal, numerical, and literal can exist in the same context (Earp, 1970). For example, Principal = \$100 × $r \cdot t$. In reading this equation, the reader shifts from alphabetic (Principal) to numerical (100), to symbolic (\$, =, ×''' ·), and finally to literal (r, t) responses.

TABLE 16.1. Some Symbols That Occur in Algebra

$=$	is equal to	$\overset{?}{=}$	is this statement true
$\neq$	is not equal to	$\surd$	yes, statement is true
$<$	is less than	$\|\ \|$	absolute value
$\not<$	is not less than	$\geq$	is greater than or equal to
$>$	is greater than	$\leq$	is less than or equal to
$\not>$	is not more than	$\mathcal{R}$	(the real numbers, 1, 2, 3 . . .)
$\{\ \}$	set	$\%$	percent
ϵ	is an element of	$\pm$	plus or minus, *or* positive or negative
$\notin$	is not an element of	$\overline{AB}$	line segment A, B
ϕ	empty set	$\overrightarrow{AB}$	ray AB
$\cdots$	continues unendingly, *or* and so on through	$\angle A$	angle A
		$m\angle A$	measure of angle A
υ	union of sets	$\overrightarrow{AB}$	vector AB
$\cap$	intersection of sets	$\#$	number
$\subseteq$	is a subset of	$\triangle$	triangle
$\approx$	is approximately equal to		
$\therefore$	therefore		
$\bigcirc$	circle		
$\ominus$	radius		

Source: The list is from Mary P. Dolciani and William Wooton, *Modern Algebra: Structure and Method.* Book I, revised edition. Copyright © 1973 by Houghton Mifflin Company. Used by permission.

TABLE 16.2. Symbols for Arithmetic Operations and Their Synonyms

$+$	and, plus, increased by, sum, add, together
$-$	less, minus, take away, decrease, subtract, diminish, reduce
$a \times b$	times, multiplied by, product of (note that multiplication of a and b is indicated by four symbols)
$a \cdot b$	
$a(b)$	
ab	
$\div$	three symbols that mean divide or find number of groups in a number
$\overline{)\ }$	$(8\,\overline{)32}$: finding number of groups of 8 in 32)
$/$	
x^2	multiply x by itself or square x ; 2 is an exponent of x
x^n	multiply x by itself as many times as is indicated in the exponent, for example, x^4 is $x \cdot x \cdot x \cdot x$
$\sqrt{\ }$	square root

technical words used to talk about the symbolic or object language (Brunner, 1977). Using metalanguage, we can say that the symbols $x + 3 = y$ represent an *equation* in which x is a *variable* to which a *constant* is *added* to obtain *values* indicated by the variable y. The underlined words are vocabulary items in the metalinguistic statement.

A third category of vocabulary that occurs in mathematics is made up of

TABLE 16.3. General and Technical Meanings of Terms Used in Mathematics

	Meaning	
Term	Alternate	Mathematical
1. arc	luminous discharge of electricity across a gap in a circuit	any unbroken part of the circumference of a circle
2. base	one of the four stations in a baseball infield	the number with reference to which a set of numbers is constructed, e.g., base 10, base 2
3. exponent	an advocate for our side	a superscript indicating the power to which a number is raised (multiplied times itself, less one, e.g., $x^3 = x \cdot x \cdot x$)
4. expression	a vivid depiction of mood on a person's face	a meaningful combination of symbols, frequently enclosed in parentheses
5. power	control, authority, influence over others	the number of times (as indicated by an exponent) a number is to be multiplied by itself
6. prime	best, first	a number divisible only by itself or 1 (1, 2, 3, 5, 7 . . .)
7. principal	the head of a school	a capital sum of money placed at interest or due as a debt or used as a fund
8. product	result of work	the number resulting from multiplying together two or more numbers or expressions
9. radical	person associated with policies of extreme change	root part; number which has been raised by an exponent
10. set	a group of at least six games of tennis	a collection of objects with identifiable common characteristics
11. square	a person with unsophisticated or conservative tastes	a quadrilateral whose sides are equal and whose angles are right angles
12. times	*The New York Times* (a newspaper)	multiplied by (2 times 2 = 2 multiplied by 2)

vocabulary terms that have special meaning in mathematics (Aaron, 1965; Collier & Redmond, 1974; Shepherd, 1978). Compare the meanings of the terms in Table 16.3.

A fourth category consists of general vocabulary terms that occur frequently in mathematical problems, such as *distance* (measurement between two points), *each* (every, as each day for a week), *difference* (result of subtraction), *total* (whole or sum), and *obtain* (find the result).

The math teacher must not assume that students know the meanings of terms in any of these four categories of vocabulary, especially in the technical, precise, and abstract way in which they are used in math textbooks. They have to be taught explicitly. We think that instruction in math vocabulary should be an intrinsic part of a math lesson so that it is more likely to be applied in problem solving. Hence, in our five strategies for meeting the wide range of individual differences in ability to learn mathematics, we consciously and deliberately include instruction in the language of mathematics.

STRATEGIES FOR TEACHING STUDENTS TO LEARN FROM TEXTS USING EXAMPLES FROM ALGEBRA

Directed Reading Activity (DRA)

Reading with comprehension involves identifying words, symbols, and signs, determining their meaning and the processes called for, and utilizing the reasoning abilities of analysis, inference, and interpretation. However, not all the information that is necessary for comprehending and solving problems is in the printed materials. Knowledge stored within the individual's memory must be retrieved and brought to bear upon the written material at the appropriate time. The DRA, a procedure for covering all these aspects of the reading-comprehension process, consists of this sequence of six steps:

1. *Readiness for reading.* The teacher determines whether students have the prerequisite store of knowledge for the particular lesson. The teacher may do so through (a) a review, (b) a formal pretest, (c) an informal pretest. Content for readiness consists of vocabulary, previously learned rules and processes, and general information, including knowledge of measurement.

2. *Vocabulary.* The teacher presents new vocabulary terms and their synonyms; clarifies general terms, technical words, symbols, and signs. These can be taught through directed study, including writing them on the board, listing them with their synonyms, pronouncing and defining them, and showing how they fit into the context of a problem. Then provision should be made for students to practice identifying the new vocabulary by locating it in problem sets and defining what a vocabulary item means either by verbal definition or by carrying out an operation; for example,

the meaning of *minus* is demonstrated by simplifying the sentence $3x - (-2x) - 10 = 0$.

3. *Purpose.* The teacher establishes the purpose of the lesson, for example, to learn the commutative axiom of addition, $A + B = B + A$. This purpose also states the objective. Consequently, students will be able to test themselves to determine whether they have satisfied the purpose of the lesson.

4. *Presentation.* The teacher does the following: (a) explains a concept or a process; for example, demonstrates a procedure for solving an equation, including transformation of an equation to show how to solve for each variable ($I = Prt$, $P = I/rt$); (b) applies it to problems: analyzes a problem (draws a picture to represent the problem whenever possible). Then divides the problem into its unknown (what is asked for) and its knowns (what is given). Shows how to solve the problem by letting $x =$ the unknown (y and $z =$ other unknowns); then states the knowns in terms of x. Sets up the equation as a sentence with terms in the sentence that correspond to the unknown and the knowns in the problem. Finally, shows how to solve the equation to find what x is equal to and how to check by substituting the solution; (c) varies ways of stating the same problem: shows syntactic transformations and synonyms that may occur.[8]

5. *Practice under teacher guidance.* The teacher assists students, either in their seats or at the board in applying new knowledge (equation, concept) to problems by asking questions such as ''What is known?'' ''What is unknown?'' Teacher-posed questions direct students' processes of thinking in logical and precise ways. As these processes become internalized, students will use them to guide their own thinking.

6. *Phase out/Phase in.* This process shifts students from dependence on the teacher (Step 5) to independence. When many students can do the problems or exercises, the teacher organizes the class into groups to do similar problems or exercises *as groups.* The group process allows cross-ability teaching and discussion to occur. When the teacher is satisfied that most students comprehend the new lesson, then homework (individual assignments) can be given with a high probability that students will do it with understanding and ease, demonstrating their comprehension by successfully solving the set of problems. Those students who are still having difficulty after the group process may get some individual help from the teacher.

In Box 16.10 is a DRA constructed by Ms. Stewart, a math teacher at Monroe High.

---

[8]When sixth- and eighth-grade gifted students rewrote math problems to make them easier to understand for students who did not do as well in math, they simplified the vocabulary and shortened the sentences, that is, they reduced the readability levels of the problems. They also drew diagrams and made the syntax of the problem consistent with the order of numerical information and separated the question sentences. The average sixth grader then performed significantly better on the math problems that had the easier format. (Cohen & Stover, 1981)

BOX 16.10. *Class: Algebra (DRA)*

"USING EQUATIONS"

1. Readiness (Ms. Stewart checks to be sure that prerequisites for the lesson are met.)
   a. Students can simplify by collecting like terms.
      Test: $5m + 10 - 4m - 4 - 3 = 0$.
   b. Students can add a number to each side of an equation. Test: $3t - 5 = 17$.
   c. Student can solve for an unknown by dividing each side of an equation. Test: $4m = 12$.

2. Vocabulary (Ms. Stewart reviews with the class key technical terms to be used in lesson.)
   Identify vocabulary terms and give their quantitative meaning. Although these terms are explained earlier in the text and are in the glossary, they need to be reviewed again in the context of the lesson.
   a. *longer than* means a length greater than a given length.
   b. *shorter than* means subtract the difference from the length being compared.
   c. *Overall length* means add the lengths together to get the total length.
   d. *Symbol:* something used to represent something else. In algebra, letters at the end of the alphabet, such as x, y, z, are used to represent unknown quantities or variables. If only one unknown is in an equation, it is represented by x.
   e. *Replacement set:* the members of a specified set; in this case, the number that can replace the unknown variable, x, in the equation.
   f. *Open sentence:* an equation that contains one or more variables.
   g. *Equation:* a statement of equality, i.e., where the variable(s) and quantities on one side equal those on the other side of the sentence.
   h. *Positive real numbers:* $1, 2, 3 \ldots n$.
   i. *Root of the equation:* the solution of the equation.
   j. *Solve:* to determine the solution set of an open sentence over a given domain.

3. Purpose (Ms. Stewart clarifies the lesson's purpose.)
   To translate the numerical relationships of a word problem that contains an unknown quantity into an equation and then solve the equation for the unknown quantity.
   Problem: The length of the service module containing the engines of the *Apollo II* spacecraft was 4 feet shorter than twice the length of the command module housing the crew. Also, one lunar module was one foot longer than the command module. If the overall length of *Apollo II* was 45 feet, how long was the command module?

4. Explanation (Ms. Stewart explains how to solve the problem step by step, working with the class.)
   a. The first step in solving this problem dealing with length, as well as other problems whose information can be depicted, is to draw a diagram. (Note: A diagram is shown in the text, but is not listed as the first step in solving the problem.) If necessary, supply knowledge of relationships among service, command, and landing modules. Draw the diagram and indicate lengths as given in the problem.

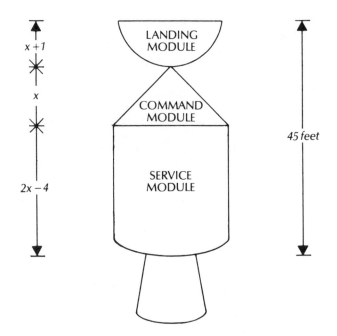

b. Information in the problem can be divided into two categories:
  (1) What the problem asks for and what is unknown. This problem asks, how long is the command module? We let a symbol, x, represent this unknown quantity and place it on our diagram to indicate the length of the command module.
  (2) What information is given in the problem: (a) Length of the service module is twice (two times) the length of the command module *(x)* less (minus) four feet or $2x - 4$. Place this length on diagram. (b) The landing module is one foot longer (+1) than the command module *(x)* or $x + 1$. Place this length on diagram.
c. Now, an equation may be written by indicating how the sum of the parts (the length of each component) is equal to the overall length of the spacecraft.

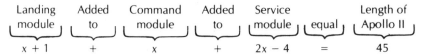

Landing module	Added to	Command module	Added to	Service module	equal	Length of Apollo II
$x + 1$	$+$	x	$+$	$2x - 4$	$=$	45

d. Now *solve* the equation, that is, find what the unknown, x, is.
  (1) Simplify the equation by collecting like terms:
      $$4x - 3 = 45$$
  (2) Add 3 to each side of the equation:
      $$4x - 3 = 45$$
      $$\underline{+3 \quad +3}$$
      $$4x \quad = 48$$

(3) Divide each side of the equation by 4:

$$\frac{4x}{4} = \frac{48}{4}$$

$$x = 12$$

∴ the unknown x, the length of the command module, is 12 ft.

e. Check results by substituting 12 for each x in the equation:

Landing Module		Command Module		Service Module		
$x + 1$	+	x	+	$2x - 4$	=	45
$12 + 1$		12	+	$2(12) - 4$	=	45

f. Now remove parentheses by multiplying 2 times 12:

$12 + 1$	+	12	+	$24 - 4$	=	45

g. Now add:

13	+	12	+	20	=	45
				45	=	45

h. Therefore:

Landing Module = 13 feet
Command Module = 12 feet
Service Module = 20 feet

Length of Apollo = 45 feet

5. Practice Under Guidance (Now Ms. Stewart gives students additional, but similar, examples to work on in class. She directs them to (a) draw diagram, if at all possible, (b) state what is known, and (c) let x represent the unknown.)

Example: As you walk past a school, you can see it is divided into a central part and two wings of equal length. The total length of the school is 500 feet. The central part is three times as long as a wing. How long is the central part?

6. Phase In/Phase Out (Ms. Stewart begins to withdraw guidance as students show signs of being able to work independently.)

a. When Ms. Stewart observes that some students know how to do the practice problem, she divides the class into groups to work together on additional problems which are representative of the homework problems: (a) finding perimeter, (b) determining area of a rectangle, (c) buying and selling, (d) time problems, (e) traveling problems, (e) money problems. She circulates among the groups, giving help to those students who are not benefitting from peer group work.

b. After Ms. Stewart sees that almost all students can now do the problems, she realizes that the class is ready for individual work, and so she assigns homework.

N.B. Steps 1 and 2 are in texts, but the presumption that students are able to recall the processes and meaning of the terms is frequently not warranted. Steps 5 and 6 are not in textbooks; these steps are left to the teacher to do.

Quoted material in this box is from Mary P. Dolciani and William Wooton, *Modern Algebra: Structure and Method*, Book I, revised edition. Copyright © 1973 by Houghton Mifflin Company. Used by permission.

Marginal Gloss

Another way to supplement a textbook is through a marginal gloss. These marginal notes in a textbook can define vocabulary or symbols, remind students of previously learned processes, provide knowledge or information that students are expected to have in their mental repertoire and that is necessary for making inferences or interpretations, or suggest strategies for solving problems.

Of course, a teacher cannot actually write marginal glosses in a text, but can either provide dittoed glosses keyed to text pages or else have students construct glosses from classroom comments. Students can use the glosses when doing their homework. In Box 16.11 is Ms. Stewart's marginal gloss for homework problems.

BOX 16.11. A Marginal Gloss for Homework Problems in Algebra

Gloss	*Homework Problem*
Given: Two numbers (b) Let x = smaller number (a) Then $3x$ = larger number (c) *Given:* Their sum is -16. Then: $3x + x = -16$. *What to find?* What are the smaller and larger numbers? (Note: The problem does not explicitly ask this question.) Solution: Solve the equation. (1) First collect like terms. (2) Then solve for x by dividing both sides of the equation by the coefficient of x. (3) What does x = ? (4) What does $3x$ = ? (5) Check by substitution of $3x$ and x in your equation. Simplify. (6) When you do, does the left of the equation equal the right?	1. (a) One number is three times (b) another number, and (c) their sum is -16.
Draw a sketch to help solve problems. In this case, draw a soccer field. *Given:* width = y, length = $y + 40$ yds. and a perimeter = 380 yds. $y + 40$	2. A soccer field has a perimeter of 380 yds, a width of y yds and a length that is 40 yds more than its width.

(1) Remember that a soccer field is a rectangle; in a rectangle, widths and lengths are equal. Therefore, the other width is y yards and the other length is y + 40 yards.

(2) Remember: Perimeter is equal to the sum of its sides. Therefore:
y + y + 40 + y + y + 40 = 380 yds.

(3) What is asked for? Implicitly the problem asks you to find the width and length in yards. Therefore, solve for y.

What is given?
_____ oxygen
_____ hydrogen
_____ grams of water
What is asked for?
What will equal x in your equation?
What will be 8 times x? What do their totals equal?
Now, set up equation and solve for x.
Check.

Givens:
What will x = ?
What does problem ask for?
(Note: This problem is a two-step problem. It first asks, what is x? After solving for x, you have to substitute in the equation the monetary equivalents of the coins to answer the second question.)

3. Water is a compound made up of 8 parts by weight of oxygen and 1 part by weight of hydrogen. How many grams of hydrogen are there in 225 grams of water?

4. Ken had 8 coins in his pocket. If he had 2 fewer dimes than nickels and one more penny than nickels, how much money did Ken have?

Problems in this box are from Mary P. Dolciani and William Wooton, *Modern Algebra: Structure and Method,* Book I, revised edition, pp. 134–137. Copyright © 1973 by Houghton Mifflin. Used by permission.

Next the teacher can phase out and phase in students through this three-stage plan:

1. The teacher or the text demonstrates some homework problems.

2. The gloss, which decreases in degree of explicit instruction on representative homework problems, is used by groups of students working together in class. Cross-ability instruction thus operates under teacher consultation. That is, the teacher moves about the room helping wherever needed.

3. Students who demonstrate they can do problems on their own are allowed to start on their homework. The rest of the students get additional teacher aid and glosses to help them do their homework. The glosses should have decreasing degrees of teacher direction and questioning.

Reading and Learning-from-Text Guide (RLT)

The reading and learning-from-text guide (RLT) helps the student (a) identify meaning of vocabulary and symbols used in explanations of equations or in problems, (b) processes used in solving equations, and (c) applications. Again, a phase-out/phase-in procedure is used with (a) teacher taking students as a class through a guide, then (b) having students work on guides in groups, and (c) using guides on individual assignments. In Box 16.12 is an RLT Ms. Stewart prepared.

BOX 16.12. RLT Guide for Equations Having a Variable in Both Members

RLT Guide	Text
Identify vocabulary and symbols (Note: check your responses against the glossary at the end of the text.) 1. *Variable* in the problem refers to (a) $2p$, (b) $5p$, (c) p, (d) $7p$. 2. Both *members of the equation* are: (a) $2p$, (b) $63 - 5p$, (c) $2p$ and $63 - 5p$. 3. *Equation* refers to: (a) $2p$, (b) $=$, (c) $63 - 5pm$, (d) $2p = 63 - 5p$. 4. *Real numbers* are: (a) 2, (b) 63, (c) -5, (d) p, (e) a, b, c, and d. 5. The symbol $\overset{?}{=}$ means: (a) is unequal, (b) is equal, (c) is this statement or equation true, (d) is unknown. 6. This symbol $\{\ \}$ means: (a) multiply, (b) perform operations inside brackets first, (c) identifies set, (d) contains answers to problems.	In the equation $2p = 63 - 5p$ the variable appears in both members. Are you allowed to add "$5p$" to each member? For every real number p, "$5p$" denotes a product of real numbers, and therefore, it represents a real number. Because you are permitted to add a real number to each member of the equation, you are also allowed to add "$5p$" to each member without changing the solution set of the equation. Thus, you may solve the equation as follows: $2p = 63 - 5p$ $2p + 5p = 63 - 5p + 5p$ $7p = 63$ $\dfrac{7p}{7} = \dfrac{63}{7}$ $p = 9$ check: $2p = 63 - 5p$ $2 \cdot 9 = 63 - 5 \cdot 9$ $18 = 63 - 45$ $18 = 18$ $\therefore$ The solution set is $\{9\}$ Answer.

True or False
Indicate whether the statement is true (t) or false (f) by writing the appropriate letter in the parentheses.
1. ( ) You can add $5p$ to each side of the equation without changing the answer or answers for which the equation is true.

2. ( ) You can add $2p$ to $5p$ to get $7p$.
3. ( ) You divide each side of the equation to find what p equals.

Processes
1. When $+5p$ is added to $-5p$ the result is:
   (a) 0   (b) p
2. The process of eliminating $+5p$ by adding $-5p$ to it is called:
   (a) additive inverse   (b) negative inverse
3. After $7p$ is divided by 7 the result is really:
   (a) $1p$ (b) $0p$ (c) 1
4. When any real number, except 0, is divided by itself, $(a \div a)$ or multiplied by its reciprocal $(a \cdot {}^1\!/a)$ the result is always:
   (a) 1   (b) 0   (c) the original number

Problem
1. A salesman offered to give a storekeeper 10 pints of an expensive liquid if the storekeeper would buy four of them for $126. After the salesman left, the storekeeper wanted to know how much each bottle would have cost if he had paid $126 for all the bottles. Was he correct when he constructed this equation?
   $4p = \$126 - 10p$
   What would each bottle then have cost him?
2. Can you make up a problem that would fit this equation?
   $2p = 63 - 5p$

Text passages in this box are from Mary P. Dolciani and William Wooton, *Modern Algebra: Structure and Method*, Book I, revised edition. Copyright © 1973 by Houghton Mifflin. Used by permission.

Another type of guide divides the information of a problem into literal (directly stated), interpretive and inferential, and applied levels (Feeman, 1973). But this type of division does not lend itself to the diagnostic categories of vocabulary, information, processes, and applications that are in the RLT guide.

Riley and Patchman (1978) help students solve problems by asking them to divide the problem into three categories: (1) facts of the problem, (2) mathematical ideas and interpretations, and (3) mathematical computations for solving the problem. This division is useful. However, the RLT guide gives much more help initially and then phases out from a maximum to a minimum.

SQ3R

This formula, originally used as a study procedure, guides the student to (a) *S*urvey the assigned reading, (b) formulate *Q*uestions to answer, (c) *R*ead to answer the questions, (d) *R*ecite the answers, and (e) finally *R*eview to check the answers. This formula could be stretched to adapt it to problem solving in math. After *surveying* the problem, the student would ask such *questions* as "What is given?" "What is asked?" "What do the unknown or unknowns equal?" "What equation do I need to set up to fit the problem?" Next, the student would *read* the problem again to see whether the equation fits. Then the student would do the equivalent of *reciting* by solving the equation. Last, he would *review* by checking the answer in the equation and by rereading the problem to see if the answer to the equation fit the requirements of the problem.

Leo Fay (1965) set up an alternative formula: *S*urvey (read rapidly to determine purpose), *Q*uestion (find out what is asked), *R*ead (read for the facts), *Q*uestion (what process is required), *C*ompute (do computation), *Q*uestion (ask: Is the answer correct?). After going through these steps, the student would check the answer by substituting in the equation and checking. Also, check solution against the requirements of the problem.

Neither SQ3R nor Fay's formula seems to fit the problem-solving situation. We think the following formula is more appropriate.

1. *Read* the problem carefully. If necessary, to determine meaning of symbols, consult table of symbols and glossary. Also, if necessary, reread explanatory material on processes.
2. *Question$_1$:* What facts are given?
3. *Question$_2$:* What do I have to find out?
4. *Question$_3$:* What shall I let x equal?
5. *Question$_4$:* How shall I represent the other information given in the problem?
6. *Set up* the equation by translating the words of the problem using the answers to 2, 3, 4, and 5, for the left and right members of the equation.
7. *Solve* the equation.
8. *Test* answer(s) or solution set for the equation by substituting the answer(s) in the equation and by checking answer(s) against the problem.

The acronym for this procedure is RQ_4S_2T. Let's apply it to a problem in Box 16.13 to see how it works.

BOX 16.13.   Application of the RQ_4S_2T Formula
to a Problem

RQ_4S_2T	Problem
1. *R: Read* carefully. Note that all quantities are in the same unit, milligrams.	A cup of (1) *coffee contains 20 more milligrams of caffeine than a cup of tea and*
2. Q_1: What facts are given? These are numbered and underlined in the problem.	(2) *85 more milligrams of caffeine than the average cola drink.* (3) *If one cup of*
3. Q_2: What do I have to find out? See the last part of the last sentence.	*tea and four cola drinks contain the same amount of caffeine as one cup of*
4. Q_3: What shall I let x equal? (x = milligrams in a cup of coffee)	*coffee, how many milligrams of caffeine are there in one cup of coffee?*
5. Q_4: How shall I represent other information in the problem?	

$(x - 20 =$ milligrams in tea$)$
$(x - 85 =$ milligrams in cola$)$

6. S_1: Set up the equation. See sentence three:

1 cup of tea	and	4 cola drinks	contains the same amount of caffeine as	one cup of coffee
$x - 20$	$+$	$4(x - 85)$	$=$	x

7. S_2: Solve the equation:

$$x - 20 + 4x - 340 = x$$
$$4x = 360$$
$$x = 90$$

8. T: Test answers:

$$90 - 20 + 4(90 - 85) = 90$$
$$70 + 20 = 90$$
$$90 = 90$$

∴ 1 cup of coffee contains 90 milligrams of caffeine.

The problem in this box was taken from Mary P. Dolciani and William Wooton, *Modern Algebra: Structure and Method*, Book I, revised edition, p. 45. Copyright © 1973 by Houghton Mifflin Company. Used by permission.

As in the preceding strategies, the teacher again handles the range of individual differences by first phasing in the strategy (taking the class through the RQ_4S_2T procedure), then dividing the class into groups to work on assigned problems with this formula as a guide, and finally having individual students use the RQ_4S_2T procedure on homework problems. Eventually, the procedure will become internalized and used automatically.

Of course, the acronym RQ_4S_2T is only a way of reminding students to apply what they have learned from explanatory material and previous classroom instruction. Since math is extremely cumulative, it is imperative that teachers pace students so that their learning can be cumulative. To do so, math teachers have to adhere closely to a teach-test-reteach instructional procedure, probably on a text section-by-text section basis or at least once a week.

We believe that our strategies for handling the wide range of individual differences will help in this process. We have organized the strategies so that their effects will be cumulative and lead toward independence in reading and learning from text. Hence, we think that students who have gone through the prior strategies will now be ready to use the project method in mathematics.

Project Method

The project method places the student in a position of even greater independence. The strategy first begins with the teacher asking students to read the explanation for a new section. Then the teacher asks, "What do you want to know about this explanation?'' The questions may cover a range of concerns from vocabulary to process to application. Students may then go ahead to find and try out answers to questions under teacher direction. When the class's questions have been answered and the teacher is satisfied that at least some students are able to apply their new knowledge to the solution of problems, then the class can be divided into groups that can try their ability on the next explanatory section in the text. More students are likely to demonstrate independence under this peer group cross-teaching and be able to go on to work individually on problems or even the next explanatory section.

Of course, not all students will be able to attain this stage of development. The instructor may not be able to use this strategy with all students. Or, use of the strategy may have to terminate at the group level for most students.

Another way in which the project method can be applied to mathematics is to find out what students would like to know about mathematics in general. Some questions that may arise are: Who invented algebra? In what ways has algebra been used to solve problems? In what fields do people use algebra? Is it useful in programming computers? Questions of this kind can then be investigated through use of the library and interviews of engineers or computer scientists. The information obtained in such ways can be organized and reported upon by the group. The teacher should direct the first project for the whole class before going on to group and individual projects.

Other projects may come to mind: searching through various texts to find out different ways of explaining the same process; investigating the lives of famous mathematicians; constructing models for various equations; or, the student may use the project method to tackle extra problems listed in textbooks.

SUMMARY

Mathematics is a hierarchically organized system that starts with numbering of objects and progresses to higher order abstractions consisting of symbols. In a meaningful curriculum, this progression is developed systematically so that the student can relate the concrete to the abstract, and vice versa. In addition to the development of this quantitative hierarchy, the student also learns grouping operations such as addition, subtraction, division, and multiplication. Additional symbols are used to represent these operations.

Supplementing the symbols are technical terms, the language of mathematics, and metalanguage (the language about mathematics). Some of these terms are also part of general, everyday vocabulary. For example, the word *radical* has a political meaning and a medical meaning as well as a technical meaning in mathematics. Hence, instruction in symbols and terminology, and differentiation of technical meanings, are an important part of math instruction, particularly when students get into algebra.

Not only must mathematical terms be taught, they must be remembered. The best way to remember something is (1) understand or learn well what is to be remembered by studying a variety of examples, specifying the features of each term, and indicating its related concepts; (2) use what was learned; use, of course, constitutes review. Hence, to help students learn and remember terms and symbols, introduce them in an appropriate context; then use them in a cumulative way (Guthrie, 1978b; Pearson & Johnson, 1978).

In addition to remembering technical terms and symbols, students must also know synonyms and syntactic transformations. We think that math texts and math instructors tend to teach formulas with only one set of technical and general terms and with one syntactic arrangement. If synonyms and syntactic transformations were taught in class, students would be more likely to have greater success with their homework and mathematics because they would know not only how to *read* the problem but also how to use syntactic and semantic knowledge to *comprehend* the problem.

A major difficulty in mathematics, particularly algebra, is having no set of procedures for systematically solving a problem. For this purpose, we believe the procedure, named by the acronym RQ_4S_2T, is appropriate. The validity of this procedure is demonstrated by applying it to several problems.

We concluded this chapter by demonstrating how our five strategies for handling individual differences in the classroom can be applied to mathematics instruction, using algebra as our example. Although the use of these strategies is time consuming initially, each prepares for a phase out of the teacher and a phase in of the student. In short, through this phase out/phase in, students learn from the teacher, then each other, and finally they internalize how to learn to read *and* learn from their math texts.

ACTIVITIES

1. Analyze a math textbook. See whether it contains formulas with problems following them that (a) require syntactic transformations of the formulas and (b) use synonyms for the terms in the formulas. Explain how you would teach students to use syntactic transformations and synonym substitutions. Hint: You can construct a plan for a directed reading activity, for a marginal gloss, or for a reading and learning-from-text guide. Perhaps you would prefer to create your own teaching plans.

2. Interview your students to determine whether they have developed a quantitative hierarchy that extends from arithmetic through algebra. Start with an algebraic equation, such as a × b = c. Ask students to supply an example in arithmetic for this algebraic equation (3 × 5 = 15). Then ask them if five 3s are the same as three 5s (no; 3, 3, 3, 3, 3 is not 5, 5, 5). Ask next how three 5s would be shown on paper (substitute five 1s for each 5). If you want to take this interview a step farther, have students substitute objects for the 1s. See the sections related to Boxes 16.2 and 16.3 for more explanation of a quantitative hierarchy.

3. Take a paragraph from a literature text. Try to express sentences, phrases, and words in mathematical language. (See Box 16.8 for examples.)
4. To individually diagnose a student's difficulties in solving word problems in mathematics, select two problems, one done correctly and one incorrectly. Ask the student to read each problem, explain the meaning of its key vocabulary, symbols, and formula terms, and then re-do the problem aloud (think-out-loud strategy).

17 The Present: Centers for Reading

CHAPTER OVERVIEW

This book began with a discussion of instructional problems that affect an entire school. It is appropriate, then, that the concluding chapters provide a description of how an entire school can deal with the vast differences in students' abilities to read and learn from text. This chapter explains how to use the results of reading achievement survey test to classify all students in a school into four categories. The rest of the chapter describes specific centers on the current scene. We describe each center and evaluate its strengths and weaknesses. We first present a composite of an elementary school reading laboratory or center. Then at the junior and senior high school level, we describe eight centers that include (a) tracking center, (b) clinical center, (c) reading laboratory, (d) functional reading program, (e) individual reading class, (f) multi-faceted reading instruction, (g) the three-stage program, and (h) the schoolwide reading program. In addition to the eight centers, this chapter discusses reading proficiency tests and the possible development of a new center—to teach students the curriculum for the proficiency tests. The next chapter deals with the future scene, an "ideal" school-wide program for reading and learning from text.

GRAPHIC ORGANIZER

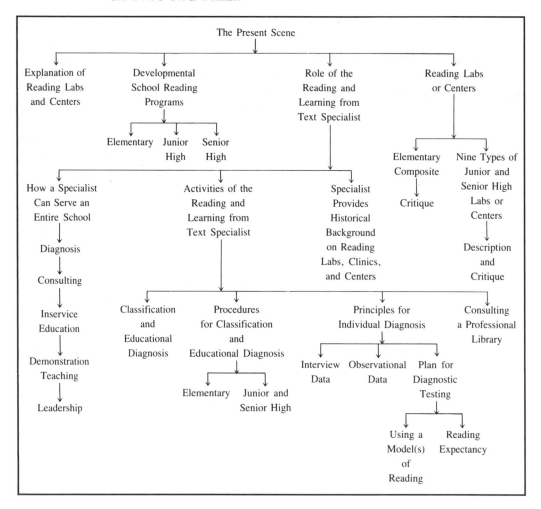

PREPOSED QUESTIONS

1. Why do reading labs and centers exist? What function do they serve?
2. How should a reading specialist allocate time and service so as to serve an entire school?
3. What are the principles for individual diagnosis?
4. How would you use survey tests to classify an entire classroom or grade level into diagnostic classifications?
5. What are the characteristics of current elementary labs or centers? What are their limitations?
6. Describe current reading labs or centers at the junior and senior school levels? How do they operate? What are their advantages and disadvantages? Which type of lab or center would you think is best for your school?

EXPLANATION FOR READING LABS
AND CENTERS

Although the range of individual differences in reading ages increases as students progress through the grades, as explained in chapter 3, the ways of handling this range, such as the widely used three instructional groups in the elementary schools and the single- and multiple-text strategies explained in chapters 6, 11, and 13–16, are adequate for most students. However, some students depart so much from the norms for their class that they require specialized instruction, particularly in reading acquisition. The reasons for these deviations are multiple. For example, some students in the first grade are 6 years old but have a mental age of 4 years. Although they can make some progress in reading acquisition, their learning rate is low (IQ 67) and their ability to deal with abstractions and symbols is limited. Nevertheless, they can make some progress in reading acquisition if they are taught in a small group of 4 to 6 students and the criterion for successful achievement is ability to identify 10 to 20 words in 6 months of instruction (Davidson, 1931). Some other students may have a mental age of 6 years, but have not had any preschool or parental preparation for reading, such as listening to stories. Some students may have visual or auditory defects, frequent absence from school, emotional disturbances, inadequate or inappropriate instruction, particularly if their home language is different from the language of instruction, or they might be students who were free of defects, deficiency, disruptions, and typical differences, but for one reason or another could not keep up with the pace of instruction (Barr, 1973–1974). On the principle that "prevention is better than a cure," these children need to be diagnosed in the primary grades and have a prescribed program under the direction of a reading specialist. At this primary level, the specialist must work closely with the classroom teacher because of the need to emphasize supplemental instruction in the reading laboratory or center and to provide case-study feedback to the classroom teacher so that the classroom teacher can also acquire diagnostic and instructional knowledge on how to teach exceptional students.

If students do not make progress in learning how to read in the primary grades, they are likely to depart even more from their peers in reading achievement in the intermediate grades. Although teachers in Grades 4 through 6 continue to group students for instruction in reading during the reading period, they are not likely to have much time for the students in the lowest group whose reading development is still at the first- and second-grade levels. These students are also likely to begin to accumulate a knowledge deficit because of their lack of free reading and their inability to learn from their knowledge deficit may still interfere with their general comprehension and their ability to learn from texts in the various content areas. Therefore, a reading specialist is also required in the intermediate grades, not only to work with students but also with the faculty on strategies for teaching students to read and learn from texts.

Students who have not mastered reading acquisition at the junior and senior high school levels have a double problem: they must still learn how to read and they also need to learn how to learn from texts in the content areas. The reading acquisition part of their problem is the concern of reading labs and centers. The learning how to learn from texts has to take place in the content area classrooms; as explained in chapters 6, 7, 11, and 13–16, single- and multiple-text strategies enable the teacher to handle a wide range of individual differences in reading achievement.

In this chapter, we describe and critically evaluate an elementary reading laboratory or center and then nine types of junior and senior high school reading laboratories or centers that are in operation on the current scene. We find that each one of them has some limitations; they usually fail to integrate reading instruction with content area material.

In the next chapter, we explain how to develop a "Reading and Learning-from-Text Center" that does integrate reading acquisition with content area materials. The Director of the Center is also a reading specialist who cannot only diagnose reading and learning from text difficulties, but can also conduct an in-service program whose objective is schoolwide instruction in reading and learning from text in each content area.

DEVELOPMENTAL SCHOOL READING PROGRAMS

Elementary Schools

Elementary schools depend upon classroom teachers for the developmental program in reading instruction. The teachers do their own instruction, diagnosis, and reading improvement. Teachers in the primary grades are likely to take into account individual differences in reading achievement throughout the curriculum. Although intermediate grade teachers group students for reading instruction in the reading period, in teaching in the content areas of social studies and science, they frequently use only a single text for the entire class and act as though the class is homogeneous in reading in these content areas. In fact, as we explained in chapter 3, the range in reading achievement in Grade 4 is about 6 years (grade equivalent 1 to 7) and in Grade 6 it has increased to 8 years (grade equivalent 2 to 10). Consequently, teachers in the intermediate grades need to use the strategies explained in chapters 6, 11, and 13–16, particularly when they have only single texts for each content area.

Junior High Schools

Some junior high schools have developmental reading instruction; that is, all students may be required to take a reading course. Other junior high schools may have a developmental reading program and/or reading laboratories or centers for students still in need of reading acquisition.

High Schools

Usually high schools have only reading laboratories or centers for students who are in need of reading acquisition instruction or whose reading achievement is 3 or more years below their grade level. However, our detailed description of

"Monroe High School" explains the need for a schoolwide program for all students: The picture at Monroe High School was beginning to look brighter, quite a contrast to that stormy faculty meeting, the one you read about in chapter 2. The principal's schoolwide committee that directed the in-depth study of the school's many problems continued on as his permanent advisory committee. The committee consisted of Ms. Jones of the social studies department, Mr. Wallace from the English department, Mr. Phelps from science, Ms. Stewart from mathematics, Ms. Jorgensen from home economics, Mr. Carter from industrial education, Ms. Williams the vice principal, and Mr. Umeki, head of the counseling department. One of the committee's recommendations was to hire a reading specialist to help solve the students' reading problems. Subsequently, the principal had the committee serve as an interviewing team to screen and recommend for hiring a new reading specialist.

The committee, chaired by Ms. Jones, screened 40 applications and interviewed 10 applicants. After much deliberation, the committee agreed to recommend Ms. Valdes for the job. She had exactly the kind of background and experience that the school needed. First of all, Ms. Valdes had taught in the science department of a senior high school for 5 years, so she was familiar with the curriculum problems of a specific content area. Second, the committee liked the fact that she had been an excellent but unusual teacher: she had enrolled in a university program so she could learn how to do something for "all those kids who had problems learning from their science textbooks." Third, her subsequent university training focused not merely upon teaching students how to read, but also on how to learn from their textbooks. The committee realized Ms. Valdes could work with the entire range of reading problems of their high school, from working with students who have severe reading problems to assisting content area teachers in making their textbooks more readable and their students more able to read and learn from them. Particularly impressive to the committee was Ms. Valdes's practical explanation of what a reading and learning-from-text specialist could do. Last of all, the committee thought Valdes was realistic about what one specialist for an entire high school could accomplish.

Here is a summary of Ms. Valdes's responses in answer to the question "How can a reading specialist serve the entire school?"

ROLE OF THE READING AND LEARNING-FROM-TEXT SPECIALIST

How a Specialist Can Serve the Entire School

Ms. Valdes began by explaining the role of a *reading specialist* in the elementary school, and then discussed the specialist's role in the secondary school.

Elementary school reading specialists could operate a schoolwide program, serving all students, with emphasis in these areas: (a) diagnosis followed up with reading improvement plans and instruction for individuals and small groups; (b) demonstration of reading and learning-from-text strategies for students in all content areas, (c) consultation with faculty on problems in reading and learning from text, (d) in-service education of faculty and (e) leadership on instruction, curriculum, and evaluation in reading and learning from text. However, in the past, most reading specialists focused on reading acquisition; they gave little emphasis to comprehension or to learning from text in the content areas. Consequently, even though the reading specialists at the elementary level have provided service to all students, they could expand the scope of the service to include more emphasis on comprehension and on teaching students to learn from texts in social studies, science, arithmetic, and literature. When they do so, elementary students will have better preparation for entry into middle school or junior high school instruction (Spache & Spache, 1977).

Typically, Ms. Valdes continued, junior and senior high school reading specialists have also had a narrow role, limited primarily to students still at the acquisition level of reading or to students whose reading achievement is two or more years below grade level. Hence, the reading specialists at junior and senior high school levels have not been providing service to all students; in general, the school has not used their expertise appropriately. If they are well-trained in reading, have majored at the undergraduate level in some academic subject, and hold a junior or senior high school credential, they are also qualified to teach in a content area and to be members of an academic department. This dual role for the reading specialist is desirable because teaching at least one academic class per semester would provide the reading specialist with credibility among the faculty and would enable the specialist to demonstrate that strategies for reading and learning from text can be combined with content area instruction over an entire semester or year. When some reading specialists did serve in this way in junior high schools, they had gained so much credibility at the end of one year that other content area teachers were willing to consult with them and invite them into their classrooms for demonstration teaching and in-service training (Singer, 1975). Thus, they were able to carry out all the functions of reading and learning-from-text specialists. However, since many specialists do not have extensive academic background in one field, they will need to rely on the expertise of all the content area teachers while carrying out these functions.

Ms. Valdes pointed out that the functions of reading and learning-from-text specialists at the junior and senior high schools are somewhat different from those of elementary reading specialists. These functions are: (a) diagnose students with reading difficulties, (b) direct or teach classes in reading acquisition in the content areas and functional reading programs, (c) demonstrate lessons in teaching reading and learning from texts in the content areas and perhaps teach at least a unit or an entire semester in a content area class, (d) advise teachers of introductory classes on strategies for teaching incoming students to learn from texts in content areas, and (e) provide in-service education and serve on a school-wide committee for developing a program for teaching all students how to read and learn from text. These five functions are time-consuming, but all of them can be conducted in a school if the school has the proper ratio of reading specialists to students.

Ms. Valdes explained how to determine the proper ratio by structuring the schedule of a reading specialist: (a) Allocate one of the five periods per day to demonstration teaching of reading and learning from text in a content area with the same number of students as any other teacher (approximately 25 to 30 students). (b) Assign two of the five periods to teaching acquisition or functional reading classes for about 20 students per class. The specialist can provide ongoing observation and diagnosis, both individual and group, within the acquisition and functional reading classes. (c) Allot one period per day for advising teachers in content areas who are offering introductory courses in reading and learning from text to incoming freshmen. (This course can be a 6-week minicourse for a group of 25–30 students enrolled in content area classes such as science, math, social studies, English, auto shop, and so forth. If these minicourses are staggered during the year, then, working together, the reading specialist and the content area teachers combine to teach students how to read and learn from texts in specific content areas. Initially, the reading specialist will do most of the instruction and demonstrate to the content area specialist; gradually the content area teacher will learn and assume sole responsibility for instruction. Eventually, if a school does not have much faculty turnover, the content area specialists will be doing their introductory minicourses on their own.) (d) Allot the last of the five periods in the teaching day for the specialist to direct inservice training, to consult with parents, or to chair a schoolwide committee on reading and learning from text.

Recognizing that one reading specialist could not provide all these services for an entire school, Ms. Valdes went on to explain to the committee that the proper ratio of reading specialists to students could be determined by estimating the number of students who need acquisition or functional reading classes. In general, about 5% of the students in an average high school will need these classes. If the school has 3,200 students, then 5% of 3,200 would be 160 students. The school would need at least four reading specialists, each responsible for 40 of these students.

If a school had only one specialist, that specialist could concentrate on the freshman class; over a 4-year period, the specialist would have served all the students and faculty in the school. In this way, one trained reading specialist could realistically carry out all five functions.

Activities of the Reading and Learning-from-Text Specialist

The principal accepted the committee's recommendation and hired Ms. Valdes in midsummer. By early fall, Ms. Valdes began work on her first problem, one that Ms. Jones brought to her. In looking over the scores on a reading survey test, Ms. Jones was surprised at the large number of her students who were reading well below grade level. In the past, Ms. Jones, occupied with other instructional problems, had only glanced at the scores. But now, as chairperson of the schoolwide committee, she believed she should consult Ms. Valdes because she wanted to know why these students had scored so low.

CLASSIFICATION AND EDUCATIONAL DIAGNOSIS

Procedures for diagnosis, whether at the school, classroom, or individual level, are the same. A survey test ascertains the students' current reading achievement. Current reading status consists of two major components: speed and power of reading. *Speed of reading* is the rate of processing printed materials. A speed of reading test, such as the Gates-MacGinitie,[1] consists of relatively easy passages with time for reading them drastically limited.

Power of reading is the ability of students to comprehend passages of increasing difficulty when given unlimited time to do so. Comprehension tests are "power" tests only when their paragraphs are arrayed from easy to difficult and students have unlimited time to work on them.[2] When students reach the limits of their power of reading, they usually stop; but if they continue on, their answers become merely guesses. A correction for guessing eliminates credit for any guesses that tend to be correct by chance. Typically, the initial paragraphs on graduated tests of comprehension are relatively easy while the final paragraphs are relatively difficult. Further discussion and examples of the speed and comprehension of reading items can be found in chapter 3.

A multiplicity of reasons can be given to explain why a student can be a fast or slow reader and a powerful or nonpowerful reader (Holmes & Singer, 1966). The task of the content reading specialist is to (a) determine the student's current reading status, (b) the cause(s) or reason(s) for this status, and (c) plan how to reduce the student's weakness and improve the student's strengths.

The initial step is to administer survey tests. A typical survey test consists of two subtests: comprehension or power of reading and vocabulary. You can also use the reading and vocabulary subtests of such comprehensive test batteries as the *Comprehensive Tests of Basic Skills, California Achievement Tests, Metropolitan Achievement Tests, and the Stanford Achievement Tests* as survey tests.

Determining Students in the Reading Acquisition vs Learning from Text Phase of Reading Development

A consensus definition determines whether students are in the acquisition phase or beyond it and into the learning from text phase of reading development. A consensus definition may determine the students, regardless of their current grade level status, who score below grade equivalent 4.5 on a reading survey test

---

[1]We are not advocating use of the Gates-MacGinitie as a school's survey test. We are merely employing the Gates-MacGinitie as *one example* of how to use survey test results for classifying readers. We could have used other standardized survey tests that assess speed and comprehension of reading equally well for classifying readers. See chapter 3 for a list of some other survey tests and *Buros Yearbook of Mental Measurements* for critical reviews of survey tests of reading achievement.

[2]When time is limited, students who are slow in speed of reading are penalized. The Gates-MacGinitie manual estimates that 20% of students who take the 45-minute Gates-MacGinitie test are penalized by slowness in speed of reading.

or the reading comprehension subtest of one of the comprehensive test batteries are still in the acquisition phase of reading development. Those students who are beyond grade equivalent 4.5 are in the learning from text phase of reading development. (See chapter 4, Silent Reading, measurement section, for more detailed information on this classification)

Speed of Reading

Some survey tests also contain a subtest on speed of reading. If they do not contain one, you can use the *Van Wagenen Rate of Reading* for assessing speed of reading for Grades 4 and up or the *Minnesota Speed of Reading* subtest. These tests can be administered to individuals or groups. They provide not only a measure of speed of reading, but they also can be used as an index of a student's mastery of word recognition. Students who can read 100 words per minute or faster are likely to have mastered word recognition. That is, they can read at least as rapidly as the normal rate of speech, the rate that radio announcers usually use. (See Buros' *Yearbook of Mental Measurements* for a detailed description of these tests and the survey and comprehensive test batteries.)

At the elementary school level, for Grades 3 to 6, use *the Gates-MacGinitie Reading Test,* Level CS; it has a speed-of-reading subtest. If a speed-of-reading test is not available, then use the individually aministered timed word recognition subtest on the Spache or the Gates-McKillop-Horowitz tests (See descriptions of these tests in chapters 3 and 4).

After you have administered the speed-of-reading test to all students in a particular grade, to students in one classroom, or even to individuals, you score the tests and find the percentile or grade equivalents for scores from the manual's table of norms. You can then classify the scores into one of four categories, as shown in tables 17.1 and 17.2. The dividing line for the four categories is at the 50th percentile or grade equivalent level for each grade. Thus, results from a speed-of-reading test place a student with a score below the 50th percentile or below the grade equivalent level into the slow category and a student with a score at or above the 50th percentile or above grade level into the fast category.

If you gave the timed word recognition test in place of a speed-of-reading test, use the norms in the test manual to classify students on these timed word recognition tests as being above or below the 50th percentile or grade level at the time of testing. For example, if a student in the third grade who is tested in October (Grade 3.2) scores at grade equivalent 3.6, the student is performing *above* grade level. Thus, a score from the timed word recognition tests will determine whether a student is above or below grade level in word recognition speed and accuracy.

Use results from comprehension tests to categorize students in the same way. If a student's score is below the 50th percentile or grade equivalent level, he or she belongs in the nonpowerful category. If the score is at or above the 50th percentile or grade equivalent level, the student belongs in the powerful reader category. Thus, you will have constructed the fourfold classification shown in table 17.1 for elementary school and 17.2 for junior and senior high school.

PROCEDURES FOR CLASSIFICATION AND
EDUCATIONAL DIAGNOSIS

Students in each quadrant of the fourfold classification scheme can be given additional tests to arrive at a more differentiated educational diagnosis. Generalizations about the kinds of students in the four quadrants and further tests for diagnosing them are given below.

Elementary

Table 17.1 shows the classification of elementary readers into four major categories. We explain each of these categories.

A. Accurate Word Recognition and Powerful Readers. These students are making rapid progress in learning how to read and comprehend or learn from text. If they are still in the primary grades, they will need further development in word recognition and comprehension; if they continue to progress at the same rate, they should become fast and powerful readers at the junior and senior high school levels.

B. Accurate but Nonpowerful Readers. These students are learning to identify printed words, but are not learning to comprehend. Test for vocabulary ability. If it is above grade level, then teach students active comprehension (see chapter 4) and make a cumulative chart for them of (a) rate of reading in words read per minute and (b) rate of reading times multiplied by percentage of comprehension questions answered correctly at each session). First have students read questions for passage, then have them try to anticipate the questions, and finally have them generate their own questions.

C. Low Accuracy but Powerful. These students may be accurate but slow in word recognition. However, they are relatively bright, as indicated by their

TABLE 17.1. *Classification of Elementary Readers into Four Major Categories*

		Power of Reading *50th %ile or Grade Equiv.*	
		Above	*Below*
	Above 50th Percentile or Grade Equivalent Level	A. Accurate—Powerful	B. Accurate Nonpowerful
Word Recognition Accuracy		*50th Percentile or Grade Equivalent Level*	
	Below 50th Percentile or Grade Equivalent Level	C. Low accurate but powerful	D. Low accurate Nonpowerful

above-average scores on comprehension. They need additional instruction in word recognition and probably lots of reading of interesting but relatively easy material so that they can develop fluency or automaticity in word recognition (See chapter 4 for information on development of fluency or automaticity).

D. Low Accuracy and Nonpowerful. These readers have relatively low ability in word recognition that is not due to slowness because their comprehension is also low. A variety of students fit into this category. They all need an individual diagnosis to determine whether their difficulties are due to a defect, deficiency, disruption, or difference. We would expect to find the entire range of intelligence represented, but positively skewed with many of the students being in the intellectual range below IQ of 90. Some students may be in this category because they are deficient in English, some may be physiologically handicapped (visual or auditory), some may have had inadequate instruction, some may have had a high degree of absence from school, some may have gotten a poor beginning in reading for various reasons, and some may not have been ready to read when instruction began (See chapter 4 for phonemic awareness).

Junior and Senior High School

The four quadrants for categorizing junior high and high school students are shown in Table 17.2. We shall explain each of these categories.

Fast-Powerful Readers. These students read rapidly and with relatively high comprehension. A specialist should scan test results to determine whether any students have "broken the top of the test," that is, responded correctly to all or almost all the items. These students should take a test at a more advanced level to determine their actual reading levels in each content area (the *Iowa Test of Educational Development,* for example) or even informal reading inventories in each content area. While their general reading ability is in the top quarter of the class, their ability to read and learn from texts in specific content areas is likely to reveal strengths and weaknesses related to their interests and curricula.

Fast-Nonpowerful Readers. These students are relatively rapid, but not powerful readers. They often enjoy reading, but tend not to adjust their speed of reading to rates appropriate for difficult materials; or they have some deficiency that interferes with their comprehension of relatively difficult material. Although they have probably mastered basic word recognition skills, they are likely to have a deficiency in vocabulary. Sometimes these students are referred to as "word-callers" because they can pronounce all the words but they do not attend to meaning. They may think of reading as pronouncing words rapidly. To test this hypothesis, examine their vocabulary scores on the survey test. If these scores are low and their general intelligence is at least average, they need vocabulary training.

An alternate hypothesis might be that some of the fast-nonpowerful readers are not flexible. To determine whether they lack flexibility, these students should be given an equivalent test, reading it slowly and doing the items more carefully. A significant improvement on scores would confirm the hypothesis.

TABLE 17.2. Classification of Junior and Senior High School Readers into Four Major Categories

	Power of Reading	
	Above the 50th Percentile	*Below the 50th Percentile*
Above the 50th Percentile	A. Fast–powerful readers Above the 50th percentile in both speed and power of reading.	B. Fast–nonpowerful readers Above the 50th percentile in speed but below the 50th percentile in power of reading.

Below the 50th Percentile	C. Slow–powerful readers
	Above the 50th percentile in power of reading but below the 50th percentile in speed of reading.
		D. Slow–nonpowerful readers
		Below the 50th percentile in both speed and power of reading.
		1. Linguistically different readers
		  a. Bilingual
		  b. Dialectal
		2. Low IQ reader
		3. Content area deficient reader
		4. Reluctant reader
		  a. Attitude
		  b. Ability
		5. Affectively alienated reader
		6. Physiologically handicapped reader
		7. Educationally underdeveloped reader
		8. Instructionally mismatched reader
		9. Word recognition deficient reader
		10. Narrow background reader

(Row axis label: Speed of Reading)

Source: Adapted from Harry Singer and Alan Rhodes, "Problems, Prescriptions, and Possibilities," in *Problems in Reading: A Multidisciplinary Perspective,* edited by Wayne Otto, Charles W. Peters, and Nathaniel Peters. Reading, Massachusetts: Addison-Wesley, 1977, p. 311. Reprinted by permission.

Occasionally some students may have emotional disruptions on the day of the test. On a retest, their comprehension scores are likely to be higher, particularly if the emotional disruptions are no longer present.

Slow-Powerful Readers. These students comprehend well what they read, if given adequate time. However, they tend to process all their reading in a time-consuming fashion. The specialist can test the following hypotheses to determine why the students are slow:

1. They have not mastered basic word recognition skills. An appropriate and quick test for evaluating this hypothesis is to administer the reading sub-test of the *Wide Range Achievement Test* (WRAT); Jastak & Jastak, 1965).
2. They prefer to read and analyze materials in depth—as though they were studying for an important exam. Test this hypothesis by having them read equivalent material to answer a few specific questions given to them before they read. Ask them to read only to answer these questions. If they maintain the same slow rate, interview them to find out how they read the material and how they feel when they are expected to read rapidly. (See Box 17.1 for an interview schedule.)

Slow-Nonpowerful Readers.   These students are slow and nonpowerful readers for a variety of reasons. The group can be divided into 10 common types. These types are not mutually exclusive, but tend to overlap. Some students may have characteristics that make them members of two or more catgories.

1. *Linguistically different readers.*
    a. *Bilingual readers.* Upon entering school, bilingual readers may have been able to speak only their native language. Consequently, they could not benefit from reading instruction in their second language. Subsequently, they may have become proficient in their second language, but were then in grade levels where initial reading instruction was no longer given. If an interview using the questions in Box 17.1 reveals this pattern of development, then, with reading acquisition instruction, they are likely to improve dramatically.
    b. *Dialectally different readers.* On the basis of oral reading tests, these students are judged to be deficient merely because their speech patterns are different. Care must be taken to determine whether their pronunciations of words are true reading errors or only dialectally different oral responses. To differentiate, put their incorrectly pronounced words into sentence context. If the context makes a difference in their pronunciations or if their pronunciations are still incorrect (but they answer questions correctly, indicating they have understood the meaning of the sentence), they are giving dialectally different responses, not making reading errors.

    Another clue to dialectally different readers is a higher percentile score on a silent reading test (such as the *Gates-MacGinitie Silent Reading Tests*) than on an oral reading test (such as the *Gates-McKillop-Horowitz Reading Diagnostic Tests*).

    Dialectally different readers may also be in this category because of (a) word recognition difficulties, (b) lack of wide reading experi-

intelligence, or (d) some combination of these factors. To diagnose, the specialist administers the *Gates-McKillop Reading Diagnostic Tests,* interviews students on their reading history and has a certified school psychologist administer an individual intelligence test, such as the *Wechsler Adult Intelligence Scale* (WAIS) or *Stanford-Binet Intelligence Scale* (S-B).

2. *Readers with low IQ.* Low scores in general reading achievement may be due to low mental ability, particularly if English is the native language. The specialist has an individually administered intelligence scale given to these students. Even if they do have low intelligence, some yearly improvement in reading is possible because their mental ages still increase from year to year. It is important to adjust the difficulty of reading material to the reading level of these students so that they can comprehend better.

3. *Content area deficient readers.* A student may have good general reading, but still have difficulty in reading material in a specific subject. The specialist can test this hypothesis by comparing the student's percentile or equivalent scores on a survey test and on specific content area tests (science, history, and so forth) that had been given to the same norm group. If the difference between the equivalent scores on the two tests is significant, then the student needs to learn the technical vocabulary, information background, and processes of reading appropriate to the specific content area.

4. *Reluctant readers.* Reluctance may be due to negative attitudes or to low ability.

   a. *Attitudes.* Although at, or slightly below, grade level in reading ability when retested on the reading test under encouraging conditions, these students still refuse to read. Further confirmation comes from interviews and attitude inventory results. The interview is likely to show that although they have the ability, they have not done much independent reading. Hence, they did not develop fluency or automaticity in word recognition processes; they have a shallower and narrower knowledge of the world; and they have a less adequate vocabulary than they could have.

   b. *Ability.* These students may refuse to read because they want to hide a lack of ability. The specialist can test their word recognition skills and word attack processes through use of *Gates-McKillop-Horowitz Reading Diagnostic Tests.* Given high-interest, low-difficulty materials, they may respond more favorably to reading assignments.

5. *Affectively alienated readers.* These students are openly hostile to reading, and perhaps have been for many years. Interviews are likely to reveal the duration of this negative attitude. They must have their curiosity rekindled and aroused and their interest in reading stimulated. The specialist should introduce short passages of high-interest, low-difficulty materials with considerable prior discussion of information and presenta-

tion of vocabulary contained in the materials. Perhaps using filmstrip stories that feature pictures with captions may awaken interest in reading. Then the specialist can progress gradually toward longer passages in which the content is more closely related to the content of the courses in which these readers are currently enrolled.

6. *Physiologically handicapped readers*. Readers in this category experience visual problems (crossed eyes, squinting or watery eyes when reading, books held too close or too far from eyes), and auditory problems. To detect hearing problems, the specialist can administer a whisper test by having a student stand 20 feet away with back to the examiner, and then having the examiner whisper, "Turn around." A correct response to this direction will indicate that the student is not likely to have an auditory acuity deficiency. Students with either of these problems or those suspected of having other physiological problems should be referred to the appropriate specialist, perhaps starting with the school nurse.

7. *Educationally underdeveloped readers*. These students have not learned one or more important components of the reading process (use of affixes, context, inference, and so forth). Tests of prefixes and suffixes are helpful here. Also, the *Reading Miscue Inventory*. Analysis of responses to comprehension tests may reveal deficiency in inferential ability. Instruction can improve these abilities and processes.

8. *Instructionally mismatched readers*. These students are not making progress because their reading materials may be too difficult relative to their abilities. Their attitudes and desire to learn may be strong, but they are frustrated by difficult textbooks. Use of strategies for meeting the wide range of individual differences advocated in this text will tend to alleviate this problem. (See chapters 6, 13, 14, 15, and 16.)

   Some students may not have the prerequisite background for courses and consequently they flounder in them. The specialist can check by administering entry level tests. If the entry level tests indicate that these students do have an inadequate background, they could benefit from counseling and program changes.

9. *Word recognition deficient readers*. The *Gates-McKillop-Horowitz Reading Diagnostic Tests* and/or the *Reading Miscue Inventory* can determine which students have not mastered basic word recognition techniques. The *Dolch Basic Sight Word Test* (220 basic words that are usually mastered by 95% of students at the third grade or earlier) also assesses word recognition ability. These words account for 75% of all primary words and 50% of all words in reading materials from fourth grade up.[3] The Dolch words should have priority in reading instruction,

---

[3]The Dolch Basic Sight Word Test and reading materials for teaching the Dolch words can be obtained from Garrard Press, Champaign, Ill. The word list can also be found in Tinker and McCullough (1975).

followed by development of technical vocabulary in content areas. Together, this combination of word recognition and technical vocabulary development would improve comprehension in content areas significantly.

Most of the students in the slow-nonpowerful category are likely to lack word recognition mastery. These students need intensive instruction in content area reading acquisition.

10. *Narrow background reader.* Students who have not done much reading outside school or much collateral reading in school are likely to be slower and less powerful than they should be relative to their general aptitudes. The performance of one of these students is analogous to someone who has learned to swim but never practiced swimming. Narrow background readers did not develop automaticity in word recognition processes, nor did they acquire an adequate informational background. Observation of their oral reading and an interview would reveal their awkward processing of print and their narrow background. A guided reading program would help these students.[4]

PRINCIPLES FOR INDIVIDUAL DIAGNOSIS

A survey test classifies students into four broad categories. To arrive at an *individual diagnosis* of the strengths and weaknesses of students in each category, the reading and learning-from-text specialist can follow the principles described under the next six headings.

Interview Data

The specialist collects information from teachers, parents, and from students themselves about behavior in class, about attitudes toward reading[5] and toward studying in a particular content area, and about procedures used in reading their texts. To obtain this information, the specialist ask teachers and parents to tell or write down what they know about the students' reading in class or at home. More detailed information can be collected from the students. Often a specialist will interview them to bring out their past reading history, their present use of time, and their interests. A specialist might use the interview schedule in Box 17.1.

BOX 17.1 Interview Schedule

1. Start by reviewing the survey test and results with students. The purpose is to find out why students made particular responses to the test. Balance correct with

---

[4]For concrete illustrations and case study vignettes of these readers and ways of working with them, see Singer and Rhodes (1977).

[5]Although the interview schedule shown in Box 17.1 is adequate, a standardized scale for assessing attitudes towards reading is available (Estes, 1971).

incorrect items. Have students redo some items aloud so that you can listen and infer what processes may have been used.

2. Have students go through their textbooks and explain how they read and study them. Ask students to read and explain sample passages from their texts.
3. Ask students about materials read at home: newspapers, magazines, books, and about current reading and type of reading done in the past.
4. Ask students to recall initial and early experiences in learning to read and in reading during elementary school, in class, and at home.
5. Ask students to tell what they would like to learn about reading and what they would like to learn from texts.
6. Discuss with students their past and future interests and their vocational plans.

Note: The interview should be informal, with the interviewer volunteering some information so that the atmosphere is conversational. Pursue additional questions and issues as they arise.

See Ruth Strang, Constance McCullough, and Arthur Traxler (1967), pp. 171, 458–472, for a thorough and revealing interview schedule and technique. See also Lou Burmeister (1974), pp. 61, 63, for a more detailed interest inventory.

Observational Data

While interviewing students, a specialist should observe clues to possible physical and physiological causes of disabilities, such as visual and auditory deficiencies. The specialist should also listen for hints of affective alienation to school, teachers, home, and particular content areas.

A Plan For Diagnostic Testing

Knowledge gleaned from observing students reading their texts and from allowing students to give their own explanations for their difficulties, attitudes, techniques, and processes used in reading will give the reading specialist sufficient information for developing reading improvement plans for students. However, some additional diagnostic tests may be necessary, especially for quantifying difficulties in reading and for determining reading expectancy levels (how well students should read). See also the material under the heading "Reading Expectancy" and the current edition of the standard reference book on tests, *Buros's Yearbook of Mental Measurement.* A new edition appears every fourth year.

Using a Model or Models of Reading. Models of reading are useful for directing the diagnostician's attention to the systems underlying speed or power of reading that may not be functioning properly or may not have been adequately developed. Psycholinguistic, affective, and developmental models are available. See Singer and Ruddell (1985).

Reading Expectancy. How well should a student be able to read and learn from texts? This question cannot be answered conclusively. Any criterion used for answering it is likely to be fallible for one or more reasons. Intelligence tests, for example, are not likely to be fair measuring instruments for linguistically different students or for students who were unable or lacked the motivation to learn general culturally determined information. Nevertheless, expectancy criteria will provide at least a qualified approximation of current performance expectations. One criterion is general intelligence, as determined by an individual intelligence test administered by a school psychologist. The assumption is that students' reading ages should equal their mental ages. One formula that is based upon this assumption is that of Harris and Sipay (1975):

$$\text{Reading grade level expectancy} = \text{Mental Age} - 5$$

Thus, a student with a mental age of 15 should have a general reading level of 15 − 5 or a grade equivalent of 10.[6]

Another criterion for determining expectancy is a listening test. The assumption underlying the use of such a test is that students should be able to read and comprehend as well as they listen (Sticht, Beck, Hauke, Kleiman, & James 1974).

A specialist can use an orally administered vocabulary test to assess expectancy. The underlying assumption is that *part* of the system's underlying comprehension (semantics) can be used to estimate the whole of comprehension. The oral vocabulary subtest of the first ediction of *Gates-McKillop Reading Diagnostic Tests* can be used for this purpose. For an informal estimate, a specialist can readminister the oral vocabulary scale of a survey test, only reading the words and choices to students while they follow along reading silently. Although the norms were not designed for interpreting the results of this informal estimate, they can nevertheless be used as a rule of thumb for this purpose; however, the norms used this way are not precise and probably represent an overestimate of expectancy.

Much of the additional diagnostic testing may be done in Reading Content Area Acquisition Classes or in Reading and Learning from Text Centers taught or administered under the direction of the specialist.

CONSULTING A PROFESSIONAL LIBRARY

The reading specialist should have a professional library to consult on problems in reading and learning from text. For example, the specialist may want to know how to teach "mapping," or the current theories or explanations of reading, or evidence for the effectiveness of a particular program or teaching strategies. The professional books, particularly their table of contents and index, will be useful

---

[6]Both the reading and the expectancy tests, however, have errors of measurement. That is, a difference between the two tests may be only a chance difference. You can use a statistical procedure to determine whether the difference between the two test scores is attributable to chance. Consult a measurement test, such as Thorndike and Hagen (1969) or Chase (1978) for further explanation on determining the reliability of the difference between two test scores.

for solving problems or obtaining answers to questions. See Box 17.2 for a selected list of professional books.

Journals are also important for a professional library. They provide current research and professional information. Some selected journals are also listed in Box 17.2.

BOX 17.2. *Selected List of Professional Books and Journals*

Elementary

Aukerman, Robert C. *Approaches to Beginning Reading,* Second Edition. New York: Wiley, 1984.

Dallman, Martha, Roger L. Rouch, Lynette Y.C. Char, and John J. Deboer. *The Teaching of Reading,* 5th Edition. New York: Holt, Rinehart and Winston, 1978.

Duffy, Gerald G., George B. Sherman, and Laura Roehler. *How to Teach Reading Systematically.* Second Edition. New York: Harper & Row, 1977.

Durkin, Dolores. *Teaching Them to Read,* Third Edition. Boston, MA; Allyn and Bacon, 1978.

Karlin, Robert and Andrea R. Karlin. *Teaching Elementary Reading: Principles and Strategies,* Fourth Edition. San Diego, CA: Harcourt Brace Jovanovich, 1987.

McNeil, J. *Reading Comprehension: New Directions for Classroom Practices.* Glenview, IL: Scott, Foresman, 1986.

McNeil, J., Elizabeth Donant, and Marvin Alkin. *How to Teach Reading Successfully.* Columbus, OH: Merrill.

Spache, George D. and Evelyn B. Spache. *Reading in the Elementary School,* 4th Edition. Boston: Allyn and Bacon, 1977.

Secondary

Cooper, Charles R. (Editor). *Research Response to Literature and the Teaching of Literature: Points of Departure.* Norwood, NJ: Ablex, 1985.

Criscoe, Betty L. and Thomas C. Gee. *Content Reading: A Diagnostic/Prescriptive Approach.* Englewood Cliffs, NJ: Prentice-Hall, 1984.

Dishner, Ernest K., Thomas W. Bean, John E. Readence, and David W. Moore (Editors). *Reading in the Content Areas: Improving Classroom Instruction,* Second Edition, Dubuque, IA: Kendall/Hunt, 1986.

Early, Margaret and Diane J. Sawyer. *Reading to Learn in Grades 5 to 12.* San Diego, CA: Harcourt Brace Jovanovich, 1984.

Berger, Alan and H. Alan Robinson (Editors). *Secondary School Reading: What Research Reveals for Classroom Practice.* Urbana, IL: ERIC Clearinghouse on Reading and Communication, 1982.

Herber, Harold. *Teaching Reading in Content Areas.* Englewood Cliffs, NJ: Prentice-Hall, 1978.

Roe, Betty D., Barbara D. Stoodt, and Paul C. Burns. *Secondary School Reading Instruction: The Content Areas,* Third Edition. Boston, MA: Houghton Mifflin, 1987.

Tierney, Robert J., John E. Readence, and Ernest K. Dishner. *Reading Strategies and Practices: Guide for Improving Instruction.* Boston, MA; Allyn and Bacon, 1980.

Vacca, Richard T. and JoAnne L. Vacca. *Content Area Reading,* Second Edition. Boston, MA: Little, Brown, 1986.

Research and Theory

Orasanu, Judith (Editor). *Reading Comprehension: From Research to Practice.* Hillsdale, NJ: Lawrence Erlbaum Associates, 1986.

Pearson, P. David (Editor). *Handbook of Research on Reading.* New York: Longman, 1983.

Purves, Alan C. and Olive Niles (Editors). *Becoming Readers in a Complex Society.* Eighty-Third Yearbook of the National Society for the Study of Education. Chicago: University of Chicago Press, 1984.

Singer, Harry and Robert B. Ruddell (Editors). *Theoretical Models and Processes of Reading,* Third Edition. Newark, DE: International Reading Association, 1985.

Journals

The Reading Teacher.
Conveys a variety of information for elementary teachers.
Journal of Reading.
Aimed for the junior and senior high school teacher.
Reading Research Quarterly.
Primarily for those interested in research on all aspects of reading.

These three journals are published by the International Reading Association, Newark, Delaware.

Journal of Reading Behavior.
Research articles on literacy.
Yearbook of the National Reading Conference.
Research reported at the annual conference.

These two journals are published by the National Reading Conference, Rochester, New York.

Index
The Education Index
Psychological Abstracts
Dissertation Abstracts

These indices are available in college and university libraries.

THE SPECIALIST PROVIDES HISTORICAL BACKGROUND

Ms. Jones was glad to get the information on classification and educational diagnosis. She felt even more definitely that Monroe could use a program in reading acquisition. However, before instituting such a program at Monroe High, Ms. Valdes thought it would be a good idea to visit some neighboring schools that offered various programs for students with problems in reading and learning from text. After doing a little investigation, Ms. Jones and Ms. Valdes located eight nearby schools offering such programs. In released time, both teachers visited the schools to observe their programs. Ms. Valdes agreed to observe each program intensively and provide thorough evaluations of each program's strengths and weaknesses. In the car enroute to the first of the eight school sites, Ms. Valdes filled Ms. Jones in on some historical background related to the teaching of reading.

High schools have been operating reading clinics, classes, and centers for over 50 years (Singer, 1970; N. B. Smith, 1965a). During World War I, the country had been shocked to learn that a large number of draftees were rejected because they were deficient in reading ability. In reaction, the country called for high schools to improve the reading performance of its graduates.

But perceiving a problem and calling for its solution were not enough to produce effective high school programs. School districts lacked tests, techniques, teaching materials; they had to design, try out, and evaluate reading programs. The educational concepts and tools were not long in being produced. Thorndike (1917) started the field in the direction of teaching students to learn from text when he pointed out that, in the mature reader, reading is reasoning, analogous to solving a mathematics problem. A few years later, Gates (1921) began to develop reading tests that differentiated students' levels of abilities in reading and learning from text; and in 1927, he established the first reading clinic for diagnosis and improvement of reading. Judd and Buswell (1922) found that the reading process is not unitary, but varies according to the reader's purposes and the kinds and difficulty of the reading material. Consistent with Judd and Buswell's implications, McCallister (1932) published a book on teaching reading in the content areas at the high school level. Bond (1938) provided specific evidence that the students' comprehension varies from one subject area to another. A student may comprehend better, for example, in literature than in science. Only recently have relevant materials for teaching reading in content areas become available (Herber, 1970a, 1976) perhaps because the demand for them has become greater.

Although the need for post-elementary reading instruction was apparent, and materials, methods, and measuring devices had been or were being developed, junior and senior high schools were still slow to establish reading programs. Indeed, the concept of a developmental reading program that would provide instruction continuously from elementary grades through high school did not take hold until the 1950s (N. B. Smith 1965a). Playing a prominent role in the establishment of this concept were Strang's research, writing, and reading demonstrations at the high school level (Strang, 1938, 1942; Strang, McCullough, & Traxler, 1946). She found that *individual* patterns of reading vary at the high school level. Other research provided further understanding of reading. Robinson and Hall (1941) discovered that reading skills for prose and nonprose are different. Later, Holmes (1954) presented evidence that a hierarchically organized set of subsystems underlies speed and power of reading. Then Holmes and Singer (1961, 1966) reported that high school readers must not only mobilize strengths and minimize weaknesses; they must also draw upon certain essential subsystems to attain speed and power of reading.

Research on high school and mature readers has continued to expand knowledge of reading. On the instructional side, Ausubel (1964) theorized that advance organizers facilitate comprehension. Similarly, some researchers found that reading guides and structured vocabulary overviews facilitate comprehension (Herber & Barron, 1973; Herber & Sanders, 1969), while other researchers discovered that teacher-posed questions before and after reading helped students comprehend. More recently, Anderson (1976a) explained that abstract concepts generate concrete scenarios that enable individuals to comprehend, that is, to assimilate, store, and retrieve information; for example, an abstract concept, such as making a sandwich, can generate a sequence of events or knowledge structures in a person's mind that can be used to assimilate a story about a person making a sandwich.

Adding impetus to the movement to improve developmental reading was the United States Army's formation of reading centers in universities during World War II. The purpose of these centers was to speed up the war effort by teaching high school and college graduates enrolled in officer training programs to improve their comprehension and speed of reading. After the war, university and college reading centers survived to serve students enrolled in regular college programs. In the 1960s and 1970s the centers were also upgrading reading achievement of minority students whose reading potential had not been fully realized. Consequently an anomalous condition existed: during the 1940s and continuing in some places even today, reading was taught in the elementary grades and in colleges and universities, but not at the levels between. Over the past 30 years, junior and senior high schools have been filling in this gap.

Pressure to eliminate the gap has also come from changes in the composition of high school enrollment. Instead of dropping out of high school for jobs in agriculture, business, and industry, high school students (especially those with low academic achievement and ability) began to remain in high school until graduation. From 1930 to 1960, enrollment of the 14- to 17-year-old age group in secondary school increased from 51.3 to 83.2% (Tyack, 1967). A more recent analysis of school holding power revealed that 85% of students enrolled in ninth grade were still attending school in the 12th grade (Jencks, 1975). Among the determinants of this holding power was the initiation of the 100% promotion policy in which students were promoted regardless of their achievement levels (Caswell & Foshay, 1950). Concomitant with this policy was the development of a more differentiated and appropriate high school curriculum that could accommodate the diverse abilities, aptitudes, and aspirations of this more heterogeneous group of students as they progressed through school. Also, pressure on students to remain in school and for schools to expand their curricula to accommodate them came from civil rights groups, buttressed by the 1954 Supreme Court decision that separate schools were inherently unequal. In the 1960s, civil rights groups not only urged integration of minority students into the schools (Singer & Hendrick, 1967), but also counseled minority students to remain in school and make schools adapt instruction and curricula to their needs and interests. The goal was to have schools provide minority students with appropriate training for development of their abilities so that they could go on to college and to jobs that required a higher level of academic education.

Thus, high schools today no longer have the highly selected group of students they had some 75 years ago when the Committee of Ten had advocated a college preparatory program as *the* high school curriculum (Tyack, 1967). High schools now have not only a more heterogeneous group of students but also a more varied curriculum with numerous electives, minicourses, and programs, Indeed, the educational system has made considerable progress towards attainment of the comprehensive type of high school advocated by Conant (1959) and the ''12 year common school'' curriculum proposed by some educators (Caswell & Foshay, 1950).

You can view the establishment of reading programs in junior and senior high schools as a concomitant of the social, economic, legal, and educational forces that have led to the curriculum of the 12-year common school. These reading programs are helping post-elementary schools provide equality of educational opportunity to their heterogeneous student bodies and to low-achieving students who are remaining in school longer to pursue elevated academic aspirations. But in solving the problem of how to provide equality of educational opportunity for students whose reading grade equivalents range from grade 0 to 12 and higher, schools have created reading programs that vary considerably.

Since Ms. Jones and Ms. Valdes were the only two staff members from Monroe High visiting the eight sites they took careful and detailed notes for a report they would give to the Monroe faculty when they returned. During their visits they noticed that, while each of the eight schools had its own basic *type* of program, a given program often shared two or more features with another program and did not quite fit into the traditional categories of developmental, corrective, clinical or remedial, content, and enrichment classes.

As Ms. Jones was led to believe, these programs represented the best current attempts of some schools to solve the reading problems of junior and senior high school students whose reading grade equivalents range from 0 to 12 or higher. Some of these programs were specific answers to the question often posed by high school content area teachers: ''What do I do with the student who can't read or learn from text?''

READING LABS OR CENTERS

A Composite Elementary School Reading Laboratory or Center

Some elementary schools have a reading specialist, a resource teacher, or a director of a reading laboratory, supported by federal funds, known as Chapter I funds. Some states may have also have a state-funded program for elementary schools. For example, California has a Miller-Unruh program that is named after the legislators who authored the legislation that initiated it. Since prevention is more effective than remediation, the program focuses on the primary grades. Teachers who pass the test to be certified for the program work with small groups of six children, either in the classroom or in a pull-out situation. The children are in the lower quarter or lower third of the class in reading achievement, as defined by a standardized test, such as the *Comprehensive Test of Basic Skills, Stanford Reading Achievement,* or the *Metropolitan Achievement Test.* The emphasis in the program is on supplementary instruction; that is, the specialists find out what the students' classroom teacher is teaching and do follow-up type of instruction. This instruction uses the same texts, assignments, and informal text-based reading inventory in current use in the classroom. Research has demonstrated that such supplementary instruction is very effective (Gates & Bond, 1936; Ellison et al. 1965). Long- and short-range objectives are established for each child, daily lesson plans are made, and separate folders are kept for each student. Box 17.3 contains a composite of an elementary school reading laboratory or center.

BOX 17.3. Composite Elementary School Reading Laboratory or Center

Referral

Based on their observations and judgment of students during instruction in the classroom or on test score results, classroom teachers refer students to the program for various reasons. The students are likely to be in the lower quartile on standardized achievement test scores, a requirement of some funding programs, such as Miller-Unruh; or below the 35th percentile, a stipulation of Chapter I funds. Some of these students have non-English language backgrounds, some have necessary skills but are slow in developing them, and some simply have gaps, particularly in decoding (use of context, blending, phonics).

Diagnosis

Acting on the principle that they should obtain their own test results so that they know the conditions under which the test was administered, some laboratory teachers administer diagnostic tests to referred students, such as the *Gates-McKillop-Horowitz Reading Diagnostic Tests* or Spache's *Diagnostic Reading Scales.* (These scales are described in detail in chapter 4.) Diagnosis also occurs through observation of students in individual or group learning tasks. For determining expectancy levels, that is, how well a student should be reading, tests such as the *Wechsler Intelligence Scale for Children (WISC)* and *Peabody Inventory Achievement Test (PIAT)* are used, if a school psychologist is making the referral. Or, the laboratory teacher can use the listening age on the Spache test as an expectancy criterion. Some laboratory specialists may also use the *Wide Range Achievement Test (WRAT)* and *Silvaroli Inventory* or the *Woodcock Reading Mastery Tests* to obtain information on students' development of reading and subskills in reading. Diagnostic information is also obtained as a result of observing students during instruction. The reading specialist uses this information to write objectives for each student.

Instruction

Students are grouped for instruction according to grade level and skill areas. First graders receive developmental, supplementary instruction, based on the readers used in their classrooms; this instruction is coordinated with their classroom teachers and with the instruction they receive in their own classrooms. Students in Grades 2 and 3 receive instruction according to their diagnostic test results. The reading specialist writes group and individual lesson plans. Students participate in setting goals and in the plans for improvement.

A progress folder is kept for each student. It contains the student's test scores, individual educational prescription, completed exercises, daily comments on the student's performance at each class session, and plans for the student's next session. The aim is to get students up to grade level or their expectancy, and then return the student to his or her class after a conference with the student's teacher.

Instructional Materials

Materials used vary from one laboratory to another. Supplementary instruction is usually based upon the same basal reader series used in the classroom. Other materials may include the *Barnell Loft* books that have exercises on particular skills, *Spring Starter* books that contain short mystery stories that children enjoy reading, a *Language Master* for teaching vocabulary. Teachers may tape stories so that children can listen to them and then reread the stories, as suggested by the method of repeated reading (See chapter 4 for an explanation of this method). Other materials used in primary grade reading laboratories are *Monster* books (written in children's language), Modern Curriculum Press materials, *Reading Concepts, Dolch Puzzle Books, SRA Kits,* and board games for motivational purposes.

Motivation

Students are rewarded usually in the form of praise and other types of feedback, such as test results and information on their strengths and weaknesses. They also get some form of tangible reward, including "stickers" on their work and certificates of achievement. Students do not get grades, but the reading specialist confers with the classroom teacher about each student's progress.

Funds

Funds for specialists come from the State and federal government (Chapter I funds). Some funds may come from the school's budget. The funds are used for purchasing materials and employing aides.

References for Some Materials Used in Reading Laboratories or Centers

Barnell Loft Specific Skill Series. Westbrook Publications, 1970.
Dolch Puzzle Books. Garrard Publishing Company, 1979.
Famous People Stories. Unigraph, 1979.
Peabody Individual Achievement Test. Circle Pine, MN: American Guidance Service, 1970.
Systems 80 kits. Borg-Warner Educational Systems.
SRA Reading Laboratory Kits. Palo Alto, CA.: Science Research Associates, Inc.

Spring Starter Books. New York: Scholastic Book Services, 1978.

Wide Range Achievement Test. Guidance Associates of Delaware, 1978.

Woodcock Reading Mastery Tests. Circle Pine, MN: American Guidance Service, 1973.

Critique of Elementary Reading Laboratories or Centers

Reading specialist instruction in Grade 1 should be primarily supplemental to classroom instruction in reading. But students referred to reading specialists in Grades 2 and above should have diagnostic testing and individual educational plans (IEP) with specific instructional objectives in word recognition and comprehension. (See principles for individual diagnosis in this chapter.) Daily lessons should include not only instruction in specific skills, but also transfer of these skills to reading narrative and expository texts (See chapter 4 on teaching reading and chapter 18 on teaching acquisition and comprehension in a laboratory setting). Students can be grouped for common instructional needs and have group instruction in comprehension strategies (See chapter 4 on directed and active comprehension).

Reading specialists should also go over each student's diagnosis with his or her classroom teacher. The teacher will then learn the student's particular strengths and weaknesses, and perhaps acquire information useful for making diagnoses within the classroom. Progress charts on skills and comprehension should be kept on each student (See cumulative charts in chapter 18) and these charts, along with the child's folder of objectives and instructional plans, should be communicated to the classroom teacher when the student has achieved at the expected level and is being returned to the classroom. Thus, the classroom teacher will learn how to diagnose and improve individual students, and the reading specialist will have provided in-service education for the teachers and perhaps will have prevented some future reading problems from occurring.

If students do not learn how to read during the primary grades, they are less likely to learn during the intermediate grades because teachers at this level profess that they do not know how to teach beginning reading or else point out that they do not have the time to do so. Hence, assignment of students to reading specialists at this level would help solve reading problems for some students before they get to junior high school.

Reading specialists in the intermediate grades should also carry out all the functions that junior and senior high school specialists do, including in-service training of teachers on teaching strategies for handling individual differences in reading achievement and for teaching all students to read and learn from texts in the content areas. We describe the functions of a reading specialist in greater detail in the rest of the sections of this chapter and in the next chapter.

Nine Types of Junior and Senior High School Labs or Centers on the Current Scene

1. THE TRACKING SYSTEM

Description

A familiar type of solution to the range of reading levels in a school is placement of low-achieving readers into a separate track in which curriculum and texts can be adapted to their levels of reading ability and reading instruction can be given to all the students in the track. An example of high school *tracking* appears in Box 17.4.

BOX 17.4. Tracking System

I. Intake
  A. Five Instructional Tracks
    1. Honors
       a. Gifted students (IQ above 132)
       b. "Very able" high achievers
    2. X section
       a. College preparatory (IQ 110 to 131)
       b. Students reading above grade level
    3. Y section
       a. College preparatory, community-college-bound (IQ 95–109)
       b. Students reading at or slightly below grade level
    4. Z section
       a. Community college, terminal (IQ 75–94)
       b. Students reading two or more years below grade level
    5. "Correlated" (IQ below 75)
       a. Mentally retarded

II. Testing
  A. *CMM: California Test of Mental Maturity/Stanford-Binet* (special request)
  B. *Otis Quick Scoring Mental Abilities Tests* (for transfer students)
  C. *Gray's Standardized Oral Reading Test/Iowa Test/Sequential Tests of Educational Progress (STEP)*

III. Description of Students
  A. Honors and X students tended to come from professional families, small business owners, and farmer-ranchers. Noted sense of humor. Lively. Volatile. Articulate. Critical, often openly. Easy access to administrative offices and counselors.
  B. Y students. Tend to come from small farms and ranches, children of blue collar workers and clerks. Difficult to motivate. Frequent discipline problems. Unparticipatory in student activities.
  C. Z students. Tend to come from parents that are in unskilled labor and unemployed. Fewer discipline problems than Y students. Easy to get into routine. Regarded any change with uncertainty.

IV. Typical Program and Materials
   A. Honors-X Program. Difficult and varied reading materials. Heavy involvement in discussion and dramatic activities. Creative projects. Essay examinations. Presentation of "college" objectives — "You'll need to know this when you get to college."
   B. Y students. Tend to come from small farms and ranches, children of blue-collar workers and clerks. Difficult to motivate. Frequent discipline problems. Unparticipatory in student activities.
   C. Z students. Tend to come from parents who are in unskilled labor and unemployed. Fewer discipline problems than Y students. Easy to get into routine. Regarded any change with uncertainty.
   Virtually no discussion or dramatics. Heavy use of films.

V. Grading
   Different viewpoints existed at the school. In general, grading standards were the province of individual teachers. Some teachers allowed Z students the opportunity to make the same number of As and Bs as X or Honors students. Other teachers felt that Z students should receive nothing higher than Bs and Cs. Some teachers felt that since Y students were going to college, they should be graded on the same standard as X and Honors students. Some teachers felt that X and Honors students should be graded most stringently since they would be attending university. In general, Honors students tended to have more As than X, Y, and Z students.

VI. Staffing
   Sectioning occurred in 9th-, 10th-, and 11th-grade English and social studies and 9th-grade Science. Other courses (chemistry, typing, bookkeeping, masterpieces of Literature) tended to section themselves. Although certain teachers were selected to teach one class of Honors students, most teachers taught a mixture of sections. In other words, faculty weren't identified as X teachers and Y teachers.

VII. Moving Up and Down Sections
   For the most part, students stayed in sections throughout high school. However, certain students were resectioned on the basis of teacher request, parent request, or new testing data (one prominent example was a young Black student who scored 86 on the *Otis Quick Scoring* and *Mental Ability Tests* and later 119 on the *Stanford-Binet*). Occasionally, students were resectioned for disciplinary reasons: a disruptive X student could be perceived as not profiting from classroom instruction and would be resectioned. Also, students who were nonachievers were frequently resectioned lower: some Honors classes contained a majority of high-achieving, nongifted students, while the X sections would have low-achieving gifted students.

Critique of Tracking System

A tracking system is not appropriate for the differentiated abilities of students.[7] Moreover, the downward adaptation of curriculum for students placed in the lower track tends to increase the achievement gap between lower and higher tracks (Balow, 1964). Although research evidence on the issue is not clear (Macmillan, Jones, & Aloia, 1974), it is possible that the lower track and special classes may stigmatize at least some students and consequently be counterproductive to effective teaching and learning.

However, some specialized instruction is required for students at the high school level, especially those students still in the acquisition phase of reading development. Although grouping students into specialized classes for specific instructional need is defensible, tracking students is not. The three-level program described in Box 17.4 groups students in a junior high school for specific reading instruction; these students are not tracked because they can and do progress from basic to more advanced levels of instruction. Other programs have ways of providing for specific educational needs *without tracking students*.

2. CLINICAL CENTERS

Description

Clinical centers tend to exist in elementary schools or in universities where they also serve as laboratories for training reading specialists. Students referred to these centers are diagnosed by reading specialists trained to use a battery of individually administered diagnostic tests. Drawing upon the diagnosis, a specialist plans a reading improvement program and then applies it to the individual, either on a one-to-one basis or in small groups. Box 17.5 contains a more detailed description of how a reading clinic operates in a school setting.

BOX 17.5. Reading Clinic

A Schoolwide Center Emphasizing
a Diagnostic and Prescriptive Program
for Reading Achievement and Self-Concept

Description: This Junior High is located in an agricultural area in transition to a suburban neighborhood with medium-priced, single-family homes. A high percentage of students come from Spanish-speaking homes. The center, located in the school's former library, is carpeted and air-conditioned, has a receptionist-secretary,

---

[7]The system of tracking students, that is, assigning them to sections for all of their course work on the basis of an aptitude test, is rapidly disappearing from American high schools. Even the high school used as an example for table 17.2 no longer tracks its students. The reason for the elimination of tracking is that the court in the base of Hobson v. Hansen (1967) declared that tracking or ability grouping is illegal when it is based on tests that may be biased and when it results in placing students against whom it may be biased in an inferior educational program.

couches in one corner in a living room arrangement, round tables seating about four or five students, and walls lined with books and materials.

The reading facility was established for a demonstration program by an annual competitive grant of $150,000 from the State of California under Assembly Bill 938, passed in 1969. Each year the least cost-effective of the 15 demonstration programs established under the Assembly Bill is eliminated from grant support. Since the program maintains a student-to-teacher ratio of 5 to 1 with a staff of 10, including a Project Director, a full-time, on-site, bilingual (Spanish and English) counselor, three reading teachers with M.A. degrees, four instructional aides, and a full-time secretary, the program can be categorized as fitting the criteria of a school-based reading clinic.

Intake: All seventh graders, except educable mentally retarded students, are programmed into the center from their English classes. During the first year of the center's operation, English teachers accompanied their classes to the center and participated in its activities. Now, half the students from two English classes are scheduled each period; after 3 weeks, the other half of the students rotate into the center. This alternation procedure continues every 3 weeks throughout the year. Thus the center has a full-sized class of some 30 students in each period and the English teachers have reduced classes of about 15 students.

Testing: All students take (in October and again in May) the *California Test of Basic Skills* which provides grade equivalents on comprehension. Those below grade equivalent 4.5 take the *Durrell Analysis of Reading Difficulty.* The *Stanford Diagnostic Test,* Levels I or II, is administered to students at grade equivalent 4.5 or above. The *Classroom Reading Inventory* by Nicholas Silvaroli is given to students entering the program later in the year for quick assessment before the diagnostic tests are given. Students take progress tests in instructional materials used at the center (*Clues to Reading Progress* for students reading at grade levels 2.0 to 4.0 and criterion-referenced testing in the Audio Reading-Progress Laboratory for students at reading levels 4.0 to 10.0). Students also take placement tests for Systems 80, controlled readers, and other programs. They take informal tests to pinpoint specific difficulties such as lack of familiarity with words on the Dolch list, consonants, vowels, blends, syllabication, affixes, and roots. Students also have auditory and visual screening and take the *Slosson Intelligence Test* and the *San Diego Interest Inventory* (Patrick Groff). Each student's test results are diagnosed and an individual prescription is written by the reading teacher. Table 1 shows the gain in achievement for a group of students after one academic year.

TABLE 1. Average Gain in Vocabulary and Comprehension
from October to May for 318 Students

Test Results CTBS, Level 3	Mean Grade Scores		
	Pretest	*Posttest*	*Gain*
Vocabulary	6.4	8.3	1.9
Comprehension	5.8	7.7	1.9

Counseling: Students initially took pretests and posttests on a "Self-concept Semantic Differential" administered on a group basis. They rated themselves through the degree of agreement or disagreement on these dimensions: I am (good *vs.* bad, useful *vs.* useless, superior *vs.* inferior, important *vs.* unimportant, failure *vs.* success, good reader *vs.* poor reader, like school *vs.* hate school, like myself *vs.* hate myself, and like to read *vs.* hate to read). But the median changes, although in a positive direction, were slight; so, the center decided to drop the test. Every student has the opportunity to participate in group counseling sessions.

Typical Program: Each student has a Student Profile Sheet that contains a list of tests taken and their results, including an estimated informal reading inventory level (Silvaroli) and a diagnostic check list of difficulties in oral communication (knowledge of English, dialect, low verbal ability), listening comprehension, visual perception (memory for words), word analysis, oral reading (processes, error types, and rate), and comprehension (vocabulary, main ideas sequence, recalling details, drawing conclusions, cause-effect relationships, inference, understanding author's purpose, silent reading (rate and comprehension), study skills (following directions, critical reading, use of reference materials, skimming and scanning), and general reading habits (insecurity, low effort, easily distracted).

A prescription/instructional plan in each area (visual perception, word attack, vocabulary, study skills, comprehension/rate, and motivation) is drawn up. Students then have a contract plan based on their instructional plan with 5 to 10 points per lesson. Under each instructional category is a list of materials in the center for instructing the student. The contract in Box 17.6 contains a partial listing: Students keep a daily record for each 3-week period of points earned, and at the end of the 3 weeks evaluate the three things learned on their contract, the lessons found to be most helpful, the skills that still need to be worked on, and their comments on the program.

How Plan Works: Each class has 18 days to complete work. Students are to earn an average of 20 points per day and minimum of 20 points for outside reading. During the first week, orientation is given on how to use the contract, responsibility for behavior, and procedures for using equipment and materials. At first, students operate in heterogeneous groups, but after orientation period, they have individual choices.

Motivation
1. Points earned. The 100 persons who earn the most points go on field trips (zoo, superior court, county museum).
2. Prize day at end of each rotation (prizes: choice of paperbacks and posters).
3. Film at end of year.
4. Immediate feedback to students.

Relation to Other Content Areas
1. Indirect: resource center; order materials.
2. Provide training for English teachers.
3. Available to work with each department.

Grades: None, but this Evaluation Sheet is filled out in a conference between teacher and student:

Learning Objectives	Most of time	Often	Sometimes	Seldom
Completes assignment				
Shows progress				
Understands what he/she reads				
Shows growth in ability to evaluate own work				
Behavioral Objectives				
Tries hard to do his/her best				
Makes good use of time				
Works well independently				
Shows consideration for others				

Conferences with Parents: Although all are invited, only about 10% come to conferences.

Staff Credentials: Director, M.A. in Reading; three teachers with M.A. One is a reading specialist.

Evaluation: Outside evaluator provides annual evaluation: analyzes pretest and post-test results; interviews random sample of students; interviews staff of center and faculty of school at beginning of year on objectives (program and personnel) and end of year on their degree of attainment; and makes suggestions for the following year.

Critique of Clinical Centers

Two assumptions underlie reading improvement programs: (1) a majority of students will make significant gains in these programs—more than one year gain for each year of instruction, and (2) gains made in these programs will transfer to produce improved performance in regular classrooms and in all content areas (Evans, 1972). Skilled diagnosis and intensive treatment can result in significant reading acquisition (B. Balow, 1965), since the task of learning to read can be mastered by all students in the normal range of intelligence, given adequate instructional time (Bloom, 1971; Carroll, 1964; Singer, 1977). But improvement in ability to gain information from texts through concentrated instruction is more difficult to attain. When it does occur, it is exceptional, as it is in the example given in Box 17.5, because there is no shortcut to attainment of the concepts, vocabulary, and particularly information or world knowledge (Winograd, 1972)

BOX 17.6.   Individual Contract

Cover page: Identification, dates, contracted points

Second page:

	Points per lesson	Date lesson completed	Points earned
Visual Perception			
EDL Tach-X	5		
Word Attack			
EDL Aud-X	5		
System 80	5		
Vocabulary			
Word Clues Series	5/7		
Language Master	5		
Study Skills			
Study Skills Library	7		
Aud-X Dictionary Skills	10		
Countdown (Scope/study skills)			
Comprehension/Rate			
Controlled Reader	10		
Go Magazine	5		
Specific Skills Series	5		
Action Units	5		
Sports Action/Skill Kit	5		
Recreational Reading			
Scope Plays	5		
Total			
Contracted total:			

All equipment and materials mentioned in this box, and throughout chapters 17 and 18, will be credited by publisher or manufacturer in Appendixes A and B, respectively.

---

that readers must draw upon to learn from texts or to comprehend in various content areas. Even under the specially favorable experimental conditions of performance contracting instruction, students did not improve significantly in reading achievement (Kelley, 1973). Moreover, when students who have been successful in the clinic are returned to regular classrooms, the disparity between their ''hothouse'' clinic instruction and the competitive classroom environment with its demanding textbooks and assumptive instruction (Herber, 1970a) overwhelms the improved readers; they become frustrated, withdraw from reading tasks, and tend to return to the clinic and the ranks of the reading disabled (Balow, 1965).

Even students who have finally mastered the closed-ended objectives of reading acquisition in laboratory or clinic reading programs are not likely to overcome deficiencies in the open-ended objectives of vocabulary development, conceptual ability, world knowledge, values, and attitudes related to reading comprehension. Indeed, if a 2- to 3-year achievement gap or more exists between such students and others in their peer group, they will not be able to compete successfully with their peers who have been developing in the open-ended objectives steadily throughout their school careers. Hence, it is essential to intervene, and hopefully prevent, disabilities in reading and learning from text as early as the primary grades. Although the outlook for significant gains in learning from text for disabled readers at the high school level is pessimistic, the possibility of significant gains in reading acquisition is enough to justify clinic centers (Lovell, Johnson, & Platts, 1963).

3. READING LABORATORY
Description
A reading laboratory is usually stocked with a variety of self-instructional materials. See Box 17.7 for a description of some self-instructional materials that are frequently used in reading laboratories. Students are either programmed into the laboratory as a result of low reading test scores or, more rarely, as a part of a schoolwide program.

BOX 17.7. A Reading Laboratory:
Developmental Reading with Motivational Emphasis

Intake: Students are referred by teachers, and evaluated by counselors and reading lab staff at weekly Friday meetings at 7 A.M. If students are reading 2 or more years below grade level on the *Stanford Achievement Test* administered at the ends of Grades 6, 7, and 8, they are taken out of English class, unless they are enrolled in Basic Skills in English. Then they are taken out of history. Some students are kept in reading lab until openings occur in other programs (Educationally Handicapped, Learning Disability Group)—usually low IQ students.

Testing: Use *Gates-McKillop Reading Tests* (oral reading paragraphs, blending vowels, consonants, and syllabication). Then assign 20–30 students/class period to work in centers to develop these subskills. Also administer placement test for *SRA Reading Laboratory Kit.*

Description of Students: Grade equivalent range 2–6. Heavy turn-over of 50% of students per year because of nearby Air Force base.

Typical Programs

1. Fill out card on each student, one for file and one for referring teacher. Card is progress report on tested Gates-McKillop subtests and comprehension *(SRA Reading Laboratory Kit* Progress Chart).
2. Each student gets work contract for Monday through Thursday at centers located in various places in the room. Centers have task card, game, or worksheet on materials related to Gates-McKillop subtests. Each center has a "Help Sign"—a Peanuts character on card students raise when they want help. Students earn points for tasks completed.
3. Students in three groups on Friday for active comprehension instruction — learning to formulate their own questions and reading to answer them. Use Scholastic Action Books or Sports Close-Up Book or SRA Pilot Library for this instruction on active comprehension.

Materials Used Frequently

1. SRA Reading Laboratory Kit
2. SRA Pilot Library — high-interest, low-difficulty paperback tradebooks.
3. *Clue Magazine*
4. Scholastic Book Services *Action Books*
5. Sports Illustrated — The Sports Illustrated Learning Program: An Interdisciplinary Approach to Education.
6. Webster Word Wheels — use for blending exercises.
7. Teacher-made task cards for syllables, vowels, consonants, affixes. Bingo games for sight words, crossword puzzles for new vocabulary. "Vocabulary Word Center" (Have list of vocabulary ranging from Grades 2–7 for each step in Scholastic's Individualized Reading Program), "Word Search": Puzzle that requires students to identify words in various spatial arrays.
8. Classic Comics Illustrated.

Motivation

1. Any holiday — have contests or prizes (free books).
2. Essay Contest — "What if you couldn't read?" Schoolwide contest.
3. Read-A-Thon—2-week contest for Mental Health Association; sponsors contribute to Mental Health Association for number of books read.
4. Once-a-Month Fun Day— No contracts that day. Unannounced surprise. Usually around a holiday. Examples:
   Magic show: Each student reads and performs magic tricks in group — had five different magic tricks.
   Valentine's Day: Origami — made animal valentine — had to read and follow directions.
   Party for graduates from lab: Receive diploma, cookies. Graduates are those students whose reading scores come up to or near grade level. Had 25 out of 200 who achieved this goal over period from September to March.
5. Earn points for each skill task, for each 10–20 pages in book chosen for free reading, complete SRA story (1 point for doing task, 2 points for 80% comprehension, 3 points for 100% comprehension.

Relation to Content Area Courses in School
1. Doesn't tie in — strictly developmental reading now, but moving to tie in with history and science. Relevant materials:
   a. Harper & Row Design for Reading: *How to Read Social Studies:* "From Falcons to Forests," "Lions to Legends," "Mysteries to Microbes," "Pyramids to Princes." Paperbacks. Teacher's Edition. Grades 2–5.
   b. *Lending Library for Teachers*
      SRA Reading Laboratory Kit
      SRA Map and Globe Skills
      Countries and Cultures (SRA Dimensions Series)
      SRA Literature Sampler
      EDL Study Skills Library: Social Studies
      SRA Reading for Understanding

Grade
1. Grade, based on effort, as assessed by progress reports in folder, goes to teacher of class from which student came and grade is prorated for semester grade in content area course according to fraction of week spent in reading lab.
2. Retested on *Gates-McKillop Reading Diagnostic* subtests and progress report sent to content area teacher.

Assistance
1. Student aides correct papers and exercises, and determine number of points earned.
2. Aide from government-sponsored aide-training program. (Train aide for 6 months who then is employed in other programs.)

Staff for Lab: Two certificated teachers, one with elementary teaching credential and M.A. degree in reading and the other with a secondary credential, an M.A. in reading, and a reading specialist credential.

Budget: $1,100 for materials per year.

In the laboratory, students sometimes take diagnostic tests. Usually, they take a test that indicates placement level in a particular set of instructional materials. The materials consist of short stories or expository paragraphs, followed by comprehension questions and perhaps some word meaning or word recognition exercises. Students read the passages, answer the questions, check their answers against the scoring key, and graph the results in a progress booklet. Occasionally, students receive help from a teacher or a teacher's aide who may be circling the room offering help. When students complete one program of self-instructional materials, they may go on to another program. Some laboratories accept students referred by content area teachers who notice the text is too difficult for them. These students may return to class after they have completed work on one set of materials. See Box 17.7 for a more detailed description of one of these programs.

Critique of the Reading Laboratory

Packaged reading programs used in reading laboratories, such as the Science Research Associate's (SRA) *Reading Laboratory Kit,* are based on excellent principles of instruction. They start students at appropriate levels of difficulty where they can successfully comprehend, allow students to progress in small increments of difficulty at their own rates of progress, provide for immediate feedback of results on exercises and tests, have students plot results for graphed evidence of progress. Moreover, the content of the reading selections are short and highly interesting.

The limitations of this approach are the following: (1) reading lab instructors do not initiate input instruction on reading acquisition and learning from text; (2) teacher diagnosis and prescription are not continuous; (3) students must determine their own difficulties and find ways to overcome them, or at least know when and on what to ask for teacher assistance; (4) the content may be useful for reading acquisition, but is not the content the students must learn to read for their content area subjects; and (5) students are not taught, and consequently do not learn, principles or processes of reading acquisition and learning from text that they can apply to their content area courses.

4. FUNCTIONAL READING PROGRAMS

Description

Functional reading programs use tests, materials, and objectives based upon an analysis of what adults actually have to read at home or at work. Students are trained to read these materials. They are taught to identify the particular words, understand their meanings, and do the related comprehension exercises, frequently the type that requires the reader to follow directions (reading and following a recipe), carrying out the directions of an instructional manual for repairing a car, or looking up prices and ordering supply items for a store. A more detailed description of two of these programs is provided in Box 17.8.

BOX 17.8. Two Functional Reading Programs

A. A Functional and Developmental
Reading Class

School: High School, 1,250 students—39.4% Chicano, 7.6% Black, 52.5% Anglo, 0.5% Asian.

Testing: Entering ninth graders tested in Grade 8 on the *Nelson Reading Test.* Those scoring at Grade 6.5 and below then take *Spache Diagnostic Reading Scales.* (Some students score low on Nelson because they don't want to take the test, but can read well, Grade 8.0 or better.) Counselors screen transfer students on mini-*WRAT.* All students take criterion-referenced test consisting of all objectives in Title I.

Description of Class: Mostly bilingual, range in reading from Grade 2.5 to 8.0. Class size: 20. Two Title I ESEA bilingual aides hired from local community (score and record exercises, keep charts and attendance, salary about $4 per hour, about $4,000 per academic year). Federal programs require records and check-off of objectives.

Time Period: 50-minute classes, 5 days per week. All students continue in class as long as they remain below reading grade equivalent 7.0, or until they become juniors when they have option of remaining in class.

Room Arrangement: Teacher's desk, six or seven round tables and chairs, library rack for paperback books, four carrels with EDL *Aud-X* headsets and tape recorders.

Functional Reading Exercises
1. Practice in writing numbers.
2. Fill out checks.
3. Complete short form of income tax.
4. Read a map.
5. Compute wages based on hourly salary and hours worked. Read and check on wage statement.
6. Cut out want ads. Answer questions: Where to go? Whom to call?
7. Read newspaper.
8. Use telephone directory.
9. Learn to use reference materials: dictionaries, encyclopedias.

Teaching Materials for Developmental Reading
1. Scholastic Action Library.
2. Barnell-Loft "Specific Skills Series."
3. Grolier's Reading Attainment Systems.
4. Science Research Associate's (SRA) Reading for Understanding, Junior Edition (Grades 3–8).
5. Scholastic Action Units.
6. Random House's Hip-Pocket Series.
7. Education Development Laboratory's Aud-X Kit.
8. Learning Trends (Globe Book) *World of Vocabulary* by Sidney J. Rauch and Zacharie J. Clements, 1974.

Typical Class Period
1. Folders for each student with objectives based on criterion-referenced test.
2. Initially, spend entire class period teaching students how to do exercises in each set of materials.
3. Occasionally, entire class works on a skill together with teacher input and instruction.
4. After initial orientation, students get three individually prescribed exercises per class period.

Relationship with Content Area Classes: Provides some support for English teacher by providing reading students with help on assignments such as capitalization.

Retesting
1. Spache in middle of year for those with reading grade equivalent 5.5 and up.
2. Year-end test: Nelson.

Grades
1. Based on point system: 10 points for daily activity, 10 points for homework turned in.
2. Letter grades: A = 90% of all points that should have been earned, B = 80–89%, C = 70–79%.

Budget
1. Aides from Title I.
2. $150/year for maintenance of kits and supplies.
3. Thermofaxing provided by central office.

Teacher's Background: B.A. at Western Michigan University, year at University of Chicago in history of religion, substitute teacher, aide at juvenile delinquent institution, teaching credential at University of California, Irvine. Set up reading program at high school as Title I teacher 3 years ago; nw certificated teacher employed by district.

B. Functional Reading with Emphasis
on Comprehension

Testing: Retest on the *Nelson Reading Test* in Grade 9, administer Gray Standardized Oral Reading Tests.

Class Description: 15 students, reading grade equivalents 3–6. One teaching aide paid from Title I funds.

Materials
1. *Scope* magazine.
2. Newspapers, *Los Angeles Times;* rewrite stories daily to fourth grade level, test with one question.
3. Combine math with reading — use supermarket ads to compute bill for shopping.
4. Read want ads.
5. Skill development: laminated Science Research Associates Reading Laboratory (3A) cards. Listen to story on tapes made by teacher and answer comprehension questions. Scored by teacher's aide.

Class Organization and Period
1. Monday–Thursday, half go to library; other half get SRA cards.
2. Class activities:
   a. Vocabulary exercises or homework: Half the students bring in homework (three words on ditto sheet—make up sentences using them).
   b. SRA Story Progress: Comprehension 0–1 errors, move up to more difficult level; 2–3 errors, remain at same level; 4 or more, move down a level.
   c. Functional activities: work in groups. Entire group completes activity on want ads, supermarket shopping, and so forth.

Gains: Some gains on specific materials, but not on standardized tests; not enough time. Students would have to read 2–3 hours per day to complete enough to gain on test.

Teacher Background
B.A. New School for Social Research.
M.A. in Psychology.
M.A. in Teaching Reading, University of New Falls.

Critique of Functional Reading Programs

Although the objectives of functional reading programs are laudable, they must be recognized as (a) only minimal requirements for operating in society, (b) the consequence of a decision to give up on trying to prepare some students for content area courses and the general academic objectives of school, and (c) relevant only to some specific adult reading requirements that are susceptible to change or modification. Although application questions, for example, have some common elements (name, age, address) which can be specifically taught, they also have variable elements that call for general, not specific, word identification abilities. However, because different words may refer to the same information, audio-taped directions are beginning to accompany application forms in various places such as government offices, reducing the necessity for reading application forms.

Although while some functional reading requirements can be specified (Harris, 1970), there is no consensus on what constitutes functional literacy (Bormuth, 1975). Vocational reading instruction is one answer, but this instruction may be as difficult or even more challenging than other content area instruction. (See chapter 10 for levels of difficulty of vocational materials.) Specific occupational reading instruction can be done on the job (Sticht & McFann, 1975), but such training can come only when people are employed or know what specific jobs they will have.

What may be most desirable in high school functional literacy classes is to use the motivational effects of adult and occupational reading materials for teaching general reading acquisition and processes of learning from text. To do so, abstract the vocabulary from these materials for teaching word identification and word meaning techniques, use the content in varying syntactic arrangements and prose organizations, and teach students to interact with printed materials, drawing upon their knowledge and experiences, particularly for making inferences and evaluations. This broader goal is likely to help students become more adaptable to changes in content and enable them to function better in diverse reading situations.

5. INDIVIDUAL READING CLASS
Description
Students, usually low in "reading" achievement, are programmed into an *individual reading "class"*; frequently these classes replace regular English courses. Some teachers of individual reading classes may administer a diagnostic test and provide some individual diagnosis and instruction (Singer & Rhodes, 1977), but in many of these classes, students simply self-select and read high-interest paperback books. The paperbacks range in difficulty, but among them are many high-interest, low-difficulty materials. See Box 17.9 for a more detailed description of this type of class.

BOX 17.9. *Individual Reading Class*

Intake: The English department at the high school has an informal tracking system. Students are rated on basis of Nelson-Denny Reading Test, given at the end of junior high school and/or counselor recommendations. Students missed through this process are referred by classroom teachers. The class is a depository for students with behavior problems, learning disabilities, and bilingual students ranging from high to low intelligence. Students reading at grade level 6.0 or below are urged, but not mandated, into a reading class. Those above 6.0, but still below grade level, get developmental reading, which is actually an English literature program with less difficult materials, high-interest, low-difficulty adolescent fiction. Those at grade level or above take the regular English curriculum. Those whose Stanford-Binet IQs are 134 or above are placed in an English honors program.

Testing in Reading Class: Individual testing on appropriate subsections of the *Gates-McKillop Reading Diagnostic Tests* or the *Gilmore Oral Reading Test* and the *Gates-MacGinitie Reading Test.*

Class Size: Maximum of 10–15 students. No aides.

Program
1. Each student gets an individual program and a file is kept (two for each student; one for student use and the other for the teacher's records).
2. Individual program stressing oral reading. While other students silently read self-selected paperbacks, one student at a time is called to the teacher's desk where he or she reads orally for 10 minutes; students thus see the teacher once every four days.
3. Treatment:
   a. Individual, choice of a wide variety of material, including some kits, but SRA is used sparingly.
   b. Much free reading. Usually, students browse or get the instructor's advice on selection of paperbacks.
   c. Typically, little is done in the way of instruction.

A Weekly Schedule

Monday: Student selects new book and reads to teacher. They discuss the passage. Teacher evaluates appropriateness of book for student. The student starts graph or chart on pages read during session.

Tuesday: Student discusses with teacher or relates what he/she read. They go over list of difficult words or new terms.

Wednesday: Student may have a writing assignment.

Thursday: Word recognition exercises, individual or group.

Friday: Reading games.

Relationship to Content Areas: Use content area textbooks based on content area teacher's message that student needs help in reading the assigned textbook; the reading teacher gives individual student instruction on reading in the particular content area.

Materials: Primarily paperbacks.

Gains: Some students showed gains but floundered when put back in regular English classes; some students did whatever they could to stay in the reading lab. Many low IQ pupils showed no gains during 4 years in the lab.

Teacher Background: Five English teachers; initially, none had experience in teaching reading. Each teacher has two sections of reading and three English classes. New teachers are usually assigned to reading lab duty.

Evaluation: Teachers work hard but feel frustrated. They have limited success with a few students. They want to change the program but no one involved seems to know what to do.

For individual counseling and instruction on problems in reading in the content areas, see Harry Singer and Alan Rhodes, "Problems, Possibilities, and Programs at the High School Level," in Wayne Otto *et al.* (eds.), *Reading Problems: A Multidisciplinary Perspective.* (Reading, MA: Addison-Wesley, 1976).

Critique of the Individual Reading Class

The individual reading class is a form of tracking because students are divided up according to levels of reading achievement and provided with differentiated instruction. That is, some low-achieving students enrolled in English classes are programmed into reading classes while the higher-achieving students get regular or accelerated English instruction (analysis of literature, composition, and grammar instruction). Regardless of the label assigned to the lower track—the individual reading class—it soon stigmatizes the students involved. The negative label tends to demoralize students with high levels of aspiration and overprotects less ambitious students who may perceive the class as a refuge from regular

English classes (Singer & Rhodes, 1977). However, research has not definitely established that "stigmatized" labels alone affect students in general (Mac-Millan, Jones, & Aloia, 1974). What may have a detrimental effect is the lowered expectations on the part of teachers with these effects: input instruction is reduced; students do not have as many assignments or classroom questions to respond to; tests may not be administered with the result that neither students nor teachers have knowledge of progress. In short, students do not obtain any of the essentials of instruction. Hence, it is not surprising to find little or no gain in reading achievement in this type of class.

Low teacher expectations of student achievement can have serious effects. Beez (1968) found that prospective teachers serving as tutors, when told their students were dull, administered only half as many words during instruction as tutors who were told their students were bright. The students were actually equal in ability. The result was an immediate gap created in words learned by the two groups.

Even if lowered expectations do not lead to differences in achievement, the change in curriculum from English to reading instruction leads to an increased gap in knowledge of English content. The gap can be avoided or at least reduced if the reading class has the same objectives and instruction as the other English classes.

Another assumption underlying the individual reading class is that the average and above-average readers do not need further instruction in reading. Although they do not need reading acquisition instruction, they do need to learn how to learn from texts in the content area of literature. Some of the instruction in English classes accomplishes this purpose, particularly if it involves teaching such aspects of literature as structure in a novel or short story, characterization, literary devices (such as irony, satire, and metaphors), paragraph and chapter organization, styles of writing, and the genres. Such instruction may even be more effective for teaching students to learn from text if it were done to help students learn from text. Furthermore, such instruction is necessary and appropriate not only for the average or better student but also for lower-than-average achievers. Otherwise, tracking would merely widen the knowledge gap (I. Balow, 1964) between the two groups.

6. MULTI-FACETED READING INSTRUCTION
Description
Multi-faceted *reading instruction* has a variety of exercises for students to do each class period. Most of the exercises are short and interesting. Frequently they are teacher-made learning packets or dittoed sheets of exercises or games. They may be done individually or in groups. Occasionally, the teacher may provide some input instruction, using magazine materials written for junior and senior high school students (Singer, 1973b). See Box 17.10 for a more detailed description of this type of program.

BOX 17.10. Multi-faceted Program for
Reading Acquisition

Test: The Nelson Reading Test plus teacher-made criterion-referenced test, administered in English or Spanish.

Class Description: Size: 15–20, reading grade equivalents 0–4. Two Title I aides (salary $4,300 per academic year).

Materials
1. Thematic units for criterion-referenced items — used on contractual basis; 20 contracts over school year
2. Scholastic Units
3. *Scope* magazine
4. Action Library Series
5. Paperbacks
6. Games
7. Language Master
8. Controlled readers — used minimally.

Class Period and Organization
1. Three or four assigned activities. Points earned for grade, arbitrary division of points.
2. Monday, Tuesday, Thursday: Activities on contracts, prescribed over 2–3 week period. Work on contracts, individually or small groups (3–4 students).
3. Wednesday, Friday: Students work on skills in sociometrically chosen groups; groups compete for prizes.

Posttest: The Nelson Reading Test; gains of 1.6 to 2 years over 9 months.

Teacher Background
1. B.A. in English and teaching credential, Bradwell University; speaks Spanish well enough to conduct class in Spanish.
2. Four years of teaching experience.

Critique of Multi-Faceted Instruction

Although multi-faceted instruction could be focused, coherent, and cumulative, often it is not. Students may work on word recognition exercises using words that are unrelated to those employed in word meaning assignments, and both the word recognition and word meaning tasks may be unrelated to any story or expository content occurring in the class. Although a variety of exercises is motivating and stimulating to students, the exercises can also be related—not only to each other but also to content area courses students are enrolled in. Moreover, the exercises can be organized into a sequence to promote cumulative learning and generalizations that transfer to the content area classes. Even the use of technical terms from content area courses in word recognition and word meaning exercises would provide some application from multi-faceted reading instruction to content area classes. For a more detailed presentation of this approach, see the section headed ''Reading Acquisition in the Content Areas,'' chapter 18.

7. THREE-STAGE PROGRAM
Description
Some schools have reading programs not only for low and average but also for high-achieving readers. These classes are often referred to as remedial, corrective, and accelerated classes, or by some other triad of terms. The remedial class may resemble the clinic or reading class and the corrective class may resemble the reading laboratory. The low achievers are given the remedial reading program, while readers closer to grade level are assigned to a reading laboratory. Students reading above grade level have an accelerated reading and study skills program designed to speed up their reading and sharpen their study skills in preparation for college aptitude tests, scholarship exams, and college-level work. The accelerated reading programs may resemble those that were developed for the Army at universities and are now offered to college students. A detailed description of a three-stage program is given in Box 17.11.

BOX 17.11. Three-Stage Program

A Junior High School Program
for All Levels of Reading

Intake: All seventh graders take reading: students are placed according to their reading grade equivalents on the *Gates Reading Survey:* Reading Lab = 0–5.5; Developmental Reading = 5.5–7.5; and Exploratory Reading = 7.5 and up. Students can progress through all three stages.

Tests
1. *Gates Reading Survey* (Grades 3–10): Levels of comprehension and vocabulary.
2. Test is given three times a year — September, December, and May — to accommodate students who transfer into the school (about one third of the students trickle in and out during a year).
3. No additional testing in Reading Lab. December testing on Gates is used for determining promotion from one reading class to another.

READING LAB CLASS

Objectives
1. Recognize and reproduce letters of alphabet
2. Sound-symbol correspondence and blending
3. Meaning of simple and long words

4. Recognize affixes — syllabication
5. Use sentences to find answers to questions
6. Find main idea in a paragraph
7. Read story and understand it

Materials

EDL Aud. X: Phonics for beginning level readers

EDL Tach. X: Word recognition and vocabulary study

The Sullivan Reading Program: Word recognition in sentence contexts (individual)

Kottmeyer: Conquests in Reading (beginner)

Readers' Digest New Advanced Reading Skill/Builders: On audio tape — students follow along; may reread. Educationally handicapped referrals use these tapes one period per day. A few are at second-grade level of reading, but majority read at grade equivalents 3–5.

Barnell and Loft's Specific Skills Series (Richard Boning, author): Comprehension exercises: Drawing Conclusions, Getting Main Ideas, Working with Sounds, Using the Context, Following Directions, Detecting the Sequence. Graded materials, some in programmed instruction format and others in multiple-choice format.

EDL Controlled Reading Program: Lessons built to reinforce word recognition and vocabulary

Go Magazine

Typical Period in Lab: Assignments made at beginning of period. Teacher keeps folder with charts for each student. Individual written assignments and materials on sheet stapled into folder — lasts for semester. Students correct own papers in skills series; turn them in weekly. Class is mostly individualized.

Motivation: Celebrate holidays.

DEVELOPMENTAL READING CLASS

Objectives
1. Use word attack through structural analysis.
2. Increase vocabulary up to grade level.
3. Use context to understand unfamiliar use of word.
4. Increase comprehension through class discussion and answering questions about material read.
5. Locate the main idea and relate it to supporting details in nonfiction.
6. Follow written directions.
7. Use subject-matter textbooks (social studies and science) effectively.
8. Separate fact from opinion.
9. Recognize tone or slant in an article.

Organization of Class
1. More like regular class than individualized Reading Lab. Partly taught as class; group instruction for class; partly as small group work and individualized instruction.
2. Students usually have a choice of assignment based on their assignment sheets

which lists book and unit to do in Barnell Loft (Richard Boning), Specific Skills Series, Magazines, Graph and Picture Skills Kit, SRA, Be a Better Reader.

Materials
1. SRA Labs and Vocabulary Kit.
2. Reading for Understanding.
3. Specific Skills Series.
4. Magazines: *Scope, You and Your World, Read.*
5. Selection of paperbacks.
6. Be a Better Reader Series A, B, C, or I, II.
7. Graph and Picture Study Skills.

Typical Assignment
1. Be a Better Reader "B," p. 67, "Pioneer Flights for Cape Kennedy." Do activity 1, 2, pp. 8–9.
2. Working with social studies words, p. 70.
3. *Scope* magazine: Read "Born Free."
4. Library research report due next Monday.

Typical Period
Individual: Make choice from assignments in folder. Self-selected reading.
Group: Vocabulary instruction.

Motivation
1. Keep track of progress.
2. Weekly grade of A to F on assignments; record on report card.

EXPLORATORY READING (Accelerated Reading Class)

Objectives
1. Read a whole book.
2. Read many different kinds of books on a variety of subjects.
3. Broaden understanding of history, geography, and social problems through reading.
4. Learn to read critically; be able to argue a point of disagreement with printed material.
5. Learn to read creatively: students should be able to apply what is read to situations in their own lives.

Organization of Class: Taught partly as class, but often individualized, depending on students.

Materials
1. Different kinds and levels of books.
2. *Success in Reading*, Bk. I and II by Robert E. Shafer, Arthur S. McDonald, and Karen Hess, California State Series, 1967.
3. Unit on using library.
4. Teacher-prepared reading guides on skimming, recognizing similes, use of graphs and maps, remembering what is read.

Grade: Based primarily on effort. Students can get As or Bs by doing work at level placed in. If work done, may get A or B. If not done, get D or F.

Assistance (In reading lab and in developmental reading)
1. One full-time aide.
2. Teaching Assistant: 8th- or 9th-grade students assist with grading; help with new children. TA is graduate of class. Works with students individually in class.

Relationship to Content Area Teachers
1. In-service training on use of kits in social studies.
2. Students in each class have different teachers — grouped not by grade but by reading levels.
3. In other subjects students are also sectioned: three sections in each content area. Sections based on reading scores and recommendations of 6th-grade teacher. Lowest 9th grade has 5th-grade social sudies materials; but lowest 7th and 8th grades have few materials in anything—teachers are working to develop their own materials.

Consultation with Parents: Only ad hoc consultation on problems.

Budget: $500 per year.

Staff: Three reading specialists, two with M.A. degrees and reading specialist with credentials from Bullock University. One teacher converted from English to teaching developmental reading, but has had no formal instruction in reading.

Critique of Three-Stage Programs

The assumption underlying the three-stage programs is that the students in the programs have qualitatively, as well as quantitatively, different instructional needs. While the quantitative assumption is likely to be true according to the criterion used in differentiating the students, it is not likely to be true on all the other skills and abilities that enter into reading and learning from texts (I. Balow, 1962).

The qualitative assumption is not true. Students at all stages need instruction in word recognition, word meaning, and learning from text, although students in the lower groups need a heavier emphasis on word identification. Indeed, the lower achievers are likely to include more subcategories of learners who need individual treatment. (See chapter 18 for a reading program for acquisition in content areas for these low achievers.) All of the tracks can use relevant content from the various content areas so that the students not only can improve in the reading classes but also can transfer what they learn and consequently improve in reading and learning from texts in various content areas.

8. SCHOOLWIDE READING PROGRAMS
Description

A *schoolwide reading program* may vary from one organized and administered by a reading specialist on an informal request basis (Thomas, 1969) to a program that involves the entire faculty in intensive in-service training. Although rare in the past, schoolwide in-service training is occurring now with greater frequency as faculties become less mobile and fewer new teachers are hired. Even more rare are the schools which in a concentrated attack on reading improvement use a particular technique, such as marginal glossing, on a schoolwide basis (Dillner, 1971).

Critique of Schoolwide Reading Programs

A reading consultant or specialist on a school faculty serving only on a request or informal basis is likely to have some helpful effects on faculty and students. However, beneficial results are more likely to follow from defined objectives and systematic development of faculty for teaching reading and learning from text to students in each content area. Then, students are likely to get instruction in reading and learning from text in all their content areas. The reinforcement in processes of reading and learning from text and instruction in various content areas for all students will be reflected as gains on standardized reading tests if improvement has occurred in each content area sampled by a general reading achievement test (Singer & Rhodes, 1976). Hence, a comprehensive inservice course and instruction in all facets of reading and learning from texts are preferable to the schoolwide use of a single instructional technique. However, the single instructional technique may be a necessary strategy for starting a faculty toward the goal of a comprehensive program.

9. PROFICIENCY EXAMINATIONS AND RELATED CURRICULUM FOR A HIGH SCHOOL DIPLOMA
Description

Before returning to Monroe High School, Ms. Valdes mentioned another type of program that they hadn't observed: a program that develops students for passing *functional* or *proficiency tests* mandated for high school graduation. She provided Ms. Jones with the following information:

In 1977, the Educational Testing Service reported (ETS, 1977) that state legislatures were mandating mastery of essential skills as a condition for high school graduation. Seven states (California, Colorado, Florida, Maryland, Virginia, New Jersey, and Washington) had already enacted such legislation, while the state boards or departments of education in nine states took action to establish minimal competency requirements. California enacted legislation in September, 1976 (Assembly Bill 3408) that was superseded by another bill (AB65) in September, 1977. The second bill requires school districts in California to assess reading proficiency by administering a district-adopted early warning, minimal competency test at the elementary level in Grades 4 to 6, then an exit level or proficiency test at the junior high school once in Grades 7–9, and twice at the high school level. Once students have passed the test they will not have to take it again. For those students who do not pass the test, the district must provide a diagnostic and prescriptive remedial conference with the student and his or her parents to determine how the student would satisfy the district's proficiency requirement. After June, 1980, students who do not meet the proficiency standards will be denied a high school diploma, even if they have met all other requirements for graduation.

In 1980, some 39 state legislatures had mandated some form of competency testing, but the specific features of the laws varied considerably from state to state. They differed in governmental level for setting of standards (7 local, 19 state, and 12 state and local); grade levels assessed (Grades 1 to 12); expected use of standards (grade promotion, 3; high school graduation, 16, and local option, 2), early exit tests (only 2, California and New York); remediation (11); and year the first graduating class was assessed (1980 to 1985) (Education Commission of the States, 1980). State control on setting of standards meant a uniform level of passing the competency test(s); for example, New York State required passing the state-adopted test or a standardized reading achievement test at the 50th percentile or higher in Grades 7 to 9. But local control meant considerable intrastate variability; for example, grade level standards for passing the reading test varied in some 10 California school districts from Grade 5.1 to Grade 8.7 (Balow & Singer, 1987).

Remediation also varied. For example, in response to the legislation, the Los Angeles School District developed its own *Senior High Assessment of Reading Proficiency* (SHARP Test) and a curriculum in the form of miniunits directly related to the reading tasks for those students who do not pass the test. As of June, 1979, only those Los Angeles high school seniors who have passed the test will receive a diploma. When the test was first administered, 24% of the district's high school students did not pass the test, which had a cutting score of 81 (67% of the items correct). Since each of the three parts of the test is worth 40 points, the cutting score requires students who want to pass to take all three parts of the test. The SHARP Test and the remedial curriculum accompanying is a new type of reading program on the current scene.

The purpose of the SHARP test is to:

Objectively assess reading skills at the high school levels that relate to the understanding of and/or appropriate responses to printed materials. These materials represent forms and documents that adults must read and/or complete continuously.

The materials fit into three categories in SHARP:

1. Can you follow directions? This category includes directions for voting, driver's tests, library cards, job and rental applications, unemployment

insurance claims, letter writing, social security documents, and change of address forms.

2. What's in it? This section deals with reading and comprehension of signs, labels, and want ads, Yellow Pages, dictionaries, newspapers, warranties, bank accounts, signature cards, credit applications, and check writing.

3. What does it mean? This part covers reading skills involved in the use of maps, area codes, cash register tapes, bank statements, TV guides, income tax forms, utility bill codes, and job resumes.

(This information came from the Second Revision of the *Senior High Assessment of Reading Proficiency*, SHARP. Monterey, California: CTB/McGraw Hill, 1975. Copyright 1975 by Los Angeles Unified School District. All Rights Reserved.).

Critique of Proficiency Examinations for the High School Diploma

The SHARP Test is an impressive device for assessing its specific domains. However, it includes content that is not specifically taught in the school (though perhaps it should be) and omits academic content that is stressed by the school. Hence, the test measures literacy in survival types of reading materials, not academic types of content.

A comparable proficiency test that also uses "real-life" situations for its content (but may be more closely attuned to the levels of reading ability stressed in the school) is the Educational Testing Service's Basic Skills Assessment Reading Test. Fifty percent of its items stress literal comprehension, 40% inference, and 10% evaluation (ability to distinguish fact and opinion, predict outcomes, and determine sequence, style, and tone). Even so, ETS states that the test is "easy for the high school population as a whole" (Harlstorne, 1977, p. 4.)

However, the ETS test is also not designed to test academic content. Presumably schools that want to assess this type of content can use one of the standardized achievement survey tests, such as ETS's Sequential Test of Educational Progress or the Stanford Achievement Test Battery. Another limitation of ETS's Basic Skills Assessment Test is that, in contrast to SHARP, it does not have a set of curricular materials accompanying it. Presumably ETS tries to key its items to existing curricular materials. An advantage of ETS's testing program is that ETS promises to revise its test every 6 months and maintain tight security over it. Hence, it is unlikely that students will have access to it before their reading proficiency is tested.

Either SHARP or the ETS test assesses basic proficiency of survival-type literacy. Although the alternative curriculum is less academic than the school's standard curriculum defined by the tests and embodied in SHARP's minicourses, at least it ensures that students who pass these or similar tests and receive a high school diploma will have a minimal level of competency.

If other states follow California's lead, the standards will vary considerably within the state. As we have pointed out, it varies in 10 districts in California from Grade 5.1 to Grade 8.7. Consequently, the public, which has clamored for a meaningful high school diploma, still has difficulty in determining what a high school diploma indicates about a student's level of reading proficiency.

What reading proficiency assessment does mean is that high schools throughout the country will at least be filling the educational gap by hiring reading specialists and initiating a reading course at the high school level. Initiation of this course may be only a beginning. High schools may expand the course into a schoolwide operation for reading and learning from texts in all content areas. Indeed, we know that the San Diego Unified School District no longer administers reading competency tests in isolation, but instead it began in 1986 to assess reading competency in all of the 23 courses it requires for high school graduation (Singer & Balow, 1987b).

Although San Diego's approach to competency assessment may not be appropriate for students still in need of reading acquisition instruction, it may be more effective than a remedial reading course for those students who are beyond reading acquisition and into the learning from text phase of reading development (See explanation of differentiating these two phases in chapter 4). We have some evidence that students who are beyond reading acquisition (beyond grade equivalent 5.5 on a standardized reading achievement test) but have failed a reading competency test that required a grade equivalent of 8.7 to pass improved significantly more on a retake of the reading competency test after a year in a regular English class that they elected to take than a comparable group of students who, in place of the English class, were assigned to a year in a remedial reading class. The English course emphasized academic content for all students and the remedial reading course stressed workbook type material on "survival skills," essentially consumer-type reading, such as reading advertisements, recipes, and governmental forms. This evidence is consistent with the basic premise of this text: after students have learned how to read, they develop their ability to learn from text by instruction in the content area courses (Singer & Balow, 1987).

The Los Angeles Unified School District has also abandoned its functional reading test (SHARP) in favor of a subset of items from the reading comprehension subtest of the *Comprehensive Test of Basic Skills* for assessing competency. In doing so, the district is not only economizing on testing but also emphasizing competency in basic skills required for *academic* success (Singer & Balow, 1987). Thus, California has dramatically changed its minimum competency program.

SUMMARY

In this chapter, we discussed how a reading and learning-from-text specialist can serve the entire school. The high school specialist functions in much the same way as does the elementary specialist. The high school specialist (a) diagnoses students with reading difficulties: (b) directs or teaches classes in reading acquisition in the content areas and functional reading programs; (c) demonstrates lessons on teaching reading and learning from texts in the content areas; (d) advises teachers of introductory classes on strategies for teaching incoming students how to learn from texts in the content areas, (e) provides in-service education and (f) participates in a schoolwide committee for developing a program to teach all students how to read and learn from text.

We also described in detail a composite elementary school reading laboratory or center and nine types of reading programs on the current scene and mentioned a potential program that teaches students to pass proficiency exams for high school graduation. Reading programs at the junior high school level tend to teach all students in the school and emphasize developmental reading. Typically an individualized approach is used: students are diagnosed; a prescription is made, and file folders for assignments and progress records are kept. At the high school level, programs are also individualized, but the emphasis is more on functional reading with a survival type of content. Hardly any instruction is given on learning from text or content area reading at the junior or senior high levels. Moreover, relationships with the content area faculty tend to be minimal.

Although the individualized programs usually supply students with materials appropriate to their reading levels, teaching practices in the programs often do not satisfy the criteria of instruction. These criteria are:

1. Diagnosing students, formulating objectives consistent with the diagnosis, and organizing materials that are appropriate for achievement of objectives and providing for feedback and evidence of progress. Most reading programs and many package programs on the current scene, such as those of the SRA Reading Laboratories, meet these criteria.

2. Input instruction, including explaining, clarifying, test trials, and additional practice to strengthen learning and to provide for individual differences in rate of learning. Some of the programs provide input instruction. The reading lab (Box 17.7) provides instruction on active comprehension in small groups once a week. But, most of the time, students have to lift themselves up by their own bootstraps as they follow their assignments in packaged programs with the directions serving as the teacher. The packaged materials, however, do not diagnose student errors. Usually, students score their own exercises and fill out their own progress charts with little teacher analysis and correction of errors.

3. Coherence is minimal in all the programs. To explain coherence, consider any paragraph. What knowledge, abilities, and processes would a reader have to mobilize to comprehend the paragraph? The following is a list of major variables or subsystems underlying comprehension:

   a. Word identification skills
   b. Word meaning (vocabulary)
   c. Morphemics (knowledge of roots and affixes)
   d. Knowledge of syntax (ability to recognize intrasentence, intersentence, inter-paragraph relationships and relationships among larger

units of organization, such as problems and solutions or parts of story structure

e. General knowledge (knowledge supplied by the reader for filling in information a writer assumes readers know; for supplying evaluative criteria; for generating major prmises; for interpretation; or for understanding literary devices such as metaphors, similes, and allusions)

f. Attitudes and values that determine how a reader processes and reacts to the material

g. Reasoning processes, such as inference, interpretation, concept formation, and conceptual ability, and evaluation.

Some materials used in reading programs on the current scene have internal coherence because they do teach some word identification skills and vocabulary that occur in passages or comprehension exercises. However, most of the assignments in the programs are not coherent. Students may have one set of materials for word recognition, another for vocabulary development, and still another for comprehension without any specific relationship among them. Apparently the programs operate on the assumption that students will develop *general* abilities in each subsystem and mobilize these abilities to solve their reading problems as they need them. This is a long-range goal that must await some relatively high level of development in each subsystem before it can be achieved. Either in the long or the short run, current programs also rely on transfer of training for application of subsystems to the attainment of reading comprehension. But the evidence from research on learning is that transfer is more likely to occur when teachers teach for it; to teach for transfer, teachers should give students instruction in those specific contents and processes immediately required for a comprehension task, demonstrated in the directed reading activities (DRA) in chapters 13–16. Using the DRA strategy, teachers are likely to be successful in teaching students to apply the subsystems, and students are more likely to gain satisfaction from successful comprehension.

4. Psychosynchromeshing facility occurs when students not only attain the necessary content and processes but can mobilize them appropriately for attaining comprehension. This facility is more likely to be attained if students can try out newly learned content and processes in literature or expository materials. An analogy can be drawn from swimming instruction: after a skill such as an arm-stroke is taught on land, the students jump into the pool to try out the stroke in the total act of swimming. Likewise, if word recognition, word meaning, and reasoning in reading process are taught, students should have an immediate opportunity to use them in the total act of reading.

5. Isolation versus Group Interaction. Most reading programs have students do their assignments in isolation. Hardly any time is allocated to group instruction or discussion. Yet students can and do benefit from group

discussions. Consequently, whenever possible, reading programs should group students whose reading levels are close and have them read the same material as is done in Steps 1 and 2 of Scholastic Units. (See chapter 13 for a description of how these units work and chapter 8 for instructional procedures on discussion.)

6. Integration of reading programs with reading and learning from texts in the content areas. Students are referred to reading programs because they usually have difficulty in comprehending the assigned texts. Classroom teachers could adopt levels of texts to students. Frequently they do not, but they do expect the reading program to do so. (See single- and multiple-text strategies throughout this text but particularly in chapters 6, 7, 11, 13–16.) Yet, most reading programs do not teach students to read and learn from texts. The next chapter, about the future scene, explains how a school can teach all students to read and learn from texts in reading programs and in courses in each content area.

ACTIVITY

Visit a nearby elementary, junior or senior high school that has a center for reading and learning from text. The program used might be similar to one described in this chapter. Interview the director of the center to find answers to these questions:

1. How does the faculty refer students, and how does the center select students for the program? What are the characteristics of these students?
2. What tests does the center use (a) to screen students, (b) to diagnose students' difficulties and to evaluate their progress during the program? What progress do students make in the center?
3. What student activities does the center have?
4. What materials does the center frequently use to improve students' performance? What is the daily and weekly instructional plan?
5. How does the center grade students? Motivate them?
6. Who staffs the center?
7. What amount of money has the principal budgeted for running the center? What is the cost per student?

   When you have compiled the information from the interview, compare it with the data other students have gathered from their interviews.

18 The Future: A Schoolwide Program

CHAPTER OVERVIEW

Now that you have read about some of the current attempts to solve the problem of handling individual differences in reading and learning from text within a single school, you are prepared to deal with the future scene, a program that incorporates the viewpoint inherent in this book. The topics in this chapter include (a) an outline of a reading content acquisition course that is based upon an explanation of word identification and comprehension or interaction between the reader and the text; and (b) in-service education that involves a sequence for acquiring and learning to use single- and multiple-text strategies, an introductory course for reading and learning from text in the content areas, and a committee on reading and learning from text.

GRAPHIC ORGANIZER

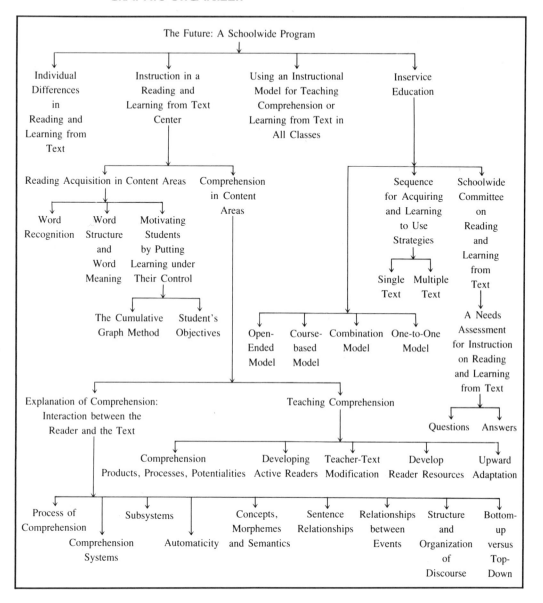

The Future: A Schoolwide Program

Individual Differences in Reading and Learning from Text

Instruction in a Reading and Learning from Text Center

Using an Instructional Model for Teaching Comprehension or Learning from Text in All Classes

Inservice Education

Reading Acquisition in Content Areas

Comprehension in Content Areas

Sequence for Acquiring and Learning to Use Strategies

Schoolwide Committee on Reading and Learning from Text

Word Recognition

Word Structure and Word Meaning

Motivating Students by Putting Learning under Their Control

Single Text Multiple Text

The Cumulative Graph Method Student's Objectives

Open-Ended Model

Course-based Model

Combination Model

One-to-One Model

A Needs Assessment for Instruction on Reading and Learning from Text

Explanation of Comprehension: Interaction between the Reader and the Text

Teaching Comprehension

Questions Answers

Comprehension Products, Processes, Potentialities

Developing Active Readers

Teacher-Text Modification

Develop Reader Resources

Upward Adaptation

Process of Comprehension

Subsystems

Concepts, Morphemes and Semantics

Sentence Relationships

Relationships between Events

Structure and Organization of Discourse

Bottom-up versus Top-Down

Comprehension Systems

Automaticity

PREPOSED QUESTIONS

1. What would you put into a lab that would integrate reading acquisition with content area materials?
2. How would you motivate students?

3. How would you explain and teach comprehension?
4. What would help learners become more confident?
5. What are some models for inservice training?
6. What would you do to bring about a schoolwide program in reading and learning from text?

INDIVIDUAL DIFFERENCES IN READING AND LEARNING FROM TEXT AT EACH SCHOOL LEVEL

We began this text by pointing out that a wide range of individual differences in reading and learning from text now exists throughout the grades (See chapter 3). However, over 75 years ago, the range was relatively narrow in high school because then most students did not go on to high school, and those who did go on tended to be high in reading achievement. But, as we explained in the beginning of this text, the high school population has changed dramatically. One of the major changes was that high school students now tend to remain to graduate. In the 1950s, some 55% of the students in the ninth grade remained to graduate; this figure went up to 87% during the 1970s, but has dropped down to about 75% in the 1980s. The reading achievement of the group that has remained in school is about grade equivalent 5.0 for the lowest reading achievers in Grade 10 to 24.0 (second-year graduate school level) for the highest reading achievers in Grade 10. This range is normal; that is, we expect to have this range in reading achievement if all students are achieving to the best of their mental capabilities.

At the primary grade level, teachers try to solve the problem within classes by grouping students. Typically, they form about three groups, which is an optimum compromise between teacher time allocation and range of reading achievement within their classes. However, they could further subdivide the lower group; if they had an aide, they might be able to manage more than three groups. In the intermediate grades, teachers still have about three groups during the reading and mathematics periods, but tend to use whole-class instruction during the social studies and science periods, which typically have single texts. The single- and multiple-text strategies would be appropriate for these classes. That is, intermediate grade teachers could use these strategies for meeting the wide range of individual differences in ability to read and learn from text in their classes. Indeed, the information in the rest of this chapter, which is addressed to junior and senior high schools, would also be appropriate for the intermediate grades.

However, organizational differences at the junior and senior high school level provide additional ways for solving the problem of trying to educate students who vary so widely in ability. We perceive three possibilities: (a) We could invoke grade level standards; that is, we could insist that students who are not reading up to grade level repeat their present grade until they meet the entrance standard for the next grade. Our proficiency reading tests are a step in this direction. If we returned to invoking grade level standards that we more or less did prior to 1950, we would have an even wider range of achievement in each grade and would discourage low-achieving students from continuing in school. (b) We could have different curricula or tracks for students according to their levels of reading achievement. However, schools have officially dropped tracking students because they have had difficulty in justifying this practice to our courts. Consequently, high schools no longer assign students to classes; instead, students can select and sign up for any classes regardless of their own achievement levels. Of course, students with low reading achievement tend to avoid classes with heavy reading assignments such as English, science, social studies, and math, in favor of vocational classes, such as auto shop, sewing, and home economics. Also, some school counselors advise students to select courses that they think will match their ability levels. Hence, we have some *self-selective* and some *guided* tracking. Nevertheless, we still have a wide range of individual differences in reading achievement in all classes, even vocational classes. (c) We could adopt teaching strategies that enable teachers to provide equality of educational opportunity for all students without stigmatizing any. This text stresses the third possible solution.

The major part of the text (chapters 6–16), explains single- and multiple-text strategies for teaching content to students who differ widely in the ability to read and learn from text. This "difference" group consists of the largest numbers of students in a school. In chapter 17, we showed how schools are currently teaching students in the other three of the four reading difficulty categories (the 4 Ds) we defined in chapter 1. These are students with defects, deficiencies, and disruptions, and students who are at the low end of the difference curve. They are attending reading labs or classes in centers where they undergo further screening, take diagnostic tests, and receive instruction based on individual or group reading improvement plans.

These two types of programs fit the four types of reading difficulties and the range of individual differences in reading achievement in high school. However, high schools do not yet use single- and multiple-text strategies in any systematic way. This is, we do not know of any school where we could find teachers throughout the school using single- and multiple-text strategies in a phase-out/phase-in sequence. We could, and did, identify some schools where teachers were using one or more of these strategies.

Most schools that have reading labs or centers do not consciously employ content area materials in teaching high school students how to read; that is, these schools do not use the kind of content that appears in courses in the high school. Hence, they do not maximize transfer of learning in the content areas.[1]

We recognize that the strategies we have advocated for reading and learning from text in the content areas are not part of the current scene. We hope they will become part of the future scene. This chapter suggests how a high school could develop its own program to bring about this future scene: a schoolwide program for reading and learning from text.

To begin, the school would have to have a reading and learning-from-text specialist who would develop the necessary knowledge and skills for teaching a content reading acquisition course and strategies for reading and learning from

---

[1]Schools would have to construct their own materials to fit their own texts. However, some commercially prepared materials are available that will at least provide ideas on how to prepare these materials. For this purpose, see "Workbook Type Materials" listed in the Centers in chap. 17. They can also use the strategies explained throughout this text for constructing these materials, particularly the strategies in chaps. 6, 13–16, and the specific suggestions contained in this chapter, beginning on p. 586.

text. We suggest in this chapter what this specialist would have to do to convert existing reading labs or centers to content reading acquisition labs and learning from text centers. Most centers currently do teach students how to learn to read, and they do include instruction in comprehension in their reading acquisition programs. What they would have to do to become content reading acquisition labs is to substitute content area materials for their current instructional materials and exercises. We think that with this change they would probably meet the criteria for a competency-based course we outline in this chapter.

The use of single- and multiple-text strategies throughout the school would require an in-service education program planned and implemented by a school-wide committee. To help this committee plan its in-service education program, we have outlined the questions committee members would probably formulate and the answers they might generate for decision making and planning. The committee would, of course, need strong administrative support for this undertaking and a timetable of about 5 years.

We describe four models of in-service training that have worked successfully. The schoolwide planning committee would want to consider them. We also suggest a sequence for teaching and disseminating to the faculty strategies for reading and learning from text that would maximize its learning and minimize its resistance.

We anticipate that some teachers would cooperate and readily support the in-service program. These teachers could then teach introductory courses in reading and learning from text in their own content areas. The courses could serve as regular classes for freshmen students and as demonstration classes for other teachers.

To communicate how this future scene may come about, we employ the schoolwide committee of Monroe High School. You will eavesdrop on meetings of this committee via five dramatic scenes presented in this chapter. In the first scene (beginning below), the committee learns about a content reading acquisition class. In the second, they get a review of in-service education models. The third scene is a continuation of the second scene. It focuses on the idea of an introductory course in reading and learning from text. A week later, in the fourth scene, the schoolwide committee finds out the questions it will have to investigate in devising an in-service education program for the faculty and decides on tentative answers to them. The fifth and final scene is a meeting with the school principal. With this background, we are ready for Scene 1.

It is 4:30 in the afternoon. Monroe High students have been out of class for one hour. The schoolwide committee is meeting in a classroom with Ms. Valdes, the newly hired reading and learning specialist, to hear the results of the visits made by Ms. Valdes and Ms. Jones to neighboring schools' reading centers. Ms. Jones has described the centers and Ms. Valdes has just finished giving her evaluations of the programs. Committee members start to react.

Mr. Wallace: I sure like the sound of the individual reading class. I think that's the one we should adopt.

Mr. Phelps: Of course you do. That's the one most like a remedial English course. How's that going to help my kids with science?

Ms. Stewart: Or with math? We need something a little more imaginative.

Ms. Jorgensen: I like the functional reading program. It's practical and task oriented.

Ms. Stewart: That has its drawbacks. It tends to focus on low-level activities. And, by the way, as Ms. Valdes has said, how do we really know what it will take for these kids to function when they get through school? The way society's changing, entire vocational areas can be made obsolete overnight. Jeb, can you vouch for that?

Mr. Carter: That's true. Sometimes I feel kind of guilty teaching shop with outdated tools that the kids may never encounter and textbooks that writers, for some reason, make too damned difficult!

Ms. Jorgensen: You know what it looks like—none of these places you visited have the answer. They don't seem right for our needs.

Mr. Wallace: I still like the individual reading class.

Ms. Stewart: (*good-naturedly*) Who asked you? Why'd they ever let you on this committee? You've been reading T. S. Eliot too long!

Ms. Jones: O.K. Enough clowning around! Both Ms. Valdes and I have said the same things all of you are saying. We are of the opinion that none of these situations are right for us. So, why not build our own program?

Mr. Phelps: That's going to take a lot of work.

Ms. Jones: It might be worth the work.

Ms. Valdes: You see, learning to read and learning to learn from text are different processes. Reading acquisition includes a set of skills that the majority of students master by the fourth to sixth grades, but some students are still learning how to read when they reach high school. That applies to a small percentage of students at Monroe. Most of the students we've been talking about know *how* to read; they just can't understand their textbooks.

Ms. Jorgensen: We still have to deal with those nonreaders.

Ms. Valdes: True, most of the programs that we visited handle the nonreader, but the problem with these programs is that they don't use content from the courses the students are taking, and they don't do much with comprehension of text material.

Ms. Stewart: Well, as Latrice just mentioned, since we still have this group of students that are still in reading acquisition, couldn't these kids be learning to read from the same materials that elementary kids use?

Ms. Valdes: No, to keep their interest and to help them with the words in the textbooks you are using, our students need content drawn from high school texts. Let's take a few minutes here for you to read something I wrote about reading acquisition in the content areas as well as comprehension strategies.

INSTRUCTION IN A READING AND LEARNING FROM TEXT CENTER

Reading Acquisition in the Content Areas:
WORD RECOGNITION

The elementary program for developing reading acquisition was explained in the first part of chap. 4, "oral reading." Although mastery of the acquisition phase of reading development is approached by most students by Grade 6, some students are still in this stage of development during junior and senior high school. Students who are slow in speed of reading and low in general reading achievement are likely to still be in the acquisition stage of development; that is, they are still learning how to read the language they use in their everyday speech.

A consensus definition would probably indicate that students below grade equivalent 4.5 on a reading survey or comprehensive subtest of widely used test batteries, regardless of students' current grade status, are still in the reading acquisition phase of reading development. (See chap. 4, "Silent Reading," for more information on a consensus definition of the boundary between the overlapping phases of reading acquisition and learning from text.)

However, it would not be appropriate to have students at the junior or senior high schools who are still in the acquisition phase of reading development use the same materials elementary pupils use, even though they have to learn the same words, syllables, digraphs, consonant clusters, letter-sounds, and blending processes (Singer, 1971). Moreover, junior and senior high school students also have to learn to identify technical words that occur in their content area instruction. The solution to teaching both basic word identification skills and technical word recognition skills is simply to use technical words for teaching the students word identification skills. Suppose you are teaching students the relationship between the initial consonant *p* (the *symbol*) and the *sound* it represents. You could select some words from physics (*power, piston, pulley, pressure*) and list them in a column to make the initial consonant *p* apparent, as follows:

*p*ower

*p*iston

*p*ulley

*p*ressure

Then begin teaching students as suggested below.

1. "What consonant letter do all these words begin with?" (*p*)
2. "Listen to the beginning sound of each word." (Then pronounce the words or have students do so.)
3. "Give me other words beginning with the same sound." (A student says *pump,* and passes the transfer test. Other students may add *population, peroxide, pendulum.*)
4. The words students volunteer are then written in the column.
5. At the elementary level, you would also have students look at the beginning letter and learn its features (Gibson, 1976). This step is probably unnecessary at the higher grade levels.

Thus, students could learn sound-symbol correspondence and other word identification processes (responses to digraphs, syllabication, recognizing affixes, and blending word components) *using content area words from their own texts* (Resnick & Beck, 1974; Samuels, 1968). They would not only learn word identification responses and processes but they would also be able to recognize content area words when they came to them in their texts. Furthermore, this type of content for word identification instruction is less likely to embarrass junior or senior high school students enrolled in acquisition classes. Although the processes and procedures for learning to read are the same for all students, regardless of age, reading acquisition classes can and should use instructional techniques, tests, and topical materials suitable to more mature students.

Functional Words Common to All Texts

Some words, particularly functional words, are common to all texts. Dolch's 220 basic words account for 50% of all words in a text, so it would be helpful to have a list of these words (Tinker & McCullough, 1975). The list consists of such words as noun determiners (*a, the, this, these, those, that, some, and*); prepositions or locative words (*to, for, from, beyond, beneath, above*); conjunctions or combining words (*and, but, nor*); and subordinating words (*while, since, although*). These functional words tie the contentives (nouns, adjectives, adverbs, verbs) together.

By the end of Grade 3, 95% of all students have learned all the functional words. Therefore, these words should have priority in the reading acquisition program for junior and senior high school students who still cannot quickly identify functional words.

Teaching Words in Context

Do not teach functional words in isolation. Teach them in the context of content area phrases and sentences because the context is necessary for signaling the semantic and syntactical properties of functional words. You should also teach content area words in context, especially in sentences and paragraphs drawn from content area texts. Context makes the syntactic properties of the words apparent and helps the reader select the appropriate meaning of a word. The context helps identify the meaning of the word *constitution* in this sentence from a social studies text: "The people voted to change the *constitution*." In this sentence from a medical text, constitution has a very different meaning, which the context helps to make clear: "The man had a healthy *constitution*." A list of some content words for use in various word identification tasks is given in chapter 4, Box 4.1. You can locate additional words for word identification and word meaning instruction in glossaries or indices of content area texts.

Teaching for Transfer to the Process of Reading

Students in acquisition classes should also practice their newly learned words in content area paragraphs. You can locate paragraphs that contain these words in students' textbooks or in texts listed in the school catalogs. (See chap. 11, Box 11.3, for school catalog information.)

Psychosynchromeshing Facility

Transfer all word recognition skills to the process of reading. This transfer process is analogous to first teaching a skill in swimming on shore and then having the student try out the new skill in the pool. The swimming pool for reading is a text or book in a content area that has passages that elicit the word identification response you just taught. If you want to teach a student to identify the sound of the initial consonant p, do not end the lesson until the student dives into a passage in the text and consciously responds with the correct sound (phoneme) each time the initial consonant p (grapheme) appears in a word. The student may accompany the response by tapping a finger or foot. The purpose of this transfer process is to develop *psychosynchromeshing facility*, the ability to mobilize appropriate phonemic responses to graphemes at the appropriate time and in the appropriate sequence.

Another technique for having students learn to use words or word parts in sentence context is the Singer Sentence Generator (Singer & Beasley, 1970). This sentence generator consists of the four basic sentence patterns shown in Box 18.1.

BOX 18.1. *Singer Sentence Generator*

USING THE FOUR BASIC SENTENCE PATTERNS

Directions: Substitute recently learned words, one at a time, for successive word slots (noun or pronoun, verb, adjective, noun determiner, noun) to generate novel sentences.

Sentence Generator 1
Sentence Pattern: Noun (or Pronoun)–Verb (NV)

Motors	run
noun or pronoun	*verb* .

Sentence Generator 2
Sentence Pattern: Noun (or Pronoun)–Verb–Adjective (NVA)

Motors	are	powerful
noun or pronoun	*verb*	*adjective* .

Sentence Generator 3
Sentence Pattern: Noun (or Pronoun)–Verb–Noun Determiner–Noun (NVN$_D$N)

Electricians	threw	the	switch
noun or pronoun	*verb*	*noun determiner*	*noun* .

Sentence Generator 4

Sentence Pattern: Noun (or Pronoun)–Verb–Noun–Noun Determiner–Noun

$$(NVNN_DN)$$

Electricity	gives	condensers	a	charge
noun or pronoun	verb	noun or pronoun	noun determiner	noun

Indeed, to guide students to the stage of reading acquisition where they are automatic in their responses to printed words and can consequently devote their attention to thinking or reasoning about meaning (Laberge & Samuels, 1976), there is no substitute for an abundance of easy, interesting materials in which recently acquired skills appear frequently. (see Strang, McCullough, & Traxler, 1967, pp. 309–310)

WORD STRUCTURE AND MEANING

Also use content area words for teaching prefixes, suffixes, and roots. Scientific terms in particular draw heavily upon these word components. A list of affixes and roots that occur frequently in content area texts is in Table 18.1.

For this purpose, content acquisition instructors should stock their classroom libraries with content area texts at various levels of difficulty. (Use the school catalogs described in chapter 11, Box 11.3 (see reference to Fidel & Bogart [1970] and Fidel & Berger [1972] for selecting content area texts at various levels of difficulty.) Thus, the procedure for developing effective and efficient skills alternates between learning skills accurately and then learning to apply them rapidly until students can mobilize their skills and use them effortlessly or automatically (Singer, 1966).

MOTIVATING STUDENTS BY PUTTING
LEARNING UNDER THEIR CONTROL
The Cumulative Graph Method

In all aspects of content acquisition, and indeed in any instruction, knowledge of results motivates students to learn. A technique for motivating students and for putting achievement under a student's control (Singer, 1971; Singer & Beasley, 1970) is to graph results that are cumulative. Figure 18.1 shows a graph of the cumulative number of pages one student read during successive sessions. The graph contains a line which shows a student has read at least the same number of pages (horizontal step) or a greater number of pages (vertical step) with each successive session. The cumulative graph cannot go down; it can only remain at the same level or go up. Thus, the graph indicates that the student read four pages the first session and an additional four pages the next day for a cumulative total of eight pages. During the third session, the student did not read any pages; so

TABLE 18.1. List of Prefixes, Suffixes, and Roots in Content Area Words

Prefix	Meaning	Word	Meaning
a-	not, without	asexual reproduction	reproduction without eggs or sperm
ad-	to	adhesion	form of attraction between unlike molecules
ambi-	both	ambivalent	simultaneous attraction toward and repulsion from a person or object
ante-	before	antebellum	before the war
anti-	against	antibody	immune substance in the blood
apo-	away from	apogee	the highest point (as of a satellite) moves away from the earth
archae-	ancient, primitive	archaeology	study of early human life
auto-	self	autoregulation	self-regulation
bene-	well, good	benefactor	one who does good, makes a gift
bi-	two	binary fission	division of cells into two approximately equal parts
biblio-	book	bibliography	list of works referred to in a text
bio-	life	biology	study of life
capt-	take, seize	capture	seize
cent-	one hundred	century	one hundred years
circum-	around	circumference	perimeter of a circle; a line enclosing a circle
co-, com-	together	cohesion	stick together
con-, contra-	against	contradiction	say the opposite
de-	down	degenerative	tending to cause a lowering of vitality to a worsened state
deci-	one-tenth	decimeter	one-tenth of a meter
di-	two	diode	two-terminal radio tube
dia-	across, through	diameter	a measure across
endo-	within	endoskeleton	hard outer covering of certain animals
epi-	on, upon, over	epidermis	outer tissue

Prefix	Meaning	Word	Meaning
eu-	well, good	euthanasia	mercy killing
ex-	out	exothermic	give out heat
hemi-	half	hemianopsia	half vision
hetero-	other, different	heterodyne	mixing two frequencies to get a different frequency
hyper-	over	hypertonic solution	contains a higher concentration of solutes and lower concentration of water than another solution
hypo-	under	hypotonic solution	contains a lower concentration of solutes and higher concentration of water than another solution
il-	not	illegal	not legal
inter-	among	internode	the space between two nodes
intro-	inside	introvert	turned inward, one who is withdrawn
iso-	same	isomers	two substances having the same molecular but different structural formulas
mal-	bad	malodorous	having an offensive odor
mono-	one	monoplane	plane with one wing
multi-	much, many	multiphase	having many phases
non-	not	nonviable	not capable of living
ob-	in front of	obstetrician	literally, one who stands in front of, a physician who delivers babies
pan-	all, every	panacea	a remedy for all ills
para-	beside	parathyroid	glands adjacent to thyroid gland
poly-	many	polymer	a large molecule made up of a monomer repeated many times in a sequence
post-	after	postnatal	after birth
photo-	light	photon	a quantum of light energy
pre-	before	preamble	an introductory statement indicating what is to follow
pro-	for	pronoun	standing for a noun

Prefix	Meaning	Word	Meaning
pseudo-	false	pseudopodium	a "false foot" of the amoeba
retro-	backward	retrorocket	rocket producing thrust in opposite direction
semi-	half, partly	semiconductor	a solid whose electrical conductivity is nearly metallic at high temperatures and nearly absent at low temperatures
sub-	under, below	sublingual	salivary gland lying under the tongue
super-	over, beyond	supersaturation	beyond saturation
syn-	together	synergic	working together
tele-	far off, distant	telephone	instrument for producing sound at a distance
trans-	across	transgress	to go over a boundary or limit
ultra-	beyond	ultrasonic	vibrations in matter beyond 20,000 vibrations/second
uni-	one	univalent	capacity of an atom to form only one bond

Suffix	Meaning	Word	Meaning
-able	fit for	workable	practicable, feasible
-age	rate of	dosage	regulation of doses
-al	relating to	mental	relating to the mind
-an	characteristic of	median	in the middle
-ance	quality or state	hindrance	something that delays action
-ant	personal or impersonal agent	tenant	one who rents or leases land or a house
-ary	place of or for	library	a place in which literary or artistic materials are kept
-ate	action in a specified way	insulate	separate from conducting bodies
-ence	action or process	emergence	action of coming out into view
-ent	personal or impersonal agent	dependent	a person who relies on another for support

Suffix	Meaning	Word	Meaning
-er	one who performs a specified action	worker	a person who works
-ive	tending toward an indicated action	motive	something that causes a person to act
-less	not having	fearless	not having fear; brave
-ment	concrete result; object or agent of a specified action	entanglement	state of being entangled, confused, or in a complicated situation
-ness	state, quality, condition or degree	kindness	quality of wanting to help or be sympathetic
-or	one who does a specified thing	actor	one who acts a part
-ous	full	famous	widely known
-y	like that of	homey	homelike

Root	Meaning	Word	Meaning
anim	life, mind	animate	give life to
anthrop	man, human	anthropology	the science of humans
chrom	color	chromatophore	a pigment-bearing cell capable of changing skin color by expanding or contracting
chron	time	chronometer	instrument for measuring time
cycle	circle	cyclone	a storm that rotates about a center of low atmospheric pressure
dem	people	democracy	a government by the people
dic, dict	speak	dictate	to speak domineeringly
duc, duct	to lead	ductile	capable of being drawn out; easily led or influenced
fac	make	facsimile	an exact copy
fin	end	finite	having definite limits
flex	bend	reflect	bend back, as a mirror reflects light
flux	flow	fluctuate	to ebb and flow in waves

Root	Meaning	Word	Meaning
gamy	marriage	polygamous	having more than one mate at a time
gen	produce	androgen	producer
gnos	knowledge	agnostic	belief that existence of ultimate reality is unknown
loq, loqy	speech	loquacious	given to excessive talking
meter	measure	ohmmeter	instrument for measuring resistance
mov, mot	move	automotive	self-propelled
ped	foot	pedestrian	performed on foot
ped	boy	pediatrics	branch of medicine dealing with the child
phil	love	philanthropy	love of mankind; active effort to promote human welfare
phon	sound	telephone	transmit sound over a distance
rupt	break	rupture	tearing apart of tissue
scrib	write	inscription	wording on a coin, medal, or seal
spect	look	spectator	one who looks on or watches
stat	stable	static	at rest or in equilibrium
tang, tact	touch	tangent	straight meeting, a curve at one point only
vert, vers	to turn	reverse	to cause to go in opposite direction
voc	to call	vocation	a divine call to the religious life; work in which a person is regularly engaged

This table includes prefixes (Stauffer, 1942), suffixes (Thorndike, 1941), and roots (Durrell, 1940) that occur most frequently in basic reading materials. Some have more than one meaning, but we have only listed the most common.

FIGURE 18.1. Cumulative pages read over a number of sessions.

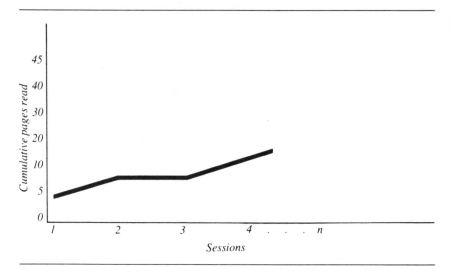

the line on the graph remained at 8 pages. At the fourth session, the student read 10 pages, which made the graph line go up to 18. The rate at which the line went up was under the student's control because the *student* decided how many pages to read each session. When we used this type of motivational procedure with a boy who was a severely disabled reader, he progressed from not reading at all to reading for a full 45-minute period in just 8 weeks (Singer & Beasley, 1970). We used similar charts for a cumulative number of words learned, for a cumulative number of grapheme-phoneme relationships acquired, and so forth, with similar results: the line went up dramatically in each graph. We call the type of instruction where the learner decides upon his or her rate of progress "learning under the student's control."

Student's Objectives

Not only knowledge of progress but also setting of goals helps to motivate students. A useful way to provide motivation is to construct a diagnostic and prescriptive index for each student. To construct this index, place survey and diagnostic test variables on the side of a chart using whatever variables are in the tests you administered to the student. Place next to each test variable the specific materials which are relevant for developing the variables that need improvement. The students' beginning level of achievement on each variable should be indicated along with student-set goals. Observe progress towards these goals via charts of achievement on the specific classroom materials; retest students on the standardized test variables after you have taught the students in enough areas of a particular domain for some generalized achievement to have occurred. Table 18.2 contains a chart of a student's objectives. The reading specialist and the

TABLE 18.2. Student Chart

				Dates as- signed and	
Student's name _____ Date tested _____ Retested _____					
	Pretest *scores*	*Objectives*	*Materials*	*completed*	*Posttest* *scores*
Gates-McGinitie Silent *Reading Tests*					
Comprehension					
Vocabulary					
Speed					
Gates-McKillop-Horowitz *Reading Diagnostic* *Tests*					
Words (timed)					
Words (untimed)					
Syllabication					
Blending					
Oral Vocabulary					
California Reading *Achievement Test*					
Vocabulary					
English					
Math					
Science					
Social Studies					
Comprehension					
Following directions					
Informal Reading *Inventory*					
Social Studies					
Literature					
Science					
Study Skills					
SQ3R					
Graphic Aids					

This form is a prototype. If you use other tests, insert them on the left. List pretest scores; inform students of test results; have students in conference with the teacher decide upon objectives and enter objectives on the chart. List materials for teaching students and dates when you assigned and students completed them. Posttest students upon completion of assignment(s) and enter scores on the chart. Use this chart for individual tests, objectives, and assignments throughout the course.

student in conference set up these objectives after they had reviewed the student's scores on the Gates Survey, Gates-McKillop-Horowitz California Reading Achievement Tests, and Informal Reading Inventory in Content Areas.

Also place on the chart the specific skills that the student can master and materials for developing each skill. Check off the skills as soon as the student masters them. Most of the skills that a student can master are in the word recognition area (consonants, blends, vowels, digraphs, syllabication), but you can also construct a mastery list for word meanings and morphemes by specifying particular words, affixes, and roots. Students can also master some study skill techniques, such as SQ3R and the reading of charts, tables, and graphs.[2] Check off these skills as the students master them. The chart will give students knowledge of their pretest results, set their objectives, and show progress towards their goals.

Teachers and students alike should know that significant gains can occur from specific instruction. Students can learn some specific skills or a specific list of vocabulary items in a short time. But to achieve significant gains on standardized tests, students require more instructional time because these tests assess general achievement or performance over an entire domain, even if the test variable seems to be specific. The timed word subtest of the Gates-McKillop-Horowitz Reading Diagnostic Tests, for example, assesses automaticity for sight words. But the words on the list are only a sample of words at successive frequency levels of the Thorndike word *frequency* list (see footnote 2; Thorndike, 1931). To improve by at least one frequency level on this subtest, a student would have to learn to recognize quickly not just words on the Gates-McKillop-Horowitz subtest, but most of the words on the next level of the word frequency list. Hence it is important to assess both whether students have learned what was taught (specific achievement) as assessed by teacher-made tests or on informal reading inventories and whether they improved in general achievement as measured by standardized tests. The chart in Table 18.2 is likely to show improvement on acquisition of *specific contents or processes* over a short term of instruction.

By using the charts, students and teachers will see that students have made specific gains. They should realize that specific gains become noticeable on standardized tests only when they have accumulated to become gains in general achievement. Thus, students can make specific gains, but they are not likely to make any gain in general achievement over a short period of instruction. If teachers administer standardized tests over this short period of instruction, they might rightfully protest that they know the students have learned but that the tests did not show it. The remedy is simple: assess students for both types of gains— specific gains over a short period of instruction (a day, week, or month) and general gains over a longer period of time (a semester or a year). Thus, the reading content acquisition class should develop, assess, and chart development for the competencies shown in Box 18.2.

---

[2]Teachers could, of course, construct a master reference list of variables, tests, and materials for developing these skills. See the appendix for a starter set of reference materials.

BOX 18.2. *Word Recognition Competencies for an Acquisition Class*

1. *Objective*
   Students should be able to respond accurately and quickly to graphemes in varying combinations (single consonants and vowels in beginning, middle, and final positions; digraphs, such as *ch, th* as functional units (Venezky, 1970); consonant clusters, such as *str;* syllables; roots and affixes.
   Test
   Given artificial words consisting of various combinations of graphemes and approximating English words, students should be able to identify 95% of them accurately in half a second per word. Repeat this process with content-area words.

2. *Objective*
   Students will be able to utilize contextual clues (syntactic and semantic) to identify missing words that have been taught in the acquisition class.
   Test
   Given sentences or passages at the student's level of general reading ability in which every 10th word is omitted, students will accurately supply 85% of the missing words.

3. *Objective*
   Student will attain automaticity for high-frequency words, such as the 220 Dolch words and 95 common nouns.
   Test
   Given relatively easy sentences in which the words are deleted, students will supply them within half a second each.

4. *Objective*
   Students will be able to use affixes and roots to identify and analyze the meaning of content area technical terms taught in the acquisition class.
   Test
   Given a representative sample of technical terms taught in the acquisition class, students will correctly identify and explain the meanings of 85% of them by defining their constituent affixes and roots.

5. *Objective*
   Students will develop fluency and automaticity in oral reading of passages that contain Dolch words, common nouns, and technical terms taught in the acquisition class.
   Test
   Given passages containing the above words, students will read 95% of them accurately at a speed of one quarter of a second per word.

6. *Objective*
   Students will be motivated to spend increasingly more time in reading.
   Test
   Cumulative charts kept of student's reading time during the acquisition class will indicate an upward slope for 85% of the students.

7. *Objective*
   Students will transfer what they learn in acquisition classes to their content area texts.

Test

Students will keep weekly logs of the number of words from their acquisition class that occur in their content area classes and/or texts. In addition, interviews of content area teachers will indicate that at least 90% of the teachers of students enrolled in acquisition classes will note that these students correctly identified and used content area terms more than previously.

8. *Objective*

Teachers in content area classes will teach their classes technical terms as they occur in assignments in the text.

Test

Observation of a random sample of content area classes will reveal that teachers teach the meanings of new technical terms, either through reading guides, glosses, oral instruction, or by writing terms on the board whenever new topics are introduced. If so, then students in acquisition classes will get additional instruction in content area classes that will supplement their instruction in reading acquisition classes.

9. *Objective*

Students will have knowledge of their goals in comprehension, vocabulary, word identification, and study skills, and will progress toward these goals.

Test

Each student will have an individual chart showing the pretest levels in general and specific content area comprehension, general and specific content area vocabulary levels, word identification skills, and specified study skills. Their objectives will be shown on these charts along with the materials specified for enabling the student to reach the objectives. Students will also have progress charts of specific achievement for each objective. At least weekly entries will have been made in the specific progress charts and at least two entries per semester will have been made in the student's general chart.

Thus, the acquisition classes will use content area words for teaching word recognition, employ these words in context, and transfer their use to actual reading situations. Since acquisition students will find these words in their content area texts, they will get not only additional reinforcement but also heightened motivation. Consequently, reading acquisition classes based upon content drawn from texts used in the content areas will probably accelerate students' development toward mastery of reading acquisition.

But acquisition of word identification skills is not enough. Students in acquisition classes also need instruction in how to comprehend and learn from texts.

EXPLANATION OF COMPREHENSION:
INTERACTION BETWEEN THE READER AND
TEXT
The Process of Comprehension

The systems involved in comprehension differ from acquisition only in a shift toward greater emphasis on the contents and processes of thinking. Russell

(1958) included in contents of thinking these components: *sensations, percepts, memories, images,* and *concepts* that an individual has acquired through direct or vicarious experience, including reading. Russell might also have listed *range of information* (Holmes, 1954) or *world knowledge* (Winograd, 1972). However, we think that *range of information* or *world knowledge* are included under *memories* in Russell's list. Russell's processes of thinking are listed in Box 18.3.

BOX 18.3. *Russell's Processes of Thinking*

1. *Concept formation* includes discrimination, abstraction, generalization, and organization of attributes and their values. *Example:* An apple has attributes of color, texture, size, taste. Each of these attributes varies in value; for example, the color of an apple varies from green to purple.
2. *Problem solving* is defined as thinking directed to a goal or a solution. *Example:* Mystery stories direct thinking to the goal of determining who committed the crime.
3. *Inference* is drawing conclusions from major and minor premises. *Example:* (Major Premise) The closing of a country's frontier necessitates conservation. (Minor Premise) The United States frontier closed in 1890. (Conclusion) Therefore, after 1890 the country became more conservative.
4. *Interpretation* involves construction of major premises and then use of a stated minor premise to infer a conclusion. *Example:* (Minor Premise Stated) Columbus left his son, Diego, behind when he set sail for the New World. (Major Premise constructed by reader) When a father goes off on an adventurous trip and leaves his son behind, his son is sad. (Conclusion) Diego was sad when Columbus set sail for the New World.
5. *Evaluative thinking* requires (a) use of standards or criteria for judging truth or falsity of propositions or (b) employment of values for making affective responses to situations. *Example:* (Statement) Creation of the Glen Powell Dam flooded a scenic area in order to provide power for electricity. (Evaluation) The dam was undesirable. (Value) Scenic areas should be protected and not sacrificed to economic motives.
6. *Creative thinking* stresses use of imagination or cognition, particularly suppositional thinking, to devise novel ideas. *Example:* (Statement) Some people do not appreciate basic elements of life: suppose the sun shone only one hour a year. Ray Bradbury wrote a short story based on this supposition.

This list of processes of thinking provides for a more comprehensive definition of reading than does Thorndike's (1917) definition that "reading is reasoning." Indeed Russell's contents and processes categories indicate the subsystems that readers mobilize at the cognitive level when they interact with text.

Box 18.4 shows seven systems that can be used for interacting with print. At any one moment during the process of reading an individual can mobilize each system by itself or in combination with other systems (Holmes, 1954, 1965; Singer 1976a). At one moment, a reader may mobilize systems for identifying a word, at the next moment retrieve a meaning, and at the next, infer, interpret, conceptualize, or solve a problem, and store or retrieve ideas from memory. (See chap. 4, substrate-factor theory, for further explanation for this dynamic process of systems and subsystems.)

BOX 18.4. *Systems Underlying Speed and Comprehension*

1. *Cognitive Systems*
    Reasoning Processes (abstraction and generalization, concept formation, inference, interpretation, evaluation, and problem-solving)
    Morphemics (minimal units of meaning, incuding inflections, affixes, and roots)
    Semantics (word meanings, concepts, denotative and connotative meanings)
    Syntactics (grammatical structures and relationships, including relationships in and among sentences, paragraphs, and larger units of discourse)
2. *General Information or World Knowledge* (fulfilling presuppositions of writers; generating major premises for interpretations, minor premises for inferences; explicating elliptical passages)
3. *Word Identification*
    Graphophonemics (symbol-sound correspondences)
    Graphomorphophonemics (division of words into morphemes, enabling graphophonemics to be used: *shep-herd, sheep · herd · er*
4. *Perceptual Processes* (processing and differentiation of print at the letter and higher units; sampling print to reduce uncertainty)
5. *Visual and Auditory Abilities* (development of functional oculomotor efficiency and speed of processing stimuli)
6. *Attention* (automaticity in processing print, which enables individual to maximize attention on comprehension)
7. *Affective and Conative Systems*
    Attitudes (criticalness)
    Values (desire to know, desire to read rapidly)
    Self-concept (confidence, independence)

See H. Singer and R. B. Ruddell, eds., *Theoretical Models and Processes of Reading,* Third Edition (Newark, DE: International Reading Association, 1985) for information on each of the systems listed in this box. See especially Irene Athey, "Reading Research in the Affective Domain," for information on affective and conative systems. David H. Russell, *Children's Thinking* (Boston: Ginn and Company, 1958), gives a definition and review of the various reasoning processes listed under cognitive systems.

Comprehension Systems

Reading and learning from text include more systems than those included among Russell's contents and processes of thinking. In Box 18.4 we have listed all the major systems with which a reader can interact with printed stimuli, such as content area texts, to produce comprehension.

Subsystems

A reader can shift not only from one system to another, but also from one level *within* a system to another. If a reader cannot identify a whole word, then he or she might mobilize subsystems for identifying each letter and blending the letters together under the influence of other systems, such as syntax and semantics. Then the reader can give a whole-word response to the printed symbol. We depict this process in Figure 18.2. Likewise, with the systems of semantics, syntactics, and perceptual oculomotor control, a reader can shift from one level to another level of response. The purpose of instruction in reading is to develop this hierarchical structure of systems and subsystems until they function automatically (LaBerge & Samuels, 1976; Singer, 1976a, 1976b).

Automaticity

Individuals first learn to be accurate in performing any skill; then, with more practice, they can perform the skill without thinking about it. At this point, they have gone beyond accuracy to *automaticity* in the skill (Samuels, 1977). In learning to identify a word, an individual might process a word letter-by-letter, then "chunk" the word, that is, respond to the printed word with a whole-word response without going through any intermediate processes. With continued practice, the response can become so automatic that the individual is almost

FIGURE 18.2. Shifting from a Holistic to an Analytic Level

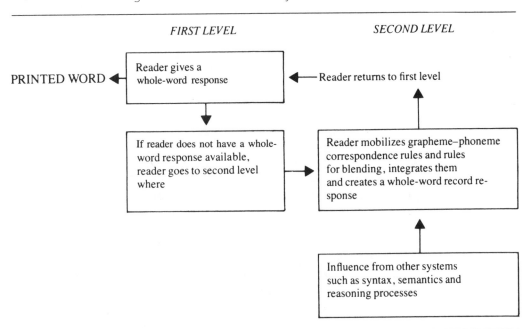

oblivious of the printed word, as such, and concentrates attention upon meaning or comprehension (LaBerge & Samuels, 1976, 1985). In short, the individual has become a lexical reader who does not have to sound out the words, but can go directly from print to meaning (Chomsky, 1970).

Students can use the method of repeated reading of a story to progress at each reading from (a) identifying printed words to (b) getting the meaning of the words to (c) comprehending the story. The method is simply to have poor readers do what some good readers did as children: read and reread the same story many times. The method of repeated reading assumes that the repetitions will result in automatic processing of words so that the reader can focus attention on comprehension (Chomsky, 1976; Samuels, 1979).

Students can develop automaticity in other ways. They can read materials that are interesting but repetitious, particularly in vocabulary. For example, series books (such as the ones about the Hardy Boys, Nancy Drew, Tom Swift, and so forth) that are prevalent in the "culture of children" (Stone & Church, 1973) help readers develop automaticity because only the plots vary slightly within each series. Automatic recognition of words, particularly functional words (conjunctions and prepositions that tie together the content words—nouns, adjectives, verbs, adverbs), is most likely to develop from repeated reading, from reading series books, or from a large amount of reading of relatively easy books.

Concepts, Morphemes, and Semantics

As individuals read and learn from text, they acquire meanings for words. When these meanings organize themselves about a word, the word becomes a label for a concept. Each concept has four general relationships of meaning associated with it: (a) class membership, that is, a concept can belong to a superordinate (a concept at a more abstract level); (b) properties or attributes, which describe what properties a concept has; (c) exemplification, lower order concepts that are examples of the concept; and (d) relationships with other concepts at the same level of abstraction. To develop a concept, explain or provide experiences that bring out its four types of relationships. Figure 18.3 depicts a concept with its four general relationships (Pearson & Johnson, 1978).

Concepts, morphemes, and semantics are generally grouped under vocabulary. Throughout Grades 1–12, vocabulary is the single most important predictor of comprehension (Homes & Singer, 1966; Singer, 1976a). Consequently, content area teachers should stress vocabulary, especially technical terms as they use them. They should teach students what the technical terms mean, how to use them in a sentence, how to pronounce them, and what morphemes they contain. For example, *motor, motion,* and *motile* contain the root *mot,* which means "to move." Teaching morphemes will reduce the complexity and magnitude of the vocabulary load in content areas. (See Table 18.1 for a list of some morphemes.)

Concepts are also organized into a semantic hierarchy. Figure 18.3 shows part of one semantic hierarchy for one state. But the hierarchy contains other states and can contain other nations. When readers interact with text, they mobilize

FIGURE 18.3. The Concept "City" Embedded in Four Types of Relationships

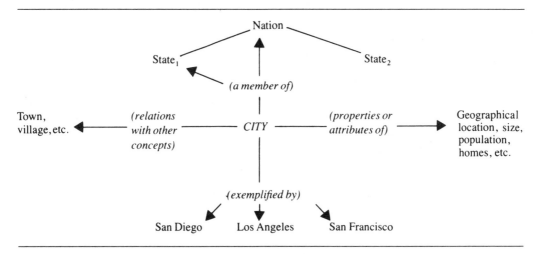

their semantic hierarchies and categorize information under the appropriate conceptual structures in their hierarchies (Anderson et al., 1977).

Sentence Relationships

Each sentence contains a verb and one or more noun phrases to depict an event. In the sentence "A steam turbine produces electrical power," we have two noun phrases, "A steam turbine" and "electrical power." The noun phrases have certain relationships to verbs within sentences (Fillmore, 1968; see chapter 4, Box 4.5a for examples of noun relationships). However, Chafe (1970) makes the opposite claim to Fillmore: he states that verbs are central and nouns peripheral to the structure of meaning. See Box 4.5b for his examples.

Knowledge of role relationships within sentences helps you comprehend simple sentences or events. For comprehension of complex sentences, you have to know *relationships between events*. Conjunctions express these relationships. A list of some conjunctions and the relationships between events that they express is in chapter 4, Box 4.6.

A larger organization exists in discourse or communication of thoughts in words. The organization consists of a structure or relationships among the parts of the passages.

Structure and Organization of Discourse

Knowledge of the structure of content areas facilitates comprehension because it provides readers with schemas, which are concepts or ideas for assimilating or categorizing information (Anderson, 1976b; Ausubel, 1964; Inhelder & Piaget, 1958). Thus, if readers know the structure of a story, they can more readily organize and store incoming information and ideas (Rumelhart, 1977). However, this knowledge structure, like all knowledge structures, has a developmental gradient. During preschool years, young children who listen to parents reading to them are likely to develop at least this simple conception of the structure of a story: a story has a beginning, middle, and end. This knowledge of structure enables these children when they enter school to read and categorize information under these three aspects of a story. Subsequently, they can use knowledge of these three parts of a story as self-directing cues in response to a request to retell the story; that is, they remind themselves to give the beginning, then the middle, and finally the end of the story. Later, children may encounter more differentiated story structure in a story that has these constituents: plot events, setting, characters, theme, conflict, and resolution (Thorndyke, 1975). Children can then use these constituents of a story for assimilating and regenerating a story in greater detail. Still later, through instruction in high school and college English courses, students get an even more differentiated structure of a story, including knowledge of genres (fables, fantasies, science fiction), symbols (purity represented by the Mississippi River in *Huckleberry Finn*), and literary devices (satire, irony, flashback). Students can then use these more abstract structures for interacting with texts and for assimilating, interpreting, constructing, storing, and retrieving the resulting knowledge.

Each content area develops it own structure and ways of thinking about its content. In chapters 13–16, we outlined the structure, modes of inquiry, and major concepts in four major content areas. These contents and processes of thinking, along with other systems of reading (such as syntactic and word perception systems), can operate simultaneously or in a processing sequence from bottom-up to top-down.

Bottom-Up Versus Top-Down Processing

In general, the systems for reading, comprehending, and learning from text are dynamic. Readers can mobilize these systems in varying combinations as they interact with the text according to their changing purposes and the changing demands of the text. They may mobilize systems simultaneously or in a "bottom-up" or "top-down" mode (Fredericksen, 1975; Rumelhart, 1976). In the bottom-up mode, the reader's systems operate in a sequence—from the level of sensations or print upon the retina of the eyes to detection and unitization of these sensations into words, syntactic organization of words into phrases and sentences, association of meaning to the sentences through use of concepts and abstract structures or schemata for assimilating the incoming information, and finally, reasoning in reading processes and storage of meaning.

In the top-down mode, a reader can use abstract knowledge structures to direct attention to printed stimuli in a selective manner, and these stimuli can then confirm or disconfirm the reader's expectations. For example, a reader may use the abstract structure "Vehicles locomote across space" which contains semantic slots and a syntactic structure for assimilating the words or ideas in such sentences as:

The cars   raced   down the hill.
(Vehicles)(locomote)(across space.)

Also, as individuals read, they may allocate attention back and forth between top-down and bottom-up modes, frequently even within the same sentence. In the incomplete sentence, "The car raced down the h_____," a shift from a bottom-up to a top-down mode may occur as the reader progresses across the sentence. At the beginning of the sentence, the reader takes in stimuli (words) and identifies them; as the reader takes in and processes more words, he or she inductively generates a semantic and syntactic expectancy and then may shift to a top-down process. In the top-down process, the reader uses abstract structures to predict or anticipate the final word (at least its meaning or idea) and confirms this prediction through perception of the initial consonant, or through perceptually sampling the letters of the last word. Or the reader may even skip the last word and get confirmation in subsequent sentences because the inserted word or meaning is consistent with meanings in the following sentences. (Also see chap. 4, schema interactive theory of reading)

TEACHING COMPREHENSION

In teaching comprehension, the teacher's task is to develop in readers all the systems that are necessary for interacting with text and to teach the readers to use them in varying combinations for different purposes and requirements in reading. Through the acquisition stage of reading, teachers stress the word identification systems of graphophonemics in conjunction with syntax and semantics. However, some development of systems for comprehension or learning from text also occurs from the beginning of reading instruction concomitantly with reading acquisition. Gradually, with progress through the grades, a shift-over takes place toward emphasis on comprehension and learning from text; but even after the shift, teachers must still give some attention to word recognition, particularly to identification of technical words, idioms, foreign words, and expressions that have only recently become part of the language. We have already presented ways of developing word identification skills in a Reading and Learning from Text Center. Now, how can we develop comprehension in this Center?

Comprehension Products, Processes, and Potentialities

A dictionary has three definitions of comprehension:

1. A product: "the knowledge gained by comprehending"
2. A process: "the act or action of grasping with the intellect"
3. A potential: "the capcity for understanding"[3]

---

[3]*Webster's Seventh New Collegiate Dictionary.* Springfield, MA: G and C. Merriam Company, 1963.

Spache and Spache, in teaching comprehension, asks questions that elicit products of thinking, such as:

1. "Who, What, Where, When, How."
2. "What conclusions can you draw?" or "Why did this happen?"
3. "Do you approve of this action?" (Spache & Spache, 1969, pp. 475–478)

However, Ruddell (1974), following Taba (1965), stresses instruction in *processes of* comprehension by using these types of questions:

1. *focusing,* which initiates or refocuses a discussion ("What did you like best about the story?")
2. *extending,* which obtains more information at a given level ("What other information do we need about the hero?")
3. *clarifying,* which obtains a more adequate explanation or draws out a student ("Would you explain what you mean?")
4. *raising,* which moves a discussion from a factual to an interpretive, inferential, abstraction or generalization level ("We now have enough examples. What do they have in common?") (Ruddell, 1974, pp. 400–402)

Thus, Ruddell uses discussion, as we do, to lead to various levels of thought. (See chapter 15 for further explanation of these discussion procedures.)

However, both Spache and Ruddell assume that the role of the teacher is to ask questions while the student's role is to answer them. This type of instructional relationship is not only recommended in textbooks on teaching reading, but is also prevalent in practice. It is directed comprehension (DC). From the viewpoint of learning, it assumes that the teacher is modeling behavior that students will imitate. Instead of hoping this kind of transfer of training will occur, we think teachers should *directly* develop this transfer by teaching a self-questioning process of attaining comprehension that we call "active comprehension." In this mode of reading, students search for answers to questions they themselves formulate as they read. (For more information, see explanation of Directed Comprehension and Active Comprehension in chapter 4).

Develop Active Learners

In teaching active comprehension, teachers first model a process of comprehension by taking a class of students through a discussion strategy to arrive at products of comprehension. (See strategies for teaching reading and learning from text, single- and multiple-text strategies, chapters 6 and 11.) Next, teachers go on from this modeling of behavior to form students into groups, then into pairs, and finally they can give individual students the assignment to formulate questions, use these questions to guide their own thinking, learn through these self-directing questions to transfer relevant information to long-term memory, and arrive at their own comprehension products which will then increase their potential for comprehending subsequent materials. In one technique to attain this transfer, a teacher divided a class into groups and had individuals take turns serving as the teacher or discussion leader for the groups as they processed a passage or a chapter in a text. Eventually, each student had an opportunity to use the questioning strategies modeled by the teacher and consequently learn to formulate questions. Then students were advised to use the questioning process on their own while reading. Thus, through phase out of the teacher and a phase in of the student, teachers can help students develop a *process of reading* which we call "active comprehension" (Singer, 1978a; R. Yopp, 1987).

Purpose in Reading. Students do have varying purposes in reading a text, and their purposes will lead them to selectively attend to and store in memory certain parts of the story. When asked to recall the story, they can only retrieve the information they stored. When asked to read a story about two boys going through a house, those readers who had the perspective of a house buyer recalled information that differed from those readers who had the perspective of a burglar (Pichert & Anderson, 1977). Hence, it is important for teachers to establish purposes in reading any assignment.

Intent to understand and remember enhances comprehension, perhaps because it leads the reader to generate responses (Marks, Doctorow, & Wittrock, 1974), or to answer independently formulated questions (Singer, 1976b). These active comprehension procedures, which put the motive for learning within the learner's control, have been described in more detail in chapter 6. However, students need instruction in content and processes of inquiry in content areas to help them form relevant questions (Herber & Nelson, 1976). Therefore, have individuals determine why they are reading a passage, formulate questions to answer as they read, and state their answers and reactions to the passage while they are reading. Then, they are more likely to store relevant information in their long-term memories, and consequently to be able to retrieve it when needed.

Textbooks have not been teaching students to be purposeful in reading. They have been emphasizing teacher control and direction over student thinking by having teachers ask students to answer teacher-posed questions. Both textbooks and teachers tend to emphasize development of comprehension products, not comprehension processes or potentials.

Processes of Inquiry. Processes of inquiry in content areas are more likely to facilitate comprehension if teachers explicitly teach them. Literature teachers, for example, may teach students to formulate hypotheses for explaining a character in a novel by noting consistencies in the character's actions, statements, inward reflections, and the reactions of other characters in the story to the character under examination. Then the teacher can have students test their hypotheses by making predictions about what the character will subsequently do. Finally, the students can gain more information (read further) to test the validity of their predictions. Of course, the predictions will have to state how the character will or will not react in contrasting situations in order to have a controlled condition. This process of inquiry in literature is analogous to use of the scientific method in science. (See chapter 15 for steps in the scientific method.)

Development of cognitive abilities and processes, purposeful reading, and curiosity are not enough in teaching students to read and learn from text. Teachers also have to develop favorable attitudes, appropriate values and self-confidence in students for them to be effective in reading and learning from text.

Attitudes, Values, and Self-Concept in Reading. Students need confidence that they can learn and understand texts (Athey, 1976). When only counseled that they could achieve, some students who had believed otherwise improved significantly in comprehension (deCharms, 1972). This counseling strategy when used with low-achieving students, especially low-achieving minority students, may have worked because it led them to mobilize the necessary abilities and stay with difficult tasks until they comprehended them. Thus, not only instruction but also the teacher's attitude can induce students to work up to the best of their capabilities and help them to develop confidence in their reading ability.

Development of Confident Learners. Teachers must first adapt materials to students so they can be successful in the attainment of comprehension and thus get the positive feedback necessary for reinforcing learning. But, as students learn, teachers should also gradually increase the difficulty level of the materials and teach the students how to comprehend these more difficult materials.

If you make materials in any content area easy enough, most students in a class can comprehend them. Indeed, Bruner (1963) stated that any idea can be taught to anyone at any age provided it is put into a thought form appropriate to the learner. How can you make materials easier? Here are some ways:

Teacher-Text Modification

Teachers can enable students to comprehend by modifying their texts. See chap. 5 for a detailed explanation of text features. Below is additional text modification strategies.

Vocabulary. Substitute common synonyms for rare words. When Marks et al. (1974) substituted such words as *boy* for *lad,* fourth-grade students were better able to comprehend a passage. Why? Samuels (1968) explained that high-frequency words have more associations to them than do low-frequency words. Consequently, when high-frequency words appear in sentences, they are more likely to elicit associations of relevant experience. This associational process, in part, explains how students "put meaning into words."

Two books are useful for constructing easier materials: *Roget's International Thesaury*[4] lists synonyms, and the *American Heritage Word Frequency Book*[5] contains frequencies and association values for 80,000 words. Teachers who

---

[4]Third edition. New York: Thomas Y. Crowell, 1962.
[5]By John B. Carroll, Peter Davies, and Barry Richman. Boston: Houghton Mifflin, 1971.

want to prepare graded materials could use these books to substitute words that will make texts more comprehensible.

Syntax. Comprehension of complex sentences is more difficult than simple sentences, not only because they have more ideas in them but also because they are longer and put a greater strain upon memory, particularly sentences that have left-embedded clauses in them. A left-embedded, or left-branching, sentence is one in which a clause comes before the main verb. Here is an example: "The man *who came to dinner* had a mustache and beard." A right-embedded, or right-branching, sentence is: "The man had a mustache and beard *which was white and long.*" Left-branching sentences put a greater strain on memory because readers or listeners have to keep all the information in short-term memory until they reach the main clause. In right-branching sentences, the main clause comes first. Readers or listeners can treat right-embedded clauses as separate sentences when they come to them and store each sentence in long-term memory (Gough, 1976). In general, to give students sentences that are easier to comprehend, (a) select texts that have simple syntax, (b) rewrite with right-embedded sentences, or (c) reduce complex sentences to simple sentences. Here is a long sentence with two embedded clauses: "A hydrogen atom has one electron, which has a negative charge, and one proton, which has a positive charge." You can turn this complex sentence into these three simple sentences: "A hydrogen atom has one electron and one proton"; "The electron has a negative charge,"; The proton has a positive charge."

Some sentences, however, are not easier to comprehend when split into two sentences (Pearson, 1974–1975). For example, divide this sentence into two sentences: "John used a lever to move the heavy rock." You get these two sentences: "John used a lever"; "He moved the heavy rock." It now requires more mental ability to comprehend the two sentences because the causal relationship between "using the lever" and "moving the rock" is no longer explicit; the reader has to infer the causal connection between the two.

Explication. *Elliptical* sentences that omit significant information usually because it is redundant or very familiar. If it is familiar, readers must draw upon their own experience and imagination in order to comprehend them. Consider this sentence: "The cigarette caused the forest fire." It does not fully explain how the cigarette caused the fire (Kintsch, 1974). The reader must fill in from experience and imagination events like the following: "The cigarette was lit. It was dropped on dry tinder which smouldered and finally caught fire. Then the fire grew larger and spread to the trees, perhaps with the wind fanning the flames." Most readers could supply the necessary information and relationships from their experience and imagination to make the sentence comprehensible. When readers cannot do so, supplying it for them will enhance their comprehension for a particular passage (Marshall, 1976). This procedure will not, of course, make them generally better readers. Neither will more illustrations or diagrams that explicate what the text only implies succeed in making students generally better readers. To become generally better readers, they will have to increase their own knowledge reservoir so that they can explicate texts on their own.

The implications for content area teachers are (a) inspect texts to determine what will have to be made more explicit, either through explanation, through addition of illustrations, diagrams, and examples, or through rewriting of material; and (b) evaluate students to determine whether they have the background information, knowledge structures, and conceptual abilities for effective interaction with the text as written, and (c) provide for broad and varied reading that will enable students to develop their knowledge reservoirs.

Instructional Devices.   Teachers can facilitate comprehension through use of such instructional devices as overview and reading guides (Herber, 1970a), preposed and postposed questions (Rothkopf, 1976), inserted questions (Shavelson, Berliner, Ravitch, & Loeding, 1974; Spring, et al., 1982; Watts & Anderson, 1971), use of chapter and subheadings (Smith, 1973), or acronymic formulas such as SQ3R—Survey, Question, Read, Recite, and Review (Robinson, 1961). See chapter 6 and 13–16 for explanations of these devices.

Organization.   The way in which the writer of a text organizes ideas may make the ideas more or less comprehensible. If the text states all the attributes of one car together (color, style, accessories), then the attributes of another car, and so forth, this organization is easier to comprehend than if the text first stated one attribute of each car, then another attribute, and so forth (Frase, 1969a).

Develop Reader Resources

Imagery.   Imagery facilitates comprehension (Bransford & Franks, 1974; Levin, 1976) because recall of images is superior to recall of words. The reason students may remember pictures better than words is because pictures tend to be unique, whereas words are quite similar. Therefore, having students transform words into images as they read. As a way of teaching the use of imagery, give them exercises to transform text into pictures and into pictorial sequences of events. In one such exercise, readers could construct a diagram of the relationships among the characters in Charles Dickens's *Tale of Two Cities*. This diagram would help readers comprehend the story better, just as Mendeleev's Periodic Table helps chemistry students better perceive relationships among chemical elements. Finally, advise students to draw their own visual aids when the text omits them. Use of visual aids is one way to make thought concrete. You can make thought more concrete in other ways, too.

Concrete Levels of Thought.   Concretizing abstract ideas enables individuals to image ideas. It also lessens the level of abstraction of the ideas and hence the difficulty of comprehending them. Anderson (1976a) found that when he added adjectives to sentences he made the sentences more memorable, observing that students recalled the second of these two sentences significantly better than the first:

1. The regulations annoyed the salesman.
2. The strict parking regulations annoyed the salesman. (Anderson, 1976a, p. 588)

The addition of the adjective *parking* makes the statement more particular and more imageable. R. Anderson et al. (1977) believe that individuals comprehend not just by imaging but by thinking of exemplars or instances for ideas and that these exemplars or instances are stored and help recall the ideas. The sentence "The woman was outstanding in the theater" elicits in readers' minds the instance of *actress* for *woman*. When the same individuals subsequently see *actress*, the word helps them recall the sentence. The implication is to teach comprehension by having students "instantiate," or think of concrete examples, as they read; that is, simply instruct students to think of examples or generate instances whenever text writers omit them.

Word Identification. Teachers want to leave technical terms in texts they modify because students have to learn to communicate in technical language. However, even students who have mastered general word identification skills still need help in pronunciation of technical terms (for example: *genre, isosceles, caveat emptor, pterodactyl, deuterium*). In General, content area teachers should not assume that students, even high-achieving readers, know how to pronounce content area terms. As a rule of thumb, teachers should model pronunciation of any terms that appear in the index to a text as they introduce these terms in class (especially terms with irregular spellings and foreign terms and phrases). Then they should use the terms in sentences, break them down into their constituent parts (prefix, affixes, roots), and explain their meanings.

Wide Reading. Teachers should stimulate students to learn from texts in classroom situations and to engage in wide reading because individuals learn through reading, and, as they read, they acquire contents of thinking. Indeed, the broader the range and depth of their reading materials, the more individuals can acquire, store, and subsequently retrieve contents of thinking for top-down processing. Moreover, as individuals acquire more information, the less they have to acquire from any new reading task. Consequently, a wide scope to the curriculum, even though not necessarily focusing on reading comprehension per se, will develop systems employed in comprehension, and consequently, will improve comprehension. Hence, the strategies we have described throughout this text for teaching students to read and learn from texts in the content areas, such as inquiry, are also ways of improving comprehension for the entire range of students.

All these strategies are ways for *teachers* to make texts more comprehensible and facilitate students' learning from them. However, these comprehension-improvement procedures involve downard adaptation of materials. Teachers should phase out such materials as students improve and can comprehend more difficult materials. Thus, procedures for making texts more comprehensible are only a means of enabling students to comprehend and learn from texts until they can develop their abilities to learn from texts that have more abstract vocabulary, complex syntax, elliptical statements, and complicated sentence structures.

The reading and learning-from-text specialist can use all these procedures for improving comprehension and for making texts more comprehensible in a Reading and Learning from Text Center. In this Center, students have to learn not only to identify words but how to use their language background to comprehend text. In Box 18.5 are the competency criteria and assessment procedures for teaching comprehension in content area acquisition classes.

BOX 18.5. *Comprehension Competencies and Assessment Criteria*

Objectives

1. Students in the Reading and Learning from Text Center who are in the reading acquisition phase of reading development will attain at least 50% comprehension on reading tasks with materials that have been adapted to their levels of ability.

   Using the informal inventory of the cloze technique, teachers in acquisition classes will have selected content materials, perhaps through use of the *school catalogs,* that meet the 50% criterion for comprehension. Questioning of students in the classes will reveal that 85% of them state they can comprehend the materials they are reading.

2. Teachers will systematically develop each of the students' systems for comprehending and learning from texts.

   Test

   Analysis of lesson plans will indicate that students have had input instruction at least once a week in one or more of the systems related to comprehension: vocabulary; sentence, paragraph, or larger units of prose structure (macrostructures); morphemic analysis; interpretation, inference, concept formation, problem solving, critical and creative reasoning; a study skill, such as SQ3R and interpretation of graphs, charts, and maps; or a comprehension technique, such as use of imagery, concretizing abstractions, knowledge of content structure, and modes of inquiry.

3. Students will be motivated to read.

   Test

   Analysis of teachers' lessons will indicate that teachers have had students establish purposes for reading connected discourse at least once a week.

4. Students will have control over their progress in reading.

   Test

   Students will have kept cumulative charts of pages read and words learned.

5. Students will be using content area words in their acquisition instruction.

   Test

   Analysis of contentives (nouns, adjectives, adverbs, verbs) used in word identification lessons will reveal that 85% of them are words that are in the students' content area texts.

6. Teachers in acquisition classes will teach for psychosynchromeshing facility.
   Test
   Analysis of lessons in word identification, word meaning, concept formation, and morphemic analysis will indicate that 85% or more of them terminate with instructions to apply the skills taught to connected discourse or to content area texts. Provision will have been made for students to do so in class, either through specially prepared sentences, paragraphs, passages longer than a paragraph, or reading assignments in students' texts.

7. As students become able to comprehend and learn from more difficult materials, they will be assigned to these materials.
   Test
   Inspection of charts or graphs of individual students will reveal that when students approached 85% comprehension on a particular level of difficulty, they were given more difficult reading tasks.

Thus, teachers in the Reading and Learning from Text Center who are teaching students in the reading-acquisition phase of development, will teach word identification, improvement in comprehension, and learning how to learn from texts. The classes will emphasize content drawn from subject matter areas and stress transfer applications in students' content area texts.

Upward Adaptation: Improvement in General Comprehension

Upward adaptation of learners to attain comprehension of more difficult material is the longer range objective. This longer range objective requires general improvement in each system necessary for reading and learning from texts, such as contents and processes of thinking plus self-confidence and deisre to know and understand. Consequently, improvement in general comprehension is not rapidly attainable, unless the student already has the necessary contents and processes of thinking in his or her repertoire of cognitive capabilities and desires to know and understand, but only needs to learn the acquisition aspects of reading. Some people—such as immigrants who can speak the language of their new country but need to learn to read it or who need to learn to both speak and write it and who read and comprehend well in their native language—can make dramatic improvements in comprehension after they learn the new language and the acquisition aspects of reading.

What is needed for improvement in general comprehension of students in addition to time to learn? Instruction in vocabulary, information, and reasoning in each content area. In short, a broad, liberal arts curriculum contributes to the development of systems necessary for improvement in general comprehension, particularly the knowledge structures, semantic hierarchies, and modes of inquiry in the various content areas. (See chapters 13–16.) Therefore, what counselors can do for students who want to improve in comprehension is to guide them into those courses where they can read and learn from texts in the content areas.

A reading and learning-from-text specialist can also guide acquisition level students toward improvement in comprehension by gradually phasing out materials that have been adapted downward and phasing in more difficult materials, including the students' own content area texts. Students in acquisition classes could then more easily make the transition back to regular course instruction in learning from texts in content areas. After students have returned to regular classes, the role of the reading and learning specialist would be to advise or instruct content areas teachers on strategies for teaching students to read and learn from texts.

USING AN INSTRUCTIONAL MODEL FOR TEACHING COMPREHENSION OR READING AND LEARNING FROM TEXT

In teaching comprehension in this chapter, we have primarily emphasized the teacher's role. Other components also have to be considered. We can best explain how to teach comprehension in all classes from the elementary through the high school level by employing our instructional model for reading and learning from text that we first presented in chap. 1, again at the end of chap. 4, and in chap. 5 where we pointed out the various components in the model and in the reader that were developed by strategies explained in the chapter. Now, we shall use the model, shown again in Figure 18.4, to explain comprehension instruction. In doing so, we shall summarize information presented in this chapter and throughout the text.

The three types of comprehension are implicit in the model. Comprehension as a *potential* is represented by the reader's resources. As a *product*, it is depicted as the goal of instruction, the construction of meaning. And as a *process*, it is shown by the arrows between the text features and the reader's resources and between the reader's resources and the goal. The feedback loop from the goal to the reader's resources is a process that enhances the reader's potential as he reads; consequently, the reader is better able to read subsequent material in the particular text and is accumulating knowledge that facilitates reading and learning from other texts. That is why wide and frequent reading is an important way

FIGURE 18.4. Instructional Model for Teaching Students to Read and Learn from Text

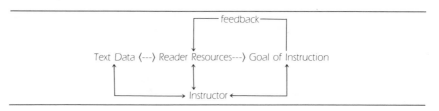

of improving comprehension: it enhances a reader's potential by increasing his or her knowledge resources.

Previous chapters provide information for improving comprehension. Chapter 4 contains explanations and instructions for teaching word recognition, oral and silent reading, and interactive processes of reading. Chapter 5 explains text features and inventories on selection of friendly texts that will facilitate comprehension and another inventory on what the instructor can do to enhance a text (Teacher-text enhancement inventory). Chapters 6 and 11 contain single and multiple text strategies for developing various components in the instructional model, including text enhancement strategies, such as marginal glosses; reader resource strategies, such as development of vocabulary; goals of reading, such as use of a reading and learning from text guide to develop a goal of remembering the literal, interpretive, inferential, and generalizeable aspects of a text. Chapter 7 demonstrates how to apply these strategies to learning chapter in different texts and the specific characteristics of texts that students have to take into account in learning from them. Chapters 8–10 have instructional procedures for developing student resources in discussion, listening, and writing. Chapters 13–16 explains how instructional that become reader-resource strategies can be used and adapted to each content area Chapter 15 contains a table of specifications that enables teachers to construct tests for instructional goals that enable teachers to construct tests that reflect the text's emphasis on contents and processes of thinking. Chapter 18 has a progress chart in Fig. 18.1 that feeds information back to students on their own cumulative learning, instead of comparing one student with another, and puts learning under a student's control, that is the student can make the cumulative learning curve progress upward as a result of effort and persistence. Instructional procedures for taking a student from dependence to independence in use of a strategy for communicated in chap. 10, a "Blueprint for instruction." We anticipate that use of these strategies will have a salutary effect upon attitudes of teachers towards teaching students to read and learn from text (chap. 2) because they enable teachers to teach all the students in a class even though students differ widely in their abilities to read and learn from text (chap. 3). Thus, the various chapters of the text can be categorized according to the components and interactional processes in the instructional model.

This model is useful for classifying instructional procedures and research, as well as planning instruction not only for students but also for in-service education of faculty. Through appropriate and effective use of the model, the instructor can make it possible for all students to make successful progress in reading and learning from text (Singer, 1987).

IN-SERVICE EDUCATION

Specialists alone cannot solve the problem of teaching strategies for reading and learning from text in all content areas. The entire faculty has to acquire and use these strategies in all their courses. They can learn to do so through an in-service education program. Some schools have conducted in-service programs in an ongoing school situation to teach teachers how to use reading-from-text strategies. The way for a reading and learning specialist to bring this in-service training about is through the support of a schoolwide committee. Scene 2 of Monroe High's schoolwide committee meeting is an ideal scenario for this step.

One week after the last meeting, just after lunch, Monroe High is on minimum day. The schoolwide committee has decided to meet again with Ms. Valdes to review what they had discussed the previous week.

Ms. Jones: Ms Valdes, I've been talking with the members of this committee and with other faculty members. The types of strategies you described last week would work well for below-grade-level students and nonreaders. But most of us are more concerned with the rest of the students, the ones that fill most of the seats in the classroom.

Mr. Umeki: It's like counseling. I tend to see the kids with problems quite frequently. But I always wonder about the majority of students that I never see.

Mr. Phelps: Ms Valdes, as you've pointed out, the school's so large that we can't expect you to work directly with all these students.

Mr. Wallace: Maybe you should be teaching us—the teachers.

Ms. Stewart: You mean, kind of like in-service education.

Ms. Valdes: That's an excellent suggestion.

Ms. Jones: What are some of the ways teachers could be trained to do some of this work?

Ms. Valdes: There are a number of ways we could proceed. One way is to include the whole faculty in a large in-service project. This would, of course, mean bringing a number of consultants to the school to focus on areas of specialization I couldn't handle. Another way is what I call the one-to-one method, that is, my working intensively with one faculty member. Why don't we take time now, and I'll explain some alternative models of in-service education.

Models

AN "OPEN-ENDED" MODEL

This model, which Herber (1970b) devised, provides knowledge and skills for teaching reading in content areas that teachers can try out and evaluate immediately. A total of 35 teachers, 5 teachers from each of seven schools, representing four different content areas received released time for an in-service training course. The course emphasized instruction in vocabulary and preparation of reading and reasoning guides for students reading content materials. Also, the teachers prepared materials in a summer session practicum on how to integrate content with reading instruction, tested the materials with summer session students in the morning, and consulted with their summer session teachers in the afternoon. In the fall, they adopted the role of content reading specialists for their departmental colleagues and continued with their in-service seminars.

COURSE MODELS

Schleich's (1971) 10-lesson course model begins with a diagnostic reading test administered to all the students in the school. Students scoring in the lowest decile take the Wide Range Achievement Test (Reading; Jastak & Jastak, 1965) to determine their basic word-recognition ability. The teacher interprets the test results for other teachers and department heads who enroll in the course. The topics in the course are general reading development, readability, informal reading inventories, directed reading activities, SQ3R, interpretation of test results, and reading skills in content areas. Then the department heads and teachers instruct students in their content areas, even students in remedial reading classes. Individual department heads and teachers receive follow-up lessons during their free periods.

Askov, Dupuis, and Lee (1978) constructed another course model, a competency-based course, that used a diagnostic-prescriptive approach, with computer printouts showing objectives that teachers in the course had mastered at three levels (cognitive, simulation, application). They taught this course over a year-long period of 15 monthly sessions, each lasting 3 hours, for volunteer teachers who received 3 to 6 hours of university credit. They used videotapes of lessons in actual courses, such as the teaching of vocabulary in social studies, to illustrate how to teach reading in content areas. Askov, Dupuis, and Lee found improvements for teachers on their attitude scale, knowledge of reading, and ratings on the use of reading skills in the classroom, but they did not assess whether the teachers' students had improved in achievement.

COMBINATION MODEL

An in-service training and consultation program (Singer, 1973b) emphasized (a) strategies for teaching for a wide range of individual differences in reading achievement; (b) patterns of writing and processes of inquiry in content areas; (c) models of reading and learning from text (chapters 13–16); (d) an instructional framework for learning from text; and (e) procedures for teaching expression (writing and discussion), and ways of assessing reading, reading difficulties, and readability of materials (all of the components of this combined program are contained in this text). The in-service training program featured at each session a workshop in applying a strategy or process to a content area; and individual consultations helped classroom teachers on specific content area problems and on adaptation of the strategies and instructional frameworks to their own classes.

ONE-TO-ONE MODEL

All of the models that we have reviewed so far try to reach the entire faculty at the same time. But we know that teachers on a faculty vary in their attitudes toward reading and learning from text and in the time they have for acquiring new teaching skills (Ruddell & Williams, 1972). What we propose is to start working with teachers who want to acquire these strategies, and then gradually spread their effects to the rest of the teachers in a school. If the initial contingent of teachers then teach incoming freshmen over a 4-year period, all students in the school will at least have had an introductory class in reading and learning from text. For this in-service education, the reading specialist can use one of the in-service models we have just reviewed, if the school can provide released time or summer-session support for teachers to participate in in-service education. If not, the reading specialist has to opt for a much slower form of in-service education: working with one content area teacher at a time during the regular school day.

The reading specialist works in a one-to-one relationship with a content area teacher in the following way. First, the reading specialist constructs a lesson plan using one of the reading and learning-from-text strategies that fits the class textbook. The content area teacher explains what content and objectives should go into the lesson plan. Then the reading specialist demonstrates by teaching from the lesson plan. Next, the reading specialist and content area teacher plan another lesson with the same teaching strategy, only this time the content area teacher uses it to instruct the class. Next, the content area teacher, using the same teaching strategy, prepares a plan alone. In this way, the reading specialist phases out while the content area teacher phases in for using the particular strategy. The process repeats until the content area teacher has acquired all the strategies for teaching students to read and learn from text.

Thus, in a one-to-one in-service education plan, a reading specialist can teach a content area teacher how to teach at least one introductory course in reading and learning from text in a particular content area. Then, the reading specialist can repeat the process with another content area teacher. This is a slow process for training an entire faculty and it is more expensive than the other models, but it is likely to end up with a content area teacher who knows *how* to teach and *is* teaching students how to read and learn from text. This teacher can then offer an introductory course for students and faculty.

The introductory course in reading and learning from text has two purposes: (a) to teach incoming freshmen how to read and learn from texts in their content area and (b) to serve as a demonstration course for other content area teachers who want to acquire strategies for teaching their own students. To find out how the schoolwide committee at Monroe High felt about this introductory course, read Scene 3, below.

Same setting as the previous scene. The schoolwide committee is reviewing what Ms. Valdes has just said about models of inservice education.

Mr. Umeki: I really like what you said about the one-to-one approach.

Ms. Williams: Yes, I like that too, but we might also want to look at something a little more far-reaching.

Ms. Jones: Do you think that we could take on the reeducation of our entire faculty?

Ms. Phelps: I wouldn't even want to take on the reeducation of my own department.

Ms. Valdes: Let me speak briefly about a couple of possibilities. If we instituted an introductory course in reading and learning from text for incoming freshmen, within 4 years, most of our students could be reached. Monroe faculty could participate in the teaching of these introductory courses. Also, we might want to have Monroe High teachers focus on one learning-from-text strategy at a time. Too much too soon can be devastating.

Ms. Jorgensen: I'd like to hear more about both of these options.

Ms. Valdes: When I'm through speaking, if there are no pressing questions, why don't we go home and think about how we want to proceed with in-service education of the faculty. But for now, let me outline an introductory course in reading and learning from text and the sequence by which students might learn single- and multiple-text strategies—as well as a step-by-step process by which the faculty could learn to use the strategies in the classroom.

In Box 18.6 Ms. Valdes's brief outline for a course in reading and learning from text. Although this course was designed for junior and senior high school, it can also be used for elementary school students and faculties.

BOX 18.6. Introductory Course in Reading and Learning from Text

Objectives of Introductory Classes

Content area reading specialists will teach regular content area classes how to comprehend and learn from text, demonstrate to teachers of these classes strategies for handling individual differences in reading and learning from text, and use a phase-out/phase-in procedure so that content area teachers can learn to incorporate strategies and techniques for teaching their own students to comprehend and learn from texts in the content areas.

Tests

1. Observe classes utilizing strategies in reading and learning from texts in a content area.
2. Observe that faculty members in the content areas plan a lesson after observing an introductory course in reading and learning from text.
3. Time sampling of the introductory classes will indicate that the content area teachers will change from observing to taking charge of the introductory courses.

Sequence for Acquiring and Learning to Use Strategies

For initiating reading and learning-from-text strategies in a content area class or for in-service education, a school can follow a sequence that progresses from easy to difficult. We can view the understanding and adoption of the strategies described in this text within a Piaget-like framework. Assimilation and *accommodation* are the two concepts Piaget has formulated for explaining how an individual takes in and organizes information. Assimilation involves information that an individual can subsume under a schema or concept already within her or his conceptual system. Accommodation occurs when an individual has to form a new schema or concept for subsuming information that concepts within his or her conceptual hierarchy cannot assimilate. For example, teachers know how to use a single textbook with a class. Consequently, a change from using one textbook to aother requires only a process of assimilation. Teachers simply use the same instructional strategy with the new text, making minor modifications to adapt the text to their usual teaching procedures. But when teachers have to modify their teaching practices, as they do when they switch from single to multiple texts, they go through a cognitive process of accommodation; that is, they must acquire concepts or schemata that will enable them to organize and subsume information that is new to them. The concepts or schemata in turn help teachers generate the necessary instructions for directing the activities of the class.

Since teachers already have a procedure for teaching with a single text, they can more readily learn alternate strategies that also employ a single text than they can acquire strategies that require use of multiple texts. Consequently, teachers (who want to expand their repertoire of teaching strategies) and reading specialists, consultants, or college instructors (who give in-service training) can ease the process of learning and facilitate transfer of what has been learned to classroom practice by starting with strategies that can be readily assimilated. Then they can progress toward strategies that require teachers to go through an accommodation process in order to acquire the new strategies.

We also recognize that knowledge alone is not enough to get teachers to try new strategies. Although teachers are willing to take risks in teaching, they would like to reduce the risks and increase their confidence that a new strategy will work for them when they try it. To increase teacher confidence, we suggest that as a teacher learns a strategy he or she should apply or test out the strategy under the in-service instructor's supervision. Starting with single-text and going on to multiple-text strategies, the instructor can increase teachers' knowledge and confidence by progressing through the strategies a step at a time. The reading specialist should spread out this process (which includes teaching not only the teacher but also the teacher's class to use the strategies) in a phase-out/phase-in procedure over an academic year. Or, if there is a college course in these strategies combined with a lab consisting of classroom experience, the instructor should spread out the strategies over the entire course. To explain how this training process can occur in a step-by-step procedure, we shall start with single-text strategies and then proceed to multiple-text strategies.

SINGLE-TEXT STRATEGIES

Teachers frequently use only a single text, and their procedure often consists of merely assigning chapters for homework. Rarely do they teach students how to read and learn from the assigned chapters. Teachers assume that instructions, discussions, and demonstrations during class will automatically transfer to students' thinking and learning processes as they read the assignment. But the evidence from experiments on the psychology of transfer is that transfer is more likely to occur if teachers teach for it by having students make the necessary applications while they are still in the classroom.

The directed reading activity (DRA) is a step toward teaching students how to read and learn from texts and consequently increases the number of students who are likely to comprehend the contents of an assigned chapter. Essentially, this strategy has the teacher explain to the class how the teacher reads and learns from the assigned chapter.[6] This process takes place as the teacher explains technical vocabulary before, or while, students take turns reading the chapter. The teacher may emphasize or clarify a process that is characteristic of the content, such as the role of allusions in literature, or the close and explicit relations between generalizations and supporting evidence in science. At another time, the teacher may point out the organization of the chapter, or the author's style of writing, or the sequence of types of paragraphs in the text. (See chapter 9 for discussion of paragraph types.) Throughout, the teacher guides the reading and discussion of the chapter by using preposed and postposed questions. Students thus acquire not only processes of reading and learning from text, but also knowledge of what the teacher sees as valuable to learn from the chapter.

After a few chapters, the teacher can phase out DRA and phase in the marginal gloss strategy, which consists of marginal notes that students can use as they read the text. These notes are essentially what the teacher communicated orally when using the DRA strategy. An assumption underlying use of the marginal gloss strategy is that students will be able to read the notes. Hence, teachers need to write notes that students can readily understand. (See chapter 9 and 10 for information on writing and readability.)

Whenever teachers use a new strategy, they should teach it to the class through a phase-in/phase-out process. They can accomplish the phase-in/phase-out process in three steps: (a) they can use the strategy with the entire class until they are reasonably certain that a majority of students understand the strategy: (b) they can then divide the class into heterogeneous groups and again use the strategy, only now knowledgeable members in each group may engage in cross-ability teaching to other members of the group who have not yet acquired the strategy; and (3) when the teachers who have been circulating among the groups as consultant, are satisfied that most of the class understands and can use the strategy, they can have individuals use the strategy alone. Those members of the class who still need help can get it through one-to-one instruction from the teacher while the rest of the class is employing the strategy. A chemistry teacher wanted to help her class by giving them programmed instruction lessons (worksheets). The assignment did not work because the teacher skipped from an explanation for the entire class of how to use the programmed worksheets to individual assignments. When the teacher went back and started over with the three-step process, first taking the class as a group through one worksheet, then having the class divide into groups to use the next worksheet, and finally having individuals do the third worksheet on their own, the students were then able to learn from programmed instruction worksheets.

---

[6]All the strategies described in this section are also presented in greater detail in chapters 6, 7, and 14–16.

Teachers who are familiar with a strategy may assume that a class will readily understand the same strategy. Such is not usually the case. Teachers may frequently jump from simply giving directions on how to do an assignment to use of cross-ability teaching as a way of handling individual differences. But note that cross-ability teaching is not the first, but the *second* step in the three-step procedure for phasing in the use of a new strategy. The first step is the one in which the teacher teaches a new strategy to the entire class, including those students who will be doing the cross-ability teaching. In other words, the teacher first teaches the student-teachers to understand the strategy. This understanding is prerequisite to cross-ability teaching.

SQ3R (survey, question, read, recite, and review) is another strategy that comes after students have learned—via a DRA strategy—how to read and learn from text, particularly a DRA strategy which emphasizes and teaches active comprehension, that is, students formulating and then reading to answer their own questions. After students have learned how to learn in a content area, particularly when they have learned to ask the kinds of questions that are relevant, they can then make better use of SQ3R. A variety of strategies for teaching self-questioning processes have been developed (Hunkins, 1976; Singer, 1978a).

The only strategy up to this point in our discussion that has required teachers to prepare teaching materials is the marginal gloss. Another single-text strategy that requires preparation of materials is the use of learning guides. The teacher begins writing the guide in a backward direction by first answering this question: "What generalization(s) do I want students to acquire or construct from this chapter?" The teacher states these generalizations explicitly. Sometimes the teacher can subsume them under controversial beliefs that the class can then debate. Next, the teacher asks, "What relationships, interpretations, or concepts are necessary for comprehending these generalizations?" The teacher also writes these statements down and then notes on a key the passages in the text from which students can make these interpretations or form concepts. Last, the teacher asks, "What details or facts support these interpretations?" The teacher then writes down the facts and prepares a key that identifies the page and line in the text where students can locate these facts. Now, the teacher can prepare a learning-from-text guide for the assigned reading, but the presentation in the learning-from-text guide is in the reverse order; the details or facts come first, interpretations next, and generalizations last. The students' task is to identify where the facts are in the text, and which interpretations, inferences, or concepts support which generalization(s).

In teaching students to use a learning guide, teachers must use a phase-in procedure. The teacher takes the entire class through the first guide, then uses groups for a subsequent guide, and finally brings students to the point where they can use guides for their own individual reading assignments. (See chapter 6 for how to expand guides for teaching students how to read and evaluate what they read.)

Next, teachers employ a phase-out procedure in which they teach students to internalize the steps in learning guides so that they can read and learn from texts without the use of guides. In this phase-out strategy, the whole class first participates as a class in constructing a guide, then the teacher forms heterogeneous groups of students to construct guides on different chapters of a text, next individual students construct their own guides, and finally the teacher has students practice reading the text for facts, interpretations, and generalizations without the use of guides. Thus, teachers can help students progress toward the goal of learning how to learn and become independent of teachers in reading and learning from text.

MULTIPLE-TEXT STRATEGIES

A strategy that provides for a transition from single to multiple texts is the *inquiry strategy*. This strategy starts with a single text. The class, under teacher direction, questions the validity of statements of "fact" made in the text. To help the students learn ways to check on the validity of the fact(s), the teacher first teaches the class how to locate information that is especially relevant in library reference books, such as the *Reader's Guide to Periodical Literature, The New York Times Index,* almanacs, and so forth. Next, the class learns how to abstract and file relevant material on index cards. The process of teaching students how to judge relevancy may consist of the teacher preparing transparencies for the overhead projector and then having the class as a group read passages. Students then identify and justify which sections or sentences contain information that helps answer a preposed question. The class can quote or paraphrase the information on cards, noting the source of the information. Subsequently, the class can learn to put the cards together to form a report. The process of writing this report is the reverse of outlining—here the class starts with information and groups the information into sections, then formulates subheadings, and finally selects a title. The teacher can phase in this process which a skeleton outline of main ideas in which students fill in the details. Gradually, in subsequent inquiry operations, as the students learn to identify, state, and organize main ideas, the teacher can phase out the outline.

The issue of the validity of "facts" in the inquiry strategy leads to additional information, some pro and some con. The teacher has to teach the class to weigh and evaluate the information. The teacher informs students that information which nonbiased observers have directly observed and which other observers independently corroborate has greater weight and credence than information that is indirect or second-hand, or that comes from observers with vested interests in the information. Students then learn to judge issues on the basis of what reasonable persons would do, say, or believe in similar situations. In short, the class acts as a jury to evaluate the information and arrive at a verdict.

Thus, the inquiry strategy teaches a class to read critically and to verify and evaluate information independently. Of course, the teacher employs a phase-in procedure for teaching the class, then groups, and finally individuals, how to use the inquiry strategy. In the process, the class learns how to use a library, judge relevant information, abstract and file information, debate and evaluate information, and finally write reports. The class can also use and apply all of these processes in the project method.

The project method starts with the arousal of the class's curiosity. Room environment (posters, newspapers, bulletin boards), a slide presentation, a movie, or a combination of these techniques serve this purpose well. In presenting these curiosity-arousing techniques, or commenting during the presentation, the teacher can ask questions that get questions, not answers, in return: *What questions would you like to ask about this event? What other questions would you like to ask about this issue, or event, or person?* Student monitors can list the questions on the board as their classmates formulate them. Then the teacher can take the class through a process of finding answers to their questions in library reference books. In the next phase, students can group questions with common categories; and students who posed these questions can form a group to answer the question *as a group*. Eventually, individuals can be led to carry out individual projects to answer their own questions.

The concept strategy is similar in operation to the project method, and may even precede its use in the sequence of teaching strategies. An English teacher may start with an anthology that deals with a particular concept such as *courage*. After going through various works that involve the concept, the teacher subdivides the class into groups according to students' interests. Then each group reads, discusses, analyses, and engages in various writing activities on a particular aspect of the concept—political courage (*Profiles in Courage*) or personal courage (*The Red Badge of Courage*). Each group can contribute to class discussion from its enriched perspective.

Next, students can use self-selection for individual projects. A commercial example of this approach is *Scholastic Magazine Units* in literature. Such materials are not readily available in other content areas, but teachers can construct their own units with the help of school catalogs. These units can include materials at different levels of difficulty, but all related to the same concept. Another example in the series of textbooks, *Concepts in Science,* edited by Brandwein, Cooper, Blackwood, Hone, and Fraser (1972), demonstrates that a clock or wind-up toy running down is a concrete instance of the concept of entropy. The series subsequently presents this concept at succeeding levels of difficulty and abstractness.

The multilevel text strategy is similar to the concept strategy except that the multilevel text strategy deals with a variety of information, concepts, and generalizations at different levels of difficulty. The teacher can use multilevel texts in various ways. He or she can introduce students to ideas in a text at a low level of difficulty and then have the class deal with particular concepts at higher levels of difficulty, progressing from easy to more difficult texts. Teachers can also use single-text strategies, such as DRA, SQ3R, and learning guides with multilevel texts.

Thus, over a year's time a teacher and a class can learn to use a wide range of strategies that involves the use of both single and multiple texts. In the process, the teacher will not only enhance students' abilities to read and learn from text, but will also (contrary to popular belief) increase the range of individual differences through this excellent instruction. (See chapter 3.)

A reading and learning-from-text specialist can teach students and faculties this sequence of strategies best. The ideal reading specialist at the elementary, junior, or senior high school can carry out five major functions: diagnosis at the individual, classroom, and school level; instruction of acquisition classes; education of teachers on how to teach incoming students to read and learn from texts in content areas; demonstration teaching and in-service training for the faculty; teaching a content area course as a member of a department in the school. To coordinate all five functions this specialist must also serve as chairperson of a schoolwide committee on reading and learning from text, as Ms. Valdes does in Scene 4, below.

One week later. It is 3:30 in the afternoon. The schoolwide committee is meeting in a small conference room at the rear of the library, since the counseling department is using Ms. Valdes's room for testing.

Mr. Phelps: I want you to know, Ms. Valdes, that you're responsible for my not getting any sleep—two nights last week.

Ms. Valdes: How's that?

Mr. Phelps: All that talk about reeducating the faculty got me thinking. I started worrying about whether we'd ever begin to accomplish it.

Mr. Wallace: You realize, don't you, that taking on Monroe's faculty is like taking on a band of guerrillas.

Ms. Stewart: Are you saying they're apes?

Mr. Wallace: No, Stewart, the other kind.

Ms. Jorgensen: I can just see me telling Bedilia Furgueson that she's got to teach reading. She'll say, "I'm lucky if the kids don't sew their arms to their aprons. How can I teach them to read?"

Mr. Phelps: I've got a couple of hotshots in my department who might want to take this all on—you know the type, masochists.

Ms. Jones: I think what we're saying, Ms. Valdes, is that some teachers won't want to cooperate, but that some might want to.

Ms. Valdes; That's human nature. One of the factors that makes a high school a fascinating place to work is the tremendous differences that exist among the faculty members.

Ms. Stewart: Maybe we could start with the ones that want to learn and gradually work our way down to the others. Maybe we could even entice Bedilia.

Ms. Valdes: You've got a good start already. The fact that we have a functioning schoolwide committee on reading and learning from text is a major plus. Let me take some time here to talk about the problems other schools face and bring up a few questions we might want to consider.

Schoolwide Committee on Reading and Learning from Text

Although schools may want to act ideally in developing a reading program, they usually have to act expeditiously, frequently because of lack of funds, time, and available personnel. Consequently, the board or administration has often employed one of three solutions to solve the problem of the wide range of individual differences in reading achievement in a school: (a) it imports or buys a commercial reading program, (b) it sends teachers to observe an outstanding reading program at another school for a day or two, bring back the ideas, and try to install the same program in their own school—without going through the process of staff and program development followed by the outstanding school, or (c) it hires a consultant to draw up a prescription for a reading program and has teachers in the school apply the prescription without providing them with any additional training. None of these solutions works very well because usually none of them fit the specific needs of the school. Moreover, they do not contain provisions for training the faculty in how to develop and implement the program nor do they take the faculty through a process of analysis of the problem, consideration of strategies for solving the problem, and finally selection or construction of an appropriate program for the school.

An ideal approach is to have the principal form a schoolwide committee of department heads or representative teachers from the primary and intermediate grades, reading and learning-from-text specialists, and the vice-principal. The function of the schoolwide committee is to advise the reading content area specialist, provide linkages between the administration and faculty, and make and implement decisions on the school's program for teaching students to read and learn from texts.

A NEEDS ASSESSMENT FOR INSTRUCTION IN
READING AND LEARNING FROM TEXT
Questions

The committee will have to do a needs assessment for instruction in reading and learning from text. It will have to start by generating a series of questions and answers to prepare for meeting with the faculty. We have posed a large number of questions in Box 18.7, among them some that we anticipate any faculty might ask.

BOX 18.7. *Questions About a School's Program in Reading and Learning from Texts*

Testing Reading Achievement and Reporting Results
1. What is the range of individual differences in general reading achievement (speed and comprehension) and in reading in the content areas?
2. Describe the school's testing program. Is it adequate: (a) Are all students diagnosed in speed and comprehension? (b) Is further diagnostic testing given to students beyond a survey test of speed and comprehension? (c) Are students assessed on reading in each content area?
3. What is done with test results? Are teachers, students, and parents informed of

test results? Do they have opportunities to consult on the results with specialists and obtain recommendations for improvement? Are the test results used for making classroom, curricular, and administrative decisions?

Attitudes of Faculty and Students

4. What are the attitudes of the faculty toward teaching students to read and learn from texts?
5. What is the attitude of students toward their texts and tests?

Classroom Materials, Strategies, and Purposes

6. What types of materials must students read in each content area (texts, library assignments, other materials)?
7. What techniques or strategies do teachers use that seem to be helpful in improving reading and learning-from-text skills in each content area?
8. What classwide strategies do teachers use for handling the range of individual differences in reading achievement? (Note: even when tracking or homogeneous grouping is used, students still vary in achievement.)
9. What is the relationship between reading improvement classes and instruction in content areas?
10. What problem(s) do individual teachers have with students' reading and learning in content areas? What suggestions do these teachers have for resolving these problems?

Role of the Reading and Learning-from-Text Specialist

11. Does the school's reading specialist(s) conduct in-service training for the faculty? Consult with content area teachers on instructional problems in teaching students to learn from texts? In general, what help does the reading specialist(s) provide for content area teachers?
12. How does the school prepare incoming students for reading and learning from texts in each content area? And for learning to study (taking examinations, learning and using library skills, writing reports, planning and organizing use of time)?
13. What should be the role of the consultant in reading and learning from texts? What questions does the faculty have for the consultant? What problems should the consultant focus on and try to solve? How should the consultant's time best be used to the advantage of the entire school?

Library Facilities and Resources

14. What is the current status of the library in relation to the content areas? Does the library have books in each content area that will cover the range of individual differences in each content area? What does the library need to adequately serve the needs of content area teachers?
15. How does the librarian coordinate with content area teachers on students' reference reading and research reporting in content areas? Does the library have a set of school catalogs?

Administration and Plans for Improving Reading and Learning from Texts

16. What plan(s) does the administration have for improving instruction in reading and learning in the content areas?

17. Does the school have a schoolwide program and committee for improving reading and learning in the content areas? How does the committee operate? What is its scope? Is the committee representative (content area teachers, reading specialists, administrators)? What has the committee done about determining and solving needs? Have individual faculty members had opportunities to state their problems and suggest solutions?
18. What provision does the school have for in-service training? How are policies on in-service training formulated? (Decisions on what training is required, who is to conduct the training, whether faculty is to get released time, whether training should be for the faculty as a whole or for departments, and whether the faculty is to get salary schedule credit for participating in in-service training.)
19. How is instruction in reading and learning from texts budgeted? Are funds distributed in many budget categories or is there a specific program budget?

Although each school has its own specific factors (such as training and interests of the faculty, characteristics of the student body, and schedule of priorities of administration) that it would have to take into account in designing and developing any program, we can give some tentative general answers, directions, or procedures to the items in Box 18.7.

Answers

Items 1–3. Review the school's testing program. If survey test results are not available, then administer a general survey test to the entire school. Follow up the survey test with individual diagnostic tests, according to our outline in chapter 17. Note that some students may perform only perfunctorily on the survey test and consequently score low, but on the individually administered test, if you properly motivate them, they will score higher. The committee is likely to discover from the results of the testing program that they can group students in three programs: (a) those students who need instruction in learning to read—they are candidates for the acquisition classes; the committee may have to subdivide some of these students further as we explained in chapter 17; (b) the same is true for the students in category 2—those students who are beyond the elementary or acquisition state of reading development, but who have comprehension levels 1 to 3 years below grade level and below the readability levels of their texts—they and their teachers are candidates for demonstration classes in comprehension and strategies for meeting the range of individual differences; and (c) those students, almost all students in the school, who need instruction in learning from texts in the content areas—their teachers are candidates for demonstration, in-service training, and for consulting on problems of teaching students to read and learn from texts in content areas.

A survey test, while closely related to a test for reading in content areas, is not sufficient for defining the students for category 3. Although some content area survey tests are standardized and published (see the list in chapter 17, Box 17.3), they do not have specific curricular validity for a particular school and their subtest reliabilities are not adequate. Consequently, teachers should construct an informal reading inventory for assessing comprehension in their own content areas. We explained the procedure for constructing such an inventory in chapter 10.

Communicate the results of testing not only to teachers but also to parents and students. If students are to improve, they need to know what their current performance is; then they need counseling on setting their goals and procedures for improvement. Furthermore, a school should use test results in decisions on classroom instruction, curricular modification, and administrative plans.

Items 4, 18. Teachers in the school can react to the attitude inventory in chapter 2. The committee can present the results of this survey to the faculty with the consequence that faculty members might then become interested in an in-service education program especially if they get released time. Following the program, they can take the attitude scale to see if their attitudes toward teaching students to read and learn from text have changed.

Item 10. The committee should interview teachers for their problems in teaching students to learn from texts and for suggestions on how to ameliorate the problems. The committee can act on faculty suggestions, particularly in areas of consensus, and can make special arrangements for unique problems.

Item 5. The committee can interview a sample of students in various content areas to assess their attitudes toward their texts and to discuss their problems in reading and learning from them in class and at home. Ask students to read passages aloud and silently and then answer informal inventory-type questions about them. The reading specialist who would conduct the interviews and observe students' reading and analyze inventory responses would then compile a list of problems.

Note: Some teachers at the high school level do not use texts—they use only the lecture method. The reading specialist could record some of the lectures and class discussions, then construct an informal inventory to administer to the class to get at problems in listening comprehension.

The problems in listening parallel those in reading, and in some ways learning is more difficult through listening because students must rely more on memory and their notes. Moreover, such oral instruction does not prepare them for the next level of instruction in which texts are used.

The committee should also interview students on their attitudes toward tests and test results. The committee may find that some students do not take tests seriously because they do not receive test results. Hence, their scores are not reliable. Consequently, when referred to clinics or labs they have to be retested.

Items 6–8. Conduct a survey to determine what types of materials and reading assignments students have, what techniques and strategies students use to help with their assigned reading, and what strategies teachers employ for handling the range of individual differences for the entire class.

The results of the survey will form a baseline for evaluating the effectiveness of subsequent demonstrations, in-service training, and consultation programs. Moreover, the survey may identify teachers' strategies and practices that the committee can disseminate in the program.

Item 9.   Make an analysis of the materials and curriculum in reading improvement classes. Describe the nature of the classes. (See chapter 17 for categories of current reading improvement classes.) A key question is whether the classes use content area materials (see section on content area acquisition classes in this chapter) for instruction in reading and learning from texts. Or, do the classes teach strictly functional reading (chapter 17)? These classes have an alternative objective to content area instruction—they simply teach survival skills in reading.

Items 11, 13.   Assess the role of reading specialists in the school. Is the school using the specialist to best advantage for the entire school? Does the specialist carry out the major functions of a specialist as outlined in this chapter? Or is the reading specialist's scope of activities focused only on teaching reading in acquisition classes? If so, what provisions can the school make for expanding the specialist's activities?

Item 12.   Does the school have a program for introducing students to reading and learning from texts? Are students learning how to study and prepare for examinations, use the library, write reports, participate in discussions, and learn to organize and budget time?

Some schools require all incoming students to take a class in reading and learning from texts in a content area. Perhaps what is preferable is to integrate reading and learning from text instruction in each content area class, instead of relying upon transfer from a special class.

Items 14–15.   Make an inventory of the school's library to determine whether the library has a range of books in each content area to meet the range of reading abilities of students. Librarians should have school catalogs (chapter 11, Box 11.3) as references for themselves and content area teachers. A possible solution to the financial problem of developing an adequate library in each school is a central library from which teachers can borrow books for units of study.

An important function of a school librarian is coordination with content area teachers. Does the librarian get course syllabi from content area teachers? Do teachers ask the librarian to arrange, borrow, or purchase books for reference reading for the particular units, or even apprise the librarian of student assignments? Does the librarian conduct orientation session in how to use the library? In general, how adequate is the collection of titles and reference materials for the school's program? What can the school or librarian do to improve the library services and collection?

Items 16, 17, 19.   Review the plan(s) of the school for improving instruction in reading and learning from text. Does the school have a plan for such improvement? What are its goals and procedures? What is the timeline for reaching the goal? What does the school consider an adequate ratio of reading specialist to students and faculty? What are its plans and budget for in-service training of faculty? What leadership is the principal providing for the program? If the principal has appointed a committee, what charge and scope of authority has he given to the committee?

Programs need time for development. As a rule of thumb, it takes about 5 years to develop an adequate program. The first year is for assessment, review, and planning. The second year is for employing reading specialists, initiating plans, courses, and in-service training. The third year is for application of the results of an in-service training program and spreading its effects to students and other faculty. The fourth year is for continued in-service training (particularly for those teachers who did not participate in the first in-service program and for faculty new to the school). The fifth year is for full-scale operation of the program and review of progress made toward the school's goal.

Although schools or consultants can devise strategies for economizing on costs and teachers' time, such as demonstration teaching in content area classes, in all probability teachers will have to have some released time for in-service training and for selection or preparation of lessons, units, and plans for implementation of new teaching strategies. If the administration has a budget specifically for the reading and learning-from-text program, then the school is likely to implement the program. In general, a specific budget item is more likely to produce results than a diffused budget for a program (Carlson, 1972).

If the school has reading specialists, the administration should decide how to use them. Interview the faculty to determine the questions and problems for the reading specialist when functioning as a consultant to the faculty. What problems does the faculty want the specialist to work on and solve? Often faculties might want to simply turn their instructional problems over to specialists. While students in the acquisition stage of development need concentrated instruction in special classes, content area teachers can also help them by teaching the technical vocabulary in their content areas. The content area teachers can provide even more help if they acquire and use strategies for teaching students in all content areas how to read and learn from texts.

In addition to answering these questions, the committee has to present some feasible solutions to the principal and gain his or her support for the project. To do so, the committee would invite the principal to its next meeting, as the committee at Monroe High does in Scene 5.

The office of Mr. Towne, the principal. The schoolwide committee has decided to approach Mr. Towne with some suggestions for effecting the future scene at Monroe High School.

Ms. Jones: Mr. Towne, as you know, the schoolwide committee has been spending a great deal of time studying the problems at Monroe High, particularly, with the help of Ms. Valdes, the problems the students are experiencing in reading their textbooks.

Ms. Phelps: Some of us are already experimenting with some of the single- and multiple-text strategies in our own classes.

Ms. Jorgensen: But we think that we're going to have to do something more far reaching than that.

Ms. Stewart: I think what we're asking is, how can we best reeducate the faculty to the needs of the students at Monroe High?

Mr. Towne: What do you propose?

Ms. Jones: Ms. Valdes has come up with a couple of good suggestions about involving faculty members in the teaching of an introductory course in reading and learning from text for our freshmen.

Ms. Stewart: Also ways of working with groups of faculty on the use of single- and multiple-text strategies, perhaps on a one-at-a-time basis.

Mr. Phelps: This may amount to some extra money. Ms. Valdes has suggested bringing in outside consultants to work with teachers in areas she feels inadequate in.

Ms. Jones: Most crucial, or course, is released time during the school year, and money for summer institutes, which would allow teachers time and support for developing classroom materials in implementing these strategies.

Mr. Umeki: Ms. Valdes seems to think that within 4 or 5 years we could have a most effective all-school program in reading and learning from text.

Mr. Towne: I would like to say that I'm most impressed with what you all have been doing. I will speak to the superintendent about funding what you propose—maybe an outside grant, or extra money in his contingency fund.

Ms. Valdes: Mr. Towne, we don't want to mislead you into thinking this is a panacea. You know Monroe's students and the nature of the faculty. It could be a long haul.

Mr. Towne: I'm willing to take the risk and I'm planning to be here for at least the next 5 years. I hope you are too. Why don't we set up a meeting for next week at this time. By that time, I'll know whether the superintendent has money. If he can't come up with money, we'll proceed as best as we can without funding. This is too important a project to let go by the wayside.

Ms. Valdes: Well, if Superintendent Ray doesn't have funds to support our in-service program, we'll still be able to go ahead at a slower rate with our one-to-one in-service model.

Mr. Towne: I'm glad you have that alternative. No matter what the superintendent does, we need to make a start on teaching all our teachers and students strategies on how to read and learn from text.

SUMMARY

To teach all the students in a school to read and learn from text, a school has to have four programs: (a) a Reading and Learning from Text Center that has a class on reading acquisition in the content areas that includes instruction not only in word recognition but also in comprehension; (b) use of an instructional model for teaching comprehension on reading and learning from text in all classes; (c) an in-service education program for content area teachers and (d) an introductory course in reading and learning from text. Teachers and students alike can acquire strategies for reading and learning from text in a sequence that progresses from single- to multiple-text strategies. This sequence fits the adaptive mechanisms of assimilations and accommodation. Students and teachers are more likely to accept single-text strategies more readily than multiple-text strategies because single-text strategies are closer to familiar concepts and methods of instruction. Single-text strategies also ease the acquisition of multiple-text strategies because they teach teachers and students alike some processes that also occur in multiple-text strategies.

But having an entire school faculty learn how to teach students to read and learn from texts is a complex operation. To administer the operation and to secure the cooperation of the faculty, the principal has to appoint a representative schoolwide committee. This committee will have a full agenda of 19 questions and will supply tentative answers to them. Even under the best of conditions, we think it will take 5 years for the development of a schoolwide program for teaching all students to read and learn from text.

ACTIVITIES

1. Attend a high school class in reading instruction. Compare the course with this text's description of a reading acquisition class. Specifically, does the class use content from texts in the school's content areas?
2. Use the set of 19 questions in Box 18.7 on a survey of a nearby high school. How many of the issues in these questions has the school resolved?

References

Aaron, I. E. (1965). Reading in mathematics. *Journal of Reading, 9*, 391–401.

Adams, M. J., & Collins, A. (April 1977, 1985). *A schema-theoretic view of reading* (Tech. Rep. No. 32). Urbana: University of Illinois, Center for the Study of Reading. Reprinted in H. Singer & R. B. Ruddell (Eds.), *Theoretical models and processes of reading* (3rd. ed., pp. 404–425). Newark, De.: International Reading Association.

Adams, M. J., & Huggins, A. W. F. (1985). The growth of children's sight vocabulary: A quick test with educational and theoretical implications. *Reading Research Quarterly, 3*, 262–281.

Agnew, D. C. (1939). *The effect of varied amounts of phonetic drill on primary reading*. Durham, NC: Duke University Press.

Aiken, L. R., Jr. (1972). Language factors in mathematics. *Review of Educational Research, 42*(3), 359–385.

Algren, N. (1965). He swung and he missed. In R. C. Pooley et al. (Eds.), *Accent: U.S.A.* New York: Scott, Foresman.

Allen, R. V. (1968). Grouping through learning centers. *Childhood Education, 45*, 200–203.

Alvermann, D. E. (1982). Restructuring text facilities written recall of main ideas. *Journal of Reading, 25*, 754–8.

Anderson, R. C. (1976a). Concretization and sentence learning. In H. Singer & R. B. Ruddell (Eds.), *Theoretical models and processes of reading,* (2nd ed., pp. 588–596). Newark, DE: International Reading Association.

Anderson, R. C. (1976b, December). *Context, knowledge of the world, and language comprehension*. Paper presented at the National Reading Conference, GA.

Anderson, R. C., & Freebody, P. (1983). Effects of vo-cabulary difficulty, text cohesion, and schema availability on reading comprehension. *Reading Research Quarterly, 13*, 227–294.

Anderson, R. C., & Freebody, P. (1985). Vocabulary knowledge. Reprinted in H. Singer & R. B. Ruddell (Eds.), *Theoretical models and processes of reading* (3rd ed., pp. 343–371). Newark, DE: International Reading Association.

Anderson, R. C., & Ortony, A. (1975). On putting apples into bottles—a problem in polysemy. *Cognitive Psychology, 7*, 167–180.

Anderson, R. C., Osborn, J., & Tierney, R. J. (Eds.). (1984). *Learning to read in American schools: Basal readers and content texts*. Hillsdale, NJ: Lawrence Erlbaum Associates.

Anderson, R. C., Pichert, J. W., Goetz, E. T., Schallert, F. L., Stevens, K. V., & Trollip, S. R. (1976). Instantiation of general terms. *Journal of Verbal Learning and Verbal Behavior, 15*, 667–679.

Anderson, R., Spiro, R., & Montague, W. E. (Eds.). (1977). *Schooling and the acquisition of knowledge*. Hillsdale, NJ: Lawrence Erlbaum Associates.

Anderson, T. H., & Armbruster, B. (1981). Content area textbooks. In R. C. Anderson, J. Osborn, & R. J. Tierney (Eds.), *Learning to read in American schools: Basal readers and content texts* (pp. 375–442). Urbana, IL: The Center for the Study of Reading.

Anderson, T. H., & Armbruster, B. B. (1986). Readable textbooks, or, selecting a textbook is not like buying a pair of shoes. In J. Orasanu (Ed.), *Reading comprehension: From research to practice* (pp. 151–162). Hillsdale, NJ: Lawrence Erlbaum Associates.

Anderson, T. H., Armbruster, B. B., & Kantor, R. N. (1980). *How clearly written are children's text-

books? Or, of bladder work and alfa (Reading Educational Rep. No. 16). Champaign, IL: University of Illinois, Center for the Study of Reading.

Armstrong, H. (1953). The relationship of the auditory and visual vocabularies of children. *Dissertation Abstracts, 13,* 716.

Askov, E. N., & Dupuis, M. (1982). *Study skills in the content areas.* Boston: Allyn & Bacon.

Askov, E. N., Dupuis, M. M., & Lee, J. W. (1978). *Content Area Reading Project* (Final Rep., Project 09-6905). Division of Adult and Community Education, Pennsylvania Department of Education. University Park, PA: The Pennsylvania State University.

Athey, I. (1976). Reading research in the affective domain. In H. Singer & R. B. Ruddell (Eds.), *Theoretical models and processes of reading* (2nd ed., pp. 302–319). Newark, DE: International Reading Association.

Athey, I. (1985). Reading research in the affective domain. In H. Singer & R. B. Ruddell (Eds.), *Theoretical models and processes of reading* (3rd ed., pp. 527–557). Newark, DE: International Reading Association. Hillsdale, NJ: Lawrence Erlbaum Associates.

Athey, I., & Holmes, J. A. (1967). *Reading success and personality characteristics in junior high school students. Reading success and a personality value-systems syndrome: A thirty-year then and now study at the junior high school level* (Contract No. S-248; Bureau of Research: No. 5-8027-2-12-1). Washington, DC: U. S. Department of Health, Education, and Welfare (Office of Education).

Athey, I., & Holmes, J. A. (1969). *Reading success and personality characteristics in junior high school students.* Berkeley, CA: University of California Press.

Au, R. (1986). *Developmental interactive word recognition hypothesis.* Unpublished doctoral dissertation. University of California, Riverside.

Ausubel, D. (1960). The use of advance organizers in the learning and retention of meaningful verbal material. *Journal of Educational Psychology, 51,* 267–272.

Ausubel, D. (1964). Some psychological aspects of the structure of knowledge. In S. Elam (Ed.), *Education and the structure of knowledge* (pp. 220–262). New York: Rand McNally.

Baker, L. (1984). Children's effective use of multiple standards for evaluating their comprehension. *Journal of Educational Psychology, 76,* 588–597.

Baker, L., & Brown, A. (1984). Cognitive monitoring in reading and studying. In J. Flood (Ed.), *Understanding reading comprehension* (pp. 21–44). Newark, DE: International Reading Association.

Balow, B. (1965). The long term effects of remedial instruction. *The Reading Teacher, 18,* 581–586.

Balow, I. H. (1962). Does homogeneous grouping give homogeneous groups? *Elementary School Journal, 63,* 28–32.

Balow, I. H. (1964). The effects of homogenous grouping on seventh grade arithmetic. *The Arithmetic Teacher, 11*(3), 186–191.

Balow, I. H., & Singer, H. (1987). Comparison of New York and California's solutions to proficiency assessment of basic skills. In H. Singer & I. H. Balow, *Proficiency assessment and its consequences* (pp. 43–54). Final Report. Project supported by California Policy Seminar, Institute of Governmental Studies, 103 Moses Hall, University of California, Berkeley (In ERIC, Number not yet assigned.)

Barr, M., D'Arcy, P., & Healy, M. K. (Eds.). (1982). *What's going on?* Montclair, NJ: Boynton Cook.

Barr, R. C. (1972). The influence of instructional conditions on word recognition errors. *Reading Research Quarterly, 7,* 509–529.

Barr, R. C. (1973–1974). Instructional pace differences and their effect on reading acquisition. *Reading Research Quarterly, 9*(4), 526, 528–54.

Barr, R. C. (1975). The effect of instruction on pupil reading strategies. *Reading Research Quarterly, 10,* 555–582.

Barrett, T. C. (1968). The Barrett taxonomy: Cognitive and affective dimensions of reading comprehension. In T. Clymer, What is "reading?" Some correct concepts. In H. M. Robinson (Ed.), *Sixty-seventh yearbook of the national society for the study of education, part II* (pp. 7–29). Chicago: University of Chicago Press.

Barrilleaux, L. E. (1967). An experiment on multiple library sources as compared to the use of a basic textbook in junior high school science. *Journal of Experimental Education, 35,* 27–35.

Barrington, K., & Rogers, I. (1968). *Group work in secondary schools and the training of teachers in its methods.* Gateshead: Oxford University Press.

Barron, R. F. (1969). The use of vocabulary as an advance organizer. In Harold Herber & Peter Sanders (Eds.), *Research in reading in the content areas: First year report.* Syracuse, NY: Syracuse University Press.

Bartlett, B. J. (1979). Top-level structure as an organizational strategy for recall of classroom text. (Doctoral dissertation, Arizona State University, 1978). *Dissertation Abstracts International, 39,* 6641A.

Bartlett, F. C. (1932). *Remembering.* Cambridge, England: Cambridge University Press.

Baumann, J. F., & Serra, J. K. (1984). The frequency and placement of main ideas in children's social studies textbooks: A modified replication of Barddock's research on topic sentences. *Journal of Reading Behavior, 16,* 27–40.

Baumann, J. F. (1986). Effect of rewritten content text-book passages on middle grade students' comprehension of main ideas: Making the inconsiderate considerate. *Journal of Reading Behavior, 18*(1), 1–22.

Bean, T. W., Singer, H., Frazee, C., & Sorter, J. (1983). Acquisition of summarization rules as a basis for question generation in learning from expository text at the high school level. In J. Niles & L. Miller (Eds.), *Searches for meaning in reading: Language processing and instruction* (pp. 43–49). Rochester, NY: National Reading Conference.

Bean, T. W., Sorter, J., Singer, H., & Frazee, C. (1986). Teaching students how to make predictions about events in history with a graphic organizer plus options guide. *Journal of Reading, 30*, 739–745.

Beck, I. L. (1986). Build-a-word. Described by A. Collins, Teaching reading and writing with personal computers. In J. Orasanu (Ed.), *Reading comprehension from research to practice* (pp. 171–188). Hillsdale, NJ: Lawrence Erlbaum Associates.

Beck, I., Omanson, R. C., & McKeown, M. G. (1982). An instructional redesign of reading lessons: Effects on comprehension. *Reading Research Quarterly, 17*(4), 462–481.

Beez, W. V. (1968). *Influence of biased psychological reports on teacher behavior and pupil performance.* Unpublished doctoral dissertation, summarized in Samuel L. Guskin & Howard H. Specker, *Education research in mental retardation.* In Norman Ellis (Ed.), *International review of research on mental retardation* (Vol. 3). New York: Academic Press.

Belden, B. B., & Lee, W. D. (1961). Readability of biology textbooks and the reading ability of biology students. *School Sciences and Mathematics, 61*, 689–693.

Benfort, A. D. (1983). Micros for reading, spelling, and self-esteem. *Journal of Reading, 26*, 638–639.

Berget, E. (1973). Two methods of guiding the learning of a short story. In Harold L. Herber & Richard F. Barron (Eds.), *Research in reading in the content areas: Second year report* (pp. 53–57). Syracuse University: Reading and Language Arts Center.

Bettelheim, B., & Zelan, K. (1982). *On learning to read: The child's fascination with meaning.* New York: A. Knopf.

Betts, E. (1947). Reviewed by W. R. Powell (1971). Validity of the IRI reading levels. *Elementary English, 48*(6), 637–642.

Betts, E. A. (1955). Reading as a thinking process. *The National Elementary Principal, 35*, 90–99.

Biemiller, A. (1970). The development of the use of graphic and contextual information as children learn to read. *Reading Research Quarterly, 6*, 75–96.

Bierce, A. (1969). An occurrence at Owl Creek Bridge. In Jay Cline, Ken Williams, Barbara Mahoney, & Kay Dziuk (Eds.), *Voices in literature, language, and composition, 4.* Boston: Ginn.

Birkmire, D. (1985). Text processing: The influence of text structure, background knowledge and purpose. *Reading Research Quarterly, 20*(3), 314–326.

Blank, J. P. (1969). Sport's worst tragedy. In Jay Cline, Ken Williams, & Don Donlan (Eds.), *Voices in literature, language, and composition, 2.* Boston: Ginn.

Bloom, B. S. (1971). Mastery learning and its implications for curriculum development. In Elliot W. Eisner (Ed.), *Confronting curriculum reform* (pp. 17–48). Boston: Little, Brown.

Bloom, B. S., et al. (1956). *Taxonomy of educational objectives: Handbook I, cognitive domain.* New York: Longman, Green.

Bond, E. (1938). *Reading and ninth grade achievement.* New York: Bureau of Publications, Teachers College, Columbia University.

Bond, G. L., & Dykstra, R. (1967). The cooperative research program in first grade reading instruction. *Reading Research Quarterly, 2*, 5–142.

Bormuth, J. R. (1966). Readability: A new approach. *Reading Research Quarterly, 1*, 79–132.

Bormuth, J. R. (1968). The cloze readability procedure. *Elementary English, 45*(4), 429–436.

Bormuth, J. R., Carr, J., Manning, J., & Pearson, D. (1970). Children's comprehension of between and within sentence syntactic structures. *Journal of Educational Psychology, 61*, 349–351.

Bower, G., Black, J. B., & Turner, T. J. (1979). Scripts in memory for text. *Cognitive Psychology, 11*, 177–220.

Boyer, E. (1983). *High school: A report on secondary education in America.* Princeton, NJ: Carnegie Foundation for the Advancement of Teaching.

Boylan, P. J. (Revisor). (1962). *Elements of physics.* (Original authors: D. L. Baker, R. B. Brownlee, R. W. Fuller.) Boston: Allyn & Bacon.

Bradbury, R. (1953). *Fahrenheit 451.* New York: Ballantine.

Braddock, R. (1974). The frequency and placement of topic sentences in expository prose. *Research in the Teaching of English, 8*, 287–302.

Braddock, R., Lloyd-Jones, R., & Schoer, L. (1963). *Research in written composition.* Urbana, IL: National Council of Teachers of English.

Brandwein, P., Cooper, E. K., Blackwood, P. E., Hone, E. B., & Fraser, T. P. (1972). *Concepts in science* (3rd ed.). New York: Harcourt Brace Jovanovich.

Bransford, J. D. (1984). Schema activation and schema acquisition: Comments on Richard C. Anderson's remarks. In R. C. Anderson, J. Osborn, & R. J. Tierney (Eds.), *Learning to read in American schools.* Hillsdale, NJ: Lawrence Erlbaum Associates.

Bransford, J. D., & Franks, J. J. (1974). Memory for syntactic form as a function of semantic context. *Journal of Experimental Psychology, 103,* 1037–1039.

Bransford, J. D., & Johnson, M. (1972). Contextual prerequisites for understanding: Some investigations of comprehension and recall. *Journal of Verbal Learning and Verbal Behavior, 11,* 717–726.

Bridwell, L. S. (1980). Writing strategies in twelfth grade students' transactional writing. *Research in the Teaching of English, 14,* 197–222.

Brinton, C. (1977). What is a revolution. In R. Ostrowski & J. Kemper (Eds.), *Echoes of time: A world history* (p. 510). New York: McGraw-Hill.

Britton, J., Burgess, T., Martin, N., McLeod, A., & Rosen, H. (1975). *The development of writing abilities (11–18).* London: Macmillan.

Brown, A. (1980). Metacognitive development in reading. In R. J. Spiro, B. Bruce, & W. F. Brewer (Eds.), *Theoretical issues in reading comprehension* (pp. 453–481). Hillsdale, NJ: Lawrence Erlbaum Associates.

Brownell, W. A. (1939). Learning as Reorganization: An experimental study in third grade arithmetic, *Duke University Research Studies in Education,* No. 3.

Brownell, W. A. (1961). Rate, accuracy, and process in learning. In T. L. Harris & W. E. Schwann (Eds.), *Selected readings in the learning process* (pp. 388–400). New York: Oxford University Press.

Brownell, W. A., et al. (1949). *Meaningful vs. mechanical learning: A study in grade III subtraction.* (Duke University Research Studies in Education, No. 3). Durham, NC: Duke University Press.

Brownell, W. A., & Hendrickson, G. (1950). How children learn information, concepts, and generalizations. *Yearbook of the National Society for the Study of Education, 49:* Part 1.

Bruner, J. (1963). *The process of education.* New York: Vintage.

Brunner, R. B. (1977). Reading mathematical exposition. *Educational Research, 18*(1), 208–213.

Buckley, M. H., & Boyle, O. (1983). Mapping and composing. In M. Myers & J. Gray (Eds.), *Theory and practice in the teaching of composition: Processing, distancing, and modeling* (pp. 59–66). Urbana: NCTE.

Burmeister, L. E. (1974). *Reading strategies for secondary school teachers.* Reading, MA: Addison-Wesley.

Buros, O. K. (1978). *The eighth mental measurements yearbook.* Highland Park, NJ: Gryphon Press.

Buswell, G. T. (1922). Fundamental reading habits: A study of their development. *Supplementary Educational Monographs,* No. 21. Chicago: University of Chicago Press.

Buswell, G. T. (1945). *Non-oral reading—A study of its use in the Chicago public schools.* Chicago: University of Chicago Press.

Buswell, G. T. (1956). Educational theory and the psychology of learning. *Journal of Educational Psychology, 47,* 175–184.

Calkins, L. M. (1980). Children learn the writer's craft. *Language Arts, 57,* 207–213.

Call, R., & Wiggin, R. A. (1966). Reading and mathematics. Eugene D. Nichols (Ed.), *Mathematics Teacher, 59,* 149–157.

Campbell, D. T., & Stanley, J. C. (1963). *Experimental and quasi-experimental designs for research.* Chicago: Rand McNally.

Capps, L. R. (1970). Teaching mathematical concepts using language arts analogies. *Arithmetic Teacher, 17,* 329–331.

Carlsen, G. R. (1967). *Books and the teen-age reader.* New York: Bantam.

Carlson, T. R. (Ed.). (1972). *Administrators and reading.* New York: Harcourt Brace Jovanovich.

Carroll, J. B. (1964). A model of school learning. *Teachers College Record, 63,* 723–733.

Carroll, J. B., Davies, P., & Richman, B. (1971). *American heritage word frequency book.* Boston: Houghton Mifflin.

Carter, G. S., & Simpson, R. (1978). Science and reading: A basic duo. *The Science Teacher, 40,* 13–21.

Carter, H. D. (1957). *California survey of study methods.* Monterey, CA: CTB/McGraw-Hill. (Out of print)

Carver, R. (1974). *Improving reading comprehension* (Final Report). Washington, DC: American Institute for Research.

Caswell, H. S., & Foshay, A. W. (1950). *Education in the elementary school* (2nd ed.). New York: American Book.

Cattell, R. M. (1886). The time it takes to see and name objects. *Mind, 11,* 63–65.

Chafe, W. L. (1970). *Meaning and the structure of language.* Chicago: University of Chicago Press.

Chall, J. (1983). *Stages of reading development.* New York: McGraw-Hill.

Chall, J. S., Conard, S. S., & Harris, S. H. (1977). *An analysis of textbooks in relation to declining SAT scores.* Princeton, NJ: College Entrance Examination Board.

Chapin, J. R., McHugh, R. J., & Gross, R. E. (1971). *Quest for liberty.* Palo Alto, CA: Field Educational Enterprise.

Charles, C.M. (1983). *Elementary classroom management.* New York: Longman.

Chase, C. I. (1960). The position of certain variables in the prediction of problem solving in arithmetic. *Journal of Educational Research, 54,* 9–14.

Chase, C. I. (1978). *Measurement for educational evaluation* (2nd ed.). Reading, MA: Addison-Wesley.

Chomsky, C. (1970). Reading, writing, and phonology. *Harvard Educational Review, 40,* 287–309, 314.

Chomsky, C. (1976). After decoding: What? *Language Arts, 53*(3), 288–297.

Christensen, F. (1967). *Notes toward a new rhetoric.* New York: Harper & Row.

Clark, H. (1977). Inferences in comprehension. In D. La-Berge & S. Jay Samuels (Eds.), *Basic processes in reading: Perception and comprehension.* Hillsdale, NJ: Lawrence Erlbaum Associates.

Clark, H., & Clark, E. (1977). *The psychology of language.* New York: Harcourt Brace Jovanovich.

Clark, L. H. (1973). *Teaching social studies in secondary schools: A handbook.* New York: Macmillan.

Clark, L. H., & Starr, I. S. (1976). *Secondary school teaching methods.* New York: Macmillan.

Clewell, S. F., & Cliffton, A. M. (1983). Examining your textbook for comprehensibility. *Journal of Reading, 27,* 219–224.

Cohen, M. R., & Nagel, E. (1982). *An introduction to logic and the scientific method.* New York: Harcourt, Brace.

Cohen, S. A., & Stover, G. (1981). Effects of teaching sixth-grade students to modify format variables of math word problems. *Reading Research Quarterly, 16*(6), 172–200.

Coleman, J. (1968). The concept of equality of educational opportunity. *Harvard Educational Review, 38,* 7–22.

Collier, C. C., & Redmond, L. A. (1974). Are you teaching kids to read mathematics? *The Reading Teacher, 27,* 804–808.

Conant, J. B. (1959). *The American high school today.* New York: McGraw-Hill.

Cook, W. W. (1951). The functions of measurement in the facilitation of learning. In E. F. Lindquist (Ed.), *Educational measurement* (pp. 3–46). Washington, DC: American Council on Education.

Cooper, C. R., & Odell, L. (1977). *Evaluating writing: Describing, measuring, judging.* Urbana, IL: National Council of Teachers of English.

Corey, N. B. (1977). The use of rewritten science materials in ninth grade biology. *Journal of Research in Science Teaching, 14*(2), 97–103.

Crismore, A. (1983). *Interpersonal and ideational metadiscourse in learning from text.* In H. Singer & T. Bean (Eds.), *Learning from text: Explanation and strategies.* University of California: Learning from Text Project. (ERIC Document Reproduction Service No. ED 239 231)

Crismore, A. (1984). *Metadiscourse as rhetorical act in social studies texts: Its effect on student performance and attitudes.* Unpublished doctoral dissertation, University of Illinois.

Cronbach, L. J. (1971). Comments on mastery learning and its implications for curricular development. In E. Eisner (Ed.), *Confronting curriculum reform.* Boston: Little, Brown.

Cuban, L. (1984). *How teachers taught.* New York: Longman.

Cusick, P. A. (1983). *The egalitarian ideal and the American high school.* New York: Longman.

Dahl, P. R., & Samuels, S. J. (1975). *Teaching high speed word recognition and comprehension skills.* Unpublished manuscript.

Dale, E., & Chall, J. (February 18, 1948). A formula for predicting readability. *Educational Research Bulletin, 27,* 37–54.

Daly, J. A., & Hailey, J. L. (1984). Putting the situation into writing research: State and disposition as parameters of writing apprehension. In R. Beach & L. Bridwell (Eds.), *New directions in composition research.* New York: Guilford Press.

Daly, J. A., & Shamo, W. (1978). Writing apprehension and occupational choice. *Research in the Teaching of English, 11,* 119–126.

Davidson, H. P. (1931). An experimental study of bright, average, and dull children at the four year mental level. *Genetic Psychology Monographs, 9,* 119–287.

Davis, F. B. (1968). Research in comprehension in reading. *Reading Research Quarterly, 3,* 499–545.

Davison, A., & Kantor, R. N. (1982). On the failure of readability formulas to define readable texts. A case study from adaptations. *Reading Research Quarterly, 17*(2), 187–209.

deCharms, R. (1972). Personal causation training in the schools. *Journal of Applied Social Psychology, 2,* 95–113.

DeMott, B. (1964). The math wars. In R. W. Heath (Ed.), *New curricula* (pp. 54–67). New York: Harper & Row.

DePillis, S., & Singer, H. (1985, December). *Reading achievement of German and American females and males at the fourth and sixth grade levels.* (ERIC Document Reproduction Service No. ED 270 737)

Dillner, H. (1971). The effectiveness of a cross-age tutoring design in teaching remedial reading in the secondary schools. *Dissertation Abstracts,* 6075.

Dolch, E. (1952). *Dolch basic sight words.* Champaign, IL: Garrard Press.

Dolciani, M. P., & Wooton, W. (1973). *Book one: Modern algebra: Structure and method* (rev. ed.). Boston: Houghton Mifflin.

Donlan, D. (1973). Implications of elementary school practice on small group instruction. *Arizona English Bulletin, 15,* 82–86.

Donlan, D. (1974). In the classroom: Nonverbal responses. *California English, 10,* 14.

Donlan, D. (1976). Multiple text programs in literature. *Journal of Reading, 19*, 312–319.

Donlan, D. (1980). Locating main ideas in history textbooks. *Journal of Reading, 24*(2), 135–140.

Donlan, D. (1985a). Teaching students to understand history graphically. *Social Education, 49*, 237–239.

Donlan, D. (1985b). Using the DRA to teach literary comprehension at three response levels. *Journal of Reading, 28*, 408–15.

Donlan, D., & Singer, H. (1979). Active comprehension of short stories. In M. Douglass (Ed.), *Claremont reading conference's forty-third yearbook* (pp. 156–162). Claremont, CA: Claremont Reading Conference, Claremont Graduate School.

Downing, J., & Oliver, P. (1973–74). The child's conception of "a word." *Reading Research Quarterly, 9*, 568–582.

Dreher, M. J. (1985). Spontaneous instantiation of general terms. In H. Singer & R. B. Ruddell (Eds.), *Theoretical models and processes of reading* (3rd ed., pp. 426–433). Newark, DE: International Reading Association.

Dreher, M., & Singer, H. (1984). Making standardized tests work for you. *The Principal, 63*(4), 20–24.

Dreher, M. J., & Singer, H. (1986, July). *Affective processes involved in reading comprehension.* Paper presented at the International Reading Association's Eleventh World Congress on Reading, London, England.

Dreher, M. J., Singer, H., & Letteer, C. A. (1987). Explicitness in sixth-grade social studies textbooks. *Thirty-sixth Yearbook of the National Reading Conference.* Rochester, NY: National Reading Conference.

Duin, A. H., & Furniss, D. (1984). *Revising expository prose from the perspective of composition instructors: An analysis and assessment.* Paper presented at the National Reading Conference, St. Petersburg, FL.

Dunbar, P. L. (1968). We wear the mask. In A. Adoff (Ed.), *I am the darker brother* (p. 86). New York: Macmillan.

Duncan, L. (1978). *Killing Mr. Griffin.* NY: Dell.

Dupuis, M. M., Askov, E. N., & Lee, J. W. (1979). Changing attitudes toward content area reading: The content area reading project. *Journal of Educational Research, 73*(2), 66–74.

Durkin, D. (1962). Reading instruction and the five year old child. In J. A. Figurel (Ed.), *Challenge and experiment in reading* (Proceedings of the Seventh Annual Conference of the International Reading Association). Newark, DE: International Reading Association.

Durkin, D. (1964). *Children who read early.* Columbia University: Teachers College Press.

Durkin, D. (1978–79). What classroom observations reveal about reading comprehension instruction. *Reading Research Quarterly, 14*, 481–533.

Durrell, D. D. (1940). *Improvement of basic reading abilities.* New York: World Book.

Dyson, A. H. (1987). *Unintentional helping in the primary grades: Writing in the children's world* (Tech. Rep. No. 2). Berkeley: University of California, Center for the Study of Writing.

Earle, R. A. (1969a). Use of the structured overview in mathematics classes. In H. L. Herber & P. L. Sanders (Eds.), *Research in reading in the content areas: First year report.* Syracuse University: Reading and Language Arts Center.

Earle, R. A. (1969b). Developing and using study guides. In Harold L. Herber & Peter L. Sanders (Eds.), *Research in reading in the content areas: First year report* (pp. 71–92). Syracuse University: Reading and Language Arts Center.

Earle, R. A. (1976). *Teaching reading and mathematics.* Reading Aids Series. Newark, DE: International Reading Association.

Earle, R., & Barron, R. F. (1973). An approach for teaching vocabulary in content subjects. In H. L. Herber & R. F. Barron (Eds.), *Research in reading in the content areas: Second year report* (pp. 84–100). Syracuse University: Reading and Language Arts Center.

Earp, N. W. (1970). Procedures for teaching reading in mathematics. *The Arithmetic Teacher, 17*, 575–579.

Education Commission of the States. (1980). Department of Research and Information. *States activity—Minimum competency testing.* Washington, DC: Education Commission of the States.

Educational Test Service. (1959). *Sequential test of educational progress: Reading. Form 1A.* Reading, MA: Addison-Wesley.

Educational Testing Service. (February, 1977). *An ETS Information report: Basic skills around the nation.*

Ehman, L., Mehlinger, H., & Patrick, J. (1974). *Toward effective instruction in secondary social studies.* Boston: Houghton Mifflin.

Elliot, S. N. (1980). *Sixth grade and college students' metacognitive knowledge of prose organization and study strategies.* Paper presented at the American Educational Research Association's Annual Meeting, Boston, MA.

Ellson, D. G., Barker, L., Engle, T. L., & Kampwerth, L. (1965). Programmed tutoring: A teaching aid and a research tool. *Reading Research Quarterly, 1*, 107–127.

Emig, J. (1971). *The composing processes of twelfth graders.* Urbana, IL: National Council of Teachers of English.

Emmer, E. T., Everston, C. M., Sanford, J. P., Clements, B. S., & Worsham, M. E. (1984). *Classroom management for secondary teachers.* Englewood Cliffs, NJ: Prentice-Hall.

Estes, T. H. (1971). A scale to measure attitudes toward reading. *Journal of Reading, 15,* 135–138.

Estes, T. H. (1973). Guiding reading in social studies. In H. L. Herber & R. F. Barron (Eds.), *Research in reading in the content areas: Second year report* (pp. 58–63). Syracuse University: Reading and Language Arts Center.

Estes, T. H., Mills, D. C., & Barron, R. F. (1969). Three methods of introducing students to a reading-learning task in two content subjects. In H. L. Herber & P. L. Sanders (Eds.), *Research in reading in the content areas: First year report.* Syracuse University: Reading and Language Arts Center.

Estes, T. H., & Piercey, D. (1973). Secondary reading requirements: A report on the states. *Journal of Reading, 17,* 20–24.

Evans, H. M. (1972). Remedial reading in secondary schools—still a matter of faith. *Journal of Reading, 16,* 111–114.

Evans, K. M. (1966). Group methods. *Education Research, 9,* 44–50.

Faigley, L., Daly, J. A., & Witte, S. (1981). *The effects of writing apprehension upon writing performance and competence.* Paper presented at the American Educational Research Conference in Los Angeles.

Farrell, R. T., & Cirrincione, J. M. (1984). State certification requirements in reading for content area teachers. *Journal of Reading, 28*(2), 152–158.

Fay, L. (1965). Reading study skills: Math and science. In J. A. Figurel (Ed.), *Reading and inquiry.* Newark, DE: International Reading Association.

Feeman, G. F. (1973). Reading and mathematics. *The Arithmetic Teacher, 20,* 523–529.

Feirer, J. L. (1975). *Wood materials and processes.* Peoria, IL: Charles A. Bennet.

Fidel, E. A., & Berger, T. M. (Eds.). (1972). *Senior high school library catalog* (10th ed.). New York: H. W. Wilson Co.

Fidel, E. A., & Bogart, G. L. (Eds.). (1970). *Junior high school library catalog* (2nd ed.). New York: H. W. Wilson Co. Annual Supplements.

Fillmore, C. J. (1968). The case for case. In E. Back & R. G. Harms (Eds.), *Universals in linguistic theory.* New York: Holt, Rinehart & Winston.

Fitzgerald, F. (1979). America revisited: History schoolbooks in the twentieth century. Boston, MA: Little, Brown.

Flanders, N. (1954). *Teaching with groups.* Minneapolis: Burgess Publishing.

Flesch, R. F. (1949). *The art of readable writing.* New York: Harper & Row.

Flesch, R. (1981). *Why Johnny still can't read.* New York: Harper & Row.

Flood, J., Lapp, D., Singer, H., & Mathison, C.

(1985). *Teacher and text feature effects upon students' comprehension.* Paper read at the Annual Convention of the International Reading Association.

Fortier, G. (1983). Reading in the future: The brain language, or how to read without the eyes. *Journal of Reading, 26,* 164–168.

Fraenkel, J. R. (1973). *Helping students think and value.* Englewood Cliffs, NJ: Prentice-Hall.

Fraenkel, J. R. (1980). *Helping students think and value: Strategies for teaching the social studies.* Englewood Cliffs, NJ: Prentice-Hall.

Franks, J. J., Nye, N. J., Auble, P. M., Mezynski, K. J., Perfetto, G. A., Bransford, J. D., Stein, B. S., & Littlefield, J. (1982). Learning from explicit versus implicit texts. *Journal of Experimental Psychology: General, 111,* 414–422.

Frase, L. T. (1967). Learning from prose material: Length of passage, knowledge of results, and position of questions. *Journal of Educational Psychology, 58,* 266–272.

Frase, L. T. (1968a). Effect of question location, pacing, and mode on retention of prose material. *Journal of Educational Psychology, 59,* 244–249.

Frase, L. T. (1968b). Some data concerning the mathemagenic hypothesis. *American Educational Research Journal, 5,* 181–189.

Frase, L. T. (1969a). Paragraph organization of written materials: The influence of conceptual clustering upon the level and organization of recall. *Journal of Educational Psychology, 60,* 394–401.

Fredericksen, C. H. (1972). Effect of talk-induced cognitive operations on comprehension and memory processes. In J. B. Carroll & R. O. Freedle (Eds.), *Language comprehension and the acquisition of knowledge.* Washington, DC: V. H. Winston.

Fredericksen, C. H. (1975). Representing logical and semantic structure of knowledge derived from discourse. *Cognitive Psychology, 7,* 371–458.

Freed, B. (1973). Secondary reading—state of the art. *Journal of Reading, 17,* 195–201.

Fry, E. (1968). A readability formula that saves time. *Journal of Reading, 11* 513–16, 575–78.

Fry, E. B. (1977). Fry's readability graph: Clarifications, validity, and extension to level 17. *Journal of Reading, 21,* 242–252.

Fry, E. (1981). Graphical literacy. *Journal of Reading, 25,* 383–389.

Fry, E. (1983). Introducing the writeability concept. In H. Singer & T. W. Bean (Eds.), *Learning from text: Selection of friendly texts* (Proceedings of Arrowhead Conference on Learning from Text, July 27–29, 1983). Riverside: University of California, Learning from Text Project. (ERIC Document Reproduction Service No. ED 251 812)

Fry, E. (1988). Writeability: The principles of writing for increased comprehension. In B. L. Zakaluk & S. J. Samuels (Eds.), *Readability: Its past, present, and future* (pp. 77–95). Newark, DE: International Reading Association.

Gagne, R. M. (1962). The acquisition of knowledge. *Psychological Review, 69,* 355–65.

Galambos, J. A., Abelson, R. P., & Black, J. B. (1986). *Knowledge structures.* Hillsdale, NJ: Lawrence Erlbaum Associates.

Gans, R. (1940). *A study of critical reading comprehension in the intermediate grades.* (Teachers College Contributions to Education, No. 811.) New York: Bureau of Publications, Columbia University.

Gates, A. I. (1921). An experimental and statistical study of reading and reading tests. *Journal of Educational Psychology, 12,* 303–314.

Gates, A. I. (1926). A study of the role of visual perception, intelligence and certain associative processes in reading and spelling. *Journal of Educational Psychology, 17,* 433–445.

Gates, A. I. (1927). *The improvement of reading.* New York: Macmillan.

Gates, A. I. (1961). Vocabulary control in basal reading material. *Reading Teacher, 15,* 81–85.

Gates, A. I., & Bond, G. L. (1936). Reading readiness: A study of factors determining success and failure in beginning reading. *Teachers College Record, 37,* 679–685.

Gates, A. I., Bond, G. L., & Russell, D. H. (1939). *Methods of determining reading readiness.* New York: Bureau of Publications, Teachers College, Columbia University.

Gere, A. R. (1985). *Roots in the sawdust: Writing to learn across the curriculum.* Urbana: National Council of Teachers of English.

Gibson, E. (1965). Learning to read. Science, 148, 1066–1072.

Gibson, E. (1976). Learning to read. In H. Singer & R. B. Ruddell (Eds.), *Theoretical models and processes of reading* (2nd ed., pp. 252–269). Newark, DE: International Reading Association.

Gibson, E. (1985). Learning to read. In H. Singer & R. B. Ruddell (Eds.), *Theoretical models and processes of reading* (3rd, ed., pp. 222–238). Newark, DE: International Reading Association.

Gibson, E. J., & Levin, H. (1975). *The psychology of reading.* Cambridge, MA: MIT Press.

Gilbert, D. W. (October, 1955). How well do you READ? *California Monthly* (Alumni magazine of the University of California, Berkeley).

Gilbert, D. W. (1956). *Power and speed in reading.* Englewood Cliffs, NJ: Prentice-Hall.

Gilbert, L. C. (1940). The effect on silent reading of attempting to follow oral reading. *Elementary School Journal, 40,* 614–621.

Gilbert, L. C. (1953). Functional motor efficiency of the eyes and its relation to reading. Berkeley: University of California, *Publications in Education, 2,* 159–232.

Gilbert, L. C. (1959). Speed of processing visual stimuli and its relation to reading. *Journal of Educational Psychology, 50,* 8–14.

Glaser, R. (1962). Psychology and instructional technology. In R. Glasser (Ed.), *Training research and education.* Pittsburgh: Pittsburgh Press.

Gleason, H. A., Jr. (1961). *An introduction to descriptive linguistics* (rev. ed.). New York: Holt, Rinehart & Winston.

Goodlad, J. I. (1983). *A place called school.* New York: McGraw-Hill.

Goodman, K. S. (1966, 1970). A psycholinguistic view of reading comprehension. In G. B. Schick & M. M. May (Eds.), *New frontiers in college-adult reading* (Fifteenth Yearbook of the National Reading Conference). Reprinted in H. Singer & R. B. Ruddell (Eds.), *Theoretical models and processes of reading* (1st ed.). Newark, DE: International Reading Association.

Goodman, K. S. (1976). Behind the eye: What happens in reading. In H. Singer & R. B. Ruddell (Eds.), *Theoretical models and processes of reading.* Newark, DE: International Reading Association.

Goodman, Y., & Burke, C. L. (1972). *The reading miscue inventory.* New York: Macmillan. (out of print)

Gough, P. (1979). Introducing children to books via television. *The Reading Teacher, 32,* 458–462.

Gough, P. (1976). One second of reading. In H. S. Singer & R. B. Ruddell (Eds.), *Theoretical models and processes of reading* (2nd edition, pp. 509–535). Newark, DE: International Reading Association.

Gough, P. (1984). Word recognition. In P. D. Pearson (Ed.), *Handbook of research on reading* (pp. 225–254). New York: Longman.

Gough, P. (1985a, Spring). Colloquium on phonemic awareness conducted at the University of California, Riverside.

Gough, P. (1985b). One second of reading. In H. Singer & R. B. Ruddell (Eds.), *Theoretical models and processes of reading* (3rd ed., pp. 661–688). Newark, DE: International Reading Association.

Graesser, A. (1983). An application and analysis of friendly text criteria: Introductory psychology texts. In H. Singer & T. Bean (Eds.), *Selection of friendly texts* (Proceedings of the Lake Arrowhead Conference on Learning from Texts). Riverside: University of California, Learning from Text Project.

Graves, D. H. (1979). What children show us about revision. *Language Arts, 56,* 312–19.

Gray, W. S., & Leary, B. (1935). *What makes a book readable?* Chicago, IL: University of Chicago Press.

Grimes, J. E. (1975). *The thread of discourse.* The Hague: Mouton.

Guest, A. (1969). Beauty is truth. In J. Cline & K. Williams (Eds.), *Voices in literature, language, and composition,* (Vol. 3, pp. 435–445). Boston: Ginn and Company.

Gundlach, B. H. (1961). *The Laidlaw glossary of arithmetical-mathematical terms.* River Forest, IL: Laidlaw.

Guszak, F. J. (1967). Teacher questioning and reading. *Reading Teacher, 21,* 227–234.

Guthrie, J. T. (1973). Models of reading and reading disability. *Journal of Educational Psychology, 65,* 9–18.

Guthrie, J. T. (1978a). Story comprehension and fables. *The Reading Teacher, 31,* 110–112.

Guthrie, J. T. (1978b). Research: Context and memory. *Journal of Reading, 22,* 266–268.

Guthrie, J. T. (1981, March). Forms and functions of textbooks. *Journal of Reading,* 554–556.

Guthrie, J. T. (1984). Literacy for science and technology. *Journal of Reading, 27*(5), 478–480.

Hafner, L. E. (1977). *Developmental reading in middle and secondary schools: Foundations, strategies, and skills for teaching.* New York: Macmillan.

Halliday, M. A. K., & Hasan, R. (1976). *Cohesion in English.* London: Longman.

Harlstorne, N. (Ed.). (1977). News of the basic skills assessment program. *Educational Testing Service, 1*(2).

Harris, A. J. (1970). *How to increase reading ability* (5th ed.). New York: McKay.

Harris, A. J., & Sipay, E. R. (1975). *How to increase reading ability* (6th ed.). New York: McKay.

Harris, L. & Associates. (1970, November 18). Survival literacy study. *Congressional Record,* E9719–9723.

Hater, M. A., Kane, R. B., & Byrne, M. A. (1974). Building reading skills in the mathematics class. *The Arithmetic Teacher, 21,* 663–668.

Hayes, D. A., & Tierney, R. J. (1982). Developing readers' knowledge through analogy. *Reading Research Quarterly, 17,* 256–280.

Heath, R. W. (Ed.). (1964). *New curricula.* New York: Harper & Row.

Heller, J. H. (1974). Learning from prose text: Effects of readability level, inserted question difficulty, and individual differences. *Journal of Educational Psychology, 66,* 202–211.

Herber, H. L. (1970a). *Teaching reading in content areas.* Englewood Cliffs, NJ: Prentice-Hall.

Herber, H. (1970b). Reading in content areas: A district develops its own personnel. *Journal of Reading, 13,* 587–592.

Herber, H. (consultant). (1976). *Scholastic's GO: Reading in the content areas.* Englewood Cliffs, NJ: Scholastic Book Services.

Herber, H. (1978). *Teaching reading in content areas* (2nd ed.). Englewood Cliffs, NJ: Prentice-Hall.

Herber, H. L. (1984). Subject matter texts—reading to learn: Response to remarks by T. H. Anderson & B. B. Armbruster. *Learning to read in American schools.* Hillsdale, NJ: Lawrence Erlbaum Associates.

Herber, H., & Barron, R. F. (Eds.). (1973). *Research in reading in the content areas: Second year report.* Syracuse University: Reading and Language Arts Center.

Herber, H., & Nelson, J. (1976). *Reading across the curriculum.* Homer, NY: Trica Consultants.

Herber, H., & Sanders, P. L. (Eds.). (1969). *Research in reading in the content areas: First year report.* Syracuse University: Reading and Language Arts Center.

Hersey, J. (1946). *Hiroshima.* New York: Knopf.

Hiebert, E. H., Englert, C. S., & Brennan, S. (1983). Awareness of text structure in recognition and production of expository discourse. *Journal of Reading Behavior, 15*(4), 63–79.

Hilgard, E., & Bower, G. (1975). *Theories of learning* (4th ed.). New York: Appleton-Century-Crofts.

Hill, W. (1971). Characteristics of secondary reading: 1940–1970. In F. P. Greene (Ed.), *Twentieth Yearbook of the National Reading Conference.* Chicago, IL: The National Reading Conference.

Hill, W. (1969). *Learning through discussion.* Beverly Hills, CA: Sage Publications.

Hobson v. Hansen. (DDC 1967). 269 F. Supp. 401.

Hochberg, J., & Brooks, V. (1970). Reading as an intentional behavior. In H. Singer & R. B. Ruddell (Eds.), *Theoretical models and processes of reading* (1st ed., pp. 242–251). Newark, DE: International Reading Association.

Holmes, J. A. (1954). Factors underlying major reading disabilities at the college level. *Genetic Psychology Monographs, 49,* 3–95.

Holmes, J. A. (1965). Basic assumptions underlying the substrata-factor theory. *Reading Research Quarterly, 1,* 5–27.

Holmes, J. A., & Singer, H. (1961). *The substrata-factor theory: Substrata-factor differences underlying reading ability in known groups* (Final Rep. No. 538). Washington, DC: U.S. Office of Education.

Holmes, J. A., & Singer, H. (1966). *Speed and power of reading in high school.* U.S. Government Printing Office, Cooperative Research Monograph No. 14, Superintendent of Documents Catalog No. FS 5.230:30016.

Horn, V. (1973). One way to read a paragraph. *Elementary English, 50,* 871–874.

Horowitz, R. (1985a). Text patterns: Part I. *Journal of Reading, 28*(5), 448–454.

Horowtiz, R. (1985b). Text patterns: Part II. *Journal of Reading, 30*(6), 534–541.

Hoskins, S. B. (1986, March). Text superstructures. *Journal of Reading,* 538–543.

Hunkins, F. P. (1976). *Involving students in questioning.* Boston: Allyn & Bacon.

Inhelder, B., & Piaget, J. (1958). *The growth of logical thinking from childhood to adolescence.* New York: Basic Books.

Irwin, J., & Davis, C. A. (1980). Assessing readability. The checklist approach. *Journal of Reading, 24,* 124–130.

James, G. & James, R. C. (1959). *Mathematics dictionary.* Princeton, NJ: D. Van Nostrand.

Jastak, J. F., & Jastak, J. R. (1965). *Wide range achievement test (WRAT).* Austin, TX: Guidance Testing Associates.

Javal, L. E. (1879). Essai sur la Physiologie de Lecture. *Annales d'Oculistique, 82,* 243–253.

Jencks, C. S. (1975). Effects of high schools on their students. *Harvard Educational Review, 45,* 273–324.

Jenkins, J. R., Pany, D., & Schreck, J. (August 1978). *Vocabulary and reading comprehension: Instructional effects* (Tech. Rep. No. 100). Urbana: University of Illinois, Center for the Study of Reading.

Johns, J. L., & McNamara, L. (1980). The SQ3R study technique: A forgotten research target. *Journal of Reading, 23,* 705–8.

Johnson, D., Anderson, R., Hansen, T., & Klassen, D. (1980). Computer literacy—What is it? *Mathematics Teacher, 73,* 91–96.

Johnson, H. C. (1944). The effect of instruction in mathematical vocabulary upon problem solving in arithmetic. *Journal of Educational Research, 38*(2), 97–110.

Johnson, O. (1950). Filming a cannibal chief. In G. Wagner, G. Person, & L. Wilcox (Eds.), *Reading skill builder, level VI, part I.* Pleasantville, NY: Reader's Digest.

Johnston, J. C., & McClelland, J. (1981). In J. C. Johnston. Understanding word perception: Clues from studying the word-superiority effect. In O. J. L. Tzeng & H. Singer (Eds.), *Perception of print: Reading research in experimental psychology* (pp. 65–84). Hillsdale, NJ: Lawrence Erlbaum Associates.

Johnston, P. (1985). Understanding reading disability: A case study approach. *Harvard Educational Review, 55*(2), 153–177.

Joyce, B., & Weil, M. (1986). *Models of teaching.* Englewood Cliffs, NJ: Prentice-Hall.

Judd, C., & Buswell, G. T. (1922). Silent reading: A study of the various types. *Supplementary Educational Monographs, 23.* Chicago: University of Chicago Press.

Just, M. A., & Carpenter, P. A. (1985). A theory of reading: From eye fixations to comprehension. *Psychological Review,* 1980, *87,* 329–354. Reprinted in H. Singer & R. B. Ruddell (Eds.), *Theoretical models and processes of reading* (3rd ed., pp. 174–208). Newark, DE: International Reading Association.

Kagan, S. (1985). *Cooperative learners resources for teachers.* Riverside: University of California.

Kantor, K. J. (1984). Classroom contexts and the development of writing intuitions: An ethnographic case study. In R. Beach & L. Bridwell (Eds.), *New directions in composition research* (pp. 72–94). New York: Guilford Press.

Katz, I. C., & Singer, H. (1982). The substrata-factor theory of reading: Differential development of subsystems underlying reading comprehension in the first year. In J. A. Niles & L. A. Harris (Eds.), *New inquiry in reading research and instruction* (Thirty-First Yearbook of the National Reading Conference). Rochester, NY: The National Reading Conference.

Katz, I., & Singer, H. (1984). The substrata-factor theory of reading: Subsystem patterns underlying achievement in beginning reading. In J. A. Niles (Ed.), *Thirty-Third Yearbook of the National Reading Conference.* Rochester, NY: The National Reading Conference.

Kelley, J. (1973). Effectiveness of a performance contracting program on reading and mathematics relative to educationally deprived secondary students. *Dissertation Abstracts,* 4567a.

Kenworthy, L. S. (1973). *Social studies for the 70's.* Lexington, MA: Xerox.

Keyes, D. (1969). Flowers for Algernon. In J. Cline, K. Williams, B. Mahoney, & K. Dziuk (Eds.), *Voices in literature, language, and composition, 4.* (pp. 25–41). Boston: Ginn.

King, J. R., Biggs, S., & Lipsky, S. (1984). Students' self-questioning and summarizing as reading study strategies. *Journal of Reading Behavior, 16*(3), 205–18.

Kintsch, W. (1974). *The representation of meaning in memory.* Hillsdale, NJ: Lawrence Erlbaum Associates.

Kintsch, W., & Vipond, D. (1974). Reading comprehension and readability in educational practice and psychological theory. In L. Nilsson (Ed.), *Proceedings of the conference on memory.* Hillsdale, NJ: Lawrence Erlbaum Associates.

Kintsch, W., & Keenan, J. M. (1973). Reading rate as a function of number of propositions in the base structure of sentences. *Cognitive Psychology, 6,* 253–274.

Kintsch, W., Mandel, T. S., & Kozminsky, E. (1977). Summarizing scrambled stories. *Memory and Cognition, 5,* 547–552.

Kintsch, W., & van Dijk, T. A. (1978). Toward a model

of text comprehension and production. *Psychological Review, 85,* 363–394.

Kintsch, W., & Yarbrough, J. C. (1982). Role of rhetorical structure in text comprehension. *Journal of Educational Psychology, 74*(6), 828–834.

Kirby, D., & Liner, T. (1981). *Inisde out: Developmental strategies for teaching writing.* Montclair: NJ: Boynton Cook.

Klare, G. R. (1963). *The measurement of readability.* Ames, IA: Iowa State University Press.

Klare, G. R. (1974–1975). Assessing readability. *Reading Research Quarterly, 10*(1), 61–102.

Klare, G. (1984). Readability. In P. D. Pearson (Ed.), *Handbook of reading research* (pp. 681–744). New York: Longman.

Knight, L. N., & Hargis, C. H. (1977). Math language ability and its relationship to reading in math. *Language Arts, 54*(4), 423–428.

Knowles, J. (1959). *A separate peace.* New York: Bantam.

Kohlberg, L. (1968). The child as moral philosopher. *Psychology Today, 2,* 25–30.

Kolers, P. A. (1975). Memorial consequences of automatized encoding. *Journal of Experimental Psychology: Human Learning and Memory, 1*(6), 689–701.

Kolers, P. A. (1979). Reading and knowing. *Canadian Journal of Psychology, 33*(2), 106–107.

LaBerge, D. (1979). The perception of units in beginning reading. In L. B. Resnick & P. A. Weaver (Eds.), *Theory and practice of early reading* (Vol. 3). Hillsdale, NJ: Lawrence Erlbaum Associates.

LaBerge, D., & Samuels, S. J. (1976). Toward a theory of automatic information processing in reading. In H. Singer & R. B. Ruddell (Eds.), *Theoretical models and processes of reading* (2nd ed., pp. 548–579). Newark, DE: International Reading Association.

LaBerge, D., & Samuels, S. J. (1985). Toward a theory of automatic information processing in reading. In H. Singer & R. B. Ruddell (Eds.), *Theoretical models and processes of reading* (3rd ed., pp. 689–718). Newark, DE: International Reading Association.

Langer, J. A. (1983). Inconsiderate text: Text properties that can inhibit the growth of meaning. In H. Singer & T. Bean (Eds.), *Proceedings of the Lake Arrowhead conference on learning from text: Selection of friendly texts* (pp. 143–149). Riverside: University of California, Learning from Text Project.

Lee, D. M. (1968). Do we group in an individualized program? *Childhood Education, 45,* 197–199.

LeFevre, C. (1964). *Linguistics and the teaching of reading.* New York: McGraw-Hill.

Letteer, C., & Singer, H. (1985). *Content analysis of the explication of sixth grade science textbooks.* Un-

published paper presented in a course at the University of California, Riverside.

Levin, J. R. (1976). Comprehending what we read: An outsider looks in. In H. Singer & R. B. Ruddell (Eds.), *Theoretical models and processes of reading* (pp. 320–330). Newark, DE: International Reading Association.

Lindille, W. J. (1970). The effects of syntax and vocabulary upon the difficulty of verbal arithmetic problems with fourth grade students. *Dissertation Abstracts International, 30,* 4310A. (University Microfilms, No. 70-7957)

Lipton, J. P., & Liss, J. A. (1978). Attitudes of content area teachers towards teaching reading. *Reading Improvement, 15*(4), 294–300.

Litsey, D. M. (1969). Small-group training and the English classroom. *English Journal, 58,* 920–927.

Lovell, K., Johnson, E., & Platts, D. (1963). A further study of the educational progress of children who had remedial instruction. *British Journal of Educational Psychology, 33,* 3–9.

Maclean, R. (1988). Two paradoxes of phonics. *The Reading Teacher, 41*(6), 514–519.

MacGinitie, W. H. (1984). Readability as a solution adds to the problem. In R. C. Anderson, J. Osborn, & R. J. Tierney (Eds.), *Learning to read in American schools: Basal readers and content text* (pp. 141–152). Hillsdale, NJ: Lawrence Erlbaum Associates.

MacMillan, D., Jones, R., & Aloia, G. (1974). The mentally retarded label: A theoretical analysis and review of research. *American Journal of Mental Deficiency, 79,* 241–261.

Mager, R. F. (1962). *Preparing instructional objectives for programmed instruction.* Palo Alto, CA: Fearon Publishers.

Mallinson, G. G., Sturm, H. E., & Mallinson, L. M. (1952). The reading difficulty of textbooks for high school physics. *Science Education, 36,* 19–23.

Mandler, J. M. (1984). *Stories, scripts, and scenes: Aspects of schema theory.* Hillsdale, NJ: Lawrence Erlbaum Associates.

Mandler, J. M., & Johnson, N. S. (1977). Remembrance of things parsed: Story structure and recall. *Cognitive Psychology, 7,* 111–151.

Marks, C. B., Doctorow, M. J., & Wittrock, M. C. (1974). Word frequency and reading comprehension. *Journal of Educational Psychology, 67,* 259–262.

Marshall, N. (1976). *The structure of semantic memory for text.* Unpublished doctoral dissertation, Cornell University.

Marshall, N., & Glock, M. D. (1978–1979). Comprehension of connected discourse: A study into the relation between the structure of the text and information recalled. *Reading Research Quarterly, 14,* 10–56.

Mauldin, B. (1968). *Up front.* New York: Norton

McCallister, J. M. (1932). *Remedial and corrective instruction in reading.* New York: Appleton.

McClelland, J. L., & Rumelhart, D. E. (1981, 1985). An interactive model of context effects in letter perception. Part I: An account of basic findings. *Psychological Review, 88,* 375–407. Reprinted in H. Singer & R. Ruddell (Eds.), *Theoretical models and processes of reading* (3rd ed.) (pp. 276–318). Newark, DE: International Reading Association.

McConkie, G. W., & Rayner, K. (1976). An on-line computer technique for studying reading: Identifying the perceptual span. In H. Singer & R. B. Ruddell (Eds.), *Theoretical models and processes of reading* (2nd ed.) (pp. 163–175). Newark, DE: International Reading Association.

McCullough, C. M. (1957). Responses of elementary school children to common types of reading comprehension questions. *Journal of Educational Research, 51,* 65–70.

McCullough, C. M. (1971). What teachers should know about language and thought. In R. Hodges & R. Rudorf (Eds.), *Learning to read* (pp. 202–215). New York: Houghton Mifflin.

McDermott, R. P. (1985). Achieving school failure: An anthropological approach to illiteracy and social stratification. In H. Singer & R. B. Ruddell (Eds.), *Theoretical models and processes of reading* (3rd ed., pp. 558–594). Hillsdale, NJ: Lawrence Erlbaum Associates.

McGee, L. M. (1982). Awareness of text structure: Effects on children's recall of expository text. *Reading Research Quarterly, 17*(4), 581–590.

McClain, L. J. (1981). Study guides: Potential assets in content classrooms. *Journal of Reading, 24,* 321–25.

McLaughlin, G. H. (1969). SMOG grading—A new readability formula. *Journal of Reading, 12,* 639–646.

McNeil, J. M., & Keislar, E. (1964). Programmed instruction versus usual classroom procedures in teaching boys to read. *American Educational Research Journal, 1,* 113–119.

Merriam-Webster. (1963). *Webster's seventh new collegiate dictionary.* Springfield, MA: G. & C. Merriam Company.

Meyer, B. J. F. (1975). *The organization of prose and its effects on memory.* Amsterdam: North-Holland.

Meyer, B. J. F., Brandt, D. M., & Bluth, G. J. (1980). A role of rhetorical use of top level structure in text: Key for reading comprehension of ninth grade students. *Reading Research Quarterly, 16*(1), 72–103.

Meyer, B. J. F., & Freedle, R. O. (1984). Effects of discourse type on recall. *American Educational Research Journal, 21*(1), 121–144.

Meyer, B. J. F., & Rice, G. E. (1984). The structure of text. In P. D. Pearson (Ed.), *The handbook of reading research.* New York: Longman.

Mickulecky, L., & Strange, R. L. (1986). Effective literacy training programs for adults in business and municipal employment. In J. Orasanu (Ed.), *Reading comprehension: From research to practice* (pp. 319–334). Hillsdale, NJ: Lawrence Erlbaum Associates.

Moffett, J. (1968). *A student-centered language arts curriculum, grades K–13: A handbook for teachers.* Boston: Houghton Mifflin.

Moffett, J., & Wagner, B. J. (1983). *Student-centered language arts and reading, K–13: A handbook for teachers.* Boston: Houghton Mifflin Co.

Moldenhauer, D. L., & Miller, W. H. (1980). Television and reading achievement. *Journal of Reading, 23,* 615–619.

Montague, W. E., & Carter, J. F. (1973). Vividness of imagery in reading connected discourse. *Journal of Educational Psychology, 58,* 707–718.

Moore, W. (1969). About reading in the content fields. *English Journal, 58,* 707–718.

Morgan, A., Rachelson, S., & Lloyd, B. (1977). Science activities as contributors to development of reading skills in first grade students. *Science Education, 61*(2), 135–144.

Murphy, H., & Durrell, D. D. (1965). *Reading readiness analysis.* New York: Harcourt Brace Jovanovich.

National Assessment of Educational Progress. (1985). *The Reading Report Card No. 15R01.* Princeton, NJ: National Assessment of Educational Progress.

National Council of Mathematics. (1977). Position statement on basic skills. *The Arithmetic Teacher, 25,* 18–22.

National Science Board Commission on Precollege Education in Mathematics, Science and Technology. (1983). *Educating Americans for the 21st Century.* Washington, DC: National Science Board.

Nelson, F. (1970). Statistics and reading: A commentary on chapters 1 and 3. *Basic studies in reading.* New York: Basic Books.

Neuman, S. B. (1984). Teletext/videotext: The future of the print media. *Journal of Reading, 27,* 340–344.

Neuman, S. B., & Prowda, P. (1982). Television viewing and reading achievement. *Journal of Reading, 25,* 666–670.

Nicholson, T. (1985). The confusing world of high school reading. *Journal of Reading, 28*(6), 514–526.

Nist, S. L., Kirby, K., & Ritter, A. (1983). Teaching comprehension process using magazines, paperbacks, novels, and content area texts. *Journal of Reading, 26,* 252–261.

Nolte, R. Y., & Singer, H. (1985). Active comprehension: Teaching a process of reading comprehension and its effects on comprehension. *The Reading Teacher, 38,* 24–31.

O'Donnell, H. (1983). Beyond computer literacy. *Journal of Reading, 26,* 78–80.

O'Donnell, M., & Cooper, J. L. (1963). *The Harper & Row basic reading program: How to read in the subject matter areas, strand II.* New York: Harper & Row.

O'Hare, F. (1972). *Sentence combining: Improving student writing without formal grammar instruction.* Urbana, IL: National Council of Teachers of English.

Olson, M. W., & Longnion, B. (1982). Pattern guides: A workable alternative for content teachers. *Journal of Reading, 25,* 736–740.

O'Rourke, W. J. (1980). Research on the attitudes of secondary teachers toward teaching reading in the content areas. *Journal of Reading, 24,* 337–339.

Otto, W., & Smith, R. (1969). Junior and senior high school teachers' attitudes toward teaching reading in the content areas. In George B. Schick & Merrill M. May (Eds.), *The psychology of reading behavior.* National Reading Conference Yearbook, *10,* 49–54.

Paivio, A. (1969). Mental imagery in associative learning and memory. *Psychological Review, 76,* 241–263.

Paivio, A., Yuille, J. C., & Madigan, S. A. (1968). Concreteness, imagery, and meaningfulness values for 925 common nouns. *Journal of Experimental Psychology, 76,* 1–25.

Patberg, J., Dewitz, P., & Henning, M. J. (1984). The impact of content area reading instruction on secondary teachers. *Journal of Reading, 27*(6), 500–507.

Pearson, P. D. (1974–1975). The effects of grammatical complexity on children's comprehension, recall, and conception of certain semantic relations. *Reading Research Quarterly, 10*(2), 155–192.

Pearson, P. D., & Camperell, K. (1985). Comprehension of text structures. In H. Singer & R. B. Ruddell (Eds.), *Theoretical models and processes of reading* (3rd ed., pp. 323–342). Newark, DE: International Reading Association.

Pearson, P. D., & Johnson, D. (1978). *Teaching reading comprehension.* New York: Holt, Rinehart & Winston.

Pepper, J. (1981). Following students' suggestions for rewriting a computer programming textbook. *American Journal of Educational Research, 18,* 159–169.

Perfetti, C. A. (1975, July). *Language comprehension and fast decoding: Some psycholinguistic prerequisites for skilled reading comprehension.* Paper presented the International Reading Association seminar on the Development of Reading Comprehension, Newark, DE.

Perfetti, C. A. (1985). *Reading ability.* New York: Oxford University Press.

Perfetti, C., & Beck, I. (December 1982). *Learning to read depends on phonetic knowledge and vice-versa.*

Paper presented at the National Reading Conference, St. Petersburg, FL.

Perl, S. (1979). The composing processes of unskilled college writers. *Research in the Teaching of English, 13,* 317–336.

Petracca, J. (1969). Four eyes. In J. Cline, K. Williams, & D. Donlan (Eds.), *Voices in literature, language, and composition, 1* (pp. 2–11). Boston: Ginn.

Pichert, J. W., & Anderson, R. C. (1976). *Taking different perspectives on a story* (Tech. Rep. No. 14). Urbana-Champaign: University of Illinois, Center for the Study of Reading.

Pichert, J., & Anderson, R. C. (1977). Taking different perspectives on a story. *Journal of Educational Psychology, 69,* 309–315.

Pooley, R. C., White, L. Z., Farrell, E. J., & Mersand, J. (1968). *Exploring life through literature.* Glenview, IL: Scott, Foresman.

Potok, C. (1968). *Beyond literacy.* Invitational address to the International Reading Association, Anaheim, CA.

Powell, W. R. (1971). Validity of the IRI reading levels. *Elementary English, 48*(6), 637–642.

Preston, R. C. (1962). Reading achievement of German and American children. *School and Society, 90,* 350–354.

Pribnow, J. R. (1969). Why Johnny can't read word problems. *School Science and Mathematics, 69,* 591–598.

Pyle, E. (1943). *Brave men.* New York: Holt, Rinehart & Winston.

Raphael, T. (1986). Teaching question answer relationships, revisited. *The Reading Teacher, 40,* 516–522.

Rasco, R. W., Tennyson, R. D., & Boutwell, R. C. (1975). Imagery instructions and drawings in learning prose. *Journal of Educational Psychology, 67,* 188–192.

Ratekin, N., Simpson, M. L., Alvermann, D. E., & Dishner, E. K. (1985). Why content teachers resist reading instruction. *Journal of Reading, 28*(5), 432–437.

Readance, J. E., Bean, T. W., & Baldwin, R. S. (1981). *Content area reading: An integrated approach.* Dubuque: Kendall/Hunt.

Redd-Boyd, T. M. (1984). *Improving the comprehensibility of expository prose: Revising expository prose from the perspective of popular magazine editors.* Paper presented at the National Reading Conference, St. Petersburg Beach, FL.

Reder, L. M., Anderson, J. R., & Bjork, R. A. (1974). A semantic interpretation of encoding specificity. *Journal of Experimental Psychology, 102,* 684–686.

Resnick, L. B., & Beck, I. L. (1974). Designing instruction in reading: Interaction of theory and practice. In J. T. Guthrie (Ed.), *Aspects of reading acquisition* (pp. 180–204). Baltimore: Johns Hopkins University Press.

Richards, I. A. (1929). *Practical criticism*. New York: Harcourt, Brace & World.

Richgels, D. J., & Mateja, J. A. (1984). Integrating content and process for independence. *Journal of Reading, 27,* 424–431.

Rieck, B. J. (1977). How content teachers telegraph messages against reading. *Journal of Reading, 20,* 646–648.

Riley, J. D. (1980). Statement-based guides and quality of teacher response. *Journal of Reading, 23,* 715–20.

Riley, J. D., & Patchman, A. B. (1978). Reading mathematical word problems: Telling them how to do it. *Journal of Reading, 21,* 531–534.

Robinson, F. P. (1961). Study skills for superior students in secondary school. *The Reading Teacher, 15,* 29–33.

Robinson, F. P., & Hall, P. (1941). Studies of higher-level reading abilities. *Journal of Educational Psychology, 32,* 445–451.

Robinson, H. A. (1975). *Teaching reading and study strategies: Content areas*. Boston: Allyn & Bacon.

Roe, B. D., Ross, E. P., & Burns, P. C. (1984). *Student teaching and field experiences handbook*. Columbus: Charles E. Merrill.

Roen, D. H. (1984). The effects of cohesive conjunctions, reference, response rhetorical predicates, and topic on reading rate and written free recall. *Journal of Reading Behavior, 16*(1), 15–26.

Roen, D. H., & Grunloh, D. (1984). *Text linguistis' revisions of Cold War text*. Paper presented at the National Reading Conference, St. Petersburg, FL.

Rogers-Zegarra, H., & Singer, H. (1981). Anglo and Chicano literal and scriptal comprension of ethnic stories. In M. L. Kamil (Ed.). *Directions in reading: Research and instruction.* (pp. 203–208) Washington, DC: National Reading Conference. Reprinted in H. Singer & R. B. Ruddell (Eds.) *Theoretical models and processes of reading* (3rd ed., pp. 611–617.) Newark, DE: International Reading Association, 1985.

Rosenblatt, L. (1976). *Literature as exploration*. New York: Noble & Noble.

Rosenthal, T. L., Zimmerman, B. J., & Durning, K. (1970). Observationally induced changes in children's interrogative classes. *Journal of Educational Psychology, 16,* 681–688.

Rosten, L. (1969). Mr. KAPLAN, the comparative and the superlative. In Cline, et al. (Eds.), *Voices in literature, language and composition, 2.* Boston: Ginn.

Rothkopf, E. Z. (1966). Learning from written instructive materials: An exploration of the control of inspection behavior by test-like events. *American Educational Research Journal, 3,* 241–249.

Rothkopf, E. Z. (1976). Writing to teach and reading to learn: A perspective on the psychology of written instruction. In N. L. Gage (Ed.), *The psychology of teach-*

ing methods (Seventy-Fifth Yearbook of the National Society for the Study of Education, Part I, pp. 91–129). Chicago: University of Chicago Press.

Rothkopf, E. Z. (1982). Adjunct aids and the control of mathemagenic activities during purposeful reading. In W. Otto & S. White (Eds.), *Reading expository material* (pp. 109–138). New York: Academic Press.

Rothkopf, E. Z., & Bisbicos, E. E. (1967). Selective facilitative effects of interspersed questions on learning from written materials. *Journal of Educational Psychology, 58,* 56–61.

Ruddell, R. B. (1965). Effects of the similarity of oral and written patterns of language structure on reading comprehension. *Elementary English, 42,* 403–410.

Ruddell, R. B. (1968). *A longitudinal study of four programs of reading instruction varying in emphasis or regularity of grapheme-phoneme correspondences and language structure on reading achievement in grades two and three:* Final Report (Project Nos. 3099 and 78085). Berkeley: University of California.

Ruddell, R. B. (1974). *Reading-language instruction: Innovative practices*. Englewood Cliffs, NJ: Prentice-Hall.

Ruddell, R. B. (1976). Language acquisition and the reading process. In H. Singer & R. B. Ruddell (Eds.), *Theoretical models and processes of reading* (2nd ed., pp. 22–38). Newark, DE: International Reading Association.

Ruddell, R. B., & Boyle, O. (1984). *A study of the effects of cognitive mapping on reading comprehension and written protocols* (Tech. Rep. No. 7). Riverside: University of California, Learning from Text Project. (ERIC Document Reproduction Service No. ED 252 811)

Ruddell, R. B., & Haggard, M. R. (1985). Oral and written language acquisition and the reading process. In H. Singer & R. B. Ruddell (Eds.), *Theoretical models and processes of reading* (3rd ed., pp. 63–80). Newark, DE: International Reading Association.

Ruddell, R. B., & Williams, A. C. (1972). A research investigation of a literary teaching model: Project delta. Final Report to U.S. Department of Health, Education, and Welfare, Office of Education, EPDA Project No. 005262. Berkeley, CA: School of Education. (Multilith).

Rumelhart, D. E. (1976, 1985). *Toward an interactive model of reading*. San Diego: University of California, Center for Human Information Processing. Reprinted in H. Singer & R. B. Ruddell (Eds.), *Theoretical models and processes of reading* (3rd ed., pp. 722–750). Newark, DE: International Reading Association, 1985.

Rumelhart, D. E. (1977). Understanding and summarizing brief stories. In D. LaBerge & S. J. Samuels (Eds.), *Basic processes in reading: Perception and comprehen-*

sion (pp. 265–304). Hillsdale, NJ: Lawrence Erlbaum Associates.

Rumelhart, D. E. (1982). Understanding understanding. In J. Flood (Ed.), *Understanding reading comprehension* (pp. 1–20). Newark, DE: International Reading Association.

Rumelhart, D. et al. (1986). Parallel distributed processing: Exploration in the microstructure of cognition. Vol. 1, Cambridge, MA: MIT Press.

Rumelhart, D. et al. (1986). Parallel distribution processing: Exploration in the microstructure of cognition. Vol. 1. Cambridge, MA: MIT Press.

Russell, D. (1958). *Children's thinking*. Boston: Ginn.

Russell, D. H. (1961). Reading research that made a difference. *Elementary English, 38,* 74–78.

Russell, D. H., & Fea, H. R. (1963). Research on teaching reading. In Nathan Gage (Ed.), *Handbook of research on teaching* (pp. 845–928). Chicago: Rand McNally.

Ryan, F., & Ellis, A. K. (1974). *Instructional implications of inquiry*. Englewood Cliffs, NJ: Prentice-Hall.

Ryan, M. (1963). *Teaching the novel in paperback*. New York: Macmillan.

Sakiey, E., & Fry, E. B. (1979). *3000 instant words*. Providence, RI: Jamestown Publishers.

Salinger, J. D. (1951). *The catcher in the rye*. Boston: Little, Brown.

Salomon, G. (1981). Communication and education: Social and psychological interactions. New York: Sage.

Samuels, S. J. (1967). Attentional processes in reading: The effect of pictures on the acquisition of reading responses. *Journal of Educational Psychology, 58,* 337–342.

Samuels, S. J. (1968). Effect on word associations on reading speed, recall, and guessing behavior on tests. *Journal of Educational Psychology, 59,* 12–15.

Samuels, S. J. (1970). Modes of word recognition. In H. Singer & R. B. Ruddell (Eds.), *Theoretical models and processes of reading* (1st ed., pp. 23–37). Newark, DE: International Reading Association.

Samuels, S. J. (1971). Success and failure in learning to read: A critique of the research. In F. Davis (Ed.), *The literature of research in reading with emphasis on models*. New Brunswick, NJ: Rutgers University.

Samuels, S. J. (1976). Modes of word recognition. In H. Singer & R. B. Ruddell (Eds.), *Theoretical models and processes of reading*. Newark, DE: International Reading Association.

Samuels, S. J. (1977, December 2). *Word recognition: Letter-by-letter or chunk—resolved?* Paper presented at the National Reading Conference, New Orleans.

Samuels, S. J. (1979). The method of repeated reading. *The Reading Teacher, 39,* 403–404.

Samuels, S. J. (1985). Word recognition. In H. Singer & R. B. Ruddell (Eds.), *Theoretical models and processes of reading* (3rd ed., pp. 256–275). Newark, DE: International Reading Association.

Sanacore, J. (1982). Using controversial materials: Bringing the forces together. *Journal of Reading, 26,* 506–511.

Sargent, E., Huus, H. & Andresen, O. (1971). *How to read a book*. Newark, DE: International Reading Association.

Sax, G., & Ottina, J. R. (1958). The arithmetic achievement of pupils differing in school experience. *California Journal of Educational Research, 9,* 15–19.

Schank, R. C., & Abelson, R. P. (1977). *Scripts, plans, goals and understanding*. Hillsdale, NJ: Lawrence Erlbaum Associates.

Schleich, M. (1971). Groundwork for better reading in the content areas. *Journal of Reading, 15,* 119–126.

Schlick, M. (1949). Causality in everyday life and recent sciences. In H. Feigl & V. Sellars (Eds.), *Readings in philosophical analysis* (pp. 515–533). New York: Appleton-Century-Crofts.

Schnabel, E. (1958). *Anne Frank, a portrait in courage*. New York: Harcourt Brace.

Scholastic Literature Units. *Series 5100*. New York: Scholastic Book Services.

Sharon, A. T. (1973–1974). What do adults read? *Reading Research Quarterly, 9*(1), 148–169.

Shavelson, R. J., Berliner, D. C., Ravitch, M. M., & Loeding, D. (1974). Effects of position and type of question on learning from prose material: Interaction of treatments with individual differences. *Journal of Educational Psychology, 66,* 40–48.

Shepherd, D. L. (1973, 1978). *Comprehensive high school methods* (2nd ed.). Columbus, OH: Merrill.

Shive, R. J. (1973). *Social studies as controversy*. Pacific Palisades, CA: Goodyear.

Shor, R., & Fidel, E. A. (Eds.). (1972). *The children's catalog*. New York: H. W. Wilson Co.

Shoup, B. (1984). Television: Friend, not foe of the teacher. *Journal of Reading, 27,* 629–631.

Simon, S. B., Howe, L. W., & Kirschenbaum, H. (1972). *Values clarification: A handbook of practical strategies for teachers and students*. New York: Hart.

Simonsen, S., & Singer, H. (1985). *Metacognition: Use of standards as a function of content familiarity versus training*. Paper presented at the National Reading Conference, San Diego, California.

Singer, H. (1962). The substrata factor theory of reading: Theoretical design for teaching reading. In J. Figurel (Ed.), *Challenge and experiment in reading* (pp. 226–232). Proceedings of the Seventh Annual Conference of the International Reading Association. New York: Scholastic Magazine.

Singer, H. (1964). Substrata factor patterns accompanying

development in power of reading, elementary through college level. In E. Thurston & L. Hafner (Eds.), *Philosophical and sociological basis of reading. Fourteenth Yearbook of the National Reading Conference, 14,* 41–56.

Singer, H. (1965). *Substrata-factor reorganization accompanying development of general reading ability at the elementary school level* (Final Rep.). Washington, DC: U.S. Office of Education.

Singer, H. (1966). Coinceptualization in learning to read. In G. B. Schick & M. M. May (Eds.), *New Frontiers in College-Adult Reading,* Fifteenth Yearbook of the National Reading Conference, pp. 116–132. Reprinted in H. Singer & R. B. Ruddell (Eds.) (1985) *Theoretical Models and Processes of Reading.* (3rd ed., pp. 239–255) Newark, DE: International Reading Association.

Singer, H. (1970). Research that should have made a difference. *Elementary English, 42,* 27–34.

Singer, H. (1971). Teaching word recognition. In M. Dawson (Ed.), *Teaching word recognition skills.* Newark, DE: International Reading Association.

Singer, H. (1973a). Measurement of early reading ability: Norm-referenced, standardized tests for differential assessment of progress in learning how to read and in using reading for gaining information. In P. Nacke (Ed.), *Proceedings of the National Reading Conference* (Abstract).

Singer, H. (1973b). *Preparation of reading content specialists for the junior high school.* Final Report. U.S. Office of Education. (ERIC Document Reproduction Service No. ED 088 003 CS 000 924)

Singer, H. (1975). The SEER technique: A non-computational estimate of readability. *Journal of Reading Behavior, 7,* 255–267.

Singer, H. (1976a). Substrata-factor patterns accompanying development in power of reading, elementary through college level. In H. Singer & R. B. Ruddell (Eds.), *Theoretical models and processes of reading* (2nd ed., pp. 619–633). Newark, DE: International Reading Association.

Singer, H. (1976b). Substrata-factor theory of reading: Theoretical design for teaching reading. In H. Singer & R. B. Ruddell (Eds.), *Theoretical models and processes of reading,* 2nd ed., pp. 681–689. Newark, DE: International Reading Association.

Singer, H. (1977a). Modifying the hypothesis, "It's the teacher who makes the difference." *Language Arts, 54,* 158–163.

Singer, H. (1966). Conceptualization in learning to read. In G. B. Schick & M. M. May (Eds.), *New Frontiers in College-Adult Reading,* Fifteenth Yearbook of the National Reading Conference, pp. 116–132. Reprinted in H. Singer & R. B. Ruddell (Eds.) (1985). *Theoretical*

Models and Processes of Reading, 3rd ed. Newark, DE: International Reading Association.

Singer, H. (1977b). IQ is and is not related to reading. In Stanley Wanet (Ed.), *Issues in evaluating reading* (pp. 44–63). Arlington, VA: Center for Applied Linguistics. (ERIC No. ED 088 004)

Singer, H. (1978a, 1979). Active comprehension: From answering to asking questions. *The Reading Teacher, 31,* 901–908. Revised version in C. McCullough (Ed.), *Inchworm, inchworm: Persistent questions in reading education* (pp. 222–232). Newark, DE: International Reading Association.

Singer, H. (1978b). *Attitudes toward reading and learning from text.* Paper presented at the National Reading Conference, St. Petersburg, FL.

Singer, H. (1978c). Research in reading that should make a difference in classroom reading instruction. In S. J. Samuels (Ed.), *What research has to say about reading instruction* (pp. 57–71). Newark, DE: International Reading Association.

Singer, H. (1979a). Attitudes towards reading and learning from text. In M. L. Kamil and A. J. Moe, (Eds.), *Reading research: Studies and applications* (Twenty-Eighth Yearbook of the National Reading Conference, pp. 254–260). West Lafayette, Indiana: The National Reading Conference.

Singer, H. (1979b). Slogans and attitudes. In J. Guthrie (Ed.), "Research Views" *Journal of Reading, 22,* 756–757.

Singer, H. (1981a). Hypotheses on reading comprehension in search of classroom validation. In M. Kamil (Ed.), *Directions in reading: Research and instruction* (Thirtieth Yearbook of the National Reading Conference, pp. 1–20). Chicago: National Reading Conference. (Contains section on Principles and Pitfalls in testing hypotheses on reading comprehension at the classroom level.)

Singer, H. (1981b). Teaching the acquisition phase of reading development: An historical perspective. In O. J. L. Tzeng & H. Singer (Eds.), *Perception of print: Reading research in experimental psychology* (pp. 9–28). Hillsdale, NJ: Lawrence Erlbaum Associates.

Singer, H. (1982). Towards an instructional theory for learning from text: A discussion of Ernst Rothkopf's adjunct aids and the control of mathemagenic activities during reading. In W. Otto & S. White (Eds.), *Reading expository material* (pp. 139–145). New York: Academic Press.

Singer, H. (1983a). Friendly texts. In H. Singer & T. W. Bean (Eds.), *Learning from text: Selection of friendly texts* (pp. 115–138). Lake Arrowhead Conference on Learning from Text. Riverside: University of California, Learning from Text Project, School of Education.

Singer, H. (1983b). Phonics first, second or not at all. In

M. Douglass (Ed.), *Reading reading: 50th anniversary perspectives* (pp. 205–217). Claremont Reading Conference. Claremont, CA: Claremont Graduate School.

Singer, H. (1983c). A critique of Jack Holmes's study: The substrata factor theory of reading and its history and conceptual relationship to interaction theory. In L. Gentile, M. Kamil, & J. Blanchard (Eds.), *Reading research revisited* (pp. 9–25). Columbus, OH: Merrill.

Singer, H. (1983d). A century of landmarks in reading research. *Journal of Reading, 26,* 332–342.

Singer, H. (1984). Teaching comprehension. In T. Husen & T. N. Postlethwaite (Eds.), *International encyclopedia of education: Research and study* (pp. 913–921). Oxford, England: Pergamon Press.

Singer, H. (1985). Comprehension instruction. In J. Husen & T. N. Postlethwaite (Eds.), *International encyclopedia of education: Research and study.* Oxford, England: Pergamon Press.

Singer, H. (1985). Stages of reading development: The next great debate. A review of Jeanne Chall's *Stages of reading development. Journal of Reading Behavior, 17*(1), 71–87.

Singer, H. (1986). Friendly texts: Description and criteria. In E. K. Dishner, T. W. Bean, J. E. Readence, & D. W. Moore, *Reading in the content areas* (2nd ed.). (pp. 112–128), Dubuque, IA: Kendall/Hunt.

Singer, H. (1987). An instructional model for reading and learning from text in a classroom situation. *Journal of Reading Education, 13*(1), 8–24.

Singer, H., & Balow, I. H. (1987a). Improving student performance for passing a minimal competency test in reading: Are remedial reading classes more effective than regular English classes? In H. Singer & I. Balow, *Final Report.* Berkeley, CA: California Policy Seminar, Institute of Governmental Studies, University of California.

Singer, H., & Balow, I. H. (1987b). Proficiency assessment and its consequences. *Final Report.* Berkeley, CA: California Policy Seminar, Institute of Governmental Studies, University of California.

Singer, H., & Bean, T. W. (1982a). *Learning from Text Project for 1981–1982: Conceptualization, prediction, and intervention* (Final Report). Riverside: University of California, Learning from Text Project. (ERIC Document Reproduction Service No. ED 223 989)

Singer, H., & Bean, T. W. (1982b). Reading and learning from text in the UC and CSU systems. *The California Reader, 15*(3), 26–28.

Singer, H., & Bean, T. W. (Eds.). (1982c). *Proceedings of the Lake Arrowhead Conference on Learning from Text,* April 14–16, 1982. Riverside: University of California, Learning from Text Project. (ERIC Document Reproduction Service No. ED 222 860)

Singer, H., & Bean, T. W. (Eds.). (1983a). *Learning from text: Selection of friendly texts.* Riverside: University of California, Learning from Text Project. (ERIC Document Reproduction Service No. ED 251 812)

Singer, H., & Bean, T. W. (Eds.). (May, 1983b). *Learning from text: Explanation and strategies.* Preconvention Institute of the International Reading Association, Anaheim, CA: Riverside: University of California, Learning from Text Project. (ERIC Document Reproduction Service No. ED 239 221)

Singer, H., & Bean, T. W. (1986). Ability to learn from text, background knowledge, and attitudes toward learning are predictive of freshmen achievement in the University of California and the California State University systems. *The California Reader, 19,* 35–38.

Singer, H., & Beasley, S. (1970). Motivating a disabled reader. In M. P. Douglas (Ed.), *Claremont reading conference yearbook* (pp. 141–160).

Singer, H., & Donlan, D. (1982). Active comprehension: Problem-solving schema with question generation for comprehension of complex short stories. *Reading Research Quarterly, 7,* 166–186.

Singer, H., Dreher, M. J., & Kamil, M. (1982). Computer literacy. In A. Berger & H. A. Robinson (Eds.), *Secondary school reading: What research reveals for classroom instruction* (pp. 173–192). Urbana, IL: Eric Clearinghouse on Reading and Communication Skills and the National Conference on Research in English.

Singer, H., & Hendrick, I. G. (1967). Total school integration: An experiment in social reconstruction. *Phi Delta Kappan, 49,* 143–147.

Singer, H., McNeil, J., & Furse, L. (1983). Relationship between curriculum scope and reading achievement in elementary schools. *The Reading Teacher, 37*(7), 608–612.

Singer, H., & Phelps, P. (1983). *The history of computers and their use in the classroom.* Paper presented at the National Reading Conference, FL.

Singer, H., & Rhodes, A. (1976). Learning from text: A review of theories, strategies, and research at the high school level. In *Reflections and investigations of reading* (Twenty-Fifth Yearbook of the National Reading Conference, pp. 22–51). Chicago, IL: The National Reading Conference.

Singer, H., & Rhodes, A. (1977). Problems, prescriptions, and possibilities in high school reading instruction. In W. Otto, C. W. Peters, & N. Peters (Eds.), *Reading problems: A multi-disciplinary perspective* (pp. 300–350). Reading, MA: Addison-Wesley.

Singer, H., & Ruddell, R. B. (Eds.). (1985). *Theoretical models and processes of reading* (3rd ed.). Newark, DE: International Reading Association.

Singer, H., Ruddell, R. B., McNeil, J., & Wittrock, M. C. (1983). *Testing achievement in basic skills, Vol. I: Executive summary and research report. Volume II. De-*

scription, Analysis, and Recommendations (Final Rep.). Berkeley: University of California, California Policy Seminar, Institute of Governmental Studies. (ERIC Document Reproduction Service No. ED 233 325 and 233 326)

Singer, H., Samuels, S. J., & Spiroff, J. (1973–1974). The effect of pictures and contextual conditions on learning responses to printed words. *Reading Research Quarterly, 9,* 555–567.

Sizer, T. R. (1984). *Horace's compromise: The dilemma of the American high school.* Boston: Houghton Mifflin.

Skoog, K. (1974). Tenth grade literature unit on medieval tales and legends (Exploring life through literature, 1968). A term paper in senior author's course in Reading in the Content Areas, University of California, Riverside.

Slater, W. H. (1985). Teaching expository text structure with structural organizers. *Journal of Reading, 28,* 712–718.

Slavin, R. E. (1980). *Using student team learning, revised edition.* Baltimore: Johns Hopkins University, The Center for Social Organization of Schools.

Smith, A. E. (1973). The effectiveness of training students to generate their own questions prior to reading. In P. L. Nacke (Ed.), *Diversity in mature reading: Theory and research* (Twenty-Second Yearbook of the National Reading Conference, pp. 71–77). Chicago, IL: The National Reading Conference.

Smith, F. R., & Feathers, K. M. (1983). Teacher and student perceptions of content area reading. *Journal of Reading, 26*(4), 348–354.

Smith, N. B. (1964a). Patterns of writing in different subject areas, part I. *Journal of Reading, 8,* 31–37.

Smith, N. B. (1964b). Patterns of writing in different subject areas, part II. *Journal of Reading, 8,* 97–102.

Smith, N. B. (1965a). *American reading instruction.* Newark, DE: International Reading Association.

Smith, N. B. (1965b). Reading in subject matter fields. *Educational Leadership, 22,* 382–385.

Smith, R. J., & Otto, W. (1969). Changing teacher attitudes toward teaching reading in the content areas. *Journal of Reading, 12,* 299–304.

Smith, W. L. (1972–1973). The controlled instrument procedure for studying the effect of syntactic sophistication in reading: A second study. *Journal of Reading Behavior, 5,* 242–251.

Spache, G. (1953). A new readability formula for primary grade reading materials. *Elementary School Journal, 53,* 410–413.

Spache, G. (1963). *Toward better reading.* Champaign, IL: Garrard.

Spache, G. D., & Spache, E. B. (1969, 1977). *Reading in the elementary school* (2nd & 4th ed.). Boston: Allyn & Bacon.

Spilich, G. J., Versonder, G., Chiesi, H. L., & Voss, J. F. (1979). Text processing of domain-related information for individuals with high and low domain knowledge. *Journal of Verbal Learning and Verbal Behavior, 18,* 275–290.

Spring, C., Sassenrath, J., Ketellapper, H., & Neustadt, S. (1982). *The effect of adjunct questions on learning from text in a college biology course* (Tech. Rep. No. 8). Davis: University of California, Basic Skills Research Program.

Stanovich, K. E. (1980). Toward an interactive-compensatory model of individual differences in the development of reading fluency. *Reading Research Quarterly, 16,* 32–71.

Stanovich, K. E. (1986). Mathew effects in reading: Some consequences of individual differences in the acquisition of literacy. *Reading Research Quarterly, 21,* 360–407.

Stauffer, R. G. (1942). A study of prefixes: The Thorndike List to establish a list of prefixes that should be taught in the elementary school. *Journal of Educational Research, 35,* 453–458.

Steiglitz, E. L. (1983). Effects of a content area reading course on teacher attitudes and practices. *Journal of Reading, 26*(8), 690–696.

Stein, B. S., & Bransford, J. D. (1979). Constraints on effective elaboration: Effects of precision and subject generation. *Journal of Verbal Learning and Verbal Behavior, 18,* 769–777.

Stein, B. S., Morris, C. D., & Bransford, J. D. (1978). Constraints on effective elaboration. *Journal of Verbal Learning and Verbal Behavior, 17,* 707–714.

Stein, J. (editor-in-chief). (1973). *The Random House dictionary of the English language.* New York: Random House.

Steinberg, E. R., & Anderson, R. C. (1975). Hierarchical semantic organization in six year olds. *Journal of Exerimental Child Psychology, 19,* 544–553.

Stephens, J. M. (1956). *Educational psychology* (rev. ed.). New York: Holt.

Sticht, T., Beck, L. J., Hauke, R. N., Kleiman, G. M., & James, J. H. (1974). *Auding and reading: A developmental model.* Monterey, CA: Human Resources Organization.

Sticht, T. G., Caylor, J. S., & Kern, R. P. (1970). *Project realistic: Evaluation and modification of reading, listening, and arithmetic requirements in military occupations having civilian counterparts.* Presidio of Monterey, CA: Human Resources Research Organization.

Sticht, T. G., & McFann, H. H. (1975). Reading requirements for career entry. In Duane M. Nielsen & Howard F. Hjelm (Eds.), *Reading and career education.* Newark, DE: International Reading Association.

Stone, L. J., & Church, J. (1973). *Childhood and adolescence* (3rd ed.). New York: Random House.

Strang, R. (1938). *Problems in the improvement of reading in high school and college*. Lancaster, PA: The Science Press.

Strang, R. (1942). *Explorations in reading patterns*. Chicago: University of Chicago Press.

Strang, R., McCullough, C., & Traxler, A. (1967). *The improvement of reading* (4th ed.). New York: McGraw-Hill.

Taba, H. (1965). The teaching of thinking. *Elementary English, 42*, 534–542.

Taba, H. (1967). *Teachers' handbook for elementary social studies*. Palo Alto, CA: Addison-Wesley.

Task Force on Education for Economic Growth. (1983). *Action for excellence: A compendium plan to improve our national schools*. Denver: Education Commission of the States.

Taylor, B. M., & Samuels, S. J. (1983). Children's use of text structure in the recall of expository materials. *American Education Research Journal, 20*, 517–528.

Taylor, W. L. (1953). Cloze procedure: A new tool for measuring readability. *Journalism Quarterly, 30*, 415–433.

Telfer, R. J., & Kann, R. S. (1984). Reading achievement, free reading, watching TV, and listening to music. *Journal of Reading, 27*, 536–539.

Terman, L. M., & Lima, M. (1929). *Children's reading*. New York: Appleton Century.

Thelen, J. (1976). *Improving reading in science*. Newark, DE: International Reading Association.

Thomas, E. L. (1969). The role of the reading consultant. In H. A. Robinson & E. L. Thomas (Eds.), *Fusing reading skills and content*. Newark, DE: International Reading Association.

Thomas, E. L., & Robinson, H. A. (1972). *Improving reading in every class*. Boston: Allyn & Bacon.

Thorndike, E. L. (1917). Reading as reasoning: A study of mistakes in paragraph reading. *Journal of Educational Psychology, 8*, 323–332.

Thorndike, E. L. (1941). *The teaching of English suffixes*. Columbia University Contributions to Education, No. 847. New York: Teachers College, Columbia University.

Thorndike, E. L., & Barnhart, C. L. (1971). *Intermediate dictionary*. Garden City, NY: Doubleday.

Thorndike, R. L., & Hagen, E. (1969). *Measurement and evaluation in psychology and education* (3rd ed.). New York: Wiley.

Thorndyke, P. (1975). *Cognitive structure in human story comprehension and memory*. Unpublished doctoral dissertation, Stanford University.

Thorndyke, P., & Hayes-Roth, B. (1979). The use of schemata in the acquisition and transfer of knowledge. *Cognitive Psychology, 11*, 82–106.

Tierney, R. (1981). Using expressive writing to teach biology. *Two studies of writing in high school science* (pp. 47–69). Berkeley: Bay Area Writing Project.

Tierney, R., & LaZansky, J. (1980). The rights and responsibility of readers and writers: A contractual agreement. *Language Arts, 57*, 606–613.

Tierney, R. J., Mosenthal, J., & Kantor, R. N. (1984). Some classroom applications of text analysis: Toward improving text selection and use. In J. F. Flood (Ed.), *Understanding reading comprehension* (pp. 139–160). Newark, DE: International Reading Association.

Tinker, M. A., & McCullough, C. (1975). *Teaching elementary reading* (4th ed.). Englewood Cliffs, NJ: Prentice-Hall.

Toffler, A. (1970). *Future shock*. New York: Bantam.

Tyack, D. B. (1967). *Turning points on American educational history*. Waltham, MA: Blaisdell/Ginn.

Tzeng, O. J. L., & Singer, H. (1982). *Perception of print: Reading research in experimental psychology*. Hillsdale, NJ: Lawrence Erlbaum Associates.

Vanderlinde, L. F. (1964). Does the study of quantitative vocabulary improve problem-solving? *Elementary School Journal, 65*, 143–152.

van Dijk, T., & Kintsch, W. (1977). Cognitive psychology and discourse: Recalling and summarizing stories. In W. V. Dressler (Ed.), *Current trends in text linguistics* (pp. 61–80). New York: De Gruyter.

Van Wagenen, M. J. (1953). *Van Wagenen rate of comprehension scale*. Minneapolis: M. J. Van Wagenen.

Vaughan, J. L., Jr. (1977). A scale to measure attitudes toward teaching reading in content classrooms. *Journal of Reading 20*(7), 605–609.

Venezky, R. L. (1970). Linguistics and spelling. In A. H. Markwardt (Ed.), *Linguistics in school programs* (Sixty-Ninth Yearbook of the National Society for the Study of Education, Part II). Chicago: University of Chicago Press.

Vosniadou, S., & Brewer, W. F. (1987). Theories of knowledge restructuring in development. *Review of Educational Research, 57*(1), 51–67.

Wade, S. (1983). A synthesis of the research for improving reading in the social studies. *Review of Educational Research, 53*(4), 461–497.

Watts, G., & Anderson, R. C. (1971). Effects of three types of inserted questions on learning from prose. *Journal of Educational Psychology, 62*, 387–394.

Weber, R. (1970). First-graders' use of grammatical context in reading. In H. Levin & J. Williams (Eds.), *Basic studies on reading* (pp. 147–163). New York: Basic Books.

Wesley, E. B., & Wronski, S. P. (1973). *Teaching sec-*

ondary social studies in a world society. Lexington: D. C. Heath.

West, J. (1954). *Cress Delahanty.* New York: Avon.

Wiener, M., & Cromer, W. (1967). Reading and reading difficulty: A conceptual analysis. *Harvard Educational Review, 37,* 620–643.

Winograd, T. (1972). Understanding natural language. *Cognitive Psychology, 3,* (whole issue).

Wolfe, H. M. (1974). A structure approach to pronouncing unfamiliar words. *Journal of Reading, 17,* 356–362.

Wong, B. (1985). Self-questioning instructional research: A review. *Review of Educational Research, 55,* 227–268.

Wooton, W. (1964). The history and status of the school mathematics study group. In R. W. Heath (Ed.), *New curricula* (pp. 35–53). New York: Harper & Row.

Wotring, A. M. (1981). Writing to think about high school chemistry. *Two studies of writing in high school science* (pp. 1–44). Berkeley: Bay Area Writing Project.

Wright, R. (1940). *Native son.* New York: Harper & Row.

Yekovich, F. R., & Walker, C. H. (1978). Identifying and using references in sentence comprehension. *Journal of Verbal Learning and Verbal Behavior, 17,* 265–277.

Yopp, H. K. (1987). *The concept and measurement of phonemic awareness.* Unpublished doctoral dissertation, University of California, Riverside.

Yopp, H. K., & Singer, H. (1985). Toward an interactive reading instructional model: Explanation of activation of linguistic awareness and metalinguistic ability in learning to read. In H. Singer & R. B. Ruddell (Eds.), *Theoretical models and processes of reading* (3rd ed., pp. 722–750). Newark, DE: International Reading Association.

Yopp, R. H. (1987). *Active comprehension: Declarative knowledge for generating questions and procedural knowledge for answering them.* Unpublished doctoral dissertation, University of California, Riverside.

Zack, J. E., & Osako, G. N. (1986). Inconsiderate text and the second-grade reader. In J. Niles & R. Lalik (Eds.), *Solving problems in literacy: Learners, teachers, and researchers* (Thirty-Fifth Yearbook of the National Reading Conference, pp. 339–343). Rochester, NY: National Reading Conference.

Zakaluk, B. L., & Samuels, S. J. (1988). Toward a new approach to predicting comprehensibility using inside- and outside-the-head information and a nomograph. In S. J. Samuels (Ed.), *Readability: Its past, present, and future* (pp. 121–144). Newark, DE: International Reading Association.

Zigler, E. (1967). Familial mental retardation: A continuing dilemma. *Science, 155,* 292–298.

Index

657